BRISTOL
AND ITS ADJOINING
COUNTIES

Bristol, 1479.

BRISTOL AND ITS ADJOINING COUNTIES

Edited by
C. M. MacINNES
AND
W. F. WHITTARD

Published
for the British Association for the
Advancement of Science
by the
Local Executive Committee

BRISTOL
1955

Republished EP Publishing Limited 1973

First published 1955

Republished 1973 by EP Publishing Limited
East Ardsley, Wakefield
Yorkshire, England

ISBN 0 85409 783 X

Printed in Great Britain by
The Scolar Press Limited, Menston, Yorkshire

EDITORIAL PREFACE

WE have intentionally refrained from confining our collaborators to those subjects which are strictly within the purview of the several sections of the British Association for the Advancement of Science and, therefore, the handbook is unusually high in its content of non-scientific matter. We believe the visitor to Bristol will discover much of vital interest outside science, and the handbook is designed to provide authoritative information to those who wish to know more of a city which once stood second only to London in importance and of a region richly endowed by history.

We wish to express our gratitude to the authors who are responsible for this book; our association with them has been happy and their co-operation not a little gratifying. Mr. H. Freke, of the Geography Department, has prepared most of the drawings for the text-figures and maps and Mr. E. W. Seavill, of the Geology Department, has made several of the photographic enlargements.

The publishers have included in this new edition an appendix including contributions from many of the original authors. These contributions outline important changes since 1955 and mention new works which have appeared since that date.

FOREWORD

by the Vice-Chancellor of the University of Bristol

MEETINGS of the British Association occur in Bristol only at long intervals. The most recent one took place as long ago as 1930. In the broad perspective of the history of the country, of Bristol and of the Association this is a short interval, but few periods of similar length in human history have seen so much or such rapid change. It is right therefore that the meeting of the Association here during 1955 should be marked by the publication of a special volume dealing with Bristol and the surrounding countryside.

The preparation of this volume has been the responsibility of a committee which has been inspired and advised by Professor C. M. MacInnes and Professor W. F. Whittard, who willingly undertook jointly the duties of editorship. Any survey of this nature must in its scale and scope reflect the breadth, variety, longevity and continuing youthfulness of the city and region which it portrays. Success could only be achieved by soliciting and obtaining the services of a considerable number of experts on various aspects of life, activity and environment of yesterday and to-day. The editors deserve praise and congratulation as well as the gratitude of the reader for their success in prevailing upon so many eminently qualified experts to make their several contributions.

It is no part of the function of a foreword to summarize or to anticipate the work which it seeks to introduce. But it is my privilege to commend this book to all who may read it and, in so doing, to call attention to a golden thread which gives an unmistakable unity to a volume of so many and such diverse chapters. It is clear that for everyone concerned its preparation has been a labour of love inspired by a warm attachment to the West of England and deep interest in its past, present and future. It is not departing too much from a becoming modesty to say that no other part of this country, or indeed of the world, has greater or more insidious claims upon the interest and affection of those who live in and serve it.

In a world in turmoil, there are to be found in the succeeding pages and in all that concerns the meeting of the British Association in Bristol this year grounds for sober optimism. The natural beauty, the architecture, the institutions, the industry and commerce of the area are all reflected not only in this volume but in the co-operation given from so many quarters in ensuring that Bristol and its region adequately and gracefully fulfil the manifold duties of a host to the guests which the meeting will bring. The initiative taken by the City and by the University could not have had a successful outcome if the willing co-operation, forthcoming on all sides, had not spontaneously expressed itself.

It is, I know, the hope of all concerned with the meeting of the British Association in Bristol that those who attend it may have their enjoyment increased and enriched by the information here presented and that when the meeting itself is only a memory this book may remain of value to the members of the Association who came to Bristol and to an even wider public.

P. R. MORRIS

It is a welcome privilege to add to the original foreword because the decision to republish this volume is clearly a very good one. Originally produced for the benefit of visitors to Bristol in 1955, it has a wide and permanent significance. The joint editors, and their many colleagues, skilfully planned an intricate tapestry to illustrate many of the varied strands in an enduring environment. Few amendments and additions to the text are necessary and those are very wisely supplied in an appendix. This book, republished in facsimile form, provides a valuable foundation for the study and enjoyment of the environment with which it deals and a pattern for other such studies. A new edition is also most opportune when an interest in conservation is more and more widespread. Conservation is a blind and empty concept unless the desire for it is informed by a wide and varied knowledge of what it is that is worth conserving. This book deals with a wide spectrum of the necessary knowledge and its widespread use can do nothing but good.

I greatly wish that all those who did so much to make this such an excellent work could have survived to join in its republication. Some of them have died but there are sure to be competent friends and colleagues still living and active who will willingly stand in for them and do what is necessary.

P. R. M.

CONTENTS

LIST OF PLATES

LIST OF MAPS AND DIAGRAMS

PART ONE

CHAPTER ONE

GEOLOGY

INTRODUCTION

BRISTOL has, perhaps, a wider range of sedimentary rocks available for inspection within a modest distance than any other British city. Within a radius of twenty miles formations ranging from the Cambrian to the Chalk may be seen, and the absence of some of the intervening divisions is compensated for by the great variety of geological phenomena displayed. No attempt has been made to lay down a rigid boundary for the account which follows, and the writers of the several parts have adopted different limits, and different modes of treatment, to suit their subjects. In the case of the Lower Palaeozoic rocks, which occur as two compact inliers whose importance is great in comparison with their area, the opportunity to give a succinct and up-to-date account has been taken. The Upper Palaeozoic rocks have recently been the subject of close scrutiny by the Officers of the Geological Survey in the primary six-inch mapping of the Bristol and Somerset Coalfields, and we are fortunate in being able to present an account of their conclusions. For this purpose it has been necessary to include some consideration of the country beyond the Severn. The description of the Mesozoic rocks, by contrast, refers to a smaller area within which features largely peculiar to the Bristol neighbourhood, and intimately connected with its previous geological history, are present in the earlier Mesozoic rocks. By the time the Upper Jurassic and Cretaceous rocks are reached, this local character is no longer present, and the exposures accessible from Bristol merely form part of the main outcrop which has often been described; accordingly, an account of these rocks has not been included.

LOWER PALAEOZOIC

(M.L.K.C.)

CAMBRIAN

The oldest rocks seen in the Bristol area are the Tremadoc shales which crop out in the Tortworth Inlier in Gloucestershire (Smith and Stubblefield, 1933) (Fig. 1). The strata consist of a great thickness of grey shales with thin siliceous bands, and were deposited in a sea which covered much of the area now occupied by the English Midlands and Wales. Although the rocks are poorly exposed in the Tortworth district the following subdivisions can be distinguished:

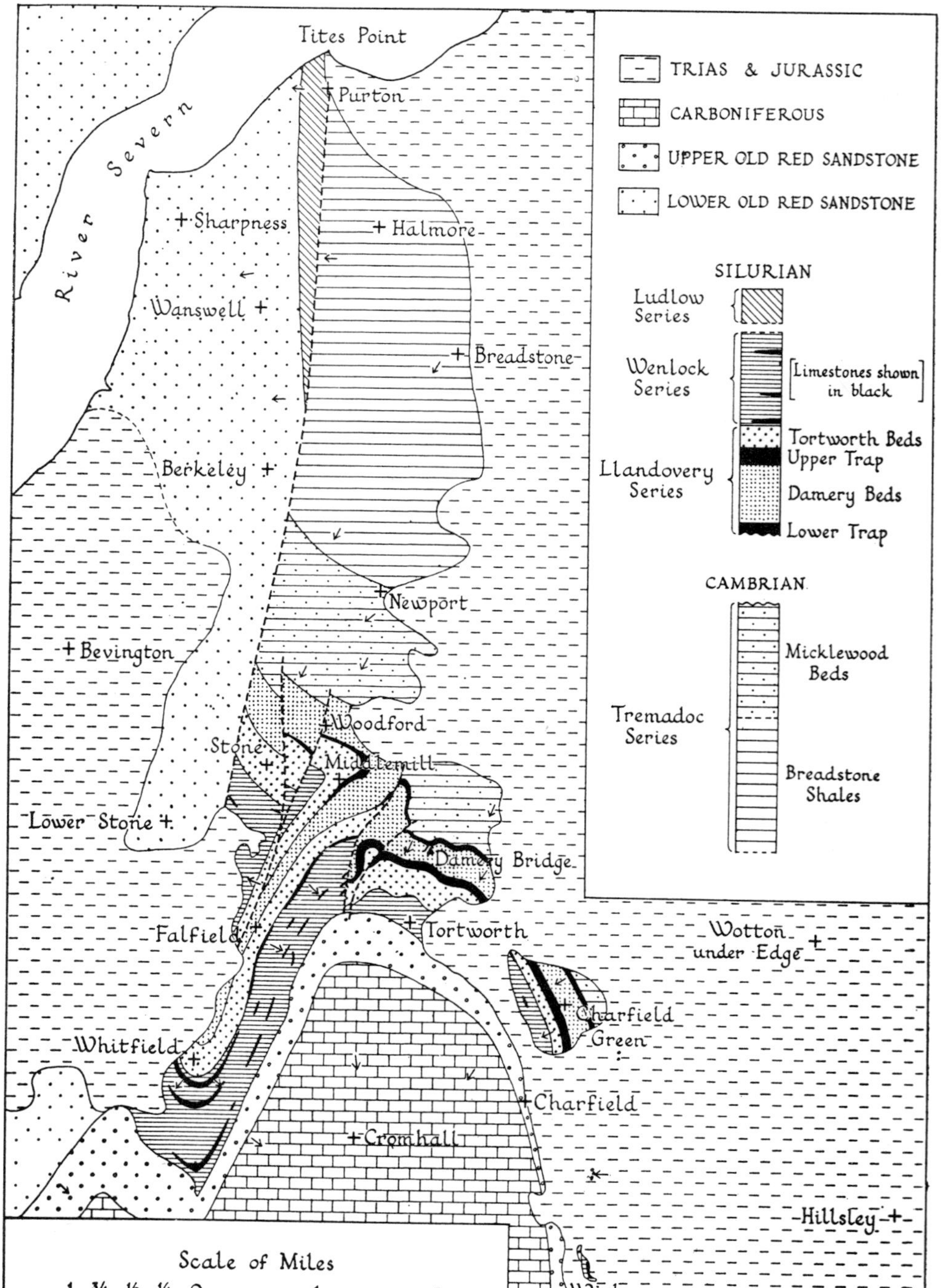

FIG. 1. *Geological map of the Tortworth district, Gloucestershire.*

(2) *Micklewood Beds*—shales with prominent siliceous bands up to a foot thick. Thickness: perhaps 1,200 ft.

(1) *Breadstone Shales*—thinly-bedded shales with thin siliceous bands. Thickness: not known, but probably to be measured in thousands rather than in hundreds of feet.

The Breadstone Shales are of Lower Tremadoc age; the fauna obtained from them at Breadstone includes *Dictyonema flabelliforme*, *Agnostus calvus*, *Bellella depressa* and *Niobe homfrayi* var. *smithi*, and shows them to belong to the *Dictyonema flabelliforme* zone. The occurrence of *Clonograptus* sp. at Mobley, near Berkeley, suggests the presence there of the *Clonograptus tenellus* zone. The Micklewood Beds are probably of Upper Tremadoc age, but have yielded no fossils apart from horny brachiopods such as *Schmidtia* cf. *crassa*, *Lingulella* cf. *lepis* and *Lingulella* cf. *davisi*. The abundance of flaggy siliceous bands in the Micklewood Beds suggests a shallowing of the sea towards the end of Tremadoc times.

SILURIAN

The Cambrian shales are succeeded unconformably by Silurian rocks. The Ordovician and a considerable part of the Lower Silurian are absent, and it seems that throughout this long period the Bristol area stood as part of a landmass which extended over much of what are now the western and midland counties of England. When, during Silurian times, subsidence occurred the whole area was invaded by a shallow sea in which corals, brachiopods, trilobites and other invertebrates abounded.

The Silurian rocks of the Bristol area are represented by sediments belonging to each of the three main divisions of the System, the Llandovery, Wenlock and Ludlow, and they include basalts and andesites which were poured out as lavas. Outcrops of these rocks occur in the Tortworth and Eastern Mendip Inliers.

The Tortworth Inlier

Llandovery and Wenlock rocks crop out in the southern part of the Tortworth Inlier (Reed and Reynolds, 1908; Reynolds, 1924), and Ludlow beds are present in the northern part where they are faulted against the Tremadoc shales (Smith, 1934, p. 119).

Llandovery Series. The Llandovery rocks consist of about 700 ft. of fine-grained sandstones and shales, and contain two igneous bands. The sediments have yielded a large fauna which shows them to belong to the topmost zones of the Upper Llandovery. Around Damery and Charfield the following succession is seen:

(4) *Tortworth Beds*—fine-grained sandstones and shales, with the *Palaeocyclus* Band at the base. Thickness: about 200 ft.

(3) *Upper Trap*—pyroxene-andesite. An extrusive lava. Thickness: about 150 ft.

(2) *Damery Beds*—fine-grained sandstones and shales with calcareous bands. Thickness: about 500 ft.

(1) *Lower Trap*—basalt. Probably an extrusive lava. Thickness: about 100 ft.

The Damery Beds are fossiliferous throughout, and among the commonest forms are *Tentaculites anglicus*, *Stricklandia lens*, *Leptostrophia compressa*, *Camarotoechia* spp., *Atrypa reticularis*, *Coelospira hemisphaerica* and *Dalmanites weaveri*. In the Tortworth Beds fossils are scarce, except at the base where the *Palaeocyclus* Band contains a large and distinctive fauna in which *Palaeocyclus porpita* and a small species of *Favosites* are particularly abundant. The igneous bands thin out westwards suggesting that the source of the lavas lay somewhere to the east. Volcanic tuffs do not occur, but at Charfield and Middlemill thin ashy limestones rest on the uneven top of the Upper Trap.

Wenlock Series. The Wenlock beds consist of some 800 ft. of shales, siltstones and calcareous sandstones, and at various horizons there are impersistent beds of limestone up to 30 ft. thick. The junction with the Upper Llandovery is apparently a conformable one, but the top of the series is not seen as the rocks are overstepped by Upper Old Red Sandstone.

The Wenlock succession is most clearly exposed in the Whitfield area where it contains three well-marked limestone bands, each about 25 to 30 ft. thick. These limestones, with the exception of the lowest, cannot be recognized with certainty in other parts of the inlier, and it appears that they wedge out laterally. The highest Wenlock rocks visible in the inlier are calcareous sandstones and shales exposed at Horseshoe Farm, south of Whitfield; fossils found at this locality have suggested to some geologists that the beds here may be of Ludlow age.

The Tortworth fauna contains many of the usual Wenlock species such as *Favosites gothlandicus*, *Parmorthis elegantula*, *Leptaena depressa*, *Meristina obtusa*, *Atrypa reticularis*, *Pterinea retroflexa* and *Dalmanites vulgaris*. Of particular interest is the rich fauna obtained from the *Pycnactis* Band which comprises the few feet of shales immediately above the lowest limestone, and in which *Pycnactis mitratus*, *Coenites juniperinus*, *Parmorthis basalis*, *Camarotoechia* cf. *nucula*, *Sphaerirhynchia davidsoni* and *Whitfieldella canalis* are abundant.

Ludlow Series. The Ludlow beds form a tapering outcrop extending southwards from Purton, and are exposed in the River Severn at Tites Point. The rocks consist of mudstones, shales, limestones and fine-grained sandstones, and are probably not less than 300 ft. thick. They appear to belong to the Middle and Upper Ludlow, and to pass conformably into the overlying Downtonian beds. The fauna is composed largely of brachiopods of which the commonest are *Orbiculoidea rugata*, *Dalmanella orbicularis*, *Chonetes striatellus*, *Camarotoechia nucula*, *Sphaerirhynchia wilsoni*, *Dayia navicula* and *Delthyris elevatus*.

The Eastern Mendip Inlier

The Silurian rocks which crop out north-east of Shepton Mallet form the core of an anticline, and are succeeded unconformably by Upper Old Red Sandstone. The stratigraphy of these beds is imperfectly understood, and the most interesting feature about them is the great thickness of andesites and associated tuffs (Reynolds, 1907; 1912*a*).

The succession, according to Reynolds (1929, p. 84), is as follows:

(3) *Wenlock.* Mudstones, often fossiliferous and with bands of micaceous sandstone. Known from temporary exposures to the south-east of Moon's Hill Quarry. Thickness: about 120 ft.

(2) Pyroxene-andesite with some interbedded tuff. Exposed in Moon's Hill, Sunnyhill and Downhead Quarries. Thickness: probably not less than 400 ft.

(1) *Upper Llandovery.* Tuffs, formerly exposed in Sunnyhill Quarry and in trenches at Tadhill and Downhead. Thickness: 110 ft. seen.

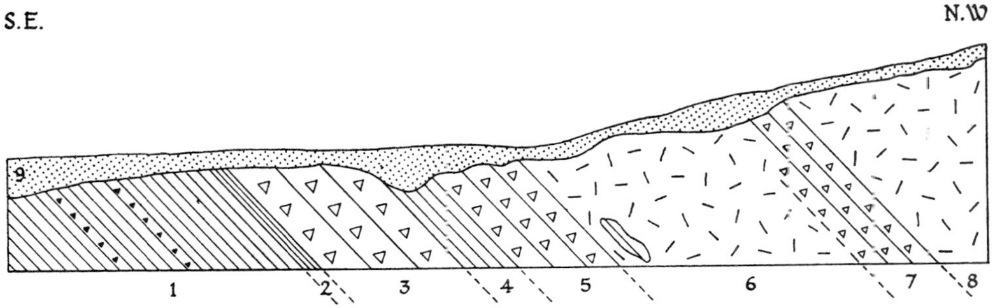

FIG. 2. *Section formerly visible in Sunnyhill Quarry, near Stoke Lane, Somerset, showing Silurian tuffs interbedded with andesite. Scale: 1 in. to 40 ft.* 1, *fine tuff with Silurian fossils;* 2, *ash;* 3, *coarse tuff;* 4, *ash;* 5, *coarse tuff;* 6, *andesite;* 7, *tuff;* 8, *andesite;* 9, *weathered rock and soil.* (*After S. H. Reynolds.*)

In addition to the above there is a fourth group of rocks comprising coarse ashy conglomerates, but their relationship to the other rocks of the inlier is unknown. These conglomerates, which crop out at Beacon Hill and to the east of Moon's Hill Quarry, contain large rounded pieces of andesite. It has been suggested that they may be coarse water-deposited tuffs, or that they may represent material filling the volcanic vents from which the lavas and finer tuffs were ejected.

The Wenlock mudstones, which apparently overlie the andesite, have provided a considerable fauna containing such species as *Craniops implicata*, *Leptaena rhomboidalis*, *Fardenia pecten*, *Meristina obtusa*, *Atrypa reticularis* and *Dalmanites vulgaris*.

The tuffs below the andesite have yielded a number of fossils of which *Parmorthis elegantula*, *Sphaerirhynchia davidsoni* and *Phacops downingiae* are among the most plentiful. These beds have generally been regarded as belonging to the Upper Llandovery, and the andesite, because it succeeds them conformably, is thought to have been extruded during Upper Llandovery times. The fauna from the tuffs is not a distinctive one, however, and it may equally well be that the whole of the Silurian succession exposed in eastern Mendip is of Wenlock age.

Silurian Vulcanicity

The presence of igneous rocks in the Bristol area is of special interest as the Silurian was, in most places, a period of volcanic quiescence. Only four other occurrences of Silurian lavas are known in north-western Europe, and all are situated along a narrow belt which extends from the west of Ireland to Bohemia. As Turner (1935, pp. 148–50) has pointed out, this was evidently a structural line of fundamental character, for it was later along the same belt that the full effects of the Armorican earth-movements were to be felt.

UPPER PALAEOZOIC

OLD RED SANDSTONE

Although there is no obvious stratigraphical break between the Silurian and Lower Old Red Sandstone in the Bristol area, there is evidence of changing conditions, for the grey Ludlow beds exposed at Tites Point, near Purton, quickly give place to red marls and sandstones. The Old Red Sandstone rocks of the area appear to have been laid down under deltaic conditions at the southern margin of a vast arid continent; a short distance to the south lay the open sea in which the Devonian sediments of Devon and Cornwall were deposited.

In the Bristol area the Lower and Upper Old Red Sandstone exist as two distinct formations, separated by a major unconformity. Outcrops of Lower Old Red Sandstone occur in the northern part of the area, and form a continuation of the much fuller development of these rocks seen around the Forest of Dean. The Upper Old Red Sandstone crops out in several localities; everywhere it is succeeded conformably by the Carboniferous Limestone, and is therefore linked, structurally, with the Carboniferous rocks rather than with the Lower Old Red Sandstone.

The unconformity which separates the Lower and Upper Old Red Sandstone shows that during Middle Old Red Sandstone times the area was raised to form land. That the land surface was undergoing severe denudation during this period is indicated by the way in which the Upper Old Red Sandstone oversteps various older formations; thus at Thornbury, as Kellaway and Welch (1948, p. 16) have shown, a considerable part of the Lower as well as the Middle Old Red Sandstone is missing, while in the Tortworth district, as in eastern Mendip, the Upper Old Red Sandstone rests directly on Wenlock rocks. Structures which are discernible in the older rocks at Tortworth and Wickwar, but which do not affect the Upper Old Red Sandstone, suggest that folding and faulting occurred during the period represented by the unconformity.

Lower Old Red Sandstone

In the country around the Forest of Dean the Lower Old Red Sandstone is represented by marls and sandstones belonging to the Downtonian, Dittonian and Breconian divisions which together attain a thickness of nearly 5,000 ft. (Trotter, 1942, p. 9).

East of the River Severn the succession is much less complete, and the Downtonian only has been identified with certainty. Rocks of this formation crop out to the west of the Tortworth Inlier, between Purton and Lower Stone, and are well exposed in the Severn at Sharpness. A considerable thickness of marls with layers of micaceous sandstone are present, and in places the marls contain curious vertically-elongated calcareous concretions. At Sharpness lamellibranchs and the remains of *Traquairaspis pococki* var. *sabrinae* and other fishes have been obtained (White, 1946, p. 213). Near Thornbury there are outcrops of similar marls and sandstones which have been termed the Thornbury Beds (Kellaway and Welch, 1948, p. 16) and which are presumably also of Downtonian age.

The Old Red Sandstone exposed to the west of Bristol is said to be some 3,000 ft. thick, and the whole succession has generally been regarded as belonging to the Upper Old Red Sandstone (Wallis, 1928, p. 763). Kellaway and Welch (1948, p. 17), however, have suggested that Lower Old Red Sandstone may be present in the core of the Westbury-on-Trym anticline.

UPPER OLD RED SANDSTONE AND CARBONIFEROUS

(G.A.K. AND F.B.A.W.)

There is no break in the sequence between the Upper Old Red Sandstone and the Carboniferous Limestone Series. West of the Severn a broad outcrop of the former runs from Magor through Tintern to Trellech. East of the river the formation crops out at Thornbury and extends around the northern part of the Bristol Coalfield to Wickwar. Another outcrop extends from Westbury-on-Trym through Portishead to Clevedon and there are occurrences in the cores of the anticlinal folds of Mendip.

The Carboniferous strata of the Bristol district occupy a roughly triangular area with the apex at Tortworth. The base, thirty miles farther south, is twenty-eight miles long from east to west, being represented by the Mendip range; the city of Bristol is almost at its geometrical centre. The triangle is margined by rocks of the Carboniferous Limestone Series and within it lie the Coal Measures. Though the Carboniferous rocks as a whole are largely hidden beneath Triassic and Jurassic deposits, the Carboniferous Limestone Series is fairly well exposed; the Coal Measures crop out in a large inlier north of the River Avon and in four comparatively small inliers south of the Avon at Pensford, Radstock, Nettlebridge and Nailsea.

West of the Severn there is a considerable tract of Carboniferous Limestone in the Chepstow area. In the Forest of Dean the upper portion of the series is predominantly composed of sandstone but the sandstone beds tongue out southwards. Recent mapping has shown that, followed southwards, the limestones themselves exhibit marked changes of facies. Between the Forest of Dean and Bristol there occur crinoidal limestone, oolite, calcite mudstone ('chinastone') and algal limestone in well-defined beds, while dolomite is also developed in the lower part of the formation. From Bristol to Mendip the facies are less well defined, the lithological types here comprise dark-grey and light-grey crinoidal limestone, oolitic crinoidal limestone, oolite and calcite mudstone. These changes indicate deposition in water on the northern edge of a basin with some minor modifications that have been caused by local earth movements that seem to have affected deposition during at least part of the Carboniferous Period.

In the Forest of Dean the main lithological divisions of the Carboniferous Limestone Series are as shown in Table 1. The name Lower Dolomite is due to Sibly (1919), those of Crease and Whitehead Limestones to Wethered (1886), that of Drybrook

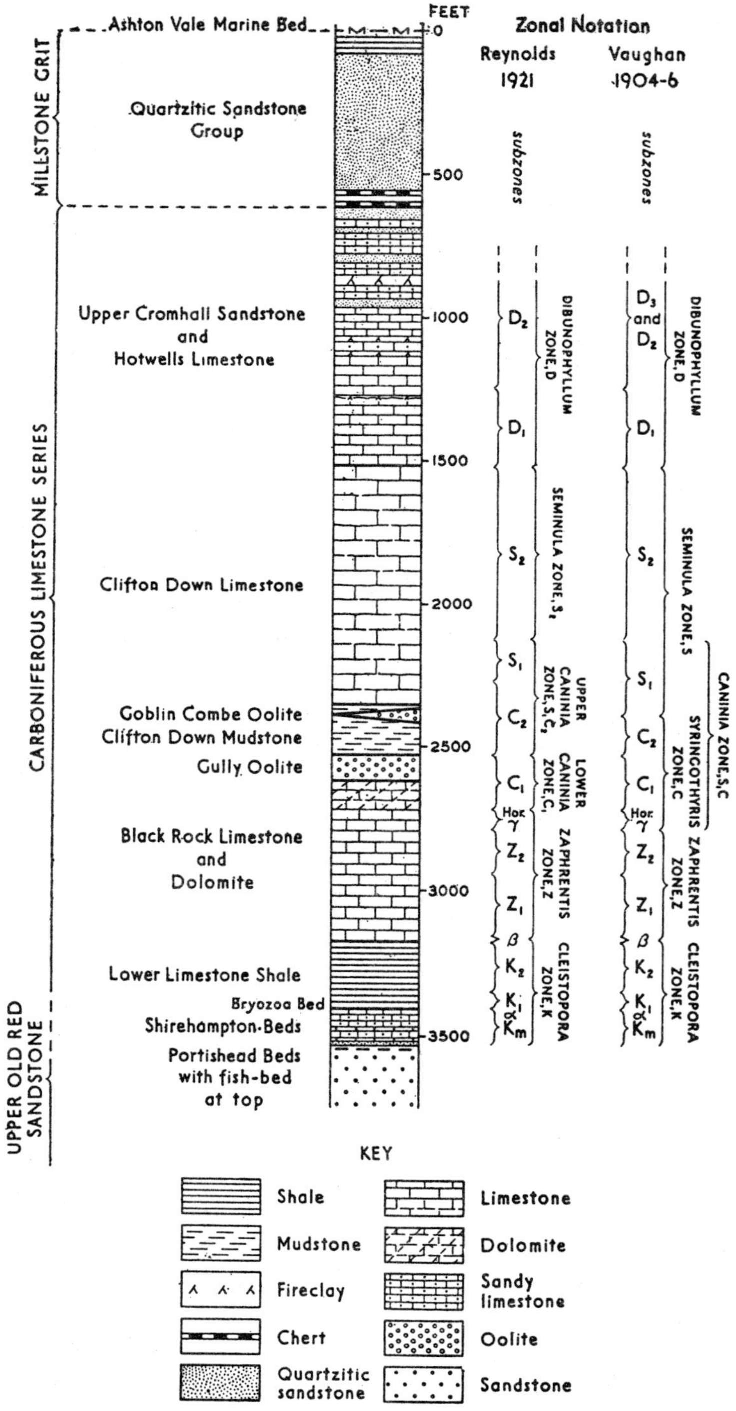

FIG. 3. *Lithological subdivisions of the Carboniferous Limestone Series in the Bristol region; thicknesses are based on the Avon Gorge Section and Ashton Park Borehole. (Crown copyright reserved. Reproduced by permission of H.M. Stationery Office.)*

Sandstone to Sibly (1919) while a limestone some 250 ft. above the base of the Drybrook Sandstone, at Clearwell, has been named Drybrook Limestone by Trotter (1940). All these names have been applied to the Carboniferous Limestone of the Chepstow district. East of the Severn, however, apart from the Lower Limestone Shale, the original names of the formations were rejected in 1905–6 in favour of zonal terms on the grounds that greater precision would result. However, for the purposes of six-inch mapping by the Geological Survey it was necessary to subdivide the Carboniferous Limestone Series on a lithological basis and to give the subdivisions so mapped appropriate names. The early names were therefore restored as far as possible and new ones selected with reference to large exposures, such as the Avon Gorge (Kellaway & Welch, 1955). These new or revived formational names applied to the Avon Gorge section are given in Fig. 3, in which the thicknesses of the formations up to the top of the Clifton Down Limestone are based primarily on detailed six-inch mapping and on information from other sources notably Reynolds (1921a) and Loupekine (1953). The thickness of the higher strata is based on the record of the Geological Survey borehole at Ashton Park (Kellaway 1967). In the Bristol and Somerset Coalfields the rocks of the Carboniferous Limestone Series can be grouped into four major divisions as shown in Table I.

TABLE I

		Forest of Dean	*Bristol–Broadfield Down*	*Mendip*
Dinantian (Carboniferous Limestone Series)	Hotwells Group	Upper Drybrook Sandstone	Upper Cromhall Sandstone and Hotwells Limestone	Hotwells Limestone
	Clifton Down Group	Drybook Limestone Lower Drybrook Sandstone Whitehead Limestone Crease Limestone	Middle Cromhall Sandstone Clifton Down Limestone Lower Cromhall Sandstone Goblin Combe Oolite Clifton Down Mudstone Gully Oolite	Clifton Down Limestone Burrington Oolite Vallis Limestone
	Black Rock Group	Lower Dolomite	Black Rock Limestone and Dolomite	Black Rock Limestone and Dolomite
	Lower Limestone Shale Group	Lower Limestone Shale	Lower Limestone Shale Shirehampton Beds	Lower Limestone Shale
Upper Old Red Sandstone		Tintern Sandstone Quartz Conglomerate	Portishead Beds	Portishead Beds

The relationship between the lithological groups set out above and Vaughan's zonal scheme (Vaughan, 1905) is shown in Fig. 3. It will be seen that in the Avon Gorge Zone K roughly corresponds to the Lower Limestone Shale Group[1], Zone Z to the Black Rock Group[2], Zones C and S to the Clifton Down Group and Zone D[3]

1 Excepting part of the Shirehampton Beds.

2 The Black Rock Group includes also part of C_1 in the Avon Gorge.

3 The highest beds now included in the Hotwells Group were not seen in the Avon Gorge and were not included by Vaughan (1905) in the Avonian D Zone.

to the Hotwells Group. In Mendip, however, the boundaries between Z, C and S zones were not defined in the same way as those of the Avon Gorge and in the Forest of Dean there is considerable difficulty in zoning the lithological groups (Trotter, 1942, p. 12).

Neither the standard coral-brachiopod zones (Vaughan, 1905, 1906; Reynolds 1936) nor the conodont zones as at present constituted (Rhodes, Austin & Druce 1969) provide a satisfactory basis for the correlation of the Dinantian rocks of Bristol and the Mendips. Both are based on extrapolated versions of the structurally disturbed and incomplete succession in the Avon Gorge where the younger Tournaisian strata of the central Mendips are probably unrepresented (Mitchell 1972) and where the upper Visean strata proved at Ashton Park (Kellaway 1967) are either concealed or badly exposed.

The best available section in the Black Rock Group is found at Burrington Combe (Green and Welch, 1965), though this may not include all the strata developed in north Somerset where the Black Rock Limestone may be up to 1100 ft. (335 m.) thick locally. On the other hand the higher Visean strata are, on the whole, poorly represented in the Mendips where they were subjected to erosion in Namurian times (Fig. 3). Thus the combined section through the Clifton Down and Hotwells groups in the Avon Gorge and Ashton Park Borehole provides the best documented and most continuous Visean section in the eastern part of the South Western Province. Individual sections in the central Mendips supply additional data, but other features are better seen in the Weston-super-Mare and Frome districts in the western and eastern Mendips respectively.

Vaughan (1905) regarded the Gully Oolite as Lower Avonian (or Clevedonian) and classified it as C_1 in the type-section in the Avon Gorge. For this reason the 'mid-Avonian break' between the top of the Gully Oolite (C_1) and the base of the Clifton Down Mudstone (C_2) has been regarded as a significant stratigraphical hiatus in this part of the succession. However, the fauna of the Sub-Oolite Bed and Gully Oolite is essentially Visean, as Vaughan (1905, p. 234) was the first to recognise. The Gully Oolite was originally included (with other Visean rocks) in the Clifton Down Group for stratigraphical reasons, but recent work has shown that the fauna of the Gully Oolite and Sub-Oolite Bed is similar to one dated as C_2 in Yorkshire (Mitchell 1972). It has therefore been suggested that the Gully Oolite should be reclassified as C_2.

This change would in many ways be beneficial, because the Burrington Oolite of the Mendips, which may in part be of the same age, has already been described as 'C_2' (Reynolds & Vaughan 1911). However, there is a question of principle involved since C_1 was first applied to the Gully Oolite in the Avon Gorge and the symbols C_1, C_{1y} and C_2 have been widely used in the South Western Province in their original sense. Some method would therefore have to be found of distinguishing the corrected from the uncorrected symbols.

Changing the significance of C_1 and C_2 in the Avon section will not, however, solve the wider problems relating to the definition of the boundary between S_1 and

S_2. The impossibility of separating C_2 and S_1 on more than a local and empirical basis is widely recognised (George 1958) and the two symbols are often combined in an attempt to group together the lower part of the Seminula Zone (S_1) and the top of the Syringothyris Zone (C_2). Unless a separation of S_1 and S_2 can be effected, the whole thickness of the Clifton Down Group has to be classified as $C_2 + S$.

Notwithstanding the additional micropalaeontological evidence which is now available there is little on which to establish a satisfactory boundary between the S_1 and S_2 subzones. Of the corals and brachiopods *Davidsonina carbonaria* is the form which is most widely favoured for this purpose. Unfortunately, its distribution is erratic, both in the Mendips (Mitchell & Green in Green & Welch 1965, p. 196) and at Bristol (Kellaway & Welch 1955; Kellaway 1967). Nevertheless it is seldom, if ever, found in the basal beds of the Clifton Down Limestone in the Bristol coalfield, though it is present locally in the middle and upper portion, and even ranges into the Hotwells Limestone above. In practice therefore it is of some local stratigraphical value even though its entry point cannot generally be relied upon as an indication of the S_2 subzone.

A rough three-fold division of the Hotwells Group can be recognised in the Bristol coalfield (Kellaway, 1967). Over a considerable part of the region between Avonmouth and Weston-super-Mare however, and in the western and southern Mendips the Visean rocks were strongly eroded and in some areas, removed, in Namurian and early Westphalian times (Fig. 3). The upper Visean succession is relatively complete at Winford, Bristol and Yate, but as the strata are traced northwards the calcareous rocks pass laterally into sandstone. This leads to the eventual disappearance of limestone bands in the Hotwells Group, together with the corals and brachiopods on which the subdivision of the Dibunophyllum Zone (D) depends.

With some adjustment of its upper limits to include the higher Dinantian rocks proved in the borehole at Ashton Park the Dibunophyllum (D) Zone can be equated with the Hotwells Group at Bristol. This leaves us with a fourfold division of the Dinantian strata in which the Lower Tournaisian is represented by the Lower Limestone Shale Group and the Upper Tournaisian by the Black Rock Group, the Lower Visean by the Clifton Down Group and the Upper Visean by the Hotwells Group (Fig. 3). Seen in this light it is doubtful whether the Avonian zonal terminology now serves any useful purpose since Tournaisian and Visean are easier to use and have a European rather than a national significance.

Zonation of the upper part of the Hotwells Group and the determination of the Dinantian–Namurian boundary is helped by the presence of goniatites of P_2 and E_1 age at Yate and Winford respectively. Brachiopods and lamellibranchs also provide confirmatory evidence and conodonts, known to be present but not so far employed for zonation, may also be of value. In 1941 it was suggested that rocks of Namurian age are present at Bristol (Moore 1941) and later work has since confirmed this. The sediments which lie between the highest Dinantian rocks and the Ashton Vale Marine Band were later given the name Quartzitic Sandstone Group (Kellaway & Welch 1955), after the intensely hard quartzitic sandstone which is the most characteristic rock type. Barren sandy and silty mudstone, mainly of non-marine origin, also makes up a considerable part of the formation. Thus the Quartzitic Sandstone Group bears little physical resemblance to the typical Millstone Grit of the North of England with which, however, it is contemporaneous.

Coal Measures occur in three main areas, namely in the Forest of Dean, Bristol and Somerset coalfields. The first coalfield is completely exposed but the others, largely concealed by Triassic rocks, are only exposed to the extent of rather more than a quarter and less than a tenth, respectively, of the total area of Coal Measures present. The natural divisions of an upper and lower shale series separated by a thick sandstone called the Pennant, have been used as a basis for classification (see Buckland and Conybeare, 1824, p. 252; Greenwell and McMurtrie, 1864, p. 19; McMurtrie, 1867, p. 48). Hitherto the scarcity of well-established marine horizons has hindered correlation with other coalfields but within the past decade the position of most of the principal marine bands has become known both in the northern and southern parts of the coalfield. Thus on the one-inch Geological Survey Malmesbury (251) Sheet published in 1970 it was possible for the first time to introduce the standard classification of the Coal Measures as defined by Stubblefield and Trotter (1957). This classification differs in several respects from the older one used on the Bristol District Special Sheet (published 1962) in which the traditional classification is employed. Other one-inch sheets (250, 264, 265, 280 and 281) published before 1970 also show the older classification.

In addition to the introduction of a classification of the Lower and Middle Coal Measures based on the distribution of marine bands the stratigraphy of the Upper Coal Measures has been reconsidered in the light of recent evidence (Kellaway 1971). The group names now proposed are in use on some of the new editions of published six-inch Geological Survey maps covering the coalfield.

The principal divisions of the Coal Measures of the Bristol and Somerset Coalfield, with generalized thickness, are as shown in Table II below:

TABLE II

			Approximate thickness in feet (metres)			
			Radstock Basin		*Coalpit Heath Basin*	
Upper Coal Measures	Supra-Pennant Measures	Publow Group	1000	(305)		
		Radstock Group	750	(229)		
		Barren Red & Farrington Groups	1400	(427)	1200	(366)
	Pennant Measures	Mangotsfield Group	1700	(518)	1400	(427)
		Downend Group	1500	(457)	300–2000	(91–609)
Middle and Lower Coal Measures		combined thickness	2200	(671)	1800	(549)

Morgan, 1885) farther south. In the Forest of Dean the bottom 25 ft. of the Crease Limestone is a crinoidal limestone, and this is overlaid by 35 ft. of oolitic limestone. In the Chepstow area the crinoidal limestone has decreased in thickness to 8 ft., giving way to the oolite, which is here 40 ft. thick. The change in thickness continues southward, and in the Bristol area the crinoidal limestone, called 'sub-Oolite' by Vaughan (1905, p. 221), though locally up to 20 ft. thick is generally much thinner, while the Gully Oolite is 90 ft. in the exposure in the Avon Gorge and 120 ft. in Goblin Combe on Broadfield Down. The crinoidal limestone, which contains abundant large orthotetids and papilionaceous chonetids, may represent the Vallis Limestone which is developed in eastern Mendip. This limestone, named after the combe of Vallis Vale near Frome, comprises a series of light-grey, coarse, oolitic, crinoidal limestones, which rest on the Black Rock Limestone. In western Mendip its development is thin, between the Black Rock Limestone and Burrington Oolite, but eastwards increases at the expense of the oolite until at Mells and Whatley the latter is not recognizable. The increasing lack of definition between contiguous facies that has been observed in passing from north to south of the region is outstandingly shown in the south-east part of Mendip at the line of junction between the Vallis and the Clifton Down Limestones. At Holwell, near Frome, interdigitations of splintery calcite mudstone containing brachiopods such as *Composita* (Clifton Down Limestone facies) alternate with coarse crinoidal limestone with large caninoid corals (Vallis Limestone facies) throughout the thickness of 220 ft. of rock. The Gully Oolite is recognizable as far south as Broadfield Down. Next above it comes the Whitehead Limestone (Wethered, 1886) in the Forest of Dean and Chepstow areas, the equivalent formation east of the Severn being the Clifton Down Mudstone. This formation was called Middle Limestone Shale by Lloyd Morgan (1885) and '*Caninia* Dolomite' (Reynolds, 1936), both of which terms are unsuitable, particularly the latter since it introduces the name of a fossil which has not yet been recognized from the stratum. The Whitehead Limestone is a pale-grey, fine-grained, calcite-dolomite mudstone and contains remarkable bands with *Garwoodia* [*Mitcheldeania*] and other calcareous algae recorded by Wethered. The Clifton Down Mudstone is of similar lithology but with fewer algal bands. In the Avon Gorge section thin bands of hard, crinoidal and oolitic limestone which are now called the Goblin Combe Oolite occur 120 ft. above the base, and above it in the section are 25 ft. of Clifton Down Mudstone. Above this, in turn, lies the Clifton Down Limestone. In places, notably in the Avon Gorge section and north of Chepstow, there is a break in sedimentation between the Clifton Down Mudstone and the Gully Oolite, sometimes referred to as the 'mid-Avonian break' but this has not been observed south of Bristol.

The Goblin Combe Oolite is distinguishable from the Gully Oolite, which it closely resembles, by the presence of *Palaeosmilia murchisoni* (olim '*Cyathophyllum*' ϕ). It increases in thickness southwards at the expense of the Clifton Down Mudstone. In Goblin Combe it is 125 ft. thick. South of Broadfield Down and in Mendip the Goblin Combe Oolite and the Gully Oolite come together and form the Burrington Oolite, a light-grey, oolitic and crinoidal limestone, well exposed in the east side of

Burrington Combe between Plumley's Den and Aveline's Hole, and here a thin band of splintery limestone may represent the last trace of the intervening Clifton Down Mudstone. Beneath the Burrington Oolite, in Mendip, a pale-grey, coarse, oolitic and crinoidal limestone, comparable with that beneath the Gully Oolite in the Bristol area, thickens eastwards as stated above to form the Vallis Limestone at the expense of the Burrington Oolite. At the top the Burrington Oolite locally interdigitates with the overlying Clifton Down Limestone making the junction indefinite, but generally in Mendip there is sufficient of the calcite mudstone facies present to fix the base of the Clifton Down Limestone. In western Mendip the Burrington Oolite contains bands with brachiopods unknown on Broadfield Down or in the Bristol area, including *Camarophoria isorhyncha* and large chonetids of the *carinata* type.

In the area south of Bristol, where Clifton Down Mudstone separates the Gully Oolite from the Goblin Combe Oolite, failure to recognize the two oolite formations caused earlier workers to regard the top of Dial Hill, Clevedon, as a *klippe* (Reynolds and Greenly, 1924, p. 458, fig. 9). Recent mapping shows that the oolite cropping out on the lower ground south-east of the hill is Goblin Combe Oolite and that the oolite on the elevated ground, once thought to be the remnant of a thrust mass, is actually Gully Oolite in normal stratigraphical position.

Locally, to the south of Bristol, basaltic submarine ashes and lavas occur in the Clifton Down Mudstone. These volcanic rocks crop out in Goblin Combe and extend eastwards to Cornwell Farm, near Butcombe Court, and other outcrops occur at Tickenham, Cadbury Camp, Uphill and Woodspring Priory, which lies north of Weston-super-Mare. Only the first three of these occurrences come within the area mapped during the six-inch survey and in each case the volcanics are found to occur between the Gully Oolite and the Goblin Combe Oolite, and not, as previously supposed, below the former (*see* Lloyd Morgan and Reynolds, 1904, p. 151; Reynolds, 1917, p. 289).

The bulk of the upper part of the Clifton Down Group consists of limestone to which the name Clifton Down Limestone has been given. Well exposed at the type locality at Great Quarry on the right bank of the Avon Gorge, this formation rests on the Clifton Down Mudstone and at its base are mudstones with more regular bedding than those of the underlying formation though continuing the same general lithological sequence; passing upwards these gradually give way to massive dark-grey limestone containing colonies of *Lithostrotion* and bands of *Productus*. The massive coral-brachiopod limestones are succeeded by oolitic, sometimes pisolitic, limestones which in places are 180 ft. thick, as at Cheddar; these frequently contain the brachiopod *Composita*. Wedging and interdigitating, the oolite is difficult to map, being developed at different horizons as shown in Plate XXXVII. This division includes local developments of oolite such as the Clifton Down (or *Seminula*) Oolite, the Brockley Oolite of Broadfield Down, the Cheddar Oolite and the Fordbury Oolite of eastern Mendip.

Silicification has occurred in parts of the Clifton Down Limestone in western and central Mendip, where, about 160 ft. above the base, the formation includes silicified *Lithostrotion* in calcite mudstone. The thickness of the silicified belt is 150 ft. in the Priddy area but it thins northwards and may be present in the Avon Gorge section as thin chert beds at the base of the Clifton Down Oolite.

Traced northwards, the Clifton Down Limestone in the northern part of the Bristol area is separated from the Clifton Down Mudstone by a thin sandstone that has been named the Lower Cromhall Sandstone (see below), a bed which is correlated with the Lower Drybrook Sandstone west of the Severn (Trotter, 1942, p. 15, fig. 3), where the Clifton Down Limestone is known as the Drybrook Limestone. This limestone around Chepstow and Tidenham Chase is up to 400 ft. thick and mainly oolite. Continuing northwards the Drybrook Sandstone thickens at the expense of the limestone until the latter is reduced to a thin band of dolomitic limestone at Clearwell in the Forest of Dean. The band here contains *Davidsonina (Cyrtina) carbonaria* which is also recorded from the Drybrook Limestone at Caerwent and from the lower part of the Clifton Down Limestone in Mendip where it occurs at two horizons 250 ft. apart.

At the top of the Clifton Down Limestone in the Bristol area and at Broadfield Down there occurs a deposit of fine-grained porcellanous limestone with wavy bedding. This was called the 'Concretionary Beds' by Vaughan (1906, p. 91) and considered by Reynolds (1921, p. 230) to be of algal origin.

Hotwells Group. The strata of this group, which succeeds the Clifton Down Group, consist mainly of limestones in the south but these are gradually replaced northwards by sandstones which eventually occupy the full thickness of the group in the Forest of Dean under the name Drybrook Sandstone.

In the district south of Bristol the poorly fossiliferous mudstone facies of the Clifton Down Limestone is in contact with the overlying oolitic and crinoidal limestone to which the name Hotwells Limestone has been given. It is rich in *Palaeosmilia murchisoni*, *Dibunophyllum bourtonense* and productids of the *giganteus* type. In places the oolitic and crinoidal limestones of this formation contain rock-types referred to as 'rubbly limestone and pseudobreccia' by Reynolds (1926, p. 25). The junction between the Clifton Down and Hotwells Limestones varies in character from place to place; thus, at Providence near Long Ashton the Hotwells Limestone rests on an irregular and bored surface of Clifton Down Limestone, in the Avon Gorge there is an alternation of calcite mudstone and oolitic crinoidal limestone, while in south-eastern Mendip, where the Clifton Down Limestone contains no mudstone but is a dark limestone, this grades upwards into the oolitic and crinoidal type. In this last area a cherty horizon, above which clisiophyllids are common, has been taken as the junction. North of Bristol the two formations are separated by the Middle Cromhall Sandstone (see below) which thickens northwards at the expense of the upper limestone. Between Emborough and Mells on the north side of Mendip are the best exposures in the Hotwells formation which show it to be up to 600 ft. thick and to consist entirely of limestone, but farther north in Broadfield Down a sandstone called the Upper Cromhall Sandstone (see below) replaces the top of the limestone in

Burrington Combe between Plumley's Den and Aveline's Hole, and here a thin band of splintery limestone may represent the last trace of the intervening Clifton Down Mudstone. Beneath the Burrington Oolite, in Mendip, a pale-grey, coarse, oolitic and crinoidal limestone, comparable with that beneath the Gully Oolite in the Bristol area, thickens eastwards as stated above to form the Vallis Limestone at the expense of the Burrington Oolite. At the top the Burrington Oolite locally interdigitates with the overlying Clifton Down Limestone making the junction indefinite, but generally in Mendip there is sufficient of the calcite mudstone facies present to fix the base of the Clifton Down Limestone. In western Mendip the Burrington Oolite contains bands with brachiopods unknown on Broadfield Down or in the Bristol area, including *Camarophoria isorhyncha* and large chonetids of the *carinata* type.

In the area south of Bristol, where Clifton Down Mudstone separates the Gully Oolite from the Goblin Combe Oolite, failure to recognize the two oolite formations caused earlier workers to regard the top of Dial Hill, Clevedon, as a *klippe* (Reynolds and Greenly, 1924, p. 458, fig. 9). Recent mapping shows that the oolite cropping out on the lower ground south-east of the hill is Goblin Combe Oolite and that the oolite on the elevated ground, once thought to be the remnant of a thrust mass, is actually Gully Oolite in normal stratigraphical position.

Locally, to the south of Bristol, basaltic submarine ashes and lavas occur in the Clifton Down Mudstone, between the Gully Oolite and the Goblin Combe Oolite. Here also the two formations were described as 'C_1' and the stratigraphy was misinterpreted through misuse of the term 'Caninia-oolite'. These volcanic rocks crop out in Broadfield Down at Goblin Combe and extend eastwards to Cornwell Farm near Butcombe. Other occurrences are known in the Clevedon–Failand ridge at Tickenham and Cadbury Camp. In each case the volcanic rocks occur above and not below the Gully Oolite as was previously supposed (Lloyd Morgan & Reynolds 1904, p. 151; Reynolds 1917, p. 289). Other volcanic rocks occur at Uphill, Worle Hill and the Woodspring promontory near Weston-super-Mare. Here there are two groups of volcanic rocks, one in the Black Rock Group as at Uphill and Middle Hope (Woodspring) the other, which occurs in the Clifton Down Group of the Worle Hill mass, as for example at Spring Cove (Reynolds 1921b), is comparable in age with the Goblin Combe volcanics of Broadfield Down.

Massive limestone forms the upper part of the Clifton Down Group in the type locality of the Clifton Down Limestone at the Great (or Tenniscourt) Quarry in the Avon Gorge. The base of the Clifton Down Limestone is marked by a thin regularly bedded sandy limestone which may represent the most southerly known leaf of the Lower Cromhall Sandstone. The succeeding rocks consist mainly of calcite mudstone with some shale bands. They are poorly fossiliferous at the base but pass up into rocks in which *Composita*, *Lithostrotion*, productids and other fossils are increasingly abundant. Some well-marked fossil beds seen in the Great Quarry include the Trilobite Bed and *Caninia-bristolensis* Bed (Reynolds 1921; Loupekine 1953). The massive coral-brachiopod limestones are succeeded by oolitic, sometimes pisolitic, limestone which in places are 180 ft. thick, as at Cheddar; these commonly contain the brachiopod *Composita*.

Millstone Grit Series

In the Ashton Park Borehole a thickness of 670 ft. of sediments lies between the Ashton Vale Marine Bed and the top of strata that can be referred with confidence to the Carboniferous Limestone Series. These beds have been called the Quartzitic Sandstone Group. In the borehole there are 440 ft. of intensely hard quartzitic sandstone overlying 50 ft. of chert beds. The base of these is taken as the base of the Quartzitic Sandstone Group. Above the 'quartzites' occur 117 ft. of sandstones, mudstones and shales with *Lingula*, resembling typical Coal Measures sediments, but, since they lie below the Ashton Vale Marine Bed, which is taken as the base of the Coal Measures, they are placed in the Quartzitic Sandstone Group. These upper beds appear to have a restricted distribution within the Bristol 'syncline' (see Plate XXXVII). In Mendip the Ashton Vale Marine Bed rests directly upon quartzitic sandstones, while to the north of Bristol the upper beds have either thinned out or have been cut out by Coal Measures.

The cherts have a wider distribution and on the eastern margin of the Bristol Coalfield, from Cromhall to Chipping Sodbury, form a recognizable band overlying the Tanhouse Limestone. At one place only, namely at Crown Hill, Winford, sixteen miles south-west of Chipping Sodbury, have the cherts yielded goniatites suggesting a Millstone Grit age. With the exception of Crown Hill and Redhill, south of Bristol, there are no exposures of the cherts south of Chipping Sodbury unless a thin desilicified band at Wick can be regarded as their representative.

The quartzitic sandstones are the most widespread and characteristic members of the series and are well exposed on the northern side of Mendip between Emborough and Mells. They also occur on the southern slope of Brandon Hill, Bristol, and on the high ground at the Royal Fort. Their succession at Wick has been described by Stanley Smith (1930).

The upper sandstone and shale bands seem to occur only in the neighbourhood of the Bristol 'syncline' and to die out southwards or to be cut out under overlapping Coal Measures. They have yielded no fossils other than *Lingula*.

The available evidence suggests that the Quartzitic Sandstone Group reaches its maximum development in the Bristol 'syncline'.

Coal Measures

The sequence and the thicknesses of Coal Measures strata are given in Fig. 4. The maximum thickness of measures occurs in the Somerset Coalfield. Four marine beds have been found in the Bristol Coalfield, namely, in upward succession those of Ashton Vale, Harry Stoke, Croft's End and Winterbourne. In addition a number of *Lingula*-bearing beds were found above the Ashton Vale Marine Bed in the Ashton Park Borehole. Details regarding the above are given by Welch and Kellaway (1955).

The Ashton Vale Marine Bed has been detected as far north as Harry Stoke, four miles north of Bristol. Farther north it may be absent due to overstep, a condition which is well marked near the line of the Lower Severn Axis, particularly in the Nailsea and Failand area where Pennant Sandstone oversteps the Carboniferous

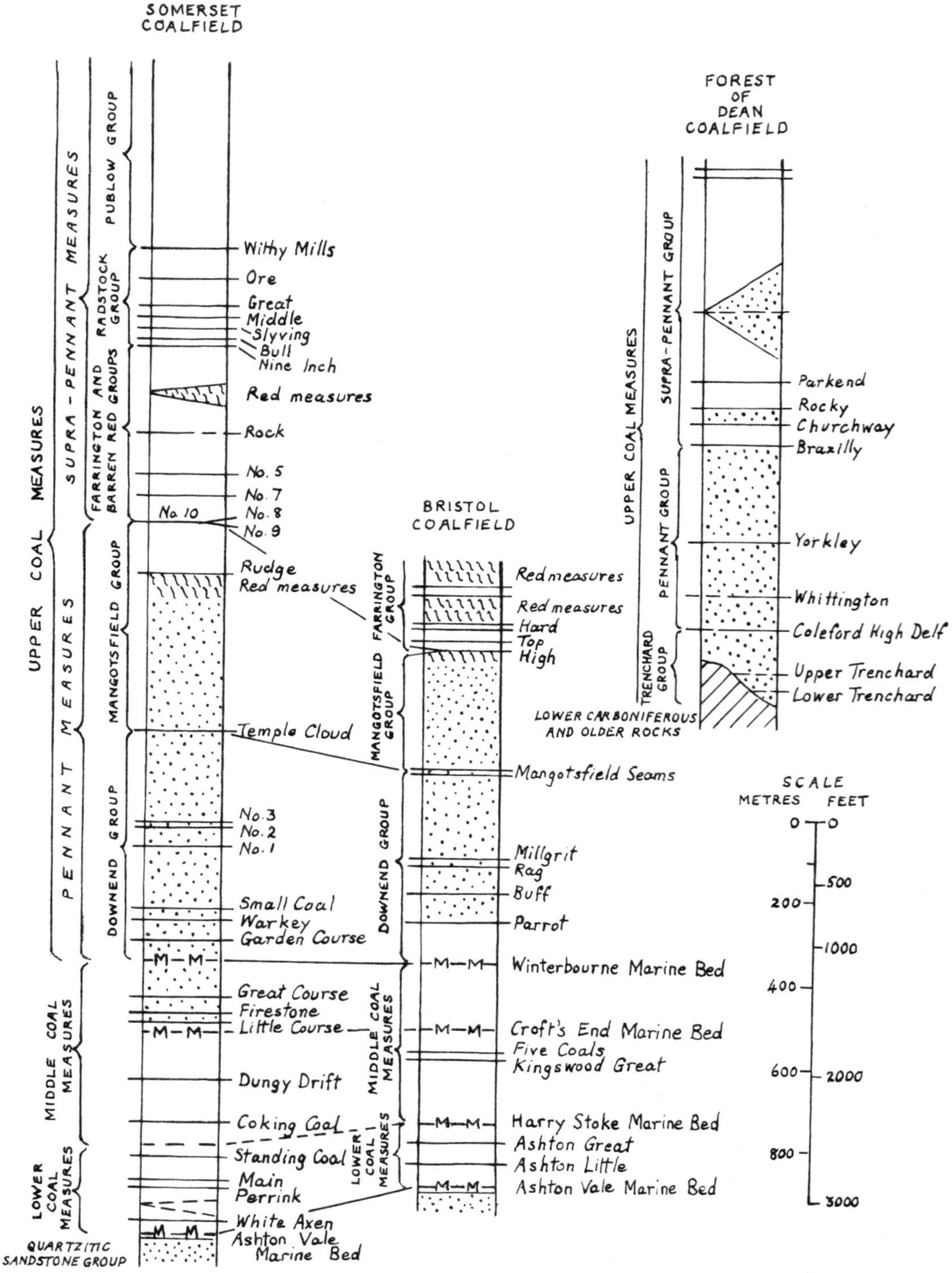

FIG. 4. *Comparative sections of the Bristol, Somerset and Forest of Dean Coalfields. (Crown copyright reserved. Reproduced by permission of the Director, H.M. Geological Survey.)*

The oolite is difficult to map continuously, being developed at different horizons. Among the more important local oolitic formations are the *Seminula*-Oolite of the Avon Gorge, the Brockley Oolite of Broadfield Down, the Cheddar Oolite and the Fordbury Oolite of the eastern Mendips.

Silicification has occurred in parts of the Clifton Down Limestone in western and central Mendip, where, about 160 ft. above the base, the formation includes silicified *Lithostrotion* in calcite mudstone. The thickness of the silicified belt is 150 ft. in the Priddy area but it thins northwards and may be present in the Avon Gorge section as thin chert beds at the base of the Clifton Down Oolite.

Traced northwards, the Clifton Down Limestone in the northern part of the Bristol area is separated from the Clifton Down Mudstone by a thin sandstone that has been named the Lower Cromhall Sandstone (see below), a bed which is correlated with the Lower Drybook Sandstone west of the Severn (Trotter, 1942, p. 15, fig. 3), where the Clifton Down Limestone is known as the Drybrook Limestone. This limestone around Chepstow and Tidenham Chase is up to 400 ft. thick and mainly oolite. Continuing northwards the Drybrook Sandstone thickens at the expense of the limestone until the latter is reduced to a thin band of dolomitic limestone at Clearwell in the Forest of Dean. The band here contains *Davidsonina* (*Cyrtina*) *carbonaria* which is also recorded from the Drybrook Limestone at Caerwent and from the lower part of the Clifton Down Limestone in Mendip where it occurs at two horizons 250 ft. apart.

In the Bristol coalfield and Broadfield Down the upper part of the Clifton Down Limestone is marked by beds of very fine-grained limestone showing algal and stromatolithic structures. These were called Concretionary Beds by Vaughan (1906, p. 91) and were considered by Reynolds (1921a, p. 230) to be of algal origin. Locally they are interbedded with shaly layers and with limestones yielding algae, polyzoa, brachiopods, lamellibranchs and *Spirorbis*. Among the corals, *Chaetetes septosus* (Fleming) is a characteristic form.

Hotwells Group. The strata of this group, which succeeds the Clifton Down Group, consist mainly of limestones in the south but these are gradually replaced northwards by sandstones which eventually occupy the full thickness of the group in the Forest of Dean under the name Drybrook Sandstone.

In the district south of Bristol the poorly fossiliferous mudstone facies of the Clifton Down Limestone is in contact with the overlying oolitic and crinoidal limestone to which the name Hotwells Limestone has been given. It is rich in *Palaeosmilia murchisoni*, *Dibunophyllum bourtonense* and productids of the *giganteus* type. In places the oolitic and crinoidal limestones of this formation contain rock-types referred to as 'rubbly limestone and pseudobreccia' by Reynolds (1926, p. 25). The junction between the Clifton Down and Hotwells Limestones varies in character from place to place; thus, at Providence near Long Ashton the Hotwells Limestone rests on an irregular and bored surface of Clifton Down Limestone, in the Avon Gorge there is an alternation of calcite mudstone and oolitic crinoidal limestone, while in south-eastern Mendip, where the Clifton Down Limestone contains no mudstone but is a dark limestone, this grades upwards into the oolitic and crinoidal type. In this last area a cherty horizon, above which clisiophyllids are common, has been taken as the junction. North of Bristol the two formations are separated by the Middle Cromhall Sandstone (see below) which thickens northwards at the expense of the upper limestone. Between Emborough and Mells on the north side of Mendip are the best exposures in the Hotwells formation which show it to be up to 600 ft. thick and to consist entirely of limestone, but farther north in Broadfield Down a sandstone called the Upper Cromhall Sandstone (see below) replaces the top of the limestone in increasing thickness towards Bristol. Thus at Ebbor upper Namurian strata rest directly on Hotwells Limestone, the lower Namurian as well as the highest Dinantian rocks being absent. In Broadfield Down notably around Winford (Kellaway 1967, fig. 4), the passage of the upper part of the Hotwells Group into Upper Cromhall Sandstone is well advanced though there is no sign of the Middle Cromhall Sandstone. These conditions continue northwards to Ashton Park and the Avon Gorge at Bristol where some massive beds of sandstone are found in the Hotwells Group. Fossiliferous limestones are interbedded with the sandstones and these include the Rownham Hill Coral Bed with its rich fauna of *Lonsdaleia floriformis*, *Cyathophyllum regium* and other simple and compound corals. Other important limestone bands in the upper part of the Hotwells Group include the Tanhouse Limestone of Yate in which Stanley Smith (1942) recorded a high Visean fauna including goniatites of P_2 age.

The sandstones at the top of the Carboniferous Limestone Series were shown on the old geological maps as Millstone Grit, but they have been demonstrated to be of Carboniferous Limestone age in the Forest of Dean by Sibly (1919) and in the north of Bristol Coalfield by Stanley Smith (1942). As stated above, three sandstone beds named Lower, Middle and Upper Cromhall Sandstones occur respectively at the base of the Clifton Down Limestone, at the base of the Hotwells Limestone and at the top of the Hotwells Limestone. Passing northwards these are first encountered at the latitude of Broadfield Down (Upper Cromhall Sandstone) and at the northern part of the Bristol Coalfield (Lower and Middle Cromhall Sandstones). Thence they expand in thickness northwards, their relationship being well seen at Cromhall. Though the sandstones pass northwards into the Drybrook Sandstone, west of the Severn, the new name has been adopted for the deposits east of the Severn since at Drybrook, the type locality, only the lower part of the sequence is present, the upper part having been cut out by the overstep of the Coal Measures.[1]

The Lower Cromhall Sandstone thickens northwards to 140 ft. at Cromhall and west of the Severn becomes known as the Lower Drybrook Sandstone. It continues to thicken northwards from 73 ft. at Chepstow to 170 ft. at Tidenham and reaches a maximum of 350 ft. at Cinderford. North of this point it merges with the main mass of the Drybrook Sandstone.

The Middle Cromhall Sandstone thickens northwards and merges with the Upper

[1] Kellaway, 1967.

Cromhall Sandstone at Cromhall. Sandy carbonaceous bands and thin coaly layers occur in this formation at Wick (Stanley Smith, 1930, pp. 349–80); and at Brentry, north of Bristol, it contains pockets of red shale and calcite mudstone with *Spirorbis*. West of the Severn at Ifton, near Severn Tunnel Junction, the upper surface of the Drybrook Limestone (the Clifton Down Limestone) is pocketed with sandstone and shale, the latter with *Spirorbis*. The deposit at Ifton, possibly of Middle Cromhall Sandstone age, has been classed as Millstone Grit (Dixon, 1921; Moore, 1941) but the sandstone overlying the Drybrook Limestone at Tidenham Chase, named Upper Drybrook Sandstone by Trotter (1942, p. 15, fig. 3), is almost certainly the equivalent of the Middle Cromhall Sandstone.

The Upper Cromhall Sandstone includes thin sandy limestones with *Buxtonia* near the Winford reddle works on Broadfield Down. Thickening northwards towards Bristol it was proved to be 320 ft. thick in the Ashton Park Borehole. At this locality it consists of grits, sandstones, decalcified limestones and thin shale bands, grey when unweathered but reddened in weathered parts by the decomposition of included pyrites.

Namurian (Millstone Grit Series)

In the Ashton Park Borehole (Kellaway 1967) a thickness of 670 ft. of sediments lies between the Ashton Vale Marine Band and the highest strata that can be referred with confidence to the Dinantian. These beds are now known as the Quartzitic Sandstone Group. They may be divided into a lower and an upper division the boundary being placed at a marine band proved at a depth of 708 ft. (238 m.) in the Ashton Park Borehole. The lower division is thought to be mainly of E_1–E_2 age and consists of basal mudstone with cherts which are equated with the *Eumorphoceras*-bearing chert of Winford (Kellaway & Welch 1955). The mudstones and cherts average about 50 ft. in thickness in the Bristol area and contain some thin quartzitic sandstones. Above them lie massive, intensely hard quartzitic and pebbly sandstones known as Brandon Hill Grit. A similar succession is found at Yate and Rangeworthy in the north-eastern part of the Bristol coalfield. Here the Tanhouse chert, overlying the (P_2) Tanhouse Limestone, forms the base of the Namurian. The Quartzitic Sandstone Group is now known to be thicker at Yate than at Bristol (Kellaway 1971) but its general character is much the same and it appears to be conformable with the underlying Dinantian rocks.

South of Bristol the basal Namurian cherts crop out at Winford and Redhill on the eastern and southern flanks of Broadfield Down. They are not present in the Mendips where the lower division of the Quartzitic Sandstone Group has not been identified. In those localities such as Ebbor Gorge where the basal Westphalian is only separated from the Dinantian by thin mudstones and sandstones of Namurian age the latter appear to be conformable with the overlying Ashton Vale Marine Band and are thought to belong to the upper division of the Quartzitic Sandstone Group. It therefore appears that there may be a major stratigraphical break between the Namurian and the Dinantian over a considerable area in the southern and western Mendips. Somewhat similar conditions characterise the western side of the Bristol and Somerset coalfield where the Quartzitic Sandstone Group is thought to rest unconformably on older rocks.

The Quartzitic Sandstone Group is seldom well exposed. It forms a number of hills and ridges in and around Bristol, notably at Ashton Hill, Brandon Hill and Royal Fort. The full thickness of the group is seen in the Wick inlier but the rocks are now poorly exposed. At Yate and Chipping Sodbury also there is little opportunity of studying either the basal cherts or the mudstones and quartzitic sandstones which crop on to the east side of the coalfield.

West of the Severn infillings and pockets of quartzitic sandstone and shale at Ifton are thought to be Namurian. Elsewhere in the Chepstow and Forest of Dean area the occurrence of Namurian rocks is problematical. It is possible that some of the quartzitic sandstones attributed to the 'Drybrook Sandstone' may be of Namurian age but no positive evidence to this effect has been recorded.

Westphalian (Coal Measures)

The sequence and the thicknesses of Coal Measures strata are given in Fig. 4. The maximum thickness of measures occurs in the Somerset Coalfield. Four marine bands have been found in the Bristol Coalfield, namely, in upward succession those of Ashton Vale, Harry Stoke, Croft's End and Winterbourne. In addition a number of *Lingula*-bearing beds were found above the Ashton Vale Marine Band in the Ashton Park Borehole (Kellaway 1967). The Ashton Vale Marine Band has been detected as far north as Harry Stoke, four miles north of Bristol and at Wick on the eastern side of the Bristol Coalfield. Here it is very thin. In Somerset however it is thicker and widely distributed from Barrow Gurney to Ebbor (Green & Welch 1965, Kellaway 1967) and eastwards to Vobster. It appears to be generally missing in the Avonmouth-Clevedon area where Upper Coal Measures rest locally on the Carboniferous Limestone and Old Red Sandstone.

On goniatite evidence there are grounds for correlating the Ashton Vale Marine Band with the *G. subcrenatum* Marine Band of South Wales and the Pot Clay of Yorkshire, and, on goniatite and brachiopod evidence, for correlating the Croft's End Marine Band with the Cefn Coed of South Wales and the Mansfield of Yorkshire. In the case of the Harry Stoke Marine Band faunal evidence is weak, but on stratigraphical grounds it seems likely that this represents the Amman of South Wales. The Winterbourne Marine Band is thought to represent the Upper Cwm Gorse of South Wales and is of great importance in defining the top of the Middle Coal Measures.

The Westphalian Coal Measures of the Bristol & Somerset coalfields were formerly divided into (1) Lower Coal Series, including the Vobster Group (McMurtrie, 1867), (2) Pennant Series including the former New Rock Group (McMurtrie, 1867) and the Upper Coal Series. These divisions have now been abandoned in favour of stratigraphical units based on the distribution of marine bands. In the Upper Coal Measures however the Farrington Group, Barren Red Group, Radstock Group and Publow Group are based partly on lithology and partly on the plants and non-marine faunas

(Kellaway 1971). Their approximate thicknesses are shown in Table II. The Radstock Group and Publow Group are not known in the Bristol coalfield and may have been removed by later erosion.

In the Forest of Dean coalfield marine bands are unknown and it is possible that most if not all of the Coal Measures are of Upper Westphalian age. The only area where marine strata have been located on the west side of the Severn is situated near Portskewett where Mr. K. Taylor has found mudstones with a *Lingula*-band beneath Pennant Sandstone. The age of the marine band is uncertain but it may represent one of the bands in the Lower or Middle Coal Measures.

The Upper Coal Measures of the Forest of Dean are divided into (1) the Trenchard Group, (2) the Pennant Group and (3) the Supra-Pennant Group, but there is no clear correlation between them and the divisions of the Bristol district.

The Bristol and Somerset coalfields are separated geologically by the Kingswood Anticline, an east-west structure of highly folded and faulted measures of the Lower Coal Series, the higher parts of the Coal Measures having been eroded.

Most of the seams worked in the Lower Coal Measures of the Bristol Coalfield north of the Kingswood Anticline are very thin or impersistent. At Kingswood and Yate the principal worked seams are now known to lie between the Crofts End Marine Band and the Harry Stoke Marine Band (Kellaway 1971). In terms of non-marine lamellibranch zones this is the lower part of the *Similis-pulchra* zone. South of the Kingswood Anticline the same group of seams, including the Bedminster Great Vein, was worked at Bedminster and Ashton but in this area Lower Coal Measures seams, notably the Ashton Great Vein, were also of economic importance. The most concentrated area of coal working is situated in east Bristol and the western and central part of the Kingswood area. Here coal working is of great antiquity and the principal seams may have been worked at the surface from Roman times onwards. Much of the built-up area of Easton, St. George's, Kingswood, Hanham, Oldland and Warmley is underlain by old mine workings, both deep and shallow. Very little coal working has taken place in the area to the north-west of Kingswood. The presence of the Kingswood Great Vein and other seams was established in the Hambrook-Harry Stoke-Stoke Gifford area in the period following the end of the war of 1939-45. In the changing economic conditions however it was found to be unprofitable to continue working and the Harry Stoke Drift Mine closed in 1963, thus bringing to an end more than 750 years of coal mining in the Bristol area. North of the anticline, the Coalpit Heath Basin is generally an area of low dip except along the eastern margin, where the inclination of the strata increases to 40^0, and at the western margin, where the beds are much disturbed. The basin is crossed by the north-south Coalpit Heath Fault, of 300ft. downthrow east, which runs approximately down its centre, and by the smaller east–west Kidney Hill Fault. Measures thought to belong to the Farrington Group, which occur near the centre of the basin and have been exhaustively worked, are overlain by Barren Red Measures.

The Somerset Coalfield, south of the Kingswood Anticline, contains the largest area of Coal Measures in the region and is roughly oval-shaped with a south-south-easterly axis terminating southwards against Mendip. There is a concealed extension westwards that becomes narrower as it passes between the Carboniferous Limestone masses of Broadfield Down and Mendip and also a small detached basin lying to the west. The presence of Coal Measures in a borehole at Westbury, Wilts., suggests a possible extension of the coalfield eastwards. The basin is affected by north–south and east–west faults and overthrusts. Those of the latter trend are the more important, and two of them namely the Southern Overthrust and the Farmborough Compression Belt, some six miles apart, divide the basin naturally into three parts. The Southern Overthrust is a belt or zone in which thrust-faulting is developed and the measures are highly inclined or inverted. It is probably the eastward extension of the great Emborough Thrust that has been traced westwards through the Carboniferous Limestone as far as Cheddar. The Farmborough Compression Belt is a zone of reversed faulting in which three or four lap-faults repeat the succession so that coals of the Radstock and Farrington Groups lie piled up on one another in a series of elongated slices; the uppermost fault is usually referred to as the Farmborough Fault. Between the Southern Overthrust and Mendip is the Nettlebridge area where coals in the Lower Coal Series and in the lower part of the Pennant Series have been extensively exploited. The incompetent shaly strata of the Lower Coal Series between the competent Carboniferous Limestone and the Pennant Sandstone have been violently upturned, overturned and crushed, as was well seen in the fantastic structures proved in the old collieries at Vobster and Edford, yet the coals in the overlying Pennant, although inverted, have suffered but little.

Between the Southern Overthrust and the Farmborough Compression Belt lies the Radstock Basin, which has been the most extensively explored and worked part of the Somerset Coalfield in the measures above the Pennant. Many of the faults affecting the strata are east–west low-angle overthrusts which cause 'overlap' and repetition of the coal seams as in the case of the Radstock Slide, which in the upper parts is steep but decreases in dip in the lower parts and may ultimately merge into a bedding-plane slip. In the Camerton area in the northern part of the Radstock Basin a series of east–west faults with northerly downthrow ranging up to over 200 ft. occurs as the Farmborough Compression Belt is approached from the south.

The chief north–south fault of the Radstock Basin is the Clandown or 100-Fathom Fault, trending north–north-west and lying immediately west of Radstock. The maximum throw is 720 ft. down west, just north of the town; the structure consists of a belt of several fractures with low dip, which southwards spreads to a width of half a mile. This fault, though of Armorican age, heaves the east–west thrusts and so slightly post-dates them. The Clandown Fault diminishes rapidly in throw south of Radstock, and the west-throwing faulting is now taken up by the Luckington Fault running half a mile to the west *en échelon* with it and on a roughly parallel course. Growing southwards, this has a vertical displacement of 750 ft. in the workings of Newbury Colliery and farther south in Mendip affects the Carboniferous Limestone.

Between the Farmborough Compression Belt and the Kingswood Anticline is the

Pensford Basin in the centre of which occurs the greatest thickness of the highest Coal Measures in the succession, the Publow Group. This group, partly arenaceous, has yielded no workable coals. Mining formerly confined to the Pensford and Bromley area in the south–west of the basin has now ceased and evidence from workings and boreholes suggests that the coals of the Radstock and Farrington Groups deteriorate along a north–south line running through the centre of the basin. The deterioration, shown by increase of dirt-partings and thinning of individual seams, is depositional in origin.

West of the main coalfields are (1) the small basin of Nailsea, where 800 ft. of Pennant Measures rest on 1,000 ft. of shales and coals of the Lower Coal Series and in which workings were abandoned late in the nineteenth century, (2) the small abandoned field at Clapton-in-Gordano, which is believed to be mainly of Pennant Measures and (3) the Avonmouth Basin, north–east of the port, where concealed Coal Measures, probably of the Upper Coal Series, contain at least two coals.

In the Forest of Dean Coalfield the Coal Measures and underlying rocks occupy a basin-shaped fold with axis running roughly north–south but it is noteworthy that the axis of the more gently folded Coal Measures syncline lies east of, but parallel to, that of the older rocks (*see* Kellaway and Welch, 1948, fig. 9, p. 32). As a result, the Coal Measures rest unconformably upon the Carboniferous Limestone Series and in places along the eastern margin overstep onto the Old Red Sandstone.

Only the southern tip of the Forest of Dean Coalfield comes within the area covered by the $\frac{1}{4}$-inch geological map, specially printed for the visit of the British Association to Bristol. The lowest Measures seen, known as the Trenchard Group, comprise a variable series of sandstones, shales and conglomerates with one coal seam (the Trenchard Seam) which splits when traced northwards. The base of the overlying Pennant is drawn at the bottom of the Coleford High Delf, the most important seam in the coalfield. This coal, averaging $3\frac{1}{2}$ to 5 ft. in thickness, extends throughout the coalfield. In the overlying 800 ft. of Pennant two smaller seams, the Whittington and Yorkley, are developed.

MESOZOIC

(D. T. D.)

CONTINENTAL TRIAS

The intensive destruction of the Palaeozoic rocks consequent upon the Armorican Orogeny for long left no sediments in our area, deposits which must often have been rapidly built up being as rapidly removed. At the very end of the continental New Red Sandstone period the continuous movement of debris was at last slowed down by reduction of relief, and from this time date the fossil screes known as the Dolomitic Conglomerate, and the red sandstones and marls which fill the basins between the Palaeozoic uplands, largely blanketing the Coal Measures.

The Dolomitic Conglomerate, often a breccia, forms a narrow but persistent margin to the upstanding outcrops of Old Red Sandstone and Carboniferous Limestone south of the Avon, namely Mendip, Broadfield Down and the narrow ridges in the area between Clifton, Clevedon and Portishead (Lean, 1888). North of the river it is less consistently developed. The composition of the Dolomitic Conglomerate varies with the rocks against which it lies; in texture it varies from tumbled masses of enormous boulders to beds of small pebbles. The matrix is often also clastic, but in many places cavities have been subsequently filled with crystalline calcite. Around Clevedon the Dolomitic Conglomerate passes laterally into a yellow magnesian limestone.

Away from the Palaeozoic uplands the Dolomitic Conglomerate gives place to the Red Marls, with sandstones locally present often in the lower part of the succession. The thickness of these deposits is quite inconstant, and no standard section can be given; but it is seldom greater than 200 ft., and usually less. At the top are 15 to 20 ft. of Tea Green Marls. The Red Marls are fine dolomitic silts, stained with haematite and, being composed largely of silica (Reynolds, 1946, p. 29), the traditional term 'marl' is a misnomer. Geodes of quartz, collected in the past as 'Bristol Diamonds', occur locally in the Red Marls. More important minerals, however, are found in the evaporite deposits at a level about 50 ft. below the top of the Red Marls. Gypsum is the usual mineral, but a local peculiarity is celestine, which occurs at a number of places and is at present exploited at Yate. Calamine, haematite and ochre have also been obtained from the Trias in the past.

The Triassic rocks are barren of fossils except for rare traces of the terrestrial fauna. In 1836 bones of the dinosaurs *Thecodontosaurus* and *Palaeosaurus* were found in the Dolomitic Conglomerate of Durdham Down, Bristol, and recently the bones of small rhynchocephalian reptiles have been collected in abundance in Triassic fissure infillings in Mendip and at Cromhall where they are associated with the ostracod *Euestheria*.

RHAETIC

The Rhaetic rocks, belonging to the closing stages of the Triassic period, show no special features in their normal development, which is that characteristic of south-western England (Reynolds, 1946; Richardson, 1904; 1911). The local succession is:

Upper Rhaetic	*Cotham Beds*. Cotham Marble at the top. Below are light-grey mudstones and marls. Horizons with the plant *Naiadites*, with *Euestheria* and with marine bivalves . .	to 11 feet
Lower Rhaetic	*Westbury Beds*. Thin-bedded black shales with a fauna of chiefly small lamellibranchs including *Pteria contorta*, *Chlamys valoniensis*, *Schizodus ewaldi*. Occasional limestone bands. At the base, impersistently, the Bone Bed with remains of *Ceratodus*, other fish and saurians	to 14 feet

The hills of the Triassic landscape remained as islands in the Rhaetic sea, towards them the Rhaetic beds become thinner, while along the shorelines they become sandy or conglomeratic. In many places the Bone Bed marks a period of wave-erosion which was the first effect of the transgression, but locally black shale deposition began earlier or later than the Bone Bed. The Westbury Beds were deposited by the sea, but the conspicuous absence from the fauna of many marine organisms, notably brachiopods, cephalopods and echinoderms, indicates abnormal, probably reduced, salinity. During the formation of the Cotham Beds lacustrine conditions prevailed, and the rocks are barren for much of the thickness. Occasional, temporary incursions of the sea allowed a fauna of fish and molluscs to enjoy a brief field-day.

The Cotham Marble is a locally famous rock, never more than about 9 in. thick but persistent over a considerable area. It has an irregular, crinkled upper surface and when broken reveals a 'landscape' pattern inside. Possible modes of origin for this have been discussed by several writers (Short, 1903; Thompson, 1894; Woodward, 1892).

JURASSIC

The rocks to be described in this section have a special interest for the stratigraphical geologist, for it was in that part of the Jurassic outcrop nearest to Bristol, namely the environs of Bath, that William Smith established the principles of stratigraphy, and here the familiar names of the Lower and Middle Jurassic formations, Lias, Inferior Oolite, Fuller's Earth and Great Oolite were first employed by Smith and the Rev. Joseph Townsend.

Marine conditions, first in evidence during the Lower Rhaetic, were fully established at the beginning of Blue Lias times, and continued throughout the Jurassic. The hilly landscape of late Triassic times continued to exert an influence, albeit steadily diminishing, on deposition in the area throughout the Lower and Middle Jurassic, and almost every formation shows important lateral variations. Attenuated or condensed sequences are prominent in the neighbourhood of Mendip, while more normal developments occur farther north.

Lower Jurassic or Lias

The earliest formation is the White Lias, alternating thin beds of shale and porcellanous limestone, which was laid down to a maximum thickness of about 20 ft. in basins north and south of Mendip, but peters out to nothing towards the Bristol Channel. A shallow-water, perhaps lagoonal deposit, it has a modest marine fauna. The summit of the White Lias is a limestone bed, up to 18 in. thick, known as the Sun Bed or Jew Stone, penetrated by U-shaped burrows and marking a slight interruption of sedimentation. The Blue Lias rests upon it and consists of darker and less pure limestones; where fully developed, as at Saltford, the Blue Lias is 60 ft. thick and shows close resemblance, both in lithology and zonal subdivisions, to the thicker development near Lyme Regis, in Dorset. Ammonites now abounded, and species replaced one another in rapid succession (Donovan, 1952). The succeeding Lower

Lias clays are seldom exposed and little known, and Lonsdale's thickness of 200 ft. (1832, p. 243), for the neighbourhood of Bath, has hardly been superseded. Northwards to Chipping Sodbury a thickness of about 200 ft. for the Lower Lias seems to be maintained. South of the Avon, however, both the Blue Lias and the lower part of the clays thin rapidly, and in a belt four or five miles wide north of Mendip almost all the Lower Lias is compressed into a series of condensed deposits seldom more than about 10 ft. thick. Above these are about 120 ft. of clays of the normal facies, belonging to the zone of *Prodactylioceras davoei*, the highest zone of the Lower Lias. The condensed deposits are often very fossiliferous and a number of successive faunas have been recognized (Tutcher and Trueman, 1925). At the beginning of Lias times, at least, some of the Palaeozoic uplands continued to form islands or shoals, and a littoral, conglomeratic facies is found at the eastern end of Mendip and at Broadfield Down. South-west of East Harptree a cherty facies of the Lower Lias spreads over part of Mendip top.

The Middle Lias is missing between the Avon and the south side of Mendip, except for a remnant of ironshot oolite, 5 ft. 6 in. thick, on Dundry Hill, a local representative of the Marlstone. Along the main scarp north of Bath the Middle Lias reappears and a thin representative is present at Sodbury. Farther north it increases in thickness.

The Upper Lias is absent in eastern Mendip. Throughout the rest of the area it is represented by fine clayey sands and ferruginous, condensed deposits crowded with ammonites. As is well known, both these facies are diachronic. Between Mendip and Bath the condensed deposit ('Junction Bed'), about 4 ft. thick, is below the sands, resting non-sequentially on Lower Lias, and is succeeded by the Midford Sands, which perhaps reach 100 ft. in thickness and fall within the *jurense* zone of the Upper Lias (Gorham, 1930). Between Bath and Sodbury the sandy facies becomes rapidly earlier, and at Sodbury the Cotteswold Sands, about 180 ft. thick, span the top of the *bifrons* and base of the *jurense* zones. They are now capped by another condensed deposit ('Cephalopod Bed') containing fossils of the *jurense* zone. Kellaway and Welch have suggested that the sandy facies along the main outcrop is due to the coincidence of the outcrop with their 'Bath Axis' (1948, fig. 20). At Dundry Hill, to the west of the axis, the Upper Lias consists of a condensed deposit representing the lower zones, capped by about 60 ft. of clay belonging to the upper part of the *jurense* zone.

Middle Jurassic

The Middle Jurassic opens with elevation of the sea-floor and perhaps gentle folding, so that erosion of existing deposits replaced deposition throughout the greater part of the area. Along the main outcrop, from eastern Mendip where is the famous unconformity of Upper Inferior Oolite on wave-planed Carboniferous Limestone, northwards nearly to Sodbury, only Upper Inferior Oolite is present, resting unconformably on the older rocks. The basal member is the fossiliferous Upper Trigonia Grit, a limestone in spite of its name, followed by other organic and oolitic limestones to a total thickness of about 30 ft. (Richardson, 1907; 1910). A little to the south of Sodbury oolites of the Lower Inferior Oolite appear, and thicken rapidly northwards. The most notable outcrop of Inferior Oolite in the area, however, is at Dundry Hill, now almost within the boundary of Bristol and only four miles south of the centre of the city. In the days when quarries were working the hill was the resort of many collectors, and was exhaustively studied by Buckman and Wilson (1896). Lower, Middle and Upper Inferior Oolite are all represented, the first two subdivisions by a total of about 12 ft. of condensed, highly fossiliferous deposits, the highest by the Dundry Freestone, from 4 to 27 ft. thick, and associated beds. The old collections contain important series of ammonites, especially of the families Oppelidae, Otoitidae and Sonninidae, besides fossils of various other classes.

In eastern Somerset the Inferior and Great Oolite limestones are separated by the argillaceous Fuller's Earth. The succession at Bath is:

Upper Fuller's Earth Clay	90 ft.
Fuller's Earth Rock	25 ft.
Lower Fuller's Earth Clay	30 ft.

the thicknesses being approximate. The Lower Fuller's Earth contains abundant fossils, including banks of *Ostrea acuminata*, and the Fuller's Earth Rock is highly fossiliferous, yielding ammonites, brachiopods and lamellibranchs. The Upper Fuller's Earth is nearly barren. Commercial Fuller's Earth forms a band near the top of the upper division, exploited on the southern outskirts of Bath. Northwards from Bath Arkell and Donovan (1952) have demonstrated that lateral changes occur; the rock-band splits in two, and shortly afterwards, in the neighbourhood of Sodbury, the Upper Fuller's Earth Clay wedges out and the upper rock-band becomes joined to the Great Oolite Limestones. Farther north still the process is repeated by the middle clay and the lower rock-band (Fig. 5).

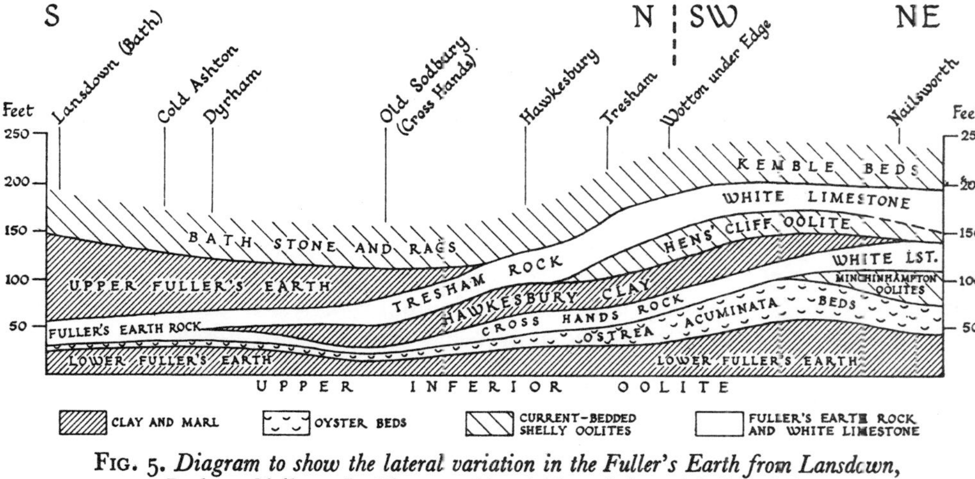

FIG. 5. *Diagram to show the lateral variation in the Fuller's Earth from Lansdown, near Bath, to Nailsworth, Gloucestershire.* (*Adapted from Arkell and Donovan.*)

In south-eastern Somerset the argillaceous sedimentation begun by the Fuller's Earth continued, with little variation, throughout the rest of the Middle Jurassic, varied near the end of that time by some shelly limestones and a sandbank (the Hinton Sands) of the Forest Marble. Around Bath and in the country to the north, however, deposition of the Fuller's Earth was ended by the formation of great banks of ooliths and broken shells, perhaps caused by a shallowing of the sea, which build the Great Oolite Limestones and include the fine freestones known as Bath Stone. The maximum thickness of the Great Oolite Limestones east of Bath, where the stone is now mined, may be of the order of 100 ft., but is doubtless variable. The limestones are succeeded by the predominantly argillaceous Forest Marble, which covers the dip slopes east of Bath and is the highest formation which will be mentioned in this account. At Bradford-on-Avon the base of the Forest Marble is marked by the famous Bradford Clay whose basal part yielded numberless calices of the crinoid *Apiocrinus parkinsoni*, as well as brachiopods and other fossils, to old collectors. Farther north there may be a more gradual passage between the two formations.

PLEISTOCENE

The Pleistocene history of the area commences with the lower reaches of the Avon flowing at a level about 100 ft. higher than to-day, and depositing gravels which at Kelston, Brislington, St. Anne's Park and Shirehampton have yielded lower palaeolithic implements. There is no associated fauna, but the industry corresponds so well with the Middle Acheulian of the Thames Valley that the gravels can be assigned to the Great Interglacial with some confidence (Lacaille, 1954, pp. 20–3). No fauna of undoubted Great Interglacial date is known from the Bristol neighbourhood, but it is possible that this period is represented in the infillings of several fissures in the Carboniferous Limestone, of which the most important are those of Durdham Down, near Bristol, and Milton Hill, near Wells. Both these fissures yielded a 'warm' fauna with *Elephas antiquus* and *Hippopotamus*, cave lion, hyaena and other species (Balch, 1937; Wilson, 1885). In the absence, however, of any animals diagnostic of such an early date, it seems more prudent to place these faunas in the Last Interglacial, while remembering that the fissures may have been open for a considerable time and all the animals in a fissure were not necessarily contemporaneous. The Last Interglacial may also be represented by the filling of Walton Bone Cave, which contained abundant remains of bear and horse and a number of rodents, including *Microtus malei* and *M. nivalis* which led Hinton (1910, p. 494) to regard the fauna as of about the same age as the Crayford Brickearth in the Thames Valley. The cave was sealed by sands and breccias probably of the Last Glaciation (Greenly, 1922; Palmer and Hinton, 1929).

At Bath, the basal beds of gravels about 100 ft. above the Avon have yielded *E. antiquus*, and may be as early as the Great Interglacial, but the majority of the Bath deposits, lying at all levels from over 100 ft. down to the flood plain and including both river gravels and solifluxion deposits, are later. They have yielded mammoth, woolly rhinoceros, *Bos primigenius*, *B. longifrons*, horse, wild boar and reindeer (Moore, 1870; Oriel, 1904; Winwood, 1886; 1888). Musk-ox has been found at Freshford seven miles up-stream (Dawkins, 1872). This series of deposits presumably reflects changes of sea-level during the Upper Pleistocene and perhaps earlier, but most of our knowledge of the deposits comes from nineteenth-century collectors who paid little attention to the sequence of events represented. It has not yet been possible to trace the later stages of the history of the Bristol Avon.

The Last Glaciation is represented by numerous cave faunas from Mendip. One of the most famous is the Hyaena Den, Wookey Hole, from which vast quantities of bones of the hyaenas and their prey have been obtained (Dawkins, 1862; 1863). The favourite food of the hyaenas was horse and woolly rhinoceros, but mammoth, cave lion, giant Irish deer, and a number of other animals were identified, including two teeth of *Diceros leptorhinus* (=*Rhinoceros hemitoechus*). An occasional occupant of the cave was man, who left flint implements of the local 'proto-Solutrean' type. Of about the same date may be the famous bone caves of western Mendip, at Bleadon, Hutton, Sandford and Uphill. A later stage of this period is represented by inhabited caves of the Creswellian culture, of which the chief is Gough's Cave, Cheddar (Donovan, 1955). The fauna had now been reduced by the disappearance of the mammoth, woolly rhinoceros, cave lion and hyaena. Cold conditions prevailed in the area during much of this time, but no correlation with the continental sub-divisions of the Würm Glaciation has yet been achieved. Frost-weathering breccias which flank some Carboniferous Limestone outcrops near the Bristol Channel, as at Clevedon and Bleadon (Palmer, 1934), probably belong to the Upper Pleistocene, and at Brean Down a series of breccias and windblown sands represents the transition from Pleistocene to post-Pleistocene time.

STRUCTURAL HISTORY

The earliest structural history of the area is not easy to discover on account of the restricted outcrops of the rocks concerned and the masking of original structures by violent Armorican movements. The first earth-movements of which we have record probably occurred during the Ordovician, and subsequent denudation followed by marine incursion gave rise to the unconformity between the Upper Llandovery and the Cambrian rocks of the Tortworth Inlier. The transgressive nature of the Upper Llandovery here recalls the situation farther north, on the Welsh Border. Little more is known about the effects of the Caledonian Orogeny, whose operations in the area are dated to about the middle of the Devonian period. There was probably folding along approximately north–south axes in the country north of the Avon, and ensuing denudation resulted in a strong unconformity between the Upper Old Red Sandstone and earlier formations, which, however, is not well seen in the area. These Caledonian movements may have been of importance in determining the trend of some of the structures developed later in the Carboniferous rocks.

Preliminary disturbances of the Armorican Orogeny occurred during the Carboniferous period, but the main episode took place after the deposition of the Upper Carboniferous rocks, presumably in early Permian time. The area was now subjected to severe compression from the south, resulting in folding, faulting and overthrusting, with a predominantly east–west strike. In the south were elevated the Mendip Hills, a series of *en échelon* anticlines showing overfolding to the north and thrusting and faulting of the limbs. The structures are most severe at the eastern end of the chain where a combination of an overfold and thrusting has resulted in *klippen* of Carboniferous Limestone lying on Coal Measures at Vobster (Welch, 1933). The next anticlinal line to the north, traceable from Worlebury Hill and Sand Point, on the Bristol Channel, to Bath, is not so closely reflected by the topography as the Mendip line, for the resistant Carboniferous Limestone and earlier rocks lie at a lower level along much of its length. The structures here are said to be less strongly faulted than in Mendip (Kellaway and Welch, 1948, p. 39). Farther north still, in the Kingswood Anticline, north of the Avon, the rocks older than the Coal Measures lie at considerable depth. West of Bristol is the Westbury Anticline, with a north-east to south-west axis, through the southern limb of which is cut the Avon Gorge. Here again overthrusts are prominent.

In the synclinal zones the Coal Measures have been preserved from denudation and mining has produced much evidence of intense disturbance. There is a contrast between the structures in the Carboniferous Limestone, which for the most part is thrown into large, simple folds, and in the incompetent Coal Measures which display all manner of contortions and repeated low-angle overthrusts. North of the Avon north–south striking elements appear in the structure, and may betray the influence of pre-existing Caledonian structures.

Tectonic activity since the close of the Armorican Orogeny has been slight, and probably confined to occasional posthumous movements along fold and fault lines already established. Many small-scale structures in the Mesozoic rocks fall principally into this category.

REFERENCES

Arkell, W. J. and D. T. Donovan. 1952. The Fuller's Earth of the Cotswolds, and its relation to the Great Oolite. *Quart. Journ. Geol. Soc. Lond.*, **107**, 227–53.

Balch, H. E. 1937. Mendip Nature Research Committee. Report for 1936. *Rep. Wells Nat. Hist. Arch. Soc.*, (1936), 41–3.

Buckland, W. and W. D. Conybeare. 1824. Observations on the south-western Coal District of England. *Trans. Geol. Soc. Lond.*, (2) **1**, 210–316.

Buckman, S. S. and E. Wilson. 1896. Dundry Hill: its upper portion, or the beds marked as Inferior Oolite (g^5) in the maps of the Geological Survey. *Quart. Jour. Geol. Soc. Lond.*, **52**, 669–720.

Cumberland, G., *in* R. Bright. 1817. On the Strata in the neighbourhood of Bristol. *Trans. Geol. Soc. Lond.*, (1) **4**, 193–205.

Dawkins, W. B. 1862. On a Hyaena-den at Wookey Hole, near Wells. *Quart. Journ. Geol. Soc. Lond.*, **18**, 115–25.

Dawkins, W. B. 1863. On a Hyaena-den at Wookey Hole, near Wells, No. II. *Ibid.*, **19**, 260–74.

DAWKINS, W. B. 1872. A Monograph on the British Pleistocene Mammalia. Part V. British Pleistocene Ovidae. *Ovibos moschatus*, Blainville. Pal. Soc., London.
DE LA BECHE, H. T. 1846. On the Formation of the Rocks of South Wales and south-western England. *Mem. Geol. Surv.*, **1**.
DIXON, E. E. L. 1921. The Unconformity between the Millstone Grit and the Carboniferous Limestone at Ifton, Monmouthshire. *Geol. Mag.*, **58**, 157–64.
DONOVAN, D. T. 1952. The Ammonites of the Blue Lias of the Bristol District. *Ann. Mag. Nat. Hist.*, (12) **5**, 629–55, 717–52.
—. 1955. The Pleistocene Deposits at Gough's Cave, Cheddar, including an account of recent excavations. *Proc. Univ. Bristol Spelaeo. Soc.*, **7**, 76–104.
GORHAM, A. 1930. The Upper and Lower Junctions of the Midford Sands at Limpley Stoke, south-east of Bath. *Geol. Mag.*, **67**, 289–97.
GREENLY, E. 1922. An Aeolian Pleistocene Deposit at Clevedon. *Geol. Mag.*, **59**, 365–76, 414–21.
GREENWELL, G. C. and J. MCMURTRIE. 1864. *On the Radstock Portion of the Somersetshire Coal Field.* Newcastle upon Tyne.
HINTON, M. A. C. 1910. A Preliminary Account of the British Fossil Voles and Lemmings; with some remarks on the Pleistocene Climate and Geography. *Proc. Geol. Assoc.*, **21**, 489–507.
KELLAWAY, G. A. and F. B. A. WELCH. 1948. British Regional Geology. Bristol and Gloucester District. 2nd ed. *Mem. Geol. Surv.*
LACAILLE, A. D. 1954. Palaeoliths from the Lower Reaches of the Bristol Avon. *Antiq. Journ.*, **34**, 1–27.
LEAN, J. 1888. Dolomitic Conglomerate of Bristol. *Proc. Bristol Nat. Soc.*, n.s., **5**, 207–15.
LONSDALE, W. 1832. On the Oolitic District of Bath. *Trans. Geol. Soc. Lond.*, (2) **3**, 241–76.
LOUPEKINE, I. S. 1953. Reversed Faulting in the Great Quarry, Avon Gorge. *Proc. Bristol Nat. Soc.*, **28**, 335–42.
MCMURTRIE, J. 1867. The Coal Fields of Somersetshire. *Proc. Somerset Arch. Nat. Hist. Soc.*, **13**, 16–21.
MARTYN, S. 1875. On Fish Remains in the Bristol Old Red Sandstone. *Proc. Bristol Nat. Soc.*, n.s., **1**, 141–4.
MOORE, C. 1870. The Mammalia and other remains from Drift Deposits in the Bath Basin. *Proc. Bath Nat. Hist. Antiq. Field Club*, **2**, 37–55.
MOORE, L. R. 1941. The presence of the Namurian in the Bristol District. *Geol. Mag.*, **78**, 279–92.
— and A. E. TRUEMAN. 1937. The Coal Measures of Bristol and Somerset. *Quart. Journ. Geol. Soc. Lond.*, **93**, 195–240.
MORGAN, C. LLOYD. 1885. Sub-aerial Denudation and the Avon Gorge. *Proc. Bristol Nat. Soc.*, n.s., **4**, 171–97.
— and S. H. REYNOLDS. 1904. The Igneous Rocks Associated with the Carboniferous Limestone of the Bristol District. *Quart. Journ. Geol. Soc. Lond*, **60**, 137–57.
ORIEL, B. 1904. The Avon and its Gravels. *Proc. Bristol Nat. Soc.*, n.s., **10**, 228–40.
PALMER, L. S. 1934. Some Pleistocene Breccias near the Severn Estuary. *Proc. Geol. Assoc.*, **45**, 145–61.
— and M. A. C. HINTON. 1929. Some gravel deposits at Walton, near Clevedon. *Proc. Univ. Bristol Spelaeo. Soc.*, **3**, 154–61.
REED, F. R. C. and S. H. REYNOLDS. 1908. On the Fossiliferous Silurian Rocks of the Southern Half of the Tortworth Inlier. *Quart. Journ. Geol. Soc. Lond.*, **64**, 512–45.
REYNOLDS, S. H. 1907. A Silurian Inlier in the Eastern Mendips. *Ibid.*, **63**, 217–40.
—. 1912*a*. Further Work on the Silurian Rocks of the Eastern Mendips. *Proc. Bristol Nat. Soc.*, (4) **3**, 76–82.
—. 1912*b*. *A Geological Excursion Handbook for the Bristol District.* Bristol. 1st ed.

REYNOLDS, S. H. 1917. Further Work on the Igneous Rocks associated with the Carboniferous Limestone of the Bristol District. *Quart. Journ. Geol. Soc. Lond.*, **72**, 23–42.
—. 1921. The Lithological Succession of the Carboniferous Limestone (Avonian) of the Avon Section at Clifton. *Ibid.*, **77**, 213–45.
—. 1924. The Igneous Rocks of the Tortworth Inlier. *Ibid.*, **80**, 106–12.
—. 1926. Progress in the Study of the Lower Carboniferous (Avonian) Rocks of England and Wales. *Rep. Brit. Assoc.*, 65–101.
—. 1929. The Geology of the Bristol District. *Proc. Geol. Assoc.*, **40**, 77–103.
—. 1946. The Aust Section. *Proc. Cotteswold Nat. F.C.*, **29**, 29–39.
— and E. GREENLY. 1924. The Geological Structure of the Clevedon–Portishead Area (Somerset). *Quart. Journ. Geol. Soc. Lond.*, **80**, 447–67.
RICHARDSON, L. 1904. Notes on the Rhaetic Rocks around Charfield, Gloucestershire. *Geol. Mag.*, (5) **1**, 532–35.
—. 1907. The Inferior Oolite and Contiguous Deposits of the Bath-Doulting District. *Quart. Journ. Geol. Soc. Lond.*, **63**, 383–423.
—. 1910. The Inferior Oolite and Contiguous Deposits of the South Cotteswolds. *Proc. Cotteswold Nat. F.C.*, **17**, 63–136.
—. 1911. The Rhaetic and Contiguous Deposits of West, Mid, and part of East Somerset. *Quart. Journ. Geol. Soc. Lond.*, **67**, 1–74.
SHORT, A. R. 1903. On the Cotham Marble. *Proc. Bristol Nat. Soc.*, n.s., **10**; 135–49.
SIBLY, T. F. 1912. The Carboniferous Succession in the Forest of Dean Coalfield. *Geol. Mag.*, (5) **9**, 417–22.
—. 1919. Iron Ores: The Haematite of the Forest of Dean and South Wales. *Min. Res. Mem. Geol. Surv.*, **10.**
SIMPSON, SCOTT, 1951. A New Eurypterid from the Upper Old Red Sandstone of Portishead. *Ann. Mag. Nat. Hist.*, (12) **4**, 849–61.
SMITH, STANLEY. 1930. The Carboniferous Inliers at Codrington and Wick (Gloucestershire). *Quart. Journ. Geol. Soc. Lond.*, **86**, 331–54.
—. 1934. The Tortworth Inlier (*in* The Geology of the Gloucester District by C. I. Gardiner and others). *Proc. Geol. Assoc.*, **45**, 114–20.
—. 1942. A high Visean Fauna from the vicinity of Yate, Gloucestershire; with special reference to the Corals and to a Goniatite. *Proc. Bristol Nat. Soc.*, (4) **9**, 335–48.
— and C. J. STUBBLEFIELD. 1933. On the Occurrence of Tremadoc Shales in the Tortworth Inlier (Gloucestershire), with Notes on the Fossils. *Quart. Journ. Geol. Soc. Lond.*, **89**, 357–78.
THOMPSON, B. 1894. Landscape Marble. *Ibid.*, **50**, 393–410.
TROTTER, F. M. 1940. *In* Summary of Progress for 1938. *Mem. Geol. Surv.*
—. 1942. Geology of the Forest of Dean Coal and Iron-ore Field. *Mem. Geol. Surv.*
TURNER, J. S. 1935. Gotlandian Vulcanicity in Western Europe. *Geol. Mag.*, **72**, 145–51.
TUTCHER, J. W. and A. E. TRUEMAN. 1925. The Liassic Rocks of the Radstock District (Somerset). *Quart. Journ. Geol. Soc. Lond.*, **81**, 595–666.
VAUGHAN, A. 1905. The Palaeontological Sequence in the Carboniferous Limestone of the Bristol Area. *Ibid.*, **61**, 181–307.
—. 1906. The Carboniferous Limestone Series (Avonian) of the Avon Gorge. *Proc. Bristol Nat. Soc.*, (4) **1**, 74–168.
—. 1915. Correlation of Dinantian and Avonian. *Quart. Journ. Geol. Soc. Lond.*, **71**, 1–52.
WALLIS, F. S. 1925. Note on an Exposure of Old Red Sandstone at St. Monica's, Durdham Down, Bristol. *Proc. Bristol Nat. Soc.*, (4) **6**, 179–82.
—. 1928. The Old Red Sandstone of the Bristol District. *Quart. Journ. Geol. Soc. Lond.*, **83**, 760–89.
WELCH, F. B. A. 1933. The Geological Structure of the Eastern Mendips. *Ibid.*, **89**, 14–52.

WETHERED, E. 1886. On the Structure and Organisms of the Lower Limestone Shales, Carboniferous Limestone and Upper Limestones of the Forest of Dean. *Geol. Mag.*, (3) **3**, 529–40.
WHITE, E. I. 1946. The Genus *Phialaspis* and the '*Psammosteus* Limestones'. *Quart. Journ. Geol. Soc. Lond.*, **101**, 207–42.
WILSON, E. 1886. The Bone-cave or Fissure of Durdham Down. *Proc. Bristol Nat. Soc.*, n.s., **5**, 31–45.
WINWOOD, H. H. 1886. List of Fossil Mammalia found near Bath. *Proc. Bath Nat. Hist. Antiq. Field Club*, **6**, 95.
—. 1888. Recent 'Finds' in the Victoria Gravel Pit. *Ibid.*, **6**, 327–32.
WOODWARD, H. B. 1892. Remarks on the Formation of Landscape Marble. *Geol. Mag.*, (3) **9**, 110–4.

GEORGE, T. N. 1958. Lower Carboniferous palaeogeography of the British Isles. *Proc. Yorks. Geol. Soc.*, **31**, 227–318.
GREEN, G. W. and WELCH, F. B. A. 1965. Geology of the county around Wells and Cheddar. *Mem. Geol. Surv.*
KELLAWAY, G. A. 1967. The Geological Survey Ashton Park Borehole and its bearing on the geology of the Bristol District. *Bull. geol. Surv. Gt. Brit.* No. 27, 49–153.
—. 1971. The Upper Coal Measures of South-West England compared with those of South Wales and the Southern Midlands. *C. R. 6e Congr. Intern. Strat. Geol. Carbonif. Sheffield 1967*, **3**, 1039–1055.
MITCHELL, M. 1972. The base of the Visean in South-West and North-West England. *Proc. Yorks. Geol. Soc.*, **39** (2), 151–160.
RHODES, F. H. T., AUSTIN, R. L. and DRUCE, E. C. 1969. British Avonian (Carboniferous) Conodont faunas, and their value in local and intercontinental correlation *Bull. Brit. Mus. London*, Supplement 5.
STUBBLEFIELD, C. J. and TROTTER, F. M. 1957. Divisions of the Coal Measures on Geological Survey maps of England and Wales. *Bull. geol. Surv.* G.B., **13**, 1–5.

CHAPTER TWO

PHYSIOGRAPHY

AS one would expect from the variety of its rock exposures and long geological succession, the Bristol region is quite distinctive from neighbouring areas to the east and west, and may well be considered as an individual unit. Two geological axes, of the Lower Severn and of Bath, are of first importance and run approximately north and south; they tend to converge to the north and finally join in the mass of the Malvern Hills. To the south the Mendip axis, trending approximately east and west, was later thrust across the direction of the northward running axes. It is probable also that during the greater part of the earlier history of the area there was a land-mass to the north. These aspects of the geology are important in separating the Bristol area from its immediate neighbours, and they further account in part for the former alternation of shallow and deeper waters and thus, in turn, for deltaic and estuarine deposits with their attendant sands and gravels, and the alternation of the latter with deposits of deeper water origin.

Later, a wide cover of newer rocks was laid down and tended to conceal the older formations, but the rock-sequence varies remarkably both in thickness and in extent in all directions, and the cover itself naturally became more complex following earth-movements in still later times.

Within short distances there are different rocks and therefore widely differing results of erosion. As time advanced and erosion proceeded the older rocks tended to be exposed, as the varied agents cut downwards to the older surfaces. But it was all a very uneven process, as the evidence suggests, and has resulted in an almost unique series of gorges, and confusion of Coal Measures and Mesozoic deposits. Throughout, the controls of the sediments and of folds are manifest as the remnants and slopes of the older landscapes were revealed.

The Severn Estuary in the past was at times of the same form as it shows to-day. It bore witness to a weaker part of the crust and around its edges a region of folding controlled the thickness of the sediments laid down on the one hand and their erosion and washing away on the other. Both the Estuary and Channel have suffered many changes and, at the present time, an elevation of one hundred feet would make them dry land as far to the west as the Swansea–Minehead line.

It is suggested by Dr. F. J. North that immediately before or early in the Glacial Period the form of the Channel was not very different from that of the present. Its earlier history was influenced by movements in Tertiary times, but he regards the

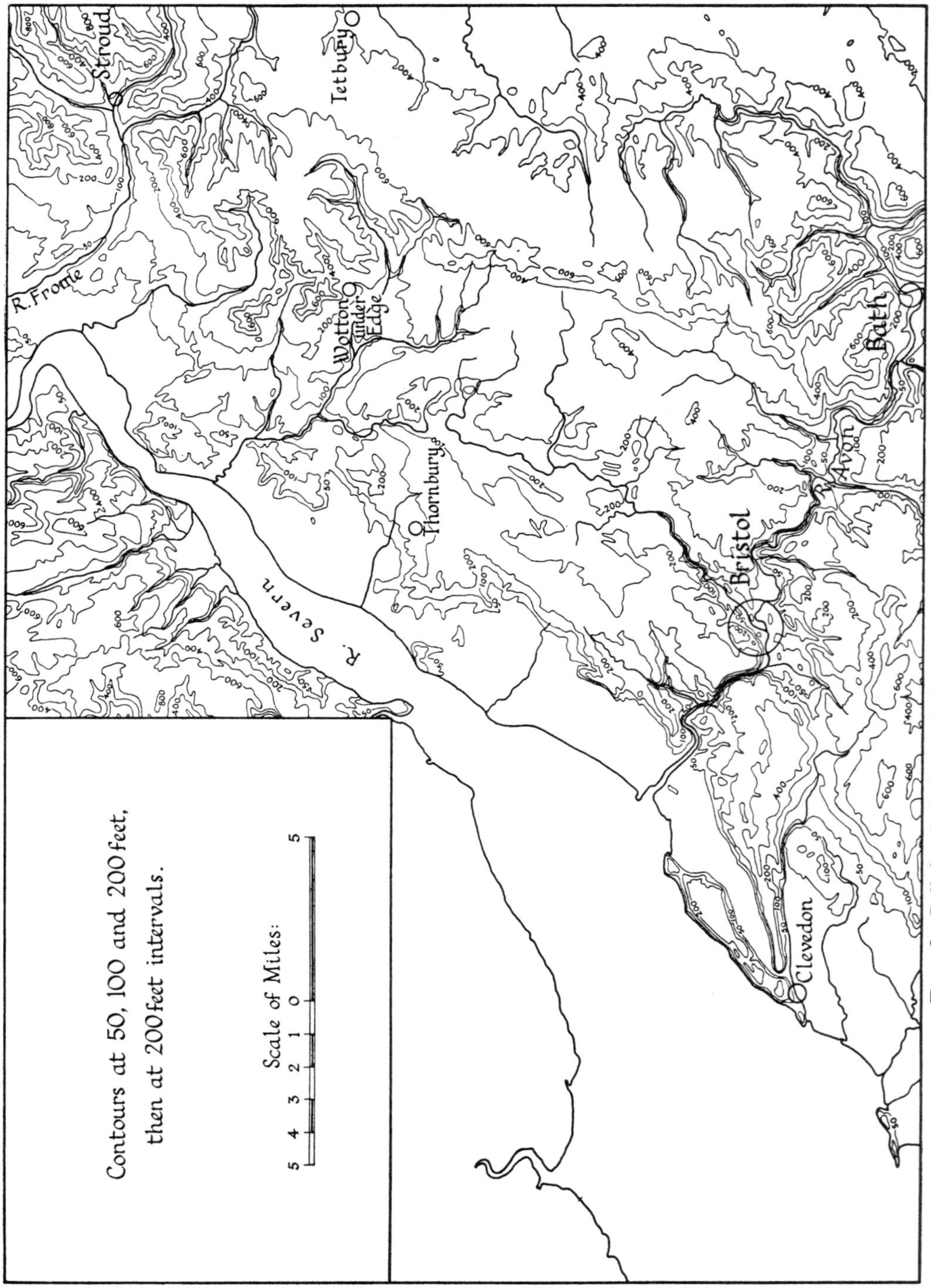

FIG. 6. *Relief and drainage of the Lower Avon and the northern Bristol area.*

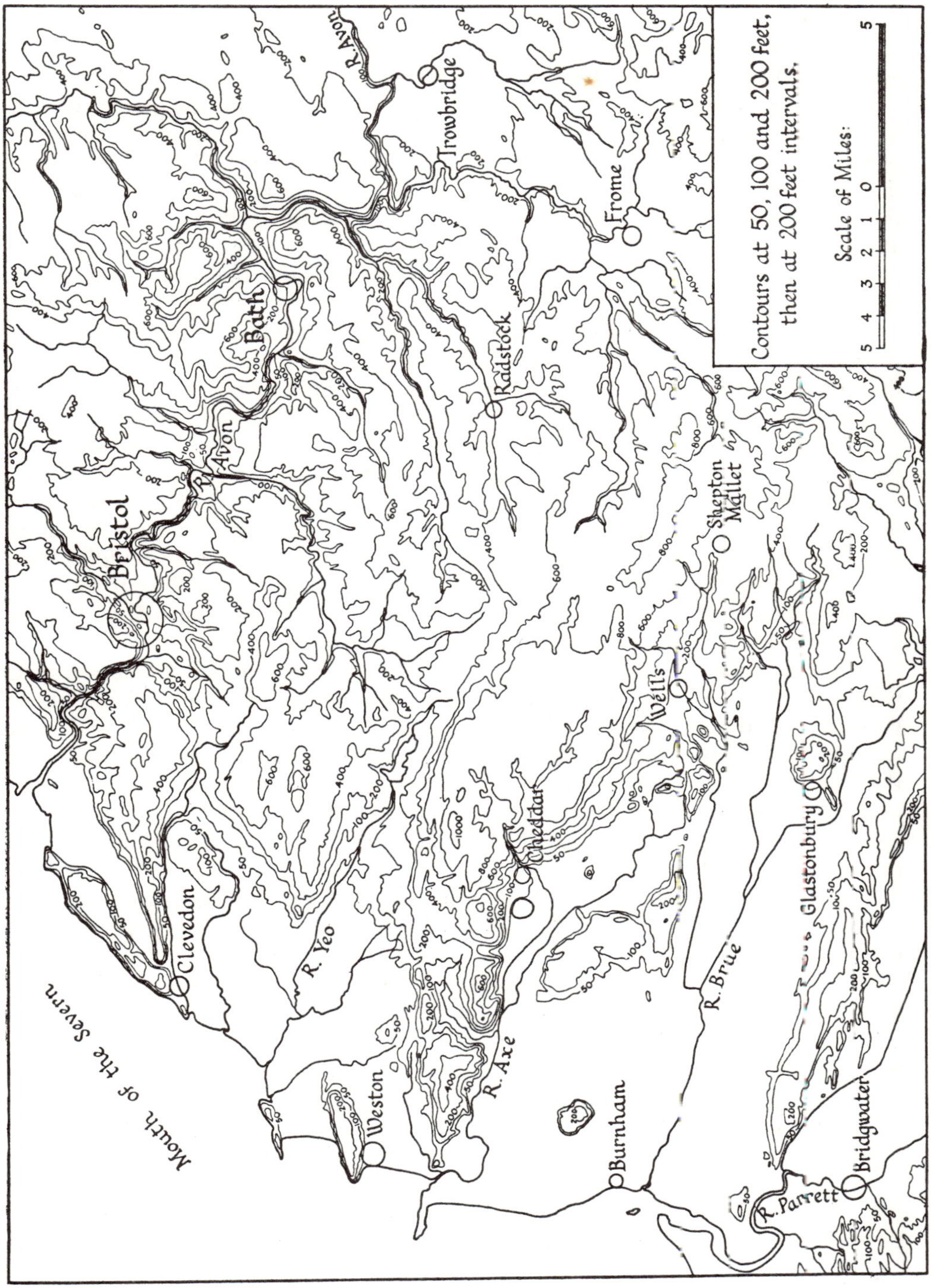

FIG. 7. *Relief and drainage of the Lower Avon and the southern Bristol area.*

present form as that of a river system that has been partly entered by the sea; the evidence afforded by raised beaches however complicates this story of subsidence.

The Severn Estuary runs in a south-westerly direction and for the greater part of its length the southern shore is bordered with alluvium. This is true also of the coast of the Bristol Channel. In the Bridgwater Bay area lines of well-established sand dunes are found in the Berrow district. The range of the tide is greater along this coast than at any other place in Europe, figures for spring tides being, Bridgwater Bar, 35 ft., Weston-super-Mare, 40 ft. and Avonmouth, 42 ft.

The muddiness of the Estuary is renowned and at low tide the rivers running into it are fringed with impressive mud banks, those of the Parrett and Brue extending vertically up to thirty feet. The great rise and fall of the tide leads to active erosion in places and the banks of the Parrett show rapid changes where unprotected as at Stert Point. Large areas of alluvium however show little change in area, the vast quantities of sediment carried by the tides making good the losses due to erosion.

The long gradually-narrowing Estuary produces tidal waves which, under certain conditions, give rise near Gloucester to the bore for which the river is so well known. This may lead to excessive erosion and in recent years there has been considerable loss of land as, for example, at Stonebench. The bore may run as a mass of water, five or six feet high along the banks and three and a half feet high in the middle of the river. The same phenomenon is present in other rivers and in the Parrett the bore reaches a height of about two feet at spring tides. Should these coincide with gales from the south or south-west, the bore may be an impressive sight.

A recent report on the coastline of England and Wales showed Gloucestershire with $34\frac{3}{4}$ miles of coast and Somerset with $80\frac{1}{4}$ miles. This survey listed three types of natural coastal scenery, viz., exceptional quality, very good quality and good quality. None of the coastline of our area ranked in the highest category, and only the Avon Gorge was marked as very good. These facts should emphasize the urgent necessity of sound planning for the preservation of the amenities of the coast, especially as certain lengths, particularly in Somerset, have already been sadly despoiled.

There are Carboniferous rocks at Clevedon and Brean Down which are continued in the islands of Steepholm and Flatholm. Patches of shingle are comparatively rare and those found are usually of insignificant proportions.

The coast is protected by dune ridges, north from Burnham to beyond Berrow, and these reach heights of fifty feet and more. Inland from the dunes, in the Somerset Levels, the height of the land is often below that of sea-level. There is evidence of wind erosion immediately north of Burnham and some 'blow outs' are very marked. In that neighbourhood a relatively new marsh with a strong growth of Spartina grass is building up and giving much-needed protection to the coast. The same kind of thing, but on a smaller scale, is repeated farther north in the Berrow district, where the dunes appear menacingly near to the church.

Bridgwater Bay is an impressive feature, hemmed in to the north by the Brean Down limestone mass and bordered to the south by the lower slopes of the Quantock

Hills. A line connecting these two highlands encloses an area along the coast made up of Stert Flats in the south and of Gore Sands and Berrow Flats in the north. These are up to four miles in width, the Gore Sand at its highest points not being covered save at high tides.

The course of the Parrett is a remarkable one, and there seems to be no obvious reason why the river should not have continued on its course at Combwich and entered the Channel in the Stolford district. Actually it runs for six miles beyond Combwich before swinging away from the coastline and out to sea between the Gore Sand and Stert Flats. The present position of Stert Point indicates that it has been built up in a north-easterly direction and the river pushed farther and farther to the east. The break between Stert Island and Stert Point however suggests that the river has, from time to time, succeeded in breaching the point and forming subsidiary channels to the sea. Those occasions have probably witnessed a critical combination of winds and storm waves. Before the days of lighted coasts, the task of approaching the mouth of the Parrett must have been difficult and even to-day it is by no means simple.

In the evolution of the shape of the shoreline the longshore drift and the dominant waves are actively concerned in the transport of material, which is drifted by the prevalent waves and piled up by the dominant waves. These two sets of waves tend to follow the same easterly direction up the Channel, and the shoreline is being slowly moulded and changed so as to face the direction of the dominant breakers, which is also that of the greatest fetch of open water.

Along the coast enclosing the mouth of the Parrett a constant struggle goes on between the waves and the wind on the one hand and Stert Point on the other. Under ordinary circumstances the point gradually makes to the north-east. The longshore drift is in that direction, and the constant supply of shingle, though small in quantity, has afforded protection for the inclusion of such areas as Fenning Island in the mainland. But the tidal currents in the area are strong, and there must be a constant danger of severe erosion by storm waves especially when they coincide with high tides. The separation of Stert Island from the mainland was probably the result of a critical combination of these elements. It is perhaps significant that the break occurred immediately opposite the mouth of the River Brue. Both Stert Point and Stert Island are unstable structures; at present the point is pushing out towards the island, and the channel between the two almost dries out at low water. The island itself is suffering severe erosion and may disappear before a junction can once more be effected with the point. Old drainage channels, once conspicuous on the seaward side of the island, are now practically obliterated but on the landward side a sandy beach to the south is still bordered by miniature dunes. Shingle on the south-west coast of the island has extended in recent years, but the supply is limited and probably does not cross the channel from Stert Point.

An unusual occurrence on the shoreline in the Bridgwater Bay area is a number of balls of clay (blue mud) which have been seen from time to time. Notice of these in literature on coastlines in this country is rare though they have previously been seen on the sandy foreshore at Uphill. They were first observed in the summer of 1934 on the west side of Stert Island, and have been noticed occasionally since that time. They then occurred in considerable numbers, and their size varies in diameter from one to six inches. Their composition is of fine blue clay, mixed with small pebbles, and they are often beautifully rounded in shape. Probably the rounding effect is due to rolling by water. Apparently they can be formed in quickly moving water only, and normally they will not be preserved. Later they were seen north of Burnham, again in considerable number, but here they were crudely rounded and had a more cylindrical form. They appeared at a time when the beach had been denuded of sand and the underlying clay exposed. Wave erosion had apparently cut grooves into this and, from the exposed edges, pieces of clay had been torn away. These pieces, constantly rolled to and fro by the waves, seemingly developed as clay balls. They probably disappear quickly and are often covered by deposition from the tide following their development.

Raised beaches in the area are usually near the present coastline and are indicated by wave-worn rock platforms. The fifty-foot beach has been traced along the coast south from Portishead to Brean Down and, inland, to the foot of the Mendip Hills, to Cheddar and west to Wookey. The ten-foot beach is distinguished by a rock platform between Portishead and Clevedon, which is covered in places by isolated conglomerates of old beach pebbles.

The Nature Conservancy, which was formed in the winter of 1948–49, has recently included some ten miles of the foreshore of the Somerset Coast in its list of Nature Reserves. This includes Stert Point, and Stert Island will be added very soon. Much of this foreshore is protected by an abundant growth of Spartina grass accidentally introduced some years ago.

There are many stories of inundation by the sea in historical times and some embankments probably date from Roman times. In Neolithic times the area suffered considerable subsidence. Ussher, discussing the submerged forest at Stolford, three miles west of the Parrett, suggested that, when the forest flourished, the land must certainly have stood forty feet higher. Boyd Dawkins, writing of the same forest along Bridgwater Bay, considered that 'the land there stood sixty feet above present level'. This was probably the last important movement along the coast. Following that movement the coastline almost certainly had an irregular outline, in marked contrast to its present even contour. It must also have been cut back relatively rapidly and the outlet of the Parrett may have been changed considerably owing to the formation of spits and bars, which would accompany the erosion of the coastline in such a manner.

The mountain-building movements of Tertiary times set up subsidiary folding and modified the then river system rather dramatically. The main course of the River Thames is a representative of the new streams then set up. The River Severn represents other streams thus initiated, but with a north-east and south-west trend. This stream system gradually cut its way north-eastwards by headward erosion and captured, one by one, the headwaters of the streams flowing in a south-easterly direction; some of the dry valleys in the Cotswolds may be of significance in this respect. It is generally accepted however that the present courses of the rivers in this area may have been decided by the kind of rocks over which they flowed. There have been many changes in these courses and the cover of Mesozoic rocks on which the rivers were initiated has been largely removed by denudation. Therefore, the rivers have been superimposed and now run over strata older and different from those on which they originated. The streams have in general continued to flow in the courses and directions which were dictated by the rocks since removed.

To the north several small streams flow east from the Cotswolds, meeting in the headwaters of the Thames. These and other streams were probably once connected to streams on the west side of the ridge, and the Severn is thus a subsequent stream, which has increased in power and so cut off the present headwaters of the Thames from their former connexions on the Welsh side of the Estuary. Many opinions have been expressed on the development of the valley of the Severn. These really depend on the extent to which the sea is considered to have played a part in the moulding of the scarp of the Cotswolds, and its attendant re-entrant valleys. The scarp is the work of sub-aerial agents in association with the lateral erosion of the river, and many outliers, such as Robin's Wood Hill, prove the greater extension of the hills to the west in bygone ages.

On the higher ground the rivers still run from west to east, often in wide valleys containing extensive woodland belts and sheltered villages. Many of the valleys are now dry and several suggestions have been put forward to account for them. Possibly they are the result of erosion by water from a melting ice cap, a suggestion which is in keeping with the manner of their grouping on the high ground. Several are hanging up to thirty feet above the present stream floor, and in some cases the step-junction is scarcely modified. There is no question that the northern parts of the hills, at the least, were covered by the Quaternary ice sheet and probably the more southern parts were all within the 'no man's land' which must inevitably have lain between the ice cap itself and the completely ice-free country to the south.

The only river of any real significance in the area is the Avon, which probably shows more anomalies than many another river of like size, and flows east, south and west before reaching the Severn Estuary. Rising on the eastern slope of the Cotswolds it breaks through the range some distance farther south after receiving a tributary from the eastern Mendip. A large part of the area is drained by the River Avon and its tributaries, and many and varied are the suggestions which have been put forward in an attempt to solve the puzzle of its course. Mackinder (1902, p. 121) writes the river 'appears to be obsequent at Bath, subsequent between Bradford and Chippenham and consequent above Malmesbury where it seems to have captured a source of the Thames'. In some respects, Trueman (1938, p. 287) finds it to be 'one of the most fascinating river systems in Britain'. The Avon starts as a small stream on the dip slope of the Cotswolds near Badminton and flows east as a consequent stream to Malmesbury, where it turns south and runs on a subsequent course through

Chippenham to Bradford-on-Avon. Before reaching Bath it makes a characteristic right-angled bend to flow through the escarpment in the beautiful gorge at Limpley Stoke and later cuts the renowned gorge at Clifton.

No explanation of this erratic course is free of difficulties and it must be remembered that several of the tributaries of the Avon show features similar to those of the main river. It may also be significant that, from Bath to the sea, the river follows a direction parallel to that of the Mendip Hills.

After leaving Bath the Avon flows through an alternation of open valleys and narrow gorges, the latter being cut through uplands which vary both in character and in height. The Avon Gorge is now usually explained as a case of superimposed drainage. Clifton Down, Durdham Down and Leigh Woods form a small plateau, immaturely dissected by river erosion and owing its level surface probably, in part, to peneplanation under desert conditions in Triassic times and, in part, to marine denudation. The course of the river was determined, not by the rocks now forming the surface but by a series of Jurassic and Cretaceous rocks now entirely removed by erosion.

'Some of the tributary streams show features very closely resembling those of the Avon. The Frome has attractive gorges where it cuts into the Pennant Sandstone at Stapleton, Frenchay and Winterbourne. The Chew and its tributaries are likewise entrenched near Pensford, while the Trym streams occupy astonishingly deep valleys cut in the Mountain Limestone near Westbury-on-Trym' (Trueman, 1938, p. 288). The branches of the Trym, like those of the Avon and its tributary the Frome, seem to flow quite out of line with the present topography and the higher ground does not act as a watershed. The ridge of limestone, which circles from Penpole Point by Henbury Hill to Durdham Down, is cut by the Henbury Trym at Blaise Castle and by the Westbury Trym below Henbury Hill. The gorge at Blaise Castle is particularly impressive and as unexpected and isolated as is the Avon Gorge. These anomalies are of similar origin and probably best explained by superimposed drainage.

Harmer's ideas were rather different but little evidence has so far been detailed to support him. He called attention to the abrupt way in which the Avon leaves the plain and avoids the Flax Bourton Valley by a right-angled bend 'going out of its way to cut laterally a narrow gorge across higher land (Clifton Down)' (1907, p. 485). He suggested that the original course of the river might well have been through this valley, a more direct route and one much easier to erode. During the Ice Age, if the valley was blocked by drifted snow or ice, a lake must have formed with an overflow across the higher land to the Bristol Channel. Here then was the commencement of the gorge and Harmer suggests that once having started to cut the gorge, the river continued in its new course after the withdrawal of the ice and did not return to the Flax Bourton Valley. He further likens the gorge to the type of the Ironbridge Gorge since it has no connexion with the natural drainage and cuts through a 'narrow isthmus of Palaeozoic rock down to the level of the Triassic plains on either side'.

Away from the immediate Bristol district the drainage is comparatively simple, and practically all the streams west of the Cotswold scarp flow into the Bristol Channel while those following the dip slope join the River Thames. The simple drainage of the Cotswolds, with relatively few tributaries, is different from the conventional and well-developed dendritic pattern of the vales particularly to the east.

The River Yeo to the north of Mendip and the Axe to the south flow leisurely to the Bristol Channel, their courses largely directed by the east and west run of the hills. At almost similar intervals south, the Brue and the Parrett enter Bridgwater Bay, the latter sweeping north to the coast and across the outlet of the Brue before swinging east to the sea. The island of Stert stands waning in the loop, scarcely separated from Stert Point where one of the few spreads of shingle in the area is encountered. These rivers all cross the Somerset Levels and here the struggle to control surplus water is not yet ended. Indeed, if the relative levels of land and sea were changed by fifty feet the area between Weston-super-Mare and Bridgwater would be flooded and arms of the sea would approach Taunton, Yeovil, Glastonbury and Wells. An extensive sea-wall, often of great age, along with major drainage schemes and canals has, however, reduced the actual marshes to relatively small proportions and wide tracts of land have been reclaimed for agricultural purposes. The last of these drainage schemes was initiated in recent years and is still in progress.

It has been suggested that in earlier times, before the days of effective drainage, the Brue possibly built up a delta, part of the water finding its way out to sea via the Parrett and the remainder via the mouth of the Axe. Be that as it may, the confluence of the river with the Parrett appears unnatural and suggests a relatively short time in its present form.

The Levels have been eroded out of soft Mesozoic sediments and their flat contour is broken only by the low ridge of the Polden Hills and solitary outliers of the surrounding higher ground (Plates II and X). A considerable part is below high-water level and across this the sluggish rivers flow between fields separated from each other by willow-lined ditches or rhines. In several places there is a rise in elevation as the coastline is approached. The great differences in the rise and fall of the tide on the coast have already been mentioned, and these points, added to that of run-off from the surrounding high ground, make the problem of draining the Levels a very difficult one.

Trueman has drawn attention to the regularity of the hill surfaces in the area which he suggests are the remains of marine or sub-aerial erosion platforms, representing varied stages of dissection. There are three platforms, first, the most widespread at a height of 200 ft. to over 300 ft., secondly, at a height of 550 to 600 ft. and, thirdly, at a well-marked higher level, 750 to 850 ft., particularly around Dundry Hill, the Avon Valley, the Yate area and the Frome Valley.

The general outline of the topography over much of the area therefore was set by the elevation of these platforms. The detail of the relief is unusually complex, and the curious flow of the rivers in open valleys and deep gorges has already been noticed. It is largely due to the geological structure and to the particular distribution of hard and soft rocks. The older ones, such as the Old Red Sandstone and the Carboniferous, have been subjected to great pressures and mountain-building movements and thus are much folded and faulted. On the other hand, the newer rocks, such as the New Red Sandstone and the Jurassic, are simpler in structure and rest with marked unconformity on the older rocks. More recent erosion has removed the newer formations in many places and as a result the present land surface is, in many places, made up of different rock-types. Hence the rivers may flow in many rock formations of different ages and hardnesses, and will generally cut gorges in the older ones and run through wide, open valleys in the newer ones. If the platforms were wave-cut, then where these were uplifted, rivers would be initiated on the old sea-floor. This would suggest some of the rivers were developed on an erosion platform and not on a cover of newer rocks. In that case the usually accepted idea of superimposed drainage in the area would require modification.

The Mendip Hills form a long narrow and relatively flat-topped ridge, at a general height of 800 to 900 ft., stretching approximately east and west for a distance of over thirty miles from the coast near Weston-super-Mare. There is considerable narrowing towards the west where the hills run out to sea at Brean Down (Plate II). Steepholm and Flatholm are island-remnants of a former greater extension of the hills to the west. Their north-eastern flanks are less distinct and the older rocks, of which they are chiefly made up, disappear under a thin patchy cover of Mesozoic strata as the Cotswolds are approached. To the east, in the Frome district, they are covered by the newer rocks which form the floors of the valleys cut into the Chalk escarpment, as in the vales of Pewsey and Warminster.

The plateau rises to its highest point in Blackdown, above Shipham, at 1,068 ft., where the Old Red Sandstone core shows through the limestone cover, and with the well-known gorges of Cheddar and Burrington to the south and north respectively. But the hills form domes, or periclines, of which Blackdown is the most westerly. The remaining ones, North Hill, Pen Hill and Beacon Hill occur in that order to the south and east and, in each case, the Old Red Sandstone is similarly revealed. These hills and their general flatness are largely due to the planation of Liassic times.

The summit of the plateau is bare and treeless and its grey masses and crags are exposed over wide areas, across which walls of the same grey rock stretch, either with or against the contours. Swallow holes are common and narrow dry gorges cut into the body of the plateau. There is no water here and scarcely any habitation either of village or farm. In many places the scars of old lead-mine workings are still in evidence and more modern limestone quarrying is rapidly cutting into the hills as, for example, near Shipham.

To the south and west the hills rise abruptly from the plain and their borders are marked by the beginnings of the gorges and of a line of towns and villages. The position of the latter is dictated by the presence of water at the limestone junctions, though the later growth of some of them such as Cheddar and Wookey has been influenced by the scenery of the gorges and the opening of the caves to visitors. As is common in limestone country, much of the scenery is hidden, and the caves of Wookey Hole and Cheddar are well known. There are however many other attractive gorges and little known caves and the number of the latter is added to year by year. The Blackdown area, particularly near Tynings Farm and around Charterhouse and Burrington Combe, is especially rich in caves and archaeological remains. and much work is still actively carried on there by the Spelaeological Society of the University of Bristol. This area is also a good illustration of the different type of country resulting from the exposure of the Old Red Sandstone, which gives a heath-covered moorland with several well-marked streams, which disappear when they reach the surrounding Carboniferous rocks. The striking scenic features are the result of the solubility of the limestone combined with its relative hardness and strong vertical jointing. Ebbor Gorge, with enormous screes, is beautifully wooded and perhaps the wildest ravine in Somerset. Several theories have been suggested to account for the gorges. Possibly they were originally the lines followed by a series of caves through which flowed underground streams. Subsequently the roofs of the caves have collapsed and have been carried away, the former streams having mostly disappeared. The River Axe and Wookey Hole cave are a possible example of a stage in this process, if the theory be correct.

The Cotswolds, built largely of oolitic limestones, extend northwards from the Bath district to Chipping Campden. Increasing in height from south to north they reach 1,070 ft. in Painswick Beacon. To the west they overlook the Severn Lowland with a steep scarp face but, to the east, slope down gently below the newer formations (Plate 1).

The name suggests a considerably wooded area, with villages here and there, but nowadays the hills are bare and carry relatively few trees save for wide and numerous shelter belts. They provide corn-growing country, in which large fields are separated by stone walls. Running from the south-west to the north-east in conformity with the natural line of the county of Gloucester they are roughly parallel to the Severn Estuary, and provide many vantage points for wide views to the west. The hills are made up of light-coloured oolitic limestones, whose browns and yellows are characteristic of the fields and of the walls of the area.

The valleys of the Cotswold edge are deeper and narrower than those of the upland and the dip slope, since the steep drop to the Estuary has enabled the streams to cut down more rapidly. The rivers in these valleys have carved out much of the present-day topography and some areas are in process of being cut off from the parent hills. There is an ever-present urge for the swiftly flowing streams of the scarp to deepen their valleys and to cut back their sources. It has been suggested that an eastward extension of this kind may explain the west-flowing anomalous courses of the Avon and the Stroud Frome. In the Stroud area there are good examples of such streams, and here the deeply cut valleys of Painswick, Toadsmoor, Nailsworth and the Slad join the Frome Valley which leads west to the Severn Estuary.

The limestone of the hills provides the material for a fine and distinguished domestic architecture, believed by many to be the finest in the country. Happily the National Trust is already in possession of several of the more noted examples such as the Arlington Row at Bibury.

In modern times the main lines of communication have deserted the high ground and are found principally along the river valleys. In Neolithic times, however, the Cotswolds were part of the route from the Salisbury Plain area to the mines of Derbyshire; along this route the people gathered in fortified camps for purposes of defence. Many examples of camps, probably of the Iron Age, are still preserved along the edge of the scarp and the plan of their layout is easy to see. Many obviously gave mutual support and all suggest a location in which the chances of surprise attack were reduced to a minimum. There are places where the road runs almost on the edge of the scarp and the view west to the Severn and beyond is not easily rivalled. Many ranges stand out and points as far afield as the Sugar Loaf, above Abergavenny, are included in a panoramic view.

In many Cotswold villages, water supply is a difficult problem, since the alternation of permeable and impermeable rocks, together with many fissures, give rise to regions of little water and in several areas there is also grave danger of water pollution.

In the south the Cotswold escarpment merges in a complex area with the Mendip axis, produces an area of indefinite topography and ends in the Lansdown Hill district, but Dundry Hill rising to a height of nearly 800 ft., although now quite separate from the ridge, is a notable outlier and shows distinct structural and geological associations with it, and is clear evidence of the former westward extent of the escarpment. This is one of the finest vantage points for a comprehensive view over a wide area. To the west and south of Dundry Hill an outcrop of Carboniferous Limestone is shown rising to 600 ft. in the dome-like mass of Broadfield Down. It is bleak and bare as in Mendip, with characteristic and picturesque valleys such as Brockley Combe and Goblin Combe.

REFERENCES

Davis, W. M. 1895. The Development of certain English Rivers. *Geog. Journ.*, **5**, 127.

Harmer, F. W. 1907. On the origin of certain canon-like valleys. *Quart. Journ. Geol. Soc. Lond.*, **63**, 484.

Jones, O. T. 1930. Some Episodes in the Geological History of the Bristol Channel Region. *Rep. Brit. Assoc.*, 57.

Kellaway, G. A. and F. B. A. Welch. 1948. British Regional Geology, Bristol and Gloucester District. 2nd ed. *Mem. Geol. Surv.*

Mackinder, H. J. 1902. *Britain and the British Seas.* London.

North, F. J. 1929. *The Evolution of the Bristol Channel.* Cardiff.

Palmer, L. S. 1931. The Pleistocene Succession of the Bristol District. *Proc. Geol. Assoc.*, **42**, 345.

Reynolds, S. H. 1927. The Mendips. *Geography*, **14**, 187.

Trueman, A. E. 1938. *The Scenery of England and Wales.* London.

—. 1939. Erosion Levels in the Bristol District, and their relation to the development of the scenery. *Proc. Bristol Nat. Soc.*, (4) **8**, 402.

CHAPTER THREE

CLIMATE

VISITORS from the northern counties and the eastern Midlands frequently comment on the enervating character of Bristol's climate. This is attributable to the fact that the effects of a warm ocean lying close to windward are funnelled towards the city by the Bristol Channel. Consequently the air is always moist, especially in winter when mild south-westerly airstreams raise the temperature, and skies are generally cloudy. Nevertheless, in spite of the fact that the climate of the Bristol region as a whole is dominated by marine influences, there are notable differences as between its several subdivisions (Fig. 13). Thus the Cotswolds and Mendip are bleaker and more snowy in winter, and cooler and more bracing in summer, than is the small basin in which Bristol lies.

Although the records of the British Rainfall Organization provide reasonably good cover, the absence of reliable long-term temperature readings over wide areas precludes any detailed study of such local differences as are undoubtedly experienced throughout the region as a whole. Consequently, the following account refers only to the climate of the city of Bristol and its immediate vicinity. Moreover, it is based on the only reliable series of meteorological observations which cover a period of sufficient length, viz., those made at the University of Bristol's Agricultural and Horticultural Research Station at Long Ashton.[1] Long Ashton lies in a shallow valley about four miles to the south-west of the city's centre and ten miles from the coast. The meteorological instruments are sited on a freely-exposed piece of level ground which stands at an altitude of 160 ft. To the north the ground rises sharply to reach an altitude of 400 ft. in a distance of half a mile, but to the south the slope is much more gentle and undulating.

WIND

A Halliwell-Dines anemometer, with its cups 24 ft. above ground-level, was installed at the Long Ashton Research Station in March 1925. From then until December 1930 observations of wind direction and strength made at 0900 hours G.M.T. were recorded on the 16-point scale, but thereafter such observations were noted on the 8-point scale. The reduction of the 16-point observations to an 8-point scale by some arbitrary method is unsatisfactory, and consequently the only

[1] The writer is much indebted to the Long Ashton meteorological observer, Mr. G. E. Clothier, for providing ready access to all the daily records.

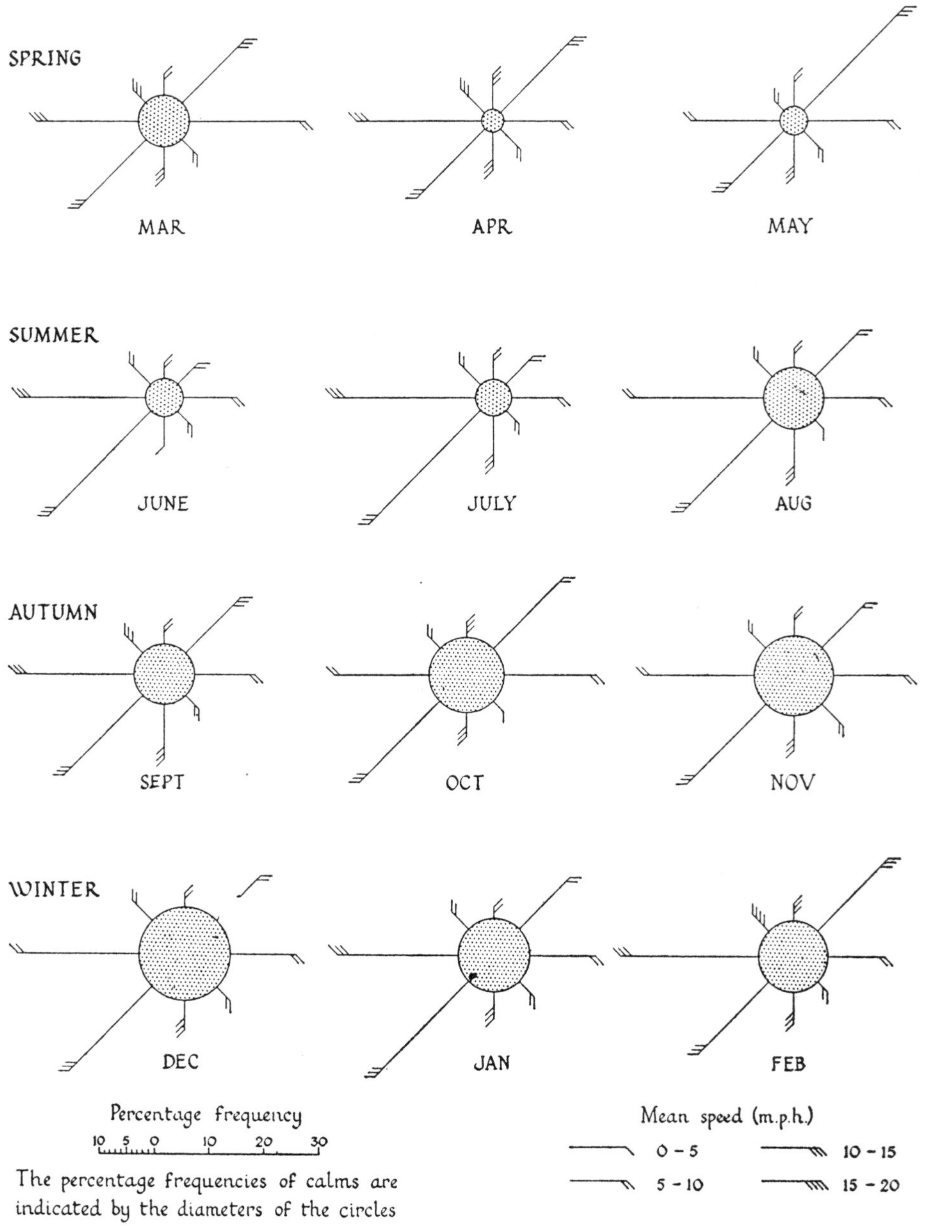

FIG. 8. *Monthly percentage-frequencies of wind directions and calms, and mean wind speeds,* 0900 *hours G.M.T.,* 1931–53.

observations here considered are those covering the period of twenty-three years from January 1931 to December 1953. In January 1947 the anemometer was replaced by a Dines Pressure-Tube Anemograph, but since the height of the cups remained unaltered the 0900-hour readings have been combined with the anemometer records in the compilation of the following summary.

Monthly wind-roses have been constructed, showing the mean percentage-frequencies of wind directions and calms and mean wind speeds at 0900 hours G.M.T. (Fig. 8). The percentage-frequencies of calms are indicated by the diameters of the circles, and the percentage-frequencies of winds by arrows whose lengths are scaled from the circle circumferences. Contrary to what might be generally expected, calms occur least often in the late spring and early summer. Their percentage-frequency figures increase steadily throughout the autumn and reach a maximum of 16·7 in December, a fact which undoubtedly has an important influence on the higher incidence of fog in that month. In all seasons except spring the winds most frequently experienced are those which blow from the west and south-west, and their predominance over those from all other directions is most marked in early summer. In spring there is a tendency for anticyclones to take up a position to the north of the British Isles. The dominant winds are then from the north-east and east, and their comparatively low relative humidity largely accounts for the fact that spring is the driest season of the year. Winds from the north-west, north, south-east and south are infrequent in all months. Although this may in some small measure be attributable to the canalizing effect of the shallow east–west valley in which Long Ashton is situated, the only quarter from which the station can derive any effective shelter is the north.

Mean wind speeds vary but little from month to month (Fig. 8). The only winds whose mean speed falls below 5 m.p.h. are those which blow from the south in June and from the south-east in August and October. On the other hand, the only winds whose mean speed exceeds 15 m.p.h. are February's north-westerlies. As is to be expected, the winds of most constant strength are those from the south-west, whose mean speed does not fall below 10 m.p.h. in any month.

Winds which exceed speeds of 25 m.p.h. (Beaufort force 6 and over) at 0900 hours G.M.T. have been recorded on only 1·8 per cent. of all occasions. Of the total of such recordings, 41 per cent. have been made in winter, 33 per cent. in spring, 22 per cent. in autumn and only 4 per cent. in summer. The percentage-frequencies of direction for these strong winds are given in Table III.

TABLE III

Percentage-frequencies of direction for winds whose speeds at 0900 hours G.M.T. exceed 25 m.p.h. (Beaufort force 6 and over)

	N.	NE.	E.	SE.	S.	SW.	W.	NW.
Percentage-frequency .	3	11	8	3	7	47	20	1

The strongest gust at Long Ashton was recorded at about 1450 hours on 16 November 1928, when the wind speed exceeded 73 m.p.h.

TEMPERATURE

Daily records of air temperature have been taken at the Long Ashton Research Station since 1920, and the following summary is founded on the years 1920–53 inclusive. The equipment comprises two standard thermometers which are used as dry and wet bulbs, with maximum and minimum thermometers of the sheathed pattern, all of which are placed four feet above ground-level in a Stevenson screen. The grass minimum temperature is recorded by a sheathed thermometer exposed over a grass surface. Readings are taken daily at 0900 hours G.M.T., at which time the sheathed thermometers are set.

MONTHLY AND ANNUAL MEAN TEMPERATURES

The monthly mean temperature does not fall below 40° in any month of the year, and in this particular respect the monthly means recorded at Bristol differ most markedly from those at inland stations situated further to the east (Table IV). The influence of the warm ocean lying close to windward is most strongly felt during the winter half of the year, and this accounts for the fact that the monthly mean temperatures at Bristol from October to March inclusive are 1° to 2° higher than those at such stations as Oxford. On the other hand, the monthly mean temperatures at Bristol during the summer half of the year are somewhat lower than the corresponding figures at inland stations in the same latitude, though the differences are now much less marked.

The greatest departures from the monthly means occur during the winter, and more particularly in January and February. Moreover, during these months the largest departures are below the mean. This is a reflection of the fact that the maritime influences, which normally prevail throughout the winter, are occasionally swept aside by a cold stream of air from the Continent. The outstanding example occurred in February 1947, when the mean temperature of 29·1° was 11·7° below the normal. Continental influences were also paramount in January 1940 when the mean temperature was 30·7°, a figure which is 9·8° below the normal. These months, February 1947 and January 1940, are the only two in the records whose mean temperatures fall below 32·0°. Positive departures from the monthly mean temperatures in January and February are considerably less, the greatest values being 7·1° in 1921 and 5·9° in 1926 for these months respectively.

During the summer months departures from the monthly mean temperatures are less pronounced. During the warmest month on record, July 1921, the mean temperature was no more than 5·1° above the normal, and only in eight years has the figure for any month from May to October shown a departure of more than ±4·0°. The least variation has occurred in May, when departures of ±3·0° cover all years

TABLE IV

Mean and extreme temperatures (°F.), 1920–53

	J.	F.	M.	A.	M.	J.	J.	A.	S.	O.	N.	D.	Year
Mean temperature	40·5	40·8	43·9	47·7	53·1	58·5	61·6	61·1	57·1	51·0	44·7	41·3	50·1
Highest recorded	47·6	46·7	48·0	51·8	56·1	61·9	66·7	65·4	61·5	56·5	49·5	47·7	52·2
(Year)	('21)	('26)	('48)	('43)	('52)	('40)	('21)	('47)	('49)	('21)	('38)	('34)	('21)
Lowest recorded	30·7	29·1	39·6	43·4	48·4	55·1	57·6	56·7	52·3	47·4	38·5	34·1	48·7
(Year)	('40)	('47)	('37)	('22)	('41)	('46)	('22)	('22)	('52)	('22)	('23)	('33)	('22)
Extreme range	16·9	17·6	8·4	8·4	7·7	6·8	9·1	8·7	9·2	9·1	11·0	13·6	3·5
Mean daily max. temp.	46·0	46·2	51·0	55·5	61·8	67·1	69·6	69·1	64·9	58·0	50·7	46·6	57·3
Absolute max. temp.	59	62	72	76	84	87	93	93	83	80	66	60	93
(Year)	('44) ('30)	('48)	('29)	('45) ('43) ('40)	('44)	('39)	('23)	('32)	('40)	('21)	('46)	('53)	(12 July 1923) (19 Aug. 1932)
Mean daily min. temp.	34·9	35·0	36·6	39·9	44·5	49·9	53·5	53·0	49·4	44·0	38·8	36·0	43·0
Absolute min. temp.	8	6	13	25	25	35	41	38	33	24	21	18	6
(Year)	('40)	('47)	('47)	('38) ('29) ('22)	('45)	('20)	('48) ('28) ('24)	('31) ('22)	('48) ('43) ('28) ('27)	('31)	('37) ('23)	('48) ('46) ('44) ('35)	(25 Feb. 1947)
Mean daily range	11·1	11·2	14·4	15·6	17·3	17·2	16·1	16·1	15·5	14·0	11·9	10·6	14·3
Absolute grass min. temp.	−2	−5	−1	16	17	28	34	30	25	16	11	8	−5
(Year)	('45)	('47)	('47)	('52) ('34)	('45)	('39)	('52) ('24)	('22)	('43) ('39)	('31)	('43)	('46)	(24 Feb. 1947)

except 1941, and even during that year the mean temperature for this month was no more than 4·7° below the normal.

Contrary to popular belief the summer months of 1954 were not the coolest on record. During that year the monthly mean temperatures for June, July and August were 56·9°, 57·8° and 59·1° respectively, figures which are in each case higher than those lowest recorded values shown in Table IV. In 1954 the average mean temperature for these three summer months was 57·9°. Cooler summers were experienced both in 1920 and in 1922, when the corresponding figures were 57·8° and 57·3° respectively.

The annual mean temperature is 50·1° and, in common with all parts of the British Isles, the departures from this figure are small. In only five of the thirty-four years under consideration have the departures amounted to more than 1·0°, the greatest being +2·1° in 1921 and −1·4° in 1922.

DAILY TEMPERATURES

Although the greatest departures from monthly mean temperatures occur in the winter months, the mean daily range of temperature is least during this season. Having reached a maximum of 17·3° in May, the mean daily range then declines slowly throughout the summer months before falling sharply during the autumn to reach its minimum of about 11° in the months of December, January and February (Table IV).

The absolute maximum temperature recorded at Long Ashton is 93·0°, a figure which has been reached on two days, 12 July 1923 and 19 August 1932. Apart from these, the maximum temperature has reached 90° on three days only, 13 July 1923, and 28 and 29 July 1948. Daily maxima of 80° and over have six times been recorded as early in the year as May and on two occasions as late as October.

The absolute minimum temperature is 6·0°, recorded on 25 February 1947 during a period in which the normal marine influences were completely ousted by exceptionally cold easterly winds from the Continent. For the same reason, daily minima of 8·0° and 7·0° were recorded on 21 January 1940 and 14 February 1929 respectively.

Certain other data concerning daily temperatures at Long Ashton are presented in Table V.

TABLE V

Means of annual temperature extremes (°F.), 1920–53

Mean of the highest maximum temperature recorded in each year	84·7
Mean of the lowest minimum temperature recorded in each year	19·0
Mean of the lowest ground minimum temperature recorded in each year	10·6
Average mean air temperature on the warmest day of each year	71·7
Average mean air temperature on the coldest day of each year	27·0

The warmest day ever experienced at Long Ashton throughout the period under review was 13 July 1923, when the mean air temperature reached 78·5° (max. 91°, min. 66°). The coldest day on record was 13 February 1929, when the mean air temperature was only 18·0° (max. 27°, min. 9°).

The warmest day of the year has occurred as early as 25 May and as late as 12 September, a total spread of 110 days (Fig. 9*a*). However, the interquartile range runs from 27 June to 3 August, and there is thus an even chance that the warmest day in any year will fall within this 37-day period. Fig. 9*b* shows that the coldest day of the year has been experienced as early as 13 November and as late as 12 March, a spread of 120 days. In this case, however, the dates are more evenly distributed, with the result that the interquartile range covers a much longer 54-day period between 19 December and 11 February.

The total numbers of cold and very cold days in each month throughout the period 1921–53 are represented by the figures given in Table VI.[1]

TABLE VI

Total numbers of cold and very cold days, 1921–53

	J.	F.	M.	A.–O.	N.	D.	Total	Mean Annual Number
Cold days	115	73	19	Nil	16	77	300	9·1
Very cold days	31	26	2	Nil	1	14	74	2·2

The very cold days are included among the cold-day figures. Thus in an average year Bristolians can expect 9 cold days of which 2 will be very cold.

FROST

Whilst air frost has been experienced in all months from October to May inclusive, the only months which have remained completely free of ground frost[2] are July and August (Table VII).[3]

TABLE VII

Mean monthly and mean annual number of days on which frost was recorded, 1923–53

	J.	F.	M.	A	M.	J.	J.	A.	S.	O.	N.	D.	Year
Air Frost	12·0	10·4	9·0	2·6	0·8	0	0	0	0	1·8	5·7	9·9	52·2
Ground Frost	16·2	15·4	14·7	9·7	3·5	0·2	0	0	1·1	5·6	11·4	15·3	93·3

[1] A day is here described as 'cold' when its mean air temperature is below 32·0°, and as 'very cold' when its maximum temperature does not rise above this figure.

[2] Ground frost is registered when the grass minimum temperature equals or is less than 30·4°.

[3] A ground frost was recorded on 26 August 1922 when the grass minimum temperature fell to 30·0° but, since the records of ground frost in that particular year are incomplete, they were not considered in the preparation of Table VII.

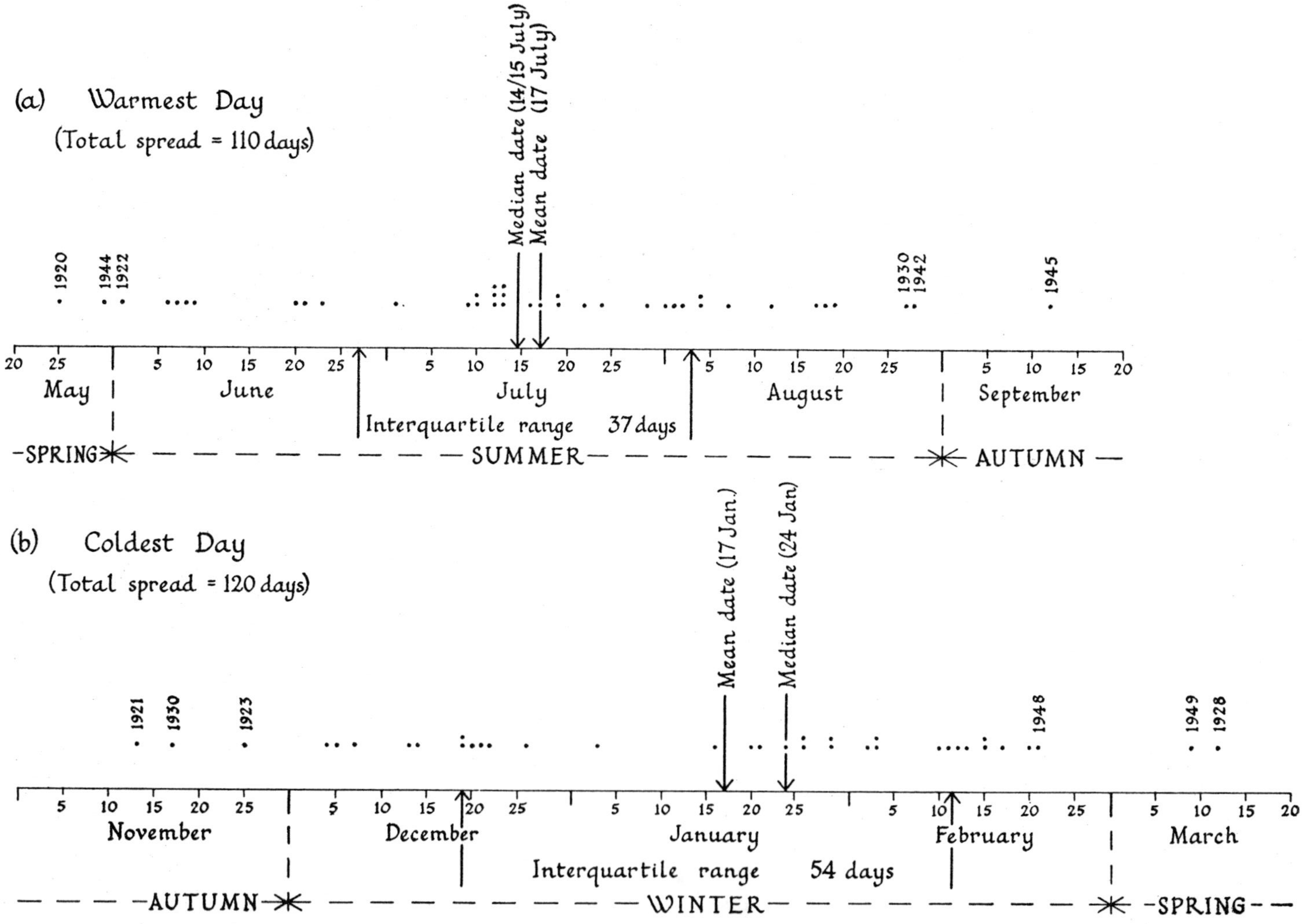

FIG. 9. *Date of (a) the warmest and (b) the coldest day (highest and lowest mean temperature) in each year,* 1920–53. (*The date of each warmest and coldest day is represented by a dot. When two dates in any one year experienced equally high or low mean temperatures, both are plotted.*)

The months with most frost, arranged in order of decreasing frequency, are January, February, December and March. The severity of the worst air and ground frost experienced in each month can be ascertained from a consideration of the absolute minimum and absolute grass minimum temperatures which are supplied in Table IV. It is particularly worthy of note that over 31 degrees of ground frost have been recorded in each of the first three months of the year, and that on 25 February 1947, following a night on which 35 degrees of ground frost were registered, the minimum air temperature fell 26 degrees below freezing-point. These figures show that in spite

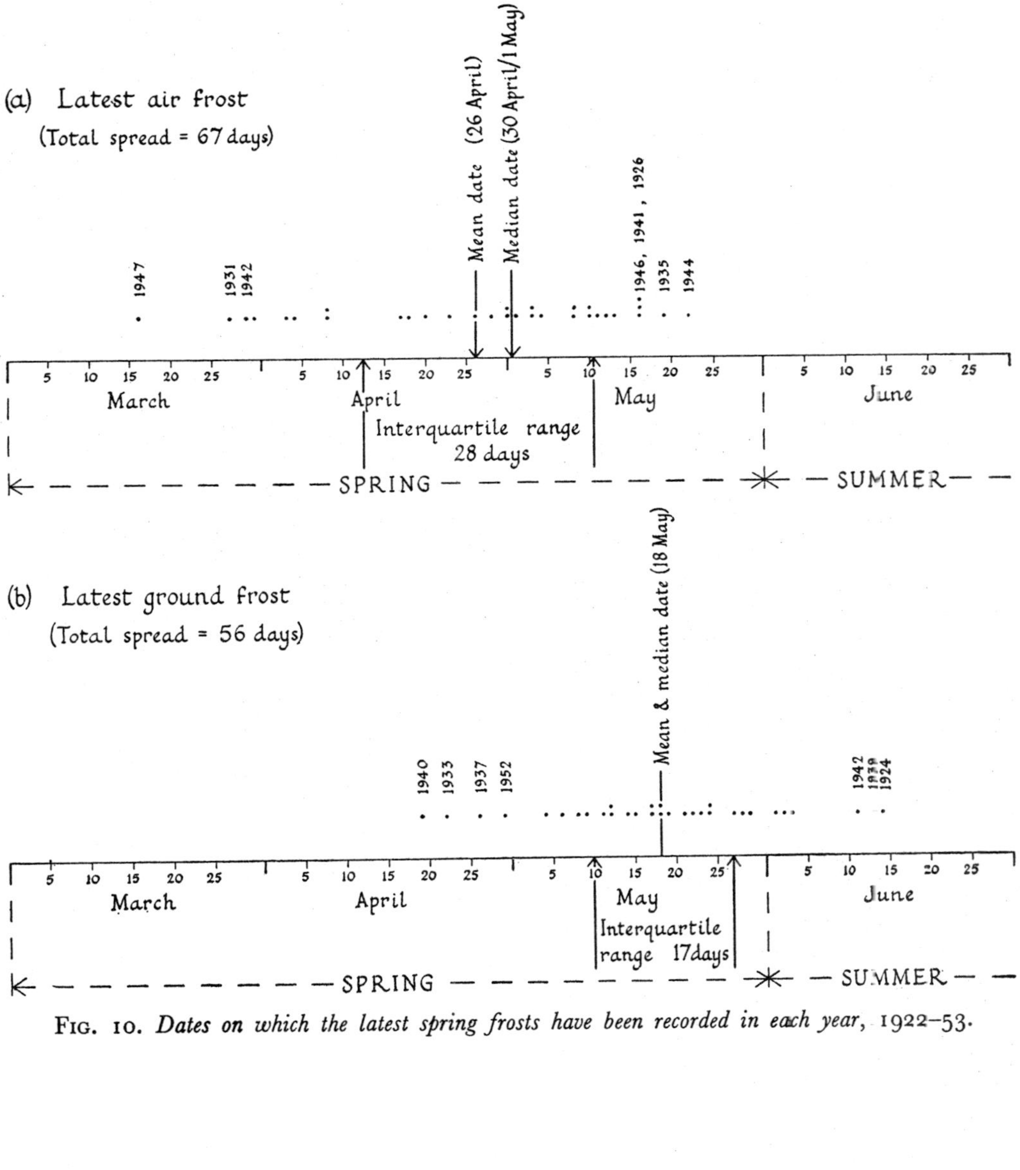

FIG. 10. *Dates on which the latest spring frosts have been recorded in each year*, 1922–53.

of the fact that winters are normally mild, low temperatures can be recorded at Bristol when the area is dominated by continental rather than by marine influences.

Following a winter of unusual severity, the latest air frost in the spring of 1947 was recorded on 16 March, a date which is considerably earlier than that in any other year under review (Fig. 10*a*). At the other end of the scale the latest air frost in the spring of 1944 was not recorded until 22 May. The dates of the latest air frost in the springs of other years are reasonably well distributed over this 67-day spread, with the result that the interquartile range covers a 28-day period extending from 12 April to 10 May. Although the latest spring ground frost has been recorded as early as 19 April and as late as 14 June, representing a 56-day spread, the relevant dates in half the years under review fall within a comparatively restricted period of 17 days extending from 10 May to 27 May (Fig. 10*b*).

The chances of an air frost are reasonably remote after the middle of May, but this statement does not apply to ground frost until the end of that month is reached. The interquartile range for the latest ground frost begins on 10 May when that for the latest air frost ends. Thus if both interquartile ranges be placed end to end they cover the 45-day period between 12 April and 27 May. There is an even chance that the latest air frost will be experienced during the first 28 days of this period, and that the latest ground frost will be recorded during its last 17 days.

The first autumn air frost has been recorded as early as 1 October and as late as 20 December, giving an 80-day spread, but there is an even chance that this will be experienced within a restricted 12-day period extending from 19 October to the end of that month (Fig. 11*a*). The dates on which the earliest autumn ground frost have been registered cover a more restricted period of 64 days extending from 26 August to 29 October (Fig. 11*b*). However, in this case the dates are much more evenly distributed, with the result that the interquartile range covers the 27-day period between 22 September and 19 October. The probability of ground frost in autumn increases rapidly after the middle of September, and of air frost after the middle of October. The interquartile range for the earliest air frost begins on 19 October, when that for the earliest ground frost ends. Thus if both interquartile ranges be placed end to end they cover the 39-day period between 22 September and 31 October. There is an even chance that the earliest ground frost will be recorded during the first 27 days of this period, and that the earliest air frost will be experienced during its last 12 days.

The mean length of the season free of ground frost for the years 1922–53 was 136 days, with maxima of 164 days in 1933 and 1934, minima of 101 days in 1923 and 1925 and an interquartile range of 120–152 days. The mean length of the season free of air frost during the same period was 182 days, with a maximum of 224 days in 1937, a minimum of 143 days in 1928, and an interquartile range of 165–193 days.

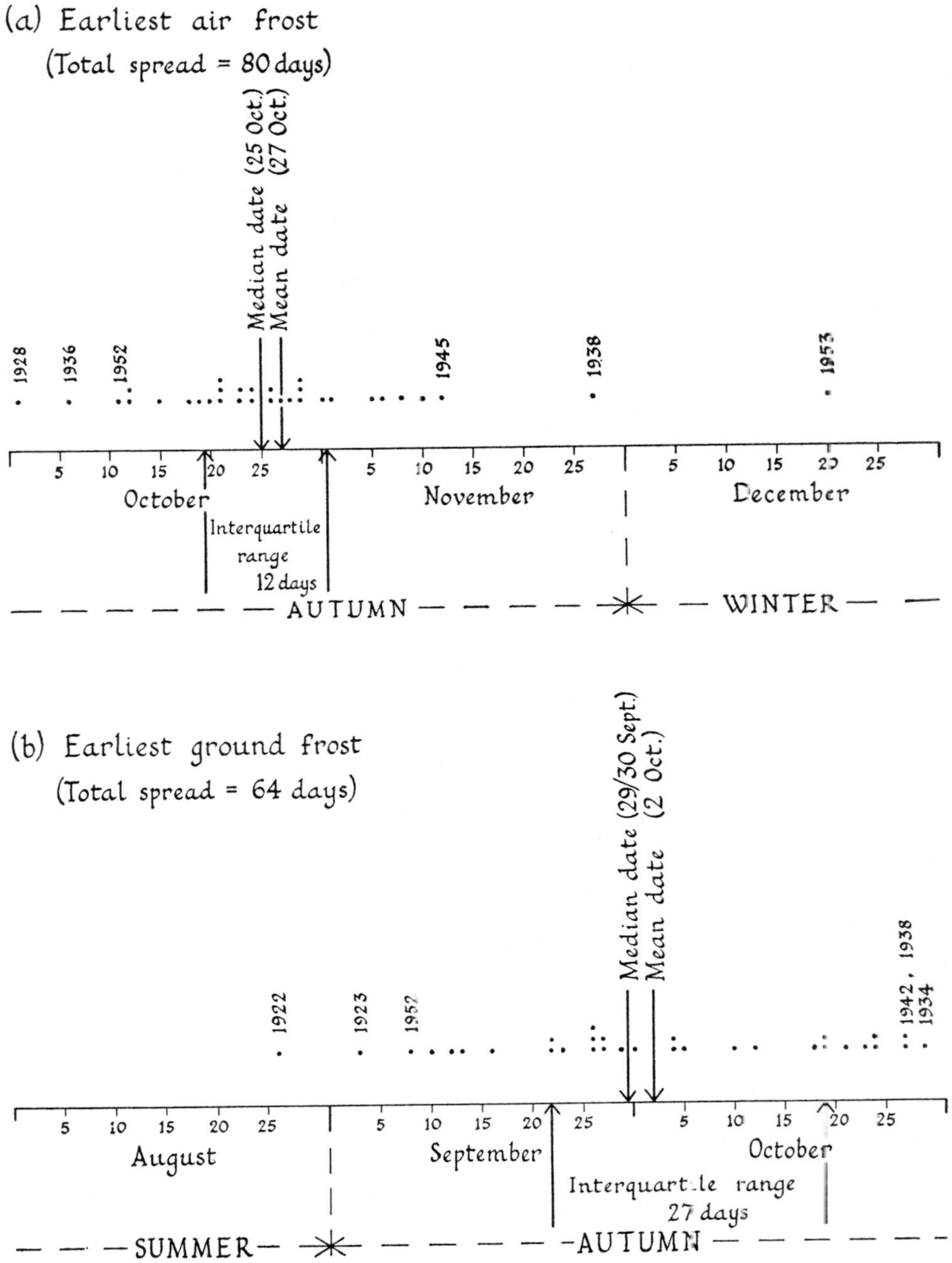

FIG. 11. *Dates on which the earliest autumn frosts have been recorded in each year*, 1922–53.

SUNSHINE

Records of daily sunshine totals in hours have been taken at the Long Ashton Research Station since 1921, and the following summary is based on the years 1921–53 inclusive. Readings are taken from a Campbell-Stokes sunshine recorder elevated on a roof-top 31 ft. above ground-level. The instrument is well situated to give an unobstructed exposure to the sun at all times of the year except during part of June and July when it is shaded by a hill to the north-west shortly before sunset.

The months with the highest and lowest mean sunshine figures are June and December respectively (Table VIII). All months with the exception of January experienced their highest sunshine totals in the 1920s or 1940s, and in seven cases the lowest totals were recorded in the 1930s. In June and July 1954 the sunshine totals were 152·5 hours and 121·8 hours respectively. Thus, although neither of these two months was the coolest on record, both were the least sunny.

From a consideration of mean sunshine values for the period 1921–50 it has been established that throughout the year as a whole the sun shines for only 34 per cent. of the total number of hours during which it is above the horizon. The corresponding figure for the months of December and January is in each case as low as 19, and even in June it does not rise above 43.[1] These figures are typical of a station in this latitude whose climate is so markedly dominated by marine influences.

PRECIPITATION

RAIN

The recording of daily rainfall totals at the Long Ashton Research Station commenced in 1914, but in order to preserve uniformity as between the periods covered by the temperature and rainfall records the following summary relates only to the years 1920–53 inclusive. The raingauge has a diameter of 8 in. and is sited such that its rim stands 12 in. above ground-level.

On the basis of mean rainfall totals March is the driest month of the year and November the wettest (Table IX). However, Fig. 12 shows that in all months except January and April the median values are less than the mean, with a maximum difference of nearly 0·7 in. in November. This at once indicates that in each of the ten months in question the mean is weighted upward by one or more abnormally heavy falls, and is therefore not suitable as a guide to average conditions. On the basis of median values March is still the driest month of the year, but the wettest is October, and both January and August have more rain than November. The interquartile range is a minimum in the months of April and September (1·55 in.), and a maximum in November (3·10 in.) All months have experienced minimum rainfall totals of less than 0·9 in., and except in April, May and June the maximum totals have exceeded 6·3 in. The rainfall totals in the wettest year (1924) and the driest year

[1] G. E. Clothier. 1950. 'Sunshine at Long Ashton, 1921–50', *Ann. Rep. Univ. Bristol Agric. Hort. Res. Station, Long Ashton,* 210.

TABLE VIII

Mean and extreme sunshine figures, 1921–53

	J.	F.	M.	A.	M.	J.	J.	A.	S.	O.	N.	D.	Year
Mean sunshine (hours)	48·2	67·5	120·2	161·2	194·7	213·0	196·8	185·0	139·3	101·2	57·5	47·0	1531·7
Highest recorded	78·4	111·5	197·3	226·0	286·3	334·8	273·9	270·8	208·0	172·1	97·0	79·0	1880·3
(Year)	('33)	('49)	('29)	('21)	('48)	('25)	('21)	('47)	('29)	('21)	('23)	('46)	('21)
Lowest recorded	24·1	20·8	71·5	104·3	127·6	157·3	124·4	137·7	88·2	62·8	15·8	17·1	1305·9
(Year)	('21)	('47)	('39)	('31)	('32)	('53)	('31)	('31)	('51)	('34)	('34)	('27)	('31)
Mean sunshine (hours per day)	1·55	2·39	3·88	5·37	6·28	7·07	6·39	5·97	4·64	3·26	1·92	1·52	4·19
Mean number of sunless days	12·5	8·2	4·4	2·6	1·9	1·6	1·5	1·5	2·1	4·7	9·8	11·8	62·5
Highest recorded	17	18	11	7	4	5	6	4	6	10	19	20	86
(Year)	('53) ('41) ('37)	('47)	('42)	('31)	('52) ('51) ('41)	('46)	('50)	('48) ('38) ('29)	('32)	('46)	('34)	('27)	('37)
Lowest recorded	4	1	0	0	0	0	0	0	0	1	4	7	47
(Year or number of years)	('33) ('22)	('49) ('22)	('27)	('48) ('45) ('21)	('21)	7 Yrs.	7 Yrs.	4 Yrs.	6 Yrs.	('47) ('41)	('25)	('46) ('29)	('25) ('21)

TABLE IX

Mean and extreme rainfall figures, 1920–53

	J.	F.	M.	A.	M.	J.	J.	A.	S.	O.	N.	D.	Year
Mean rainfall (in.)	3·45	2·49	2·08	2·38	2·62	2·13	3·09	3·55	3·09	3·75	3·91	3·29	35·83
Highest total	6·37	7·12	6·30	4·85	5·93	4·45	7·92	7·45	7·88	7·96	9·92	8·08	49·07
(Year)	('48)	('23)	('47)	('35)	('32)	('24)	('40)	('50)	('35)	('49)	('29)	('29)	('24)
Lowest Total	0·74	0·05	0·46	0·25	0·89	0·03	0·77	0·19	0·50	0·55	0·53	0·56	25·20
(Year)	('53)	('32)	('38)	('38)	('39)	('25)	('52)	('40)	('41)	('47)	('45)	('26)	('21)
Mean rainfall per 10 days (in.)	1·11	0·88	0·67	0·79	0·85	0·71	1·00	1·15	1·03	1·21	1·30	1·06	0·98
Mean number of rainy days	19·2	14·8	14·0	15·0	14·2	12·3	15·0	15·6	15·2	16·6	18·1	18·0	188·1
Highest total	28	24	25	23	21	22	28	25	26	26	27	30	225
(Year)	('48)	('23)	('47) ('27)	('32)	('45) ('32) ('24) ('23)	('46)	('36)	('24)	('50)	('32)	('26)	('29)	('30)
Lowest Total	6	2	5	6	8	1	6	3	3	7	10	10	150
(Year)	('53)	('21)	('44)	('38)	('28)	('25)	('52) ('51)	('47) ('40)	('41)	('47) ('22)	('34) ('20)	('33)	('53) ('21)
Mean rainfall per 10 rainy days (in.)	1·79	1·68	1·48	1·59	1·85	1·73	2·05	2·27	2·03	2·26	2·16	1·83	1·90
Total number of occasions on which thunder heard (1922–53)	8	12	14	32	65	50	70	75	31	29	15	15	416
Total number of occasions on which over 1 in. of rain fell in 24 hours (1922–53)	2	2	0	1	8	4	8	17	8	14	14	3	81
Heaviest fall of rain in 24 hours (1920–53)	1·79	1·34	0·88	1·22	1·68	2·21	2·32	1·86	1·81	2·32	2·35	1·32	2·35
(Date)	1/'26	24/'33	12/'47	30/'39	1/'32	13/'52	15/'37	29/'53	14/'27	5/'29	2/'40	19/'22	2 Nov. 1940

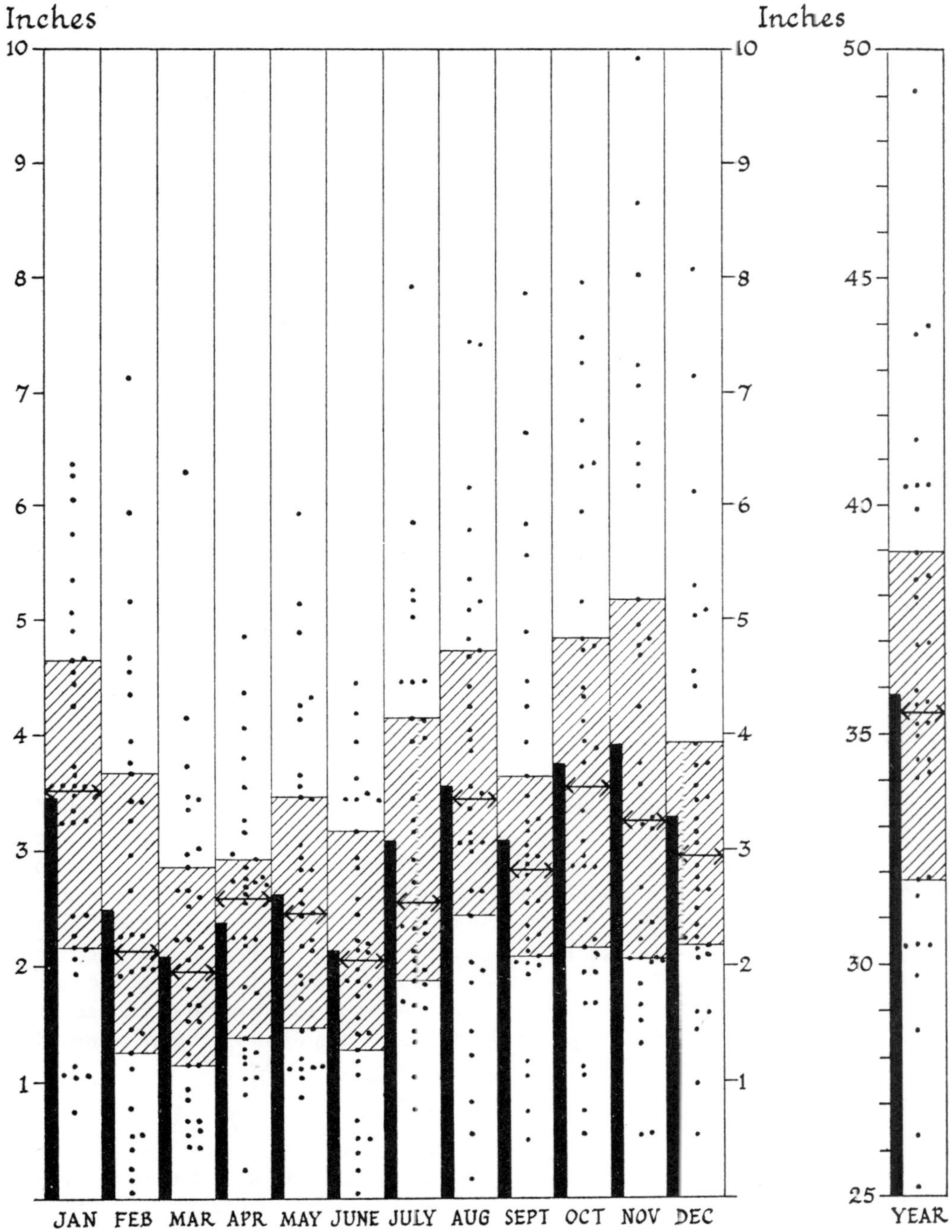

FIG. 12. *Rainfall dispersion diagram for the period* 1920–53. *Individual monthly totals are shown by dots. Median values are shown by arrows and mean values by the tops of the narrow black columns. Interquartile ranges are shaded.*

(1921) were 37 per cent. above and 30 per cent. below the mean respectively. Variations of this magnitude are however quite exceptional, as is indicated by the fact that throughout the 34-year period under review the annual rainfall has deviated from the mean by plus 20 per cent. and minus 20 per cent. in only four and three years respectively.

The mean annual rainfall total is well distributed throughout the year, 20 per cent. falling in spring (March–May), 24 per cent. in summer (June–August), 30 per cent. in Autumn (September–November) and 26 per cent. in winter (December–February). The mean number of rainy days[1] is 14 or more in every month with the exception of June, and all months have experienced maxima of at least 21. No month has ever been completely free of rainy days, and in neither November nor December has the minimum fallen below 10. July has never failed to produce at least 6 rainy days, and the corresponding figure for May is as high as 8.

During the summer half of the year the heaviest falls of rain are associated with thunder. This is heard most frequently in August, the month in which the mean rainfall per 10 rainy days and the total number of occasions on which over one inch of rain has fallen in 24 hours are highest. Thunderstorms are more frequent in May than in April or June, which results in a higher mean rainfall per 10 rainy days and in a greater number of occasions on which over one inch of rain has been recorded in 24 hours. With the exception of March, all months have experienced over one inch of rain in 24 hours, and in June, July, October and November over 2 in. have fallen in that time. The most intensive fall of rain in the period under review occurred on the night 14–15 July 1937, when 3·02 in. were recorded in 11 hours.

The distribution of mean annual rainfall over the Bristol region, as in all parts of the British Isles, is closely related to relief (Fig. 13). The Brendon Hills south of Minehead reach elevations of over 1,300 ft., and here the mean annual rainfall during the period 1881–1915 exceeded 50 in. The figure for the Mendip summits, which exceed 1,000 ft. in height, was over 45 in., and more than 40 in. were recorded in that portion of the Forest of Dean which lies above the 650-foot contour. The only other part of the region which experienced a mean annual rainfall of over 40 in. during this period was that centred on the chalk hills south of Frome whose summits rise above 800 ft. Apart from these heavy local increases over areas of high ground, the mean annual rainfall totals represented in Fig. 13 show a steady decline in a north-westerly direction, as is to be expected from the fact that most of the rain is brought by south-westerly winds. In the Vale of Severn to the north of Gloucester mean annual totals fall below 25 in., and are thus less than half the figure recorded on the Brendon Hills.

SNOW AND SLEET

The mean annual number of days on which snow or sleet falls is 12·0. Snow is said to be lying when at least half the ground visible from the raingauge site is

[1] A rainy day is one on which at least 0·01 in. of rain is recorded.

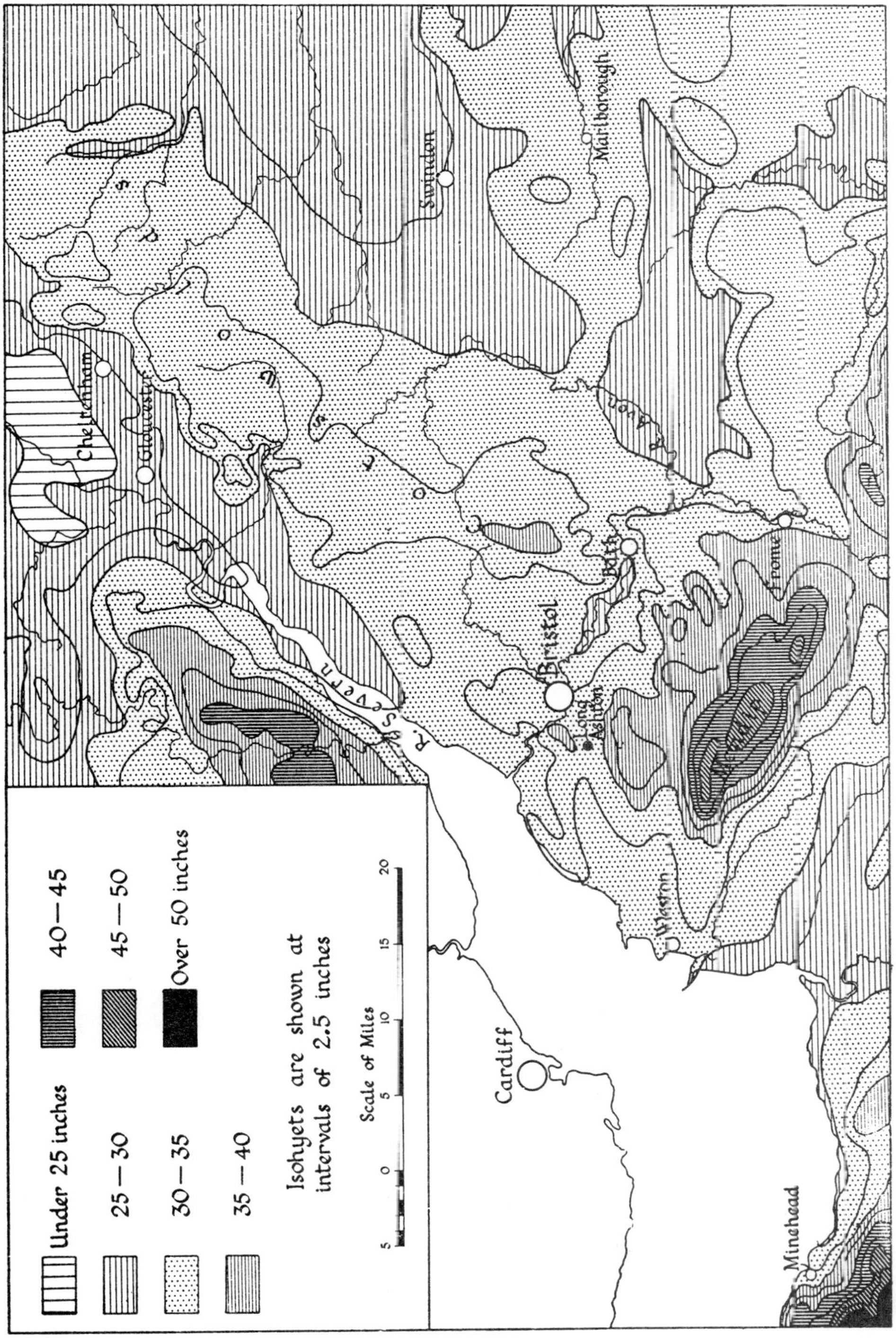

FIG. 13. *Mean annual rainfall, 1881–1915.*

TABLE X

Snow and fog, 1922–53

	J.	F.	M.	A.	M.	J.	J.	A.	S.	O.	N.	D.	Total	Mean annual number
Total number of days on which snow or sleet fell . .	98	119	66	29	3	0	0	0	0	2	11	55	383	12·0
Total number of days with snow lying at 0900 hours G.M.T.	63	70	25	1	0	0	0	0	0	0	8	35	202	6·3
Total number of days on which fog was recorded at 0900 hours G.M.T. .	72	48	55	6	2	0	0	4	13	53	78	90	421	13·2

snow-covered at 0900 hours G.M.T., and the mean annual number of such occasions is 6·3. Thus snow is less frequent at Bristol than at such inland stations as Oxford, where the corresponding figures are 18·5 and 10·5 respectively.[1] Snow or sleet has fallen in all months except June–September inclusive (Table x). About 57 per cent. of the total number of days on which falls have been recorded occur in January and February, the latter being the most snowy month of the year.

FOG

The mean annual number of days on which fog is recorded at Long Ashton at 0900 hours G.M.T. is 13.[2] In this respect Bristol compares favourably with such inland stations as Stratford-on-Avon and Oxford, where the corresponding figures are 29 and 39 respectively.[3] Fogs are most often recorded in December (Table x), due at least in part to the fact that the percentage-frequency of calms reaches a maximum in that month (Fig. 8). Personal observations suggest that on many occasions when the city is shrouded in fog its higher outskirts remain comparatively clear, and that the fog is often thickest in the vicinity of such railway stations as Temple Meads and Stapleton Road, where smoke pollution is highest and where the close proximity of the rivers Avon and Frome increases the vapour content of the air.

[1] C. G. Smith. 1954. 'The Oxford Region', *Handbook Brit. Assoc. Adv. Science*, 47.

[2] Fog is recorded when the visibility is less than 1,100 yards.

[3] C. G. Smith: op. cit., 48.

CHAPTER FOUR

SOILS OF GLOUCESTERSHIRE, SOMERSET AND WILTSHIRE

SOILS result from the action, over longer or shorter periods, of chemical, physical and biological processes on the parent material, which is derived from the weathering of rocks. The processes involved are largely controlled by factors of climate, vegetation, relief and the nature of the parent material and, since similar effects are produced all over the world by certain combinations of these processes and factors, it is possible to refer a great many soils to a few categories which, in Britain, are termed major soil groups.

In the three counties, the most extensive major soil group is that of 'calcareous soils' or 'rendzinas'; under grassland, these soils have a dark-coloured, highly humose A horizon overlying the C_1 horizon, which consists of white or grey, highly calcareous loam intermingled with numerous fragments of soft limestone and passes into the weathering rock. Shallow rendzinas are found where the rock is harder and more ferruginous, but generally 'red and brown calcareous soils' occur in which a less humose A_1 horizon overlies a more or less brown-coloured, calcareous B horizon before the weathering rock is reached.

When the parent material is not highly calcareous but has a good reserve of bases and plant nutrients, a luxuriant deciduous vegetation is found which, by its leaf-fall, maintains the base status, while the abundant soil fauna incorporates organic matter and the mineral soil so that they are mechanically inseparable (mull humus). Products of mineral decomposition largely remain *in situ* and there is little loss of material from the soil. Soils such as this are termed 'brown earths' and have a dark-coloured, mull humus A horizon which passes to a B horizon of a colour similar to that of the parent material but with a brown tint. Brown earths are delicately balanced in their environment and a change in climate or vegetation (including that caused by man) may have disastrous results which are not apparent for many years. Hard, massive limestones only yield a small amount of non-calcareous parent material and shallow brown earths as well as rendzinas occur on such rocks.

More acid parent materials are usually colonized by plants whose leaf-fall is insufficient to maintain the base status and by a soil fauna which does little to incorporate mineral and organic matter. As a result, material is lost from the profile and 'podzolized soils' are formed. In these soils, which are rare in the region, a layer of decomposing leaf litter (raw humus)—the A_0 horizon—rests on a grey-coloured A_1 horizon where mineral grains are coated with organic substances; this grades into an almost white A_2 horizon. From all these A horizons most of the plant nutrients and iron compounds are lost. Underneath the A horizons is a dark or rusty-brown B horizon where the iron compounds accumulate to form the B_2 horizon which may or may not be differentiated from the more highly organic B_1 horizon which usually lies above it.

The soils so far described are developed under free drainage conditions but many soils, either because of their situation or because the parent material is close-textured, are formed under poor drainage conditions and are classified as 'gley soils'. The more or less permanently wet zone may occur either near the surface or at some depth below it; in the former circumstance the diagnostic characters become less intense and, in the latter, more intense with depth. In both cases, there is a zone, where the water-table fluctuates, characterized by pale-grey, orange and rusty-brown spots and blotches. Where the water-table is stationary the soil-mass is predominantly grey. The remains of vegetation are not well incorporated because faunal activity is low and they therefore accumulate to form a dark-coloured humose or peaty A horizon. There is considerable variation in the characters of gley soils and their characteristics can be impressed on those of other major soil groups.

Peats and peaty soils belong to the major group of 'organic soils' and occur typically in two sites, viz., in basins or on elevated land. In the first site vegetation grows in ponded water and decays beneath it. The type of vegetation is controlled by the nutrient status of the water and peats can be classified according as to whether they are produced from vegetation grown in base-rich water or otherwise. When the surface of the peat becomes raised above the water, plants growing on it become dependent on the slightly acid rainwater, and mosses eventually predominate. Hummocks of acid 'raised moss' may thus form, surrounded by the original 'basin peat'. Peat is acidic on elevated land and is formed by the slow decay of such plants as can withstand high rainfall, low evaporation and low temperatures. Such peats are classed as 'blanket peat' and cover large areas in northern England and in Scotland.

The soils in the three counties are more closely related to the underlying geological formations than those of many other parts of Britain. There is considerable variation in the strata exposed because extensive mountain-building processes and subsequent erosion have resulted in the exposure of a succession of rocks ranging from Cambrian to the younger Eocene. Although the region was outside the limits of the great Quaternary ice sheets there are large areas of recent and superficial deposits which originated under periglacial conditions.

While major soil groups provide a broad picture of the soils of large areas they are not suitable for more detailed mapping and smaller units are used. The basic mapping unit in Great Britain, the United States and many other countries is the soil series which refers to a group of soils developed from a common parent material and having a similar succession of horizons; the textures of the surface soils may vary, and on these textural differences the series are further divided into soil types. Parent material is dependent on geology and in Britain the boundaries of many of the major soil groups and soil series coincide roughly with those of certain geological formations.

On the other hand, owing to the interplay of soil-forming factors and processes, a geological formation may give rise to soils in different soil series; however, a major group may occur on a number of geological formations.

About 50 per cent. of Wiltshire consists of an elevated mass of Chalk dissected by many streams and forming a distinct landscape-unit. It is a good example of geological and pedological boundaries coinciding, for the soils on the Upper, Middle and Lower Chalk can be considered as rendzinas in varying stages of development although, of course, the profile is frequently modified by cultivation. The arable soils typically have a grey, calcareous, clay-loam surface which overlies a whiter, soft, highly calcareous clay-loam in which the pieces of chalk increase in number and size with depth until the weathering rock is reached. Under old grassland, the profile is essentially similar, but the surface soil is darker, due to a higher content of organic matter, and may be almost completely decalcified; the lower horizons are similar to those under arable cultivation. Such soils are mapped as the Icknield Series. The Lower Chalk Marl contains a higher proportion of clay; the soils, therefore, are correspondingly heavier in texture and have better water-holding properties. They are considered to be rendzinas and are mapped as the Wantage Series which, under grass, has a dark-grey, humose and calcareous clay horizon above grey calcareous clay which persists to the weathering rock or marl. In depressions, the water-table may not be far below the surface and, in addition to the characters of the Wantage Series, signs of imperfect or poor drainage appear. Such a soil is mapped as the Burwell Series and is classified as a gleyed rendzina.

Many of the highest parts of the Chalk are capped by the remains of the superficial Clay-with-flints deposit, the soils on which give rise to several problems. In general, the deposit is a compact, orange or red clay and, where it is close to the surface, as on the shoulders of escarpments or slopes, the soils are mapped as the Winchester Series. The opinion has been advanced that these deposits are the remains of soils formed in Miocene or Pliocene times and should, therefore, be regarded as parts of fossil or relic soils, developed under former sub-tropical conditions, on which the present soil is being formed. Elsewhere, the deposit is covered by material the geologists map as brickearth and where this is sufficiently deep the soils are mapped as the Batcombe Series; here the profile is a slightly humose loam passing into a pale-brown silt-loam which rests on the orange-coloured (and often grey-mottled) clay of the Clay-with-flints. It is possible that such soils are derived from the Clay-with-flints entirely by eluviation of clay and could therefore be considered as grey-brown podzolic soils.

Another example of the close relationship between pedological and geological boundaries is presented by the great mass of the limestones of the Inferior and Great Oolite and the Cornbrash which traverse Gloucestershire and Somerset from north-east to south-west. These limestones form a landscape-unit sharply delimited on the western side by the sudden fall from the crest of the ridge to the flat land in the low-lying plain. The eastern edge is less clearly defined because the limestones dip beneath the Oxford Clay which, together with the Kimeridge Clay, forms the wide valley between the Oolite and the Chalk. A number of series occur on the limestones which can be grouped and classified as red and brown calcareous soils. The commonest series is the Sherborne which, under grassland, has a thin, slightly calcareous or acid mull-humus horizon of a clay-loam, or clay, texture overlying a variable thickness of brown, or reddish-brown, calcareous clay-loam, or clay, often containing numerous fragments of limestone, which passes into the cream-coloured weathering rock. There are some points of resemblance between this and the rendzina and, indeed, soils of the latter group occur under woodland and in other situations on the limestones. Again, on some sites, the more usual red colour is intensified; the soil is friable when dry but plastic when moist, and has lost so much of its carbonate that it can almost be considered as a terra rossa or a soil normally associated with limestone in sub-tropical climates.

A landscape-unit found scattered in Gloucestershire, but also comprising large areas in Somerset, is that associated with the Carboniferous Limestone. The hills are often sparsely covered with vegetation but in Somerset, on Mendip, with a somewhat higher rainfall, vegetation is more luxuriant. The parent rock is hard and, on weathering, yields a red, almost non-calcareous, fine sandy clay which forms the parent material of the thin, brown-red, slightly acid, loamy soils mapped as the Lulsgate Series. There appears to be a thin, fine sandy, superficial deposit on many parts of Mendip which gives rise to the Nordrach Series with 2 to 3 ft. of slightly acid, brown or pale-brown, fine sandy loam overlying reddish clay. It might be expected that, with a moderately high rainfall and acidic parent material, podzolized soils would be frequently found on Mendip, but this is rarely so and most of the soils fall into the group of brown earths. Although the red colour of the soils indicates iron oxide in plenty, the oxide is probably not in a form to permit easy and extensive mobilization by solution and reduction; furthermore, it may be too aged to react easily, because the source of the iron oxide may not be the recent weathering of ferruginous minerals, but the particles that were reddened in Triassic times. The scarcity of podzolized soils where they might be expected on red-coloured rocks of Triassic and Devonian age probably has a similar explanation.

Brown earths, not of great extent in the three counties, are not confined to any particular geological horizons, although in this group also the boundary of a soil series may coincide with a geological boundary. Furthermore, brown earths often occur in situations where, locally, gleying conditions may also be found. For these reasons, soil series included in the brown earths are subdivided according to the drainage conditions and base status. Brown earths are found on the Middle and Upper Lias Sands (Atrim, Martock, Petherton Series), Keuper and Permian Sandstones (Bridgnorth Series), Devonian rocks (Bodley and Blackmore Gate Series on Hangman Grit and Morte Slates respectively) and on several other formations and superficial deposits; intermingled with these well-drained soils are others in which the influence of ground water is apparent and these are considered as brown earths with gleying. Soils which, by definition, might be considered as belonging to the grey-brown podzolic group are also found where brown earths are common and it is frequently difficult to decide whether the heavier-textured B horizon is of pedological or geological origin. On account of their properties brown earths provide farmland of high quality. Their nutrient status is easily maintained, their water-retaining power is good though their internal drainage is free, usually their texture is such that they are easily cultivated and maintain their tilth, and they frequently occur on land with relief suitable for cultivation. They are sought after for arable land, market gardens, orchards and nurseries so that, in planning the use of land, every effort should be made to retain them for agricultural purposes. Probably soils of this group are most extensive in the Vale of Taunton Deane, in the area north-east and south-west around the Quantock Hills, on the Old Red Sandstone and Coal Measures in the vicinity of the Forest of Dean and they also occur on the red sandstones of the latter formation north-east and south-east of Bristol. The Worcester Series developed on Keuper Marl, and the Bromyard Series on marly beds in the Old Red Sandstone are brown earths in which slight gleying may or may not be present. These series are extensive in Somerset and Gloucestershire.

Completely gleyed soils are, fortunately, rare in the region, but in many soils the water-table remains sufficiently high for a long enough period of time to produce the effects of gleying. As might be anticipated, gley soils are commoner on heavy-textured materials and in low-lying land, but they are not confined to either. In Gloucestershire and Somerset, adjacent to the coast and often extending several miles inland, the alluvial flats are occupied by gley soils of the Wentlloog Series in which the pale-grey, silty clay-loam is mottled with yellow, orange and brown colours at variable depths. A rise of a few feet in the land-surface in these areas, causing an increase in the depth of the better-drained surface soil, may determine whether the soils are used for arable crops or permanent grass.

The Evesham Series, developed on Lower Lias clay, may be regarded as a calcareous gley soil, though its classification is still under consideration, for it frequently displays signs of moderate gleying in and below the subsoil. Owing to the fact that the soil cracks deeply and widely in dry weather and often has a high content of calcium carbonate which assists in the maintenance of a good structure, water can move fairly readily through these heavy-textured soils. On the same formation, the Charlton Bank Series is often much less calcareous and occurs in situations where water is not easily removed, hence gley phenomena, though difficult to recognize in the grey-coloured soil, are more pronounced and the soils are considered as gley soils. The usually non-calcareous, heavy clays of the Denchworth Series, associated with the Oxford and Kimeridge Clays in all three counties and occupying the clay vale between the Oolite beds and the Chalk, are also recognized as gley soils and, though sometimes cultivated, are usually under grass. It is notable that the red Keuper Marl, when gleyed, becomes a dull blue-grey colour indicating that under stringent conditions the solution-reduction process can operate on aged ferric oxide; such soils are mapped as the Birtsmorton Series, but are not of great extent in the region.

Superficial deposits, laid down by streams at the close of the Glacial Period, are extensive in the lower land of the three counties and the classification and mapping of the associated soils is difficult. In the widespread Badsey Series, calcareous, and often water-bearing, gravelly beds of variable thickness lie on a bed of clay and are themselves covered by a variable thickness of a deposit of differing texture. The water régime in this and several similar series depends on the thickness and position of the gravel as well as on the texture of the surface soil, so that brown earths and gley soils are often inextricably intermingled. Where the gravel occurs at a depth below the surface, such that its influence on the upper layers is almost negligible, the soil is mapped as the Honeybourne Series and classed as a slightly gleyed brown earth. In the Podimore Series, however, developed on a similar sequence of deposits, gleying predominates.

Owing to the lack of suitable conditions for their development, podzolized soils are infrequent in the region and are mainly confined to the higher parts of Exmoor, and the Brendon and Quantock Hills, all composed of Devonian rocks. The Ilkerton and Kentisbury Series, developed on the Hangman Grits and Ilfracombe Beds respectively, are podzolized soils in which gley effects are also more or less prominent and they are therefore considered as gley podzolized soils. It is notable that both brown earths (Bodley Series) and podzolized soils are developed on the Hangman Grits—a further instance of different major soil groups occurring on one geological formation. Areas of peat on Exmoor are not sufficiently extensive to merit the term blanket peat, but are formed under similar conditions and are also found in depressed sites on these hills.

Basin peat covers large areas in central Somerset where inland waters were ponded against the marine alluvium which now forms the Somerset Levels. The Sedgemoor Series is the commonest and consists of a considerable depth of dark-brown, waterlogged peat which has grown in the inflowing base-rich waters. Extensive flooding in the past has resulted in the surface being enriched with some mineral matter. In places, raised moss has formed and was probably more extensive before drainage and cutting reduced its area. The few surviving areas are mapped as the Westhay Series.

A complete survey of the whole region has not yet been made, but an area around Glastonbury, Sheet 286, 3rd ed., has been surveyed in detail, and a memoir and map published. Work on the adjoining Sheet 280, 3rd ed., around Wells is proceeding and the results will be published in due course.

The practical use of soil surveys may be illustrated by one example, viz., the problem of the 'teart' land. For many years it had been known that in some areas of central Somerset, on soils developed from the Lower Lias, young cattle and dairy cows were liable to lose condition, scour badly and even die if grazed on apparently good feeding pastures, particularly in spring and autumn; such land was said to be teart. Mapping the soils and recording districts and fields reputed to be teart established a correlation between certain soil series and the incidence of the trouble. Further investigation by spectroscopic analysis of herbage from teart and non-teart fields showed that the former contained excessive amounts of molybdenum. Tests on animals revealed that excessive molybdenum could cause the symptoms and, further, that the addition of a small amount of copper sulphate to the feed prevented the trouble. As a result of these investigations farmers are now able to use this valuable grazing land which was formerly considered dangerous to cattle.

CHAPTER FIVE

FAUNA

THE BRISTOL CHANNEL AND SEVERN ESTUARY

A VISITOR to the port of Bristol might suppose that the area supported a good marine fauna. This is not the case. The beaches at Portishead and Weston (Fig. 14) yield a much impoverished estuarine fauna and for a good marine assemblage the naturalist must travel fifty miles or more down the coast.

PHYSICAL CONDITIONS

It is usual to consider the Bristol Channel and Severn Estuary, which meet at Avonmouth, as separate entities but for biological purposes the two form a single tapering waterway some 130 miles long in which brackish water floods to and fro with the changing tide-level. At Porlock Weir there is a marine invertebrate fauna of over 140 macroscopic species but this does not represent the full variety of a good marine habitat. A sudden drop in the number of species occurs above Porlock Weir although a large number still extend to Portishead. Above this point the conditions deteriorate rapidly and the rate of dying out increases, until at Epney no marine species are found. A brief description of the physical factors will illustrate the nature of the adverse conditions.

The Tide-wave

Starting at Ilfracombe and Swansea with a range of not more than 27 ft. the tide-wave advances at about 50 knots. A maximum tidal range of up to 50 ft. is attained at Aust, whereafter the rising bed of the Estuary reduces the range although the crest continues to increase in height slightly. Above Sharpness the wave-front becomes so steep that the flood only occupies one hour whilst the ebb takes 11½ hours. In this region the foot of the wave moves at not more than 12 to 14 knots and is termed the bore-wave, which develops on suitable tides; a good bore occurs only on the best tides at the equinoxes.

While the wave is still rushing up the higher reaches of the Estuary, the water at Aust and below has long since turned and is flowing seawards. As the tide-wave dies out in the upper regions the whole body of water in the river, estuary and channel ebbs seawards for a period of at least three hours before the flood tide sets in once more at Ilfracombe and Swansea.

The actual movement of a body of water on one tidal sweep may be 35 miles but usually the distance travelled is much less. The currents produced are low in the

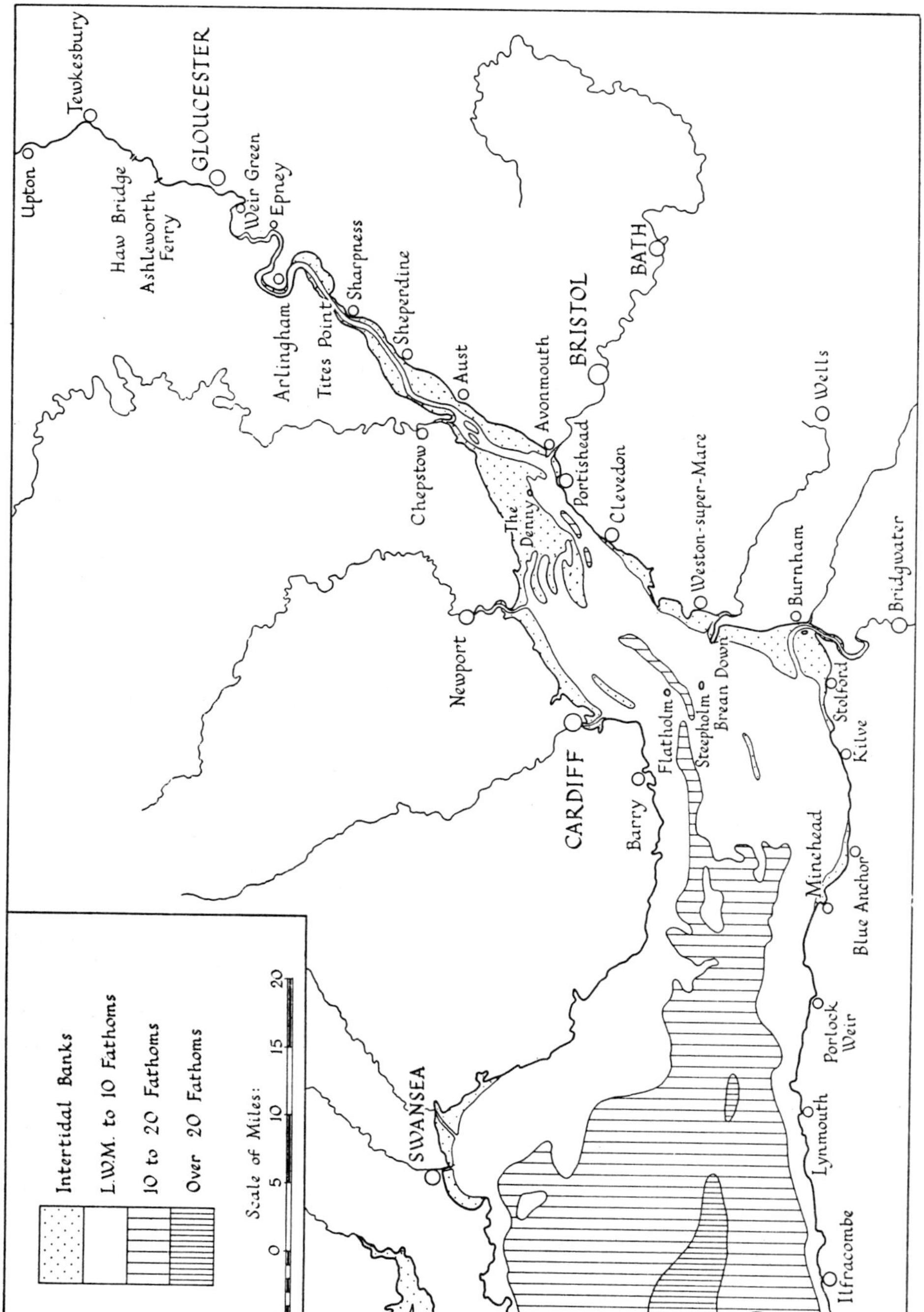

FIG. 14. *Sketch map of the Bristol Channel and Severn Estuary.*

Channel and increase to a maximum of 6 or 8 knots at Severn Beach and Aust, falling at Sharpness to 4 or 5 knots (Gibson, 1933).

High water in the Irish Sea and English Channel coincides with low water in the Bristol Channel. As the water ebbs out of the Irish Sea and English Channel some turns and enters the Bristol Channel to create high tide there. Thus the Welsh shores are bathed in Irish Sea water whilst the Ilfracombe coast receives Atlantic water from the mouth of the English Channel (Matthews, 1913). It is not yet known whether this phenomenon produces any differences in the fauna of the two coasts.

Salinity

Sea water contains 35 grams of salts per litre, that is, it has a salinity of 35. Fresh water usually contains one-hundredth of this amount and the characteristic salts are of calcium rather than of sodium. The Severn fresh water is unusual in showing more salts and more sodium than is normal and this is probably due to drainage from the Droitwich Spa area.

The fresh water from the drainage area mixes with the sea and creates a brackish zone, which ebbs and flows with the tide, the higher the tide rises the farther the brackish zone penetrates the Estuary. The greater the flow of the Severn the more the zone is held back. Thus on very high tides in summer, when the river is low, slightly saline water flows almost to Gloucester, but on poor tides in the winter flood season, it only just reaches Arlingham. Extreme conditions for 1940 are shown in Fig. 15 and may be illustrated by considering the effects at particular places.

At Porlock Weir the salinity rarely falls below 30.

At Weston the seasonal range is greater than the tidal range. In summer, although the vast body of water sweeps upstream for 6 hours, the salinity changes only from say 28·3 to 28·5. As winter approaches the salinity falls steadily, until early in the year the low-tide salinity is 22 and rises only to 23 at high tide.

At Aust the changing seasons bring wider variations. Summer salinities are about 24 and alter by no more than 3 or 4 on the tide. In winter, however, a tidal range of 10 or more is not uncommon and the low-tide salinity may occasionally fall to zero or the high-tide salinity rise to 17.

It is at Arlingham that the salinity changes reach their maximum. Here the tide floods for only one hour and ebbs for $11\frac{1}{2}$ hours. In summer, animals living in the river channels, if such were present, would be subjected one day to a salinity of 10, rising in one hour to 25, and falling in a few hours to 10 again; seven days later the maximum salinity would be 1, with a low-tide salinity of zero except for the fresh-water salts; in winter the maximum salinity would be 9. Together with fast currents and turbid water these salinity variations represent extremely arduous conditions and few animals live here.

At Epney neap tides are without effect and the river flows seawards all the week. During spring tides the river floods for a short period and sometimes, particularly in summer, salt water appears.

In the region of Gloucester the river is tidal only on the highest tides of the year

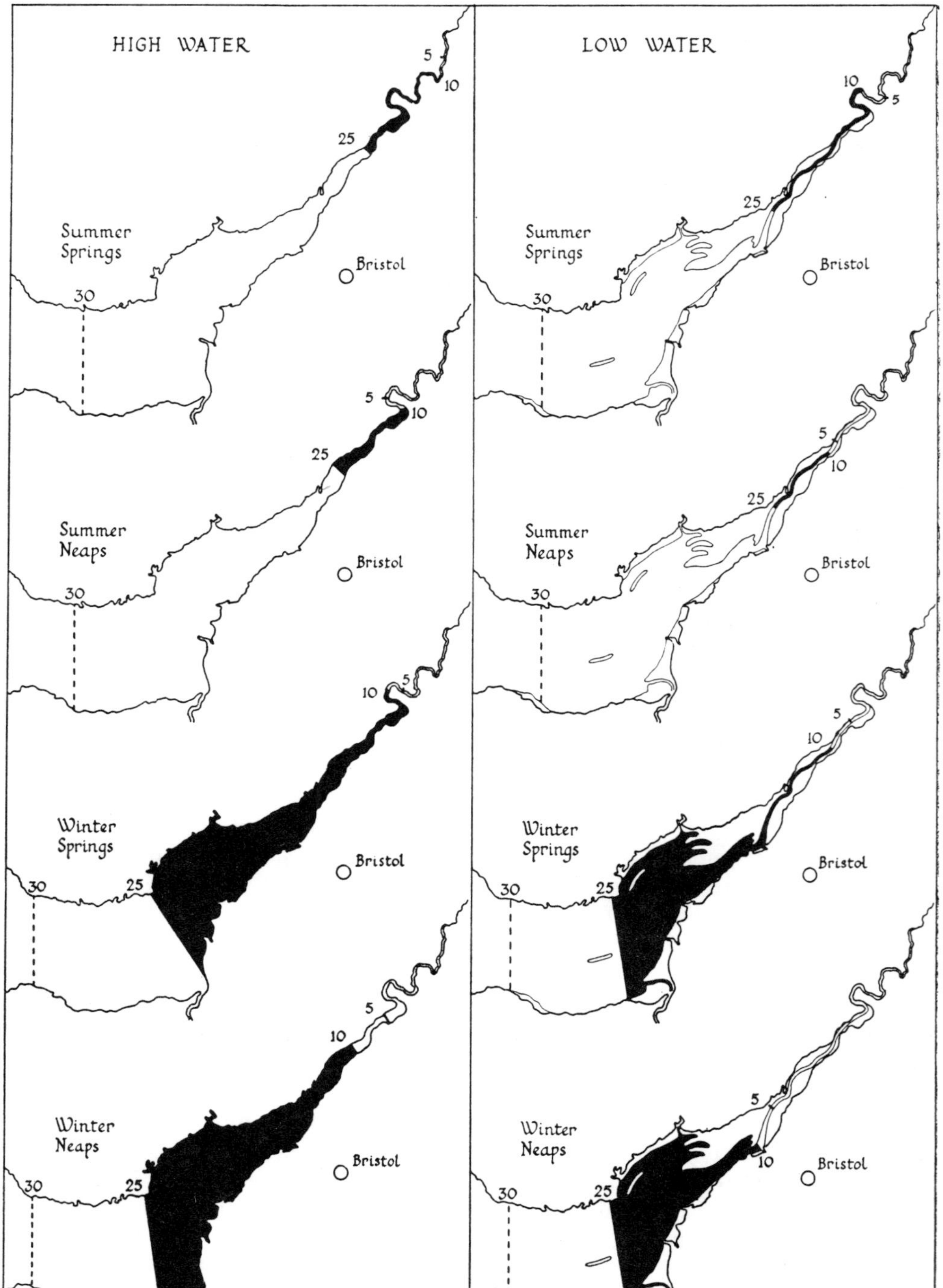

FIG. 15. *Salinity in the Bristol Channel and Severn Estuary.*

and salt water does not penetrate. Above this is a stretch of river which rises and falls a few inches on the highest tides but the current never reverses.

Turbidity

The waters of the Severn Estuary are notoriously muddy and measurements up to 5·7 grams of sediment per litre have been recorded (Purchon, 1937). The turbid zone is associated with the fastest currents, moves up and down with the tide and probably elongates as it is squeezed into the narrower reaches. On the flood tide, the zone extends beyond Sharpness and it follows that most sediment is present during the flood; on the ebb, the lower end of the turbid zone falls back to Aust and Portishead where the greatest amount of sediment occurs about low tide.

The distribution of the muddy water is a function of the current system and, accordingly, the turbid zone is found in winter in less saline water than in summer.

Approximately two million tons of sediment are carried past Severn Beach on the ebb of a spring tide. The combined efforts of all the rivers draining into the Estuary produce less than one million tons per annum, representing a layer of 0·036 inches when spread over the bed of the Estuary. The rivers could thus contribute the movable sediment of the turbid zone in about three years (Gibson, 1933).

There is more sediment in suspension during spring tides than during neaps, and in winter than in summer, and it follows that there are periods of temporary sedimentation every fortnight when the tides are taking off and also every season when summer approaches.

Even under these conditions of turbulent currents, muddy water, and periods of sedimentation the shore at Aust includes in its fauna good growths of the hydroids *Tubularia indivisa* and *Sertularia cupressina*.

ESTUARINE FAUNA

Invertebrates

An estuarine fauna consists of four main types of species—first, true brackish-water species not found outside that environment: secondly, euryhaline species which have such efficient mechanisms for controlling the content of salt and water in the body that they live in water of a wide range of salinities; this group includes forms which pass rapidly through the Estuary usually on a spawning migration: thirdly, freshwater species which show a tolerance to increased salinity and, fourthly, marine species which show a tolerance to reduced salinity.

There are few truly brackish-water species and most of the estuarine fauna is comprised of tolerant marine species. In the Severn the most notable members of the first group are *Nereis diversicolor* and *Gammarus zaddachi*, but the salt-marsh pools contain other species like *Corophium volutator* and *Sphaeroma rugicauda*. These last two, living in a habitat isolated from the main estuarine channel, are subject to violent fluctuations in temperature and salinity quite different in character from the conditions of the Estuary, and are really not estuarine but salt-marsh forms. The worm

Nereis diversicolor lives in immense numbers in burrows on the extensive mud flats which are characteristic of the coast from Blue Anchor to Sharpness. The amphipod *Gammarus zaddachi* occurs from Kilve to at least as far as Ashleworth Ferry. There are three more or less distinct forms of this species which differ in the number of spines and hairs on the body. Form *A* occurs near Kilve but may spread in summer as far up river as Sharpness; Form *B*, the most abundant, lives from Kilve to Sharpness all the year round but shows some reaction to the combined effects of low temperature and low salinity; Form *C* exists in the upper reaches and indeed is found both here and elsewhere in fresh water. Despite adaptation to variable conditions this amphipod is regarded as a true brackish-water species.

Among euryhaline species are the ordinary three-spined stickleback and the flounder, both of which are at home in the sea and in fresh water. Species of this second type do not contribute much to the variety of the Severn fauna but they may be of considerable importance to the fisheries, as is the case with the salmon and eel.

It is a notable fact that fresh-water species of the third type are not very tolerant of increased salinity so that few spread down into estuaries. Why this should be true of species whose ancestors were marine and which in some cases have become adapted by passage through estuaries or swamps to fresh water is difficult to understand. In the Severn, any penetration down river involves extending the distribution into the turbulent and muddy environment of the Arlingham region where the conditions militate against such an invasion. But even in quieter and more stable brackish waters the invasion of fresh-water species is limited.

Species of the fourth type often show a surprising tolerence to reduced salinity and turbid waters. Not all marine species recorded are included in Table XI because some, like the common shrimp, are washed to and fro by the tide and are not subject to the arduous low-tide conditions of the up-river localities.

Sponges, starfish, sea-urchins and sea-squirts are intolerant of estuarine conditions but whether this is a response to reduced salinity or to increased turbidity is a debatable matter. The absence of hydroids at Porlock Weir has been attributed to the nature of the beach. Shingle is obviously rolled about and seaweeds are poorly developed and damaged. Hydroids probably suffer in a similar way. The anemone that persists to Aust is *Tealia felina* but the specimens are of the pallid variety. The carnivorous nemertine worm *Lineus gesserensis* penetrates to Sheperdine where it is most abundant. After a hard winter the species withdraws from Aust and Sheperdine but reappears later. A feature of the up-river specimens are their dark, almost black, colour whereas the individuals at Blue Anchor show the usual green and rose colour.

Polychaete worms are usually abundant on the sea-shore and although the variety of species falls gradually from Porlock Weir to Portishead it is above this place that most of the remaining species die out, leaving only *Nereis pelagica* and *Amphitrite johnstoni* to persist as far as Aust.

Few barnacles can withstand estuarine conditions but *Balanus improvisus* extends as far as Sharpness where, as happens in other estuaries, the specimens are large for the species. Although not recorded in the table (p. 79), the New Zealand barnacle

Elminius modestus has been found at Blue Anchor (Bassindale, 1947) and at Weston and Portishead (R. Brehaut, private communication). Apparently brought to this country on ships and first recorded at Chichester in 1945, this species has subsequently spread, and is now found up to the Blyth Estuary on the east coast and as far as the Solway and Loch Ryan on the west (Crisp and Molesworth, 1950).

TABLE XI

The numbers of species of non-motile invertebrate marine animals along the southern shores of the Bristol Channel and Severn Estuary

	Collecting Station									
	Porlock Weir	Blue Anchor	Kilve	Weston	Portishead	King Road	Aust	Sheperdine	Sharpness	Arlingham
Distance from King Road (Avonmouth) in miles	43	34	28	18	2	0	8	11	20	30
Sponges	4	1	1	—	—		—	—	—	—
Hydroids	—	4	6	3	5		4	—	—	—
Anemones	2	3	2	2	2		1	—	—	—
Nemertine worms	1	1	1	1	1		1	1	—	—
Polychaete worms	19	13	7	11	10		2	2	—	—
Barnacles	6	2	2	2	1		1	1	1	—
Slaters	6	5	5	5	7		5	5	4	1
'Shrimps' (Amphipoda)	15	10	13	8	8		5	3	3	1
Crabs and Prawns	12	3	3	3	2		1	1	—	—
Snails	28	13	10	28	7		4	4	2	—
Mussels	9	4	3	21	4		2	2	2	—
Polyzoa	34	6	6	4	3		4	2	1	—
Starfish and Urchins	4	1	1	—	—		—	—	—	—
Sea-squirts	x	—	—	—	—		—	—	—	—
Total:	140	66	60	88	50		30	21	13	2

The sea-slaters, or Isopoda, are not abundant but they extend a long way into the Estuary, *Sphaeroma rugicauda* having been found as far as Arlingham. Amphipod shrimps are present in great variety at Porlock and die out gradually; *Bathyporeia pilosa* has been recorded from Arlingham but it probably represents a temporary invasion.

Among the crabs and prawns the dog-crab *Carcinus moenas* shows its usual versatility by reaching up to Sheperdine, but few other species extend past Porlock Weir. There are many prawns, shrimps and mysids, which are washed to and fro and cannot be regarded as low-tide inhabitants of the places at which they are taken in the commercial nets.

The snails, like the amphipods, show a gradual decline in variety as the Estuary is ascended and the records illustrate two features. The first is the extension of *Littorina rudis* (*saxatilis*) to Sharpness. Now *L. rudis* occurs in the upper part of the tidal zone; it is clearly not subject to the low-tide salinities of the channel and, indeed, is only covered by water of reasonable salinity even in winter; in the summer breeding and growing season the salinities to which it is exposed are probably always over 15, that is, half sea water. The second feature of the records of the snails, and also of the mussels, is the abundance of species at Weston, which directly correlates with the habits of malacologists, more collecting having been done at Weston than elsewhere. Apart from this peak at Weston the records for bivalve molluscs show a gradual decline from nine species at Porlock Weir to two only, *Tellina crassa* and *Macoma balthica*, at Sharpness. The latter is a characteristic inhabitant with *Nereis diversicolor* of estuarine mud flats and occurs in enormous numbers at Blue Anchor, Weston, Aust and Sheperdine.

The Polyzoa are little known except to sea-shore microscopists. There is a surprising number of species at Porlock Weir and, of the few which extend into the Estuary, one is *Electra hastingsae*, known to be tolerant of reduced salinity, and the other, *Electra crustulenta* var. *fossaria*, found only at Aust, Sheperdine and Sharpness, is apparently a brackish-water species. Two other species from Aust are *Bowerbankia imbricata* and *Membranipora aurita*.

Insects of various species are often recorded from the shore but usually from the debris at the high-tide level. For example, the interesting beetle *Eurynebria complanata* has been taken at Burnham. Nevertheless, the extent of the invasion of the shore by insects is still little appreciated. At Portishead, Dr. H. E. Hinton has discovered the larva of a tipulid, *Geranomyia unicolor*, to be one of the commonest animals in the intertidal mat of short algae and he believes this is by no means an exceptional phenomenon on British shores.

Fisheries[1]

Fishes are usually so mobile that an estimate of their penetration into an estuary is difficult because they can so easily avoid temporarily difficult conditions by local migration. Nevertheless, many species are commonly found and, apart from migrants like the salmon and eel, there are species which regularly enter estuaries to feed sometimes at particular seasons. The winter fishery at Weston is founded on such a

[1] Information regarding the Fisheries has been taken mainly from Matthews (1933); additional accounts are available in Waters (1947) and Taylor (1953).

habit in the sprat. Similarly, there are species of invertebrate, like the common shrimp and certain mysids, which are carried up and down by the tide and form the basis of a seasonal or all-the-year-round fishery. In the case of the Severn Estuary the fast currents and extreme range of tide over the extensive intertidal banks permit the use of fixed nets for fishing purposes. Below Avonmouth, traps made of netting have been in use for centuries but, above Avonmouth, the currents are so fierce that netting is not adequate and basketwork traps are employed. There can be few tools of mankind that have survived unchanged from prehistoric times and these basketwork traps are probably examples.

Salmon are fished in two ways; by hand net from salmon pools and by trap. Salmon pools are simply large intertidal lakes left on the banks by the receding tide. The salmon pool at Oldbury-on-Severn is about two miles long, 15 ft. or more in depth at the upper end, and 3 to 4 ft. deep at the lower, where there is a weir or bench of stones over which the water flows. About 20 ft. from the bench are two large stones upon which the fishermen stand clear of the water in the pool. A large triangular dip or lave net extended on poles about 9 ft. long is used (Plate III). A footrope 9 ft. long joins the ends of the poles, while a short yoke near the apex of the triangle spreads them apart. A handle about 3 ft. long is also fixed at the apex. When not in use the poles are swivelled round so that the frame is closed, and the net is rolled up round them.

The salmon cruise up and down the pool and when they reach the lower end they attempt to get over the bench with the stream of water flowing over it. As the water on the bench is too shallow for them they turn and swim back again. As they turn in the shallows they create a wash and frequently show the back above water, when the waiting fisherman plunges his net in and dips out the fish. As the water is not clear, but very muddy, the fishermen face downstream when waiting for fish, for they can only see them when they turn in the shallows, except on a 'black tide', or dead calm, when the wash caused by the fish swimming down the pool can be seen on the surface. Three or four fish are reckoned a good average catch. Fishing is, of course, only possible at low water, and the fishermen have to move off quickly when the tide starts flowing, as it rushes in with great force and velocity.

Salmon traps, or putchers, are conical openwork wicker baskets, 5 ft. 6 in. long and 2 ft. wide at the mouth. They are lashed, by withy bands, in four long rows one above the other, to vertical stakes set in rows at right angles to the shore; the open end faces downstream. Salmon ascending the river meet the putchers, become jammed into the head part and are drowned; it is surprising how firmly they wedge themselves. The putchers only last two seasons, as the fish can smash and burst out of old and weak ones. All the putchers are made locally from withies grown on the marshes adjoining the Severn. Some fishermen have tried using putchers made of galvanized wire, but they caught no fish. Concrete posts have been tried instead of wooden ones, but they also were unsuitable, being easily broken, and not having the spring and elasticity of wooden ones. The stakes on muddy ground are driven in; on rock or stony ground they are wedged into holes excavated in the bottom. At Aust two ranks of putchers are connected by a wall of wire-netting so that fish shall not escape between them. A good average tide's catch for a rank of 650 putchers is six fish, though up to twenty-four have been taken on one tide. The season is from 15 April to 15 August. Many other animals besides salmon are occasionally caught in the putchers and these include lampreys, sturgeon, small sharks and even porpoises.

Kypes are basketwork fish-traps, conical in shape, which are set on stakes with their open end facing upstream; fishing is done on the ebb tide. They are set in rows at right angles to the bank from fifty to one hundred and fifty in a row. Kypes consist of three parts having different sizes of mesh in the basketwork (Plate IV). The first part, the 'putt', is made of open basketwork with the mouth about 5 ft. in diameter, is about 5 ft. in length and tapers towards its inner end, where it is jammed into the mouth of the second part, or 'butt'. The butt is composed of a closer mesh basketwork, has a ring of backwardly directed withy spikes projecting on the inside near the mouth, is about 5 ft. long and tapers towards the end, where it is jammed into the mouth of the third part, the 'forewheel' or 'firwell', in which the catch is retained. The forewheel is made of closely woven fine basketwork, is about 2 ft. 6 in. long and tapers from the front backwards; a non-return valve of projecting spikes joined by basketwork fills a constricted part towards the fore end, while into a construction at the hinder end is jammed a wooden plug to retain the catch.

Kypes are fastened to stakes with the mouths just clear of the ground. The putt and butt are fixed permanently with withy bands, but the forewheel is removable. The front end of the forewheel is jammed onto the back end of the butt, and the after end is supported by a short forked stake. The hinder construction is held by the arms of the fork and a withy band, fastened to one arm and slipping in a loop over the other arm, holds it in position. When the fisherman visits the kypes at low tide he removes the forewheel, takes out the plug at the after end, and shakes out the catch. Kypes, like putchers, are all made locally from withies grown on the adjoining marshes. About five years is their maximum length of life.

The kypes catch large quantities of shrimps; fishermen say that about once in ten years the Severn shrimps appear in enormous numbers; however, apart from exceptional years, large quantities are taken regularly. The fish caught in the kypes are occasional salmon, flounders in quantity, dabs, large numbers of small soles, small cod, whiting, conger, also freshwater eels, sprats and lampreys. Windy and wet weather usually produce the best catches. Kypes are fished in the Bristol district at Hallen, Oldbury-on-Severn, Sheperdine and off Berkeley.

Stow nets are bag-shaped nets which are hung on stakes on the foreshore; the ebbing tide carries the fish into them and they are visited and emptied at low water. The mouth of the net is 12 to 18 ft. square, and the bag of the net is about 30 ft. long. The net, with two stakes on either side of it, is called a 'stall' and the row of stakes is known as a 'hang'. The small end of the net, the 'cod end', is untied when the net is visited and the fish are shaken out. On the flood tide the cod end drifts upstream under, or to the side of, the net but on the ebb the net is opened like a bag and thus

---

PLATE I. *Cotswold escarpment from near Frocester looking towards the Dursley gap.*

PLATE II. *Sedgemoor, Brent Knoll, Bridgwater Bay and the southern flank of Mendip from above the Cheddar Gorge.*

traps the inswept fish. The chief catch of the stow nets is sprats, but many other sorts of fish are taken as well, mainly whiting, codling, flounders, dabs and thornbacks.

At Weston-super-Mare there is a hang of some fifty or so stalls between Birnbeck Island and the mainland, but there are now not more than about half this number in use. Before the pier, connecting the island with the mainland, and the landing-stages for the pleasure steamers on the western side of the island were built, there was a further extensive hang on the seaward or western side of the island. This fishery was at its height from about 1830 to 1880. The fishermen had a thatched hut on the island in which two men called 'gull-yellers' lived during the fishing season. Their job was to scare the gulls from the nets as the tide ebbed. Before the pier was built fishermen waited until the tide had ebbed low enough for them to cross to the island on stepping-stones over the causeway, or 'stepway', which dries out at low water, before they could visit the nets; hence the necessity for gull-yellers. One man looked after the western nets and the other after the eastern ones. They were both paid £1 a week, each fisherman paying according to the number of stalls he rented. Catches of five to six tons of sprats were made each tide and the fish were sent to Bath, Bristol and other towns by rail.

Swing nets are similar in size and shape to stow nets but are buoyed and moored in the tideway, and not fixed to stakes. The net is extended by two spars at the mouth, the upper one of wood and the lower one of iron, which by its weight keeps the mouth open. The spars are made fast by bridles to a mooring line, fixed to a length of chain, held to the bottom by concrete sinkers, and buoyed at the surface. The net swings with the tide and fishes on both the ebb and the flood. A tripping line is made fast to the lower spar and runs through a thimble on the upper spar to its attachment on the buoy. When the net is visited by boat at low tide, the tripping line is hauled up thus closing the net, and the fish are emptied from the cod end where the net is of smaller mesh than nearer the mouth. The chief catch of the swing nets is sprats, with numbers of whiting, small cod, dabs, flounders, thornback, conger and some shrimps. The fishing season, as with the stow nets, lasts from early October to the end of January, occasionally longer. The nets last about four seasons, but are only put out for about a week at a time, and are dried between each spell of duty.

Shrimp nets or hose nets are similar in shape to the stow nets, but the tail end of them is supported by two withy hoops, and a funnel-shaped piece of netting, forming a non-return valve, is fastened to the first hoop. A line from the first hoop to a third short stake behind the net holds the tail clear of the ground. The nets are about 6 ft. square at the mouth and are set on the stakes well clear of the ground. The shrimp nets are fished from about the end of August to March, and take both brown and pink shrimps, as well as some quantities of flat fish, whiting and so on. These nets are set singly or in batteries of twelve or more on the mud-flats at Burnham-on-Sea, while at Weston-super-Mare a row of shrimp nets is worked on the foreshore opposite Birnbeck Island below the pier.

PLATE III. *Lave-net fishing for salmon from standings, Oldbury-on-Severn.*

PLATE IV. *Weir of shrimp kypes about half a mile offshore between Oldbury-on-Severn and Sheperdine.*

Other nets are, or were, used in the district but with the decline of inshore fisheries some have gone out of use and others are not so common as formerly.

The difficulties of working nets situated at some distance from the shore across banks of soft mud have been solved by the use of 'mud horses' which vary in design at different places but which consist of a basal skid or sledge, to carry the gear, with handles or rails on which the operator leans as he pushes rapidly across the mud.

The migratory habits of the common eel form the basis of the Epney elver fishery. The elvers, after a three-year journey across the ocean, ascend European estuaries into fresh water and although small (about one thousand to the pound) their enormous numbers make them worth fishing; many years ago the Germans established at Epney a collecting station from which some seven million living elvers were despatched annually to all parts of Germany to provide larger numbers of eels than would ascend their rivers naturally. The fishing only lasts a few weeks in the spring. In its heyday the night fishing, when each fisherman had a bright flare to attract the elvers, converted the river into the semblance of a lighted city street and the special dip net used was peculiar to the district (Lloyd, 1940; Matthews, 1942). However, improvised nets are sometimes utilized and a meat-safe tied on to a long pole often proves satisfactory. Apart from the export of living elvers, the catch is eaten fried or cooked in the form of a pressed dried 'cake'—a delicacy of local interest, like the wall-fish (*Helix aspersa* or the common garden snail) which is still eaten in Bristol.

The commercial traps described above capture a wide variety of fish and occasionally rare species are taken. The salmon forms the basis of a valuable fishery while cod, whiting and sprats are abundant. A hundred years ago the winter sprat fishery of the Weston area not only provided the poor with a good source of winter food but was worth £10,000. Lloyd (1941) gives a detailed account of the much-reduced fishery of the 1940–41 winter and also gives a list of the 112 species of fish taken in the nets. The large lamprey, *Petromyzon marinus*, esteemed by Royalty, seems now to be rare as is also the sturgeon. The records of flying fish, sea-horses and *Maurolicus* (a small fish with luminous organs) add somewhat exotic items to the lists; the records of the burbot and the leptocephalus larva of the conger are noteworthy.

An investigation of the bionomics of the shrimp (Lloyd and Yonge, 1947) showed the individuals live for five years and the effect of the reduced salinities in the Estuary is to shorten the breeding season as compared with that of the Bristol Channel. There is also a migration from the Estuary, particularly by the males during the winter when low temperatures increase their susceptibility to the low salinities. Among the ordinary, or brown, shrimps taken in the Channel nets in summer are large numbers of a pink or white shrimp, *Pasiphae sivado*, which is better described as a primitive prawn, more characteristic of deep oceanic, than of tidal, waters.

Marine mammals do not constitute a prominent feature of the local fauna except at the seaward end of the Bristol Channel although, in an account of sixteen species recorded locally, there is evidence that the common seal is settling in the area (Matthews, 1941).

Waterfowl

The extensive intertidal banks and saltings serve as feeding and resting grounds for both resident and migratory water-birds. The numbers of species and of individuals to be found on these banks, and also on the Barrow Gurney and Blagdon reservoirs, is impressive (Davis, 1935; 1947; Tetley, 1935; 1937). Nesting grounds for some of these waterfowl are of course to be found on the mainland but interest centres on the islands, notably Lundy and Steepholm. Lundy, on which a field station has been available for many years, is remote from Bristol but Steepholm, just off Weston-super-Mare, is well within the area. Local naturalists have recently combined to establish a small field station on Steepholm from which it is possible to observe not only the island's fauna and flora but the sea-birds and also many land-birds which use the island as a stepping-stone in their migrations. Particular attention is already being paid to the herring gull (Poulding, 1954). Specimens marked on Steepholm have been recovered from France, proving a wider range for the individuals than was expected.

The value of ornithological work by local naturalists is well known but it has been emphasized in this district by the discovery in Bridgwater Bay by Mr. D. Perrett of a moulting-ground of the shelduck. Earlier it was believed that British shelduck flew across the North Sea to moult in the Heligoland Bight. These birds drift back in January and February in time for the next breeding season. Now it is known that thousands of individuals collect in Bridgwater Bay to moult and leave there early in November, but the problems of where they come from or why they leave so early remain unsolved.

The activities of the Bristol Waterworks Company have recently resulted in the production of a new waterfowl resort, the Chew Valley Lake. The popularity of the Blagdon and Barrow Gurney reservoirs with both resident and migratory waterfowl led to a watch being kept on the developing lake. It was found that the aquatic birds immediately adopted the lake in large numbers, thereby reorganizing the local bird-life. The best example is the development of a rookery of immature blackhead gulls, which, after feeding inland, now roost on the Chew Valley Lake instead of returning to the more distant coastal rookeries as heretofore.

Despite these varied facets of waterfowl life the main interest is undoubtedly concentrated on the flocks of thousands of whitefront geese which arrive each winter in the Slimbridge area (Davis and Tetley, 1943). Here Mr. Peter Scott has chosen the site of the headquarters of the Wild Fowl Trust, and he has assembled a collection of living geese and ducks of incomparable value. This collection is displayed in a well-arranged system of paddocks and, together with the wild flocks on the adjacent saltings, provides material for investigations which are adding much to our knowledge of these birds. Not the least interesting experiment is the attempt to perpetuate by breeding in captivity the almost extinct Hawaiian or Sandwich Island goose.

LAND AND FRESHWATER FAUNAS

The late Mr. H. L. F. Audcent left a well-documented collection of about 4,000 species of Diptera, now housed in the Zoology Department of the University, of which 2,200 species are recorded as local (Audcent, 1945; 1949). The Proceedings of the Cotteswold Naturalists Field Club include lists of Gloucestershire Orthoptera, Hymenoptera, Lepidoptera and Carabidae (Fletcher, 1936; Fletcher and Clutterbuck, 1943; 1937–43; Townsend, 1945) and the Proceedings of the Bristol Naturalists' Society give annual accounts of local Lepidoptera (Peach, 1938). The Bristol City Museum houses good collections of insects. Twenty-four species of dragonflies have been recorded within fifteen miles of Bristol in recent years. All but three species breed regularly in the district and Moore (1952*a* and *b*; 1953; 1954) has shown, in his investigations of a half-mile stretch of the Portbury River in the Gordano Valley, that densities of more than 13 males per 100 yards of stream are infrequent and never maintained, whether one or more species are present. The evidence suggests that the density of adults is controlled by the migratory behaviour of the insects themselves.

There seems to be no specifically local list of spiders but these are abundant, varied and include interesting species like the long-legged *Pholcus phalangioides*, the water and raft spiders *Argyroneta* and *Dolomedes*, the spinner of a fine hedgerow web, *Agelena laybrinthica* (which lays its eggs on August Bank Holiday week-end) and also, in Bristol itself close to the University, a thriving colony of *Segestria florentina* which, besides being our longest spider, has a distribution like that of the black rat, being restricted to seaports.

Eighteen species of slug and sixteen of earthworms have been listed by Bacchus (1925) and Davis (1950). Swanton's (1912) list of the Mollusca of Somerset is comprehensive. The slugs include *Testacella*, the earthworm predator with the vestigial shell, and perhaps the most local record is Woodland Road.

There are four recent records of local interest which concern a leech, a jelly-fish, a worm and the chaffinch.

The leech is *Trochaeta subviridis*. In Britain leeches are, perhaps fortunately, aquatic animals but *Trochaeta*, which has been recorded from few localities, was recently taken from a garden in Portishead. It is an amphibious species reaching a resting length of four inches; it feeds on earthworms.

The freshwater jellyfish, *Craspedacusta sowerbii*, and the freshwater worm, *Branchiura sowerbii*, have a curiously similar history of discovery. Both were originally described from the lily ponds in Kew Gardens, and subsequently from similar tropical lily ponds in European botanical gardens. *Craspedacusta* has never been found in its native haunts (which are believed to be in South America) but it has occurred in sporadic outbursts, of one sex only, in artificial lakes and reservoirs all over Europe and the U.S.A. It was reported from the Exeter Canal in 1931 and 1947, from Monmouthshire in 1933, and from the reservoirs of the Gloucester Waterworks at Witcombe in 1947 (Bassindale, 1947), but has not appeared again at Witcombe. *Branchiura* has been discovered in natural habitats in India and beyond and so may be regarded as a tropical Asiatic species. Its main feature of interest is a series of paired filamentous gills which give the appearance of a delicate fin at the posterior end; the form has been taken by Miss P. M. Jenkin in 1954 in the canal above Bath.

The chaffinch, our commonest bird, attracted the attention of bird watchers of the Bristol Naturalists' Society during observations made as part of a nation-wide survey of passerine migrations. Observers on the cliff at Aust, on 18 October 1953, recorded nearly 10,000 chaffinches migrating north-eastward into the wind in a five-hour period early in the day. As this was against the general trend of migration at this time of the year the status of such an accumulation and migration is unknown. It might represent a local temporary response to the weather conditions but illustrates clearly that the behaviour of our commonest species is still little understood (P. Chadwick, private communication).

Lizards, grass-snakes, adders and blind-worms are common, and the three species of newt are sometimes to be found in the same pond.

Of the local mammals, Tetley (1940) has recorded thirty-seven species of which ten are bats. Leisler's bat has been added subsequently (Matthews and Mayes, 1945*b*). The otter is common enough, the pine martin does occur and the badger and fox are to be found within the city boundaries, but so also is the common seal (Matthews, 1932). The fox has even been seen within the University precincts, if the gardens of Burwalls could be so described. Attention has recently been directed to the badgers and otters of the district in two widely separate ways. Neal's book on the badger (Neal, 1949) is based on observations made near Taunton. The otter has been shown by Dr. H. D. Crofton and Miss P. Fraser to be an important alternate host for a tape worm, *Diphyllobothrium*, which in its other host, the trout, produces disease and poor growth often seriously affecting angling prospects in many British and Continental waters.

All three varieties of the black rat have been recorded from the Bristol Docks but the normal variety has recently overcome its earlier restriction to the dock warehouses and is to be found all the way up Whiteladies Road to the Downs. Rats trapped in the University are usually black rats and at one time this marked the limit of their spread from the docks.

Somerset is noted for its caves and besides those open to the public there are numerous others which are visited regularly, and have been mapped and photographed by members of the local spelaeological societies. Some attention has been paid to cave faunas and a comprehensive account is to be found in the chapter, contributed by Miss Hazleton and Brigadier Glennie, in Cullingford's book on *British Caving* (1953). The account of the fauna of Read's Cavern is perhaps the most comprehensive of local investigations so far published (Walton, 1938). Although Walton found no animals restricted to caves his list of fifty-five species includes twenty-two spring tail insects (Collembola). These were not only zoned with reference to depth of penetration into the cave but some were found to be feeding on a species of the fungus *Penicillium*, which was itself growing on the candle droppings of cave explorers. It was found possible to grow the *Penicillium* on laboratory paraffin wax and to keep the Collembola alive on the fungus.

Bats are characteristic of some caves (Hooper and Hooper, 1953) and the local caving societies have recently used ringing to help in investigating the habits of bats in the area. Mr. P. Bird of the Bristol City Museum (who would welcome information about any colonies of bats in this area) has described the techniques employed and reports that interesting facts have already emerged (Bird, 1951). Attention is being directed mainly to the greater horseshoe bat, which clusters during hibernation, and the lesser horseshoe bat, which does not cluster. Neither species shows a segregation of sexes during hibernation as was earlier believed to be the case and neither species wanders very much. The maximum recorded range is twenty-six miles for the greater and nineteen for the lesser horseshoe bat, but movements from one colony to another, even in winter, are usually of only a mile or so. Winter flights are not uncommon and, so far, no bat ringed in Devon has been found in Somerset nor a Somerset bat in Devon. Sometimes bats are found low down in a cave instead of high up and they may be discovered in moist places; one colony had water trickling over the sleeping bats. The greater horseshoe bat has already been shown to live up to four years and further knowledge will undoubtedly be added as the experiments continue.

REFERENCES

AUDCENT, H. L. F. 1945. Bristol Insect Fauna. Diptera (Orthorrhapha). *Proc. Bristol Nat. Soc.*, **27**, 409–70.

—. 1949. Bristol Insect Fauna. Diptera (Cyclorrhapha). *Ibid.*, **28**, 45–132.

BACCHUS, A. D. R. 1925. List of Slugs Found in the Bristol District. *Ibid.*, (4) **6**, 229–31.

BASSINDALE, R. 1941. The Invertebrate Fauna of the Southern Shores of the Bristol Channel and Severn Estuary. *Ibid.*, (4) **9**, 143–201.

—. 1942*a*. The Distribution of Amphipods in the Severn Estuary and Bristol Channel. *J. Anim. Ecol.*, **11**, 131–44.

—. 1942*b*. An Account of Collecting Stations, and Corrections to the Fauna List. *Proc. Bristol Nat. Soc.*, (4) **9**, 304–15.

—. 1943*a*. The Physical Environment and Intertidal Fauna of the Southern Shores of the Bristol Channel and Severn Estuary. *J. Ecol.*, **31**, 1–29.

—. 1943*b*. A Comparison of the varying Salinity Conditions of the Tees and Severn Estuaries. *J. Anim. Ecol.*, **12**, 1–10.

—. 1943*c*. The Intertidal Fauna of Porlock Bay. *Proc. Bristol Nat. Soc.*, (4) **9**, 386–99.

—. 1946. The Fauna of Skomer Island. A preliminary Sketch. *Ibid.*, **27**, 109–20.

—. 1947. Zoological Notes. *Elminius modestus* and *Craspedacusta sowerbii*. *Ibid.*, **27**, 223–4.

BIRD, P. F. 1949. Additions to Fauna List of Caves in the Mendip Hills. *Proc. Spelaeol. Soc. Bristol*, **6**, 23–6.

—. 1951. The U.B.S.S. Bat-ringing Scheme. *Ibid.*, **6**, 205–7.

BOYCOTT, A. E. 1936. The Relation of Slugs and Snails to Man in Britain. *Proc. Cotteswold Nat. Fld. Cl.*, **26**, 73–82.

BOYD, H. 1945. Terrestrial Isopoda of Steepholm. *Proc. Bristol Nat. Soc.*, **27**, 483–5.

—. 1952. Leach's Petrel in Great Britain in the Autumn of 1952. *Ibid.*, **28**, 343–50.

CRISP, D. J. and A. H. N. MOLESWORTH. 1950. Habitat of *Balanus amphitrite* var. *denticulata* in Britain. *Nature, Lond.*, **167**, 489.

CULLINGFORD, C. H. D. 1953. *British Caving*. London.
DAVIES, H. 1950. A Note on the Lumbricids found in the Bristol District. *Proc. Bristol Nat. Soc.*, **28**, 197–8.
DAVIS, H. H. 1935. Waders in the Bristol District. *Ibid.*, (4) **8**, 106–13.
—. 1947. A Revised List of Birds of the Bristol District. *Ibid.*, **27**, 225–68.
— and H. TETLEY. 1943. The Severn Geese. *Ibid.*, (4) **9**, 494–509.
DONOVAN, C. 1941. A Catalogue of the Macrolepidoptera of Gloucestershire. *Proc. Cotteswold Nat. Fld. Cl.*, **27**, 153–86.
FLETCHER, T. B. 1936. Notes on Orthoptera and their allies found or likely to be found in Gloucestershire. *Ibid.*, **26**, 87–90.
— and C. A. CLUTTERBUCK. 1943. A rough list of the Aculeate Hymenoptera of Gloucestershire. *Ibid.* **28**, 50–7.
— and —. 1937–43. Microlepidoptera of Gloucestershire. *Ibid.*, **26**, 183–204, 298–317; **27**, 34–53, 93–108, 136–52; **28**, 15–29, 58–66.
GRACE, S. F. 1936. Friction in the Tidal Currents of the Bristol Channel. *Mon. Not. R. Astr. Soc. Geophys. Suppl.*, **3**, 388–95.
GIBSON, A. H. 1933. Construction and Operation of a Tidal Model of the Severn Estuary. *Severn Barrage Committee Report. Economic Advisory Council*, 63–78–2. London.
HARDISTY, M. W. 1944. The Life History and Growth of the Brook Lamprey (*Lampetra planeri*). *J. Anim. Ecol.*, **13**, 110–22.
—. 1954. Sex Ratio of Spawning Populations of *Lampetra planeri*. *Nature, Lond.*, **173**, 874–5.
HAZLETON, M. and A. E. GLENNIE. Cave Fauna and Flora. *In* Cullingford, 1953. Ch. 9, 247–83.
HOOPER, W. M. and J. H. D. HOOPER. Cave Dwelling Bats. *In* Cullingford, 1953. Ch. 10, 284–302.
LLOYD, A. J. 1941. The Marine Fish Fauna of the Southern Shores of the Bristol Channel. *Proc. Bristol Nat. Soc.*, (4) **9**, 202–30.
—. 1942. A Survey of the Fishing Industry of Weston-super-Mare during the Winter of 1940–41. *Ibid.*, (4) **9**, 316–27.
— and C. M. YONGE. 1947. The Biology of *Crangon vulgaris* L. in the Bristol Channel and Severn Estuary. *J. Mar. Biol. Assoc.*, **26**, 626–61.
MATTHEWS, D. J. 1913. The Salinity and Temperature of the Irish Channel and the waters south of Ireland. *Fisheries, Ireland Sci. Invest.*, **4**.
MATTHEWS, L. H. 1932. Denny Isle. *Proc. Bristol Nat. Soc.*, (4) **7**, 371–8
—. 1933. Sea Fish and Fisheries of the Bristol District. *Ibid.*, (4) **7**, 442–62.
—. 1941. The Marine Mammals of the Bristol District. *Ibid.*, (4) **9**, 231–50.
—. 1942. The Catches of a Somerset Fish Weir. *Ibid.*, (4) **9**, 328–34.
—. 1943. Elvers in the Severn. *Ibid.*, (4) **9**, 400–5.
— and W. E. MAYES. 1945*a*. Occurrence of the Pine Martin near Bristol. *Ibid.* **27**, 121–2.
— and —. 1945*b*. The Occurrence of Leisler's Bat at Bristol. *Ibid.*, **27**, 486–8.
— and others. 1938. A Survey of Steepholm (Historical, Geological, Botanical, Zoological). *Ibid.*, (4) **8**, 438–78.
MOORE, N. W. 1952*a*. On the so-called 'Territories' of Dragonflies (Odonata-Anisoptera). *Behaviour*, **4**, 85–100.
—. 1952*b*. On the Length of Life of Adult Dragonfiies (Odonata-Anisoptera) in the Field. *Proc. Bristol Nat. Soc.*, **28**, 267–72.
—. 1953. Population Density in Adult Dragonflies (Odonata-Anisoptera). *J. Anim. Ecol.*, **22**, 344–59.
—. 1954. On the Dispersal of Odonata. *Proc. Bristol Nat. Soc.*, **28**, 407–17.
NEAL, E. A. 1949. *The Badger*. London.
PALMER, M. A. (editor). 1946. *Ilfracombe Fauna and Flora*. Ilfracombe Field Club, Ilfracombe.

Peach, A. H. 1938. A List of Lepidoptera from Leigh Woods. *Proc. Bristol Nat. Soc.*, (4) **8**, 435–7.
Poulding, R. H. 1954. Loss of Rings by Marked Herring Gulls. *Bird Study*, **1**, 37–40.
Purchon, R. D. 1937. An Ecological Study of the Beach and Dock at Portishead. *Proc. Bristol Nat. Soc.*, (4) **8**, 311–29.
—. 1947. The Littoral and Sub-littoral Fauna of the Northern Shores near Cardiff. *Ibid.*, **27**, 285–310.
Richardson, A. 1944. Supplement to Donovan's Catalogue of the Macrolepidoptera of Gloucestershire. *Proc. Cotteswold Nat. Fld. Cl.*, **28**, 76–107.
Swanton, E. W. 1912. *The Mollusca of Somerset*. Som. Archaeol. Nat. Hist. Soc., Taunton.
Taylor, J. N. 1953. *Illustrated Guide to the Severn Fishery Collection*. Folk Museum, Gloucester.
Tetley, H. 1935. Gulls of the Bristol District. *Proc. Bristol Nat. Soc.*, (4) **8**, 99–103.
—. 1937. Bird Life on Barrow Gurney Reservoirs. *Ibid.*, (4) **8**, 330–47.
—. 1940. Land Mammals of the Bristol District. *Ibid.*, (4) **9**, 100–42.
Townsend, C. C. 1945. A List of the Carabidae of Gloucestershire. *Proc. Cotteswold Nat. Fld. Cl.*, **29**, 149–58.
Tucker, B. W. 1935. The Rookeries of Somerset. *Proc. Som. Archaeol. Nat. Hist. Soc.*, **81**, 149–240.
Walton, G. A. 1944. The Fauna of Read's Cavern. *Proc. Spelaeol. Soc. Bristol*, **5**, 127–37.
Waters, B. 1947. *Severn Tide*. London.
Yonge, C. M. 1937. Studies on the Biology of the Bristol Channel. General Introduction. *Proc. Bristol Nat. Soc.*, (4) **8**, 310–11.
— and A. J. Lloyd. 1939. The Shore Fauna of Steepholm. *Ibid.*, (4) **8**, 474–8.

CHAPTER SIX

VEGETATION

THERE are good reasons for botanists with Bristol as their centre to count themselves fortunate. The varied geology leads to a diversity of vegetation-types which is augmented by the presence of a coastline. The regional flora is a rich one, notably in its content of rarities. About eight species are not found elsewhere in Britain, and several occur in few other British localities. From the sixteenth century onwards the flora has attracted botanists of the calibre of William Turner, John Ray, J. J. Dillenius and Sir Joseph Banks. The records until 1912 are incorporated in a regional *Flora* (White, 1912) which is widely regarded as one of the best works of its kind; many of the entries, moreover, make entertaining reading. It covers relatively little of Gloucestershire, but this county is now handsomely provided for by the recent *Flora of Gloucestershire* by Riddelsdell, Hedley and Price (1948), which gives an ecological account of the main vegetation-types as well as plant records.

New records in the Bristol region are listed annually in the *Proceedings* of the Bristol Naturalists' Society. Besides the addition of new localities for species already known in the region, there have been a few notable additions since 1912 to the 1,178 species given in White's *Flora*, among them *Centaurium capitatum*, *Epipactis sessilifolia*, *Ranunculus ophioglossifolius*, *Viola lactea* and *Wolffia arrhiza*. In 1952 Mrs. C. I. Sandwith found the colourless saprophytic liverwort *Cryptothallus mirabilis* on the Somerset peat moors.

The Port of Bristol and its surroundings carry a rich adventive flora which includes plants from many parts of the world, the majority of them Mediterranean in origin (Sandwith, 1932).

The only extensive ecological study in the region is the pioneer investigation by Moss (1907) in Somerset. This and other publications have provided useful material for the present account, but our primary source is a recent first-hand study of some of the communities.

For the present purpose the limits of the region are approximately the following: to the north, the Stroud gap; to the east, the boundaries of Gloucestershire and Somerset; to the south, Frome—Shepton Mallet—Glastonbury and the Polden Hills; to the west, the coast.

A high proportion of the area is under cultivation, but grassland is of much greater extent than arable. The woodlands, chiefly in the hilly districts, are rarely extensive. Only one of the major vegetational groupings of southern England is poorly represented, namely lowland heath and associated acid woodland. No attempt can be made to consider all the vegetation-types of the region, and attention is directed to those which are here of particular interest. The Somerset peat moors are unique, but the botanical attraction of longest standing has been the flora of the Carboniferous Limestone, on account of the rare plants, whose occurrence is restricted locally and in Britain as a whole. The richest site of all for plants of this kind lies within the city of Bristol.

MARITIME VEGETATION

Much of the low-lying coastal area of the Bristol region, especially the part in Gloucestershire, is fringed with mud flats and salt marshes; between Clevedon and Portishead and on several headlands the shoreline is rocky; there is one stretch of sand dunes.

The rocky sites, although often rising suddenly from sea-level, support a number of common salt-marsh species together with plants of maritime cliffs such as *Crithmum maritimum* and *Asplenium marinum*, the latter usually hidden in rock clefts. The three Carboniferous Limestone islands in the Severn Estuary have an interesting maritime vegetation. For example, the rich flora of Steepholm contains *Allium ampeloprasum, Inula crithmoides, Lavatera arborea, Plantago coronopus* var. *sabrinae* and the naturalized *Paeonia mascula. Smyrnium olusatrum* is unusually abundant (Skene, 1938).

Sand dunes are limited to the five and a half miles stretch of coast facing west between Burnham-on-Sea and Brean Down. The northern (Brean) half is a narrow belt of marram sandhills, but the southern part (Berrow) reaches a width of nearly half a mile in places. Although in some parts there is a succession of parallel ridges, these are not separated by clearly defined low-lying 'slacks'. However, a number of zones dominated by different plants may be recognized. The low fore-dunes, as well as many small, isolated ridges on the beach, bear almost pure *Agropyron junceiforme*. The *Ammophila arenaria* zone behind merges into a dense and almost ungrazed dune pasture in which *Festuca rubra* and *Carex arenaria* are important components. Species found here which are not of regular occurrence on British dunes include *Anthyllis vulneraria, Elymus arenarius, Oenothera* spp., *Saponaria officinalis, Trifolium arvense*, and *Viola canina* var. *macrantha* in showy abundance. *Iris foetidissima* is plentiful. Some of the irregularly distributed damp hollows contain a fairly rich flora which includes *Epipactis palustris, Hydrocotyle vulgaris* and numerous mosses, of which the commonest is *Acrocladium cuspidatum.* Many of the sandhills carry a dense growth of *Hippophaë rhamnoides*, first planted here about sixty years ago; this scrub now extends over a considerable area, in some places reaching almost to the shoreline. An account of the dune vegetation has been given by Boley (1942).

Salt marshes, with mud flats below them, occur along the banks of the Severn, and also at the mouths of the rivers Parrett, Brue, Axe, Yeo, Kenn and Avon. In the Somerset marshes the zonation is often not well defined. On some parts of the coast, such as that illustrated (Plate v), there is a sharp drop averaging 4 to 5 ft. from a primary marsh to a secondary one. The mode of formation of such an escarpment has been described by Yapp, Johns and Jones (1917). Erosion of the face by tidal undercutting results in the fall, onto the secondary marsh, of large turves whose plants form centres of colonization for the highest levels of the secondary marsh. The tides of the Bristol Channel are the highest in Europe and ebb and flow with great velocity, so that the plants have to withstand considerable tidal forces. The primary marshes support an almost closed turf of *Puccinellia maritima* with locally abundant *Festuca rubra.* Other characteristic plants are *Artemisia maritima, Aster tripolium, Atriplex hastata, Glaux maritima, Juncus gerardi, Plantago coronopus, P. maritima, Salicornia ramosissima, Spergularia marginata, S. salina, Suaeda maritima* and *Triglochin maritima.* The secondary marshes have a poorer flora, being now dominated, often almost to the exclusion of all other plants, by *Spartina townsendii,* which has spread rapidly along the coast of the region in recent years. This vigorous grass does not, however, colonize the primary marshes, except along the banks of drainage channels. *Puccinellia maritima* sometimes occurs in dense Spartinetum; the only other plants doing so regularly—and often quite abundantly—are algae, chiefly *Cladophora* spp., *Enteromorpha* spp. and *Ulva lactuca. Fucus spiralis,* attached to eroded rootstocks of *Spartina,* is locally abundant in Somerset salt marshes. In small areas of secondary marsh not yet colonized by *Spartina* are to be found *Aster tripolium, Atriplex hastata, Festuca rubra, Plantago maritima, Salicornia stricta, Spergularia marginata* and *Triglochin maritima.*

The salt marshes on the banks of the Severn, described by Priestley (1911), often show as many as three or four flat zones, at different levels, separated by sharp erosion faces varying in height from ½ to 5 ft. Here the lower zones, at one time dominated by *Salicornia* and *Puccinellia,* are now densely covered by *Spartina.*

One salt marsh, adjoining the southern part of the Berrow dune system, has special interest because its site is distinctive and history known (Thompson, 1922, 1930; Kendall, 1938; Boley, 1943). The marsh began to develop on the mud flats about 1910, and by 1922 covered approximately one hundred acres, with *Puccinellia maritima* as the dominant plant and *Salicornia* spp. locally abundant. In 1922, a few other species were present in small quantities, those noted being *Aster tripolium, Spartina townsendii, Suaeda maritima, Triglochin maritima* and *Zostera marina.* Subsequently the vegetation became much richer, forty-four species being recorded in 1942; some of these species are fresh-water aquatics which occurred mostly adjoining the sand dune system and probably received fresh water by drainage. By 1942, *Spartina* dominated much of the marsh and at present is even more extensive and has apparently led to the extinction of *Salicornia stricta.* The level of the marsh has no doubt risen in recent years and sand dunes, forming to the west, may ultimately enclose the area. Plants now growing in the marsh include the fresh-water species *Alisma plantago-aquatica, Apium graveolens, A. nodiflorum, Carex acutiformis, Catabrosa aquatica, Iris pseudacorus, Oenanthe lachenalii, Phragmites communis* and *Samolus valerandi,* together with salt-marsh species, such as *Aster tripolium, Carex distans, Juncus gerardi, Puccinellia maritima, Scirpus maritimus, Spergularia marginata* and *Triglochin maritima.*

SOMERSET PEAT MOORS

The extensive Somerset Levels consist of the low-lying flats to the north-west and south-west of Mendip, with a further division (King's Sedgemoor) south of the

Polden Hills. In addition, a small, detached area of similar character (the Gordano Valley) lies north-east of Clevedon. The botanical interest of the Levels is centred on one or two of the areas covered by peat. One area is of outstanding interest because it is the scene of intensive investigations, chiefly by Dr. H. Godwin, into the nature and sequence of the peat layers and the prehistory whose traces they preserve. Much information is now available concerning the changes in the character of the vegetation of this area since the Ice Age.

The peat surface is largely confined to the inland half of the Levels; the coastal half is covered by marine alluvium. One indication of a shoreline inland of the modern coast is provided by the sandy Burtle Beds, for example at Edington Junction and Middlezoy, which date from Pleistocene times.

Changes of relative sea-level and of climate since then have had a decisive influence on the vegetational history of the peat area. The main events can be summarized as follows (Table XII).

TABLE XII

Date (approx.)	Period	Main events
B.C. 10000	Beginning of Post-glacial	End of Ice Age
5500	Late Boreal—Atlantic	End of sea-flooding; beginning of peat-building (reedswamp→fen→raised bog)
1000–500	Sub-boreal—Sub-atlantic transition (Bronze Age—Iron Age)	Dry→wet climate; river-flooding widely reconverted the bogs to fen
B.C. A.D. 50–350	Romano-British	End of primary peat-building Sea-flooding (to several miles inland of modern coast) and retreat

The marine transgression after the melting of the great ice sheets deposited, within the broad valleys now forming the Levels, a floor of clay on which a brackish reedswamp developed as the sea retreated. The *Phragmites* peat formed in the swamp made a foundation for sedge fen of *Cladium mariscus*, which was in turn succeeded by carr, largely of birch. Some of the peat area may have remained as fen or carr until cultivated or converted to pasture after human settlement. Other developments, however, occurred in the area between the Wedmore and Polden ridges, where 'heaths' extend from near Glastonbury coastwards for about six miles. This remnant of the great peat moors has escaped pasturing and cultivation but is exploited vigorously for peat, which, on Shapwick Heath, reached a depth of nearly 18 ft.

Although peat-cutting destroys the existing plant communities and evidence of past vegetation, it has been responsible for interesting archaeological finds of great value in correlative dating. On the 'heaths' the growth of peat outstripped the ground-water level, and the developing surface, watered only by rain, turned acid and became a large raised bog or group of bogs, composed of *Sphagnum*, *Calluna* and other typical bog plants. Excessive surface water, held by *Sphagnum*, was no doubt responsible for destroying the woody carr.

At the close of the Sub-boreal Period, a great climatic deterioration affecting all western Europe led to important changes on the peat bogs. During Sub-boreal times the climate was relatively dry; on Shapwick Heath, for example, peat shown by the pollen profile to be of this age contains much cotton grass (*Eriophorum vaginatum*) and *Calluna*, rather than a rapidly-built *Sphagnum* matrix. The sudden onset of a much wetter climate was marked by a wide recurrence of *Cladium* fen, a community known to develop only in the presence of base-rich water. Its recurrence therefore implies flooding from the swollen rivers (Clapham and Godwin, 1948). The effects may be visualized from the condition of the area recently, when the River Brue burst its banks and some parts were flooded by over a foot of water (Plate VII) while others remained above the flood. Likewise the prolonged flooding of 3,000 years ago swamped some parts but not all, as indicated by differences between peat profiles at different sites. Some of them lack the fen peat which marks a return of eutrophic conditions (good mineral supply); instead they show a recurrence of *Sphagnum* as an active dominant, accompanied by abundant *Scheuchzeria palustris*, which testifies to continued oligotrophic conditions (low mineral supply) under a pronounced increase in rainfall. A further striking confirmation of the wetter climate is provided by the buried trackways of this period. Clapham and Godwin have shown that they must have been built across the bog to fortify hitherto firm routes as they became increasingly swampy, but before long even these wooden tracks were abandoned; they were waterlogged and overgrown so rapidly that they show little wear from use or decay from exposure on the surface.

Raised bogs are now known to have extended over a much wider area than that of the present 'heaths'; along the recently cut Huntspill River bog peat has been found barely three miles from the coast (Godwin, 1943). Here it is overlain by about 10 ft. of marine clay, the product of renewed sea-flooding which stopped short of the Meare-Shapwick 'heath' area. Archaeological finds both below and above the clay have shown that this marine transgression began and ended in the Romano-British Period. The clay left behind forms the present surface of the coastal area.

The peat surface farther inland, although largely unaffected by this episode, ceased active growth at about the same time. This has been deduced from the position of late Roman hoards buried on Shapwick Heath (Godwin, 1941). Senescence of the bog may possibly have had a climatic cause, or its own convexity may have become so pronounced that natural drainage halted the accumulation of peat, or artificial drainage and peat-cutting may by then have begun. The drier condition allowed succession to woodland including birch, oak, pine and sallow.

Woodland is still the climax vegetation, although it now consists largely of birch (*Betula pubescens*) and sallow; alder is plentiful but not widely dominant. Peat-cutting and drainage are responsible for the conspicuous occurrence, especially on well-drained sites, of species alien to growing peat, such as bracken and willow-herb (*Chamaenerion angustifolium*). In recent peat cuttings, open water leads to local dominance by *Typha latifolia*, *Eriophorum angustifolium* or other species, according to the age of the cutting, until a secondary peat-building succession more or less fills the hollow. Unfortunately little or none of the primary peat surface now remains.

The existing communities show features of both bog and fen, and in this respect parallel those of Sub-atlantic times when active bog and fen grew side by side and, in some places, alternated on the same site. The mixed flora established then may be regarded as ancestral to that of the present day, but the modern mixed communities have been determined by peat-cutting; surfaces of acid peat remain, but calcareous water drains into some of the cuttings and ditches. In the mosaic of areas that now occupy different levels or represent different subseral stages, the nearest approach we have seen to the bog vegetation of prehistoric times is a community dominated by *Calluna* and *Molinia*, and also containing *Erica tetralix*, *Eriophorum angustifolium* (both abundant), wide cushions of *Sphagnum* (*recurvum* and *papillosum*), *Salix repens* (local) and occasional small plants of *Osmunda regalis*, but very few other species. Here the ground water showed a pH, as determined by glass electrode, of 4·3 to 4·7. Nearby, the reaction was somewhat more acid, although the vegetation, a scrub of birch and *Myrica*, lacks *Sphagnum* and contains, together with *Molinia* and the same two heaths, *Potentilla palustris*, *Valeriana officinalis* and *Peucedanum palustre*; the last is normally a fen plant, but is here quite frequent although much more poorly grown than in fenland. Other species common in the same neighbourhood include *Carex paniculata*, *C. pseudocyperus*, *Epilobium palustre*, *Lotus uliginosus*, *Scutellaria galericulata* and *Thelypteris palustris*. Along some of the droves the attractive *Wahlenbergia hederacea* is locally abundant. In the watery hollows and rhines there is often a dense vegetation; some of the conspicuous plants are *Alisma plantago-aquatica*, *Glyceria maxima*, *Hydrocharis morsus-ranae*, *Phragmites communis*, *Sium latifolium*, *Sparganium ramosum* and *Utricularia* spp.

At the eastern extremity of the 'heaths', two miles from Glastonbury, the ground water was found to be almost neutral with a pH of 6·6 to 7·1. Base-rich water has had easy access to this locality. In places the vegetation altogether lacks characteristic bog species. One area of less than an acre yielded, without exhaustive recording, a list of about 80 species, including seven *Carices* and four *Junci* (one, the notably eutrophic *J. subnodulosus*) and typical fen plants like *Rhamnus cathartica*, *Eupatorium cannabinum* and *Symphytum officinale*, with *Orchis praetermissa* nearby. The community has closely followed the clearance of carr and, on this account as well as in its composition, is equivalent to the showy 'mixed fen' recognized by Godwin and Tansley (1929) at Wicken near Cambridge.

Many of the plants at one time abundant on the peat moors have now become very rare or extinct. *Cladium*, which played a leading part in the initial fens of 7,000 years ago, and again in the swamping period which began 4,000 years later, is now very local on the moors. Likewise, *Andromeda polifolia* has been reduced in the past hundred years from abundance, at least locally, almost to extinction. *Scheuchzeria*, whose conspicuous remains are so plentiful where bog growth was renewed in the cold rain of Sub-atlantic times, disappeared from the moors before botanical recording began, and now persists, in Britain, only as a Scottish rarity. *Oxycoccus palustris*, also quite often found in the Sub-atlantic bog peat, is now at best extremely rare in the locality. On the other hand the bog myrtle, *Myrica gale*, a fen as well as bog plant, appeared with the earliest onset of bog conditions and for several millennia has shown here a distinctive abundance which is still maintained. It occupies old peat cuttings extensively, whereas some of the plants now very rare, including *Carex dioica* and *Hypericum elodes* as well as *Oxycoccus* and *Andromeda*, apparently cannot do so.

GORDANO VALLEY

The peat of the Gordano Valley, about seven miles from Bristol, is enclosed between two narrow ridges diverging north-east and east from Clevedon, and reaches a depth of at least 15 ft. The vegetation is of natural aspect and is fen with sallow carr; together with most of the common fen plants there are present *Juncus subnodulosus* (abundant), *Achillea ptarmica*, *Orchis praetermissa*, *Platanthera bifolia* and *Valeriana dioica*. The two British species of *Cyperus*, *C. fuscus* and *C. longus*, both rarities, have been found in this locality. At least some of the fen is of secondary origin, a reversion from former cultivation. Nothing is yet known about the primary development of the peat. The likely origin is one of reedswamp leading to fen. The modern vegetation is certainly fen. There may, nevertheless, have been some development of acid (bog) peat, as at Meare and Shapwick. The present ground water, despite the close proximity of the surrounding calcareous slopes, is sometimes slightly acid although usually about neutral (pH 5·3 to 7·4).

LIMESTONE COUNTRY

The two hard limestones which occur over large areas in the region, the Carboniferous Limestone and the Oolite, lie in contact just west of Frome; from here they run respectively westwards and northwards to form the Mendip and the Cotswold Hills. As shown in Fig. 16, the Carboniferous Limestone is represented by several hilly areas besides the main range of Mendip; the latter is broken by a number of gaps between Axbridge and the coast. The terms 'Mendip' and 'Cotswold' usually refer only to the main hill ranges of the two limestone formations, the former from near Frome to Brean Down and the latter from Bath northwards. Here the terms are sometimes employed in a more general sense for the country occupied by the limestones, and 'Oolite' is used to mean both the Great and Inferior Oolites, or either of these.

LIMESTONE WOODLAND

The woods at the northern and southern extremes of the limestone country are distinctly different. The difference is not, however, simply between Oolite and Carboniferous Limestone woodland, for the intervening woods show wide variations in character, particularly in the dominant trees.

The central Cotswolds around Stroud are well known for their beechwoods. On the Carboniferous Limestone in Somerset, the semi-natural woodland was considered by Moss (1907) to be fundamentally ashwood, although he recognized that oak was by no means absent. Between these two types a transition might be expected in the southern Cotswolds, and has been tentatively recognized (Tansley and Adamson, 1913).

Further information is evidently needed concerning the proportions of the tree components of the limestone woods. The predominance of ash on the Carboniferous Limestone may easily be exaggerated, the tree being distinctive in appearance and vigorous as a colonist, so that it forms a conspicuous fringe around the margins of many woods. But other trees form much of the timber in the Carboniferous Limestone woods. A stronger basis of fact is also needed about the nature of the woods immediately south of the beechwood country, a question which has more than a local bearing, for it relates to the general problem and rather sharp limits of beech dominance in Britain.

In a recent survey we have selected about twenty woods on the limestones and assessed subjectively the abundance of the component trees. The aim has been to choose woods which are natural or semi-natural, but information as to past planting and exploitation is often lacking. However, there is little doubt that some of the facts presented by an aggregate of some twenty woods reflect the natural ecological relationships of the tree species. The woodlands studied are almost entirely on hillsides, usually with a slope of 20 to 30°.

In the limestone woods as a whole, the five most important trees are oak, ash, beech, wych elm and lime. Some or all of these five nearly always form more than 70 per cent. and sometimes almost 100 per cent. of the tree layer. In Fig. 16 their relative frequencies are shown for eighteen of the woods examined.

The most distinctive distributions are those of beech and lime. Beech, the dominant in Cotswold woods around Stroud, is much less frequent on the Oolite farther south, and almost lacking on the Carboniferous Limestone. On the other hand, the lime (*Tilia cordata*) is almost confined to Carboniferous Limestone woods where in some places, such as Cheddar Wood, it is an important component of the tree layer. The oak of the region is largely *Quercus robur*, although in some woods in Somerset, notably Leigh Woods in and above the Avon Gorge, there is much *Q. petraea* together with forms intermediate between it and *Q. robur*. In Fig. 16 the two oak species, where both are present, have been grouped together. Oak, which is often as abundant as ash in woods on Mendip, is usually much less common on the Oolite, although present in some quantity in the Bath district. On the Cotswolds some of the oak which has been planted is of poor quality, many of the trees being stunted and malformed.

PLATE V. *Salt marsh between Clevedon and Middle Hope, the distant headland. Grazed primary marsh in foreground, indented by tidal drainage channels. Fallen turves lie below the eroded cliff, here 5 ft. high.* Spartina townsendii *dominates the lower, secondary marsh and forms colonies on the mud beyond* (7 September 1954).

PLATE VI. *The south slope of Brean Down, mostly covered by limestone grassland.* Ammophila *dune in foreground* (6 October 1954).

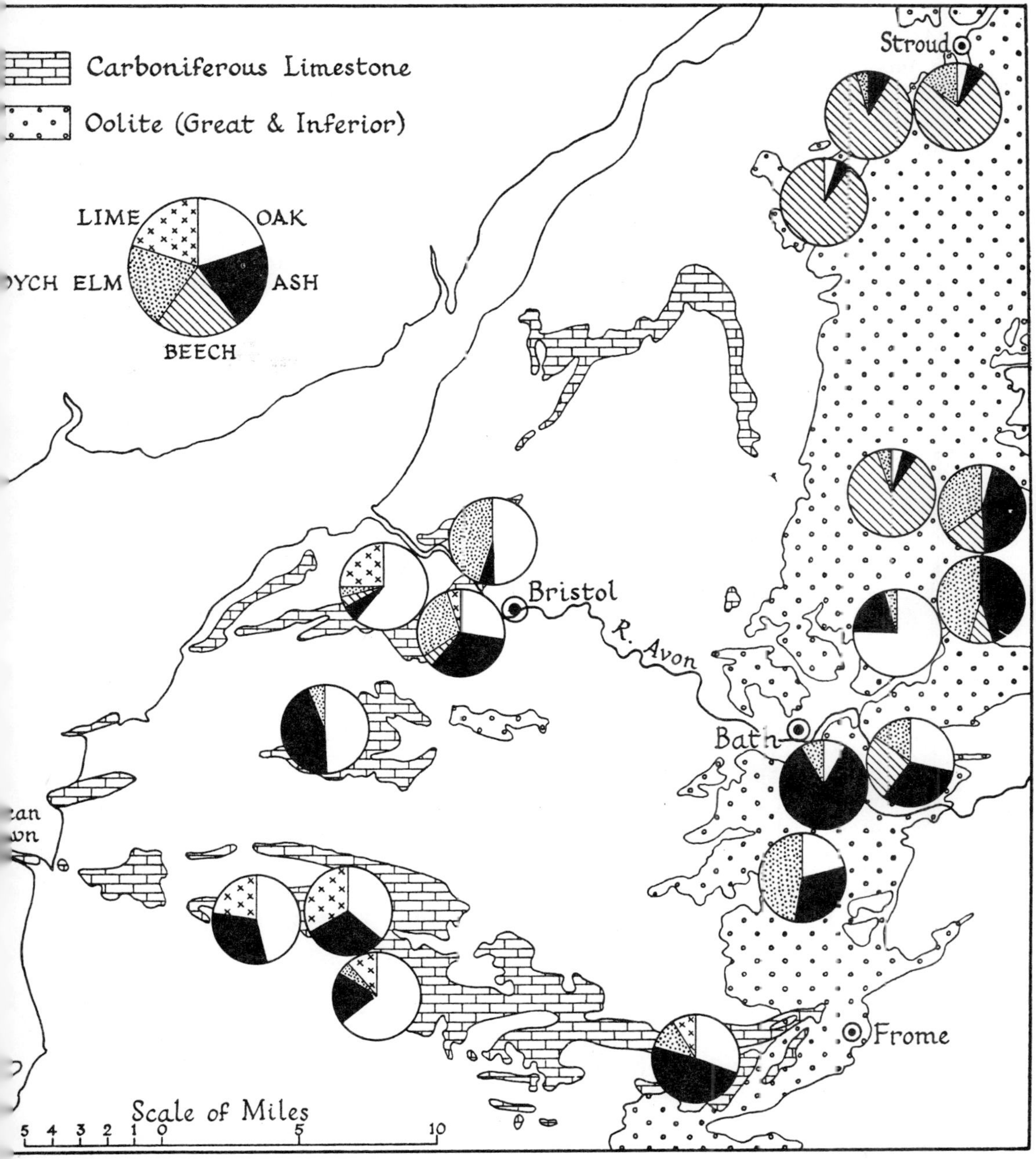

. 16. *The tree composition of woodland on Carboniferous Limestone and Oolite. Each circle represents one woodland. The sectors indicate by their size the relative abundance of the five important trees.*

ATE VII. *Grazed peat moor at Sharpham, near Glastonbury, under flood. Natural carr, here mostly sallow, on left* (19 August 1954).

ATE VIII. Linosyris vulgaris *in flower, in front of bare rock, on Carboniferous Limestone near Weston-super-Mare. Much of the grass is* Koeleria vallesiana (15 October 1954).

Ash is usually dominant or abundant in Mendip woods, and is also a conspicuous component of some Cotswold woods, where growth is often good. It is the only tree present in all the woods and copses studied. The wych elm (*Ulmus glabra*), although never extensively dominant on the limestones, is often abundant locally on both Carboniferous Limestone and Oolite.

From earlier studies and from our own observations the following summary can be given about the woodland dominants. On the Carboniferous Limestone slopes the natural woodland seems to be balanced closely between ashwood and ash-oak wood, ash being conspicuous as a pioneer and probably forming a climax consociation on the steeper, rockier sites with shallower soils. On the Carboniferous Limestone plateaux, however, oakwood is sometimes well developed, and might indeed be the natural climax. On the steep slopes of the Oolite, where the soils are often shallow, the beech climax of the Stroud region gives way towards the south to ash and oak together with wych elm. Price (Riddelsdell, Hedley and Price, 1948) points out that beechwood is largely restricted to slopes of the Inferior Oolite. He also mentions that rainfall is relatively high in the region of climax beechwood. Obviously much remains to be explained about the relationships of beech and the other dominant trees of the Oolite.

Besides the trees considered above, several others and a number of calcicolous shrubs are often present in the limestone woodlands. On the Carboniferous Limestone, the following species appear in at least five out of eight woodlands examined:

Acer campestre	*Ilex aquifolium*
Clematis vitalba	*Ligustrum vulgare*
Cornus sanguinea	*Lonicera periclymenum*
Corylus avellana	*Prunus spinosa*
Crataegus monogyna	*Sorbus aria*
Euonymus europaeus	*Viburnum opulus*

In some places, for example Cheddar Wood, the privet forms a thick, half-dead undergrowth whose density and height of 6 to 8 ft. were evidently attained during a scrub-phase after the wood was coppiced. In addition to the species listed above, *Rhamnus cathartica* and *Daphne laureola* are present in some of the Mendip woods. The corresponding list for the Oolite—species present in at least eight out of thirteen woods—contains only:

Acer campestre	*Crataegus monogyna*
Corylus avellana	*Viburnum lantana*

The common elm (*Ulmus procera*) is an Oolite woodland tree, although a less constant one, being locally abundant in three of the woods examined. Less constant shrubs on the Oolite are *Daphne laureola* and *Rosa arvensis*; the latter occurs fairly regularly and plentifully in the beechwoods of the Dursley neighbourhood. Three other woody species found on both limestones call for brief comment. Hazel is abundant and often sub-dominant, except in the beechwoods. Yew, although widespread, is rarely plentiful and is absent from many of the woods. Hornbeam (*Carpinus betulus*) is of special interest in this region, where it occurs as a rarity on the limestones and on other soils. In unfrequented woods hornbeam has the appearance of a native, although isolated from its region of abundance in south-east England. When Miller Christy (1924) doubted its native status near Bristol, the *Carpinus* pollen buried in Sub-atlantic peat in Somerset had not been discovered (Godwin, 1941).

The ground flora of the limestone woods is usually dominated by *Mercurialis perennis*, and in some woods, especially those on the southern Oolite, dog's mercury is abundant almost to the exclusion of other herbs. In herbaceous as well as subordinate woody species, the Carboniferous Limestone woods are generally richer than those of the Oolite, especially those where abundant beech monopolizes the surface soil and casts a heavy shade. Herbaceous species characteristic of the Carboniferous Limestone woods, found in at least five out of eight studied, are[1]:

Ajuga reptans	*Mercurialis perennis*
Carex sylvatica	*Tamus communis*
Circaea lutetiana	*Teucrium scorodonia*
Endymion nonscriptus	*Viola riviniana* and/or *reichenbachiana*
Euphorbia amygdaloides	*Dryopteris austriaca*
Fragaria vesca	*D. filix-mas*
Galeobdolon luteum	*Phyllitis scolopendrium*
Geum urbanum	*Polypodium vulgare*
Hypericum hirsutum	

The only Oolite species of equivalent constancy are four of the above, *Fragaria*, *Mercurialis*, *Viola* and *Dryopteris filix-mas* together with *Epilobium montanum*. Other fairly common herbs are *Asperula odorata*, *Sanicula europaea* and *Viola odorata*. Less frequent species found on both limestones include *Campanula trachelium*, *Epipactis helleborine*, *Helleborus foetidus*, *H. viridis*, *Paris quadrifolia*, *Polygonatum multiflorum* and, in moist situations, *Dipsacus pilosus*. *Allium ursinum* is often abundant but sometimes absent. *Convallaria majalis* is locally abundant in a few unfrequented woods on both limestones, especially where rocky.

Two herbaceous species, *Rubia peregrina* and *Lithospermum purpurocaeruleum*, are highly characteristic of the Mendip woodlands, for in them or their borders they are fairly common, whereas on the Cotswolds one (*Rubia*) is very rare and the other (*Lithospermum*) is absent. In Somerset *Lithospermum* does, however, occur on formations other than Carboniferous Limestone, being known in a few places on and near the Polden Hills. Growing with it in one Mendip hedgerow, in very small quantity, is *Carex depauperata*, an extremely rare sedge with only one or two other British habitats.

Examples of Carboniferous Limestone woodlands with a rich ground flora are provided by Leigh Woods and Asham Wood. The former, adjoining Bristol, contains *Aquilegia vulgaris*, *Cardamine impatiens*, *Carex digitata* and *Hypericum androsaemum*. Asham Wood, on eastern Mendip, has *Convallaria*, *Dipsacus pilosus*, *Polygonatum*

[1] The records for both limestones were made in late summer and are incomplete for vernal species.

multiflorum and the hybrid between *Geum rivale* and *G. urbanum*, growing near its parents; *Colchicum autumnale*, which also occurs here, is fairly common in moist woods on the Carboniferous Limestone, but has various other habitats including Oolite woodland (Butcher, 1954).

Of the rarer woodland herbs characteristic of the Oolite, two are especially associated with the Bath neighbourhood: *Ornithogalum pyrenaicum*, the Bath asparagus, which is locally abundant, and the beautiful but sporadic flowerer *Gagea lutea*. Other uncommon plants of the Oolite, characteristic of the Cotswold beechwoods, are the saprophytes *Monotropa* and *Neottia*, growing where the humus is thick, and *Hieracium exotericum*, *Hordelymus sylvatica*, *Pyrola minor*, *Cephalanthera damasonium* and the very rare *C. rubra*, whose British occurrence is limited to the Stroud neighbourhood. *Stachys alpina*, which has only one other British locality, also grows in the district in a few woods and at their margins.

The fern flora of the Oolite woods is much poorer than that of the woods on Carboniferous Limestone. In the damp rocky parts of Asham Wood, at least eight fern species, including *Cystopteris fragilis* and *Polystichum lobatum*, may be found readily. The valley slopes of Leigh Woods also are rich in ferns, among which are *Blechnum spicant*, *Dryopteris spinulosa*, *Polystichum setiferum* and *Thelypteris phegopteris*.

One noticeable difference between the Oolite and Carboniferous Limestone woods of the Bristol district concerns the abundance of bryophytes, which are richly represented in some Mendip woodlands. Rock surfaces are extensively occupied by many of them, including *Camptothecium sericeum*, *Ctenidium molluscum*, *Ditrichum flexicaule*, *Frullania tamarisci*, *Grimmia apocarpa*, *Madotheca platyphylla*, *Neckera complanata*, *N. crispa* and *Plagiochila asplenioides*. These and other species may form an almost complete cover. On the Cotswolds bryophytes are generally much less abundant. This difference and some of the others mentioned previously may be related to the character of the soil on slopes, which on the Oolite is loose, rubbly and unstable, whereas that on the Carboniferous Limestone usually has a firm surface.

LIMESTONE GRASSLAND

Bristol lies within easy reach of all three principal types of British calcareous grassland—those of the Carboniferous Limestone, the Oolite and the Chalk. The fullest knowledge of such grasslands has been obtained on the Chalk. Near Warminster chalk grassland occurs scarcely twenty-five miles from Bristol, but it lies outside the scope of this chapter, because it cannot usefully be considered in isolation from the broadening expanse of chalk country which extends far beyond our region.

The semi-natural grasslands of the other two limestones make an interesting comparison. In floristic content they often match each other closely. They share the familiar constant plants of calcareous grassland, for example, *Festuca ovina*, *F. rubra*, *Briza media*, *Helictotrichon pratense*, *Carex flacca*, *Poterium sanguisorba*, *Lotus corniculatus*, *Linum catharticum*, *Cirsium acaule*, *Thymus drucei*, *Hieracium pilosella* and *Plantago lanceolata*. There are probably not more than one or two grassland species characteristic of both limestones in the region, as distinct from calcareous grassland elsewhere.

This description might apply to *Linum bienne*, although it is considerably rarer on the Oolite than on the Carboniferous Limestone. William Turner made the first record (published 1562) of this species as a British plant 'wythin a mile of Welles'.

The broadest contrast between the two types of grassland is seen in the different range of sites which they occupy. Grassland of typical calcicolous composition is found on oolitic slopes of any angle or aspect, and on flat sites where spared by the plough. On the Carboniferous Limestone only the slopes of drier aspect regularly bear an entirely calcicole flora; the plateau sites bear limestone heath or at least some species alien to strongly calcareous grassland. So do most slopes of more or less northerly aspect, although here the heathy element is often masked or replaced by dominant bracken.[1] Characteristic plants of limestone heath, growing intermixed with more or less calcicolous species, include *Calluna vulgaris*, *Erica cinerea*, *Potentilla erecta*, *Agrostis tenuis*, *Hypericum pulchrum* and *Viola canina*. On these sites the surface soil lacks free carbonate and is acid. Absence of free carbonate is also, however, a usual feature of south-facing Mendip grasslands of purely calcicole appearance. The Cotswold grasslands almost always have free carbonate in the surface soil.

The above differences between the two types can be related with confidence to lithological rather than climatic factors. Of the latter, rainfall is probably the most relevant to this grassland comparison. The Gloucestershire Cotswolds receive an average of 30 to 35 in. annually; a similar amount of rain falls on the lower parts of Mendip, but the main massif east of Axbridge gets amounts up to, and locally more than, 45 in. There is thus no Cotswold–Mendip difference greater than that within the Mendip Hills themselves. Yet even the drier parts of Mendip, from Axbridge to the coast, with an annual rainfall like that of the Cotswolds, show the grassland features which are distinctive of the Carboniferous Limestone as compared with the Oolite.

Examination of the soils and the subsoil weathering of the two limestones shows how the texture and composition of the parent rock account for the heathy tendencies on the Carboniferous Limestone and their absence from the Oolite. The hard, homogeneous Carboniferous Limestone weathers at its subsoil surface without much fragmentation; the softer, heterogeneous Oolite becomes riddled with fissures and crumbles into fragments which get mixed with the soil, where they act as a dispersed source of free carbonate. On the Carboniferous Limestone, therefore, it is only on sites where erosion keeps pace with soil-formation that the rooting layer remains within reach of limestone or, at least, that the soil remains permanently immature and therefore rich in calcium. These conditions are almost restricted to slopes where a dry aspect supplements steepness, for perennially moist conditions allow a thicker vegetation cover that reduces the rate of erosion.

Oolite heath is at best extremely rare, and there is none on record in the southern Cotswolds (Knight, 1912). Here the plateau sites, unlike those of the higher-lying Mendip plateau with its patches of rocky ground, are almost entirely cultivated;

[1] On part of the Cotswold escarpment near Dursley there is a conspicuous cloak of bracken, here, however, growing on the Cotteswold Sands (Upper Lias) underlying the Inferior Oolite

even if they were not, the natural factors already described would probably make for very slow development of Oolite heath.

The different incidence of leaching on the Carboniferous Limestone and the Oolite thus accounts for one group of grassland species—the calcifuges or near-calcifuges—which are differential in their occurrence. A comparison limited, however, to the most calcareous grasslands of the Carboniferous Limestone, and Oolite grassland, shows other differences. Maritime species, present in coastal Carboniferous Limestone grassland, lack suitable sites on the Oolite. *Erodium maritimum* is of some interest in this connexion, being locally frequent on some Mendip sites as far as nine miles inland. Most of these inland localities were maritime in the periods of marine transgression referred to earlier (p. 94). *Plantago coronopus* is likewise a member of short turf on Carboniferous Limestone but not on Oolite. The Carboniferous Limestone also supports several rare or local species, not inherently maritime, which are unknown on the Oolite. These are found particularly in rocky habitats, and are considered later. Four of them, however, *Carex humilis*, *Helianthemum apenninum*, *Koeleria vallesiana* and *Potentilla tabernaemontani*, also occur in grassland swards adjoining rocky sites.

On the other hand the few grassland species limited to the Oolite seem independent of rocky ground. Notable species in this group are *Anemone pulsatilla*, *Astragalus danicus*, *Polygala calcarea* and *Thesium humifusum*. All four reach a western distributional limit within twenty-five miles of Bristol. That *Anemone* and *Astragalus* extend thus far on the Oolite is interesting when considered beside the fact that on the Chalk their occurrence stops well short of the west Wiltshire downs, and indeed shows a strong eastern tendency.

The most conspicuous Cotswold–Mendip difference is one of dominance. *Festuca ovina*, the usual dominant on Mendip, is commonly replaced on the Cotswolds by *Zerna erecta* or *Brachypodium pinnatum*. On Mendip Brachypodietum and Zernetum are both rare, although the former is abundant locally and *Zerna* does occur on roadsides and elsewhere. Quantitative differences also appear among the subordinate species. *Koeleria gracilis*, for example, is much more regular and plentiful on the Carboniferous Limestone than on the Oolite. That such differences are shown by other species common to both limestones has become clear from a recent comparative study by Mr. G. E. D. Tiley, of the University of Bristol, whose knowledge has been a valuable help at several points in this account.

MENDIP PLATEAU

Not all the semi-natural vegetation of the Mendip plateau is leached limestone grassland or limestone heath. There are three or four tracts of upland heath on outcrops of Old Red Sandstone and possibly on part of the Lower Limestone Shale. Podsol is sometimes present where the heath association is well developed. The latter has the customary dominants, *Calluna* and *Erica cinerea*, locally accompanied by abundant *Molinia* and *E. tetralix*; typical associates include *Juncus squarrosus*, *Nardus stricta*, *Polygala serpyllifolia*, *Ulex gallii* and *Vaccinium myrtillus*. *Deschampsia flexuosa* is common but restricted to banks and mounds. In one or two places this vegetation is accompanied by wet heath or rudimentary valley bog. The most conspicuous bog encroaches on a pond formed by an artificial dam. Much of its area is covered by stands of one or other of the following: *Carex rostrata*, *Equisetum fluviatile*, *Eriophorum angustifolium*, *Molinia caerulea*, *Sphagnum* spp. A pH determination of the bog water here gave a value of 5·1.

Abandoned lead-workings are common on Mendip. On their banks, but also elsewhere, grow two rare species which occur in similar habitats on the Carboniferous Limestone of northern England, namely *Minuartia verna* and *Thlaspi alpestre*. The Mendip race of the latter is distinctive. The old lead-workings also form an inland habitat for *Silene maritima*.

CARBONIFEROUS LIMESTONE ROCKS

The rocky habitats of the Carboniferous Limestone include cliffs, screes and hillsides. Some are hidden by woodland, and others are partly occupied by scrub. Their chief interest, however, is the open herbaceous vegetation, which contains several species rare or absent elsewhere in Britain. An interesting account of them has been given by Lousley (1950).[1]

Some such habitats are extensive, especially the Avon and Cheddar Gorges; many are much smaller. Here attention is confined to those known for their rare species, but it must be emphasized that there are similar sites, such as Burrington Combe and Cleeve or Goblin Combe, where rarities are very sparse or absent.

Within the boundary of Bristol stand the west-facing cliffs of the Avon Gorge. They have attracted botanists for centuries, and St. Vincent's Rocks, now spanned by Clifton Suspension Bridge, are quoted frequently. On the Somerset side of the gorge, unshaded rock exposures are much less extensive and do not carry so rich a flora. The vegetation on the Bristol side is a mixture of scrub, merging into woodland where the cliffs give way to slopes, and open herbaceous growth, with more grassy expanses on some of the wider ledges. The scrub includes *Acer campestre*, *Cornus sanguinea*, *Crataegus monogyna*, *Fraxinus excelsior*, *Ligustrum vulgare*, *Lonicera periclymenum*, *Rosa* and *Rubus* spp., *Taxus baccata*, *Ulex europaeus*, *Viburnum lantana* and more than one species of *Sorbus*. Only *S. aria* is common, but *S. bristoliensis*, endemic to the Avon Gorge, is also present in the scrub and on both sides of the river in woodland. Besides these and *S. aucuparia*, two other *Sorbi* are recorded for the Avon Gorge. *S. eminens*, commoner in the Wye Valley, is apparently very rare on the Clifton side; *S. torminalis* is present but where known now is not on limestone. Several alien species of trees and shrubs have been planted near the Suspension Bridge, among them *Cotoneaster frigida*, *Garrya elliptica*, *Laurus nobilis*, *Quercus cerris* and *Q. ilex*; the last regenerates abundantly. In the scrub, *Rubia peregrina* is often plentiful, as is *Orobanche hederae* growing on trailing ivy. Herbaceous species which are widespread and often plentiful on the rocks include the following:

[1] We are indebted to Mr. J. E. Lousley and to Mr. N. Y. Sandwith for answering queries about the limestone flora, and to Dr. E. F. Warburg for information about *Sorbus* spp.

Campanula rotundifolia	*Kentranthus ruber*
Centaurea scabiosa	*Origanum vulgare*
Ceterach officinarum	*Pimpinella saxifraga*
Chrysanthemum leucanthemum	*Poterium sanguisorba*
Dactylis glomerata	*Scabiosa columbaria*
Festuca ovina	*Sedum acre*
Helianthemum chamaecistus	*Solidago virgaurea*

The list does not contain any of the species which give distinction to the Avon Gorge flora. Two or three of the latter, however, are quite abundant. *Veronica spicata* ssp. *hybrida*, with handsome blue spikes, is plentiful on ledges and in crevices, where it appears to spread by creeping stems as well as by seed; a white-flowered plant has been seen recently. *Potentilla tabernaemontani*, of distinctly local occurrence in Britain, is widespread here as elsewhere on the Carboniferous Limestone of the region. *Carex humilis* is locally plentiful in short closed turf, and on rocky ground where *Trinia glauca* is often present as well. *Geranium sanguineum*, although localized, forms a few large patches near the cliff-top; small plants also grow in the crevices below. A much more recent find is *G. purpureum*, a close ally of *G. robertianum* with which it may well have been confused. *G. purpureum* is centred in the Mediterranean region and in Britain is restricted to the south-west (Baker, 1955). Spring-flowering annuals are represented by *Hornungia petraea* and *Cerastium pumilum*, the former a limestone rarity and the latter also found, uncommonly, in other calcareous habitats. All of the rarest species on record still survive, although at least two of them have been in considerable danger of extinction. *Scilla autumnalis*, inhabiting turf as well as rock, is exceedingly restricted. So is *Allium sphaerocephalon*, an extreme rarity whose only other occurrence in the British Isles is in Jersey. *A. carinatum* and *A. siculum* are also present; they are planted aliens which, like some others, now maintain themselves. Apart from *Sorbus bristoliensis*, only one other Avon Gorge species is as rare in Britain as *Allium sphaerocephalon*; this is *Arabis stricta*, which may also exist as a native in one locality in Wales. At Bristol it is occasionally fairly plentiful on some of the rocks. Although plants have been known to grow for as long as ten years, many of the rosettes are small and may be confused with *A. hirsuta* which sometimes occurs nearby. *A. stricta* is remarkable for its limited world distribution, being known for certain only in south-west Europe and Bristol. Here the species has been on record since 1686. By then half of these rare plants had been recorded; *Trinia* was known here as early as 1562.

The Cheddar cliffs are most famous for *Dianthus gratianopolitanus*, the Cheddar pink, which is found nowhere else in Britain. Some of the shady rock-ledges bear *Saxifraga hypnoides*, a northern plant here in its southernmost British locality. Conspicuous plants of the Cheddar Gorge include *Chrysanthemum leucanthemum*, *Meconopsis cambrica* and *Thalictrum minus*. Several *Hieracia* are known in the Cheddar locality, among them *H. britannicum* var. *stenolepiforme*, *H. cyathis*, *H. lachenalii*, *H. maculatum*, *H. angustisquamum* and *H. lima*. The last two species are endemic to Cheddar. On the limestone screes the fern *Thelypteris robertiana* is frequent; in the gorge also occur

Asplenium adiantum-nigrum and *Cystopteris fragilis*. Associated with *Sorbus aria* on the rocks and cliffs are *S. anglica* and *S. porrigentiformis*.

The rocky, south-facing slope of Brean Down (Plate VI) is subject to maritime influences, and to some degree the same may be true of the less extensive slopes at Uphill. With a few important exceptions, however, even the Brean Down flora resembles that of similar habitats inland. One maritime feature is a population of wild carrots containing, with *Daucus carota* ssp. *carota*, intermediates between this and the maritime *D. gingidium*. Two of the abundant plants on Brean Down, *Helianthemum apenninum* and *Koeleria vallesiana*, are extremely rare as members of the British flora. *K. vallesiana* is known only on Brean Down and in rocky limestone grassland inland of this neighbourhood, including Uphill (see Chapter 8, p. 126). Apparently growing best on open, rocky ground, it is also plentiful, together with a lesser quantity of *K. gracilis*, in grazed closed turf adjoining. The white rockrose, which dominates some areas on Brean Down, occurs also at one nearby site inland but, elsewhere in Britain, only near Torquay in Devon. *Carex humilis* is plentiful on some of the rocky southern slopes, and also forms an extensive closed turf comparable with the Festuco-Caricetum humilis of the Wessex chalk. *Trinia glauca*, which grows on several neighbouring inland sites, has not been found on Brean Down.

In one locality near Weston-super-Mare the very rare *Linosyris vulgaris*, restricted in Britain to five scattered sites on western coastal limestone, has a somewhat precarious foothold on the rocks (Plate VIII). It was previously known at two other places nearby. The vegetation of the existing colony of *Linosyris* includes *Anthyllis vulneraria*, *Cirsium acaule*, *Festuca ovina*, *Koeleria vallesiana*, *Pimpinella saxifraga*, *Scabiosa columbaria* and *Trinia glauca*.

PROBLEMS OF THE LIMESTONE RARITIES

The occurrence in the Bristol region of some of the rarities of limestone rocks is shown in Table XIII. Apart from the Avon Gorge, the localities given form a series from Cheddar Gorge westwards, ending with Brean Down. These species and a few others make the region a source of valuable information relating to the general problem of rarity in plants.

The number of species involved is too great to be a chance concurrence. The grouping of rarities, well known elsewhere, implies that the localities concerned are unusual in past or present environmental features. This might apply particularly to the Avon Gorge, whose wealth of rarities is outstanding.

In some instances the differing content of rare species in the various sites listed may be partly due to the chances of dispersal. The element of chance might account for the distribution of *Helianthemum apenninum*, which is present on Brean Down and Purn Hill but absent from the intervening and apparently similar site at Uphill. The same explanation may also hold in the case of *Trinia*, unrecorded from Cheddar cliffs and Brean Down.

TABLE XIII

Occurrence in the Bristol region of some rare plants of Carboniferous Limestone
(*Doubtful records are not shown*)

	Avon Gorge	Cheddar Gorge	Crook Peak	Purn Hill, Bleadon	Uphill	Brean Down
Allium sphaerocephalon	+	.	.	.	.	.
Arabis stricta	+	.	.	.	.	.
Hornungia petraea	+	.	.	.	.	.
Scilla autumnalis	+	.	.	.	.	.
Veronica spicata ssp. *hybrida*	+	.	.	.	.	.
Geranium purpureum	+	+	.	.	.	.
Dianthus gratianopolitanus	.	+	.	.	.	.
Saxifraga hypnoides	.	+	.	.	.	.
Helianthemum apenninum	.	.	.	+	.	+
Carex humilis	+	.	.	.	.	+
Geranium sanguineum	+	+	.	.	.	+
Koeleria vallesiana	.	.	+	+	+	+
Trinia glauca	+	.	+	+	+	.
Cerastium pumilum	+	+	+	+	+	+

A contrasting type of distribution is shown by *Koeleria vallesiana*, which occurs in several adjoining but in no outlying sites; here a controlling factor, perhaps connected with proximity to the coast, may operate only in the area occupied by the species.

The restriction of the rare species to so few localities does not have a single explanation for all the species. The endemic microspecies of *Hieracium* and *Sorbus* of Cheddar and the Avon Gorge are a special case. In the latter genus the forms in the region require further study; apparently there are other *Sorbi* besides those already mentioned. In both genera the restriction of the species concerned may be closely connected with their apomictic reproduction and the spatial isolation of their habitats. The restriction of other rare plants may be interpreted on the lines indicated by Pigott and Walters (1954). They emphasize, as did Griggs (1940), that such species frequently depend on habitats where closed communities are not readily formed. Lasting habitats of this kind are provided where hard rock is exposed, and for species which are also calcicolous—as British rarities often are—the combined conditions are found on the Carboniferous Limestone. It has recently been shown beyond doubt that many species now rare in Britain had a much wider distribution during and following the close of the Ice Age (Godwin, 1953). The rare plants of the Bristol region belong to several different elements, or geographical groups, including alpine, continental, sub-Mediterranean and oceanic, which probably gained access to the region in different epochs. The authors quoted above point out that such plants, mostly growing in open communities, would have been extensively overrun by the subsequent spread of forest and peat, persisting only where these could not develop. The rocky sites of our region are often difficult or impossible habitats for woody plants. Where inaccessible they also provide protection from grazing, from trampling by heavy animals and from human interference. Where the soil is exposed, unstable or very stony, herbaceous competition often appears to be slight. Some of the rare species, however, like *Koeleria vallesiana*, *Carex humilis*, and, in woodland, *Lithospermum purpurocaeruleum*, also grow in closed communities. In these instances and many others, ecological understanding of the rare plants is far from complete.

REFERENCES

BAKER, H. G. 1955. *Geranium purpureum* Vill. and *G. robertianum* L. in the British Flora: I. *Geranium purpureum*. *Watsonia*, **3**, 160.

BOLEY, G. M. 1942. The Vegetation of Berrow, North Somerset. I. The Salt-marsh Community. *Proc. Bristol Nat. Soc.*, (4) **9**, 427.

—. 1943. The Vegetation of Berrow, North Somerset. II. The Sand Dune Succession. *Ibid.*, (4) **9**, 510.

BUTCHER, R. W. 1954. *Colchicum autumnale* L., in *Biological Flora of the British Isles*. *J. Ecol.*, **42**, 249.

CHRISTY, MILLER. 1924. The Hornbeam (*Carpinus betulus* L.) in Britain. *Ibid.*, **12**, 39.

CLAPHAM, A. R. and H. GODWIN. 1948. Studies of the Post-glacial History of British Vegetation. VIII. Swamping Surfaces in Peats of the Somerset Levels. IX. Prehistoric Trackways in the Somerset Levels. *Phil. Trans. Roy. Soc.*, B, **233**, 233, 249.

GODWIN, H. 1941. Studies of the Post-glacial History of British Vegetation. VI. Correlations in the Somerset Levels. *New Phytol.*, **40**, 108.

—. 1943. Coastal Peat Beds of the British Isles and North Sea. *J. Ecol.*, **31**, 199.

—. 1953. British Vegetation in the Full-glacial and the Late-glacial Periods. *The Changing Flora of Britain* (ed. J. E. Lousley), p. 59. Bot. Soc. Brit. Is.

— and A. G. TANSLEY. 1929. The Vegetation of Wicken Fen. *The Natural History of Wicken Fen*, Part V. Cambridge.

GRIGGS, R. F. 1940. The Ecology of Rare Plants. *Bull. Torrey Bot. Club*, **67**, 575.

KENDALL, O. D. 1938. The Coast of Somerset. II. *Proc. Bristol Nat. Soc.*, (4) **8**, 497.

KNIGHT, H. H. 1912. The Distribution of *Calluna* on the Cotteswolds. *Proc. Cotteswold Nat. Field Club*, **18**, 69.

LOUSLEY, J. E. 1950. *Wild Flowers of Chalk and Limestone*. London.

MOSS, C. E. 1907. *Geographical Distribution of Vegetation in Somerset: Bath and Bridgwater District*. Roy. Geogr. Soc. London.

PIGOTT, C. D. and S. M. WALTERS. 1954. On the Interpretation of the Discontinuous Distributions shown by certain British Species of Open Habitats. *J. Ecol.*, **42**, 95.

PRIESTLEY, J. H. 1911. The Pelophilous Formation of the Left Bank of the Severn Estuary. *Proc. Bristol Nat. Soc.*, (4) **3**, 9.

RIDDELSDELL, H. J., G. W. HEDLEY and W. R. PRICE. 1948. *Flora of Gloucestershire*. Arbroath.

SANDWITH, CECIL I. 1932. The Adventive Flora of the Port of Bristol. *Bot. Exch. Club Rep.*, **10**, 314.

SKENE, M. 1938. A Survey of Steep Holm. III. Botany. *Proc. Bristol Nat. Soc.*, (4) **8**, 452.

TANSLEY, A. G. and R. S. ADAMSON. 1913. Reconnaissance in the Cotteswolds and the Forest of Dean. *J. Ecol.*, **1**, 81.

THOMPSON, H. S. 1922. Changes in the Coast Vegetation near Berrow, Somerset. *Ibid.*, **10**, 53.

—. 1930. Further Changes in the Coast Vegetation near Berrow, Somerset. *Ibid.*, **18**, 126.

WHITE, J. W. 1912. *The Flora of Bristol*. Bristol.

YAPP, R. H., D. JOHNS and O. T. JONES. 1917. The Salt Marshes of the Dovey Estuary. Part II. The Salt Marshes. *J. Ecol.*, **5**, 65.

CHAPTER SEVEN

AGRICULTURE AND HORTICULTURE

AGRICULTURE

WITH such a wide variation of soil type, farming method, and physical character in the West of England, it is necessary to consider the various counties comprising it individually. Some basic statistics are given below.

	Total Area '000 acres	*Area of Crops and Grass '000 acres*	*Area of Rough Grazing '000 acres*	*Number of Holdings*
Gloucestershire . .	805	599	31	8,500
Somerset	1,032	796	58	12,700
Wiltshire	860	616	86	6,000
Dorset	623	440	49	5,000

Despite the large farms on the Cotswolds, in Wiltshire and in parts of Dorset, the region is predominantly one of relatively small farms; in Somerset nearly 60 per cent. of all holdings are under fifty acres.

Farming in Gloucestershire falls into three main geographical areas (*a*) the Cotswolds, (*b*) the Severn Vale and (*c*) the Forest of Dean.

The Cotswolds. The Cotswolds extend to some 400,000 acres and form an oblong plateau most of which lies between 400 and 1,000 ft. above sea-level. The predominant soil is shallow, overlying limestone brash, and is inherently poor, being notoriously deficient in phosphates and inclined to 'burn' in a dry summer.

The past twenty years have brought great changes in the Cotswolds. The large number of progressive farmers has had a most profound effect on the general standard of farming and techniques they have introduced have been major factors in bringing about a remarkable increase in productivity. Farming economy is now based essentially on the production of cereals for sale; on the better-managed farms, average yields of 30 cwt. per acre of grain are common and individual yields in excess of this figure can be expected with confidence (Plate XI). New cereal varieties, generous and intelligent use of fertilizers, and improved methods of maintaining fertility have all contributed to this achievement. Yields and cost of production compare favourably with the more fertile corn-growing areas in Britain, and ever the search for greater economy in production goes on, often by increasing the size of farms though these are already large.

A typical rotation is winter corn, spring corn, one-year ley and roots, corn, corn, three-year ley. Into such a rotation, herbage seed production, principally Cocksfoot and red clovers, seed potatoes (a recent innovation) and Brussels' sprouts (in the north), all fit to provide a high proportion of cash crops. A recent trend is to increase the proportion of corn still further by reducing the ley from three to two years, a step which will require a high degree of skill if yields are to be maintained.

Leys are based on Cocksfoot with Meadow Fescue and Timothy as companion grasses, and are grazed by ewes and beef stores. Although lack of water and inadequate fencing present difficulties, there have been appreciable increases in ewe flocks over the past two years.

Ewes are either Kerry or Clun type and although most of the lambs, sired by Down rams, are sold as stores or wintered on the arable land, many farmers now aim to sell them fat off the ewes. Beef stores are Hereford crosses usually bought as calves and multiple suckled, but breeding herds of beef type are being introduced. To an increasing extent these cattle are sold fat off the better leys.

Milk production seems to be a matter of individual preference but tends to be concentrated on the smaller farms. Pigs are scattered throughout the area with little specialization, and poultry, in deep litter and hen yards, are increasing in number.

The Severn Vale. The soil in the vale is derived mainly from Lias clay. Its heavy nature and the liability of the area to flooding seriously limit the acreage that can be cultivated and so grassland dairying on 'family farms' predominates.

In recent years the traditional permanent grass system has been superseded by an increase in ley farming and in intensive grassland utilization, and these changes have increased greatly the stock-carrying capacity. Since stock have to be wintered inside, the main problem to-day is the efficient conservation of summer grass for winter feeding. Subsidiary enterprises are pigs and poultry.

The Forest of Dean. This area presents a complex pattern of forestry, mining and farming. Agricultural holdings are small and, while sheep and cattle rearing are the main enterprises, milk production is also practised. A large proportion of the sheep grazed on the common land in the forest is owned by miners holding grazing rights. The flocks vary in size from 10 to 150.

The soil is of low inherent fertility, sometimes marginal in productive capacity, but in the north-west near the border of Herefordshire there is an area of soils derived from the Old Red Sandstone which is farmed intensively, cash crops such as sugar beet and potatoes being prominent features. Beef, sheep, and milk are all produced in this small region.

Four main areas may be distinguished in Somerset, viz., (*a*) West, (*b*) the Central Plain, (*c*) the Mendip Hills and North and (*d*) South.

(*a*) *West.* The western part of the county is dominated by Exmoor (two-thirds of which is in Somerset) and by the Brendon and Quantock Hills. Much land lies at an elevation of 1,000 ft. or more and is devoted to stock rearing with the emphasis on sheep. Exmoor Horn and Devon Closewool breeds, formerly supreme, now have to meet competition from the Scotch Half-Bred and the Kerry Hill. Although traditionally a store-rearing area, the use of lime and phosphate and the establishment of better leys now makes it possible for a proportion of the lambs to be sold direct to the fatstock market. The Devon breed of cattle still predominates, but on many farms some milk is produced for sale. Exmoor ponies are not now bred in large numbers.

Many hill farms deteriorated between the wars but improvement schemes under the Hill Farming and Livestock Rearing Acts, and the Hill Cattle and Sheep Subsidy Schemes have done much to bring new equipment and new life to these farms.

Features of the west are the beech hedges on banks and the relatively small fields, except on the moor, which provide shelter and prevent soil erosion on steep slopes. Much of the soil is derived from red sandstone but soils from Devonian shales also cover a wide area. Lime deficiency is common and available phosphate tends to be low. Corn growing is precarious so there is dependence on roots, some mangolds and cabbage for young cattle, but mostly turnips and swedes for sheep; the latter need roots in times of snow, and some make silage.

Between the Brendons and the Quantocks, between the Brendons and the sea, and also between Minehead and Porlock lie relatively small areas of fertile lowlands. Here are grown barley and other arable crops.

The Central Plain. Eastwards from the Quantocks to Mendip, but principally east of the River Parrett, is a low-lying grass area of some 150,000 acres of which at least 20,000 acres are liable to flooding or waterlogging. The Somerset Moors cover much of this area, the best known being Sedgemoor (Plate x). Rhines and ditches replace as boundaries the beech and earth banks of the west.

Soils are mainly alluvial types, of estuarine origin near the coast and for some way inland; they consist mainly of silt-clays and rank as heavy loams; farther inland are found medium clays and silt-loams and also alluvial soils with textures varying from heavy clay to sandy loam. There are also fairly large areas of peaty soils of low agricultural value, and west of Glastonbury are smaller areas of pure peat of considerable depth, which are cut for fuel and for horticultural purposes.

Although the rainfall is not high, ranging only from 28 to 33 in., the soils usually lie wet since, with only a few exceptions, such as the Polden Hills and a number of low mounds, the whole area is below the high-tide level and depends on pumping stations for drainage and on coast and river works for protection. Flooding is specially liable to occur because of the slow discharge of the rivers into the Bristol Channel and of the downflow of rainwater from the surrounding hills. Ten pumping stations at least function in the area, draining some 25,000 acres.

Villages and farms are on the higher land and access to the fields is by 'droves' or unstoned roads. These are normally unfit for use in winter, consequently the moors are used mainly for summer grazing and hay production. From May onwards water is 'penned up' for fencing and drinking purposes in the ditches and rhines by means of sluices. Growth of grass is lush and much summer milk is produced. Cows are milked in the fields, frequently by machine in a bail.

In certain areas, particularly in west Sedgemoor, the growing of 'basket' willows or osiers (known locally as 'withies') is of importance. Typical 'beds' which are productive for ten years or so may be seen alongside the railway line west of Langport and from the road between Taunton and Glastonbury. In all some 2,000 acres of withies are grown.

Mendip Hills and North. The Mendip Hills rise steeply from the central plain and north of them towards Bristol and Bath lies a large area of undulating country; westwards towards the coast there is low-lying grassland, similar to Sedgemoor.

The Mendip country and the north are almost wholly devoted to milk production. While permanent grass predominates, leys are being used to a greater extent than formerly. Milk production is specialized and on the larger farms modern milking parlours are common features. Comparatively few sheep are kept.

South. From the Wiltshire border near Wincanton to east of Wellington lies a large area of diversified farming with considerable arable land. Oxford Clay soils occur along the Wiltshire border and slightly west of it there are brashy soils where arable farming is practised in conjunction with milk production. A broad belt of Lias clay runs from east to west and some of the permanent grass on this formation at times causes scouring in cattle, particularly in cows in milk and young stock. Such land is known as 'teart', a condition due to excess molybdenum, and its effects are countered by the use of small amounts of copper sulphate generally fed along with cattle cake. Red cattle tend to lose colour on teart pastures. Further west the Lias clay soils provide conditions suitable for growing a most unusual crop, the teazle, which is used in the woollen industry. This crop is found only in small acreages at Fivehead and in the nearby parishes.

Perhaps the most notable farming in south Somerset is that on the Midford Sands and Marlstone around South Petherton. Here fertile soils are highly farmed and market gardening is practised. Sheep flocks of Dorset Horn and Dorset Down breeds are close-folded over arable crops.

Along the Dorset border and farther west there is a belt of soil derived from Clay-with-flints, which is almost wholly devoted to milk production. It embraces the Blackdown Hills, which rise to 800 ft. above sea-level and where the rainfall averages 40 in. per annum compared with 30 in. elsewhere in south Somerset. In contrast to the high Blackdown country, with its beech hedges and banks, there is to its north the Vale of Taunton Deane extending over some 30,000 acres. In the vale are rich red fertile soils derived mainly from the New Red Sandstone, including the Keuper Marl. This is traditionally an area of mixed farming but the dairy cow has largely

PLATE IX. *Wiltshire Downs near Stonehenge—early agricultural features and modern usage.*

PLATE X. *Sedgemoor landscape with typical peat land.*

replaced the beef animal and sheep numbers have fallen. In 1791 Collinson remarked that 'the lands are rich and fertile and all the environs of Taunton seem profusely furnished with the munificence of nature'. To-day the vale around the county town still retains its proud place in the forefront of British farming.

Few counties have seen greater changes in farming practice during the past fifty years than have occurred in Wiltshire. Sheep were the mainstay of its agriculture, and industries and even towns were dependent on wool. Towards the end of the last century as many as 800,000 sheep were kept and at that time few horned stock were to be seen. Large flocks shepherded on the open downs by day were close-folded on arable land at night. The land, so enriched, could then grow large acreages of corn. Along river valleys well-kept water meadows provided early grass and abundance of hay.

To-day corn growing remains a major enterprise but sheep have been replaced by dairy cows. The woollen industries have reduced in importance. Water meadows are rarely 'drowned' and temporary leys are relied on to keep the land in good heart.

Between the wars the poor returns from cereals and sheep led to much of the arable being sown to grass. During the 1939–45 war this land once again came under the plough and, with corn production continuing to be attractive, has remained as arable. This development has been possible because most chalkland farms are large, often extending to 500 acres and exceptionally to as much as 5,000 acres, and a high degree of mechanization is economic (Plate IX).

Every modern technique is adopted. Corn is grown for three or four years in succession and thereafter the land is sown to grass for a corresponding period. The use of fertilizers and the newer varieties of grasses and clovers give high production, and this in turn permits a high density of animal stocking which results in a build-up of organic matter. In recent years new varieties of wheat and barley, increased use of fertilizers, fertilizer placement in combine drills and selective weedkillers have helped to increase further the high yields of cereals obtained by this system. Yields of the order of twenty sacks of spring wheat and more rarely of twenty sacks of spring barley per acre have been reported. Such yields were unheard of in the 'sheep' era. Straw, often previously disposed of by burning, is now collected by pick-up balers and utilized by the greater number of livestock carried under this system.

Development of milk production, although less spectacular, has none the less been real, some 60 million gallons being sold off farms annually. Since 1947 the average yield per cow has increased from 550 to 665 gallons per year, a figure calculated by dividing total sales of milk by the number of cows and heifers in milk and cows in calf but not in milk. In the same period dairies producing T.T. milk have increased from about 500 to just under 2,000, rather more than half of all milk-producing farms. Dairy Shorthorns, formerly supreme, now increasingly meet competition from Friesians and other breeds.

The grassland farmer has made his land more productive and has become less

PLATE XI. *Corn-growing in the Cotswolds—a ploughing scene near Cirencester.*

PLATE XII. *Blacksmith and thatcher, Tarrant Gunville, Dorset.*

dependent on purchased feeding stuffs by adopting greatly improved methods of grassland management. More fertilizers are used, silage making has become a recognized practice, controlled grazing is practised and the benefits of short-term leys are well understood. All this has posed the problem as to which are the best livestock enterprises to exploit. It is doubted whether dairy cattle should be increased and indeed shortage of labour and lack of sufficient fixed equipment make expansion difficult. To some extent the problem is being solved by the use of colour-marking beef bulls on the poorer-yielding dairy cows for the production of beef-type animals.

Since 1947, dairy cows have increased by about 8 per cent. and beef production by no less than six times. The Wiltshire farmer has thus chosen an expansion of cattle stock rather than a return to the traditional sheep of his forefathers. Just as mechanization has extended cereal production, and leys and milking bails have increased milk production, so to-day the farmer is seeking ways and means of increasing output of beef at lower costs. The largest possible use of grass and grass products is probably but the first step.

Rapid studies are being made in the eradication of tuberculosis throughout the county.

No record of Wiltshire farming would be complete without reference to Wiltshire bacon, so called because of a particular type of cure developed by several factories. It is not surprising therefore to find pigs on nearly every farm. Wessex Saddleback sows predominate and they are well suited for the somewhat rigorous conditions that obtain on dry chalkland. Invariably they are crossed with Large White boars to produce the ever popular 'blue' pig. Here also the Wiltshire farmer is alive to the need for economic production and greater attention is being paid to housing arrangements.

Early writings on agriculture in Dorset abound with references to the large sheep population of those days. In the time of Charles II it is recorded that 'the chiefest help that the hill country hath for their corne ground is their great flockes of sheeps which they constantly fold upon the land'. As in Wiltshire, that early pattern of husbandry has virtually disappeared and to-day, apart from a limited amount of arable sheep farming, the dairy cow, ley farming and mechanized corn growing hold the field on the chalklands.

A wide range of soil types occur. The Chalk area, extending to over 350 square miles, with its uplands, downs, and narrow valleys, gives a unique character to the Dorset scene. Here soils vary from sticky acid clays, black earth and Clay-with-flints to the thin Chalk soils of the hillsides and the richer soils in the valleys.

To the west of the Chalk lies the delightful, variable and undulating countryside of west Dorset, through which runs the Marshwood Vale with its strong wettish land. An area of small farms this, with a former reputation for Dorset Blue Vinny cheese and cider.

To the north and north-west lies the famous Blackmore Vale, the best soils of which produce first-class grassland. Small dairy farms predominate. To the east of the Chalk lie the heaths, much of which are afforested. In the extreme south-east is the Isle of Purbeck, which is a high-lying, rather bleak, dry upland.

Since 1939 cattle numbers have increased by over 45,000 to 168,000 and the great majority are dairy cattle. There are 3,049 milk producers, of whom 60 per cent. hold T.T. licences, and it is estimated that about 80 per cent. of the milk produced is tuberculin tested. Although little farmhouse cheese is made, cheese manufacture is important and at Bailey Gate is the largest cheese-making factory in the world.

Despite the large area of cereals grown, of which barley is the main cash crop, grass still occupies some 74 per cent. of the total, and ley farming is widely practised. Indeed ley farming is the basis of milk and cereal production. Much downland had fallen into a low state of production prior to 1939. During the 1939–45 war many areas were brought into cultivation and skilled operators, using similar methods to those in Wiltshire, have since transformed the scene. Well over 300 combine harvesters are in use compared with only a few in 1939. To-day the downlands are producing more than ever before.

Dairy stock are now dominant; only 47,000 sheep remain (100,000 fewer than in 1939) and tradition has been broken by the introduction of grassland flocks. The native breeds, Dorset Horn and Dorset Down, have a high reputation. The ability of the former to produce lambs in the autumn is unique and enables high-quality, early lamb to be marketed. Pigs and poultry are kept in numbers exceeding those of pre-war days. There is widespread interest in light and thoroughbred horse breeding and a section of the National Stud is maintained at Gillingham.

HORTICULTURE

The area of land in Gloucestershire used for horticultural crops is approximately 6,800 acres, including 76 acres under glass. The holdings are many and varied, and range from small mixed market gardens to extensive fruit plantations, the latter producing some excellent quality fruit.

The nature of the soil and conditions in the county vary greatly and these variations have given rise to the localized development of specialist crops, in particular Brussels' sprouts and early cauliflowers. About 4,000 acres of sprouts are normally grown, by far the greatest proportion on the high land, covering some 20 square miles, contained in a triangle formed by Chipping Campden, Burford (Oxfordshire) and Andoversford. Here there is a shallow limestone soil overlying brash and, although the hills reach a height of 850 ft., some of the finest quality sprouts are produced in this area, giving average yields of $3\frac{1}{2}$ tons per acre. A complete contrast is seen in the early cauliflower crops grown on the flat low-lying ground round Mickleton, a small village lying close to the northern border of the county. The soil in this area varies from a heavy clay-loam to a light, almost sandy loam. The light soils are apparently well suited for the production of early cauliflowers, of which around 400 acres are planted each year, one grower alone being responsible for 25 per cent. of this figure.

Another specialist crop is forced rhubarb which is grown in small areas near Cheltenham and Paxford in the centre and north, and Bristol in the south; the total area is about 20 acres. Special forcing sheds have been built in the two former districts but most of the Bristol growers still use the tall earthenware pots which are said to have originated in this locality.

Mixed market-garden holdings occur mainly in the Cheltenham and Bristol areas but there are also some around Willersey near Broadway, where asparagus is a specialist crop. Onions, carrots and celery are mostly grown on the lighter soils round Bristol, Newent and at Cheltenham; some excellent crops of parsnips are produced at Mickleton. Of the remaining vegetables, brassicae and green peas for market form the bulk, with acreages of 650 and 500 respectively.

Although the distribution of glasshouses is fairly widespread, there are four main concentrations, namely, in the south round Willsbridge (near Bristol), Cheltenham, Newent, and in the Chipping Campden–Mickleton district. The chief crops are tomatoes, cucumbers, lettuces and chrysanthemums, smaller areas being given over to bulbs and bulb-forcing. A few growers specialize in carnations, the best being found in the Willsbridge area. In addition, Dutch lights and cloches figure prominently throughout market-garden districts, early lettuces being the predominating crop.

Fruit orchards and plantations are a characteristic feature of the countryside but much of the fruit area consists of old orchards containing cider and perry fruit. The more modern fruit-growing areas are to be found in the west between Newent and Dymock where some excellent crops of Cox's Orange Pippin, Worcester Pearmain and other dessert apples are harvested, along with plums, raspberries, strawberries and blackcurrants. Another important fruit area is centred round Chipping Campden. Cherries are a feature here, but other fruits are also grown and of late years extensive plantings of apples, plums and cherries have been made. In addition, there are several hundred acres of fruit in the Toddington and Tewkesbury area where the chief crops are apples and plums, with smaller plantings of pears. Soft fruits are cultivated in most of these areas, but an interesting feature is the growing of strawberries on the exposed heights at Clapton and Little Rissington, climatic conditions being such as to reduce considerably the incidence and spread of virus.

The 1951 fruit tree census showed a total area of tree fruits of 14,146 acres including some 5,000 acres of cider fruit; to this, 611 acres of bush fruits and strawberries should be added to complete the fruit-production picture.

In Somerset there are 18,000 acres of orchards, mostly on farms and mainly consisting of cider fruit. There is not a great deal of information available concerning the origin of apple orchards attached to mixed farms in the south-west, but it is probable that the development occurred at the same period throughout Devon, Somerset, Gloucestershire and Herefordshire. From the evidence of existing orchards, it can be presumed that the greatest interest in the cider-apple orchard occurred between 80 and 150 years ago, when most of the farm orchards seen to-day were planted. From then until thirty years ago, cider was drunk extensively on the farms and vied closely with beer in all the local public houses, particularly in areas of comparatively low-paid industries. Most farmers produced cider for supplying to their own workers, and those with larger orchards sold cider to public houses in the area. With the stopping of free cider on farms and the tying of public houses, interest in farm-cider making diminished and to-day only the makers on the larger farms remain together with the cider factories which have developed in the county.

Interest in farmers' orchards has fluctuated much throughout these years, and has been mainly influenced by the ruling price for cider fruit. There was also much interest aroused during the 1914–18 war in the production of cooking apples and, with the advent of the variety Bramley Seedling, many hundreds of acres were planted or grafted to this variety. There was also a good deal of 'dual-purpose' apple planting at one time, using varieties which could be sent to market in scarce seasons and made into cider in years of abundance. The early apple Morgan Sweet was extensively grown for marketing in South Wales where miners took them to work for refreshment in the pits.

Except where good management can be maintained and a market apple of good quality produced, the general farmer is now encouraged to produce cider fruit only in his orchard. It is thought that in the future the traditional West Country farm orchard may be largely replaced by the specialized cider apple-growing industry on some of the most suitable farms. Meantime farmers with derelict or unproductive orchards are being encouraged to grub them, aided by grants from the Marginal Land Production Scheme, but it is costly and slow work. It is estimated that some 3,000 acres of these farm orchards could be spared without detriment to the cider industry.

During recent years, there has been a substantial development in the production of high-grade dessert apples by specialist fruit growers. The growers of these apples are mainly newcomers to the county with little general agricultural knowledge. The orchards, which consist mainly of Cox's Orange Pippen, are mostly situated in the lower rainfall areas. The quality of fruit produced compares favourably with that from the east of England.

In addition to top fruit, blackcurrants have been found to be a suitable crop in Somerset, particularly where good supplies of farmyard manure are available. Most of the currants are grown on a long-term contract scheme for a firm of fruit-juice processors.

Strawberries, which are also an important crop, are mainly produced in the sheltered Cheddar Valley. Here there are about 250 growers who produce early berries for the dessert-fruit market. Another crop now being grown on a considerable scale in the Cheddar district is the winter-flowing anemone.

Some of the other important horticultural crops in the county include glasshouse tomatoes grown in the summer and followed by chrysanthemums in the autumn. These occur over a wide area though there are several concentrated groups in the northern part of the county. Market-garden crops are obtained around the large centres of population at Bath, Bristol and Weston-super-Mare, and vegetable growing is also practised on extensive lines in the South Petherton district where extremely favourable soil conditions make for excellent production from most crops. Another specialized area for vegetables is the North Petherton district with an extension round the southern end of the Quantock Hills. Here green peas for direct marketing have been a popular crop for many years. The acreage during the last ten years has declined partly through the popularity of processed peas, and the labour of shelling the green pea, but there is still a considerable interest especially in the early varieties, which are normally picked in June. Broad beans for market are also grown in this area.

Wiltshire may be counted as one of the better of the 'minor' counties from the point of view of commercial horticultural production. General market holdings are well distributed on the lighter soils, about one-fifth of the growers being concentrated in the Bromham district. The soil of the Lower Greensand of that area is particularly suitable for the production of heavy crops of high-quality root vegetables—carrots, parsnips, beetroots—though a wide range of other vegetables is cultivated for the local markets of the west Wiltshire industrial towns, and for Bath and Bristol. The Upper Greensand area round Easterton at the west end of the Vale of Pewsey is also noted for the production of high-quality root vegetables. One of the country's best-known intensive salad and vegetable holdings is a 'French' garden situated at Sutton Benger to the north of Chippenham.

Most of the glasshouse holdings are in the west of the county occupying sites between Malmesbury and Mere, where one old-established family of growers has upwards of twelve acres of heated glasshouses.

Two leading fruitgrowers have plantations, mainly of dessert apples, in the Pewsey and Devizes district on the Upper Greensand, and other plantations have been established since the war. Watercress is grown in the Chalk valleys of the Pewsey Vale, and at Bradford-on-Avon an extensive area of caves, from which Bath Stone was quarried, is used for the growing of mushrooms.

Apart from a limited number of holdings which cater for the local markets of Lyme Regis, Weymouth and Swanage, together with the inland market towns, the horticultural industry in Dorset is, in the main, established in the areas adjacent to Poole and Bournemouth. Poole is the most important market for the county's horticultural produce, which consists chiefly of glasshouse tomatoes, cucumbers, watercress and, to a lesser extent, flowers. Most of the cider fruit grown is used within the county.

Commercial horticultural production in Dorset is linked closely with the geological regions. One of these, the heathland, extends from the New Forest almost to Dorchester and includes the eastern portion of the county where specialist glasshouse, frame and field crops are all grown. The land, being level, lends itself to intensive work and is suitable for the use of rotary cultivators. Initially, it needs lime and additional organic matter to raise the fertility to the high level required. Rainfall is about 30 in. and irrigation is often desirable; for this mains-water is generally available. In this area, special emphasis is placed on earliness of the produce. Commonly grown crops include frame and field lettuce, celery, spring and early summer cabbage, bunching beets and carrots, winter brassica and peas; there are also small areas of tree fruits and strawberries. Some of the acid soils are particularly well suited for the production of decorative trees and shrubs, for which there is a national demand and also a considerable export trade. Orchids, in particular Cymbidiums, are also exported from the county.

The second geological region which has influenced horticultural development is that of the Chalk uplands where watercress production is the major horticultural activity. The industry was established about fifty years ago, and there are now approximately eighty-four acres under this crop. The water supply for the greater part of this acreage is obtained from artesian wells, but some of the water comes from natural streams running on the Chalk. The green type of cress is now superseding the brown owing to the greater susceptibility of the latter to a disease known as Crook Root. Much of the watercress goes to the markets of South Wales, the Midlands and the North.

The third geological region where horticulture is practised comprises the hilly area of heavy soils which fringes Somerset and Devon. Here cider apples grown in farm orchards are the chief crop, but in recent years a few plantations of dwarf pyramid apples have been established.

CHAPTER EIGHT

SCIENTIFIC ACTIVITY IN THE BRISTOL REGION IN THE PAST

IN LOOKING back over the years preceding 1800 there emerges a picture of a world in which there was an intense curiosity among people in all walks of life about the works of Nature, particularly following the founding of the Royal Society in 1660. By the time we enter the eighteenth century the mathematical and physical sciences were relatively advanced, but the biological sciences much less so, and chemistry only began to take on a modern look at the end of this century. Apart from a few university posts the day of the professional scientist had not arrived, still less that of the specialist, and the advancement of science was carried on almost entirely by amateurs. The state of knowledge was such that these amateurs could be, and often were, well informed in more than one branch of knowledge. The scientific world was a small one, whose members did not work in watertight compartments, but kept in touch by reading and contributing to the *Philosophical Transactions of the Royal Society*, and by frequent correspondence, much of which, fortunately, has been preserved. There was also a surprising amount of travelling about from place to place, on systematic tours in search of knowledge or to meet other scientists, under conditions which would hardly be tolerated to-day. It may be worth recalling that at the first Bristol meeting of the British Association in 1836 members had to travel to the meeting by coach or on horseback. Towards the end of the eighteenth century local societies, such as the Philosophical Society of Bath, began to spring up in the provinces, marking the transition to present-day conditions. The picture presented here of scientific life in the Bristol region before the nineteenth century may well be typical of what went on in Britain as a whole, outside London and the university cities.

We may start our account most appropriately by recording that some five hundred years ago Bristol had its own alchemist, Thomas Norton, whose father was Sheriff of the city in 1401, and Mayor in 1413. Thomas composed three alchemical works, only one of which, *The Ordinall of Alchemy*, has been published. The alchemists were the forerunners of to-day's chemists, and Norton's *Ordinall*, which was written in English, gives an interesting picture of the average alchemist and his activities in the fifteenth century. It was composed in the form of a long poem, in a somewhat lighthearted vein, and has rather more to recommend it than most of the productions of the early alchemists. The Norton family lived in a house on the site of the picturesque old half-timbered mansion, known latterly as St. Peter's Hospital, which was so familiar to Bristolians until destroyed by enemy action. It is believed that the *Ordinall* was written here in 1477. A taste for alchemy seems to have run in the family, for Thomas Norton's great-grandson Samuel, who lived at Abbot's Leigh, just outside Bristol, also wrote several alchemical treatises, which were published at Frankfurt in 1630.

The story of the development of the study of botany in our area commences far back in the middle of the sixteenth century. The richness of the Bristol flora must have become widely known at an early date, because for centuries it acted as a magnet to famous herbalists and botanists, a succession of whom, both British and foreign, were attracted to the district and have often left records of their visits. Not infrequently they made notes about other matters, such as the archaeology and geology of the country they passed through.

We know now that the character of the flora depends on ecological factors, but it is improbable that such questions exercised the minds of the early botanists to any extent. In fact, they were often physicians, and until the middle of the seventeenth century the botanical texts were usually herbals, in which the authors were much concerned with the medical properties of the plants they described.

Possibly the earliest British botanist with a local connexion was the famous and much-travelled Protestant clergyman, Dr. William Turner (*c.* 1515–68), who published *A New Herball*, the first part of which appeared in 1551. Turner was appointed Dean of Wells in this year, and on taking up his appointment he could not obtain immediate entry into the Deanery. He wrote, in May, that he was 'pened up in a chamber of my lorde of bathes w^{t} all my ho[use]holde servantes and Children as shepe in a pyndfolde. . . . i can not go to my booke for ye crying of childer & noyse y^{t} is made in my chamber. . . .' However, he brought out the book that year, and in the preface wrote 'I have in this boke taught the latine name, the greke, the englysh name, ye duche, and the frenche name, most commōly of every herbe that I write of. I declare also the vertues of every herbe, & shew the place where I have sene it, lest it shuld seme to be on of them which wryte of thynges whyche they never saw.'

Turner was the first British botanist to exercise the beginnings of scientific judgement in discriminating one plant from another. He also wrote knowledgeably about birds. Later British floras are founded on the 238 native plants described in Turner's *Herball.* A dozen or so of the rarer ones he lists were collected near Bristol. The following entries are typical: 'Mustarde . . . it that groweth in the corne in Somersetshyre a little from Glassenberrye [Glastonbury] is much shorter than the gardine mustarde is, but nothynge behynde it in byting and sharpness',[1] and 'Peucedanum. . . . I found a root of it at Saynt Vincentis rock a little from Bristow. But it was nothynge so great as it of Germany.'[2]

Two Flemish botanists visited Bristol about this time. One, Matthias de l'Obel (1538–1616), also known as Lobelius, settled in Britain in 1566, becoming physician

[1] According to J. W. White, p. 152, *Sinapis alba*, the introduced White Mustard.

[2] According to J. W. White, p. 334, the Honewort, *Apinella* (= *Trinia*) *glauca*.

to James I. He first visited Bristol between 1566 and 1570, and again in 1581, and he published first records of as many as eighty British flowering plants, ten of which came from near Bristol or Bath. One interesting record is that of *Euphorbia pilosa*, the Downy Spurge, from Prior Park, Bath, where, at least up to the early decades of this century, it was still growing; and l'Obel recognized two species of the rare prickly-headed poppy in the Somerset cornfields. On his second journey he was accompanied by a compatriot, Charles de l'Escluse, known also as Clusius (1526–1609), who had translated into French a famous Dutch herbal, R. Dodoens' *Cruÿde Boeck*. Towards the end of the sixteenth century, in 1578, there appeared an English translation of this herbal made, it is interesting to note, by a Somerset man, Henry Lyte (?1529–1607), a botanist and antiquary of some repute, and a member of a family long resident at the old Manor House at Lytes Cary,[1] about two miles north of Ilchester. John Aubrey (1626–97), the antiquary, a Wiltshire man born near Malmesbury and famous as the author of '*Brief Lives*', was related to the Lyte family, and he records that Henry Lyte 'had a pretty good collection of plants for that age, some few of which are yet alive 1660'.

Later herbalists who visited Bristol were John Gerard (1545–1612) and John Parkinson (1567–1650), both of whom record plants from the Bristol district. The former published his *Herball, or general Historie of Plantes* in 1597; while Parkinson produced in 1629 a book with the title *Garden of all sorts of pleasant flowers which our English ayre will permitt to be nourished up*, and also his *Theater of Plants, or an Herball of a large extent*, in 1640.

Sometimes these old herbalists were sent on a fool's errand, and Gerard records that 'Meum groweth . . . (as it hath been told me) upon Saint Vincents rocke by Bristowe, where I spent two daies to seeke it, but it was not my hap to find it, therefore I make some doubt of the truth thereof.'[2] However, Gerard found four of the 182 British species that receive first mention in his *Herball* in the Bristol district; and Parkinson records twenty-eight species for the first time as natives of Britain, including *Lavatera arborea*, the Tree Mallow, and *Hypericum montanum*, the Mountain St. John's Wort, from this area.

To the Bristol botanist, however, the most interesting seventeenth-century figure is Thomas Johnson (*c.* 1600–44), apothecary and Royalist soldier who died bravely in the Siege of Basing House in Hampshire. He edited a revised edition of Gerard's *Herball*, which was published in 1633, and Bristolians may like to know, since their city has been a centre for the importation of the banana for many years, that in this edition of Gerard the fruit is figured and carefully described. The bunch arrived green, as they do to-day, but was hung in the shop until the fruit ripened. The next year Johnson published a work entitled *Mercurius Botanicus* which contains a detailed description of a botanical expedition to the neighbourhood of Bath and Bristol. Johnson, whilst acting as medical attendant to a lady of wealth at Bath, met a party of physicians and apothecaries from London and Oxford who were 'not less learned

[1] Now belonging to the National Trust.

[2] Meum—the plant of which Gerard was told was, no doubt, *Trinia glauca* (see footnote, p. 124).

than agreeable', with whom he investigated the flora round Bath. A visit to the garden of a Bath surgeon, George Gibbs, who had visited Virginia, from which he had brought home plants, was included. Thence the party proceeded by way of 'Mangersfield' [Mangotsfield], where they were hospitably entertained at Rodway Hill Manor House, to Bristol. Here the learned and jovial apothecary John Price welcomed them, accompanying them to an inn, where they rested until eight the next morning. They then visited St. Vincent's Rocks and the banks of the Avon where, in addition to the plants, they examined the spars, crystals and 'Bristol diamonds' to be found there. This sociable excursion sounds very like those made by our botanical and other societies to-day! Johnson, in his edition of Gerard's *Herball*, added about 170 flowering plants to the British flora, some of which resulted from observations made in the Bath and Bristol districts.

Another botanist of the period who claims our attention is Dr. Christopher Merrett, F.R.S. (1614–95), who was a west-countryman, born at Winchcomb, in Gloucestershire, a few miles from Cheltenham. Though mainly interested in medical matters he published a small herbal in 1666 which, in addition to giving upwards of 1,400 species of British plants, contains lists of indigenous animals and the first list of British birds ever published. It includes, too, a list of native rocks, fossils and minerals. For this reason the book, which bears the title *Pinax rerum naturalium Britannicarum*, has some historical interest.

The next botanist to visit Bristol was the learned and accomplished naturalist John Ray, F.R.S. (1627–1705), who, incidentally, wrote in 1667 that 'the world is glutted with Dr. Merrett's bungling *Pinax*'. Ray was much interested in geology and zoology, but is best known for his botanical works, which include *Catalogus Plantae Angliae*, first published in 1670. His writings and those of some of his contemporaries mark the commencement of the era of scientific botany. During the extensive excursions he made through Britain Ray passed through Gloucestershire and Somerset in 1662, and again in 1667. Helped by correspondents he added about five hundred new forms to the British flora, the majority being permanent additions. He recorded most of the rarer Bristol plants that had escaped earlier observers, and was the first to notice in print the famous Cheddar Pink, *Dianthus gratianopolitanus* [*caesius*]. In Britain this attractive flower is confined to a limited area near Cheddar. Ray lists it under the name *Armeria* and records the locality as 'on Chidderroks'. The plant was first found by a Wiltshire botanist of some repute, Samuel Brewer of Trowbridge, who supplied the record to Ray. Brewer, who seems at one time to have been head gardener to the Duke of Beaufort at Badminton House, Gloucestershire, corresponded with many contemporary botanists.

Ray was followed by Jacob Dillenius, F.R.S. (1687–1747), the first Sherardian Professor of Botany in the University of Oxford. In the summer of 1726 he toured Somerset and Gloucestershire in the company of Samuel Brewer, visiting the Mendip Hills, and Uphill and Brean Down, near Weston-super-Mare. He added at least one species, *Koeleria vallesiana*, Dillenius' Hair Grass, to the list of rare species confined to the west of England, though, by a curious circumstance, it was not until the specimen collected by Dillenius was found in the Sherardian Herbarium at Oxford in 1904, by Mr. G. C. Druce, that this record came to light. In the interval it had not been rediscovered but, on visiting Uphill and Brean Down, Mr. Druce confirmed its existence there, after nearly two hundred years.

So one might continue indefinitely the tale of the travellers who headed for Bristol to study, collect and often to discover new plants. The chronicle may fittingly close with a mention of the visit of Sir Joseph Banks (1742–1820), later President of the Royal Society, and a great patron of the sciences, especially botany. He first visited Bristol in his twenty-fifth year, in 1767, and wrote an account of this tour. The manuscript came into the hands of a Bristol naturalist, S. G. Perceval, and was published in the *Proceedings of the Bristol Naturalists' Society* in 1898. Banks' interests were catholic and, in addition to examining the plants at St. Vincent's Rocks, Cheddar and elsewhere in the district, he visited Wookey Hole and the Cheddar caves. He also spent two hours with the Rev. A. S. Catcott, inspecting his collection of fossils (see p. 132). He records, too, a visit to the brass and spelter works of William Champion at Warmley, between Bath and Bristol, mentioning that two 'fire' engines were in use there for raising water.

After his voyage with Captain Cook in 1768–71, Banks again visited Bristol in 1773. This time he was accompanied by the Rev. John Lightfoot, F.R.S. (1735–88), a Gloucestershire man, and one of the earliest members of the Linnean Society, who is now chiefly remembered as the author of *Flora Scotica*, published in 1777. Although by this time it must have been difficult to find new plants around Bristol, two new ones were recorded by Banks and Lightfoot. These were *Tragopogon porrifolius*, commonly known as salsify, 'from a meadow by the River's Side beyond the new wellhouse towards Cook's Folly', which is near Clifton Downs; and *Bromus madritensis*, the Upright Annual Brome-grass, 'upon the Rocks above the Well' [Hotwells]. Lightfoot also recorded *Potentilla tabernaemontani* [*verna*], the Spring Cinquefoil, 'plentifully near the May-pole at Clifton'. It still blooms thereabouts, but the maypole, alas, has vanished.

We must retrace our steps in time to obtain a picture of the part the Bristol district played in the development of geology. It is perhaps as well to mention that though the existence of organic fossils, or 'figured stones' had been noted and commented on for centuries, their true nature and origin was not generally accepted until about the beginning of the eighteenth century. Early references to fossils in the district, possibly the first record, can be found in the account of the tour through England of the antiquary and topographer John Leland (*c.* 1506–52). He noted in the Jurassic rocks of the Cotswolds, south-east of Wotton-under-Edge, 'Stones clerly fascioned lyke cokills, and myghty shells of great oysters turned into stones'; and between Bristol and Bath, 'Stones figurid like serpentes wound into circles . . . about Cainsham' [Keynsham].

Moving on to the latter half of the seventeenth century, there is a Bristol naturalist about whom one would like to learn more than is known. This is William Cole

(d. 1701), a Surveyor of Customs in Bristol, who owned a small estate near Malmesbury, Wiltshire, close to the home of John Aubrey, to whom Cole was known, at least by repute. We first hear of Cole's activities in a long letter to the great scientist Robert Hooke, which is dated from Bristol, 30 September 1669. In this letter, which is of considerable botanical interest, Cole describes his discovery 'that all kindes of species of Ferns together with all the like Capillary Plants their Congeners are more prolifical in Seeds than any other Plant'; and he proposes to 'draw the figures of them all as they appear by the Microscope', an early record of the use of the microscope for scientific purposes. Hooke refers to Cole, in 1677, as 'a very good friend of mine at *Bristol*, the Ingenious and Inquisitive Mr. W. C.'

Some little time elapses before we hear again of Cole's activities, this time in the letters of other prominent members of the Royal Society and the closely connected Philosophical Society of Oxford. These records span the time between 1684 and 1701, the year of Cole's death. Cole sent natural history specimens to Oxford at least as early as 1684, and they were there exhibited to the members of the Philosophical Society, to membership of which Cole was elected in 1685, much to his pleasure.

Cole's chief claim to notice is that he spent some fifty years gathering together a museum of miscellaneous 'natural curiosities', including fossil shells and plants, minerals and zoological specimens. He used his position as a Customs officer to import some of them from abroad, among the sources mentioned being Virginia and the West Indies. He also seems to have used the 'Kings Wherries', attached to the Customs, to examine the shores of the Bristol Channel in search of objects for his museum. Whilst on duty at Minehead he scoured the neighbourhood for fossils, and reported in a letter to Robert Plot, Keeper of the Ashmolean Museum in Oxford, that he had 'sent away neere 5 hundredweight of stones etc. found on theise Coasts within 2 leagues of this Port excepting some few from the Welch shoar.' After describing some of the fossils he says: 'Theese and more such Phænomena . . . will puzle Mr. Hooke and the rest of those ingenious Gentlemen who will have them to be petrified shells of fishes.'

Another matter in which he was greatly interested was the fast purple dye to be obtained from a living mollusc, which he called *Purpura*, and which he found on the shores of the Bristol Channel. He sent specimens of cloth dyed with the extract from *Purpura* to the Philosophical Society, and these were later shown to Charles II. In pursuing his enquiries on this subject it is interesting to know that he made use of Bristol's early public library, founded in 1613. He describes the occasion as follows: 'I was lately told by a Gent that he had read in ven: Bede of a larg shell on ye Engl shores wch gives the purple dye, uppon wch I repayred to our Library in Kings Streete, but found only ye 2d 7th & 8th Tome where he writes of ye Purpura, but only by way of alusion.' Cole's account of the 'Purple Fish' was published by the Royal Society in 1685.

At various times Cole was visited by Plot, with whom he corresponded extensively, and by Edward Lhwyd, Welsh archaeologist and geologist, author of the first catalogue of English fossils, who succeeded Plot as Keeper of the Ashmolean Museum. Lhwyd records seeing fossil plants in 'that excellent Musæum of Natural Bodies, collected by Mr. William Cole'. Cole also visited Hooke in London, in 1689. Another celebrity with whom he corresponded was John Ray, though they do not seem to have met. Ray, in a letter to Lhwyd, dated 1693, judges from his correspondence with Cole that the latter 'is a little infected with an immoderate desire of honour, & apt to think well, it may be too well, of his own abilities & performance & loath to be defrauded of the reputation of his discoveries. To give him his due, he hath deserved well of the ingenious, as you also acknowledge; and therefore is to be pardoned. . . .'

During the last few years of Cole's life Oxford University negotiated with him with the intention of taking over his museum, Cole's terms being that it should be separately housed, and that the University should accept responsibility for publishing a work on Natural History he was preparing. Unfortunately no agreement was reached before Cole's death in 1701, and his museum was sold by his executor to a Bristol physician, Dr. Lane; nor was his Natural History published.

A distinguished friend and correspondent of Cole who also lived in the Bristol district for a time was Sir Robert Southwell, who, in addition to being a diplomatist and occupying other high offices in the State, became President of the Royal Society from 1690 to 1695. He bought Kings Weston Manor, just outside Bristol, in 1679 and resided there at intervals, corresponding with John Evelyn the diarist about planting yew and holly hedges in his garden to shelter the mansion house.

Another collector who was living in the district at this time was John Beaumont, F.R.S. (d. 1731), who lived in the Somerset village of Ston Easton, on the northern slopes of Mendip, twelve miles south of Bristol. Though Beaumont made no outstanding contributions to science, he is perhaps typical of his age, a country gentleman, widely read, actively interested in natural history, and an accurate recorder of facts; yet singularly credulous, or so we should regard him if he lived to-day. In 1676 he described and figured in the *Transactions* of the Royal Society fossil 'trochites', that is, crinoids, that he had collected from the Carboniferous Limestone, though he erred in regarding them as the remains of plants. He also published tracts criticizing contemporary geological works. In 1692 John Ray wrote of him that he 'hath been very diligent in searching out and collecting, & curious in observing of petrified shells and other bodies, and I suppose well qualified to write concerning them. I heard that he once threatened to write something in contradiction to Mr. Burnet's Theory of the Earth,[1] which piece I could wish to see.' This letter was in answer to one to Ray from Dr. Hans Sloane,[2] in which the latter mentions having seen Beaumont's 'collection of petrifactions'.

Ston Easton lay close to the Mendip lead mines, then working, and Beaumont must have visited them frequently. He contributed another paper to the Royal Society entitled *A New Way of Cleaving Rocks*, in which he describes the use by the Mendip miners of gunpowder to blast rock underground. Previously the method in

[1] Published a few years previously.

[2] Later Sir Hans Sloane, and President of the Royal Society.

use had been to heat the rocks by fire and then cause them to split by quenching with water. There is only one earlier record of the use of explosives in British mines, that being in Staffordshire by German miners who had imported the practice from the Continent. Beaumont figures the tools used for the purpose.

Among other experiences, Beaumont records a descent of one of the Mendip caves, Lambs Lair, at the end of a rope held by miners, and he was probably the first to explore this cave. He also published an account of Wookey Hole and other Mendip caves in the *Philosophical Collections* of the Royal Society, so that he has a distinct claim to be regarded as a pioneer spelaeologist.

Regarding Beaumont's credulity, it is perhaps sufficient to mention the title of a book he published in 1705, *Treatise of Spirits, Apparitions and Witchcrafts, and other Magical Practices*, in which he states that his own experience of spirits, good and bad, was long and varied, and that in their frequent visitations 'all would disswade me from drinking too freely'. Beaumont died in 1731, and is buried at Ston Easton.

A better-known geologist of Beaumont's period is John Woodward, F.R.S., M.D. (1665–1728), practising physician, archaeologist, botanist and author of an *Essay Toward a Natural History of the Earth*, published in 1695. Born in Derbyshire, he is said to have come of a family originating in Gloucestershire, but our justification for mentioning him here is that it was the richly fossiliferous Jurassic rocks of Gloucestershire that first attracted his attention to the study of geology, which became, for him, a lifelong interest.

When little more than a boy he was apprenticed to a London doctor, Peter Barwick, who married a daughter of Sir Ralph Dutton of Sherborne, a little village close to Northleach in the Cotswolds. Whilst still quite young he accompanied Barwick on a visit to Sherborne, and what happened then is best told in his own words: 'I began my Observations and Collections in Gloucestershire. . . . I had here likewise opportunity of carrying on my Botanic Studies, of which being then young, I was very fond. . . . Not that I confin'd my self so much to this part of Natural History, as not to be ready, forward, and desirous to look into any other; and the Country about Sherborne . . . and the neighbouring parts of Gloucestershire, to which I made frequent Excursions, abounding with Stone, and there being Quarries of this laid open almost every where, I began to visit these, in order to inform myself of the nature, the situation, and the condition of the Stone. In making these Observations, I soon found there was incorporated with the Sand of most of the Stone thereabouts, great plenty and variety of Sea-Shells, with other marine Productions. . . . This was a Speculation new to me; and what I judg'd of so great moment, that I resolved to pursue it through the other remoter parts of the Kingdom; which I afterwards did. . . .' Not very long afterwards, in 1690, we have evidence of Woodward carrying out his resolve. Edward Lhwyd, writing to the Yorkshire naturalist Dr. Martin Lister, recorded that 'One Mr. Woodward a young gentleman that lives with Dr. Barwick can give you ample satisfaction about the resemblance of plants in cole mines in ye Mendip hills (but perhaps it may be noe news to you). That gentleman gave Dr. Plot, some patterns of cole-slat having ye draughts of the common

---

PLATE XIII. *Reproduced from John Strachey's 'An account of the Strata in Coal-Mines, &c.'*, Phil. Trans. Roy. Soc., 1725, **33**, 395.

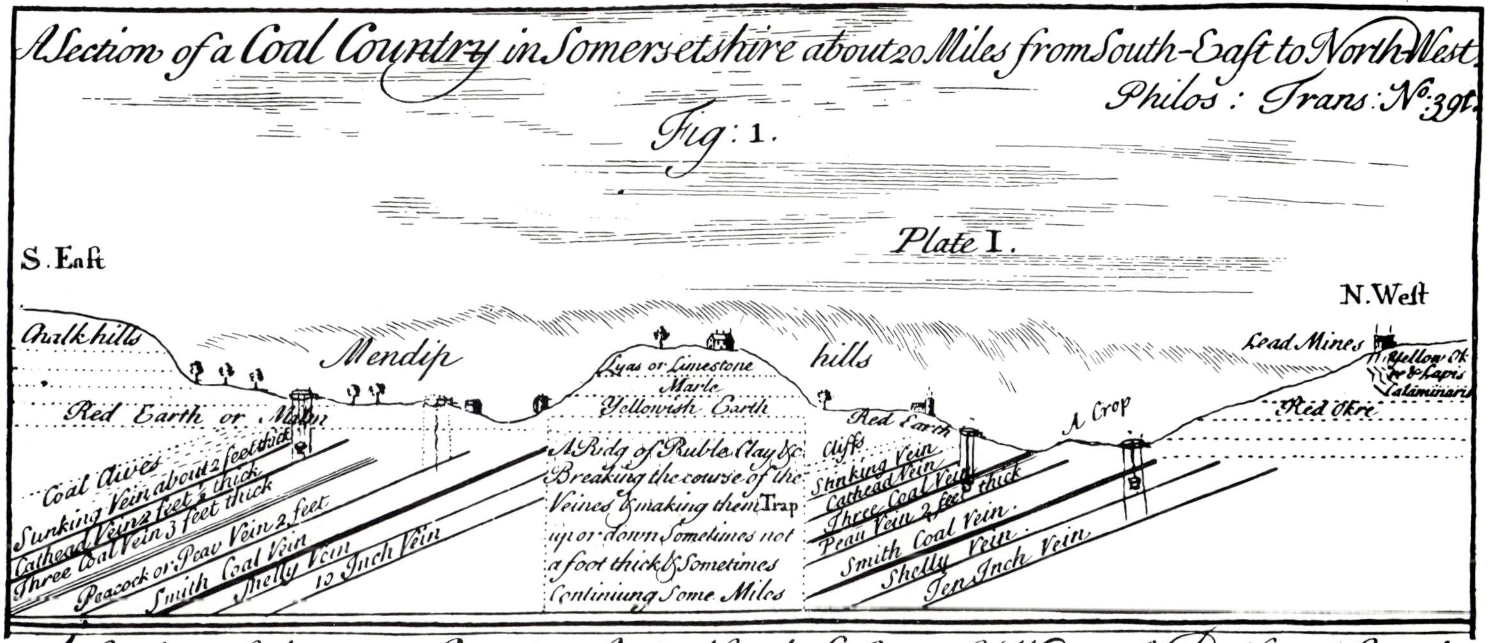

A Section of the same Country from North East to S.-W.: on ye Drift or Level of the Coal & at right Angles with ye Former

female fern. He seems to have made a wonderfull progresse (considering his age) in several sorts of knowledge. He has lately made a collection of form'd stones in Summersetshire & Glowcestershire; & told me he does not much qestion but he has found out ye causes of those productions; & added that they seem soe plain yt he wonders no body thought of it sooner. What notions he has therein I know not; but it seems qestionable whether he be sufficiently experienced in such *observations*, as to be able to satisfie mens curiosities in soe nice a phenomenon.'

Woodward became one of the greatest geologists of the period, as a result of his chance visit to Sherborne, publishing several books, notably his *Attempt Towards a Natural History of the Fossils of England*, which was a catalogue of his own extensive collections, now preserved in the Woodwardian Museum at Cambridge. The term 'fossil' at that time included minerals as well as organic fossils, and Woodward's collection includes rare minerals from the Mendip lead-workings. Woodward was the founder of the first Chair of Geology in Britain, the Woodwardian professorship at Cambridge. He also made not unimportant contributions to botany, carrying out experiments on water-culture, and he was the first Englishman to notice transpiration.

The next local geologist who must be mentioned is one of considerable importance, John Strachey, F.R.S. (1671–1743), who was a neighbour of Beaumont, living in the ancient manor house of Sutton Court, in the parish of Chew Magna, about eight miles south of Bristol, which, incidentally, was the same house in which John Leland paused for a while during his travels.

Strachey examined the local coal mines, situated almost on his doorstep, and they seem to have aroused his interest in geology. His publications, though few, show him to have been one of the earliest English geologists who was an observer and recorder of geological facts, rather than a theorist. He made what were, for the time, outstanding contributions to stratigraphical geology, in two papers published in 1719 and 1725 by the Royal Society. The first was entitled *A curious Description of the Strata observ'd in the Coal-Mines of Mendip in Somersetshire*[1], and the second *An Account of the Strata in Coal-Mines, etc.* In these papers he discusses two important geological concepts, unconformity and faulting, and also has something to say about fossils. His papers are illustrated by sections of the strata between Bishop Sutton and Farrington Gurney, four miles to the south-east. These show horizontal strata, including 'Lyas or Limestone, Marle and Yellowish Spungey Earth', which we now know to be of Jurassic (Lias) age; and beneath the Lias 'Red Earth or Malm or Loom', that is, red Triassic rocks, overlying steeply inclined Coal Measures with seven named coals. In other words he clearly indicates what is now well recognized, that in this part of the country younger rocks lie with marked unconformity on the Coal Measures (Plate XIII). It is also obvious that Strachey (and the miners) understood the effects of faulting, for he mentions that when the colliers met with a 'ridge', as they termed a fault, 'a parting of Clay, Stone or Rubble; as if the Veins by some violent shock were dis-

[1] The two together were issued as a separate pamphlet, in 1727, with the title *Observations on the Different Strata of Earths, and Minerals. More particularly of such as are found in the Coal-Mines of Great Britain.*

PLATE XIV (top) *Humphry Davy* and PLATE XV (bottom) *Thomas Beddoes. From the original pastel drawings by James Sharples, of Bath, in the collection of the City Art Gallery, Bristol.*

jointed and broken' . . . 'it causeth the Coal to trap up', or to 'trap down' if the fault were penetrated from the opposite direction.

Strachey knew of the occurrence of fossils—'cockle shells' and 'fern branches'—in the Coal Measures. While he did not forestall William Smith in grasping their full significance, he recorded their occurrence in the shale above a particular coal, the Peaw Vein, stating that, when they are found it 'is a certain Indication that they are coming to this Vein'. Thus, he anticipated the present-day technique of correlating coal seams by means of associated fossil bands.

Strachey's interest in geology was no passing one, for he visited several coal mines in Northumberland and Scotland, recording observations of dip and strike, and noting that at many mines in Scotland they 'land' the coal on 'Girls Backs'. Strachey seems to have had Scottish connexions, possibly through his first wife, Elizabeth Ellotson, who bore him eighteen children. He retired to Edinburgh for the latter part of his life, leaving his eldest son at Sutton Court, which is still the family seat.

Interest in local geology was maintained during the eighteenth century, and in 1754 a book was published in London dealing solely with the geology of the Bristol district, the first of its kind. It was entitled *Observations on the Earths, Rocks, Stones and Minerals, For Some Miles about Bristol, and on the Nature of the Hot-Well and The Virtues of Its Water.* The author was one Edward Owen, about whom nothing is known except the fact his book must have been based on a visit to the district. The text shows Owen to have been a good observer, familiar with contemporary ideas on rocks and minerals; and it also gives a few glimpses of the social activities of Bristolians at that time, and for these reasons is worth reading.[1]

Soon after the publication of Owen's book another contribution to geology of local interest appeared, this time written by a Bristolian, the Rev. Alexander Catcott (1725–79), Vicar of Temple Church, and son of a former headmaster of Bristol Grammar School. This was a book entitled *A Treatise on the Deluge,* and it was sufficiently well received to require a second edition in 1768. It is typical of its period, a 'theory of the earth' of what has been termed the 'physico-theological' school. Nevertheless, its contents show that Catcott had read widely, and that he was something more than a theorist, having studied geological phenomena in the field. He had visited the mines of Mendip, then working, and also its caves, from which he disinterred the bones of the mammoth, and other animals. These with other specimens collected by Catcott were preserved by the Bristol Museum, until destroyed by enemy action. Belief in the reality of a Universal Deluge was then so strong, however, that it is hardly surprising to find that certain geological phenomena such as the widespread distribution of scattered isolated boulders, for example the 'Grey-Wethers' of the Marlborough Downs, and the finding of bones of animals not indigenous to the countryside in Mendip caves should be accepted by Catcott as strong evidence of the action of a former deluge. Catcott left behind manuscripts entitled 'Diaries of Tours in England and Wales' and 'Papers on Fossils, the Deluge

1 For an account of Owen's book *see* S. Smith, 'Owen's Observations', *Proc. Bristol Nat. Soc.*, 1945, **27**, 93.

etc.' which are now in the Bristol Central Library. They contain a historically valuable account of the Mendip lead mines.

Next on our list is the great William Smith (1769–1839) about whom much has been written, but no account of past scientific activity in the Bristol district would be complete without some mention of his work. Smith, it is true, was an Oxfordshire man, but his contributions to geological science resulted from observations made in the High Littleton area, just south of Bristol, where Strachey had preceded him. Smith's claims to fame are twofold. He constructed the first large-scale detailed geological map of England and Wales, published in 1815, an outstanding achievement in itself. Still more important, however, is the fact that he was the first to establish one of the basic principles of geology, the value of fossils as indexes of the age and position of rocks in the stratigraphical succession. This was a discovery of such importance that it completely revolutionized geological thought. The facts are well known, but it may be of interest to recall the circumstances that brought Smith to Somerset, and led him to make his contributions to the science of geology.

William Smith started his career in 1787, at the age of eighteen, as an apprentice to a land surveyor, Edward Webb, of Stow-in-the-Wold, Gloucestershire. In 1791 he was sent to survey an estate at Stowey, near High Littleton, and shortly afterwards he was engaged to make an underground survey of the local collieries. Smith records that it was in this year, 1791, that he made his first observations on the stratification of rocks. His interest grew as his work progressed and, in 1793, according to a memorandum he made at the time, he contemplated constructing 'a model of the strata of earth and coal at High Littleton', the model to be 'divided into sections, that may be taken apart to explain the method of mining for coal.' Soon after Smith was appointed surveyor for a new project, the Somerset Coal Canal, which was to link High Littleton with the Kennet and Avon Canal. In 1795, while superintending the construction of the canal, Smith began to realize that the fossils occurring in the varied strata exposed by the excavations differed from one bed to another, even though some of the beds were alike in appearance. In fact, he found that, where doubt existed, particular fossils might be used to determine the position of particular beds in the local succession, a matter of importance to a civil engineer. Smith realized the significance of his discovery, but how important it was to prove perhaps even he did not appreciate then. However, on 5 January 1796, while living at the Swan Inn, Dunkerton, he wrote down the following statement: 'Fossils have been long studied as great curiosities collected with great pains treasured up with great care at a great expence and shown and admired with as much pleasure as a child's rattle or his hobby horse is shown and admired by himself and his playfellows—because it is pretty And this has been done by *Thousands who have never paid the least regard to that* wonderful order & regularity with which Nature has disposed of these singular productions and assigned to each Class its peculiar Stratum.' Though, to-day, the significance of fossils is accepted as axiomatic, it must be remembered that no such knowledge existed at the time Smith wrote this statement, and it was then a very true one. Perhaps it was because he had received no formal education in these matters, and approached them with an open mind, that he arrived at the truth. No doubt he had read all he could on the subject, but he has left little record of what books he consulted. It is known, however, that he possessed a copy of Strachey's account of the Somerset Coalfield. This, certainly, would have helped him to understand the geological structure of the High Littleton area, but no literature existing at that time could have assisted him in reaching his conclusion as to the significance of fossils.

Two local clergymen, the Rev. Benjamin Richardson of Farleigh Hungerford, near Bradford-on-Avon, and the Rev. Joseph Townsend, Rector of Pewsey, Wiltshire, were the first to recognize the importance of his discovery. After accompanying Smith on a series of excursions to test his statements, they decided that a written record ought to be made. Accordingly, in 1799, in Townsend's house at 29 Great Pulteney Street, Bath, Smith dictated to Richardson a list of the strata from the Coal Measures to the Chalk, together with a record of the fossils characterizing the different beds in these formations. Smith did not himself publish his conclusions until long afterwards, but copies of this historic document were widely circulated, and his ideas became common knowledge. They laid the foundations of modern stratigraphy, and formed one of the main corner-stones in the structure of geological science as we know it to-day.

For a number of years the new concepts of geology arising out of the discoveries of Smith and others were not universally accepted and aroused opposition, particularly among the clergy, who conceived they might be destructive of their teachings. As an example of the sort of tract that continued to be published we may mention one, because it has a local interest. This was a book entitled *The Geology of the Avon, being an Enquiry into the Order of the Strata and Mineral Productions of the District washed by its Streams* (Bristol, 1822). The author was the Rev. Joseph Sutcliffe, a Yorkshireman, whose connexion with Bristol is not apparent, unless, as a Wesleyan Methodist minister, he resided here for a time. He expounds his subject with great assurance, but his book is without value, even allowing for the state of geological knowledge at the time, except as a curiosity.

An amateur of a different calibre came on the scene soon afterwards, William Sanders, F.R.S. (1799–1875). He was a prominent citizen of Bristol who developed a serious interest in geology early in the nineteenth century, an interest which was stimulated by contacts with H. T. de la Beche, the first Director of the Geological Survey, and with John Phillips, the distinguished nephew of William Smith. Sanders is remembered especially for the valuable large-scale geological map of the Bristol coalfields which he published in 1862, after carrying out a detailed survey of the ground himself over a period of many years. This map has, in fact, remained the only detailed geological map of an area of about 720 square miles of Gloucestershire and Somerset that has been available for nearly one hundred years.

Sanders was one of the founders, and for long President, of the Bristol Naturalists' Society, established in 1862, which has carried on the tradition of the amateur in natural history up to the present day, long after the arrival of the professional scientist.

Although there has been much to say about the activities of the early botanists and geologists in and around Bristol, other sciences make interesting additions to the story. One of the most famous men born near Bristol was John Locke, F.R.S. (1632–1704), the philosopher, who also practised as a physician, and became interested in science through close association in Oxford with the great seventeenth-century scientist Robert Boyle. Locke was born in Somerset at Wrington, but the family home, with which he maintained contacts during his lifetime, was at Pensford, some five miles south of Bristol. Physicists may like to hear of a local incident in which Locke figured, in 1666. Early that year Locke wrote to a friend, John Strachey of Sutton Court, Somerset, intimating that he hoped to pay him a visit soon. This John Strachey was the father of John Strachey the geologist whom we have already mentioned. Strachey senior and Locke were neighbours, for Sutton Court lies only a mile or two south-west of Pensford. The proposed visit must have taken place, for in a letter, dated May, 1666, addressed to Boyle, Locke recounts certain happenings in the area. Boyle's scientific interests were very varied, and at that time he was making enquiries about mining operations and minerals, as well as continuing his studies on the pressure of the atmosphere, and its effect on the newly invented mercury barometer. He seems to have requested Locke to take a barometer to Somerset to make observations in the Mendip mines. In his letter, Locke gives some interesting particulars of mining activities, but reports that the physical difficulties of descending a mine on the end of a rope encumbered with a barometer were too great for him to attempt. In any case, he states, the mining fraternity were suspicious of his intentions, 'do what we could', he relates, 'they would think us craftier fellows than we were', and they would not help him. However, he made some barometric readings outside the house in which he was staying, and again at the top of a nearby hill, recording the pressure at the foot of the hill as $29\frac{1}{8}$ in., and at the top of the hill as $28\frac{3}{4}$ in. Locke retained an interest in meteorology for some years, and other barometric observations of his, related to weather conditions, were published by Boyle. He also took away from 'Minedeep some ore, and some stones' which he informed Boyle were 'so inconsiderable, that I shall not judge them worth sending, unless you please to command them.' Locke was not too much of a philosopher to be interested in the domestic side of life for, some years later, his patron and friend the Earl of Shaftesbury, wrote him 'Somersetshire, no doubt, will perfect your breeding; after France and Oxford, you could not go to a more proper place. My wife finds you profit much there, for you have recovered your skill in Cheddar cheese, and for a demonstration have sent us one of the best we have seen.'

Another physicist whom we may claim as a Somerset man is the erudite Quaker, Thomas Young, F.R.S. (1773–1829), who was born at the Old Bank House at Milverton, eight miles west of Taunton. Young is especially remembered for his contributions to physical and physiological optics, but he was also a practising physician and, for a time, a civil servant in his capacity as Secretary of the Board of Longitude. He was, too, an exceptional linguist, being one of the pioneers who first succeeded in deciphering Egyptian hieroglyphs from the Rosetta Stone. The encomium engraved on the tablet commemorating him in Westminster Abbey, 'A man alike eminent in almost every department of human learning', seems well deserved.

Another West Country scientist who carried the tradition of the amateur well on into the nineteenth century was the versatile William Henry Fox Talbot, F.R.S. (1800–77). He was born at Lacock Abbey, near Chippenham in Wiltshire. His name is especially associated with the early developments in photography for which he was responsible, but he was also eminent as a mathematician. He, like Thomas Young, has an achievement as a linguist to his credit, for he was one of the first to decipher the cuneiform inscriptions of Nineveh.

The Bristol district can also claim a distinguished astronomer, the Rev. James Bradley, F.R.S. (1693–1762), for a time Savilian Professor of Astronomy at Oxford, and later successor to Edmund Halley as Astronomer Royal. He was a Gloucestershire man, born at Sherborne, the Cotswold village visited by John Woodward, the geologist, when he was a youth (see p. 130). Bradley is chiefly noteworthy for having discovered the aberration of light, and the nutation of the earth's axis. Most of his life was spent outside the county, but he is buried at Minchinhampton, where a brass tablet in the church commemorates him.

A story of much more direct interest to residents in the Bristol district is that of the great astronomer Sir William Herschel, F.R.S. (1738–1822), and this is worth relating in some detail.

In December 1766 a talented young German musician arrived in Bath from the north of England to take up a post as organist in the new Octagon Chapel in Milsom Street. This curious institution was then being built to meet the needs of the fashionable visitors who thronged to Bath each winter to take the waters. It was a place where, as one writer has put it, 'the Quality could converse with their Maker without being forced into objectionable proximity with the lower orders', whom they could not avoid if they attended divine service in the Abbey.

The new organist was none other than Frederick William Herschel, who was to carry out in Bath those astronomical studies which brought him fame. Whatever we may think of the institution he served, it provided him with a living, so that during the years that followed he was able to devote much of his immense energy and outstanding ability to the study of astronomy in his spare time. In 1772 he was joined by his sister Caroline, then an uneducated girl, who became his lifelong assistant and collaborator; and, indeed, qualified as an astronomical observer of distinction in her own right. Herschel had taught himself mathematics and optics in his spare time, but it was only after his arrival in Bath that he took up the study of astronomy seriously. He then found that good telescopes were not to be bought, and realized he would have to construct his own. This he learned to do, casting, grinding and polishing the reflectors, and constructing eyepieces in a crude workshop in his own house, with the assistance of his sister and a young brother, Alexander. William's concentration on his work was matched only by the devotion of his sister who records that when 'in attendance on my Brother when polishing, that by way of keeping him alive I was even obliged to feed him by putting the Vitals by bits into his mouth—this was once the case when at the finishing of a 7 feet mirror he had not left his hands from it for 16 hours together.'

Such was his skill, patience and perseverance that he succeeded ultimately in constructing telescopes of much greater magnification than the London astronomers had at their disposal, superior, in fact, to any possessed by the Royal Observatory at that time. Indeed, when he described his observations, it was thought at first he was greatly exaggerating the power he claimed for the telescopes he had used. Whilst still at Bath he discovered a new planet, Uranus, though at first he thought it to be a comet. In Bath, too, Herschel's earliest scientific papers, which dealt with a variety of subjects other than astronomy, were read before the short-lived Philosophical Society of Bath. His labours gained him recognition, for he was elected a Fellow of the Royal Society and awarded its Copley medal in 1781, before he left Bath.

Herschel's life and his contributions to astronomical science have been well chronicled. It is sufficient to state here that this great astronomer, whose earliest work was carried out during sixteen years' residence in Bath, was the founder of stellar photometry and the greatest astronomical observer of all time. He left Bath in 1782 to become private astronomer to George III.

The final incidents in this chronicle are concerned mainly with developments in medical science, but they have some interest for the chemist, particularly, and ornithology receives a mention.

First we must mention the work of Edward Jenner, M.D., F.R.S. (1749–1823), who spent most of his life as a country doctor in Gloucestershire. His discovery of vaccination as a preventive of smallpox is one of the most outstanding events in the history of medical science. It is difficult to realize, now that this terrible disease occurs so rarely, the world-wide interest his discovery aroused at the end of the eighteenth century, and the extent to which mankind benefited.

Jenner was born sixteen miles north of Bristol in the country town of Berkeley, the son of the vicar of Berkeley. As a boy he showed an interest in natural history and, at the age of twenty, was apprenticed in London to the famous surgeon-anatomist John Hunter. Pupil and master had common interests and became lifelong friends. In 1771 Jenner was given the task of arranging the specimens collected by Sir Joseph Banks during his first voyage with Captain Cook. He carried out the work so successfully that he was offered the post of naturalist to the second expedition. About the same time time Hunter suggested a partnership, but Jenner was not ambitious and refused these offers. He loved the quiet country life of his Gloucestershire home, and returned to Berkeley in 1773 to set up practice. Here he gained the confidence and esteem of patients and friends. He took part in the activities of local medical societies, one of which met at the Fleece Inn, Rodborough, near Stroud, in north Gloucestershire. This Jenner called the Medico-Convivial to distinguish it from the Convivio-Medical which foregathered at the Ship, Alveston, between Berkeley and

Bristol. This inn is familiar to Bristolians, for in an adjoining field many a good innings was played by the famous cricketer, W. G. Grace.

Jenner caused some local excitement in 1783 when, following the example of the French pioneer Montgolfier, he constructed a balloon filled with hydrogen which travelled several miles over the neighbouring countryside.

He maintained his interest in natural history, particularly ornithology and geology. In 1788 the Royal Society published his memorable account of the habits of the cuckoo, which included the observation, for long disbelieved in some quarters, that the cuckoo, whilst still only a few days old, deliberately heaves the eggs and young of its foster parent out of the nest. Jenner was elected a fellow of the Royal Society in 1789, and later on, in 1809, he became a member of the newly formed Geological Society of London.

In spite of all these activities another, and more important matter had occupied Jenner's thoughts for a long time. He had never forgotten the remark of a young countrywoman in Chipping Sodbury, made whilst he was still a student, that she could not take smallpox because she had had cowpox. It seems to have been common knowledge in country districts that cowherds and milkmaids were generally immune from smallpox, and Jenner had been collecting evidence on the subject for years. It was not until 1796 that the opportunity occurred for him to test his idea that vaccination with lymph from a cowpox vesicle might produce immunity from smallpox. In this year he vaccinated a healthy boy, whom he later inoculated against smallpox.[1] The boy proved to be immune to the effects of inoculation. This success convinced Jenner that his views were sound, and in 1798 he published his historic pamphlet *An Inquiry into the Causes and Effects of Variolae Vaccinae. A Disease discovered in some of the Western Counties of England.* Henceforward the practice of vaccination came into use, at first slowly and with some opposition and ridicule, but soon with enthusiasm throughout the world. Jenner received many honours, foreign as well as British, and deserves to be remembered always as one of Gloucestershire's most famous sons.

We now move finally to Bristol itself where, at the close of the eighteenth century, there occurred within the city a chapter in the history of science which, at any rate to Bristolians, is of such interest as to merit description at considerable length.

In 1793 there arrived in Bristol a remarkable character, Thomas Beddoes, a man of wide attainments, already known as a chemist, a skilled linguist, well versed in geology, mineralogy and botany, and an M.D. of Edinburgh (Plate XV). Beddoes was, in addition, a man of unusual political views, something of a poet, and a prolific writer on medical, social and political subjects. Soon he was to become even better known as a physician and the founder of the Bristol 'Pneumatic Medical Institution' for treating diseases by the inhalation of gases.

A year previously Beddoes had retired from the post of Reader in Chemistry at

[1] Inoculation with the virus of a mild form of smallpox had been practised in Britain since the beginning of the eighteenth century, and did not go out of use for some forty years after Jenner's discovery.

Oxford on account of the unpopularity he had incurred through expressing sympathy towards the French revolutionaries.

At this period modern chemistry was developing rapidly and, following the discovery of various gases during the eighteenth century, what has been termed 'pneumatic chemistry' had become fashionable. Beddoes, already interested in this branch of chemistry, became imbued with the idea that the inhalation of specific gases might prove beneficial in the treatment of various diseases. On leaving Oxford he turned his thoughts towards putting his ideas into practice. Such a course must have appealed to a man of his benevolent disposition who was anxious to serve humanity, especially those in humble circumstances.

The choice of Bristol as a place in which to set up practice may have been made because of the presence there of many invalids hoping to be cured at the Hotwells. Beddoes carried letters of introduction, probably from Erasmus Darwin, to another remarkable character, Richard Lovell Edgeworth, educationalist and father of Maria the novelist, who had lately come to stay in Clifton.

Beddoes established a laboratory for preparing gases in a house in Hope Square, which opens off Hope Hill leading up from the River Avon to Clifton. His chemical activities at first alarmed the neighbours, but Edgeworth calmed their fears, and Beddoes rapidly built up a practice among both the humbler classes and the residents of fashionable Clifton. Soon he counted among his patients and friends, members of the distinguished literary circle then resident in Bristol, which included Coleridge, Southey and Wordsworth.

Beddoes' friendship with Erasmus Darwin and his Birmingham associates, among whom was James Watt, the great engineer, led to the latter placing his consumptive son Gregory in Beddoes' care. Watt also designed for Beddoes some simple and efficient apparatus for preparing gases, which was made in the famous Soho factory of Boulton and Watt. A description of the apparatus is included in the book *Considerations on the Medicinal Powers and the Production of Factitious Airs* (1794–96), of which Beddoes and Watt were joint authors. This book also contains an account of the more important investigations carried out by the former on the therapeutic effects of gases.

Beddoes continued his work in Hope Square for a few years, but the results were inconclusive, and he decided to establish a small hospital for the relief of diseases by gases, in which patients would be under constant observation. It was this hospital that became known as the 'Pneumatic Medical Institution'. Subscriptions were solicited from various sources, including members of the medical profession, but not everyone asked was sympathetic to the project, and some medical men opposed him as a quack. In the book mentioned above Beddoes included some rhymed couplets which were probably intended to illustrate the scornful attitude of the scoffers. The following are examples:

> Proceed, high toned enthusiast! Coax mankind
> With Idiot mouth to gape and suck the wind;
> To each forsaken belle and faded beau
> In Hope's gay glass alluring visions show

Nor boast *thy airs* cosmetic powers alone:
Disease and vanquished Time their virtues own.
Pneumatic art unfixes cancer's claw,
And shields the victim doomed to Phthisis' maw,
See Palsy dance! his hollows macies fill,
And Asthma pace without a puff uphill!

In 1797 Beddoes commenced to plan his 'Pneumatic Medical Institution'. His intention was to establish a small hospital for in-patients, with a large out-patient department attached. There was also to be a laboratory equipped with the most modern apparatus for studying pneumatic chemistry and its application to man and animals in health and disease. At Hope Square Beddoes had used what help came to hand, even, it is said, training his maid servants to prepare gases. Now he required a qualified staff of physicians and nurses, and a superintendent for the hospital and laboratory. The latter, he decided, must be a chemist who would be responsible for the experimental work.

The superintendent, appointed in 1798, was none other than Humphry Davy, then an unknown youth of nineteen, but destined to become, before long, one of the most celebrated chemists in Europe (Plate XIV). Previously Davy had been apprenticed to a doctor near Penzance, and such chemistry as he knew he had taught himself. His aptitude for the subject had come to Beddoes' notice as a result of two remarkable coincidences. The first was that Beddoes' patient Gregory Watt had just previously spent a winter in Cornwall, lodging, whilst there, with Davy's mother; the second that Davy's interest in chemistry had attracted the attention of a Cornish landowner, Davies Giddy,[1] a former pupil and friend of Beddoes.

Davy arrived in Bristol in October, 1798, and went to live with Beddoes, now married to one of Edgeworth's daughters. Before a suitable house for the new Institute was found he set to work in the Hope Square laboratory.

About this time a chemical discovery of some interest to Bristolians was made in this laboratory by one William Clayfield, about whom little seems to be known except that he worked in Beddoes' laboratory as a chemist, and lectured locally on chemistry. Clayfield attempted to prepare barium chloride from a crystalline mineral occurring in quantity at several localities near Bristol, believing the mineral to be sulphate of barium (barytes or heavy spar). A few years previously the existence of compounds containing a 'new earth', strontium oxide, had been established by several chemists, using naturally occurring carbonate of strontium (strontianite). Clayfield showed that the Bristol mineral was actually strontium sulphate (celestine). This was the first recognition of the new mineral in this country; and it led to the establishment later on of an important, if minor, industry in the Bristol district. For many years, up till 1939, a very large proportion of the world's output of strontium minerals, used in the sugar and pyrotechnics industries, came from the Bristol mines, which are still being worked. In passing, it is worth mentioning that, following Clayfield's

[1] Later, having changed his name to Davies Gilbert, a President of the Royal Society.

discovery, Davy himself experimented with strontium salts in the Institute, and he was the first to isolate metallic strontium, though this was after he had left Bristol.

However, the main object of Beddoes' laboratory was the preparation of 'factitious airs', as artificial gases were then called, and the investigation of their therapeutic effect. In 1799 the new Institute was established in a house in Dowry Square, Hotwells, and here Davy, with more enthusiasm than knowledge, entered into what has been called 'the boldest series of experiments ever undertaken by man'. He demonstrated, by experimenting upon himself, that nitrous oxide, or 'laughing gas' as it came to be called as a result of his experiments, could be inhaled in quantity without danger. In fact, he anticipated its possible use in surgery, as an anaesthetic, for he actually stated in print, in 1800, that it might be used with advantage during surgical operations since it appeared capable of destroying physical pain. Had the Institute been a surgical rather than primarily a medical one, possibly Davy's suggestion might have been tried out at once, but some forty years were to pass before anaesthetics came into use.

Davy tested the effects of laughing gas on Coleridge, Southey, and some young lady friends with results that were amusing, though Davy himself was very much in earnest. He went on to experiment on himself with other, more lethal gases, including even mixtures containing carbon monoxide, often with unpleasant results. In fact it is remarkable that some of his experiments did not terminate his career.

Beddoes continued to test the effects of gaseous inhalations on his patients but to-day, it must be confessed, he is most often remembered for his treatment of consumptive patients with cow's breath; the cow, it is related, being installed in the patient's bedroom with her muzzle inserted within the bed curtains, and left there all night. Medical science was not then sufficiently advanced for Beddoes' experiments to have any permanent value. It has been stated by an historian of medicine, however, that his concept of treating certain diseases by placing the patient in a special atmosphere is one that has found vindication in the modern open air treatment of phthisis, and in modern chest surgery; and that Beddoes' plan for the treatment of respiratory troubles with gaseous inhalations is now standardized as aero- or pneumo-therapy.

Davy's activities were of more lasting importance, scientifically, and in 1800 he published an account of his work in a book entitled *Researches Chemical and Philosophical, chiefly concerning Nitrous Oxide*. Meantime his interest had been aroused by an announcement, made in July 1800, that water could be decomposed into hydrogen and oxygen by means of a voltaic current, and he immediately started, in the Institute, a series of experiments on the changes accompanying the 'electrolysis' of various compounds. By January, 1801, he had published six papers on the subject, and this was the start of his famous researches in electrochemistry. In February, 1801, Davy left Bristol on appointment as lecturer to the Royal Institution in London. Henceforward his rise to fame was meteoric, but it should not be forgotten that his few years in Bristol gave him just the opportunity he needed to make his abilities known.

After Davy's departure the life seems to have gone out of the Pneumatic Institution. Though it continued in existence for a few years longer, until about 1809, nitrous oxide was only administered occasionally. Beddoes was a skilled physician, in spite of his predilection for pneumotherapy, and genuinely concerned about the care and cure of the sick. About 1803 he established a second medical institution, near Broad Quay, for the treatment of the poor and needy. He was, in fact, a pioneer in preventive medicine, having sound ideas on the subject, which he discusses in several books, and he deserves to be remembered for this side of his activities. In closing, mention may be made of the suggestion that the present Clifton Dispensary, founded in 1812, and at least as early as 1823 occupying premises in Dowry Square, may be the lineal descendant of the Pneumatic Institution.

Towards the end of his life Beddoes seems to have renewed his interest in geology, for after his death a number of rock specimens on which he had been carrying out experiments were found in his laboratory. John Loudon McAdam had recently settled in Bristol, and it has been suggested that Beddoes was experimenting on his behalf with material likely to be suitable for 'macadamizing' roads. Beddoes died on Christmas Eve, 1808, at the age of forty-eight, and so closed one of the most interesting chapters in the history of scientific activity in Bristol.

ACKNOWLEDGEMENTS

In conclusion, the author would like to acknowledge with gratitude the assistance given him by his wife in assembling the materials on which this article is based. He is also grateful to Dr. J. F. Hope-Simpson for checking points in the botanical section.

PRINCIPAL REFERENCES

Alchemy:

The Ordinall of Alchemy by Thomas Norton of Bristol. 1928. London. This edition contains an interesting introduction by Dr. E. J. Holmyard, formerly of Clifton College.

Botany:

White, J. W. 1912. *The Bristol Flora.* Bristol. Especially the chapter entitled 'History of Bristol Botany'.

Geology:

Gunther, R. T. 1925–45. *Early Science in Oxford.* Oxford. Especially Volumes IV, VIII, XII and XIV.

—. 1928. *Further Correspondence of John Ray.* London. Ray Society.

Lankester, E. 1848. *Correspondence of John Ray.* London. Ray Society.

Cox, L. R. 1942. New Light on William Smith and His Work. *Proc. Yorks. Geol. Soc.*, **25**, 1–99.

Smith, S. 1945. Owen's Observations. *Proc. Bristol Nat. Soc.*, **27**, 93–101.

Astronomy:

The Herschel Chronicle. 1933. Cambridge. Edited by his grand-daughter Constance A. Lubbock.

Medicine and Chemistry:

CARTWRIGHT, F. F. 1952. *The English Pioneers of Anaesthesia.* Bristol. (For Beddoes and Davy.)

KENDALL, JAMES. 1954. *Humphry Davy, Pilot of Penzance.* London.

DREWITT, F. D. 1933. *Life of Edward Jenner*, 2nd ed. London.

Physics:

BOURNE, H. R. FOX. 1876. *The Life of John Locke.* London.

PART TWO

CHAPTER NINE

THE PREHISTORIC ARCHAEOLOGY OF THE BRISTOL REGION

THE BRISTOL region is hard to define geographically and so arbitrary boundaries have been selected as will be seen from the maps. There is a wealth of material for study in the field but a very large proportion of the prehistoric material collected in the Bristol City Museum and in the University of Bristol Spelaeological Society's Museum was destroyed by enemy action. Other important museums of the area are at Wells and Cheddar (Gough's Caves).

LOWER AND MIDDLE PALAEOLITHIC (FIG. 17)

There are terraces of gravel on the Bristol Avon and its tributaries. They correspond to the 100-ft. and 50-ft. terraces of the Thames. There is also a spread of high-plateau gravel in places. The terraces have yielded animal remains of the period and at some sites artefacts. The fauna reported is scanty and at times poorly identified. On the seaward side raised beaches occur of which the best known is at Birnbeck, Weston-super-Mare. It seems probable that the steepness of the flanks of the hills in the southern part of the area may often have resulted in a wave-cut platform and cliff, as at Walton, near Clevedon, and not a raised beach. The extent of the incursion of the sea in terrace times can be judged from Fig. 17. On the south flank of Mendip in a number of places a terrace can be located at about 100 ft. It is probable that the deposit on it has been derived by sub-aerial denudation and that it rests on a wave-cut platform. There are also terraces on the smaller rivers, while to the north just outside the area are such rivers as the Little Avon, the Cam (where extensive gravel deposits are being worked), and the Stroud Frome. All of these demand investigation.

The fauna reported from various sites includes both warm and cold types. Cave sites do not help much in the elucidation of the problems involved, as the oldest fauna from them need not be earlier than the warm or early Mousterian. In each case where a warm fauna has been found, such as in the Durdham Downs Fissure, Hutton Bone Cave and Milton Hill near Wells, the methods of excavation and the records still remaining are inadequate. The first two sites had a cold fauna as well. The quarry fissure at Milton Hill yielded a warm fauna. A number of the bones show evidence of burning bespeaking the presence of man. Lacaille has recently described a series of implements of Acheulean date from the terraces of the Bristol Avon. The most important sites are on both sides of the river at Shirehampton.[1] No cave site dug in recent years has yielded anything older than the Upper Palaeolithic.

The gradual elevation of the land indicated by the successive river terraces continued through the Middle Palaeolithic till the rivers had cut their beds down to 60 ft. below their present level. Deposits began to accumulate on the now-exposed rock platforms so that the base of these deposits can be as old as the late Middle Palaeolithic. The deposits extend upwards into the Holocene. The best exposures of them are to be seen at Brean Down, Uphill and Walton (Clevedon). They are composed of hill wash of limestone debris and blown sand. Towards the base larger material is the rule and finer material towards the top, but there are bands of coarser material and also of almost pure blown sand. At Brean Down the sands are particularly thick. The whole appears to have been formed under periglacial conditions. Minor changes of climate are indicated by the changes in the nature of the deposits at each site. Variations between sites are in part due to their location in relation to the coast and the prevailing winds of the time.

THE UPPER PALAEOLITHIC (FIG. 17)

The elevation of the land seems to have reached its maximum about the beginning of this period. Bridgwater Bay and other lowlying areas eventually carried extensive forests. The Somerset Levels and other low areas formed part of a plain intersected by shallow valleys with fairly swiftly flowing streams. The Bristol Avon alone remained unaffected by the continued elevation of the land because in the gorge, approximately below the site of the Suspension Bridge, a sill of rock kept the waters back at much the same level as now. Downstream from this point the river behaved as its neighbours.

The Uphill Bone Caves, now quarried away, Hutton Cave, now lost, and Banwell Bone Cave contained, and in the case of Banwell still contains, a fauna that may be as old as Aurignacian. Hutton Cave also had an earlier fauna. A few flint implements from one of the Uphill Caves and some alleged to be from Banwell tend to confirm this dating. The hyaena den, known as the bone fissure, at Almondsbury, with a fauna including cave lion, may be as old as this too.

A strong Solutrean influence is manifest in the implements from the deeper levels of several caves. The basal layer of the hyaena den at Wookey Hole has yielded a fine proto-Solutrean implement.[2] The adjacent Badger Hole has yielded several more.[3] The lower levels at Soldier's Hole, Cheddar, yielded implements that could almost be termed true Solutrean[4] and a few implements from the large series at Gough's Caves, Cheddar, also show Solutrean influence.

The Creswellian is represented by fauna, man and his implements from a number of sites, all in caves. Gough's Cave has a large series of implements covering a period

[1] 1954. *Ant. J.*, vol. 34, 1. Full references are given in this paper.
[2] The implement is in the Bristol Museum.
[3] Implements in Wells Museum.
[4] Implements in Gough's Caves Museum.

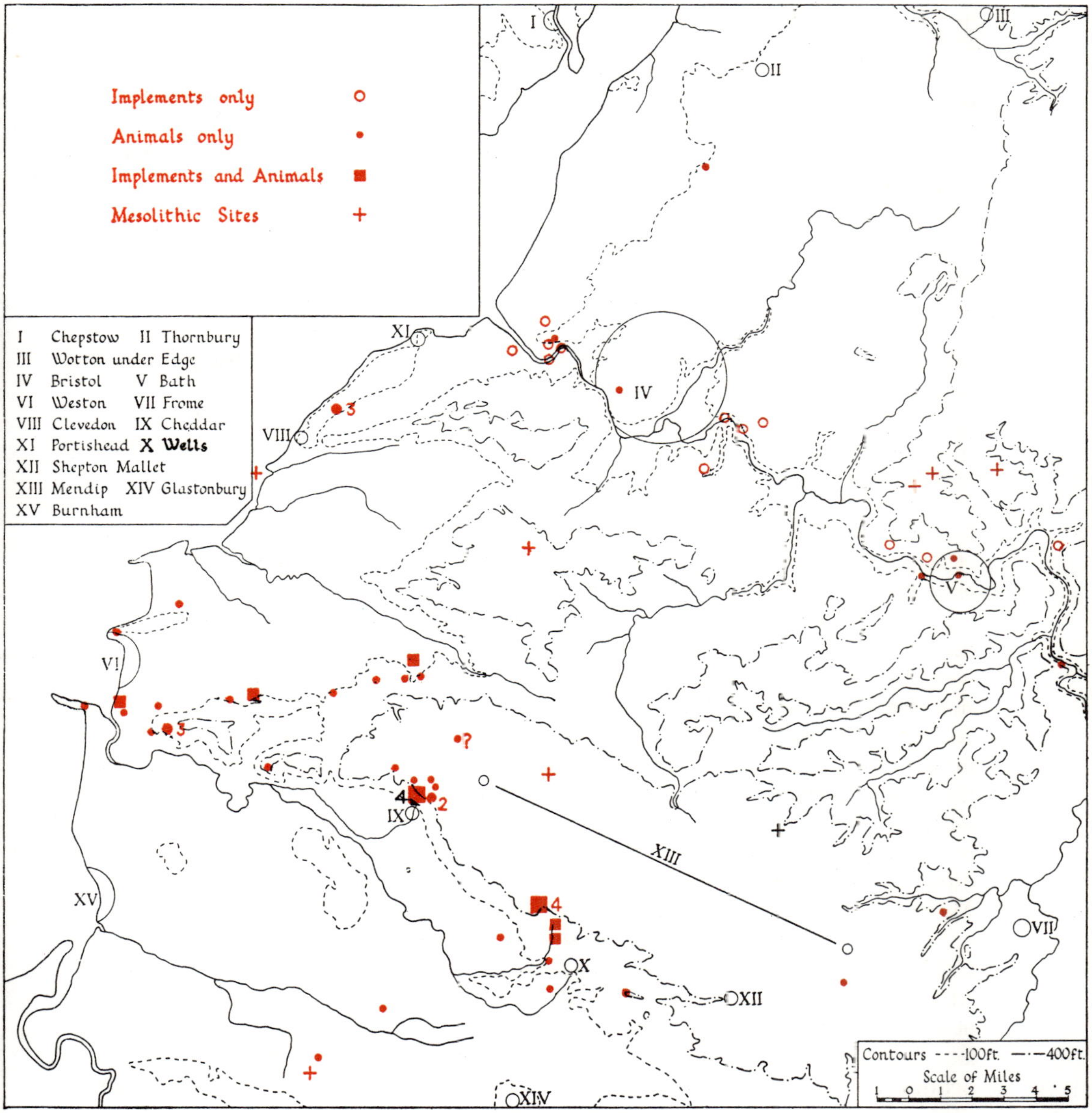

FIG. 17. *Palaeolithic (Pleistocene) and Mesolithic records.*

nearly up to the end of the Palaeolithic. The fauna includes bear, reindeer, horse, and lemming. The only evidence of mammoth is in the form of two ivory rods, if microscopical examination shows them to be truly of mammoth ivory. These should be regarded as derived fossils, in the absence of any other evidence of the presence of mammoth during the occupation of the cave. Rhinoceros and hyaena are also absent. Indeed the Mendip caves provide evidence that these beasts disappeared, from southern England at least, somewhere about the beginning of the English equivalent of the Magdalenian.

Gough's Cave Pleistocene levels have also yielded two 'bâtons de commandement', an ivory bead, a piece of amber, a stone with incised lines upon it and a bone used as a tally. Parts of several individuals were found. The skeleton of a youth, aged about twenty-two, was found almost complete, in a partially flexed position in a side passage where he must have been buried. The skull of this youth and the skull and jaw of two other persons all show marks indicating that the flesh had been removed from the bones before burial or disposal, but whether as the result of cannibalism or ritual cannot be stated. Physically they were short to medium in height, slender and long-headed but with short broad faces.

Somewhat later in general facies were the contents of Aveline's Hole, Burrington Combe, where only Pleistocene remains were found. A double-rowed antler harpoon of Magdalenian 6B type (Breuil) was found in the first-foot level. In all, parts of at least fifty individuals have been found but most of these were taken away and lost by early excavators.[1] Two ceremonial burials were found but unfortunately they had both been extensively disturbed by early excavators. Ornaments associated with these included fossils foreign to the district,[2] teeth of animals drilled for suspension, sea-shells likewise drilled, and a perforated bone. A tally bone was also found. Alongside one burial was a child's skull which had had the vertex cut off and placed upside down in the base. The flint implements showed great economy in the use of the material; every tiny scrap seems to have been utilized, unlike Gough's Cave, where there appears to have been no shortage. Perhaps the growth of forests was restricting movements and therefore opportunities for replenishing the supply of flint. The long-headed individuals from the cave closely resemble Cheddar man. Mesocephalic and even brachycephalic individuals were also present.

Still later than the Aveline's Hole series of implements is the small series from Sun Hole Cave at Cheddar,[2] and from various small shelters and caves in Ebbor Gorge.[3] At Sun Hole the deposit has obviously accumulated rapidly and has the character of a solifluxion material. At its top occurs a thin layer of soft stalagmite less than a foot in depth, in the top of which lies embedded a Beaker deposit. A similar stratification has been found at a number of cave sites. These have as yet yielded no evidence of occupation of the area by any newcomers in the Mesolithic and Early Neolithic times. The evidence from cave excavations and from such sites as Brean

[1] A few remains survived enemy action and are in the University of Bristol Spelaeological Society's Museum. One skull, formerly at Oxford, is now in the British Museum (Natural History).

[2] In University of Bristol Spelaeological Society's Museum.

[3] In Wells Museum.

Down and Walton strongly suggests that the closing phase of the Pleistocene was climatically cold and wet. The population was small, still dependent upon a food-gathering economy and perhaps forced by growth of forests to restrict their wanderings. At the end there was, geologically speaking, a rapid amelioration of the climate to warmer but still wet conditions, which were followed by the various climatic phases of the Holocene.

THE MESOLITHIC (FIG. 17)

The number of known sites is still few. The evidence of cave deposits clearly indicates that the Late Palaeolithic and Mesolithic civilizations coexisted in the area and must have had considerable influence upon each other. Perhaps the smallness of some of the implements from Aveline's Hole and from Sun Hole is a reflection of this influence. New sites are steadily being found. Sykes has reported several sites but all appear to have some later admixture. The most interesting one is that at Black Stone Rocks, Clevedon. This site is submerged at high tide but still yields Mesolithic implements as well as later types. It suggests that one possible cause of the absence of Mesolithic sites is the transgression of the sea, submerging extensive areas of sand dunes and lightly wooded land liked well by these folk. Gardiner has reported a number of sites from the Bath Downs. More recently Taylor[1] has reported two more, one at Barrow Hill, near Bristol, and the other on Mendip. Another has been found recently near Birdcombe, Nailsea.[1]

THE NEOLITHIC (FIG. 18)

At what point in time the Mesolithic may be said to end and the Neolithic to begin in the Bristol area cannot be stated. Undoubtedly the Neolithic peoples and cultures penetrated the area but there are no established sites that can be stated to belong to the opening phases. A considerable number of polished stone axes has been found in the area and several living-sites are known but none need be earlier than about 2000 B.C. The problem is further complicated by the use of polished flint axes as a source of raw material for refabrication during the Bronze Age and the survival of the Mesolithic flint tradition into the same period.

A number of stone axes has been found on the Failand ridge west of Bristol. One would expect similar finds from the high ground of Bristol itself and to the northward, but such finds are wanting even though there is a living-site at Crab Tree Slip near Sea Mills. This site yielded polished stone axes and pottery.[2] A considerable proportion of the material is thought to be in the Percival collection at Cambridge. Other living-sites were at Chelm's Combe and Rowberrow Cavern. Both yielded typical pottery and implements of the later phases of the Neolithic. Polished stone axes are sometimes found at lowlying sites such as the Marine Lake, Portishead, when this was dredged. There is evidence that the coastline differed

[1] Personal information given to the author.
[2] Account given to the author by the late Mr. A. Selley.

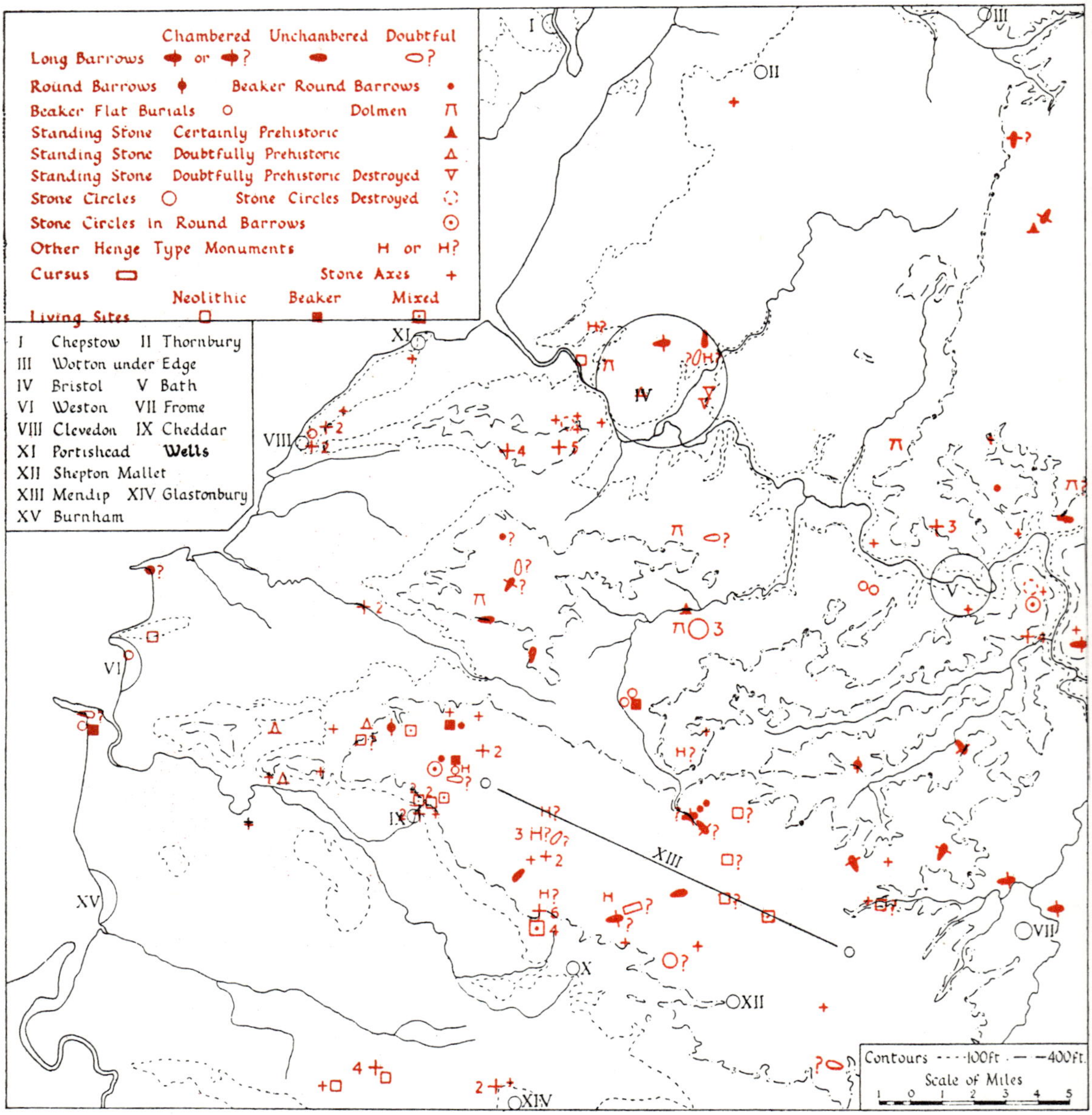

FIG. 18. *Neolithic-Beaker (Megalithic) records.*

considerably from that of the present day. The land was going down but it had not reached its present level.

The petrological examination of stone axes found in the area indicates wide trading relations with various factory sites, chiefly in Cornwall. Flint also had to be imported. Some of it came in as finished implements. A hoard of large Neolithic blades was found at the Bridged Pot Hole Shelter in Ebbor Gorge.[1] Occasionally fairly large nodules of flint turn up as surface finds such as the one from Slab House and Horrington, north of Wells, and the one found near Nordrach, on Mendip. They could of course be earlier or later in date than Neolithic. Recently at Gough's Old Cave, Cheddar, evidence has been found that flint was imported in quite small nodules.

In the later stages of the Neolithic and up to and including the beginning of the Beaker period there is the impact on the area of the megalithic cult. The main examples of this are the long barrows and dolmens of the area. Any consideration of these structures must involve consideration of the relationship of the chambered structures to the unchambered ones of either earth or stone. If the two types are to be regarded as being of different origins, as is believed by Piggott, then the fact that both types occur in the area shows a mixture of related groups of peoples and ideas. Others would regard the earthen unchambered ones as being degraded and therefore late examples of the chambered ones.

Glynn Daniels has concluded from the distribution of chambered tombs that this aspect of the megalithic cult was sea-borne. Others have suggested that the route for the chambered long barrows was by sea up Southampton Water and thence to Salisbury Plain and on to the Cotswolds–Severn area, with a southerly extension on to Mendip. Though there are chambered tombs, so located as to fit Daniels's theory, in the area there are others not so located and their density increases towards the Frome gap in the thick forests. They have an easterly directed grouping at variance with Daniels's theory but in keeping with the landward route. Further if the Bristol Channel was the main sea route for the primary settlement of the area by megalithic cult people, then it is truly remarkable that there are no long-chambered tombs at the western end of Mendip and other areas of high land adjoining the coast right up to the Bristol Avon and neither are any known north of Bristol in the area between the Channel and the Cotswold escarpment. The detailed evidence for the area does not support Daniels's theory.

Other megalithic structures consist of standing stones, stone circles and other henge-type monuments. Very little is known about them in the area. Two stones used to stand not so far from each other on relatively low ground near Loxton and Banwell. It has been suggested that they were boundary stones of uncertain date but each of them had the usual traditional stories attached to them which suggests that they were true megaliths. At Star, near Shipham, is the Wimble Stone. It stands on a little rise in a field and there is a number of larger-than-usual stones in the adjacent hedge banks. They probably formed part of a megalithic arrangement, perhaps a

[1] Mr. H. E. Balch the finder considers this hoard to be of Solutrean date.

long barrow. In Bristol two separate stones used to exist about 400 yds. apart, one in Armoury Square and one in Stapleton Road. Both were large but nothing further is known about them, or of the large stone on Redland Green save that it is reputedly a megalith.

The three stone circles and associated structures at Stanton Drew are well known. The twin avenues that run from the two northern circles meet close to the River Chew, and end at the edge of an old channel. More circle stones are present under the turf. The differences in form of the stones in some cases seem to be analogous to those at Avebury and the same conclusion may be drawn. No serious excavations have as yet been made at this very important site, which is remarkably low lying, being below the 200-ft. contour, and as the level of the valley floor of the Chew is eventually controlled by the sill in the Avon Gorge, the valley floor level at the time the circles were erected must have been very much as it is now. To the south-west at Chew Stoke (Nat. Grid Ref. ST55996161), in the hedge on the north side of the road used to stand twelve 'largish' stones, obviously not in their original position. It seems likely that they once formed part of a small stone circle. The sites of these circles fit in well with the discoveries by Rahtz of Neolithic and Early Bronze Age living- and burial-sites in the Chew valley bottom.

Wicks has recorded a small stone circle at Crapnell but an element of doubt must remain as to its authenticity, pending excavation. Lloyd Morgan[1] records the presence of a small stone circle at Abbot's Leigh but repeated attempts to locate it have failed. Scarth has recorded stone circles and an avenue in relation to Bathampton Down Camp but not a trace now remains.[2]

The four circles at Priddy are at present an enigma. They are ring mounds composed of stone and earth and now grass-grown. The ditch is in each case outside the ring, which is without a break or entrance. There is no surface evidence of any internal structures though the most northerly one of them has inside its northern portion at least one, if not three, low, round barrows. A single line can be made to coincide with a diameter of each of the three southern circles but not with the most northern one, which is separated from the others by a gap just sufficient to have contained a fifth circle. Through this gap passes the Roman road from Charterhouse. Where stones are exposed all seem to be of silicified limestone. The careful selection of this stone for Beaker Age monuments on Mendip has been noted at other sites. The gap for the Roman road suggests a Roman date for the circles. The use of the special limestone suggests a Beaker Age date for them. Only excavation can give the actual date.

There is an incomplete circle of earth and stones with a flat central area and a ditch outside the mound ring overlooking Westbury-sub-Mendip. It may be a henge-type monument. Gorsey Bigbury, Charterhouse, is a well-known henge-type monument with the ditch inside the bank and a single causeway to the north. It seems never to have been finished and fairly soon after it was abandoned 'A'-Beaker

[1] Letter to Dymond in the latter's book on Stanton Drew.
[2] 1857. *J. Brit. Arch. Assoc.*, vol. 13, p. 105.

people used the ditch both as a living- and burial-site. Recently another possible henge-type monument has been found east of Priddy. It is almost identical in form and size with Gorsey Bigbury. It lies in the floor of a very shallow valley. The circle on Beacon Hill, north of Shepton Mallet, is almost certainly not prehistoric in origin. There is a low earthen circle with a ditch outside on Kings Weston Hill and part of a circle and avenue on Purdown, both in Bristol. Only excavations can date these structures, which may not be of prehistoric date. At Knowle Hill in the Chew Valley is a circle round the top of the hill. On the slope below, air photographs show ancient field systems but, for all that, the circle may not be of prehistoric date.

THE BEAKER PHASE

It has long been established that the Late Neolithic and the Beaker periods overlapped in the Mendip Hills and adjacent territories. In a number of cave and rock-shelter sites Beaker pottery occurs unmistakably in the same horizon as typical Neolithic ware and must be contemporary with it. One may expect the same evidence from excavations of megalithic sites and henge-type monuments. Living-sites of the period are little known other than from caves. Gorsey Bigbury is an exception and recently an open living-site has been found at Bos Swallet, Burrington. There is an extensive Beaker horizon at Brean Down dipping steeply down below the present beach level.

A few barrows are known to be originally of Beaker date. Others may be of that date to judge from their special appearance. No large barrows of Beaker date are as yet known but they probably exist. Simple cyst burials occur as at Corston, and at Brean Down, where Dr. Taylor found a burial exposed by the tide well below the present high-water level.

THE BRONZE AGE (FIG. 19)

The multitude of tumuli belonging to, or by analogy belonging to, the Bronze Age testifies to the presence of a large population, far larger than in the preceding period. It is from burials and chance finds, including hoards, that our knowledge of the period in the area is based. Practically no living-sites have been proved and excavated. Rowberrow Cave has a Bronze Age level in it but has yielded remarkably little in the way of finds of the period. Other cave sites give remains indicating temporary occupation from time to time. Probable living-sites are inferred from the concentrations of flint implements of Bronze Age types on the surface. For at least a century collectors have searched the Mendip Hills for flint implements. Thousands have been found but, except for showing the types of implements, the collections are, by modern standards, virtually useless as the location from which the implements came is either not stated or stated in such general terms as to be useless. It is imperative that present-day collectors should keep proper records for from them it will be possible to plot with some accuracy the location of numerous Bronze Age living-sites. If proper records had been kept the sites could be plotted now. Every collector of flint

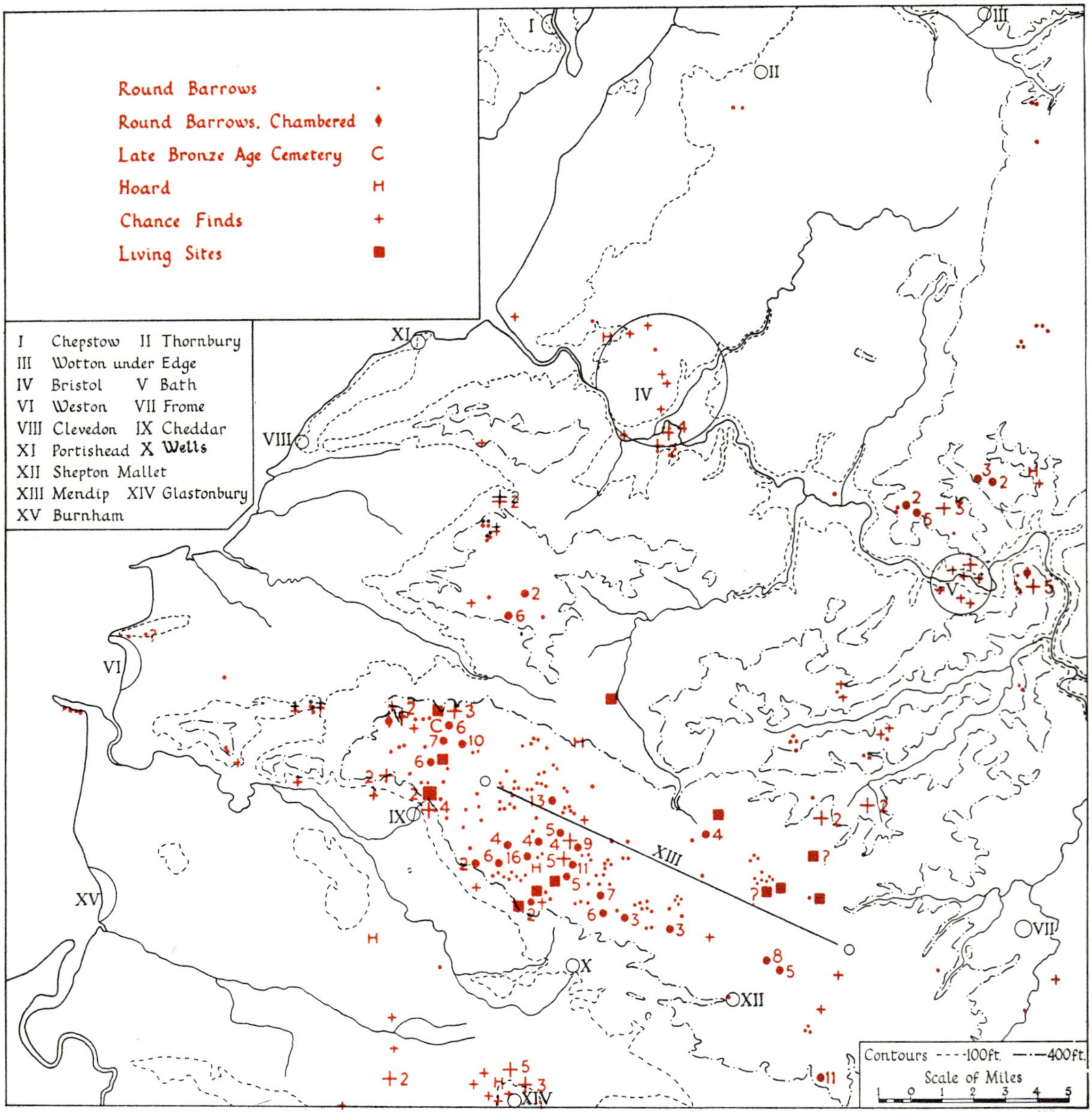

FIG. 19. *Bronze Age records.*

implements from the naturally flintless Mendip and similar areas in fact destroys valuable evidence for the location of living-sites. I would make an urgent appeal to collectors to record their finds properly or to stop collecting. The National Grid reference system provides an easy way for keeping records of location.

There are quite a number of hoards of bronze implements recorded for the area but as usual most of them have been lost to us. One such hoard is described as 'two wheelbarrowsful'. This was from near Priddy and the whole was sold for two gallons of cider. The distribution of chance finds in the Somerset Levels indicates that these were extensively populated with the actual settlements on the slightly higher ground of minor ridges and hills. The section at Brean Down helps to confirm this conclusion of Godwin and Dewar. It has also been shown by these same workers that the Bronze Age closed with a much wetter period and a rise in the level of the sea leading to extensive flooding of the low lands. Attempts were made to maintain communications by the construction of corduroy roads and this itself bespeaks a dense population and therefore the necessity of maintaining as much land under use as possible. Supporting evidence for the late date of this rise in the sea-level comes from Avonmouth Docks. Here part of a sword was found on 'a sandy stratum' covered by forty feet of mud. Though the weapon may have been dropped from a boat when the area was already permanently submerged, it was dropped while the Avon Estuary into the Severn still had a clean sandy bottom. Submergence had not gone far enough at this time for silt to accumulate here.

Bronze Age tumuli are widely distributed, and by far the greatest concentration is to be found on Mendip. The majority are on high ground but by no means always on the highest local ground. The height above sea-level varies substantially. On Mendip there is a notable grouping around Priddy, another, though not so dense, round Charterhouse and a third round Blackdown. Mendip is in general a waterless area as the drainage is underground, and it is worth noting that all three concentrations are related to zones in which surface springs are available. All types of barrows are found in the area. The great majority belong to the simple bowl type. Few of this type appear to have ditches but the excavations at Tynings Farm have shown that ditches, with or without a causeway in the henge style, may exist and only be demonstrable by excavation. Even air photographs and detailed examination from the air will often fail to show ditches on Carboniferous Limestone and this may also be true for the oolitic limestone in the north of the area. Though many of the tumuli have been disturbed few have been dug properly.

Of the tumuli that are not on the highest local ground two groups call for special mention. One group of six at Tynings Farm has been admirably excavated by Dr. Taylor[1] and lies at the head of a long and important valley leading up to the Mendip plateau from the coastal plain. The range of date of this group is from early Bronze Age to late in the period (Deverel-Rimbury pottery). The second group lies at the head of Goblin Combe, which provides an easy route from the coastal plain north of

[1] Models of these barrows and some of the finds are in the University of Bristol Spelaeological Society's Museum. Many of the finds were destroyed by enemy action.

Mendip on to the next area to the north of high ground. The Goblin Combe group originally consisted of at least five of which only one is to be clearly seen at the present day. Both groups probably mark well-used trade routes.

THE EARLY IRON AGE (FIG. 20)

'A' Period

Little is known of this period for want of suitable excavations. The distribution of finds both within and without the area shows that the whole was affected. Pottery of the period occurs in small quantities in a number of the Mendip caves, indicating temporary occupation from time to time. On the eastern fringe is Solsbury Hill Camp, near Bath. It has been encroached upon by quarrying. In the section of the ditch so exposed were to be found quantities of pottery of the period.[1] Blaise Castle Camp, Bristol, was occupied during the period, as is shown by the fact that rabbits turn up typical pottery. However, the relationship of the 'A' period people to the many camps of the area is uncertain, and excavations are needed. It is reasonable to assume that at least many of the major works attributable to the Early Iron Age were founded in this period.

Burials are known from three small tumuli on Kings Weston Hill, Bristol. Two of the three may date from the very end of the Bronze Age but the third contained a cremated burial associated with a typical carinated bowl, an iron bridle cheek piece and unburnt bones of domestic animals, including the horse. Other burials were found at Weston-super-Mare.

'B' Period

In the south of the area in the Somerset Levels are the well-known 'B' period lake villages of Glastonbury and Meare. The former has been completely excavated and described. The latter is still in course of excavation but publication of the completed portion is in hand, two volumes having already appeared. The villages provide a picture of a well-to-do agricultural population with their homesteads protected by the shallow waters of the marshes. Many of the huts of the villages were reconstructed from time to time and new hearths made but as yet no attention seems to have been paid to building up from such magnificently stratified sites a sequence-dated series of pottery styles. Such a series is urgently needed for the interpretation of finds from other sites. According to the late Dr. Bulleid there is another untouched village in Godney Moor.

Wookey Hole and Read's Cavern are both well-known habitation sites of the period. The former continued to be occupied well into Roman times. Rowberrow Cave close to Read's seems to have been a major smelting site for iron ores and this is true, to a lesser extent, for the rock shelter at Chelm's Combe. But except for these four sites caves seem only to have been inhabited occasionally for short periods,

[1] Some of this is on exhibition in the University of Bristol Spelaeological Society's Museum.

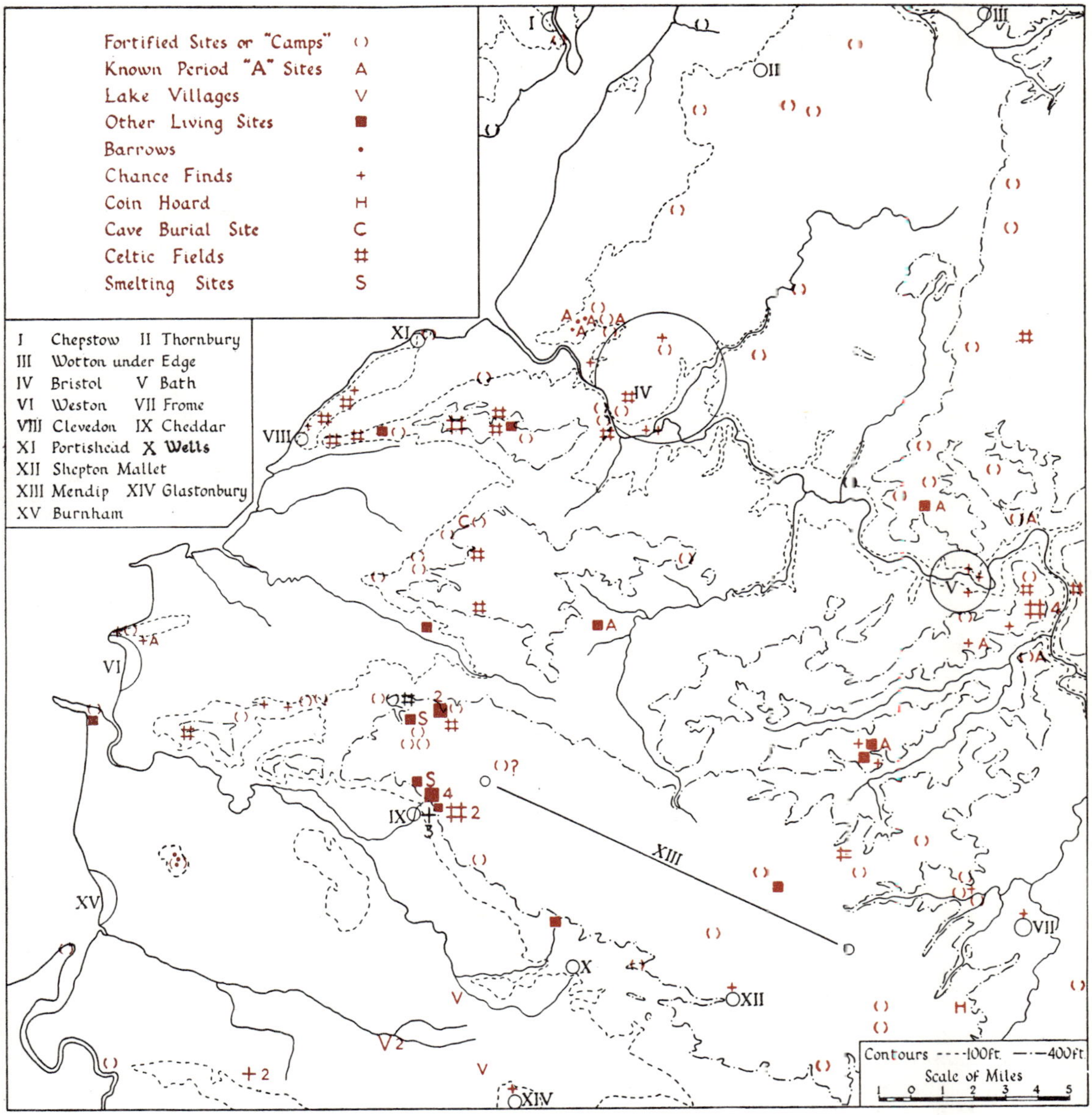

FIG. 20. *Early Iron Age records.*

until quite late in the Roman period when resort was once more made to them by the indigenous population.

There are many hill forts in the area. Some of them have been partially excavated but on the whole with rather meagre results. It is a fair assumption from these excavations and by analogy with sites elsewhere that at least all the major works belong to this period, even if many were founded in the earlier period. Their number and close proximity to each other tell of a considerable population and of troubled times. At the west end of Mendip is the camp at Worlebury, at the north end of Weston Bay, with its weaker brother at the south end at Brean Down. Inland there is the series: Banwell, Dinghurst with Dolebury, one on either side of the major pass from the coastal plain up into the Mendip Hills; Burrington Camp dominating Burrington Combe and the narrowing Yeo Valley; and eastward again is Burledge Camp guarding the watershed between the rivers Yeo and Chew. This camp with Maes Knoll to the north and Maesbury to the south-east forms a connecting link between the first series and those near Mells and Frome and thence northwards to the Bath group. It will be noted from this brief account that the first series of works is situated on the northern flank of Mendip from the coast eastwards. There are no major defensive works along the whole of the southern flank until east of Wells. The works are sited to meet an attack from the north or directly across the Severn. The Mells–Frome–Bath series seem to be sited to meet attacks from the east or south-east across what seems to have been a tribal frontier.

Near the coast north from Worlebury are the two Cadbury camps (Wrington and Clevedon), dominating the coastal plain north of Weston and guarding the approaches to two more areas of high land. Wains Hill Camp at Clevedon and Portishead Camp still farther north completes the coastal series up to the Avon. Up this river from its mouth the first ford is at the sill of rock in the Avon Gorge. This ford is guarded by a trio of camps, Clifton or Observatory Camp on the Bristol side, and Burwalls and Stokeleigh on the Somerset side. On the Clifton side there is only one feasible route to the ford. On the Somerset side there are two and hence, probably, the necessity for two camps. Control of the ford also included control of the large freshwater spring running into the very muddy and brackish waters of the Avon. It would seem that this route with its ford was very important in the period. Certainly on the Somerset side it led to the Failand ridge with its numerous areas of Celtic fields and on the Bristol side there were, till quite recently, traces of similar field systems on Durdham Downs. A few miles north of this trio is the ridge of high ground terminating at Pen Pole Point above the Avon. The ridge is pierced by the deep narrow gorge of the River Hen. This passage must also have been of great importance as it is guarded by three camps; one on either side of the gorge on Combe Hill and Blaise Castle, which is supported by the third, just to the west across a low col, on Kings Weston Hill. Perhaps the actual route turned up from the gorge and crossed the col. It is not certain if this trio marks the continuation of the route across the Avon or an independent route from the north or even from across the Severn.

The series of fortresses outlined above is continued eastwards and northwards to connect with those on the Cotswold escarpment, Buryhill Camp at Winterbourne being one of these links. The excavations there showed its main structures to be very late in date. Between Bristol and Wotton-under-Edge is a number of works of varying strength. Abbey Camp is a large work lying east of Thornbury and there are several others, some quite large, between the Severn and the Cotswolds. Perhaps the most important of these is the one in the extreme north-west of the area at Oldbury-on-Severn on the banks of a navigable pill. The camp presents several interesting features, including ditches on the landward side which were probably left stopped so as to hold water permanently and not be tidal. There is on the east side of the camp a levelled area which looks as if it may have been the original quay. On the opposite side of the Severn, a little way up on the right bank of the Wye, is another camp similarly situated, and not so very far south is yet another at Sudbrook. It looks very much as if these were the trading ports of the area in Iron Age times.

In this brief account major works have been described. There are other works of varying strength and size which are so sited as to be tactically indefensible. Perhaps they were in the nature of cattle kraals for the seasonal round-up of the herds, as has been suggested for similar types of works in Devon and South Wales. Into this category fall the works at Elborough Hill, near Hutton, the one north of Rodney Stoke Woods, the ones in Long Bottom and on the south slope of Rowberrow Warren, Blackdown and perhaps one of the two works at Charterhouse. Some of the feebler works round Bath probably belong in this category. Another series of works lies between Cadbury Camp (Wrington) and Backwell overlooking the road from Bristol to Weston on the spurs of the high ground east of that road. At the northern end is Cheston Combe with a small but strongly sited work. At the bottom of Badger Combe close by is a small rock shelter that yielded a number of burials of the Iron Age. Next in the series is Tap's Combe Camp with its rather feeble single rampart tactically poorly sited and its most unusual projecting funnel-shaped entrance. Brockley Combe, a major valley, has no defensive works at all but next again is Cleeve Combe with a feeble work on each side poorly sited. Then comes the real fortress of Cadbury Camp. This series has something in common with those between the Severn and the Cotswold escarpment and excavations will probably prove them to be all of one date.

'C' Period

Belgic influences are clearly discernible in the later stages of the 'B' period. Glastonbury village was burnt about this time but it is possible that this was accidental. It is generally assumed that the village was sacked by the Belgae, but Dr. Bulleid was at pains to point out that the distribution of the human remains did not support the theory of the village's having been sacked and the inhabitants slaughtered. Perhaps the Romans arrived in time, established peace, and brought to an end further movements of the Belgae into the area and also the necessity for lake villages and fortified camps.

ACKNOWLEDGEMENTS

In the preparation of this chapter the gazetteer contained in Mrs. Dobson's *The Archaeology of Somerset* has been a useful source of references. Dr. Taylor and Mr. Sykes have helped by giving me information about sites not yet published and Mr. Grinsell has helped me in discussions on the subject-matter. To all these I wish to express my thanks.

BOOKS FOR FURTHER READING

CHILDE, V. GORDON. *Prehistoric Communities of the British Isles*. London, 1949.
CLARKE, J. GRAHAME. *The Mesolithic Age in Britain*. Cambridge, 1932.
—: *Prehistoric Europe*. London, 1952.
DOBSON, D. P. *The Archaeology of Somerset*. London, 1931.
PIGGOTT, STUART. *Neolithic Cultures of the British Isles*. Cambridge, 1954.

PLATE XVI. *Part of a wooden tablet bearing traces of writing in ink found at Chew Park Farm, 1954. (Crown copyright reserved, Ministry of Works.)*

PLATE XVII. *Mosaic pavement in dining-room at Chedworth Villa showing figure depicting one of the Four Seasons.*

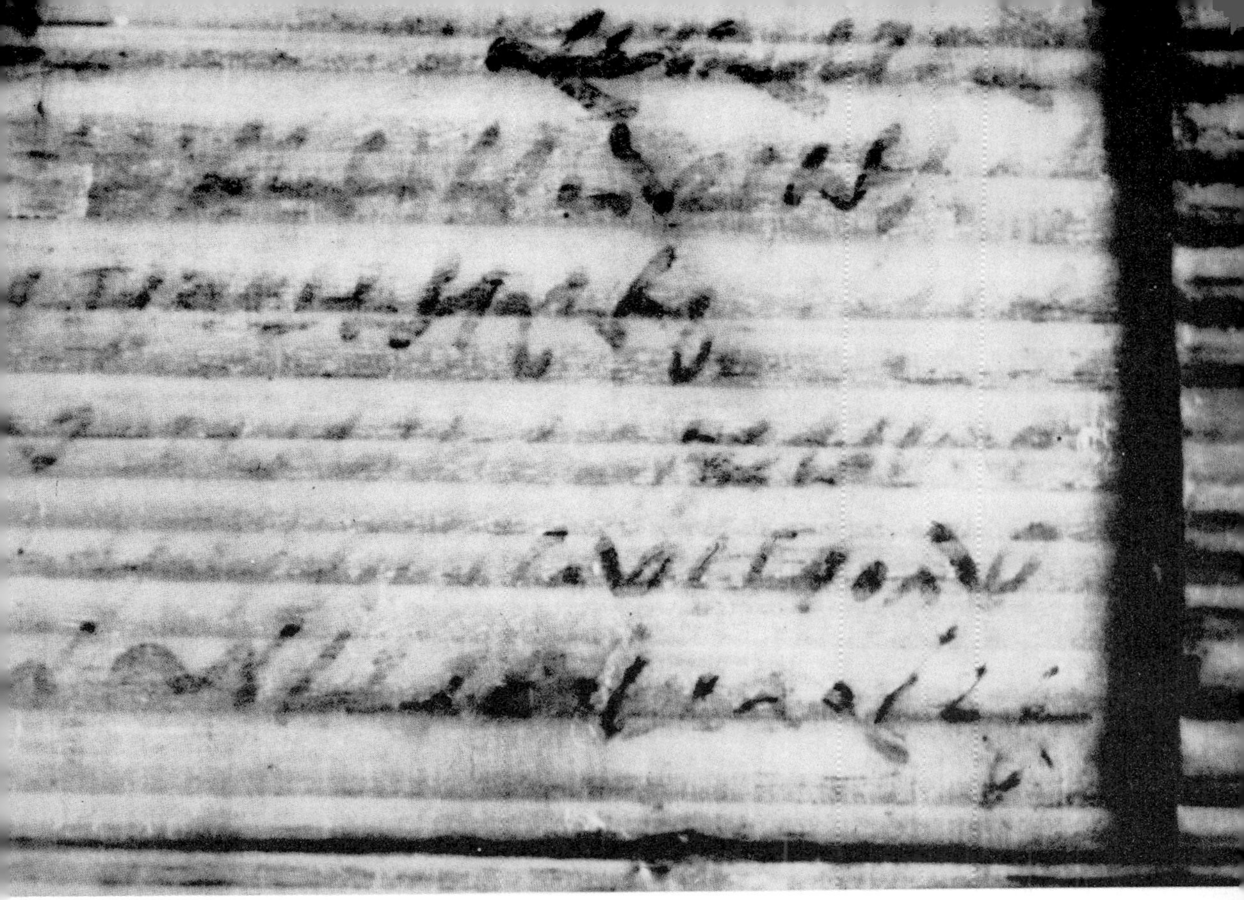

[*By permission of The Society for the Promotion of Roman Studies.*]

CHAPTER TEN

THE BRISTOL REGION IN THE ROMAN PERIOD

'FORTIFIED so near the close of the Roman era in Britain, and having a city (Aquae Solis) graced with beautiful temples and possessing every luxury, within half a day's march, it is not surprising that Bristol cannot—like her sister city—point to her architectural relics as proof of her Roman origin.' Nicholls and Taylor, who published this statement as recently as 1881 in their book, *Bristol: Past and Present*, must not be blamed too harshly for attempting, like their predecessors, to find for Bristol a pedigree comparable with that of Bath. Needless to say, their attempt failed: there is no evidence that Bristol was the site of a Roman town.

On the other hand, what may be regarded for the purposes of this chapter as the Bristol region contains a rich variety of Roman sites. This region consists of south Gloucestershire and north and east Somerset. References will be made also to the Monmouthshire shore of the Severn because it was closely linked to the Gloucestershire side of the river. But for the Roman army's activities beyond the Severn, it is possible that no Roman trunk road or Roman port would have existed in the immediate neighbourhood of Bristol.

The region thus defined includes the sites of one or perhaps two tribal capitals, a military colony, a legionary fortress, a spa, a mining centre, and numerous villas. These provide an illuminating commentary on many phases and aspects of the Roman occupation of Britain, and their place within the history of Roman Britain will be indicated, so far as is possible, in the following summary.

Aulus Plautius' first campaigning season in Britain ended late in A.D. 43 with the entry of the Emperor Claudius into Colchester. The army was then divided into three groups; and in the following season one of these, the Second Legion (Augusta), commanded by the future Emperor Vespasian, set out to subdue the south-west. The legion and its auxiliary troops fought thirty pitched battles, overran the Isle of Wight, and stormed more than twenty hill-fortresses, including the greatest of all, Maiden Castle, near Dorchester. In the Cotswolds, several oblong camps, such as those at Rodborough, near Stroud, and on Lansdown, outside Bath, may have been used by the Romans at this time. Although little is known of the details of Vespasian's campaigns, it is clear that within a few years much of what we have described as the Bristol region was in Roman hands. By 47 the Second Legion was close to the Severn; and shortly after this a base-fortress seems to have been established by it at Kingsholm, in the northern outskirts of Gloucester.

PLATE XVIII. *Mosaic pavement from a Roman villa at Low Ham, Somerset, depicting scenes from the story of Dido and Aeneas.*

Occupation was rapidly followed by more settled conditions. By 49, the date of the earliest inscribed pig of lead from Mendip, the mines there were working under Roman management; and the earliest Roman town in the region, Cirencester (Corinium), appears to have been founded before the end of Claudius' reign (A.D. 54). Cirencester was intended to serve as the capital and market-town of the Dobunni, the largest tribe of the region, with territories covering Gloucestershire and parts of Oxfordshire, Wiltshire, and possibly Somerset. As the administrative and commercial centre of this wide area the town prospered. Roman Bath (Aquae Sulis) probably came into existence somewhat later: the earliest dateable inscription belongs to the year 76. Bath was simply a spa and compared with Cirencester was small. Its reputation, however, grew and visitors came to it from overseas.

Meanwhile the road system, that most typical of Roman institutions, was taking shape. At an early stage Cirencester and the fortress at Gloucester must have been linked to the rest of the province by a road which left the highway from London to Exeter at Silchester (Calleva) in Hampshire. Long stretches of this road are still in use. At Speen, close to Newbury, a road diverged from it leading to Bath by way of the small town of Mildenhall (Cunetio). These two roads were intersected at Cirencester and Bath respectively by the Fosse Way running on a south-westerly course from Lincoln to Devonshire. The Fosse Way in its turn was crossed sixteen miles south-west of Bath by a road from the Mendip mines, and at a similar distance beyond this point passed through a Roman settlement at Ilchester, which may have become the capital of a local tribe.

The date and purpose of the Fosse Way are disputed. There is a theory that it was built about A.D. 47 as a patrolled barrier for the protection of those parts of Britain already overrun. In its extant form, however, it seems to be antedated by the ground-plans of several Roman towns lying on its route, namely Bath, Cirencester and Leicester. On balance it appears probable that the Fosse Way was constructed in several sections, all or most of which were laid out towards the end of the first century or later to serve civil, not military, needs.

Doubt also attaches to the date of the road which led from Bath by way of the northern suburbs of Bristol to a port on the Avon at Sea Mills (Abona), three miles from the mouth of the river. From here points on the Monmouthshire side of the Severn could be reached by ferry. The site has yielded coins and pottery which suggest that it may have already been occupied during the reign of Claudius. In this case, the road and port would have been used in support of the desultory and largely indecisive operations carried out by Ostorius Scapula against the Silures of South Wales in the years A.D. 49–52. The Romans may have exploited this approach to Monmouthshire from the first so as to avoid the awkward terrain of the Forest of Dean and the lower reaches of the Wye. The road which took this route branched off from one which led from Gloucester towards Monmouth and must therefore have been an afterthought. It is not unlikely, then, that Sea Mills and the road connecting it with Bath came into use in the middle of the first century. What is almost beyond doubt is that both port and road were an indispensable adjunct to the permanent occupation of South Wales by Julius Frontinus.

This began in A.D. 75. In that year, the Second Legion, after a period of inactivity, proceeded to settle accounts with the Silures. Soon it established itself in a permanent fortress at Caerleon-upon-Usk (Isca). Here the ramparts were originally of clay and the buildings of wood; but some twenty-five years later the buildings were reconstructed in stone and the ramparts faced with a stone wall, and in this form both are partly visible to-day, along with the impressive amphitheatre outside the fortress. Traces of a flourishing civil settlement which was laid out not far away have recently been revealed by excavation.

Soon after the occupation of Caerleon a town was founded eight miles to the east at Caerwent (Venta Silurum). This was to be the tribal capital of the conquered Silures and to introduce them, on however small a scale, to such amenities as a civic centre, stone houses, and baths.

The establishment of the legionary fortress at Caerleon meant the abandonment of that at Gloucester. However, during Nerva's reign (A.D. 96–98), a settlement for retired legionaries was founded on a site which was to be the nucleus of the modern city. This new military colony (Gleuum) remained small in comparison with the three other 'coloniae' of Britain (Colchester, Lincoln, and, later, York), and seems to have been less prosperous than they were, perhaps because of the proximity of Cirencester.

Cirencester, indeed, became the second largest town in Roman Britain, and its outstanding progress helps to explain why no Roman Bristol came into being to make the dreams of local antiquarians a reality. There was little scope for further urban development within the region. Indeed, by the end of the first century most of the region's major features can be traced, and the last three centuries of Roman rule may be treated more briefly.

During the second and third centuries, life in the region must for the most part have been settled and secure. Many villas arose to bear witness to the well-being of the country estates administered from them. In the north of the region villas are numerous in the districts of the Cotswolds around Cirencester, Gloucester and Stroud; and again farther south, in the Avon Valley near Bath and Bristol and along hillsides and valleys to the west and south of Bristol. To the north-east of Bristol, in an area which may have been thickly wooded, they are rare. Still farther south, there are many villas in the neighbourhood of Ilchester and Somerton. Three that are among the largest in the country lie within the region, at Woodchester near Stroud, Chedworth near Cirencester (See Plate XVII), and Keynsham near Bristol.

Two discoveries of exceptional interest have been made at villas in recent years. At Chew Park Farm, ten miles south of Bristol, wooden tablets bearing the earliest writing in ink so far known in Britain were found in 1954 in a well. These are thought to be legal documents. A clearer, indeed a unique, link with Latin literature came to light in 1945 at Low Ham, near Langport, in the form of a remarkable mosaic depicting scenes from the story of Dido and Aeneas based on Virgil's narrative (See Plate XVIII).

The building of villas reached its climax in the last half of the third century. But already there were signs of trouble. Ten coin hoards found in north Somerset and dated to the years 287–96, when the usurpers Carausius and Allectus controlled Britain, indicate that at that time the Bristol Channel was threatened by raiders from Ireland. On this occasion, effective measures, such as the establishment of a naval station at Cardiff, were taken; just as similar stations were built on the east and south coasts to repel Frankish and Saxon pirates. The danger passed, and the countryside flourished for another half-century. Then in 367 Britain was attacked on three sides by the Franks, Saxons, Picts and Scots, and plundered far and wide. Many villas were ruined or abandoned. The one at Kings Weston, near Bristol, was inhabited only by squatters after this date. Some that survived, like that at Hucclecote outside Gloucester, may have escaped merely because they lay close to a town.

This was a heavy blow to the villa and its economy. As for the towns, many of them had long been decaying as the countryside prospered. But their decline was by no means simultaneous or universal. Cirencester appears to have retained some of its vitality in the fourth century, possibly as the capital of one of the small provinces into which Britain was now divided. Late in this century the inhabitants of Ilchester still had enterprise enough to build a town wall.

But soon the ties that linked Britain to Rome were breaking as troops were withdrawn to meet attacks elsewhere or help usurpers stake their claims. In 410 the Emperor Honorius told the communities of Britain that they must arrange for their own defence. This may not have been the end of the Roman occupation, but at least it foreshadowed the end, and all western Britain must soon have been left to its own devices.

Thus the history of the region in the Roman period runs a hesitant course from one uncertainty to another. And yet, these uncertainties are luminous when they are seen against the darkness of the succeeding age.

From this brief historical account of Roman Britain, we pass to a survey of the Roman sites in the Bristol region. Urban settlements, beginning with Ilchester in the south, and ending with Cirencester in the north-east of the region, will be considered first.

Ilchester lies on the Fosse Way thirty-three miles south-south-west of Bath. The earliest settlement, dating from A.D. 55–60, was one of wattle-and-daub huts surrounded by a ditch and an earth bank. Before the end of the first century, the huts and the bank were removed, and the ditch filled in to make way for a new layout with paved streets and solidly built stone houses. At an unusually late date, towards the end of the fourth century, 32 acres of the site were enclosed within a Lias wall 3 ft. thick. Coins indicate that the occupation may have continued into the fifth century.

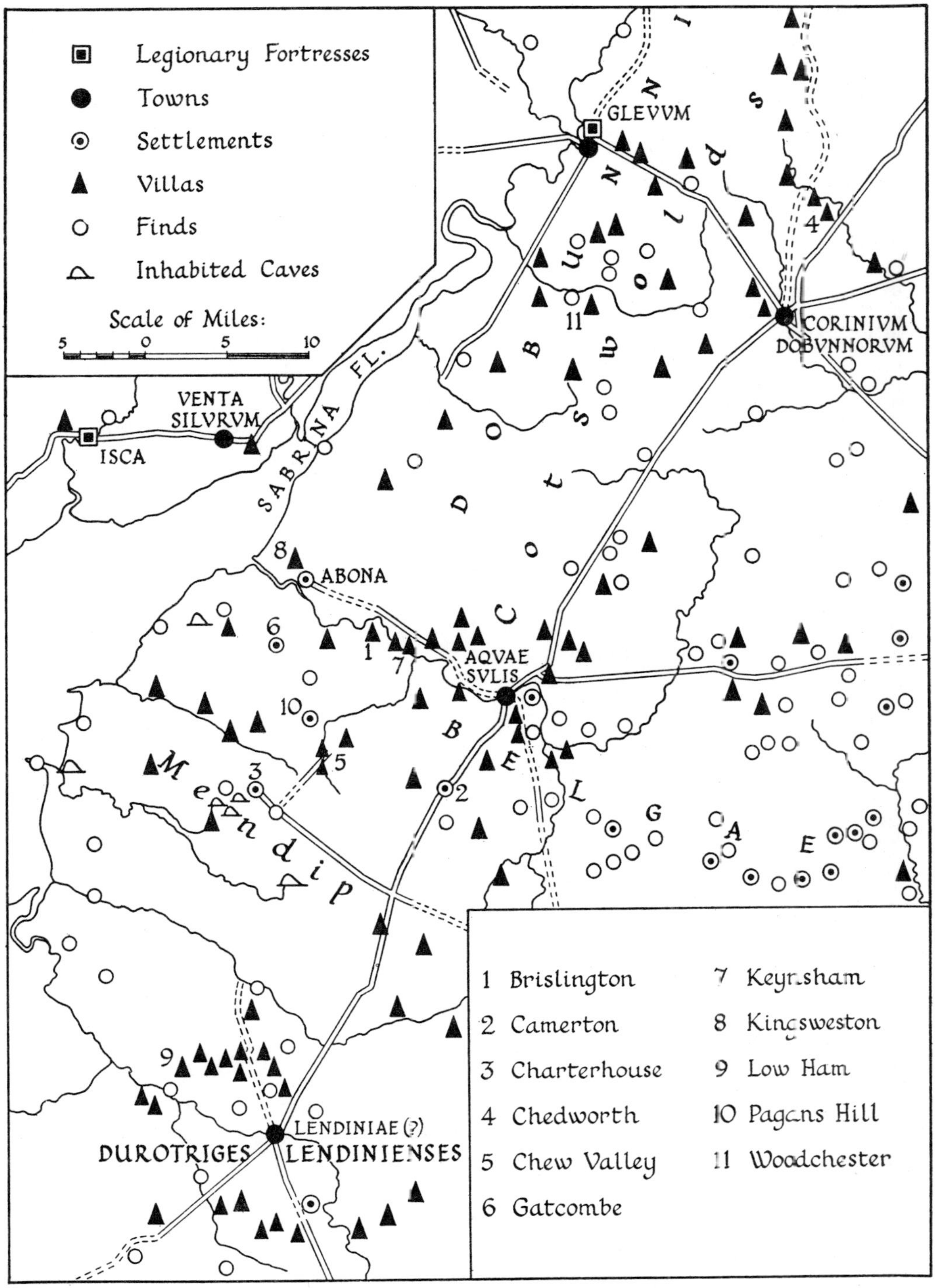

FIG. 21. *The Bristol region in the Roman period.*

The Latin name, sometimes given as Iscalis on the strength of a reference in Ptolemy, is now thought to have been Lendiniae. The town may have become the capital of a section of the Durotriges, namely the Durotriges Lendinienses, who are mentioned in two inscriptions from Hadrian's Wall, while Dorchester, to which a road ran south-south-east from Ilchester, remained the capital of the rest of the tribe.

Some twenty-six miles north-north-east of Ilchester and seven miles from Bath a British settlement lay on a limestone plateau close to Camerton. The site was first explored in 1814. Recent excavations have shown that the settlement became romanized during the first fifty years of the occupation of Britain, and that it continued to develop on either side of the Fosse Way. The earliest stone houses were built about A.D. 120. Rather more than a century later, simple rectangular houses were built for workers engaged in iron-smelting and the making of pewter. Two other buildings belong to the late fourth century. Thus the site appears to have been occupied throughout the Roman period.

From Camerton the Fosse Way continues to Bath (Aquae Sulis: the better manuscripts of the Antonine Itinerary give 'Sulis' and not 'Solis').

It seems probable that in general the outline of the walls of Roman Bath coincides with that of the medieval walls. They would thus have enclosed an irregular area of less than 23 acres. If with this we compare the 32 acres of the walled area of so modest a settlement as Roman Ilchester, and if we bear in mind that no remains of important buildings have emerged save those of the baths and a temple, it becomes clear that Roman Bath was primarily a spa presided over by the goddess Sul (or Sulis), as its name implies.

The date of the first settlement is not known; but two inscriptions, one of which probably belongs to A.D. 76 and the other certainly to A.D. 71–85, show that the spa was already well established in the early years of the Flavian period.

Neither the baths nor the temple have been precisely dated. The remains of both have been described by F. Haverfield[1] and by D. P. Dobson[2] and can here be treated only briefly and inadequately.

The baths, still unsurpassed among the antiquities of Roman Britain, were modified in important respects during their existence. Their central and most familiar feature, the Great Bath, was at first unroofed, except for the sidewalks and alcoves. Later, its twelve piers were strengthened so that the whole structure could be covered. A fountain appears to have provided only fresh cold water: the standard treatment was by immersion. To the north-west of the Great Bath are the hot springs; the main entrance to the buildings lay to the west and faced south, away from the modern Pump Room. To the east a conventional suite of vapour baths and cold douches was built at a date subsequent to the earliest period, and was later rebuilt on a larger scale. Possibly it was found that bathing in the hot waters was harmful unless it was followed by cold douches and massage, a precaution which is recommended by Pliny.[3]

[1] Haverfield, F. *Victoria County History of Somerset*, vol. i, pp. 229f.
[2] Dobson, D. P. *The Archaeology of Somerset*, pp. 145f.
[3] Pliny. *Nat. Hist.*, xxxi, 59.

The temple of Sul probably stood close to the west end of the baths. Sul was identified with Minerva, as we know from the third-century writer Solinus,[1] who also tells us that the everlasting fire in the temple did not form ash, but stony lumps. These were almost certainly coal, which could be readily obtained from outcrops near Bitton and Keynsham, a few miles west of Bath.

The temple was built on the classical model, a rarity in Britain. Its triangular pediment, resting on four columns, was decorated with carvings of Minerva's owl, helmet and shield, the last of which formed the centrepiece and was supported by two winged Victories. The most remarkable fragment is the boss of the shield. This is a Gorgon's head, duly equipped with snakes and wings in its hair, but also embellished, despite the usual notion of its sex, with a curling beard and moustache. Classical in its technique but far from classical in its spirit, it no doubt appeared barbaric, terrifying, and yet fascinating to many of the original visitors. For modern tastes its vigour and sense of form make it a memorable masterpiece.

According to Ptolemy, Bath lay within the territory of the Belgae, whose capital was Winchester (Venta Belgarum). They were probably a conglomeration of small Belgic tribes who pressed westwards in the period preceding the Roman occupation, and were then incorporated by the Romans into a single canton.

From Bath a road which formed part of Iter XIV of the Antonine Itinerary led to Sea Mills, near the mouth of the Avon. The text of the Itinerary here presents difficulties, which are discussed by F. Haverfield.[2]

The road left the London road at Walcot and ran westwards, first through Weston and then over the saddle between Kelston Round Hill and Lansdown, to Bitton. From here to St. George (two and a half miles east of the centre of Bristol) its route was that of the modern road. Its course for the next three miles through the northern suburbs of Bristol is uncertain. It probably crossed the main road to Gloucester at or near Arley Hill (one and a half miles north of the centre of the city), and followed approximately the line of Lower Redland Road and Elm Lane to the corner of Durdham Down at the top of Blackboy Hill. It then passed the site of the reservoir and continued in a straight line towards the house on the farther side of the Downs known as The Old Halt. Excavations carried out on this open stretch in 1900 showed that the road was from 20 to 25 ft. wide. Beyond this, the route, as it leaves the high ground, can be traced at the bottom of Pitch-and-Pay Lane and along Mariners' Path, a bridle track which ends close to Sea Mills. Directions are given on a board at the junction of Pitch-and-Pay Lane and Julian Road, so named from the title 'Via Julia' which was applied to the route from Bath to Caerleon by Bertram of Copenhagen in the eighteenth century.

To the Romans Sea Mills was known as Abona, the familiar reading of the Antonine Itinerary, Abone, being intended for the locative Abonae, 'at Abona'. The site lies on a sloping platform above the River Trym, where it flows into the Avon. It is three and a half miles from the centre of Bristol and three miles from the

[1] Solinus. *Collectanea*, xxii, 10.

[2] Haverfield, F. *Victoria County History of Somerset*, vol. i, pp. 347–8.

mouth of the Avon, from which its Latin name is taken. The foundations of a small building on the east side of the Portway are preserved, but most of the site is covered by prefabricated houses. Excavation has necessarily been limited. Nevertheless many objects have been found and are to be seen in the Bristol City Museum. These include a stone (inscribed SPES C SENTI and possibly a Christian tombstone), much pottery, and upwards of 650 coins belonging to all periods from the Late Republic to Honorius.

The importance of Sea Mills as a ferry station and the date of its earliest occupation, which may fall within the Claudian period, have been discussed in the historical summary (see p. 164). Below the settlement the creek formed by the mouth of the Trym provided an adequate harbour. From here ships could reach the wharves at Caerleon or a landing-place at Caldicot Pill, two miles from Caerwent, on the ebb and flow of the tide. Much of the traffic was no doubt with Caerleon, even though a single stamped tile of the Second Legion is perhaps the only evidence of this, but Caerwent must have had its share since the route of the Antonine Itinerary makes the crossing to Sea Mills from there.

The history of Abona is uncertain. There is some evidence of an intensive occupation from the Flavian to the end of the Hadrianic period. Here there may be a connexion with the presence of the Second Legion at Caerleon, before a large part of it was transferred to the north about A.D. 120. Coins indicate that the occupation of the site lasted for a considerable part of the fourth century.

Sea Mills may conceivably have been the starting-point of the road that entered Roman Gloucester from the south. There are, however, no certain traces of such a road within twenty miles of Sea Mills, although Cribbs Causeway, three miles away, bears a name that is suggestive. From the neighbourhood of Stroud Water, the course of the road is followed by the main Bristol Road, and in places by parish boundaries, for ten miles or so until it reaches Gloucester.

The earliest allusion to Gloucester (Gleuum, Colonia Neruia Gleuensium) belongs to the years A.D. 48–49. Among the events of these years Tactius[1] mentions that the warlike Silures had to be overawed by the building of a legionary fortress. Recently it has become clear that this semi-permanent base of the Second Legion was at Kingsholm, about half a mile north of Gloucester 'Cross'. The road from London by way of Cirencester is likely to have led at first straight to the Kingsholm site, its present course along London Road from Wotton to Northgate Street being a later diversion. The existence of the fortress has been deduced mainly from objects found at the site. Of its structure little is known. It was abandoned about A.D. 75, when Julius Frontinus advanced against the Silures and established the Second Legion at Caerleon.

At Gloucester there followed the building of a quay as a ferry station close to Lower Quay Street in the western quarter of the modern city. The diversion mentioned above seems originally to have led to this quay. At one point, in the neighbourhood of Northgate Street, the route passes a hillock, which became the site of a small civil settlement. This was the forerunner of the colony.

[1] Tacitus. *Annals*, xii, 32.

The foundation of the colony is dated by an inscribed tombstone at Rome, which gives its official title as Colonia Neruia (or Neruiana). This can mean only that it was established under the Emperor Nerva, in A.D. 96–98.

The walls enclosed a rectangular area of some 46 acres. Only those forming the eastern half of the rectangle can be traced with certainty. Gloucester 'Cross' seems to have been the main street-crossing of the colony: Roman paving lies beneath three of the streets (Northgate, Westgate, and Southgate) that radiate from it. In Westgate Street remains of a colonnade 200 ft. long have been found, but the position of the forum has not yet been established.

The citizens of the colony were time-expired legionaries who were settled there to afford security to the Dobunni, encourage obedience among the Silures, and further romanization in all directions. These aims the colony no doubt achieved. Economically, however, it did not match Cirencester, which at a distance of only seventeen miles, may even have flourished at its expense. Moreover, it lacked the vitality of the three other 'coloniae' of Britain. Of these Lincoln was at first slightly smaller, but eventually doubled its size. Yet Gloucester's simple mosaics point, if not to luxury, at least to comfort; and it was no doubt soundly administered by men such as the magistrates whose initials appear on the tiles made in the municipal workshops, and by others like the town councillor whose death at the age of eighty-six was recorded on a tombstone at Bath.

Cirencester (Corinium Dobunnorum), the tribal capital of the Dobunni, seems to have been founded before the death of Claudius (A.D. 54). Two tombstones of auxiliary cavalrymen, now in the Corinium Museum, may indicate that in the early period there was a short military occupation. Roman Cirencester was an important road-centre. Ermin Street, the highway from Silchester to Gloucester, ran through it from south-east to north-west. The Fosse Way and Akeman Street enter the town on the north-east, and the former leaves it at what was the south-west angle of the walls on its way to Bath. But the town tended to develop along Ermin Street, so that when, presumably in the second century, the town walls were built, they enclosed an irregular elongated area of 240 acres, measuring at its maximum 1,500 yds. by 900 yds. Thus among the towns of Roman Britain, Cirencester was second in size only to London. Its prosperity, which it owed to its position as the commercial centre of a large and flourishing area, is strikingly illustrated by numerous elaborate mosaics, some of them figured, as well as by the size of its basilica, or town hall. This was no less than 320 ft. long. Outside the walls to the south-west is an earth amphitheatre ('The Bull Ring'), the arena of which measures 148 ft. by 136 ft.

In the fourth century Cirencester may possibly have become the capital of Britannia Prima, one of the later subdivisions of Roman Britain. This is suggested by a dedication inscribed in the name of the governor on a stone which may have been the base of a sacred column. This inscription is preserved in the Corinium Museum. Here too is a relic of early Christianity, a piece of plaster incised with a word-square ROTAS OPERA TENET AREPO SATOR. The solution is as follows: PATER NOSTER should be written horizontally and vertically so as to form a cross, at the four extremities of which are placed the letters A O A O (alpha and omega repeated).

Of the villas in the region only a few can be described in a short survey. Those selected, together with certain other sites of special interest, are in the neighbourhood of Bristol.

The Kings Weston villa lies two miles north-west of Sea Mills and was discovered in 1947 when roads were being prepared for the Lawrence Weston estate. The eastern building, one of two separate structures, was excavated in 1947–48 and is partly preserved. It was built about A.D. 280 and was effectively occupied until the raids of A.D. 367–68, after which the site was taken over by squatters.

Little is known of the main block, which lies under a road. The wings, which project beyond the road, each consist of two rooms and were linked on the further side of a courtyard by a portico with a colonnade. This colonnade was later rebuilt as an arcade owing to a subsidence. Other alterations came to light. On the west side a small bath suite, originally consisting of two heated rooms, was equipped with a cold-bath chamber and a dressing-room; in the east wing, one room was provided with a hypocaust and the other partitioned to take a furnace. A room was also added on this side to balance the bath suite. These embellishments show how the prosperity of the countryside continued during the first half of the fourth century, only to be shattered by the disaster of 367.

The Brislington Villa was found and excavated in 1899 on a building estate two miles from the centre of the city, to the north-west of the junction of the Bath Road and Wick Lane. The building consisted of a main range of five rooms, the central room being paved with flagstones and treated as a small court. The two rooms to the east had mosaic floors, which are preserved in the Bristol City Museum, together with pewter jugs found in a well, and other objects. In front of the main range was a tessellated corridor, flanked at each end by slightly projecting wings. At the rear a second range of rooms, not completely recovered, included a bath suite. A few coins found on the site seem to show that the villa was built towards the end of the third century and ceased to be occupied some time after the middle of the fourth century. Burnt roof tiles indicate that it was destroyed by fire, perhaps during the raids of A.D. 367–68.

Near Keynsham, five miles south-east of Bristol, a villa, most of which lies beneath a cemetery and the adjacent road from Bristol to Bath, was partially excavated in 1922 and 1923, and was found to be one of the largest in Britain. It was built about A.D. 300 round three sides of a rectangle, the north and south wings being 206 ft. long, and the west wing 202 ft. The last was probably the main wing of the building. At each end of the west corridor there was a large hexagonal room paved with rich mosaics forming a complicated geometrical pattern. Some sections of these mosaics are preserved in Messrs. Fry's museum at the entrance to their Somerdale factory. Two panels depicting doves and fruit trees are particularly pleasing. The establishment was as opulent as it was large. In the Bristol City Museum there is a gold signet ring with a Greek inscription, 'Lucky is the wearer'. The ring must have fitted its prosperous owner in more senses than one.

In 1922 a second house was discovered three-quarters of a mile to the north-east, while the foundations of the Somerdale factory were being excavated. This building

FIG. 22. *Suggested reconstruction of the Roman temple at Pagans Hill, Chew Stoke.* (*By permission of the Somerset Archaeological and Natural History Society.*)

has been laid out close to the museum, where two coffins found near the original site are also to be seen. The house measures 54 ft. by 51 ft. For a villa the plan is unusually square, and for a private dwelling of this size the bath-suite is unusually large. Possibly it was a bath-house.

At Gatcombe Farm, Flax Bourton, five miles west of the centre of Bristol, preliminary investigations carried out in 1954 exposed one room of a building and what appeared to be the massive foundations of a wall which were 15 ft. thick. The wall was thought to be part of the defences of a small Roman town, the area of which was estimated at 12 acres.[1]

Seven miles south of Bristol and a mile from Chew Stoke is Pagans Hill. This version of the name is modern and has nothing to do with the temple excavated there in 1949–51.

The ground-plan of the temple was found to be similar to that of other Romano-Celtic temples, in that it forms two concentric figures, which in this case are octagons. There was thus an inner area, the maximum diameter of which was 26 ft., surrounded, however, not by the usual veranda, but by a closed ambulatory, 9 ft. wide. This is a rare feature. To the left and right of each of the eight corners of the ambulatory stood a buttress; and to each of these eight pairs of buttresses a pair of arches springing from a pier or a pillar at the adjacent corner of the inner area may be supposed to have transmitted the thrust of the high central roof (Fig. 22).

The temple seems to date from the late third or early fourth century. By about A.D. 340 part of it had collapsed, and the debris was deposited in a nearby well, which has also yielded pottery, coins, and an unusual specimen of glass. Thirty or forty years later, the temple was repaired and a substructure placed in the central area, possibly to serve as a mounting for the object of worship. The occupation extended at least to the end of the fourth century. The temple had some facilities of its own. Two buildings, each 75 ft. long, flanked the pathway leading to the temple. The arrangement of these buildings suggests an unusually ambitious attempt to provide an impressive approach to the precinct.

About three miles to the south of Pagans Hill, several Roman sites which will eventually be inundated by a new reservoir, the Chew Valley Lake, have been excavated since 1953.

The largest of these, at Chew Park Farm, had been occupied before the Roman period, and in the Roman period was intensively settled from a time soon after the conquest until about A.D. 300. In the first and second centuries, there existed here several wooden buildings, including a large farmhouse, as well as drainage ditches covering the 20 acres of the site. In the third century, there were more wooden buildings, these being associated with iron-smelting; and towards the end of the same century, a lime-kiln was built, possibly to supply lime for a simple stone villa of the corridor type which was soon to be constructed. This villa was occupied effectively for only a short time, although it was used as a shelter throughout the fourth century. In the adjacent well many objects were deposited, and these have been recovered in an excellent state of preservation. Among them are such rarities as fruit, seeds, leaves, leather, and uncorroded ironwork. Here too were found the wooden tablets which were mentioned elsewhere (p. 165) as bearing the earliest traces of writing in ink known in this country. These are thought to be legal documents of the early third century (see Plate XVI).

[1] *Bristol Evening Post* and *Bristol Evening World*, 20 October 1954; *Western Daily Press*, 21 October 1954.

At Herriotts Bridge, one mile south of this site, there was a Roman settlement of 15 acres which, like the neighbouring settlement, contained wooden buildings and was drained by ditches. Here, however, the occupation was less intensive, and in the third century the dwellings were merely huts or tents. A third Roman site, at Golds Cross, also appears to have been a large farming establishment.

It is possible that the farms in the Chew Valley supplied the mining settlement at Charterhouse-on-Mendip, which lay five miles to the south-west. There are indications that a road running by way of Stratford Lane and the Mendip slopes to the Fosse Way–Charterhouse road connected the two areas.

The site at Charterhouse lies on both sides of the modern road from Blagdon to Cheddar, to the north of the old school house. Here, at a height of more than 800 ft. above sea-level, a bleak hillside falls gently in an easterly direction to the Blackmoor Valley, the bottom of which is full of modern mining refuse. In this valley the ore was mined and washed. There is no evidence of underground workings; and this is hardly surprising when we remember that according to Pliny[1] Britain possessed the richest surface-deposits of lead in the Roman Empire.

The houses and smelting-furnaces, or some of them at least, lay to the west of the valley on the further side of the modern road. Our knowledge, such as it is, of this part of the site comes largely from the exploitation by a mining company of refuse, impregnated earth, and lumps of ore in the Town Field from 1867 onwards. During these operations, rough furnaces and the foundations of buildings were found, but not surveyed. However, among the objects discovered were numerous brooches, a long series of coins, several engraved gems, three fragments of inscribed stones, and a miner's lamp of lead. To the north of this area a Roman field-system was recently found.

Two earthworks may be mentioned. One of these, a rectangle, lies in Town Field and, to judge from a recent aerial survey, seems to have surrounded some kind of structure. The other, the so-called amphitheatre, lies to the north-west of the Town Field on the lower slopes of Blackdown, and within its bank measures 105 ft. by 80 ft. The bank still stands about 5 ft. high. In it there are three gaps, of which two, to the east and west, may be original. This bank may have been constructed in the Roman period. It may, however, be a cockpit of a more recent date.

Of the lead produced at Charterhouse, some was no doubt exported from Britain: a pig of lead found in northern France will be mentioned later. But some of it seems to have been used locally on a lavish scale. At Bath, the lead sheets of the Great Bath, each measuring 5 ft. by 10 ft. and weighing 30 lb. to the square foot, were probably made of Mendip lead. The same may well be true of the thick lead lining of one of two stone coffins found at Somerdale.

The Romans, however, valued the lead-mines of Britain as a source not only of lead, but also of silver. The inscription on a pig found at Charterhouse and weighing 171 lb. includes the words EX ARG(entariis), which imply that the lead from which the pig was cast had been treated for the extraction of silver. This practice must

[1] Pliny. *Nat. Hist.*, xxxiv, 164.

have been general since other pigs which do not bear this guarantee have proved on analysis to have been treated in the same way.

From inscribed pigs such as this something can be learnt of the history of the Charterhouse settlement. One pig, found between Charterhouse and Blagdon, bears the name of Britannicus, the son of Claudius, and the initials of Veranius and Pompeius, who were consuls in A.D. 49. From this we may suppose that the mines were working under Roman administration within six years of Aulus Plautius' landing. The same year, A.D. 49, was the date of another pig found over four hundred years ago near Wookey Hole and lost some time after its inscription had been published by Leland in 1544.

During the early phases of the conquest, the mines may have been under military control. A pig discovered at St. Valéry-sur-Somme, where it had probably been brought from Mendip, bears the names of Nero and of the Second Legion. Later, when the Legion was stationed in Wales, the mines were no doubt placed in charge of an imperial overseer (procurator).

The latest inscribed pigs from Charterhouse belong to the years A.D. 164–69, but the coins show that the settlement was occupied at least until the early part of the fourth century.

Some mining was carried out in other parts of Mendip. Near Hunter's Lodge Inn, four miles south-east of Charterhouse, excavations recently brought to light rough masonry, pieces of smelted lead, and—an obvious pastime in such isolation—gaming counters.

The chief link with the rest of the province was the road leading from Charterhouse to the Fosse Way, which was reached at Beacon Hill, two miles north of Shepton Mallet. Whether the road extended eastwards from the Fosse Way as far as Old Sarum is not fully established. West of Charterhouse no traces of a Roman road have been found. Lead exported to Wales may normally have travelled by way of the Bristol Avon; and indeed two pigs were found in its tributary, the Frome, at Wade Street, Bristol, in 1865. With these, perhaps the most interesting of the Roman discoveries made in Bristol itself, this chapter may close.

ACKNOWLEDGEMENTS

The writer thanks Professor W. Beare and Mr. G. C. Boon for their helpful suggestions, Messrs. J. Stevens Cox, I. D. Margary, P. A. Rahtz, and W. J. Wedlake for supplying him with information, and Mr. Frank Walker for his assistance in preparing the map.

BOOKS FOR FURTHER READING

General:

DOBSON, D. P. *The Archaeology of Somerset*. London, 1931, pp. 130–60.
HAVERFIELD, F. *Victoria County History of Somerset*, vol. 1. London, 1906, pp. 206–371.

Charterhouse:

GOUGH, J. W. *The Mines of Mendip*, Oxford, 1930, *passim*.

Pagans Hill:
Proc. Somerset Archaeological Society, vol. 96 (1951), pp. 112–142.

GLOUCESTERSHIRE

Cirencester:
Archaeologia, vol. 69 (1917–18), pp. 161–209.

Gloucester:
Proc. Bristol and Gloucestershire Archaeological Society, vol. 55 (1933), pp. 55–104.
Journal of Roman Studies, vol. 32 (1942), pp. 39–52.
Archaeological Journal, vol. 103 (1946), pp. 68–74.

Sea Mills:
Proc. Bristol and Gloucestershire Archaeological Society, vol. 66 (1945), pp. 258–295; vol. 68 (1949), pp. 184–188.

Kings Weston:
Proc. Bristol and Gloucestershire Archaeological Society, vol. 69 (1950), pp. 5–58.

PLATE XIX. *The Admiralty seal of Bristol,* 1446 *(actual size). (Bristol Corporation.)*

PLATE XX. *The first city seal of Bristol, late thirteenth century (actual size). (Bristol Corporation.)*

Edwardus dei gra Rex
Anglie & ffranc & dns hibn. Ar-
chiepis Epis Abbtibz Priorbz Du-
cibz Comitibz Baronibz Justic Vice-
comitibz ppositis Ballis ministris & omibz aliis fidelibz
suis salutem. Sciatis qd cum p cartas nuper progenitorum
nrorum quondam Regum Anglie quas ad clausula licet
confirmavimus ... libertates & quietan-
cie dilcis nobis Burgensibz ville nre Bristoll
et eorum heredibz & successoribz put in eisdem cartis
plenius continet imppetuu sint concesse. Nos
ad supplicacoem dilcorum nobis maioris & coitatis
ville predce nobis asserancm eandem villam ptim
in com Glouc & ptim in com Somers situat
existere et licet villa pdca a villis de Glouc &
Ivelchestr ubi comitatus Assie Jure & Inquisitiones
coram Justic & aliis ministris nris in com predcis

CHAPTER ELEVEN

BRISTOL IN THE MIDDLE AGES

THE tall ship which rides proudly on the civic seal and arms of Bristol has more than symbolic significance in its history. No city of comparable importance in English life owed its rise to prominence more exclusively to successful commercial activity, and it was primarily economic enterprise which, before the Middle Ages ended, caused an observant Italian visitor to rank Bristol with London and York as one of the three important towns in the realm.[1] As has been seen in the previous chapter, Bristol lacked the Roman ancestry which made York and Canterbury already ancient and famous before we have any reliable evidence that this city was more than a settlement by the crossing of the Avon—the 'place by the bridge' which its name 'Bricgstow' implied. It owed nothing, as did Lincoln, to ecclesiastical connexions, for it was not the seat of a medieval bishop; nor was it, like Gloucester, the administrative centre of a shire. Strategically, and therefore politically, Bristol was not unimportant, especially in the century following the Norman Conquest, but it was essentially the geographical advantages of its situation exploited by the trading enterprise of its citizens which enabled it to overtake and outstrip its nearest counterparts, seaports like Southampton, Boston and Lynn, long before the discovery of the New World opened new horizons.[2]

The earliest evidence that Bristol was becoming in some sort a centre of commerce and exchange comes from the reign of Ethelred II (978–1016) when coins minted there suggest the presence of a royal mint within the township. The settlement in Ireland of the seafaring Norsemen acted as a stimulus to trade, and by the eleventh century Bristol men were making money from the export of slaves to Ireland. The vigorous intervention of St. Wulfstan of Worcester put an end to this trade in human flesh, but the connexion with Ireland remained a prop of Bristol's prosperity, and trade with that country formed a nursery of its overseas enterprise. As the natural point of departure for central and southern Ireland, the city played a large part in the preparations for Henry II's invasion of 1171. Bristol men were rewarded with special privileges in Dublin, which was given the liberties and customs of Bristol. In Dublin and Ulster, however, Bristol soon faced the commercial rivalry of Chester and the infant Liverpool, and it was rather with the great ports of the west and south that Bristol's economic connexions were closest. Bristol merchants had few English

[1] *An Italian Relation of England* (Camden Society, 1847), p. 41.

[2] The development of Bristol's overseas trade in the Middle Ages has been ably surveyed by E. M. Carus-Wilson, in her *Medieval Merchant Venturers*, 1954, pp. 1–98.

PLATE XXI. *Enrolment of Edward III's charter of* 1373 *in* Ricart's Kalendar (*reduced size*). (*Bristol Corporation.*)

competitors in their trade with the Irish ports of the west, such as Galway and Limerick, and with Cork, Ross, Kinsale, and above all the proudly free city of Waterford, they had profitable relations throughout the Middle Ages. Fish was the commodity in greatest demand with English importers, and from Ireland there came a great quantity in wide variety, from the humble herring in all its forms—fresh, salted or smoked (these last were the 'red herrings' of the Middle Ages)—to rarities such as porpoise, the tongues of which were a delicacy popular with royalty, and seals, by contrast regarded as fit only for sailors' stomachs. Hides, the raw material of the flourishing Bristol leather industry, corn, timber, cheap Irish cloth, and the already famous Irish linen were among the principal Irish imports to Bristol. But Ireland was richer then than she has been since, and Bristol found a ready market there not only for necessities such as salt and iron, but also for fine English cloth, worked leather, and a number of re-exported luxuries, especially spices.

A new direction was given to Bristol trade in the twelfth century, when the union of Gascony with the English crown opened south-western France to English traders on particularly favourable terms. It seems likely that Bristol merchants were prominent from the first among the English dealing with Bordeaux and Bayonne. Moreover, by contrast with the Irish trade, this was a commerce in which English vessels predominated. By 1350 Bristol had become the chief port of the Gascon trade, and was sending half or more of the whole English export of cloth to Gascony. In return Bristol men imported raw materials for the cloth trade, such as woad, alum and potash, a variety of delicacies for the table, and, above all, Gascon wine. Both in volume and value imports of wine bulked large in English commercial balance sheets: at the height of the trade, around 1440, some 3,000,000 gallons annually were shipped to England, or nearly one-third of the whole value of English imports, and in this staple trade Bristol occupied a commanding position.

It was but a natural extension of the Gascon trade for Bristol merchants to develop also useful commercial connexions with the western ports of the Iberian peninsula. Trade with Castile was often affected by that country's political alliance with France in the later Middle Ages, and this hostility gave every encouragement to piracy and privateering. Despite the risks, trade between Bristol and the seaports of Biscay and Santander remained brisk, increasing in volume after the end of the Hundred Years War brought improved relations between England and Castile. By Henry VII's time Bristol was evidently regarded as one of the chief ports for Spain. Castile had much to offer the Bristol merchant: wine, oil, foodstuffs, iron and a variety of raw materials were in considerable demand. Bristol ships carried thither their characteristic bolts of cloth, corn, and, not uncommonly, pilgrims going to the famous shrine of St. James of Compostella. Vessels from Bristol seem to have formed part of the Crusading fleet, which, *en route* for the Holy Land in 1147, paused to help capture Lisbon from the Muslims. Thus were begun the friendly relations between England and the kingdom of Portugal which greatly assisted the development of trade, and here too, from an early date, Bristol seems to have claimed a large share. Portuguese ships were soon a familiar spectacle in the Bristol quays, bringing their cargoes of port, cork (for long obtainable only from Portugal) and sugar from Madeira, still an expensive rarity in the fifteenth century. From Portugal came also the 'grain' used to dye the brilliant scarlet cloth for which the West Country was justly famed; the dye was obtained from the cochineal-like insect called *kermes* found in the great oak trees of Portugal. Trade with Portugal expanded further during the check to the Gascon trade in the fourteen-fifties, and more was carried in Bristol ships as Portugal became increasingly concerned with her colonial ventures.

Bristol seamen thus early acquired an experience of the open Atlantic and its many perils. In their cogs and caravels, rarely of more than 500 tuns burden, and usually only half that size or less, they were not afraid of distant ventures and considerable risks. Such familiarity helps to explain their enterprising search for new markets and new horizons. In the early fifteenth century, they had much to do with reopening commercial connexions with Iceland and its valuable fisheries,[1] and when Columbus visited Iceland in 1477 in an attempt to find out what lay beyond, he found Bristol merchants predominant among the traders there. It has been suggested as not wholly unlikely that Bristol ships may have reached Greenland before 1494.[2] To the south they had hopes of establishing a direct trade with the Levant, despite the jealousy of the Italian cities, which regarded the Mediterranean as an Italian lake. The two adventurous voyages to the Mediterranean organized by the pioneer Robert Sturmy in 1446 and 1457 betray a novelty in conception and a bravery in execution which deserved a better fate than the shipwreck of the first expedition and the seizure of the second by the hostile Genoese. More than half a century was to pass before Bristol shared with London and Southampton in regular trade with the Mediterranean. Still more striking as an anticipation of the future was the remarkable venture launched from Bristol in 1480, when the *George* and the *Trinity* sailed out into the ocean in search of the 'Island of Brasylle' thought to lie to the west. After two months' search in the Atlantic, they were driven back to Ireland. Yet here was a direct inspiration for the voyages, similarly largely financed by Bristol merchants, of John Cabot, which resulted in 1497 and 1498 in the discovery of the continent of North America.

If these ambitious schemes brought little immediate profit to Bristol, the city's prosperity none the less owed much to the Atlantic outlook dictated by its geographical position, which directed its efforts away from the older centres of commerce towards new markets along the Atlantic coasts of western Europe. For this good fortune Bristol had reason to be grateful in the fourteenth and fifteenth centuries. For the traditional English overseas markets—the Baltic, Flanders and the Mediterranean lands—suffered during that period from war and political rivalry, with their attendant embargoes, protective customs barriers, and occasional confiscations.[3] Moreover, English trade with these regions was largely in the hands of powerful foreign merchants, particularly the Hansards and Italians, who used

[1] E. M. Carus-Wilson, 'The Iceland Trade', op. cit., pp. 98–142.

[2] J. A. Williamson, *The Voyages of the Cabots*, 1929, ch. 3.

[3] Power and Postan, *Studies in English Trade in the Fifteenth Century*, 1933, ch. I and ch. III.

their financial power to obtain favourable conditions from needy English kings at the expense of native traders. Bristol was fortunate, too, in that from an early date her principal export was cloth rather than raw wool, for the increasingly heavy taxation on the wool export of the eastern and southern ports combined with the labour troubles of Flemish and Italian cloth manufacturers to inflate the selling price of foreign cloth in the markets of Europe. Cloth of English manufacture, almost untouched by taxation, was thus able to compete on very favourable terms with foreign goods. It is in the operation of such economic factors that there lies the key to Bristol's rapid rise at the expense of its competitors. Apart from the temporary shock to the Gascon trade caused by the French conquest of Gascony in 1453, Bristol was able in large measure to avoid the depression from which much of English commerce suffered in the fourteenth and fifteenth centuries. By 1500 its position as the second seaport of England, inferior in the volume and wealth of its trade only to London, was unquestioned.

Bristol's prosperity, however, did not rest solely on its overseas trade. It soon became something of a regional metropolis, acting as entrepôt and centre of distribution for a wide area ranging from the far west of England to the upper Severn basin and from Wiltshire to South Wales. Wool and hides, coal and timber from Wales fed the industries as well as the commerce of Bristol; tin and fish were shipped from Cornwall for home consumption. It was of particular importance that the whole hinterland of the city became, after the invention of the water-powered fulling-mill in the late twelfth century, a thriving industrial area producing fine cloth, for which Bristol was the natural place of export. In like manner the foreign produce imported by Bristol was distributed through the channels of this thriving inland trade. As was natural in an age when overland transport was both slow and costly, it formed a great highway for this commerce: thus Gascon wine brought in by ocean-going ships to the 'Key' by the Frome was later transferred to the barge-like Severn trows for transport to Gloucester and Worcester, and thence often on by cart to Shrewsbury, Warwick and Coventry. Much of the produce of Bristol's own industries, too, found a home market in this regional empire: church bells and cannon from its foundries and soap and leather goods travelled along the same paths. There were commercial connexions also between Bristol and London and Southampton, where Bristol merchants bought and sold with the agents of the Baltic and Italian towns.

The economic expansion we have reviewed proved a potent factor alike in the topographical expansion of Bristol and in the development of its urban liberties.[1] Trade and commerce attracted a growing population to the city from Wales and Ireland as well as from the surrounding English countryside, and the profits of trade provided the inducements by which legal and commercial privileges were obtained from Bristol's feudal lords. The original settlement of the town lay upon the narrow

[1] Of the older general accounts of Bristol's domestic history, the most useful are S. Seyer, *Memoirs, Historical and Topographical, of Bristol* (1821–23), J. F. Nicholls, *Bristol Past and Present*, vol. i (Bristol, 1881) and the able sketch by W. Hunt, *Bristol* (1895). Bryan Little, *The City and County of Bristol: A Study in Atlantic Civilisation* (1954) is the most recent summary.

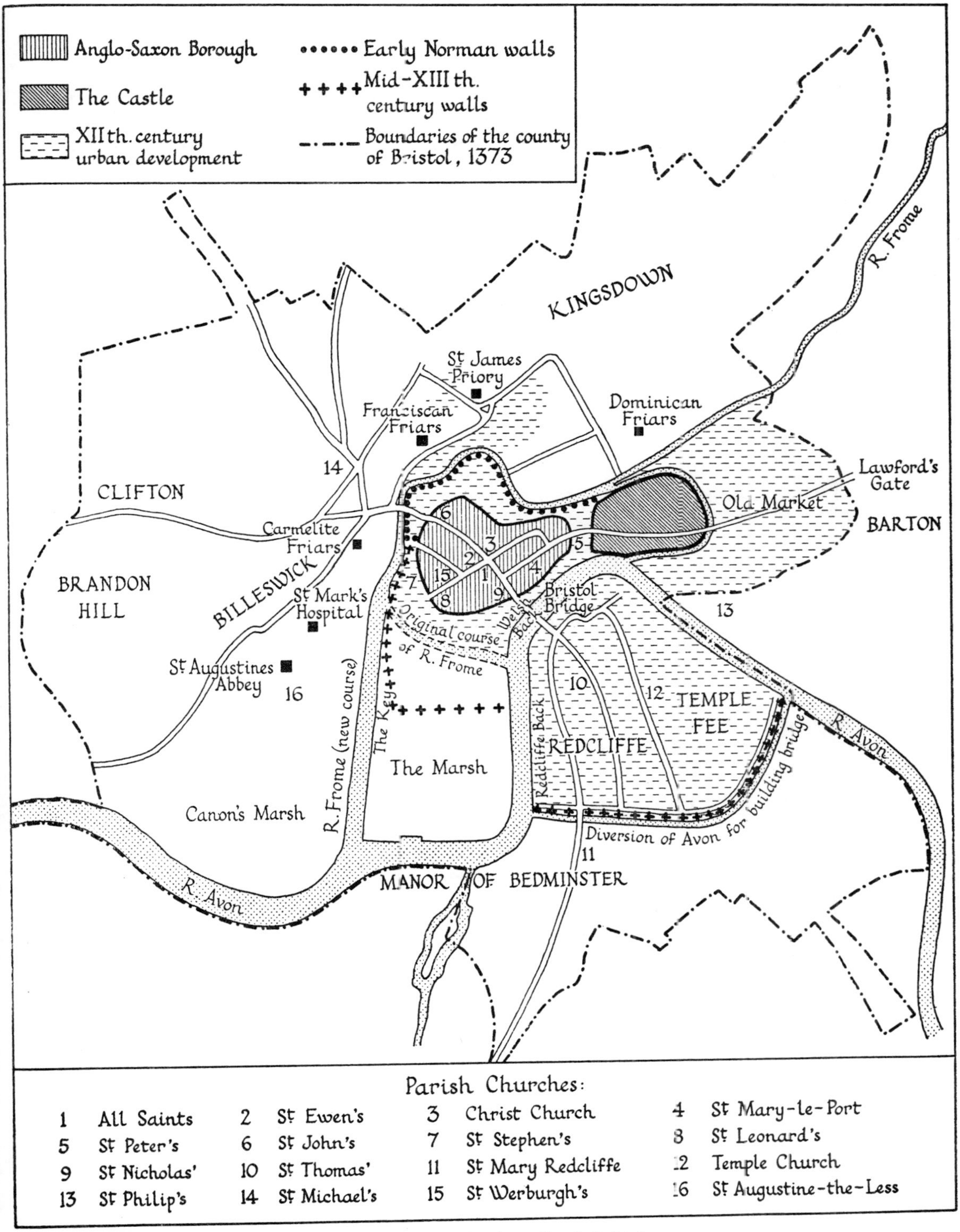

FIG. 23. *Growth of medieval Bristol.*

peninsula rising between the Avon on the south and the sweeping curve of the little River Frome where it was turned from its course to join the Avon by the triangular hill now called College Green. This area, rising sharply from the river banks, and surrounded on three sides by water, was well suited to defence, and commanded the lowest point at which the Avon could be conveniently bridged. The *burh* or borough which grew up there, fortified probably during the Danish wars, was strong enough to resist an attack by a fleet from Dublin, led by the sons of Harold, in 1068. The inhabited area formed a site less constricted than the Roman station at Sea Mills in the Avon Gorge had been, but which probably did not exceed twenty acres in the early eleventh century. It possessed also the great advantage of a good natural harbour, which, if not altogether easy of access, yielded safe anchorage and was served by strong tides; further, the harbour, once reached, was comparatively immune from attack by pirates and from foreign raids. Bristol's position on the frontier, as it were, between the western midlands and the western peninsula of England, combined with its access to the highway of the Severn and its proximity to Wales, enabled it, as we have seen, to aspire to a hopeful commercial future.

To the Norman conquerors of England, however, it was the strategic advantages of Bristol's situation which caused them to reinforce its defences by erecting a powerful castle filling the narrow neck of land between the *burh* and the higher ground to the north, like a stopper in a bottle. The castle lay just outside the walls of the borough, and to round off the defences the Normans built a further wall along the bank of the Frome enclosing the whole area behind fortifications.[1] Begun by the formidable Geoffrey, Bishop of Coutances, in the Conqueror's reign, the castle was held by him during his rebellion against William Rufus. On his death it passed with the lordship of Bristol to one of the most powerful of Norman lords, Robert fitzHamon, founder of Tewkesbury Abbey, and conqueror of Glamorgan, and from him by marriage to Henry I's natural son, Robert, Earl of Gloucester (d. 1147). Robert was the builder of the great stone keep of the castle, which became the administrative centre of his Honour of Gloucester. This in itself gave Bristol a certain importance; but since Robert was also the most powerful supporter of the Empress Matilda in the struggle for the throne during Stephen's reign, Bristol came to be the headquarters of the Angevin cause in the west. Here King Stephen was imprisoned in 1141, and here also Matilda's heir, the future Henry II, spent some years of his boyhood. Thus began a close and favourable connexion with the Angevin dynasty which was of considerable value to Bristol in the later twelfth century.

Except for a short period during the reign of Edward II, Bristol never again in the Middle Ages enjoyed such political prominence as it saw during the century following the Norman settlement. But the castle long remained a notable factor in the city's life. It was much used for the confinement of important political prisoners, such as John's potential rival, Eleanor of Brittany, and the deposed Edward II.

[1] The site and foundations of the castle were excavated recently after the bombing of 1940–41 demolished modern buildings above them: *see* K. Marshall, 'Excavations in the City of Bristol, 1948–51', *Trans. Bristol and Gloucs. Arch. Soc.*, vol. 70, (1951), pp. 5–50.

Furthermore, the authority wielded by successive constables as representatives of the king could not be ignored. In fact it was an alliance between Edward II's constable, Bartholomew Lord Badlesmere, and 'The Fourteen', the oligarchical clique which ruled the city, which fanned the resentment of the majority of the citizens into open insurrection. The so-called 'Great Rebellion' of Bristol was directed against the authority of Badlesmere: the citizens built a wall to protect them from the castle garrison and to cut off its supplies, and from 1314 to 1316 they defied all attempts to bring them to order. An attack by land from an army commanded by the Earl of Pembroke and a naval blockade conducted by Lord Berkeley were necessary to force their capitulation.[1]

Political disturbances, however, do not obscure the less ostentatious but steady growth of the borough of Bristol. The mid-eleventh century, it has been aptly said, witnessed the city's vigorous infancy.[2] Even the meagre entries in the Domesday Survey leave no doubt that by 1086 it was already, apart from its feudal connexions, a trading town of some importance.[3] By this date the walled borough contained four parish churches, St. Mary-le-Port, Trinity or Christ Church, St. Ewen's, and All Saints: a fifth, St. Peter's, stood just without the walls next to the castle, and had perhaps served as the parish church of the royal manor of Barton, of which Bristol itself was a part. But this limited area soon proved inadequate for the growing town, and population began to spill over into the surrounding countryside. The earliest suburb seems to have been immediately to the east of the castle, around the Old Market and Lawford's Gate, and the church of SS. Philip and Jacob was built to minister to the needs of the people there. Another settlement probably grew up close to the Benedictine priory of St. James, founded by Earl Robert of Gloucester about 1137. The fair granted to the monks soon became famous, attracting traders from all over the country. Of greater importance was the twelfth-century development to the south in Redcliffe in the parish of Bedminster. Here the flat, open land between the bridge and Redcliffe Hill offered a larger site than the walled borough, and the anchorage along the south bank of the Avon was deeper through the natural working of the current than at Welsh Back on the Bristol side. For a time indeed, Redcliffe, encouraged by its Berkeley lords, bade fair to rival Bristol itself. By 1158 a church dedicated to St. Mary, occupying a commanding position on Redcliffe Hill, was already serving the new suburb, although the earliest relics of the existing fabric are no older than 1190. The rapid development of Redcliffe may be measured in its liability to taxation: when King John demanded a special aid in 1210, the men of Redcliffe were assessed at 1,000 marks, exactly the same sum as Bristol itself. To incorporate these suburbs into the jurisdictional framework of the borough of Bristol presented its citizens with a formidable problem not finally solved until 1373, and then only after protracted struggle.

[1] Some aspects of the rebellion still require further investigation: the best account is by E. A. Fuller, 'The Tallage of 6 Edward II and the Bristol Rebellion', *Trans. Bristol and Gloucs. Arch. Soc.*, vol. 19, pp. 191f.

[2] H. A. Cronne (ed.), *Bristol Charters, 1378–1499*, Bristol Record Society, vol. xi, 1945, Introduction, p. 22.

[3] The probable farm which it paid to the king, £84, may be compared with the £300 of London and Middlesex, the £100 of York, the £76 of Chester, and the £60 of Gloucester, as testimony to its relative wealth.

Like other medieval trading communities, the men of Bristol continually sought from their feudal lords the special privileges and facilities necessary to allow a commercial organism to function in a society still predominantly agrarian in rhythm and outlook. There is good reason to suppose that successive Norman lords of Bristol, with the shrewdness characteristic of their race, were sufficiently aware of the advantages to themselves of a thriving trading town upon their domains to make some concessions to the burgesses' demands. Bristol's first royal charter, granted by Henry II in 1155, was no more than a just reward for the townsmen's loyal support of the Angevin cause. Its most important concession was the valuable privilege of freedom from toll for all Bristol burgesses throughout Henry's dominions in England, Wales and Normandy. The continuing good relations of Bristol with the Angevin house are reflected in the great charter of John, as Count of Mortain and Lord of the Honour of Gloucester, in 1188.[1] Stated in broad terms, John's charter exempted the citizens from the jurisdiction of all courts outside the walls of the borough, except in some aspects of royal jurisdiction and for matters concerning their property outside Bristol: they were now answerable primarily to their own borough courts, and were free of the delays and encumbrances of litigation in the feudal courts. Their guild merchant was officially recognized, their rights in mercantile matters assured, and restrictions were placed upon merchants from without. Finally, the nature of their tenurial rights was defined, and they were freed from the more burdensome aspects of seignorial control over their persons and tenements. So comprehensive were these privileges that, with some exceptions noted below, later charters added little;[2] and John's grant is rightly regarded as the foundation stone of Bristol liberties.

The charter of 1188 contained a clause defining the area in which these privileges were to be enjoyed: it included not only the borough but all the suburbs. Yet this extension of borough jurisdiction ran counter to powerful vested interests. The whole Bristol area once belonged to the king; the castle and the manor of Barton were retained by the crown after John's accession and in the later Middle Ages they became, together with the annual farm of Bristol, a part of the apanage of successive English queens. But the land immediately to the west and north-west of the walled borough, and that to the south side of the Avon, passed into private hands. Robert, Earl of Gloucester, gave the land near the modern Temple Meads railway station to the Knights Templar. This Temple Fee was speedily settled, as was the adjacent Redcliffe, and became a particular centre for weavers. Redcliffe itself, with the royal manor of Bedminster, passed by grant of Henry II to a man of humble origin but considerable wealth, Robert fitzHarding, founder of the second house of Berkeley in Gloucestershire. In addition to substantial estates around Berkeley Castle,

[1] Printed, with translation, in N. Dermot Harding (ed.), *Bristol Charters* 1115–1373, Bristol Record Society, vol. 1, (1930), pp. 8–13. Its significance is discussed by Professor Cronne, op. cit., pp. 57–70.

[2] The more important later royal charters were those of 1373, creating the county of Bristol, of 1396 limiting the power of the royal purveyors in the city, and of 1446, when the city was exempted from the jurisdiction of the court of admiralty: maritime cases were to be tried by special commission of which either the mayor or recorder should be a member. The citizens' long struggle for control of the farm of the borough is discussed by Cronne, op. cit., pp. 41–56.

FitzHarding also acquired the suburb of Billeswick by Bristol—now College Green—where he founded the Abbey of St. Augustine. FitzHarding and his successors defended their rights in Redcliffe and Bedminster with vigour against the pretensions of the Bristol burgesses, not without support at times from the men of Redcliffe and Temple, who were not wholly anxious to be absorbed by Bristol. The problem was further complicated by the way in which the crown continued to tallage Redcliffe and the Temple separately from Bristol, and by a conflict of county jurisdiction, the sheriff of Somerset claiming that the transpontine area lay within his jurisdiction, and the Bristol burgesses counter-claiming that Redcliffe and the Temple should answer Bristol before the king's justices in Gloucestershire.

What converted the technical unity of north and south Bristol into reality was the growing realization of common interests, especially in matters of trade, and their co-operation, not always voluntary, in large-scale joint enterprises. The early years of Henry III's reign saw the undertaking of three schemes of public works. Not without disagreements, the men of Redcliffe and the Temple worked with the Bristolians in the erection of a new wall enclosing all the inhabited area to the south of the river. About the same time, in 1239–40, the men of Bristol, perhaps with the intention of attracting trade from Redcliffe Back, decided to provide themselves with a new harbour. Their Avon anchorage suffered from the great difference in height between high and low tide, which often left ships stranded or capsized. To this end they negotiated with the Abbot of St. Augustine's for the purchase of his marsh to the west of the Frome's curve. Across it a new channel was dug for the river, deep and straight, due south to the Avon. This new anchorage, the 'Key', fortified with stone, became the usual mooring for ocean-going ships, and the Welsh Back and Redcliffe Back now took coasting and river vessels. Completed by a stone wall enclosing the new suburb in the marsh, this major venture cost the vast sum of £5,000. This also was a co-operative work, but it needed a royal order before the unwillingness of the men of Redcliffe to take their share could be overcome. Finally, the two halves of the city were drawn closer by the construction of a new stone bridge over the Avon. This, too, involved heavy labour, for the Avon had to be diverted through a new channel on the south side of the Redcliffe wall while the operation was in progress. Even if we had no other evidence, the successful completion of these undertakings would provide telling proof of the wealth and enterprise of thirteenth-century Bristol. Their value in unifying the city is evident, and we hear little more of rivalry between the citizens and the men of the suburbs after 1250.

The Berkeleys alone now obstructed the jurisdictional unity of the city, but it was not until 1331, after much litigation and violence, that a settlement was reached with these influential lords.[1] The issue was put beyond doubt by the charter of 1373. By this grant—the first of its kind—Edward III converted Bristol into a shire incorporate, with its sheriff and county jurisdiction. The citizens were now exempt from the control of the county courts of Gloucester and Somerset and their sheriffs.

[1] The fullest account of the connexion of the Berkeleys with Bristol is by John Smyth, *Lives of the Berkeleys* (ed. J. Maclean, 1883).

The boundaries of the new county included Redcliffe and the Temple, and the channel of the Avon out to the Steep and Flat Holms in the Severn Estuary. Among its other provisions, the charter of 1373 gave defined powers to the Common Council of the city, an elective body of forty, who were intended to act as counsellors to the mayors. Yet it would be a mistake to suppose that there was anything democratic in the city government of the Middle Ages. Effective power rested with the chief merchant families, leading members of the guild merchant: Bristol's mayors (the list of mayors begins in 1214), sheriffs, aldermen (who first appear in 1344) and members of parliament were chosen from and by this group. Municipal government under the Plantagenet kings remained essentially oligarchical.

We are fortunate in possessing a detailed description of the city of Bristol in the time of Edward IV from the pen of William Worcester, who was born here in 1415 and devoted much of his later life to a study of the topography and architecture of his native town.[1] Worcester, a scholar of distinction, has been unduly neglected, and has a better claim than John Leland to the title of 'Father of English Antiquities' usually bestowed on the Tudor scholar. It is clear from his account that by 1480 Bristol had not grown greatly in area, and the land enclosed by the thirteenth-century walls still housed most of its people. Indeed, as late as 1568, the pictorial map of William Smith (see Plate XXIV) shows the town as still essentially within these limits. The marsh between the Key and the Welsh Back had been largely built over, and a new parish church, St. Stephen's, had been erected to serve its inhabitants. North of the Frome, the houses had begun to climb a little way up the slopes of College Green and Kingsdown. Much of this hillside was occupied by the precincts and gardens of several religious houses, especially the great garden of the Carmelite Friars, which ran up as far as the modern Red Lodge. The open land called Lewin's Mead along the Frome's banks was probably built over at an early date; behind lay the modern Christmas Steps, which the Middle Ages more simply and aptly called 'Stepestrete', climbing towards St. Michael's Church, where the fifteenth-century tower points to a growing population in the late medieval period. A similar increase in population made it necessary to create a new parish in 1374 round St. James's Priory. The people of Billeswick in the precincts of St. Augustine's Abbey were provided with a new parish church, St. Augustine-the-Less, immediately against the east end of the abbey: here too the surviving fabric is mostly of the fifteenth century.

There are some indications that nearby villages—Clifton, Brislington and Stapleton—were enlarged from Bristol's growing population, but it is likely that the overspill was slight. Medieval townsmen did not insist on privacy and were not afraid of congestion, and proximity to a man's place of work was more important to him than it is to-day. There was as yet small tendency for the great merchants and tradesmen

[1] Ed. J. Nasmith, in *Itineraria Symonis Simeonis et Willelmi de Worcestre* (Cambridge, 1778). There is also a wealth of information on the social and religious life of Bristol in the fourteenth and fifteenth centuries in the city's two great medieval books of record, *The Little Red Book* (ed. F. B. Bickley, 1900, 2 vols.) and *The Great Red Book* (ed. E. W. W. Veale for the Bristol Record Society, 4 vols.) and in the mayor's register, *The Maire of Bristowe is Kalendar, by Robert Ricart*, ed. L. Toulmin Smith (Camden Society, 1872).

to move into the outer suburbs, still less to buy country seats, although some of them invested in land in adjacent counties. Almost all lived in the town, many in the fashionable area of Redcliffe, where they had space for gardens running down to the river. Here the celebrated William Canynges built his great house, timbered with Elizabethan elaboration, which impressed observers both by its size and by the novelty of its 'Bay-wyndowes', reflecting the latest taste of the time for light and air. Nearby Vyell Place, described by Worcester as a 'mansion of great stones', was also notable, for most houses were still of timber. Other merchants lived in towers upon the city walls, from which projecting chambers were built out—a practical use for fortifications now largely ornamental.

Congestion was greater still in the heart of the city, where narrow streets were made darker by the protruding fronts of houses built high for want of space, and the roads were made unsafe by the excavation beneath them of great cellars for the storage of wine and other merchandise.[1] When a merchant's widow, Alice Chester, built her house in High Street about 1472, its specifications allowed for a frontage of no more than 10 ft. 5 in. with a depth of 20 ft. Above the ground-floor shop was a hall with one of the new oriel windows, above this a chamber also with an oriel, and the fourth floor contained yet another chamber. To judge from the long series of surviving Bristol wills,[2] the interiors of these merchant houses were elaborately equipped with rich tapestries, expensive and ornate beds, quantities of linen and gold and silver plate—evidence of the wealth and rising standards of comfort of their owners. Few, however, of these secular buildings of the Middle Ages have survived to us: the Tolzey Court, built out on wooden pillars over the Old Market pavement, is an almost isolated exception.

To the modern observer from the heights of Kingsdown or Brandon Hill the most striking visible memorial of medieval Bristol is still the cluster of church spires and towers in the heart of the city. Despite the ravages of intervening centuries, these still contest the Bristol skyline with the gaunt modern office-blocks and factories, and are testimony to the vigorous and varied religious and social activity of the medieval community. Close-packed as these churches are, Bristol was notably less rich in parish churches than other cities of comparable importance: its sixteen churches compare poorly with the thirty-nine of fifteenth-century York or the forty-three of Norwich. But it possessed its full complement of religious houses—an abbey, two priories, four houses of friars (excluding the short-lived foundation of Friars of the Sack) and seven hospitals.[3] Credit for these foundations may be divided fairly equally between aristocratic patrons, who were responsible for most of the religious houses, and merchants and citizens, whose religious life centred mainly on the parish churches, although as in other towns the local friars benefited greatly from their patronage.

[1] E. M. Carus-Wilson, *Medieval Merchant Venturers*, pp. 73f.

[2] *Notes or abstracts of the wills in The Great Orphan Book and Book of Wills*, ed. T. P. Wadley (Bristol and Gloucs. Arch. Soc., 1886); *Somerset Wills*, ed F. W. Weaver (Somerset Record Soc., vol. xxi, 1905).

[3] Admirable accounts of Bristol's religious houses may be found in the articles by Rose Graham in *Victoria History of the County of Gloucester*, vol. ii (1907) *passim*.

We have seen that the Benedictine Priory of St. James was founded about 1137 by Earl Robert of Gloucester, who also rebuilt St. Ewen's Church; Robert fitzHamon performed a similar service for St. Peter's, and Earl William for St. Mary-le-Port. King John, while still Count of Mortain, established a Hospital of St. Lawrence for lepers near Lawford's Gate, but this remained small and poor despite its royal patronage, and in 1465 was given to the Dean and Chapter of the collegiate church of Westbury for the augmentation of their revenues. Pride of place among the ecclesiastical patrons of Bristol belongs, however, to members of the Berkeley family. By far the most notable religious house of medieval Bristol, the Abbey of St. Augustine, owed its origin to Robert fitzHarding, perhaps with some assistance from Henry II, who was later regarded as co-founder. FitzHarding's wife, Eva, made a parallel foundation for women in or about 1173, when she provided lands for a house of Augustinian canonesses dedicated to St. Mary Magdalen. The hospital of St. Mark, near St. Augustine's (its surviving church is now the Lord Mayor's Chapel on College Green), was founded early in the reign of Henry III by FitzHarding's grandsons, Maurice and Henry de Gaunt, and the former joined with Matthew de Gournay about 1227 in establishing the Dominican or Black Friars in Bristol. Berkeley patronage was responsible, too, for three hospitals, St. John's for the 'sick poor', St. Catherine's, Brightbow, and St. Mary Magdalen's for female lepers, all of which lay in the Berkeley manor south of the river.

It would be rash to claim that any of these houses enjoyed a particularly distinguished history. The small Priory of St. James was little more than a minor source of revenue to its mother-house of Tewkesbury. Its income in 1534 did not exceed £57 p.a., and it housed probably only three or four monks. Like most cells, it had an almost uneventful history. The Abbey of St. Augustine, by comparison, pursued a chequered career of litigation and recurrent financial embarrassment. Following the fashion of his day, Robert fitzHarding gave his support to the regular canons patronized by Henry I, and his new foundation was given to the Victorine branch of the Augustinian canons, who were distinguished for their learning and piety.[1] Consecrated about 1173, Bristol became the mother-house of a small group of Victorine abbeys in Somerset, the Abbey of Keynsham among them. St. Augustine's, unlike many other houses of regular canons, was neither too small nor too poor to maintain a satisfactory religious life. With extensive estates in Gloucestershire and Somerset, which yielded an annual income of £700,[2] it ranked among the 'greater abbeys' as they were defined by Henry VIII. So far as is known, however—for much of its history remains obscure—the Bristol house did little to maintain the Victorine tradition, and was often in trouble with its episcopal visitor, the Bishop of Worcester. None of its abbots after 1200 were notable except for their building activities. Edmund Knowle, abbot from 1306 to 1322, carried through the reconstruction of the choir

[1] The full story of the foundation of St. Augustine's, Bristol, has recently been set out by J. C. Dickinson, 'English Regular Canons and the Continent in the Twelfth Century', *Transactions of the Royal Historical Society*, 5th series, vol. i, (1951), pp. 71–9.

[2] *Two Compotus Rolls of St. Augustine's Abbey, Bristol (for 1491–2 and 1511–12)*, ed. G. Beachcroft and A. Sabin, Bristol Record Society, vol. ix.

in the manner of a continental 'hall-church', which earned for him a permanent place in the history of European architecture: his success in creating a sense of breadth and space in a comparatively small church, and the beauty of his decorative scheme for the eastern Berkeley chapel reveal him as a designer and architect of distinction. A number of tombs, and some heraldry, in the present cathedral church show the continuing connexion of the abbey with its patrons, the Berkeleys.

The most important friar foundation in Bristol was the Franciscan convent: founded before 1234 in Lewin's Mead, it became the administrative centre of the regional custody of the order. The Black Friars, whose house lay near the castle, benefited from royal patronage, and many Bristol citizens requested burial there. The Bristol Carmelites could also claim royal patrons: it was founded by the Lord Edward (later Edward I) in 1267 on the site of the modern Colston Hall, and for a time was evidently among the most flourishing houses of the order, distinguished by its great church, with a spire 200 ft. high. We know little of the history of Bristol's medieval hospitals, save for the wealthiest, St. Mark's. Originally founded as an almonry for the feeding of one hundred poor persons daily, under the direction of St. Augustine's, St. Mark's Hospital was re-endowed by Maurice de Gaunt's nephew, Robert de Gournay, about 1230. It was made independent of the abbey, and converted into a college of priests, clerks and poor scholars living under a modified Augustinian rule. It continued to perform its charitable duties not discreditably until its dissolution in 1539, when the property passed to the mayor and corporation of Bristol.[1]

If the centuries before 1300 belong to the nobility as patrons of religion, the initiative passed in the later Middle Ages to the urban middle class. The profits of trade flowed into the rebuilding and beautification of the parish churches. Individual munificence was sometimes on the grand scale. The patronage of St. Mary Redcliffe Church by the Canynges family transformed it to its present cathedral-like proportions, and the younger William Canynges (d. 1474) was a generous benefactor of the collegiate church of Westbury-on-Trym. But there are many other, if less princely examples, such as the rebuilding of St. Stephen's Church about 1470 by the Shipward family. Some of this flow of charity was diverted to educational and charitable purposes, as, for instance, the almshouse founded by John Foster in 1481 in Colston Street, with its unfamiliar dedication to the Three Kings of Cologne.

Parish churches were the centre of much corporate as well as individual religious life. Some of Bristol's numerous guilds were primarily religious in purpose, such as the guild associated with the Chapel of the Assumption built over Bristol Bridge in the mid-fourteenth century. Many more were craft guilds, but each of these had a connexion with a local church. Few Bristol guilds are known to have built halls of their own, as was done in London, but all maintained chapels or chantries. The weavers had a chapel in the Temple Church dedicated to their patron saint, St. Catherine, in 1392; the bakers' chapel was in the Black Friars' church. The profusion of chapels and chantries of all kinds born out of late-medieval piety doubtless made

[1] W. R. Barker, *St. Mark's or the Mayor's Chapel*, (Bristol, 1892). An admirable short history was published in 1950 by Elizabeth Ralph and Henly Evans.

many churches uncomfortably congested: thus the fraternity of St. John the Baptist, which developed into the merchant tailors' guild, could find no room in its own church, and had to have its chapel in the aisle of St. Ewen's. Surviving Bristol fifteenth-century churchwardens' accounts give a vivid picture of the intense interest in their parish churches which late-medieval parishioners displayed. The tangible results of this devotion are to be seen to-day in the predominance of fifteenth-century work in the fabric of Bristol parish churches. Few escaped enlargement and reconstruction and several were provided with the rich towers characteristic of the region, of which the best example is the tower of St. Stephen's in the city centre. The addition of ornate upper staging to the tower of the Temple Church caused it to lean noticeably but securely. It is not unfitting that Bristol merchants financed the reconstruction about 1480 by the designer of St. Stephen's tower of the little church of Dundry, from which village came most of the fine, clean stone for the Bristol churches: the tall and elaborate tower dominating the southern horizon of the city provides their memorial.

By modern standards Bristol was a tiny city, although it increased five-fold in population between the Norman conquest and the Tudor period. Estimates of medieval population are necessarily approximate, but it seems likely that the Domesday borough contained few more than 2,300 people. By about 1500, on a conservative calculation, Bristol's population had risen to over 10,000 and was perhaps as much as 14,000, the total population of England at this date being some two and a half millions. Yet the wealth and economic importance of Bristol were out of all proportion to the number of its people. The Middle Ages in Bristol provided a sound foundation for its coming overseas expansion, and in its citizens the self-confidence which enabled them to seize their opportunity.

CHAPTER TWELVE

CREDIT AND THE BRISTOL MERCHANT IN THE LATER MIDDLE AGES

TO CONSIDER the legal developments which are the subject of this chapter without an attempt to set them against their proper background, would be to tell only part of a story and, perhaps, not the most important part.

At the risk of stating the obvious, it must be emphasized that Law is not an end in itself but is the result of forces social, economic, political or otherwise which, because they set up stresses in society, have to be relieved in some way or another; legal development is one of the methods by which this comes about and so it is profitable to assign to it the cause of which it is the effect.

There is no doubt that all the forces mentioned were operating in Bristol and elsewhere during the later Middle Ages but, of them all, pressures arising from economic developments were certainly the most important from our present point of view, and to justify this statement as far as Bristol is concerned, it is only necessary to summarize the conclusions of scholars who have studied the subject. It is not suggested that Bristol was unique in this respect or that similar forces were not operating in other places similarly situated.

Although judged by modern standards medieval Bristol was small, its mercantile activities challenged comparison with almost any borough except London. Miss Carus-Wilson has given us a very full picture of these[1] during the fifteenth century. She points out that the junction of the rivers Frome and Avon provided a sheltered tidal harbour which was easily defensible and that the great inland waterway of the Severn, with which the Avon communicates, enabled Bristol to command the commerce of an area noted for its fertility so that, in fact, it was a great collecting and distributing centre, not only for overseas but also for inland trade.

In addition to its inland trade, Bristol, she tells us, carried on an extensive export trade with Ireland, Gascony and the Iberian peninsula. A glance at the figures extracted from the customs accounts set out in the appendix to *English Trade in the Fifteenth Century*[2] shows that Bristol, with the exception of London, was the largest exporter of broadcloths in England and, in exchange, imported fish and hides from Ireland, wine pre-eminently from Gascony and wines, fruit, oil and other luxuries mainly from the Iberian peninsula.

[1] *Medieval Merchant Venturers*, pp. 1f.
[2] Ed. Power and Postan, pp. 333–5.

The exports of broadcloths during the fifteenth century would, even if they stood alone, justify the statement that Bristol was then a thriving centre of mercantile activity involving operations which, for the time, were on a large scale; but of course, the story does not stop there because the cloth which was exported had to be manufactured and the wine that was imported had to be sold.

Miss Carus-Wilson also points out[1] that although the introduction of the fulling mill with its need for water power tended to reduce the activities of Bristol as a manufacturing centre for cloth, the numerous craft guilds in Bristol with their manifold activities and with such an outlet for their products justified the statement that 'Bristol in the fifteenth century was one of the leading manufacturing cities of England'.

As regards the manufacture of cloth in Bristol in the fourteenth century, reference may be made to the ordinances of the weavers', dyers' and fullers' guilds. The first two[2] are referred to as restarted on the 25 March 1346 and the last is stated to be newly made at the same time. The latter set of ordinances named twelve persons as the most notable persons of the fullers' guild and seventy-six as 'the commons of the said mystery'. There can be no doubt that this was a guild of considerable importance and since cloth had to be made before it could be fulled it gives a plain indication of the importance of the other guilds also.

The importance of Bristol's trade in cloth during the fourteenth century is confirmed by Gras[3] who shows from the customs account for 1348–49, that between 29 August and 4 September 1349, nine hundred cloths were exported from Bristol. This rather unexpectedly large figure is no doubt accounted for by the fact that it was a suitable time to send cloth to France in exchange for wine.

We are told by Miss James,[4] that the import figure of less than two thousand tons of wine for Bristol in 1300–01 was even then far short of the normal trade of the port, for prior to the Anglo-French War of 1294 and again in 1307, Bristol's annual imports of this commodity reached and indeed surpassed three thousand tons.

The Little Red Book contains, in addition to the guild ordinances already referred to, ordinances showing a number of important guilds operating in the fourteenth century and although most of these ordinances were made in the early fifteenth century, they clearly relate to guilds which were already in existence.

The general conclusion is that although trading operations in Bristol may have been on a smaller scale than in the fifteenth century, precisely the same kind of commercial activities were being pursued in the fourteenth century and it may safely be concluded that, during both, Bristol was a centre of great mercantile importance and activity.

The reader may wonder why a writer on legal history should venture into the perilous region sacred to the economic historian. He does so merely to show that an

[1] *Medieval Merchant Venturers*, pp. 183f.

[2] *The Little Red Book of Bristol*, ed. Bickley, pp. 6, 7 and 10f. Other ordinances relating to these guilds are to be found in the same volume.

[3] *The Early English Customs System*, pp. 419f.

[4] *Economic History Review*, 2nd series, vol. 11, p. 175.

economic situation developed in Bristol, and elsewhere, which created problems some of which could be solved only by changes in the law.

Enough has been said of its mercantile activities to make it quite certain that, for the times, transactions of considerable size were undertaken by Bristol merchants and it is equally certain that at some stage or other these demanded the giving of credit.

According to Postan[1] there is no topic in the economic history of the Middle Ages with more evidence to elucidate it than credit; the bulk of this consists of records of recognizances (that is, debts acknowledged before judicial tribunals and entered on their rolls) although after the Statute of Acton Burnell (1283) the type of recognizance created by the statute was differently acknowledged and entered on a roll of its own. Other evidence, according to the same author, consists of proceedings for debt in the courts.

If a system of credit is to work there must be legal remedies available which are sufficiently effective to make it reasonably certain that the expectations of the creditor will be fulfilled, and it only remains to consider what these remedies were; the purpose of this essay is to consider the various expedients mentioned by Postan and, in the light of Bristol evidence wherever it is available, to estimate their usefulness. That some remedy or combination of remedies was effective in practice is proved by the fact that trading on credit continued not only to persist but also to expand.

The legal machinery for making credit effective as suggested by Postan is (*a*) the recognizance, (*b*) the Statute Merchant and (*c*) the action for debt brought in some tribunal or other,[2] and in considering these it must always be borne in mind that a recognizance or the judgement of a court was useless unless by some form of execution it could be enforced against either the person or property of the debtor. It is also clear that no form of execution could be effective unless the person of the debtor or his property or both were, as lawyers say, 'within the jurisdiction'; this may obviously raise serious problems where debtor and creditor are not inhabitants of the same place. This legal machinery will now be examined in detail.

(*A*) *Recognizance*

According to a passage in *Liber Albus*[3] the Sheriffs of London were wont to take recognizances of debt to any amount and if default were made on the date fixed for payment, all the goods and chattels of the debtor *in the city* could be appraised and delivered to the creditor up to the amount of his debt, and at the expiration of the year a writ could be issued against the debtor calling upon him to show cause why execution of his goods should not be made. This rather curious procedure follows closely, as we shall see, the process of an action of debt in a court governed by Law Merchant, except that the admission of the debt and subsequent default in payment

[1] *Economic History Review*, vol. 1, pp. 314f.

[2] The Writing Obligatory did not offer a remedy; it merely recorded a debt and had to be sued upon if the debtor made default.

[3] Ed. Riley, p. 190.

put the creditor in the same position as if he had started an action for the debt in the court and obtained judgement upon it.

A large number of these London recognizances are mentioned in *Letter Book A*[1] between the years 1275 and 1289. It is noticeable that these entries almost cease after the latter date, probably because this type of recognizance was largely superseded by a new type of recognizance known as a Statute Merchant, records of which were kept in a roll of their own.

When we turn to the Bristol records for evidence of a similar procedure we encounter one of those gaps which are only too familiar to students of the history of the city. Although such unique records as *The Little Red Book* and *The Great Red Book* are fortunately still available, many others of vital importance have been lost or destroyed; these losses include not only the medieval records dealing with recognizances but also the medieval court rolls and the rolls in which Statutes Merchant were recorded.

There is, however, the well-known passage in *Ricart's Kalendar*[2] which states that Bristol 'hath take a grete president of the noble Citee of Londone in excerciseing their laudable customes' and that it was therefore necessary that the officers of Bristol should know what these customs were. After this general statement particulars follow and one of these is that the Mayor and Aldermen or the Mayor and Chamberlain of London could take recognizances of debt, with the consequences stated above if the debtor made default.

There is also an actual recognizance enrolled in *The Great Red Book*[3] which precisely follows the form usual in cases of this kind. Apart from this isolated piece of evidence there is no actual proof that the recognizance of debt was used in Bristol but it was a well-known procedure and it is almost inconceivable that it was not.

It will have been observed that the London custom allowed only goods of the debtor in the City of London to be seized which must, of course, have limited the effectiveness of the remedy considerably. It will be seen that the Statute Merchant did not possess this disadvantage.

(*B*) *The Statute Merchant*

This was a much improved form of recognizance and was first introduced by the Statute of Acton Burnell (1283); the preamble is important and reads as follows:

> 'For as much as Merchants which heretofore have lent their goods (i.e., sold them on credit) to diverse persons be greatly impoverished because there is no speedie law provided for them to have recoverie of their debts at the day of payment assigned, and by reason hereof, many Merchants have withdrawne to come into this Realm with their merchandise . . . the King for himself and by his Council have ordained and established that the Merchant which will be sure of his debt etc. . . .'

[1] *Calendar of Letter Book A*, ed. Sharpe, pp. 4f.
[2] Ed. Toulmin Smith, p. 93.
[3] Bristol Record Society. Ed. Veale. Text, Part I, p. 237.

This passage serves to show that the courts were regarded as offering an unsatisfactory remedy and as we shall see, if the merchant had to rely on the common law procedure his distrust was well founded. The question of how far the Law Merchant procedure had penetrated into the local courts at that date will be considered later; even if it had, it would certainly seem that the Statute Merchant possessed great advantages.

The provisions of the Statute of Acton Burnell may be summarized as follows:

(*a*) The creditor caused his debtor to appear before the Mayor of London or York or Bristol or before a mayor and clerk appointed by the king, to acknowledge his debt and the day of payment thereof.

(*b*) The acknowledgement must be entered on the roll kept for this purpose.

(*c*) The clerk must with his own hand, make out a bill obligatory which must be sealed first by the debtor and secondly by the mayor with a special seal provided for the purpose. This document was handed to the creditor.

(*d*) If the debtor made default in payment on the day named the creditor could come before the mayor and his clerk with the bill and the mayor would cause the debtor's merchandise to be seized to the value of the debt; this would be sold and the proceeds paid to the creditor; if a buyer could not be found the goods would be handed to the creditor.

(*e*) If the debtor had no goods within the jurisdiction of the mayor but had some elsewhere, the mayor was required to send the writing to the Chancellor, who would direct a writ to the sheriff in whose bailiwick the goods were alleged to be. It will be remembered that in this respect the Statute Merchant differed from the London recognizance in the case of which the debtor's goods could be seized only if within the city.

(*f*) If the debtor had no movables on which the debt could be levied he was arrested and imprisoned until he came to terms with his creditor. If the debtor could not maintain himself in prison the creditor had to provide him with bread and water the cost of which was added to the debt.

The procedure on the making of a Statute Merchant was modified by a Statute passed two years after the Statute of Acton Burnell and the procedure on default by the debtor was also modified by a provision that, in case of non-payment, the debtor should forthwith be arrested and imprisoned, there to remain until the creditor was satisfied. If the debtor was not within the jurisdiction of the mayor, the Statute would be sent to the Chancellor, who would direct a writ to the sheriff in whose bailiwick the debtor was, ordering his arrest.

Within a quarter of a year of his arrest his goods and chattels and lands would be delivered to the debtor so that out of them he might raise the amount of the debt. In default of payment within the quarter the goods were delivered to the merchant to be held by him until the debt was paid. If the debtor could not be found his goods and lands were delivered to the creditor to the extent of the debt.

There is also the extremely drastic rule that all the land which a debtor owned at the time a recognizance was made, was liable to be seized for the debt even though he had alienated it before he made default in payment.

From this sketch of the procedure under a Statute Merchant it is quite apparent that it provided a creditor with a most drastic remedy against his debtor, a remedy so drastic that many a debtor must have hesitated before assuming so onerous an obligation. Its rigour was, to some extent, mitigated by the Writ Audita Querela.

This writ attracted a considerable amount of litigation referred to in the Year Books, the first reference being in the year 43 Edward III; it is fairly certain that the writ had an earlier origin than that and, in fact, a case as early as 15 Edward III is mentioned in the Natura Brevium next referred to.[1]

The Natura Brevium in French (1557 Edition) gives a fairly full account of such proceedings starting with the writ, which was as follows:

> 'Rex Justiciariis suis de Banco salutem. Ex Gravi querela J accepimus quod cum idem J nuper coram J. de W. tunc maiore ville W. et T. de S. tunc clerico etc. recognovisset se debere P. C li. ad certos terminos in dicta recognitione contentos solvendas et idem P. post modum per quandam indenturam inter dictos P. et J. concessit quod si predictus J. solveret predicto P. singulis annis ad quatuor anni terminos per equales porciones quendam redditum XLS exeuntem de terris et tenementis predicti J. . . . ad totam vitam ipsius P. quod tunc predicta recognicio . . . penitus afferetur et pro nullo haberetur . . . [the writ goes on to allege that the rent was duly paid but none the less P. sought to enforce the Statute Merchant]. . . . et quia eundem J. injuriari nolumus in hac parte vobis mandamus quod visa altera parte indenture predicte et vocatis coram vobis partibus predictis auditisque hinc inde earum rationibus ulterius in hac parte fieri facias quod de jure et secundum consuetudinem regni nostri Anglie fuerit faciendum Teste etc.'

The author tells us that the writ lay where *A* was bound to *B* in a sum certain to be paid at a specified date, and before the date arrived the creditor released the debtor or varied the terms of payment by an indenture made between them but none the less sought to enforce the Statute. The justice of such an application is apparent but of course, the proceedings lay in other cases as well and, in fact, in the course of the centuries, a considerable amount of learning gathered round the writ. Brooke's Abridgement refers to forty-six cases reported in the Year Books.

If, however, the cases in which Audita Querela lay are examined it would appear that the efficiency of the Statute Merchant as a remedy was not seriously impaired and indeed that the writ merely rationalized something which, applied strictly, could produce great injustice. The Statute Merchant, although clumsy and rigid according to modern notions, was not an unsuitable type of remedy at a time when credit was not the complicated thing that it now is, and would obviously be effective as between an English debtor and creditor or between an English debtor and a foreign creditor who, in such a case, would proceed through an attorney. The only cases in which it could not be effective would be that of an English creditor and a

[1] Fo. 65 (*d*).

foreign debtor if neither the person nor property of the latter were within the jurisdiction and that of an English debtor who absconded without the jurisdiction, but the latter case needs no serious consideration since whatever procedure was available the creditor would be helpless and would make a bad debt.[1]

(C) Remedy by Action

Although a debt is frequently treated as a valuable asset this is so because the creditor has a reasonable expectation that it will be paid. In cases where the debtor makes default, payment can be enforced only by execution against the debtor's property or person following a judgement by a court or something which, like a Statute Merchant, itself takes the place of a judgement. This statement lacks complete accuracy because it disregards the possibility of self-help, of which distress for rent is an example, but it is sufficiently accurate for our present purpose.

The debtor who voluntarily pays his debt creates, of course, no problem; it is the defaulting debtor who creates the difficulty since he is attempting to evade responsibilities which it is the function of the law to enforce. To do this, an effective procedure is necessary, the most important ingredients of which are speed, and machinery for

[1] The records of Statutes Merchant enrolled in Bristol commences in 1606 and, choosing a period beginning with the 8 May 1607, we find the following:

Date	*Debtor*	*Creditor*	*Amount*
8 May 1607	James Speke, Grandon, Frome, Som., Generosus.	Ralph Loversage, Same Place, Generosus.	£200
30 May 1607	John Flower, Morton, Wilts., Generosus.	Abel K., Bristol, Merchant.	£1,000
30 May 1607	Henry Lymsel, Wilts., Generosus.	John Flower, as above.	£500
5 June 1607	John Boultinge, Wedmore, Som., Yeoman.	Richard Wykis, Wells, Som., ? Occupation.	£150
9 Oct. 1607	Richard Lyall, Monmouthshire, Yeoman.	Wm. Thomas, Caerleon, Mon., Merchant.	£60
14 Oct. 1607	David Phillips, Monmouthshire, Generosus.	Charles Phillips, Monmouthshire, Generosus.	£40
27 Oct. 1607	William Aubry (Doctor of Law) and Another, Glamorgan.	Meredith Morgan, Carmarthen, Archdeacon.	£300
8 April 1608	Richard Griffin, Warwickshire, Knight.	Wm. Chatwodde, Northamptonshire, Knight.	£6,000

It seems obvious that the Statute Merchant was not at that time used in connexion with mercantile transactions.

enforcing the debt against a debtor who, as the lawyers say, makes default in appearance. In both these respects the common law completely failed.

Pollock and Maitland have this to say of the process in an action preceding trial:

> 'Our readers would soon be wearied if we discoursed of mesne process. Its one general characteristic is its tedious forbearance. Very slowly it turns the screw which brings pressure to bear on the defendant. Every default that is not essoined is cause for an amercement, but the law is reluctant to strike a decisive blow.... Law must be slow in order that it may be fair.... One thing our law would not do; the obvious thing. It would exhaust its terrors in the endeavour to make the defendant appear but it would not give judgement against him until he had appeared.'

It is not difficult to understand the preamble to the Statute of Acton Burnell when confronted with such a piece of legal machinery as this, nor is it difficult to see that some new kind of legal procedure had to be devised if the needs of the mercantile element in the population were to be met.

Before considering what this new machinery was, it is worth describing proceedings for debt in a county court which will amply satisfy the reader that Pollock and Maitland's statements are well founded. The case dealt with is taken from the rolls of the County court of Bedfordshire[1] for the years 1332–34.

Digne v. William son of Roger de Ekendon

Action of Debt

9 Oct. 1332	The plaintiff appeared, the defendant did not. Bailiff ordered to attach him by pledges to appear at next Court. The bailiff reported that he was already attached by two quarters of corn and rye, etc.
11 Nov. 1332	Plaintiff appeared, defendant did not. The pledges for his appearance were fined and the bailiff ordered to distrain again.
6 Dec. 1332	Plaintiff appeared, defendant did not. Bailiffs reported that the defendant had been distrained by one cow. Bailiff ordered to distrain again.
1 Jan. 1333	Plaintiff appeared, defendant did not. Bailiff reported that he was already distrained by one cow and is ordered to distrain again.
2 Feb. 1333	Plaintiff appeared, defendant did not. Bailiff reported that he was mainprised by four persons. These were fined and the Bailiff was ordered to distrain again.
24 Feb. 1333	Plaintiff appeared, defendant did not. Bailiff reported that the defendant had nothing more to distrain on. Bailiff ordered to distrain again.
25 April 1333	Plaintiff appeared, defendant did not. Bailiff ordered to distrain again.

[1] *Quarto Memoirs of the Bedfordshire Historical Record Society*, vol. iii, pp. 55f.

At this point the entries, which have covered a period of six months, cease and the plaintiff is no nearer recovery of his debt than when he started. He does not get the corn or the cow or the fines inflicted on the pledges and in spite of the fact that the debtor obviously had assets, the creditor made a bad debt. These entries are taken at random and similar cases can be found over and over again in the records of the Borough courts.

It is quite unnecessary to point out that the Statute Merchant offered a creditor a much more attractive remedy, as did the Law Merchant procedure, which can now be described in outline.

The Law Merchant

One of the most important entries in *The Little Red Book of Bristol*[1] is a tract giving a description of the Law Merchant procedure. The learned editor states that the handwriting is that of the fourteenth century but from internal evidence it seems clear that the original document is of an earlier date.

At the end of the tract is a section dealing with the form of letter to be written to other courts and in a specimen letter written from York to London the following passage appears:

> 'Quia Adam Bernard mercator attachiatus est . . . ad respondendum Bernardo Ade . . . de placito quod idem B. reddat ei XL libras quas ei debet pro quodam equo badio quem idem A eidem B. . . . die veneris XV die marcii anno regni regis Edwardi filii Regis Henrici X° vendidit. . . .' (There are other references to the same king.)

The tract commences with the statement that the Law Merchant was found to arise from a market therefore in the first place it must be known where a market of this kind was held and it was to be noted that a market of this kind was held in five places only, that is to say in cities, fairs, seaports, market towns and boroughs . . . since in Cities and fairs purchases and sales of merchandise were continually made.

It will be remembered that the tract appears to date from the latter part of the thirteenth century and although it is true that the Law Merchant must have been applied at a much earlier date in the Fair courts, it is doubtful, at any rate so far as Bristol is concerned, if the procedure was also used in the Borough courts then.

There were two or possibly three Borough courts in Bristol at the end of the thirteenth century; the Hundred Court, the Tolzey Court and, possibly as a separate court, the Market Court.

There is a clear reference to the use of Law Merchant procedure in the Tolzey Court in the year 1286,[2] as appears from the following entry:

The plaintiffs alleged a debt for goods sold to the defendant and a demand for it from the latter . . . 'et hoc parati sunt probare versus eum secundum legem mercatoriam de libertate ville Bristollie'.

[1] *The Little Red Book of Bristol*, ed. Bickley, vol. 1, pp. 57f.
[2] *The Great Red Book of Bristol*, ed. Veale, Text (Part 3), p. 13.

It is not however until the reign of Henry IV that we get a clear statement that the Tolzey Court was a Law Merchant court. This statement[1] is as follows: 'Placita tenta in Curia Tols' ville Bristollie secundum legem mercatoriam et consuetudinem eiusdem. . . .'

It seems clear from the evidence that the Law Merchant procedure was used in the Tolzey Court at the end of the thirteenth century although possibly not much earlier. It was introduced into the other Borough courts, which increased in number after Edward III's charter of 1373, at a considerably later date; but for a reason which will presently appear, it is only the Tolzey Court which is important for our present purpose.

The tract gives a very full account of the Law Merchant procedure but it will suffice for our present purposes if an account is given of a typical action conducted in Bristol according to that procedure, so that it may be compared with the common law procedure already referred to:

[2]*John Sampson executor of the Will of John Sampson the elder v. Edward Courtenay the younger, Robert Cary and Robert Weyd administrators of Philip Courtenay. Claim debt £250. 4s. od.*—(1407).

(*a*) The Water Bailiff who was the Sergeant of the Court ordered to summon defendants to appear on following Monday. This order given on the Friday before the Feast of St. Matthew (21 September).

(*b*) Defendants did not appear and the Water Bailiff ordered to attach defendants by gage and pledge to attend on a day which is unfortunately illegible in the manuscript.

(*c*) Defendants did not appear and the Water Bailiff reported that he had attached a ship and its gear; he was ordered to distrain the defendants again and to have the defendants before the Court on the following Friday.

(*d*) Defendants did not appear and the plaintiff asked permission to prove his debt, which he did, and the Court ordered that the plaintiff should recover his debt with £10 damages.

(*e*) The Court ordered that the ship should be valued by honest and lawful men of the bailiwick and this was done and the valuation returned at £140 on the Monday before the Feast of St. Patrick (17 March).

(*f*) The plaintiff was ordered to find security that he would return the ship if the defendants appeared within a year and a day—if he had given security the ship would have been handed over to him; as he did not it remained in the custody of the Water Bailiff.

(*g*) At the end of a year and a day plaintiff asked that the ship should be handed over to him without security and this was done.

[1] Ibid., p. 11.
[2] Ibid., p. 35.

Here we have a typical case showing the plaintiff's method of recovery when the defendant failed to appear. If, of course, he did appear and judgement was given against him, a writ of execution was issued at once.

At first sight a remedy which could be pursued on these lines seems to be entirely satisfactory from a plaintiff's point of view but, in the case of an action pursued in the Tolzey Court, it was subject to the serious limitation that goods could be seized by distraint or execution only if they were within the jurisdiction of the court, that is, the City of Bristol, which would set very definite limits to the usefulness of the action if the defendant was not a Bristolian (it will be remembered that this difficulty did not apply to the Statute Merchant).

It must also be borne in mind that the Court had no jurisdiction unless the cause of action arose in Bristol.[1] This would also have very much limited the usefulness of the Court since Bristol merchants, especially when acting as buyers, must often have made their bargains outside the town. If a cause of action arose outside the jurisdiction of the Tolzey Court the Bristol Merchant could sue or be sued in the local court having jurisdiction but, in all probability, the remedy would be subject to the same disadvantages as those already mentioned.[2]

It should be remembered also that the jurisdiction of the Royal Courts[3] was excluded by Edward III's charter of 1373 in any matters concerning contracts, covenants, accounts, and debts, arising in the town and, even if it had not been, these courts used the common law procedure.[4]

Reference has continually been made to the Tolzey Court, but of course, this was not the only court sitting in Bristol. Excluding private courts and before Edward III's charter of 1373 apart from the jurisdiction of the King's courts, cases were dealt with not only by the Tolzey Court but also by the Hundred Court and, after it was constituted, the Staple Court.

The charter added the Mayor and Sheriff's Court and the County Court, but, as mentioned above, the jurisdiction of the king's judges was excluded.

In spite of this galaxy of local courts, however, it is certain that the jurisdiction of the Hundred Court in actions of debt was excluded. A document known as Consuetudines Bristollie[5] and dated by Miss Bateman at 1240 provides that no Burgess should answer a Burgess in any plea *except pleas of debt* elsewhere than in the Hundred Court and that burgesses as between themselves or as against a foreigner, or foreigners between themselves, could plead debts big or small from day to day according to the custom of the town.

[1] The appropriate plea is referred to in *The Practice of the Tolzey Court* (1848) J. A. Homes, p. 111, and is as follows:

'The defendant C.D. in his own proper person saith that the Court ought not to have cognizance of the plaint aforesaid, because he saith that the cause of action arose and accrued to the said plaintiff at *X* and not within the City and County of Bristol.'

[2] In volume vii of the Bristol Record Society's publications, p. 57, Miss Carus-Wilson refers to a case in which a Bristol merchant sued in Bayonne.

[3] *The Great Red Book of Bristol*, ed. Veale, Text (Part 3), pp. 46 and 47.

[4] In the Assize Rolls (which were, of course, prior to 1373) only one action of debt is recorded.

[5] Ibid., p. 8.

After the charter no case has been found in which an action of debt was tried in the Mayor and Sheriff's Court, and the matter was settled without question in an ordinance made in 1449 which provided that only actions of trespass and deceit should be taken in the Mayor and Sheriff's Court and (except in the limited number of cases in which the Staple Court had jurisdiction) actions of debt '*as it hath been of olde tyme usyd*' and all other actions should be tried in the Tolzey Court.

This being so, the Tolzey Court was the Bristol court in which debts would be recovered if we leave out of account the Fair courts.

It is probably incorrect to say that during the period under consideration the importance of the fairs had declined, but the merchant who wandered from fair to fair as described by Pirenne, must have played a very small part in the manifold trade activities of Bristol Merchants during the fifteenth century as these are described by Miss Carus-Wilson and, of course, the justice administered in the Fair courts would be intermittent, limited as it was to the times of the fairs.

It is unfortunate that no records of any of the Bristol Fair courts have been discovered prior to the reign of Edward VI when the court was quite obviously unimportant as will be seen from the following extracts from a court roll of 1547.

Plaintiff	*Defendant*	*Amount sued for* £	*s.*	*d.*
Thomas More, Grocer	George Hoper, Grocer	12	18	0
ditto	John Mekyn, Turner	1	10	5
Richard Golde, Weaver	Patrick Lang, Carpenter		2	2
Patrick Lang	William ( ) Organmaker		5	11
John Davys	Agnes Atwater, Widow		6	0
Alice Hopkyns, Spinster	Margaret More, Widow	3	6	8
Robert Alen, Mariner	Thomas Hyscokis, Brewer.		10	10

The position of a Bristol merchant in the fifteenth century who suffered the misfortune of a defaulting debtor can now be considered in the light of the description of his possible remedies as already described.

Since the recognizance by way of Statute Merchant was so obviously superior to the other type of recognizance his choice would appear to lie between the Statute Merchant and an action for debt or covenant if he held a sealed writing obligatory.[1]

To take the latter first. Reasons have already been given for the assumption that the court in Bristol would be the Tolzey Court and no other, if the Fair court (which as we have seen, was of diminishing importance with the disappearance of the peripatetic merchant) be left out of account. We have seen that the Tolzey Court suffered from the two serious limitations, that in the first place it could not be used unless the cause of action arose within the town and that in the second place execution could be levied only against goods in the town. It is difficult to see that a remedy so circumscribed could be of much value to the type of merchant described by Miss

[1] There was, of course, the petition to the Chancellor and these were not uncommon.

Carus-Wilson. If the cause of action arose outside Bristol and an action were brought elsewhere it would probably be subject to the same disadvantages.

This conclusion is amply borne out by the evidence of one of the two earliest action books which have been preserved, from which we observe that, in the year 1480, out of 512 actions brought, 439 were actions of debt, of which 239 were in respect of claims under one pound, 153 in respect of claims under five pounds, 25 in respect of claims under ten pounds, 12 in respect of claims under twenty pounds and only 10 in respect of claims over twenty pounds. In the face of this evidence it could hardly be suggested that, in that year at any rate (which according to the custom accounts was one of considerable prosperity), the merchants of Bristol used the court as a forum suitable for enforcing debts of any magnitude. In point of fact it is exceptional to find a merchant named as either plaintiff or defendant.

It may be suggested that although this was so towards the end of the fifteenth century, it by no means follows that the position was the same at an earlier date. This argument is somewhat discounted by the fact that the limitations of the court's usefulness existed just as much at an earlier date as at the later but the absence of court rolls or court books renders proof impossible.

This leaves us with the Statute Merchant which offered an effective remedy except against a debtor whose person and property were outside England. This statement should be qualified by the reflection that it was a clumsy device and one completely lacking in that flexibility which would become necessary when credit transactions became complex, and that it could be entered into only in a place where the necessary official seal was available.

The records of Statutes Merchant created in Bristol during the medieval period have unfortunately been lost so that it is impossible to say to what extent they were then employed.

In the face of the evidence it seems clear that the Bristol merchant was certainly not habitually using the Statute Merchant at the beginning of the seventeenth century, but by this time a new technique in commercial transactions was rapidly developing.

In this chapter we have been concerned with remedies available to a creditor as opposed to methods by which an obligation could be created or recorded and, with all their limitations, the alternative of Statute Merchant or action in the appropriate court seems to have satisfied our trading ancestors during the Middle Ages.

The giving of credit in the Middle Ages must have been a more risky proceeding than at the present day when, in addition to a fully developed banking system, negotiable securities and modern methods of communication, there is a fully developed and centralized system for the administration of justice. It would certainly have behoved a merchant of the Middle Ages to take every precaution before giving credit and this he could do to some extent either by availing himself of set off, which would follow if he bought goods from the same person to whom he sold, or if he conducted his export transactions through a partner or trusted agent on the spot.

CHAPTER THIRTEEN

BRISTOL SINCE 1497

IF CABOT could return to the port from which he sailed in 1497 on that momentous voyage which Bristol enthusiasm and Bristol capital had made possible, he would find the little walled town which he knew in the late fifteenth century transformed into a great modern city. Medieval Bristol, with its population of a few thousand people clustered north and south of Bristol Bridge, has grown into an urban concentration of nearly half a million, living in an area of some 26,000 acres. Yet neither the slow changes of four and a half centuries nor the rapid destruction of modern war have entirely broken the links between the medieval and the modern city. St. Mary Redcliffe and other parish churches still preserve physical continuity with the past. The Cathedral of the Holy and Undivided Trinity would not appear altogether unfamiliar to someone who knew it when it was the Abbey of St. Augustine; and there is perhaps a community of spirit between the Bristol that sent out the *Matthew* in 1497 and the Bristol that put the *Britannia* into the air in 1952.

The history of Bristol's development since 1497 is by no means one of even or uninterrupted progress.[1] Physically it grew little, if at all, in the sixteenth century, in spite of the splendid opportunities presented by secularization of the ecclesiastical property by which it had hitherto been surrounded. There was in Bristol no parallel with the remarkable growth of Tudor London, and the population was probably little more than 10,000 at the close of the century.[2] The Age of the Stuarts, on the other hand, was one of expansion, particularly in the years after the Restoration, and much new building was required to meet the needs of a population which doubled between 1600 and 1700. Yet London grew even faster, and we can better understand the continual complaints against the domination of the over-mighty capital if we consider that at the end of the century, when Bristol had become the second city in the kingdom, it could muster only 20,000 inhabitants[3] against London's 750,000.

Bristol's rate of increase was much greater in the eighteenth century, and so conscious were its inhabitants of its growing size and importance that they confidently

[1] For an account of early maps of Bristol, *see* John E. Pritchard, 'Old Plans and Views of Bristol,' *Trans. Bristol and Gloucestershire Arch. Soc.* vol. 48, pp. 325–53.

[2] Estimates of population before 1801 must be treated with caution. Some of the evidence is noted by John Latimer in the various volumes of his *Annals of Bristol*. *See* also Bryan Little, *The City and County of Bristol*, 1954, Appendix 1; H. A. Shannon and E. Grebenik, *The Population of Bristol*, Cambridge University Press, 1943.

[3] D. V. Glass, 'Gregory King's estimate of the population of England and Wales 1695', *Population Studies*, vol. iii, 1951, p. 347.

expected the census of 1801 to show a population of over 100,000. They were disappointed. The population had more than trebled in the course of the century, but it was still less than 70,000.[1] Although the city had pushed out its tentacles into the surrounding countryside, its layout and appearance still in many ways called to mind the medieval foundation from which it sprang.

The changes in Bristol in the nineteenth century, measured in terms of population and built-up area, were far more revolutionary than anything that had taken place in the three centuries before 1800. Even in the first half of the period, which is often considered to be one of stagnation, the number of inhabitants increased from some 68,000 to nearly 160,000. Bristol might not be advancing as rapidly as other cities, but the addition of over 90,000 inhabitants shows that it was not standing still. Population had more than doubled between 1801 and 1851. In the second half of the nineteenth century it doubled again, reaching the figure of 337,000 in 1901. After that, the rate of increase was less rapid, but the first half of the twentieth century nevertheless added another 100,000, and the population is now not far short of half a million, an increase of nearly fifty-fold since the time of Cabot.

The increase in population in the nineteenth and twentieth centuries was accompanied by, and is in part explained by, continual extension of the urban boundaries.[2] It would be tedious to relate in detail the stages by which Bristol gradually absorbed such places as Hotwells, Clifton, Westbury, Fishponds and other parishes which once enjoyed a separate existence. Generally speaking, the boundaries were extended in ever-widening circles round the old city. As a result of these changes not only did Bristol increase its size; it also changed its character. The City Docks are still of considerable importance, but the real centre of trade is no longer the old port of Bristol but the new port of Avonmouth, seven miles down the river. Cabot would have difficulty in recognizing a city whose boundaries stretch to Whitchurch, Kingswood, Mangotsfield, Filton and the mouth of the Avon.

Behind these four and a half centuries of change lies a story of political vicissitudes and economic fluctuations which cannot be examined in detail here. Each period had its own characteristics, its own contribution to make to a rich and varied history. Within each period there were contrasting factors. The age heralded by the voyages of discovery proved in many ways disappointing and ended on a note of depression; the prosperous eighteenth century contained within it the seeds of its own decay; the century in which Bristol grew most rapidly was one when it neglected many of its opportunities. Concern for the public good was often found in times of narrow oligarchic corruption; smug self-satisfaction often rubbed shoulders with farsightedness and vision. Many varied ingredients went to the making of modern Bristol, and slaves, cigarettes and aeroplanes are only part of its story.

The Age of the Tudors, so important in national history, was not one of the most

[1] The population of the area under the jurisdiction of the Corporation of Bristol was just over 40,000, but there were another 28,000 living in the suburbs, and they can be justifiably included in the total, since they formed part of Bristol considered as an economic and social unit.

[2] There were major extensions of the boundaries in 1835, 1897, 1904 and 1933–35.

notable in the history of Bristol. Yet the Tudor legacy is still with us. It was in the sixteenth century that Bristol first became a bishopric. It was then that the Corporation acquired the chapel of the Gaunts, one of the few municipally owned churches in the country. Bristol Grammar School and Queen Elizabeth's Hospital are Tudor foundations, and the colourful uniform of the scholars of the Hospital can still be seen in the streets of the city. It was on 'the fower and twentithe daye of August in the yere of our Lorde God A thousand fiv hundreth three score and nyne' that the city received from the College of Heralds as supporters for the city arms the fabulous unicorns, representations of which can be seen delicately pawing the air at either end of the long roof of the new Council House. In the sixteenth century, too, the Society of Merchant Venturers, still happily with us, first obtained a royal charter giving it the right to exclude non-members from overseas trade.[1] But although there was gain as well as loss in this period, in the main the city played only a minor rôle in the great events that shaped the nation's destiny. It accepted placidly the religious revolutions. There were few martyrs, Protestant or Catholic, nor was the port used by seminary priests or Jesuits. If it produced a certain number of Elizabethan sea-dogs, they sometimes embarrassed the government by failing to distinguish between enemy ships and neutrals.[2] Bristol's contribution to the fleet that sailed against the Armada was very modest—three ships and a pinnace, although in fairness to Bristol it must be added that that was all the government asked it to send.[3] The city seems to have declined from its medieval greatness, and the statue of an Elizabethan seaman standing a little weak at the knees before the Council House is perhaps symbolic of an age in which Bristol was unsure of itself. The half century which followed the incorporation of the Merchant Venturers was one in which Bristolians as a whole were not particularly venturesome.

Comparatively little is known about the economic background of sixteenth-century Bristol. Roger Barlow's comments in 1540 that it was 'a noble town of great trade and many ships'[4] certainly does not suggest that it was declining under the early Tudors, and indeed as long as it enjoyed undisturbed its trades with Spain, Portugal, Ireland and France there was no reason why it should decline, particularly as foreign trade was supported by a considerable regional trade and a well-developed industrial economy. There were indeed over a hundred different occupations to which Bristolians could be apprenticed.[5] In the second half of the sixteenth century, however, the position with regard to overseas markets deteriorated considerably. It is permissible to interpret the charter of the Merchant Venturers in 1552 as

[1] 18 December 1552. For a discussion of the relations between the Society and earlier associations of merchants in Bristol, *see* Patrick McGrath, *Records Relating to the Society of Merchant Venturers of the City of Bristol in the Seventeenth Century* (Bristol Record Society, vol. xvii, 1952).

[2] *See* J. W. Damer Powell, *Bristol Privateers and Ships of War*, Bristol, 1930, pp. 49, 50.

[3] *Acts of the Privy Council*, 1588, pp. 29, 30, 312.

[4] Roger Barlow, *A Brief Sumarie of Geographie*, 1540–41, (Hakluyt Society, 1932), p. 47.

[5] D. Hollis, *Calendar of Bristol Apprentice Books 1532–1542* (Bristol Record Society, vol. ix) gives a total of 1,449 apprentices bound to 76 different trades. The Elizabethan Apprentice Books, however, show an even greater variety of occupations.

evidence not of expansion but of decay, as the attempt of a group of merchants to monopolize a trade that was shrinking in volume. Relations with both Spain and Portugal were interrupted from time to time, and after 1585 there was a period of nearly twenty years of war. The Irish market also suffered from the attempts of the English to conquer the country and impose the new religion, and France was torn by civil war. These markets were vital to Bristolians, who could not, like the Londoners, find compensation elsewhere. We must not take too seriously the statements of those anxious to avoid taxation, but there is perhaps some truth in the words of the mayor of Bristol in 1595 who told the Privy Council that his fellow citizens had carefully considered 'the many exquisite reasons' put forward by the government for making a further contribution to the war effort, but found the burden too heavy for 'this now poor place'.[1]

Yet even for Bristol the Elizabethan Age was not one of unrelieved depression. Its share of the national cake was probably smaller than in the later Middle Ages, but a number of Bristolians fed well enough. There were men of substance in the city like John Carr who left the money to found Queen Elizabeth's Hospital, John Whitson who was busy laying the foundations of a considerable fortune later to be used to endow numerous charities, and John Browne who published in the year after the Armada a little work called *The Marchants Avizo* which became a standard textbook on foreign trade for more than fifty years.[2] These men were probably not in the same rank as the Canynges in the fifteenth century, but they were not poor. Depression is relative.

A period of arrested development under Elizabeth I was followed by one of rapid growth under the Stuarts, growth not so much in size as in importance. More than once in the seventeenth century the national destiny was closely bound up with the fate of Bristol. The city stood two sieges in the Civil War, and at one time the king conferred upon its merchants those valuable monopolies hitherto held by Londoners.[3] Bristol was not in fact large enough to compensate the king for the loss of the vast recruiting area and enormous taxable wealth of the capital, but she nevertheless counted for a great deal. Forty years later, if Monmouth had managed to take this western metropolis his fortune might well have been different. With Bristol in his hands, he would have been a very formidable rebel indeed.

The growing importance of the city in the seventeenth century is reflected in the admiring comments of numerous visitors. Since a number of them came from London, their testimony to Bristol's greatness is all the more striking. There is no reason to think that they were unduly influenced by the Bristol Milk with which they were entertained. They found a flourishing up-and-coming port; they noted the crowded harbour, the fine quays, the substantial merchants, and the spirit of enterprise. 'It

[1] Records of the Society of Merchant Venturers of Bristol: *Book of Trade*, p. 3.

[2] First printed in 1589. There were new editions in 1590, 1591, 1607, 1616 and 1640.

[3] By a charter granted at Oxford in 1643 Charles I permitted Bristolians to trade to areas hitherto monopolized by the Merchant Adventurers of England, the Russia Company, the Eastland Company, and the Levant Company.

PLATE XXII. *Temple Meads, Bristol. The railway link between Bristol and London was completed in 1841. The old G.W.R. station is still in use but has been greatly extended.*

PLATE XXIII. *Old and new in Corn Street showing All Saints' Church, medieval, with later additions; the sixteenth- and seventeenth-century 'nails' or brass pillars on which merchants transacted business: the eighteenth-century Exchange built by John Wood the Elder.*

CORN STREET
INSURANCE

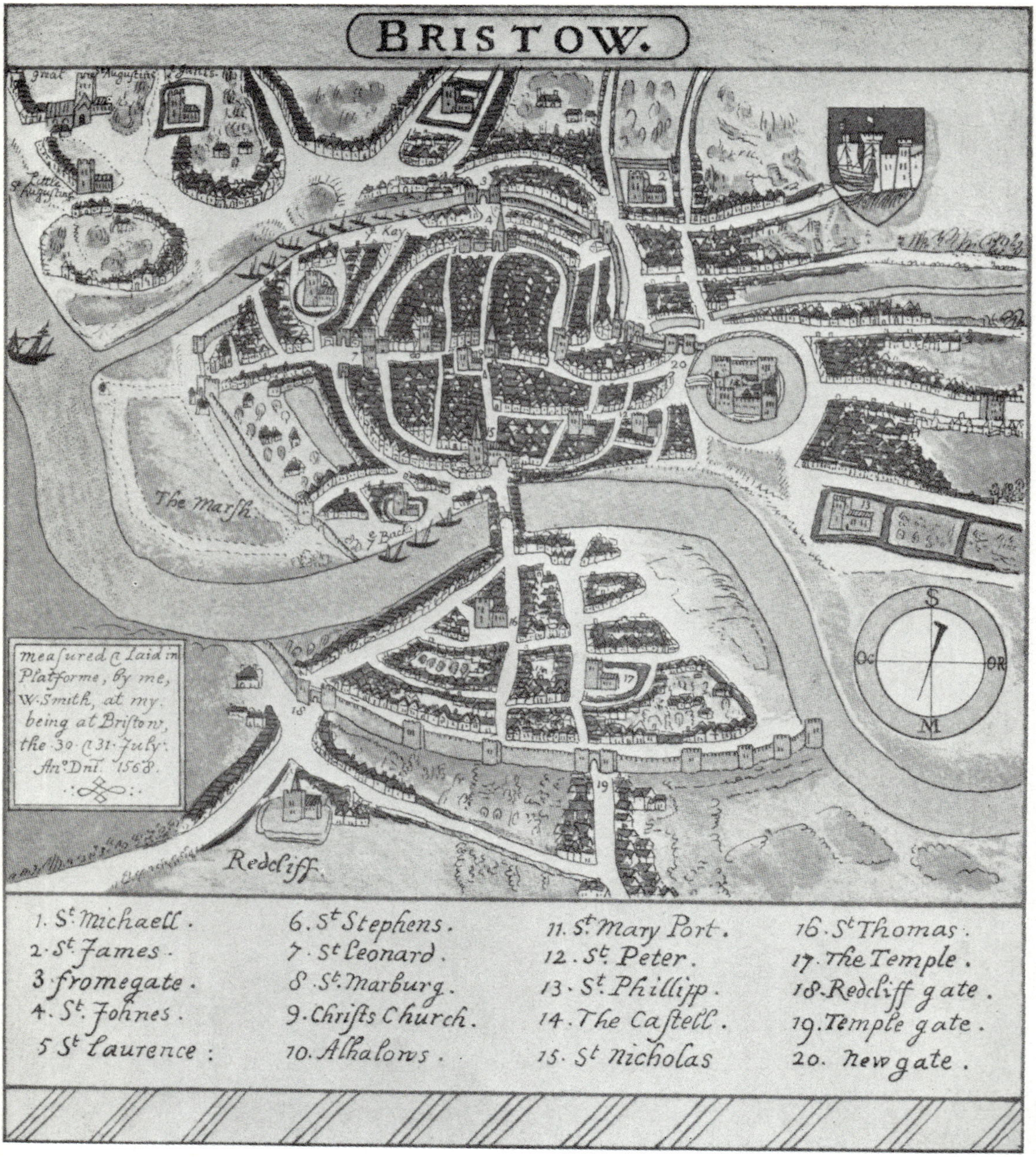
BRISTOW.
The Marsh
Redcliff
measured & laid in Platforme, by me, W. Smith, at my being at Bristow, the 30 & 31 July. An° Dni. 1568.
S
M
1. St michaell.
2. St James.
3 fromegate.
4. St Johnes.
5 St laurence:
6. St Stephens.
7. St leonard.
8. St Marburg.
9. Christs Church.
10. Alhalows.
11. St Mary Port.
12. St Peter.
13. St Phillipp.
14. The Castell.
15. St nicholas
16. St Thomas.
17. The Temple.
18. Redcliff gate.
19. Temple gate.
20. newgate.

is a second London', said one visitor in 1634. 'No city in England, London excepted, hath in so short a time bred more brave and bold seamen,' remarked Thomas Fuller in 1662, adding, perhaps not altogether without justice, 'they have been not only merchants but adventurers, possessed with a public spirit for the general good.'[1] And it was no small achievement for Bristol to win high praise from Samuel Pepys, who knew about ships and ports and was well qualified to judge Bristol in relation to the greatest of all English ports. Seventeenth-century London might have bigger plagues and better fires, but the sober substantial merchants of the western city certainly impressed the Secretary for the Navy.

The men who lived in Stuart Bristol became increasingly conscious of their own importance, 'rather admiringe themselves, soe that an ordnary fellow that is but a freeman of Bristoll, he conciets himselfe to be as grave as a senator of Rome, and very sparinge of his hatt. . . .'[2] A number of Bristolians were eager to acquire pedigrees and coats of arms, to build country houses, and to aspire to knighthood. As early as 1681 there was a demand that Bristol's chief magistrate should be a Lord Mayor.[3] Londoners might laugh at Bristolians quarrelling fiercely over the relative precedence of the wife of a knight and the wife of an alderman;[4] Roger North could sneer at the elaborate funeral arrangements;[5] but there was no doubt that the city was becoming increasingly important and increasingly rich. Before the century was out it was not merely the second port but the second city in the kingdom.

This seventeenth-century expansion was reflected in new building. Bristol Castle was demolished after the Civil War, and the Corporation arranged for the development of a considerable part of its precincts. Leases were granted which laid down certain building standards and insisted on a measure of uniformity. King Street grew on similar lines after the Restoration, and the visitor to Bristol does well to see at least the outside of the Llandoger Trow. Millerd's fine map of 1673 bears witness to growth in many directions, and at the end of the period Bristol, conscious of its new dignity, began to imitate the London fashion of laying out squares.

The prosperity of Bristol was based on industrial as well as on commercial expansion, and new industries were added to the long list of older occupations. The first sugar refinery was opened early in the seventeenth century by a distinguished merchant, Robert Aldworth, and three sugar loaves were incorporated in the design of his splendid monument in St. Peter's Church. In the second half of the century a number of new sugar houses sprang up to handle increasing imports from the West Indies. Tobacco rolling, tobacco cutting, pipe making and glass making were other indications of a changing world, and in 1695 William Bonny set up Bristol's first printing press. One of the first productions of this press was John Cary's *Proposals*

[1] Thomas Fuller, *The History of the Worthies of England*, London, 1840, vol. iii. p. 116.

[2] *The Life of Marmaduke Rawdon*, (Camden Society, 1863), p. 173.

[3] John Latimer, *Annals of Bristol in the Seventeenth Century*, Bristol, 1900, p. 406.

[4] Ibid., pp. 312–5.

[5] *The Lives of the Norths*, ed. A. Jessopp, 1890, vol. i. pp. 156–7. '. . . pride and ostentation are publicly professed. Christenings and burials pompous beyond imagination. A man who dies worth three hundred pounds will order two hundred of it to be laid out in his funeral procession.'

PLATE XXIV. *William Smith's plan of Bristol,* 1568. *The earliest authentic plan of the city. Note the walls, the gates, the castle, the Chapel of the Assumption across the middle of Bristol Bridge, and the Marsh on which Queen Square was later built.*

for the better Maintaining and Imploying the Poor in the City of Bristol. Public interest was aroused in his scheme for improving poor law administration, and in 1696 an act 'for the erecting of Hospitals and Workhouses, in the City of Bristol' made possible the establishment of one poor law authority for the whole city in place of a number of independent parish authorities. The new guardians were elected. Hopes that the poor would be made self-supporting by organizing their labour in a workhouse proved illusory, but administratively the Bristol experiment was a success and was widely imitated in other towns in the eighteenth century (see Chapter 20, p. 297).

Seventeenth-century London acted as a huge magnet attracting goods from the most distant parts of the country. Bristol could not compete with the capital, but if it was not a national market, its favourable situation enabled it to act as a collecting and distributing centre for the agricultural produce, the raw materials and the manufactured goods of a wide region. The commodities arriving by land and water were extremely miscellaneous in character, for Bristolians, like Londoners, acted as general merchants and were not forced to specialize as were merchants in smaller ports. The coastal ships and river barges were loaded at Bristol with such goods as iron, lead, nails, leather, soap, sugar, candles, salt, grocery, cloth, wool, butter, tobacco, beer, earthenware, coal, hops, glass bottles, oranges and lemons, wine and oil for the ports of the Severn, South Wales and the south-west, and they returned with equally miscellaneous cargoes, including wheat, oats, butter, cheese, linen and an immense variety of English and Welsh cloths. At the same time a well-organized carrier service to the major towns, including London, enabled Bristol to bring within its orbit a considerable area of England.

Expanding industries and growing regional trade played their part in swelling the volume of overseas commerce which made Bristol no ordinary city. It was an age when the merchants acted on the motto of their Society 'indocilis pauperiem pati'. The period between the conclusion of peace with Spain in 1604 and the outbreak of the English Civil War was one of solid comfortable prosperity. Then came a serious but only temporary setback, followed by recovery in the sixteen-fifties, and Bristol rode high on the tide of national prosperity under the later Stuarts.

For the first half of the seventeenth century Bristol merchants were interested mainly in their traditional markets in the Iberian peninsula, France and Ireland. In 1619, for example, out of 146 ships arriving at the port, 82 came from Ireland, 25 from France, 15 from Spain, 8 from Portugal, 5 from the Canaries, 6 from Newfoundland, 1 from Madeira and 1 from Algiers.[1] In 1636–37, when 176 ships arrived, the general pattern was much the same, although four ships from St. Christopher's and one from New England indicated the shape of things to come. The customs accounts show an amazing variety of goods coming into Bristol, including almonds, aquavita, baskets, battery ware, brooks and morkins, cinnamon, ginger, oranges and lemons, brown pepper, white pepper, sarsaparilla, conyskins, barrel staves, woad and Spanish wool. Outgoing cargoes were equally miscellaneous, but cloth dwarfed

[1] These and other figures for shipping are based on an examination of the Bristol Port Books in the Public Record Office.

everything else, cloth in every variety from the industrial hinterland of the port and from distant parts of the country—single bays, double bays, bridgwaters, dunster reds, filasellos, friezes, fustians, northern dozens, northern plains, penistones, perpetuanoes, stockbridges, wadmoles, polonia cloth and westphalia cloth.

Up to the middle of the century it was for Bristol largely a question of business as usual, although admittedly it was bigger business. After 1650, however, Bristolians became more than ever aware of the splendid opportunities available across the Atlantic. 213 ships arrived in 1659–60, and of these 14 came from Virginia, 10 from Barbados, 5 from Nevis, and 2 from New England. The rolls of tobacco and the butts of sugar which were seen in increasing quantities on the quays were to be the foundation of many a Bristol fortune, just as Spanish sherries and Bordeaux wines had been in earlier times. Of the 267 ships arriving in 1685–86, 70 were from the West Indies and America. Two and a half million pounds of tobacco and nearly 5,000 cwt. of sugar were imported in 1671, and many other new commodities figured in the customs accounts—molasses, indigo, ginger, cotton wool, lime juice, tortoise shells and racoon skins. In the shipping lists there began to appear among the older names like the *Unicorn*, the *Charity* and the *Hopewell* new names indicative of a new age—the *Blackamoor*, the *Maryland Merchant*, the *New England Merchant*, the *Jamaica Merchant*, and the *Nevis Merchant*.

Thus Bristol grew rich by adding new trades to old at a time when the old trades were themselves expanding. There were two flies in the ointment: the growing industrial and commercial prosperity of Ireland was thought to be a serious challenge to Bristol; and the slave trade was a monopoly of the London-controlled Royal African Company. Before the century was over, Parliament, with enthusiastic support from Bristol, had taken steps to stop the direct trade between Ireland and the plantations and had destroyed the Irish woollen industry. In 1698 it permitted any one to trade with Africa provided he paid a tax of ten per cent. on imports and exports, the proceeds of which were to maintain forts on the African coast. The prospects were bright, and Bristol prepared for a Golden Age.

Eighteenth-century Bristol expanded rapidly and has left a splendid legacy of building to delight the eyes of a later age (see Chapter 17, p. 261). The fine new Customs House in Queen Square, subsequently burnt down in the Bristol Riots; the reconstruction of the Merchants' Hall, which survived until the air-raids of 1941; and the building of the Exchange in Corn Street (see Plate XXIII), were symbolic of the growing wealth which added beauty to the city. If 'progress' demanded the removal of the medieval High Cross to a new site, and if lack of interest in the past led to the Cross's eventually passing into private hands, modern Bristolians, who have allowed the great trees to go from College Green and a replica of the High Cross to be taken to the scrap-heap, cannot afford to be too critical of the uncivilized behaviour of their ancestors. Modernization also unfortunately required the destruction of the ancient medieval bridge with its narrow arches and its tall houses, but on the other hand it provided Bristol with its Infirmary, one of the earliest eighteenth-century hospitals to be established in the provinces (see Chapter 20, p. 300).

Although Bristol was little affected by the new techniques which revolutionized eighteenth-century industry, it nevertheless experienced considerable industrial growth.[1] Commerce might be king in Bristol but it found in industry a noble consort. So accustomed are we to think of the city's eighteenth-century greatness in terms of foreign trade that it is with a feeling of surprise that we read a contemporary comment that Bristol even at the end of the century was 'not more a commercial than a manufacturing town'.[2] Yet numerous brass-works, copper-works, soap-works, glass-works, sugar refineries, distilleries, ship-building yards, potteries and iron foundries gave point to the remark. In 1729 Walter Churchman took out a patent for making chocolate by means of an engine—a patent which he later sold to Joseph Fry. Henry Overton Wills came to Bristol in 1786 to join an existing tobacco business. The names of these eighteenth-century Bristol industrialists were not without significance for the future.

Eighteenth-century Bristol continued to enjoy its very favourable position at the centre of a great regional and coastal trade. The full development of the canal system was in time to rob it of some of its advantages, but in the meantime industrial development, even in distant parts of the country, contributed to its prosperity, since often it was the most convenient market. Wheat from the Midlands, barley and oats from Wales, peas and beans from Gloucestershire and Somerset, cattle from South Wales and cheese from Cheshire, found their way by sea and river to the western metropolis. Timber from the Forest of Dean, tin from Cornwall, coal from Kingswood, copper from Anglesey, all added to the entrepôt trade of the city. Some ninety-four regular carrier services plying to and from the city to Leeds, Nottingham and other distant towns indicated the importance of Bristol in the national economy.

Another reason for the importance of this western metropolis was that it offered various services to the neighbouring areas. The first Bristol bank was established in 1750 and six more were added before the end of the century. This banking system was of more than local importance. Earlier, in 1718, there had been set up in the city the first provincial fire insurance company. In addition, Bristol capital played a significant part in the development of industry in South Wales.

Nevertheless it was its great foreign trade that made Bristol second only to London, and the words Slaves, Sugar, Tobacco and Rum are writ large across the pages of its history in this period. Africa, the West Indies and America provided splendid opportunities for making—and losing—fortunes. The emotional and romantic issues raised by these trades have perhaps tended to obscure the fact that even in the eighteenth century there was still great variety in Bristol's overseas trade. Of the 485 ships arriving in 1787, 179 came from Europe and 161 from Ireland. Only 71 came from the West Indies.

Even before the eighteenth century had run its course, the golden age was drawing

[1] For an excellent discussion of Bristol's economic importance in this period, *see* W. E. Minchinton, 'Bristol—Metropolis of the West in the Eighteenth Century', *Transactions of the Royal Historical Society*, 5th series, vol. 4, 1954, pp. 69–89.

[2] F. M. Eden, *The State of the Poor*, vol. ii, p. 183.

to a close. Never again was the city to occupy such a prominent place in the national scene. Its population in 1801 was under 70,000. Manchester by that time already had 84,000; Liverpool 78,000; and Birmingham 74,000. The tide was no longer running as strongly at Bristol as elsewhere, and man-made difficulties were added to the natural disadvantages with which the city faced the new century.

The period began hopefully, for in its first decade the Bristol Dock Company, a private enterprise, turned part of the Avon and the Frome into a floating harbour which provided far better facilities for shipping than had hitherto been available. Unfortunately, capital expenditure was heavy and the Company tried to recoup itself by charging much higher port duties than were levied elsewhere. Those who were not financially interested in the Company protested loudly. It certainly was something of a scandal that the Bristol-built *Great Western*, which was intended to help Bristol capture the American market, soon found it uneconomic to use the home port. A local poet did not miss the opportunity of commenting on Bristol's rôle as an unnatural mother. Not until 1848 was the Company taken over by the Corporation, and even that did not quickly lead to the great improvements that were expected. Elected town councillors are often nervous of doing anything that may have the immediate result of raising the rates.

The damaging effect of the Company's policy on Bristol's development must not be exaggerated. The trade of the port did not decline, although it probably grew less rapidly than it otherwise might have done. There were more fundamental causes at work than the policy of a particular Company. The old port of Bristol was obviously inconvenient for the large ships that the nineteenth century produced. In the long run Bristol's future as a great port was assured not by a more progressive policy in relation to the City Docks but by the construction of new ports at Avonmouth and Portishead. Changes in the national economy had in any case ensured that Bristol could no longer play the same dominant part as in the eighteenth century. The development of canals, roads and railways enabled many industrial areas which had hitherto perforce to use Bristol to find better service nearer home. There was no reason why Welsh produce should continue indefinitely to go through Bristol rather than through Cardiff, Newport and Swansea, and by 1850 Bristol was no longer the Welsh metropolis. The decline of the great textile industries of the south-west was yet another blow to Bristol; while the abolition of the slave trade and decreasing importance of the West Indies deprived her of two more of the props on which her former greatness had rested.

Thus Bristol moved through the first half of the century at a slower, more dignified pace than the hustling industrial cities which made England the workshop of the world. Considering the legacy these towns left to future generations, we may perhaps be grateful that Bristolians were not in quite so much of a hurry, although we must regret that the city fathers were not a little more active when the mob got out of hand in the Reform Bill Riots of 1831 and sent up in flames the Mansion House, the Customs House and the Bishop's Palace. The historian may well feel that a city government which failed to protect historic buildings and historic documents deserved its fate at the hands of the municipal reformers in 1835. He might feel bound in justice to add that the little closed Corporation which had governed Bristol since the later Middle Ages had, on the whole, not done too badly, in spite of the fact that on occasions it was guilty of the most amazing sharp practice.

The Municipal Reform Act of 1835; the launching of the *Great Western* in 1838; the plans to link London with Bristol by rail, finally complete in 1841; the building of Temple Meads station (see Plate XXII); and the acquisition by the Corporation of the City Docks were in their different ways indications that Bristol was moving with the times; and in the second half of the century a new spirit began to stir in the city. Bristol ceased to live so much in the past, and began to face the challenge of a new age. Tempers were roused and friends divided by fierce controversies over the relative merits of new docks at Avonmouth and Portishead; and there were ambitious plans to turn the whole of the Avon into a Floating Harbour. Distinguished engineers were ready with contradictory advice and had in common only the considerable fees they drew. In the end, private enterprise went ahead with work at both Portishead and Avonmouth, and eventually both were acquired by the Corporation. In spite of many set-backs Avonmouth prospered, and the building of the great King Edward Dock early in the next century showed the world that Bristol was once again in the front rank of English ports.

In the second half of the nineteenth century the population and the trade of Bristol more than doubled. It was fitting that in 1899, in the last of a long succession of charters dating back to the Middle Ages, Queen Victoria should confer upon the chief magistrate the title of Lord Mayor.

Bristol now ranks as the fifth port in the Kingdom. Its prosperity is based, as it always has been since the Middle Ages, on its overseas trade, its regional trade, and those varied industries to which the twentieth century has made such a notable addition. If the name of Bristol is now so closely associated with the making of aeroplanes, it is because Sir George White in 1909 was quick to grasp the significance of what was still little more than an interesting new toy. The year after the first cross-channel flight he established at Filton the company now known as the Bristol Aeroplane Company whose products are as well known as those of J. S. Fry and W. D. and H. O. Wills. Industrial and commercial expansion went hand in hand, and in the nineteen-twenties it was necessary to double the extent of the Royal Edward Dock which had been considered adequate for the needs of Avonmouth at the beginning of the century. The broad basis of the city's economy has enabled it to face the crises of modern times with greater confidence than many other large towns. In the Second World War it had a distinguished part to play, and it paid the price in considerable damage from air-raids and irreparable loss of many historic buildings. Only gradually is the new Bristol rising from the ruins of the old.

In the year 1955 it is still possible to discern in the layout of the modern city the framework of an earlier Bristol, but even in recent times a great deal has disappeared. The Frome, which once carried ships into the heart of the city, has been largely covered over, and in the process Bristol lost much of its earlier character. A major road driven diagonally across it has transformed the spacious Queen Square into two triangles; the historic College Green has been lowered over four feet and denuded of its trees; and in the Horsefair bodies were removed from an ancient burial ground to make way for a vast departmental store. The outlying villages are becoming suburbs and losing their identity, Charlton had to be destroyed to extend the Filton runway. What the city will look like at the end of the twentieth century is not for the historian to predict, but he can at least hope that it will not eat too much into the surrounding countryside or lose those characteristics which make it one of the most romantic of English cities.

CHAPTER FOURTEEN

BRISTOL AND OVERSEAS EXPANSION

IN the third quarter of the fifteenth century Bristol was already much concerned in the search for new lands to the westward. The wealth of the city, her powerful merchant class and her geographical position seemed to mark her out for westward exploration. The recurring obstacles which she encountered in her trade with Iceland and the refusal of the Portuguese to allow any foreigner to share in the trade of the new lands and islands discovered by them rendered the need for this search urgent. Here in Bristol the two chief streams of information relating to lands beyond the Atlantic came together. Bristol sailors returned from Iceland with stories of the Norse discoveries of the eleventh century—Helluland, Markland and Wineland the Good. Indeed, it is just possible that some of them may have seen old maps of these ancient explorations. Here in Bristol these men encountered other sailors lately returned from the Iberian peninsula. They, too, had surprising stories to tell of strange logs of wood, curiously fashioned boats and the bodies of men belonging to a race hitherto unknown in Europe, which had been washed up on the shores of the western islands.

The merchants of Bristol were stimulated by these stories and in the second half of the fifteenth century sent out an unknown number of expeditions to search for islands to the westward. All that we do know for certain is that a ship owned by John Jay the younger, commanded by a Welshman named Lloyd, sailed in 1480 in search of the island of 'Brasylle'. There was another expedition in the following year. Beyond the fact that it consisted of two ships, the *George* and the *Trinity*, that it was probably looking for new fishing grounds and that it accomplished nothing, little is known.[1] There is a tradition that, in 1477, Christopher Columbus in the course of his wanderings arrived in Bristol, but whether he came here because he knew that he could find a ship in this port to carry him to Iceland or because he was aware of the enthusiasm of Bristol merchants for western exploration we have no knowledge.

In view of this interest of Bristol it can therefore be assumed that John Cabot did not arrive here by accident. Almost certainly he came to this city because he had heard of these expeditions and also because he was aware that here there existed more information about lands to the westward than was to be found in any other port in Christendom.

[1] E. Carus-Wilson, *The Overseas Trade of Bristol*, (Bristol Record Society Publications, vol. vii), pp. 157–8 and 161–5.

John Cabot seemed to the Bristol merchants to advocate a more promising proposal than anything they had before considered. He was not anxious to search for an island but for a continent and he argued that if he kept on sailing westward long enough he was bound to make a landfall some time. The fact that he believed that this land would be Asia does not lessen the soundness of his argument, and so he enlisted the support of the Bristol merchants. Cabot must have been a remarkable person, but he remains one of the most baffling figures in history. We have some slight knowledge of his early life, but it does not carry us very far. By birth he was a Genoese and a Venetian by adoption. Before he came to Bristol he had travelled much in the Near East and was a skilled and learned geographer. In the 1480s he arrived in Bristol with his family and within ten years was accounted one of its principal citizens. Even if he had done nothing else, this in itself would have been a sufficient achievement to entitle him to immortality, since in Bristol it is usually considered that several generations must elapse before a family can be counted Bristolian. This man, then, steps suddenly on to the stage of history and after leading two successful voyages, which were destined to alter the whole course of English history, he disappears as completely as the Pied Piper of Hamelin after his second and less meritorious performance. Whether it was Newfoundland, Cape Breton or Nova Scotia that Cabot discovered on his first voyage is a question which may safely be left to Newfoundlanders, Cape Bretoners and Nova Scotians to decide among themselves. Unquestionably it was land first seen by Englishmen, land newly found.[1]

Bristol may have lamented Cabot's sudden disappearance but of this we have no record. She was, however, highly satisfied with his achievement. He discovered rich fishing grounds which Bristolians, as well as others from the West Country, proceeded to exploit. Bristol's interest in exploration was kept alive after Cabot's disappearance not only by the Newfoundland fisheries but also because of her trading relations with the Iberian peninsula. In the early sixteenth century her merchants who traded with that region sometimes had representatives of their families permanently established in the port with which they had business. These expatriates were continually hearing of fabulously rich countries beyond the ocean, discovered by the Spaniards. This news they duly reported to their principals in Bristol, and it would be surprising if in retelling these tales the wealth and glory of the new lands were not exaggerated. It was natural that Thomas Tison, a Bristolian, should be the first Englishman to land in the West Indies, to which he had gone on the look-out for trade, and it was also natural that a fellow citizen of his, Master Andrew, should be the only Englishman to sail with Magellan.

During the opening decades of the sixteenth century such families as the Thornes kept the idea of western exploration before their fellow citizens, but they received little support either from Bristol or from the country at large. Henry VII was not inclined to risk any considerable sums in such hazardous undertakings, though he must have felt that he had reaped a reasonable reward from the meagre monetary

[1] *See* J. A. Williamson, *The Voyages of the Cabots.*

recognition which he had given to Cabot. It is true that in 1501[1] and again in 1502[2] the first of the Tudors issued letters patent to Bristol merchants which allowed them to carry on the work of exploration, but the nature of these grants appears to be vague. His son, Henry VIII, had little or no interest in such schemes. Indeed, almost the only immediate substantial consequence of Cabot's discoveries was the establishment of the Newfoundland fishing industry.

Robert Thorne the younger, co-founder of Bristol Grammar School, was deeply interested in this subject, and helped Sebastian Cabot in financing his expedition for the discovery of a north-west passage in 1526. Later Thorne and his fellow citizen Roger Barlow, who had been one of Sebastian Cabot's companions on this fruitless voyage to the north, addressed their now famous *Declaration of the Indies*[3] to King Henry VIII. In this remarkable document they urged that monarch to turn his mind from traditional European entanglements, which had cost England so much blood and treasure in the past, and to lead his country along what they believed to be its destined path. Beyond the ocean lay rich lands, waiting to be discovered and claimed for England, and by taking a northerly route a sure and easy way to the Pacific and Cathay would be discovered. Thorne and Barlow greatly underestimated the rigours of polar travel, though they were ready enough to believe that it might be cold for a few days on either side of the Pole. This scheme was believed to be fantastic at the time, but it is interesting to remember that in our own day airmen are establishing routes to the Pacific and to the Orient not very different from that recommended by these two Bristolians over four hundred years ago. Henry VIII, however, was unconvinced and save for the enthusiasm of a few such far-seeing men as Thorne no-one in England during the first half of the sixteenth century was seriously interested in overseas exploration.

From about the middle of the century onward great changes took place in public opinion on this subject, and in national policy. This period was in fact a time of active preparation for the great achievements that were to come and in these preparations Bristol also shared. In 1552 the Merchant Venturers of Bristol received their charter from Edward VI. This event was of great importance in the city's history since it so largely enabled her to play the great part she did in the story of English overseas exploration, trade and colonization. The existence of such a body here meant that capital could be mobilized for great undertakings, experience could be pooled and, when the need arose, powerful influence could be brought to bear on Parliament and Court in furtherance of objects of which the Society approved.

Though Bristol went through a period of comparative stagnation in the reign of Queen Elizabeth I, a number of her citizens took a hand in privateering and exploration in the New World. Thus Thomas Chester, Thomas Kelke and Thomas Aldworth helped to finance the first voyage of Martin Frobisher; the Wynters and

[1] J. A. Williamson, op. cit., pp. 46–54.

[2] Ibid., pp. 57–66.

[3] Printed as a chapter *in* Barlow, R., *A Brief Summe of Geographie*. Edited with an introduction and notes by E. G. R. Taylor. London, printed for the Hakluyt Society, 1932.

other citizens were associated with the later expeditions of that redoubtable captain to the far north. But the north-west passage was not discovered and Frobisher's treasure turned out to be fools' gold. The Wynters also helped to finance Drake's great expedition in the course of which he circumnavigated the globe, and one of them sailed with him. In 1582 Hakluyt implored the merchants of Bristol to fit out two vessels to accompany Sir Humphrey Gilbert on his voyage to establish a colony in Newfoundland. At first the local response was satisfactory, but when the merchants learned that the men of Southampton would probably reap a richer reward from this undertaking than they would, their enthusiasm cooled. They therefore supported Carlisle in his projected venture which, however, never materialized. In 1594 the *Grace* of Bristol, commanded by Captain Rice Jones, set sail for the Gulf of St. Lawrence in search of whales and train-oil. Thus, before the close of the century, the city had become fairly accustomed to the sailing of such expeditions, avowedly for the development of trade or for the exploration of new lands, but not infrequently intended for raids on the Spanish colonies. Before the close of the sixteenth century, in fact, the eloquent and prolonged advocacy of the younger Hakluyt, now prebendary of Bristol, had convinced some of the merchants of the city of the desirability of establishing permanent English colonies overseas.

Individual Bristolians took some share in the foundation of the East India Company. Others participated in the early voyages of this new body. Thus, Captain Edmund Marlowe of Bristol was in command of the *James* on the ninth voyage, Thomas Aldworth sailed in the tenth voyage and was responsible for the establishment of a permanent English trading factory at Surat. Martin Pring was admiral of the fifth voyage and Captain Haynes, Paul Canning and other Bristolians went out to India in the Company's service. But the city as a whole took no part in the Indian trade until it was thrown open in 1813.

In the meantime, the New World, from the Arctic to the Caribbean, provided Bristol with an ample field for the enterprise of her citizens. In 1601 Hakluyt was energetically pushing his proposals for the establishment of a permanent English colony in the New World. He now urged the Society of Merchant Venturers to take this task up in earnest by fitting out ships and dispatching the expedition. When in the following year Robert Salterne returned from Virginia with favourable accounts of the country he had seen, a group of Bristol merchants at last decided to act in the manner which Hakluyt had been pressing upon them for twenty years. In 1603, therefore, a ship, commanded by Martin Pring, sailed for the northern parts of Virginia. Perhaps it should be pointed out here that the boundaries of Virginia at that time were vague and included much of the eastern seaboard of North America. After a successful voyage, Pring and his companions landed and were the first Englishmen to inhabit, though but for a few months, and to plant corn in a country that was later to become famous as New England. On his return Pring reported favourably on the nature of the land he had visited and brought with him various commodities in support of his contention that it was a suitable place for the establishment of a permanent colony. Nothing was done immediately, and three years passed by before another ship from Bristol sailed for the northern parts of Virginia. It was under the nominal command of Captain Thomas Hanham, but the real leader was Pring. These beginnings, however, did not lead to any permanent settlement at that time. Moreover, Bristol's main interests were still concentrated in Newfoundland and in the discovery of a north-west passage to the Pacific.

The first serious attempt of this city to establish settlements in the New World took place in Newfoundland, the island in which Bristol had been interested since the end of the fifteenth century and whose fisheries had already enriched her people. By a grant from the Privy Council made in May 1610, a powerful group of Bristol and London merchants were authorized to proceed with the colonization of that island. Ships were got ready and when the prospective settlers were collected the expedition sailed in June 1610 under the command of John Guy, a former sheriff of the city. A colony was established at a place now known as Cupids, but it never prospered. Guy, though brave and energetic, lacked many of the qualities necessary for a successful leader of so hazardous an undertaking. He was strict in his discipline, arbitrary and not always wise in his decisions. Moreover, from the beginning there were constant bickerings between the members of the Company in England and between them and their chosen governor. In Newfoundland, fishermen, both English and foreign, refused to acknowledge Guy's authority; the first winter was a severe one and some settlers died of scurvy. When spring came the whole colony was disheartened, supplies brought out from England were insufficient and, later, a powerful body of pirates who came to Newfoundland to refit their ships defied Guy's authority and compelled the settlers to work for them. Though he battled bravely with the difficulties that beset him and carried out extensive explorations of the coast, he finally gave up his task in disgust, the colony lost ground rapidly and in 1618 the Merchant Venturers of Bristol bought a piece of land from the impotent Company and founded the Colony of Bristol Hope at Harbour Grace. At first this place flourished,[1] but in a few years it also languished and in due course ceased to exist. In 1910 the Merchant Venturers erected a monument at Cupids to commemorate the close association of the city of Bristol with this ill-fated attempt to establish a permanent English colony in Newfoundland.

After this unfortunate experience Bristol turned her colonizing activities once more to New England. Since the voyages of Salterne and Pring, much had happened. The Pilgrim Fathers landed in 1620 and among them was a Bristol citizen, Francis Easton, and his wife, Dorothy. Two years later the Council of New England issued letters patent to Robert, son of Sir Ferdinando Gorges, enabling him to establish the first colony in Massachusetts Bay. Other Bristolians also received grants and during the twenties and thirties of the seventeenth century Sir Ferdinando Gorges spent large sums of money in the promotion of colonies in New England, and as a result of his efforts many settlers were successfully established in that area. In 1635, in recognition of his notable services to the cause, he was appointed Governor of New England, but he never took up the appointment.

[1] S. Purchas, *Purchas his Pilgrims*, vol. xix, pp. 441–5.

While Bristol was attempting to colonize Newfoundland and New England she never forgot the great project of discovering a north-west passage. Trade was still her first love and the gorgeous East still beckoned. When, therefore, in 1629, it was reported in Bristol that London was fitting out a ship which was to search for this elusive way to the Pacific the old zest for this project, which had fired the imagination of Bristol captains for over a century, revived. It is clear from the documents that Bristol was very jealous of London and she was also none too certain about the reliability of promises made by Charles I.[1] Great care was taken, therefore, to ensure that Bristol's position should be made abundantly clear. The city was determined to share to the full in any economic advantages that might result from the discovery of a suitable navigable channel through to the western ocean. After much looking about, a satisfactory ship was found. She was rechristened the *Henrietta Maria*, in honour of the Queen, and refitted. The merchants stocked her with everything which at that time was considered needful for northern exploration and the command of the expedition was entrusted to Captain Thomas James.[2] Like Cabot, James emerges from the shadows for a short time during which he plays a memorable part in English exploration and then returns to obscurity. By profession he was a barrister-at-law, but what we know of his career proves that he was also a highly skilled and daring navigator. Judging by the record of his voyage that he has left behind,[3] it is evident that he was in addition a man of culture who possessed considerable literary talent. There is a tradition, amounting almost to a probability, that the young poet, Coleridge, over a century and a half later, read this book in the Bristol library and that he drew on it for some of the imagery of the *Ancient Mariner*.

And now there came both mist and snow
And it grew wondrous cold:
And ice, mast-high, came floating by,
As green as emerald.

And through the drifts the snowy clifts
Did send a dismal sheen:
Nor shapes of men nor beasts we ken—
The ice was all between.

The ice was here, the ice was there,
The ice was all around
It cracked and growled, and roared and howled,
Like noises in a swound!

[1] *Merchant Venturers' Book of Trade*, fol. 185.
[2] Adams's *Chronicle of Bristol*, p. 226.
[3] *The Strange and Dangerous Voyage of Captain Thomas James*, printed in L. Foxe and T. James.

Be this as it may, the work undoubtedly contains some fine pieces of descriptive writing and some passages of simple eloquence. The account which James gives of the submergence of the *Henrietta Maria,* to prevent her from being carried away by drifting ice or smashed to pieces, has a quality about it to be found in the writings of few explorers.

'Our men that were ashoare stood looking upon us, almost dead with cold and sorrowes, to see our misery and their owne. We lookt upon them againe, and both upon each other, with woefull hearts. Darke night drew on, and I bade the Boate to be haled up, and commanded my louing companions to goe all into her, who (in some refusing complements) expressed their faithful affections to mee, as loth to part from me. I told them that my meaning was to goe ashore with them. And thus, lastly, I forsook the ship.'[1]

Unlike Guy, James was a true leader and it was mainly due to his courage and resource that the majority of the crew survived the winter. Even James, however, could not prevent losses. When spring came the carpenter and some of his comrades had died. The ship was successfully refloated as soon as the ice had cleared away, and to the great joy of the men it was found that the beer which had lain in ice through the winter was in perfect condition. When the *Henrietta Maria* was once more seaworthy James proceeded on his explorations for another season. During the two summers he spent in the north he explored much of Hudson Bay and discovered James Bay, gave names to various promontories and mapped the region he had visited. He returned to England in the autumn of 1632 and the only evidence that was left behind of this gallant attempt to unlock the mysteries of the north was a few lonely graves on a small eminence near James's winter quarters, which the homesick and lonely men had named Brandon Hill.

While James was thus vainly trying to find the north-west passage, more promising fields of endeavour farther south were already attracting the attention of Bristol merchants. By now, Virginia was firmly established. The colony of New Plymouth had struck roots and the Massachusetts Bay Company had recently established another colony in New England. In 1632, when James was still in the far north, a patent was granted for the foundation of Maryland. Bermuda was now flourishing and Englishmen had laid claim to Barbados, St. Christopher and Nevis. Year by year the commerce of these places was of increasing importance to the city. Tobacco, denounced by James I and loathed by Charles I, was nevertheless increasing in popularity and already the Virginia variety had won a special reputation for excellence. It was much easier, and certainly paid better, to trade in this commodity and in other colonial products than to squander money and valuable lives in the fruitless search for a western passage which might in fact not exist. When, therefore, the *Henrietta Maria* dropped anchor in Bristol the zeal for northern exploration was virtually extinct and the merchants' attention was already becoming concentrated on these new attractive sources of wealth. In the thirties, ship after ship carried out

[1] *The Voyages of Captain Luke Foxe and Captain Thomas James,* vol. ii, p. 520.

hundreds of people to the plantations, together with quantities of household goods and stores of all kinds, and the colonial trade grew steadily in importance.

In 1655 the most distinguished Bristolian of his age, Admiral Sir William Penn (see Plate XXXIII), with General Venables, captured the rich island of Jamaica and so opened up a new source of wealth for his country. This distinguished seaman, of whom Bristol has every reason to be proud, has the right to rank with Nelson, Blake, Drake, Rodney and Hood. He lies in St. Mary Redcliffe Church, a fitting resting place for so illustrious a Bristolian who, like William Canynges, its pious restorer, drew his greatness from the sea. Admiral Penn's son, William, the founder of Pennsylvania, was well known in Bristol. Here he lived for some time and was warmly supported in his colonizing project by his fellow Quakers. It was in Bristol that he married his second wife, Hannah Callowhill, and such Bristolians as James Logan were among his closest associates. After Penn's death there was a fairly constant connexion maintained between this city and Pennsylvania and so Bristol can with some justice claim to be the mother of that famous state.

Early in the eighteenth century another Bristolian of an entirely different kind played a notable part in maritime and colonial history. Woodes Rogers has never received the recognition he deserves, but by his great privateering exploits he proved that the Elizabethan spirit was still alive in England. He is often referred to, by those who have never taken the trouble to find out anything about him, as if he were merely a bloodthirsty pirate, but this is far from the truth. In the book[1] which he wrote on the completion of his voyage round the world he shows himself to have been a far-sighted patriot who held that it was unreasonable for Spain to claim for herself permanent possession of the trade and the uninhabited lands and islands of the Pacific. Though his voyage was in part intended as a privateering raid on the old enemy it was also sent out to discover, in fact, what trade possibilities the Pacific held. With his two ships he entered the Pacific and attacked Spain at her 'back door' as he had intended and with considerable success for he not only captured many ships but the important town of Guayaquil as well. Then, having achieved his purpose, he struck out across the Pacific and, after three years of privation and adventure, he returned to England with a greater booty than any privateer hitherto had brought safely home. Some years after his return Woodes Rogers was appointed to the governorship of the Bahamas. These islands were at that time infested by pirates who preyed upon the trade of the West Indies. The new governor scattered the pirates and destroyed their bases, but never received the assistance from the Royal Navy or the home Government which was his due. The closing years of his life were identified with the Bahamas, where he died in 1732 and lies buried in an unknown grave in Nassau.

About the middle of the seventeenth century a revulsion in public opinion on the subject of emigration occurred. Down to the outbreak of the Civil War the outward movement of people was on the whole encouraged, though even in the thirties it is evident that some of those in authority were disturbed by the exodus that was going

[1] Woodes Rogers, *A Cruising Voyage Round the World.*

PLATE XXV. *View looking up river from below the Rope Walk, Wapping,* 1825, *from a watercolour by Rowbotham.* (*Bristol City Art Gallery.*)

on. Thereafter emigration of free citizens was viewed with less and less approval and by the time of the Restoration, in 1660, it was denounced as a cause of national weakness. The traders of Bristol, therefore, had to look elsewhere for the labourers that were required by the colonies and so long as the Civil War went on and sectarian zeal continued to burn they had no difficulty in filling their ships. Cavaliers and Roundheads, Nonconformists and Churchmen in turn punished their unfortunate enemies by forcible emigration, and so from the port of Bristol there passed out to the plantations thousands of these labourers whose lives thereafter were miserable, but for the most part mercifully short. When religious zeal died down and the supply of victims failed, Bristol skippers turned to kidnapping and the city acquired an infamous reputation for the share it took in this wicked traffic. But still the appetite of the plantations for labour was unappeased and as a result the merchants felt that they were losing valuable opportunities of amassing wealth. Sugar had by now become the staple crop of the West Indies and its successful production demanded an abundant and cheap labour supply. The work was heavy and for Europeans under the tropical sun it was deadly.

So it came about that in the second half of the seventeenth century Englishmen, with Bristolians well to the fore, turned to the traffic in negro slaves, a commerce which their countrymen in earlier generations had despised. When the rich possibilities of this trade came to be recognized, London, true to her nature in the opinion of Bristol, attempted to monopolize it and the royal charters under which the trade was organized after the Restoration gave the London Company a monopoly. Bristol, however, had always been opposed to the enjoyment of monopolistic trading privileges by London merchants and thus, despite the law, her ships in growing numbers frequented the Bight of Benin. In due course they returned to the Avon from the colonies with valuable cargoes of sugar, molasses, rum, tobacco and other colonial products. Since this trade was illicit it is impossible to give any exact estimate of its extent, but there is enough evidence to prove conclusively that during the reigns of Charles II and James II it became of prime importance to the city. There were, it is true, some Bristolians, like the great Edward Colston and Nathaniel Pinney, who were members of the Royal African Company. But for the most part Bristol traders on the West African coast were interlopers until, in the last decade of the seventeenth century, the trade was thrown open. When this event occurred Bristol vigorously extended the slave business and the result is that to-day her citizens derive a macabre delight from the contemplation of the presumed iniquities of their forebears and their alleged preponderance in this wicked trade. In fact, Bristol never was for any considerable period of time the first slave port of the kingdom, but unquestionably she came second, first to London and later to Liverpool.

With good fortune, this trade might yield great profits. Indeed, if the voyage was successfully completed a merchant might expect to derive a profit from three distinct transactions. He would exchange the goods sent out from Bristol for slaves and make a profit. He would exchange the slaves in the plantations for colonial products at a profit, and he would dispose of these on his return to Bristol for cash, at a profit.

PLATE XXVI. *Lucea, Jamaica, from a line engraving published in 1770. (National Maritime Museum.)*

But it was always a risky business. Between 1688 and 1807 England was frequently at war and so her commerce was often exposed to enemy attack. Pirates infested the African coast and there were freebooters beyond the Atlantic. A pestilence on a slave ship, a mutiny, shipwreck, a poor market for slaves, these and a dozen other things might occur, any one of which was liable not only to destroy hope of gain but to entail a total loss of all the capital sunk in the venture. Because of all of these things and also because of the growing competition of Liverpool, Bristol's interest in the slave trade greatly declined during the second half of the eighteenth century. The writer of *The New Bristol Guide* in 1799 preened himself on the virtue of his city which unlike evil Liverpool took little part in this infamous traffic.[1] But he failed to confess that, though the righteous city was now so little concerned in the direct slave trade itself, her pious merchants did not scruple to buy negroes in the colonies from their wicked northern neighbours in order to supply their own plantations with labour.

While Bristol's interest in the slave trade declined during the second half of the eighteenth century, her connexion with the colonies generally, but with the West Indies in particular, steadily grew. It was common for her West Indian merchants to have plantations of their own in the sugar islands, and between the Restoration and the close of the Napoleonic Wars these men took a direct share in local colonial politics and, in England, they watched over colonial interests, which, as interpreted by them, were their own. The West Indian Society and the New West India Society busied themselves with colonial demands and complaints so long as these coincided with the interests of the members of these bodies. But when colonies pursued ends that were deemed detrimental to the city's interests, the attitude was entirely different. To these Englishmen, as to their countrymen at large, colonies existed mainly for the benefit of England. They were sources of raw material and closed markets for English products and their development must be determined by the overriding importance of the mother country's good. In the main, however, during the first six decades of the eighteenth century, though there were from time to time disagreements between individual colonies and the merchants of Bristol, there was no violent conflict of interest. Throughout this prosperous period Bristol ships went out to the sugar and tobacco islands either by way of the African coast or direct. They traded with the mid-Atlantic colonies, New England and Newfoundland as well. Sometimes, as in the case of the Newfoundland ships, a triangular commerce developed. The ships would sail for the Banks with men and supplies for the season's fishing and while some returned home direct with their cargoes others carried the salt cod to the Iberian peninsula. There they exchanged the fish for wine and fruit and so returned to Bristol.

When trouble began to develop with the continental colonies at the close of the Seven Years War (1763) Bristol was enthusiastic for American rights. She was bitterly opposed to the Stamp Act and hailed its repeal with jubilation. For several years thereafter the colonial cause continued to enjoy the warm advocacy of this

[1] *The New Bristol Guide*, p. 66.

city, whose merchants roundly denounced the Government's American policy. It should not be thought that this indicated any special concern for political theories, for the plain fact was that the city was interested in imperial relations and colonial political rights only in so far as these affected her economic position. The Merchant Venturers presented a number of petitions to Parliament complaining of the disastrous effects upon trade which were the direct results of the Government's restrictive policy.[1] When the Sugar Bill was under discussion (1766) Bristol pressed for a moderate policy, but by that time the pro-Government group had become powerful. The city generally remained faithful to the American cause down to the outbreak of war and indeed there was a pro-American party in the city for some time after hostilities began. The fact that in 1774 Edmund Burke, the eloquent champion of American rights, and Henry Cruger, an American by birth, were elected as the city's representatives in Parliament made Bristol's position in this long-drawn-out contest abundantly clear.

Throughout 1775, though the anti-American party was gaining strength, the Merchant Venturers continued to petition the Government against its policy. Once the war had started in earnest the two parties in the city became more clear-cut and they filled the press with their acrimonious correspondence.[2] As late as December 1775 the Merchant Venturers petitioned the Government against the Bill then before Parliament which was designed to prohibit all trade with the Americans. A year later, December 1776, the Bristol Whigs feasted at Burke's expense on a day appointed by the King as a national fast because of the American dispute. But by then, public opinion in the city was beginning to swing more rapidly to the Government side. In January 1777 a general meeting of citizens congratulated the King on his success in America. In 1780 both Burke and Cruger were rejected by the city's electors, but by that time the tide was already flowing in the other direction. It was not long before the accumulated disasters of this mismanaged war led to bitter attacks upon the Government and in January 1782 the Corporation petitioned the House of Commons against the continuance of hostilities. When, finally, North fell from power the city sent its congratulations to the new Government and a special letter of thanks to Burke; Cruger was elected Mayor that year.

When the anti-slave trade campaign opened the abolitionists were supported by Quakers, Free Churchmen and others from the beginning and there seems to have been little justification for Clarkson's apprehensions as he set out on his first journey to Bristol in 1787. On the whole he was well received here. The Merchant Venturers allowed him to examine their papers and in 1788 the first petition from Bristol against the slave trade was sent up to London. A year later, however, the pro-slave trade party set up a strong committee in the city which contained several former Masters of the Society of Merchant Venturers, ex-mayors, mayors-to-be and other important people. From then on till the final emancipation of the slaves in the

[1] *Merchant Venturers' Book of Petitions*, fol 1.

[2] *Felix Farley's Bristol Journal*, July–September 1775.

thirties of the nineteenth century the city was divided on the subject of slavery. But as years went by the champions of the old system grew fewer.

At the end of the eighteenth century and for some time after that the city's commerce was unduly concentrated in the West Indian trade. It is not suggested here that there were no other branches of commerce in which Bristol participated but it seems fairly clear that too much money was sunk in sugar. As late as 1830 Charles Pinney declared that five-eighths of Bristol's trade was with the West Indies, so it can scarcely be denied that the decline of West Indian prosperity, which occurred about the middle of the nineteenth century, adversely affected the fortunes of this city.

With the decline of the West Indian interest Bristol ceased to play a principal role in colonial affairs. During the nineteenth century she retained an interest in the West Indies and in the new West African trade. Occasionally she petitioned the Government against some particular measure that seemed to threaten her interests. Meanwhile the old Newfoundland fishing industry was declining and ceased altogether just before the outbreak of the 1914–18 war.

Bristol opened up some commerce with South Africa and Australasia and in the third quarter of the nineteenth century she was once more an important emigration port. It is sometimes declared that because the *Charlotte Jane* was a Bristol-built ship this city had a share in the foundation of New Zealand, but it would be hard to sustain this claim. In the present century the city has recovered from its nineteenth-century lethargy and is once more vigorous and forward-looking. The Imperial Tobacco Company, one of the giants of British industry, has widespread commitments throughout the Commonwealth; the flourishing chocolate industry of the city is largely dependent for its chief raw material on Empire sources of supply, and so the African trade is still important in the Bristol economy. Lastly, the vast aircraft industry, which has come into existence during the past forty-five years, not only plays a great part in Empire communications but has ramifications of growing importance in the Dominions. In all these ways the links that unite Bristol to the Queen's territories overseas are strong, and will, so Bristol believes, endure.

BOOKS FOR FURTHER READING

FOXE, L. and T. JAMES. *The Voyages of Captain Luke Foxe of Hull, and Captain Thomas James of Bristol in search of a North-West Passage in* 1631–2. Ed. by Miller Christy. 2 vols. London, Printed for the Hakluyt Society, 1893.

MACINNES, C. M. *A Gateway of Empire.* Bristol, 1939.

PARES, RICHARD. *A West-India Fortune.* London, 1950.

ROGERS, WOODES. *A Cruising Voyage Round the World.* Introduction and notes by G. E. Mainwaring. London, 1928.

WILLIAMSON, J. A. *The Voyages of the Cabots and The English Discovery of North America under Henry VII and Henry VIII.* London, 1929.

CHAPTER FIFTEEN

BRISTOL SOCIETY IN THE EIGHTEENTH CENTURY

IN contemporary opinion the social organization and amenities of Bristol in the eighteenth century suffered by comparison with those of Bath. The comparison was unreasonable but inevitable, for at that time each city reached the peak of its particular type of urban development—Bristol as the city of business, Bath as the city of leisure. It was natural for those visiting Bath to make the short journey to see Bristol as well, but the transition was too violent for their judgement not to be in some degree unbalanced. Bath was the duchess among cities, with a setting of contrived and conscious elegance in which there was no taint of trade. Bristol was the sweaty workman, in leather breeches and shirtsleeves, fairly reeking of the tannery, the soap vats or the docks. Bath was essentially a holiday playground for the nobility and the ever-widening circle of the rich, where the empty, formal, social round of Assemblies, card parties, tea drinking, calls, visits to the Pump Room, constituted an elegant nothingness to be executed in the highest style of manners. This was sheer anathema to Bristol, for if there was one thing that busy place could not stomach it was foolery and fashion. For eight hundred years she had been a great trading city and in 1700 was about to become the second in the kingdom, inferior to London alone in size and wealth and trading importance. And that economic triumph had been won precisely by eschewing the fooleries of Bath. The values that her merchants prized were those inculcated by trade—hard work, honesty, alertness, seriousness of purpose. Hers, in short, was an essentially Puritan society, and the hackles of any honest Bristol man instinctively rose at the sight of some trifling idler from Bath tittupping round the docks and warehouses, holding his nose against the honest smells of industry.

Contempt for luxury and leisure had been pushed to the point where any concession to civilized living was suspect. As late as 1700 the city was substantially medieval, and by then a desperately overcrowded tangle of narrow lanes and courts and alleys, filled with some four thousand buildings in the architectural style of 1450 or 1500 which was still followed by builders late in the seventeenth century. Houses were for trade first and dwelling afterwards, and even the richest merchants were content to live over their business premises in homes innocent of planning, and replete with every Tudor inconvenience. Affluence was exhibited only in the overloading of the living-rooms with crudely vigorous panelling, plaster work, and carving both in wood and stone. Middle-class homes were dreary with unpainted wainscoting, floors stained with soot and small beer in lieu of carpets, a few oak chairs without upholstery, a table or two, and some coarse woollen hangings on the walls. The hovels of the workers were the merest dens. As time went on, some of the richest people migrated to the handsome Georgian streets and squares built just outside the old city area, suburbs in which housing and street conditions were much better; but still more remained faithful to their familiar alleys, and it cannot be said that much improvement took place in the old city during the eighteenth century. In the narrow cobbled streets (and even the principal ones rarely reached 20 ft. in width) there accumulated the malodorous refuse of private households, of the numerous street stalls and markets for food and animals, the slaughter-houses, and the awful by-products of such places as tanneries and dye-works—all of which was thrown out into the central gutter—while the traffic struggled to force its way through the wretched lanes. Pedestrians, porters, sedan-chair-men, horsemen, drivers of private carriages, hearses, carts, vans, drays of all sizes and descriptions, iron-shod sledges (peculiar to Bristol), stage coaches and country carriers' waggons, all strove together through the garbage and the swarms of dogs, cats, goats and domestic pigs which, as late as 1800, were allowed to roam the streets in search of food. To this bedlam must be added the bawling of street hawkers, of the market people at their stalls, of apprentices and shopmen 'barking' at their doors for custom, of the incessant banging and clanging from hundreds of smiths' forges, coopers' yards, carpenters' shops and shipbuilders' slips. The night was likewise unquiet, for important funerals were held then, preceded by as much as six or even twelve hours' continuous tolling of the bells in the parish church of the deceased. The street manners of Bristolians were notoriously fierce, for the battle went to the strong; fights were innumerable and accidents too common to claim much attention. John Wesley was very nearly Bristol's most distinguished victim, for in 1747 he and his horse were borne down by a huge van and he escaped death under its wheels only by inches.

This tornado of noise and activity astonished and disgusted visitors. Defoe, in the reign of Anne, said that though Bristol was but fourteen miles from Bath, 'by the different manners of the people (it) seems to be in another country'. The brusqueness of those busy people, with no time to waste on idlers from Bath, was resented as 'monstrously rude and uncivil behaviour'. Thirty years after Defoe, Alexander Pope damned the whole place: 'The city of Bristol is very unpleasant . . . unlike any scene you ever saw . . . and no civilized company in it.' Certainly the organization of society here was commercial, not aristocratic. At its head stood the oligarchy of great merchants, rich, uncouth, and apart from the minimum requirements of business substantially illiterate, but dominating the government and the economic and social life of the city. Then came a middle class of shopkeepers and small tradesmen, with a few allied professional men like attorneys. Below was a huge and disorderly mob of labourers, artizans, street traders, dockers, seamen, and the criminal element. Education and the Church were meanly regarded as professions, and medicine not much more highly. Schoolmasters were expected to prepare their boys for the shop and the counting-house, not to waste time on educating them; and the ill-paid clergy were tolerated while they gave spiritual support to the morality approved by the merchant rulers, but never respected as spiritual leaders. The arts and artists were heartily despised. The city attracted no wealthy visitors, no class of 'retired money', and produced no native class of leisured wealth. Thus there was no sort of leisured group within the city to demand organized social pleasures such as existed in other more civilized communities. Here even the wealthiest worked with admirable energy. The business day, in 1700, began at 5 or 6 a.m. and continued till 6 p.m. Then came supper, an hour or so at the tavern, and then bed. The beer-houses shut at 9 p.m. in winter, at which late hour the curfew rang from St. Nicholas. It was dangerous to be abroad at night, for the wretched lighting of the streets (when there was any at all) made them the haunt of thieves and footpads, prostitutes and drunken brutes ready for mischief. At home the lack of comfort, the wretched light of tallow candles, and the worse lack of amusements, drove people early to bed. Card playing was banned in sober homes, there were then no newspapers, no circulating libraries, the theatre did not exist and concerts were almost unknown. Sunday was a day of formal churchgoing, hideous with the constant clamour of bells from seventeen parish church steeples in the small city area, and distinguished by all the Sabbath gloom beloved of Cromwell's major-generals.

Escape from this grimness was not through formal social diversions but through conviviality which expressed itself in drunkenness among all classes and on a huge scale. The grandees did not count this a vice in their own class, but they strongly reprobated it among the lower orders—without, however, any effect. The Corporation led the way (since their junketings were paid for by the community) with feasts upon every conceivable national, local, public and traditional occasion; and their excessive love of turtle and port long made them a national butt. Nor were they allowed to escape until *Punch*, in the 1840s, replaced them by the city fathers of London. Prices encouraged drinking, with port and sherry costing no more than 5*s*. a gallon throughout most of the century, and Madeira 7*s*. 6*d*. Many vintners' shops and about thirty inns flourished by their sale; but all this wine-bibbing was a trickle compared with the flood of beer-drinking. By 1754 there were 625 licensed alehouses alone, or one to every nine dwellings in the city, to supply them with the best beer at 3*d*. a gallon. Beer at least supplemented the meagre diet of the working class, but to it must be added probably an equal consumption of cider, with perhaps less dietetic justification, and a huge consumption of bad gin, with none at all.

Drunkenness is incompatible with the politer forms of social entertainment, but not with one—the public dinner. Feasts were held, usually in a Company's hall or one of the major inns, by numerous bodies such as the Merchant Venturers' Society, the charitable organizations like the Colston, Grateful, Dolphin, Anchor or Parent Societies, the political clubs like the Loyal and the Union, county fellowships like the Gentlemen of Gloucestershire or Somerset or Wiltshire, as well as miscellaneous bodies like the Sons of the Clergy, on every occasion for which tradition, national or local patriotism, piety, politics or just *bonhomie* could invent an excuse. But particularly was this so in the hectic weeks of preparation for a general election—as Burke found to the cost of his health in 1774.

Almost the only other reason for public gatherings was provided by sport. The horse races on Durdham Down were a local fixture before 1700 though they did not grow into an important annual race-meeting until much later. Boxing was particularly associated with Bristol, which contributed many famous fighters to the prize ring, including Slack and Belcher and Hen Pearce the Game Chicken. Fights were the delight of all classes and were usually held in the yard of an inn, or a riding school or tennis court, but sometimes in public. A tepid affair on College Green in 1756 resulted only in one boxer suffering eight broken ribs, one eye beaten out, one shoulder-blade smashed and a jaw broken in three places, while his opponent had a collar bone broken and one ear torn off. Death was not unknown in these bare-fist fights which sometimes lasted for hours. Women fought too—with half-crowns clenched in their fists to prevent them scratching one another or pulling hair. Bull-baiting had not entirely disappeared in 1700, wrestling, backsword, cock-throwing and duck-hunting were popular, but best loved by all classes was cock-fighting. There were cockpits in Pithay, Back Street, Redcliffe and Temple, but the most important, where the biggest mains were fought, was at the Ostrich on Durdham Down. One of the century's greatest patrons was Dr. Creswicke, Dean of Bristol, whose enthusiasm was such that when promoted to the Deanery of Wells he built himself a private cockpit and had the windows of his dining-room lowered so that he and his guests could watch the fights without having to leave the table and the bottles. Many private houses had bowling greens in their gardens, there are references to tennis and billiards, and the favourite game of young men of the upper classes seems to have been fives. Swimming was an accompaniment of the Sunday excursions into the countryside, so much beloved of the middle and lower classes, for whose entertainment a whole chain of 'road houses' developed. These were a combination of tavern, coffee-house, eating-room, bowling green and swimming pool, and they appeared in many villages within walking distance of the city.

The local appetite for the coarser joys of the bottle, the table and the prize ring never waned, but the mercantile aristocracy gradually learned to enjoy, as well, more civilized entertainment. This was largely because their wealth greatly increased between about 1730 and 1780, which was also the heyday of the Bristol spa at the Hotwell and its fashionable company. Their great wealth, and the desire to show it, progressively lulled the Puritan instincts of many of the trading grandees, while the example of the polite indicated to them all sorts of new means of enjoying that wealth. The old conservatives of course denounced their surrender to fashion; while the fashionable meanly sneered at their efforts to imitate. The sight of ruffled shirts, embroidered waistcoats and gold-trimmed hats roused the puritans to cry out for the honest days when God-fearing Bristol men were content to dress (apparently) like mutes at a funeral. On the other hand, the smart visitors were very merry. 'Their laced waistcoats and clumsy carcasses,' wrote one, 'ought to be drawn by Hogarth. I have frequently seen a brocade waistcoat giving directions to a porter about the delivery of a hamper of bottles.' But in fact, though Bristol grew notably more civilized, it became neither the second Babylon of the Puritans nor the city of Calibans preposterously aping their masters pretended by the visitors.

The Hotwell could never be a major English spa, partly because the medical value of its waters was trifling, partly because of its inconveniences. The St. Vincent Rock spring flowed at the foot of the highest wall of the gorge; so that the Pump Room and Assembly Rooms and other public places essential for a spa would have to be strung out along the narrow shelf of land between the river and the 300-ft. rock face, while sites for hotels and lodging houses were hard to find near the spring. Yet to lodge in Bristol was inconvenient, for the road thither was a wretched track, muddy in wet weather and dusty in fine, which crept along at the base of the cliffs. As the spring flowed below high-water level in the River Avon, the main sewer of Bristol, it was fouled at every high tide and had to be pumped clear until the tide receded—a problem which even the great engineer Smeaton failed to solve. But still, from about 1720 the spa developed rapidly, and by the end of the century the completed layout along the fine river frontage compensated for many disadvantages. Then the Pump Room, which projected over the river and terminated the road from Bristol, was linked with other units by a graceful crescent of shops over which a single residential story projected, supported on pillars, to provide a covered walk before the shops. Between crescent and river extended a gravelled promenade, with trees lining the water front. Of the two Assembly Rooms one was built out on pillars over the water, like the Pump Room which it balanced. During the summer months which constituted the season, public breakfasts were held, followed by dancing, in the main Assembly Room; there was card-playing every night, and full-dress balls twice a week, and a Master of Ceremonies presided in imitation of Bath. He saw that gentlemen did not appear in the Room in swords or spurs, or in boots at a ball—where a row of seats was reserved for 'Ladies of Precedence and Foreigners of Fashion', who were permitted, as others were not, to appear without hats. The dancing began at 7 p.m. and as the dancers were supposed to be invalids it terminated at 11. Though their doctors protested, the ladies insisted on dancing both morning and night, for there was not much else to do except read the newspapers provided or borrow books from the circulating library run by Bristol's own poetess, the milk-woman Ann Yearsley. The small Vauxhall Gardens started in the 1760s offered public breakfasts with music, and at night dances, occasional concerts and firework displays, in grounds illuminated with lights hung in the branches of the trees. But it was rather vulgar, the resort of the bolder young Bristol tradesmen and their women; it had something of the fun-fair about it, and there were liable to be rowdy scenes. Hotwell patrons did not wish to rub shoulders with Bristol, and frankly said so. In his Guide (1751) Owen assured them that the crowds who came from Bristol on a fine Sunday to drink the waters 'go in a back way and do not disturb the better sort of company'.

As the Hotwell lacked the range of indoor amenities offered by Bath, its charms lay mostly out of doors—one reason why its season could not last the year round—

and above all in its romantic situation. Though the river at low tide bared great stretches of mud to the sun, nothing could really diminish the excitements of the gorge. Even now it is impressive, but then, before it was savagely tamed by extensive quarrying, it was much more precipitous and heavily covered with beautiful foliage. Nearly as effective as the gorge itself was the sudden revelation of a peaceful landscape as the river swung round the last bend in the ravine and the cliffs sank rapidly down to the charming meadows through which the Avon then flowed to its junction with the Severn. The gorge was vastly admired, and 'terrifying', 'sublime', 'marvellous', 'majestic' were tributes paid to this miniature Grand Canyon by generations yet unfamiliar with the Alps. Despite the horrid river, it was delightful to set off on a water picnic to Portishead or elsewhere, with a band of musicians following in another boat, and to listen to the echoes of their music reflected by the cliffs. This always produced ecstasies of admiration; and then one dined on land in the cool of the evening. Another admired performance was the thunder of blasting, for even then large quantities of rock were blown up and burned for lime; and guide books declared that 'the sublime effect of the explosions re-echoed from side to side by the lofty cliffs is such as no words can paint.' The prospects from the heights above the spa were delightful in every direction—across the Severn to the Welsh hills, across the Somerset valley to the Mendip Hills, across Redland to distant Gloucestershire. One could ride for miles, or just to the Ostrich on the Downs, and play bowls while waiting for a turtle dinner to be dressed; or to see Lord de Clifford's pictures in his fine Vanbrugh house at Kings Weston; or to Shirehampton for the river views. In fine weather the spa was a wonderful place to escape from.

The leisured life of the Hotwell was not for busy Bristol merchants, but its demands in accommodation, entertainment and everything else affected the city. Local builders, for instance, had to provide houses far more elegant than were previously demanded by their Bristol clients—had to evolve, in fact, from master builders into trained architects. And their increasing knowledge of the formal art of architecture is reflected in successive stages of Bristol building, from the charming but amateurish Queen Square of the first decade of the century, to the accomplished Great George Street or Berkeley Square, of its last. With them rose a whole race of excellent local carvers, masons and—particularly—plaster workers, to embellish the interiors of both public and private buildings. Local furniture survives, as well as the products of the great Bristol china and glass makers, to illustrate the great refinement of taste which occurred within two generations. In 1733, for the first time, it occurred to the Corporation that to entertain royalty on pewter plates was unworthy of the second richest city in the kingdom, and they hired china for the Prince of Orange. Thirty years later they could entertain the Duke of York at tables magnificent with fine silver borrowed from individual aldermen.

Admittedly social education was spreading to all provincial cities, but the spa was directly responsible for two of Bristol's most important social institutions, her Assembly and her theatre. Before 1756 the city had no Assembly Room and the rare gatherings were held in a dreary building on St. Augustine's Back which served many public purposes—including tightrope displays by strolling acrobats.

A mean 'Assembly Room', absurdly built,
Boasted one gorgeous lamp of copper gilt,
With farthing candles, chandeliers of tin,
And services of water, rum and gin.

But in 1756 a new Room, patently inspired by that at the Hotwell, was opened in Prince Street, in the heart of the wealthy district. This was truly handsome, with its Great Room 85 ft. long, crowned with a beautifully coved ceiling, its fine chimney-pieces surmounted by great matching mirrors in frames of carved and gilded wood in the Chinese Rococo manner, its great organ with gilded pipes, its exquisite decorative plaster work, and the huge central chandelier—this time of crystal. The total effect was very fine, and the destruction of the building in the present century was unforgivable. Here winter Assemblies were held fortnightly, at a subscription of two guineas for the season. Dancing began at 6.30 with the minuets, which lasted until 8, when they gave place to country dances. One could also play cards—a shocking declension from the standards of 1700. Here, as at the Hotwell, a Master of Ceremonies prevented ladies from wearing hats and children in frocks from dancing in the minuets and preserved a novel decorum after the hurly-burly of the St. Augustine's Back rooms,

Where in the dull solemnity of wigs
The dancing bears of commerce murdered jigs,
Where danced the dowdy belles of crooked trunk,
And often, very often, reeled home drunk.

Even now, of course, the fashionable visitors sneered. 'They endeavour to be polite,' said one, 'and 'tis only then they are eternally ridiculous.' And, 'As to their hours, they are most damnably sober. Their Assemblies break up at exactly ten. Quadrille, long out of fashion in the polite world, is the only game their women understand.' If he had come later in the century he could have been bored until eleven, for the hour was extended.

The spa likewise provided a home for the only art for which there was a keen local appetite—the drama. It had been indulged here as much as in other cities until the conquest of Bristol by aggressive puritanism in the mid-seventeenth century caused the drama to be outlawed as a vice. After the Restoration the occasional attempts of strolling players to perform here met with fierce resistance. The Grand Jury in 1704, for instance, declared that 'in all AGES acting of PLAYS and INTERLUDES hath been attended with all manner of PROFANENESS, LEWDNESS, MURTHERS, DEBAUCHINGS and RUINING OF YOUTHS of both SEXES, infusing principles of IDLENESS AND EXTRAVAGANCE into THEM and all people who resort to them.' The clergy gave their hearty support to such protests, the terrible Rev. Mr. Arthur Bedford, Vicar of

Temple, producing in 1719 a huge work showing how 7,000 extracts from recent plays offended against over 1,400 texts of the Bible, and that both *Macbeth* and *The Tempest* were impious because they attributed storms to other than the Divine Agency. Bigotry was sufficient to prevent a theatre in Bristol, but the growth of the spa brought visitors who would certainly not submit to this provincial prejudice. The situation became suddenly urgent in 1728 with the unprecedented furore which greeted the original production of Gay's *Beggar's Opera.* The whole country clamoured to see it. The London production was quickly followed by one in Bath, whence the company came to Bristol and played in a booth in Bridewell Lane. The Grand Jury raged, the clergy thundered, but at last the Bristol public refused to be cowed or saved. They wanted to see the *Beggar's Opera.* With the company was the original Peachum, John Hippisley, a celebrated London comedian but a Somerset man by origin, who probably had local connexions. At any rate he contrived to borrow £300 from a group of citizens with which to build Bristol's first permanent theatre; and in the summer of 1729 the Jacob's Well playhouse was opened.

There was an endearing air of lunacy about this miniature theatre. Its site seemed preposterous, for it was halfway up the very steep and rough track, now Jacob's Wells Road, which climbed from river level to the heights of Clifton in the ravine between Brandon and Clifton Hills. The approaches from both city and spa were thus equally painful, always rough and dirty and, on a dark night, dangerous. Linkboys were a necessity for the patrons, and every actor prayed for a full moon on his benefit night. Winstone once, when lucky in this respect, advertised that 'Madam Cynthia will appear in all her glory'. The gallery thought this meant some great Continental star, and when she failed to appear they started a riot. But there was method in Hippisley's madness, for the playhouse was carefully sited just a few yards beyond the city boundary and the magistrates' jurisdiction, so that it was as near as it could legally be to both city and spa. Another advantage was that immediately adjoining the house was a little beershop, The Malt Shovel, and Hippisley was able to cut a hatch through his side wall to allow a continuous service of drink to be handed through to actors and audience. The theatre was square in shape (not the modern semicircle) and though tiny was complete, with a ground-floor tier of boxes up to the proscenium arch, before which the stage considerably projected; a pit sunk below stage level; and a first-floor tier of open seats. Those facing the stage formed the gallery, those at the sides the balconies, each of which terminated in a small box (called a 'pigeon hole') over the doors in the proscenium arch. Extra seats were often tiered up at the rear of the stage, right to the back wall of the building. This meant of course no scenery, and a fearful reduction of the stage space, and many times the cast had to do their best with *Macbeth* or *Venice Preserv'd* on an acting area the size of a dining-table, with the stage boxes and back seats almost literally breathing down their necks. It also meant that an actor who needed to leave the stage on one side and re-enter on the other could not cross discreetly behind a back-cloth. He had to go right outside the building and run round the back.

All this delighted the Bristol crowds. On summer evenings they congregated on

Brandon Hill, which faced the building, to comment on the arrival of the smart audience. Then they adjourned to Clifton Hill, behind it, to watch the actors racing round the back in full war-paint, encouraging them with loud cheers and helpful suggestions. One infuriated actor used to take a loaded gun with him, to quell them. Not that life was much easier inside, for the gallery was normally rowdy and the swells in the boxes very often so. Actors were never too proud to leave the stage and fight it out with their tormentors; and if the Archbishop or Tamerlane got a black eye he could always have a quick pint on returning to the stage. The annual season was in June, July and August, when the London theatres were closed and their actors at liberty. The playhouse was so small that with box seats at 3*s.*, pit at 2*s.*, balconies and pigeon-holes at 1*s.* 6*d.* and the gallery at 1*s.* the manager was happy if he took £100 a week. That meant that the great London stars could not be paid enough to lure them to Bristol, though Macklin came for one season and the great Mrs. Pritchard for seven, apparently out of friendship for Hippisley. But the companies always consisted of well-known and highly competent London actors of the second rank, some of whom—like Woodward or Shuter—later achieved the front rank. Their entertainment was infinitely superior to anything Bristol had known before, and in the lavish tradition of the period consisted of prologue, the main play (with singing or dancing by individual players between the acts), a farce, more singing and dancing, often a short one-act pantomime, and then the epilogue. And, of course, very often a free fight.

It was this rowdiness which finally closed Jacob's Well. Its many inconveniences had become intolerable to the polite by 1764, and in that year the worst of all its riots substantially wrecked the building. Thereupon a group of rich citizens, advised by the master of works at Drury Lane, Saunders, built the present King Street theatre—like the nearby Assembly Room, in the heart of the wealthy district. Fortunately it survives comparatively little changed, to flourish to-day as the unique survival of a Georgian town theatre, still retaining in the lovely soft green and gold of its ceiling the last trace of the original splendour of its colour scheme. Just before its opening night Garrick inspected it and pronounced it 'the most complete theatre in Europe'. The scene on that occasion in 1766 was so brilliant that one enthusiast said: 'Malice herself, had she been present, must for that night at least have put on a smile of approbation.' But not so the Puritans. From the moment a new theatre was suggested they flooded the local press with letters, poems, diatribes, sometimes lachrymose, sometimes threatening, but always illiberal. They reprinted with approval the Grand Jury charge of 1704; they invoked the 'rogues and vagabonds' penalty of the Act of 1737 against the players; they persuaded the Grand Jury to present the company (though no further legal action followed); and for twelve years they blocked every effort to get the theatre licensed. But now the tide was running against them and in 1778 Letters Patent from George III recognized 'the theatre in King Street' as 'The Theatre Royal'; while its baffled opponents awaited the tidal wave of rape, arson, robbery and murder due to engulf the Gomorrah of Gloucestershire.

The new theatre from the start was very grand and formal. With a capacity of £229 a night a longer season of playing was possible, and every great actor and actress of the last half of the century at some time played in King Street, with the single exception of Garrick—and he gave it his blessing. Behaviour was much more genteel, and dress rules were as severe as for an Assembly. Boots were banned in the boxes, and no gentleman would dream of attending the theatre until the barber had come to dress his hair. Ladies were not allowed to wear hats in the boxes, a prohibition which pleased them as the fashion then ran to the most elaborate *coiffures*, two or more feet high, incorporating festoons of artificial fruit and flowers and even less appropriate ornaments. On any fashionable occasion the crowd of a hundred or more private carriages in King Street constituted another traffic problem. All this was very grand and civilizing, no doubt, but the Theatre Royal was never half as much fun as Jacob's Well had been.

Otherwise the arts stirred very few. One or two private musical groups existed, and there were occasional festivals of music in the Cathedral, or the Assembly Room after 1756. Handel was the favourite composer, *The Messiah* and *Judas Maccabeus* the favourite works. Professional concerts were sometimes organized, but the attempt to arrange subscription concerts to alternate with the Assemblies in Prince Street died for lack of support. Literature was likewise languidly cherished, but in 1772 a group of wealthy citizens formed the Bristol Library Society on a private subscription basis, and obtained leave to use the City Library for their own books. In fact it became their private preserve for many years; but as the public had hardly entered their library since 1613 and the librarians had long been allowed to use the premises for their private purposes, the deprivation was not severe. The atmosphere of the city was not literary. Chatterton's isolation here is well known, and he was the only literary genius produced (and rejected) by Bristol. Hannah More cannot be taken seriously as a writer, the local poets, like Ann Yearsley, Lovell and Thorne, are a poor joke, and the supposed influence of Bristol upon Southey, Coleridge, Wordsworth and the Romantics, though strenuously claimed by local patriots, is highly dubious.

The century closed in unhappy circumstances. New economic developments in the country and the Empire shattered the traditional bases of Bristol's wealth, and the robust self-confidence of a proud community was badly shaken. The spa declined for the worst of reasons—its patients lost faith in it. Ignorant and dishonest doctors had long attributed to its waters the most preposterous curative powers in a vast range of complaints, but particularly consumption and chest diseases. Bogus learning reached, perhaps, its height in Dr. Strother's solemn pronouncement that the waters were AEQUEOSALINOCALCALINOCETACEOALUMINOSOCUPREOVITRIOLIC. The legend could not survive if they continued to send hopeless cases here, and at last 'it became all over the kingdom a source of horror and despair, instead of hope and confidence, to be ordered to the Hotwell, from whose awful bourne no traveller now returned.' The spa survived, shrunken in state and reputation, for a generation or so more, on the basis of much more modest claims.

The future belonged to Clifton, not the Hotwell. Before 1800 people had discovered that the heights, once incidental to the spa, were in themselves delightful for permanent residence, not just as an escape from river level. Building had begun in earnest round the little village of Clifton, and the Mall, Boyce's Buildings, the handsome houses in Rodney Place, all supplemented the individual mansions like Goldney House and Manila Hall; schemes were mooted for great terraces of houses to rise one above another on the cliffs overhanging the river; Clifton was to be 'another Montpellier.' The outbreak of the French war in 1793 stopped all such activity for a generation, but the character of Clifton had been determined. It was to be what neither Bristol nor the spa could ever be, the home of a wealthy class seeking retirement in beautiful surroundings. But that phase belongs to the next century.

One is conscious that Bristol itself had not perhaps changed very greatly by 1800. Manners had softened and the social outlook had widened for some, but even in its more amiable state it remained a curiously unsocial city. The young, particularly the poets, vented their feelings in fierce satires. Chatterton's charge that:

> Lost to all learning, elegance and sense,
> Long had this famous city told her pence

was repeated with equal irritability down to the year 1800 by his successors, and in milder terms was admitted even by the local guide-book writers. One such, while ecstatically praising everything Bristolian, was constrained to admit that by comparison with other provincial cities Bristol was poorly provided with social diversions; and suggested that the superfluity of Dissenters here accounted for it. The Puritan elements remained very strong throughout, and were reinforced by the Evangelical revival of the later years of the century. The Bristol printer Matthews, in his Guide published in 1796, happily assured visitors that 'there is every gratification and amusement in Bristol that a rational person can desire'; but one's confidence in his judgement of joy is shaken by his immediately instancing the daily delivery of sermons as an outstanding pleasure. This survival of its historic Puritanism is appropriately balanced by an equal survival of its old earthiness: for in the last years of the century (a period of great distress owing to the war) the annual allowance to the Mayor for entertainment was raised to the unprecedented figure of £2,000, the Colston Society dinner ran to thirty separate toasts and drinking continued until breakfast the next morning; and the last entry in Latimer's *Annals of the Eighteenth Century* is the mention of a fight by Jem Belcher, the greatest of all Bristol boxers.

CHAPTER SIXTEEN

THE ARTS IN BRISTOL SINCE 1800

THE City of Bristol has long looked like a fit haunt of the Muses. By 1800, when Clifton had risen in new-built glory, the double town must have been an inspiring sight with its older nestling brick, its new lines of proud freestone, its dense population of steeples, and its many trees; and sensitive minds have recorded the exhilaration that they found by being there. Since then, it is true, this lovely setting has known some disasters; buildings, or their proportioned neighbourliness, have been destroyed, or falsified, or masked, and Victoria Street was affectionately called The Ugliest Street in Europe—a status for which, since its wartime destruction, it no longer qualifies. But the Nine, amplified (on a birth-qualification) by the lady Kinema, have never quitted the city, and even the occasional philistinism of the place has been of a sturdy, English, reasoning quality that has brought out the best tactics on the angels' side. When Chatterton, who must be regarded as a hostile witness, destroyed himself in 1770, some of his last snarls were against the materialism, the narrow commercialism, and the poor sensibility, of his city; Alfred de Vigny, in the next century, took up this cue, and gave France and the Continent, in his astonishing play *Chatterton*, a picture of the little suicide as a martyr crushed by a society of grasping Yahoos—a picture made even less accurate by the arrival in the poet's digs of a typical English meet, composed of *lords pleins de rosbif.*

However, there really has been some unappreciative behaviour. One of the first examples was the eighteenth-century treatment of the ancient High Cross, which was first removed from the intersection of the chief streets, then re-erected on College Green, and then sold away to grace a Wiltshire estate; its imitation, which took its place in 1850, is now likewise dismantled, but clear voices in the city are urging its recall. And its advocates can take heart: when Queen Victoria (in very pretty lace) was whisked away from the apex of the Green a couple of years ago, and clad in tarpaulin, public opinion played a big part in her triumphant return. Still, it was in her reign that, for the reredos of St. Mary Redcliffe, Hogarth's unsuitable canvas was replaced by Godwin's less suitable foreign stones and mosaic. Some wit has been expended on the prodigal hand with which Bristolians fired their own Colston Hall without enemy help, and the audiences at certain concerts will remember Sir Thomas Beecham's sprightly remarks on the rumour that the new hall was to be of restricted size; but the result has been happy. And then there were the dark days of the 1831 riots; on this occasion, the grossest citizens, with the aid of some Irish visitors, tried to ignite their own cathedral, which was saved by a resolute band led by the sub-sacrist with an iron bar. The most recent clash on the delicate subject of Taste concerned a bronze torso by Henry Moore, which was to be bought by the city; some of the people's representatives demurred, however, and it was democratically placed in the Art Gallery for approval. The approval not showing itself, the torso shook the dust of Bristol from its flanks; but not before a doughty citizen dipped his vest in concrete, let it set, photographed it, and through the press offered it to his city for a nominal sum.

It has been as well to show some frankness over Bristol's response to the *passé* and the *outré*. What follows will be more cheerful, but it must be admitted that by 1800 the great days of the city, in certain fields, were ended. Bristol china, one of the earliest true hard-paste porcelains of the eighteenth century in England, ceased production in 1777, though an odd testimonial to its qualities was seen a hundred years later, when it emerged from a fire at the Alexandra Palace that had engulfed its colleagues of Worcester, Chelsea, and Bow. The days of Bristol glass were nearly over, too, and the many glass-houses, which Pope noticed on his visit, had stopped blackening the churches of Temple and Redcliffe. The art lingered on only in its derivative, the glass made out at Nailsea, where after 1810 the familiar forms emerged of gaily striped and looped jugs and flasks, walking-sticks, tobacco-pipes, and rolling-pins with endearing mottoes; and stained-glass windows are still locally produced by Joseph Bell and Son of Park Street, whose work may be seen in the Cathedral and the University. But, saddest of all for the city, in 1800 it had just ceased to be the headquarters of the Romantic movement in our poetry; Wordsworth and Coleridge, as well as Southey and Lamb, had received their first effective publication here, but, having once flown, they rarely returned, and Coleridge's visits in 1807 and 1814 were marked chiefly by his struggle against laudanum.

Clifton and the Hotwell had been a natural centre for a society of wits and thinkers, and the claim has been made for Dr. Beddoes that he was a natural leader of it. By marriage he was connected with the literary Edgeworths; his son, Thomas Lovell Beddoes, born in Clifton in 1803, owed less to Bristol than to Germany, and, after long indulgence of a morbid Gothic fancy, poisoned himself by way of illustration to his own *Death's Jest-Book*; and the father's fellow-scientist, Humphry Davy, used to stroll over the Downs sniffing stimulant gases from a bag in order to bring on the poetry that was his sideline.

Another group revolved, more decorously, round Hannah More; until her retirement to Bristol, she was only a seasonal migrant from Somerset, but she brought to the city her genteel memories of the circle of Johnson and Garrick, and it shared in the glory of her best-sellers. It is hard now to account for the dozens of editions of her *Coelebs in Search of a Wife* (1809), and for the success of her other mealy-mouthed books; but it is a fact that this blue-stocking was a woman of charm and sweetness, greatly charitable on her own autocratic terms. With a character of such contradiction, it is not surprising that her chief beneficiary was also her chief victim—Ann Yearsley, the Bristol milk-woman and poetess, who began by being grateful when Miss More had her poems published, but turned resentful when the resulting £500 was invested for her beyond her control; she eventually got the money, but with it the name of an ingrate, and in later ruin and bereavement crept away to Melksham, whence her corpse returned for burial in 1806. 'Holy Hannah' could be lavish, however, when subordinates kept their places; and Macaulay, whose mother taught happily at the Mores' school, speaks with the utmost gratitude of her kindness to him, and revisited her old home when he was staying at 16 Caledonia Place in 1852. One who liked her less was Thomas de Quincey, who came to Bristol in 1807 in hopes of meeting Coleridge—a meeting fraught with advantage to the opium trade—and gave the murder of Mrs. Ruscombe at College Green a prominent place in his *Murder Considered as a Fine Art*; his memoirs of Hannah More stress her arrogance and snobbery, illustrated by her ejection from her drawing-room of her old friend Joseph Cottle, the publisher of *Lyrical Ballads*, on the arrival of a real prince and princess.

Belatedly, Bristol paid tribute to Chatterton in the definitive edition of his works edited by Southey and Cottle in 1803; but too often the younger Romantics, forgetting how their elders had won a reputation as republicans and pretty free Christians, saw only the passing of Coleridge into pietism, of Wordsworth into high-churchdom, and of Southey into toryism, and the city looked tainted with their lapse in the lordly eyes of Byron (though his friend Hobhouse was born here). His onslaught on Bristol, in *English Bards and Scotch Reviewers*, repeats Chatterton's old charges of money-grubbing and gluttony, and is no more accurate; in fact, a new literary generation had arisen here, though it partly consisted of those who had come for the 'cure' or for a holiday, and not to found a 'school'. Landor was one who halted here for a time on his wanderings; his friend Southey, back on a grateful visit to his childhood home, helped him to appreciate something of the scene and its tradition, and Thackeray's adored Mrs. Brookfield remembered bowling her hoop in Royal York Crescent as the two poets came strolling along. Landor's verses on Clifton are approving, if nothing else:

> Clifton! in vain thy varied scenes invite,
> The mossy bank, dim glade, and dizzy height;
> The sheep that, starting from the tufted thyme,
> Untune the distant church's mellow chime,
> As o'er each limb a gentle horror creeps,
> And shakes above our heads the craggy steeps.
> Pleasant I've thought it to pursue the rower
> While light and darkness seize the changeful oar,
> The frolic Naiads drawing from below
> A net of silver round the black canoe.
> Now the last lonely solace must it be
> To watch pale evening brood o'er land and sea,
> Then join my friends and let those friends believe
> My cheeks are moisten'd by the dews of eve.

Clifton gave the aged Crabbe 'strength and . . . spirits', cured Carlyle of being a 'determined anti-view hunter', and stamped itself on the memory of Ruskin and F. D. Maurice; Mary Russell Mitford wisely saw Bristol as a 'warm, glowing, and picturesque' place; but Kingsley chiefly remembered the riots, and the dying 'Ingoldsby' Barham merely recorded that his doctor at Hotwells had enough jaw for Samson to lay waste 'all Mesopotamia, let alone Philistia'.

A more essentially Bristolian writer was John Addington Symonds, he who believed that 'These things shall be'; he lived at Clifton Hill House, and though he exiled himself to Italy and devoted his best powers to work on the Italian Renaissance, he wrote with feeling of Bristol as a formative influence on his life. In 1954 a memorial was set in Redland churchyard to T. E. Brown, the chief Manx poet, who spent his best years as a master at Clifton College, where he died on a later visit. It is to be hoped that the garden which he found 'a lovesome thing, God wot', was elsewhere than in Clifton; according to age and temperament, a stirring of the soul or a cynical snigger will greet the discovery that the close where the 'breathless hush' fell, in Newbolt's *Vitai Lampada*, was likewise at the College.

To many modern readers, Bristol is familiar from a number of novels, mostly historical, produced in the last few years, especially those of Marguerite Steen (*The Sun is My Undoing, Twilight on the Floods*), E. H. Young (*Chatterton Square*), and Lewis Wilshire. And there has been a long, if loose, connexion between Bristol and the course of English fiction, from the time when the original Robinson Crusoe walked its streets and Gulliver set out from its port. Scott claimed that his Waverley Novels derived ultimately from *The Scottish Chiefs* (1810), by Jane Porter, who lived in Portland Square, Bristol. Few novels of the last century can have sold better than 'Hugh Conway' of Bristol's *Called Back*; and Sydney Horler, the writer of mystery fiction, was (like Chatterton) educated at Colston's. Conan Doyle used Bristol in *Micah Clark* and *Rodney Stone*, and Stanley Weyman used it in *Chipping*, and fugitive appearances of the city in fiction have been cheerful enough: the Spy-Glass Inn in *Treasure Island*, for instance, and the adventures of Mr. Winkle in *Pickwick Papers*; but Thorpe's description of Blaise Castle, in Jane Austen's *Northanger Abbey*, must not be taken as authentic!

Two Bristol residents whose work of anthologizing has helped later writers were Dr. Peter Roget, who had worked with Beddoes and who compiled the *Thesaurus of English Words and Phrases*, and Vincent Stuckey Lean, whose *Collectanea* (1902–04) of proverbs and folk-lore crowned a life of scholarship and travel. The city has also contributed much to the popular and enduring art of hymnology: Chatterton Dix composed *As with gladness men of old* and *To Thee, O Lord, our hearts we raise;* Sir John Bowring, educated in Great George Street, wrote *In the Cross of Christ I glory;* and Catherine Winkworth (of 31 Cornwallis Crescent) gave the English-speaking world, in her *Lyra Germanica*, translations of German hymnody like *Praise to the Lord, the Almighty, the King of Creation.* A. M. Toplady, curate of Blagdon, composed *Rock of Ages* in (and of) Burrington Combe. Finally, Bristol played a curious part in the revival of Portuguese literature, in that Jose Maria Eça de Queiroz was at 33 Queen

Square as Portuguese Consul in 1876, and wrote from here some of his *Letters from England*; returning to Portugal, he became unquestionably its greatest novelist.

Bristol has in recent years become an important centre of the drama. 'Perdita' Robinson, who died in 1800, was a native, but the great tradition was by then established. The *Theatre Royal* in King Street is the oldest in Britain (see Chapter 15, p. 239); a Garrick prologue opened it in 1766, and during the last century-and-a-half it has thrilled to Sarah Siddons, Fanny Kemble, Macready, Madge Kendal, Ellen Terry, Henry Irving, and others of their generations. It suffered a lean period, and Bristolians can remember the playing of trivialities and the throwing of fruit therein; but since 1942, when it was bought for the city and leased to the Arts Council, it has been a good influence on the national drama. Names now famous have appeared as beginners or visitors in the Bristol 'Old Vic' Company; and the patrons, a loyal and enthusiastic body, take pride in the passing of young talent to spheres bigger though not necessarily better. For a long time these patrons willingly endured discomfort, hard and cramped (but historic); all this has now been reformed—though some of the original seating has been left as a rueful exhibit—but there is still no theatre with such an atmosphere of centuried excitement. To many, the happiest *Royal* memories will be of Shakespeare, and especially of his comedy; but the year reaches its peak in the home-made Christmas pantomimes, a triumph of the brain rather than of the leg, and the delightful 'comedy with music' idiom of Dorothy Reynolds and Julian Slade. Their older brethren, G. & S., require the vaster resources of the *Hippodrome*, which also houses grand opera, ballet, and entertainment harder to classify. The *Empire*, before it closed in 1954, had rollicked with George Robey, Harry Lauder, Marie Lloyd, Vesta Tilley, Albert Chevalier, Wee Georgie Wood, and pretty well *omne* of *hoc genus* that Thalia deigns to own. The *Little* shows 'straight' plays, and the city has plenty of the usual dramatic groups; the Old Vic runs a serious school and a club, and when the University established Britain's only Department of Drama, the art of the theatre was given a new status in the city.

The claim has often been made for the luckless William Friese-Greene, born at Bristol in 1855, that he invented cinematography; the claim is intemperate, or at least a simplification, but he *was* the first to patent certain inventions on which the art depends. His early experiments were carried out in his home behind Christ Church, Clifton; but his mature work was done at Bath and elsewhere. His native city has treated his gift in the usual palatial way, but two smaller cinemas offer programmes variously sophisticated, foreign, horrid, blushful, artistic, or intellectual. (Photography in general owes much to another resident, Mungo Ponton, who died at 4 The Paragon in 1880; his discovery 'that the action of sunlight renders bichromate of potassium insoluble' was basic to the production of permanent photographs.)

No great name from Bristol springs to mind when one considers the musical endeavours of our period, save that Dame Clara Butt's splendid contralto voice was first heard here, and that the great organist Samuel Wesley was a native. But the late Victorian records suggest that there was no lack of teamwork, even if the presence of real celebrities (like Paganini in 1831) was rare. From the Bristol Catch

Club and the Cecilian Society of the eighteenth century developed a number of societies, which flourished in the mid-nineteenth century with the aid of professionals and the use of the Assembly Rooms in Prince Street and the Hotwell. They concentrated on 'the finest orchestral symphonies and overtures', and on oratorios, and their pioneer work sounds laudable enough, though it gives us pause to see that they had 'a complete and highly efficient band'. The opening of the Victoria Rooms and of the Colston Hall stimulated the forming of other choirs and orchestras, but the far earlier Madrigal Society (1837) was more promising; one of its members, R. L. Pearsall, even eternized the Downs in his charming part-song *Oh, who will o'er the Downs so free?* (though *which* Downs—Durdham, Winterbourne, or Kings Weston—has never been determined). At its very first meeting, the Society sang madrigals by such English and Italian masters as Orlando Gibbons, Weelkes, Morley, Festa and Croce; in 1850, Bach motets were added to the repertory. The choir was all-male until after the Second World War, when ladies replaced Cathedral choristers in the soprano and alto parts. Parry, Stanford, C. H. Lloyd, Basil Harford and Walford Davies have written works specially for the Society. The much larger Bristol Musical Festival Society (1873) inaugurated a series of great triennial festivals, lavish in their programmes, studded with notable performers, graced by composers conducting their own specially-composed works, and normally attracting about 12,000 people. Hallé conducted the first nine festivals; at the last (1912), a concert performance of Wagner's tetralogy, *The Ring*, was given, but the First World War killed the series.

There were chamber concerts, too, but no orchestra was formed comparable with those of Manchester, Birmingham, and Liverpool, and this lack is still regrettably evident. We must deplore the collapse in 1953 of the Bristol Philharmonic Society, which since 1901 had given adventurous programmes, deliberately exploring the by-ways of sixteenth- and seventeenth-century music and modern choral works not given by the more traditionally-minded—and still flourishing—Bristol Choral Society; Elgar was particularly associated with the 'Philharmonic', and Holst and Vaughan Williams came to conduct their own works.

At the present time, indeed, music-making in Bristol depends rather on the enthusiasm of private persons and on the centralizing force of the University and of the great churches, especially the Cathedral and St. Mary Redcliffe; Dr. Edmund H. Fellowes, the famous discoverer and editor of so many glories of the English Tudor School, vocal and instrumental, was Precentor of the Cathedral early in this century. The old Colston Hall heard international artists from Kreisler and Paderewski to present-day celebrities; its new successor is capacious and acoustically excellent, and will soon have an enormous organ, but its most attractive concerts are those of visiting orchestras. Two of the more promising signs have been the swift rise of the Paragon String Orchestra (1952), which specializes in rarely-performed chamber music, and the many activities of the young Music Department of the University, which runs or assists scholarly performances from masses to madrigals.

Of individual Bristol musicians, none is more memorable than Philip Napier

Miles (1865–1935), who inherited the large Kings Weston property and devoted himself to music; he studied at Leipzig, Dresden, and London, with Parry and Dannreuther, and became the best sort of amateur musician. He fostered amateur music in the city, and in Somerset and Gloucestershire; he composed for the stage, and was responsible for notable opera festivals at the Victoria Rooms and the Theatre Royal, including the first English performances of Falla's *Master Peter's Puppet Show* (1924) and Vaughan Williams's *The Shepherds of the Delectable Mountains* (1926).

But, among the musical endeavours of the city, the Bristol Music Club, with its own concert-room in Clifton, has a select pre-eminence. It is over fifty years since the then 'Men's Club' was formed for 'the encouragement and performance of Music' (especially with chamber music in mind), and since 1920 it has been a self-supporting company, whose shareholders often plough back their dividend for up-keep and improvements; the Women's Club, originally founded in 1905, was amalgamated with it in 1937. In 1953 it celebrated its jubilee of music-making, and its long tradition of artistic integrity and corporate endeavour is further honoured by the great names of its associates: Joachim, the great violinist, who consented to become its first president in 1906, while visiting Bristol with his quartet; among presidents and members, many who have been knighted for their services to music—Sir Hubert Parry and Sir Hugh Allen (both directors of the Royal College of Music), Sir Henry Hadow, Sir Reginald Thatcher (Principal of the Royal Academy of Music), Sir William McKie (organist of Westminster Abbey), and Sir Charles Stanford; Dame Myra Hess is a co-president with Mr. Ivor James the 'cellist, and Dr. Vaughan Williams is an honorary member. Yet, since 10 November 1903—when the first programme was given in the sitting-room of a Clifton hotel (the Dvořák Piano Quintet and the Beethoven Quartet, Op. 18, No. 4)—continuity has rested with the loyal body of local enthusiasts, and single families (like that of Mr. Gerard Fox) have faithfully sustained a long part in keeping musicians' music alive. Not all the members are performers, either amateur or professional; but the mere listeners are trained and critical listeners. The links at once set up with the Music Department of the University have benefited both bodies.

Before we pass on to painting, no better link between letters, music, and the visual arts could be found than the Bristol Savages, a society to which the solecism 'very unique' could almost be applied. Sixty years ago, a Bristol artist called Ernest Ehlers proposed to his fellow-painters that they meet for an evening, of work and talk, in his studio; thereafter, for seven months of the year, they met once a week—evolving rules and their promising name as they proceeded—at first in the various members' studios, then in a hired place in Corn Street, and, after 1906, by the generosity of Alderman J. Fuller Eberle, at his Brandon Cottage and eventually at the lovely Red Lodge, which he bought. By 1920 they had built for themselves the new 'Wigwam' adjoining, a great hall of medieval aspect with the magnificent addition of a seventeenth-century heraldic stone fireplace from the Goat in Armour Inn on the Quay, another of the same century with the arms of Richard Stubbs (Sheriff in 1671), and a third of hectic wood, dating from the sixteenth century and formerly in the

Canynges mansion in Redcliffe Street. In this handsome atmosphere, reinforced as it is by the drifting cigar, by *bonhomie*, and by what commonly promotes it, the privileged and astonished guest will spend a Wednesday evening entertained by the music, the verses, the oratory, and the sketches, of the working and 'lay' members and the visitors. The practising artists are pre-eminent, and these will have met for two hours beforehand, to execute the sketch on the evening's topic, which has just been sprung on them; the best sketches find their way into a permanent collection. Of their more leisurely work, the first annual exhibition (in 1905) resulted in sales of over £100; there have now been forty-five, and £1,000 has been topped.

To an older generation, Bristol's contribution to painting would be summed up in the name of Sir Thomas Lawrence, born at 6 Redcross Street in 1769. He was a precocious genius whose fortune and facility never deserted him; he was about our last painter to earn a rich living by full-time portraiture, and on him have been heaped the unthinking sneers that a portraitist often wins—that he flattered, overdressed, ennobled and canonized his wealthy sitters. Apart from Sargent, he is our last painter in the Grand Manner. His swift skill has been put down as flashiness and meretriciousness; but Aristotle in the *Poetics* allowed the subtle ennobling of the sitter, and Lawrence brought to his portraits a love of privileged life, a vitality, and a Regency glitter. Histrionic and superb himself, he chose and stressed such qualities in his sitters, who face us boldly as the positive, absolute people they were —their dress gorgeous, their fine limbs poised, their eyes brilliant, their background a sweeping panorama and an opulent curtain. Bristol is not yet a very good place to study him, but his *Viscount Cremorne* and *Viscountess Cremorne* stare down at us with luminous orbs in the Art Gallery, while the Council House has his *Duke of Portland* (along with Reynolds's *Burke*, Gainsborough's *Lord Clare*, and Van Dyck's *Earl of Pembroke*, which the Corporation were willing to sell to the Pembroke family for as many sovereigns as would cover its surface—*edgewise*!).

The city was once very proud of its landscape-painter W. J. Müller (1812–45), who faithfully recorded Nature but languished in the hot colour of Greece and Egypt. At his best deriving much from Constable, anticipating the French orientalists in their 'glamour', and certainly inspiring David Cox, he died too early for any real fulfilment; his Bristol scenes will merely strike the beholder with their bright, oily assurance, caught as they were in the perpetual sunshine of nineteenth-century merchant prosperity.

Other Bristol painters of the last century will attract us less; but, largely self-taught, they appealed to the bourgeoisie of the time. There were various portrait-painters (Branwhite, Vandyke, Hancock), whose subjects are more exciting than their execution, and the deserving but little-known miniaturist James Fisher (?1814–94?), who exhibited at the Royal Academy; R.A.s like P. F. Poole (*Edward III and the Burghers of Calais*) and Edward Bird (whose *Chevy Chase* made beholders weep), with his portraits, theatrical subjects, and story-pictures like *The Reading of the Will Concluded* (exhibited 1811); the Russian émigré's son, F. P. Stephanoff, who died at Hanham; Francis Danby, with his pot-boiler landscapes and his sudden flights into the sphere of Turner; Nicholas Pocock's naval battles, Joseph Walter's marine subjects, and E. V. Rippingille's portraits of Victorian childhoood. The Sharples family deserve praise for their enterprising tours to the United States to take the likenesses of the heads of the constitution, and J. B. Pyne for being an exponent of Turner—who, accompanied by Girtin, painted at the Hotwell and Redcliffe. Samuel Jackson gave us topographical water-colours in the eighteenth-century tradition, and Alfred and George Fripp were competent Victorian raconteurs of the Grand Tour. Ernest Board (1877-1934) produced colourful canvases that would make topping jig-saw puzzles—a fine anachronistic group of great Bristolians, and *The Departure of John and Sebastian Cabot* (Royal Academy, 1906). And Roger Fry (1866–1934), artist and critic, deserves the highest praise; with Bristol connexions, and educated at Clifton, he virtually introduced nineteenth-century French painting into England by his great Post-Impressionist exhibition at the Grafton Galleries in 1910, and was our chief interpreter of Cézanne.

Less reputable is the megalomaniac Sir Robert Ker Porter, whose *Storming of Seringapatam* was 120 ft. long, and who married a Russian princess. Porter and others may have set the fashion for Bristol's possession of vast pictures; the Art Gallery has some of great acreage, including a veritable tennis-court of reposeful heather which is apparently the most popular painting in Bristol. In 1884, when the Leigh Court collection was dispersed, Bristol's great paintings were indeed few; by now, she has built up not only her twentieth-century collection, but a residuum of Academy pictures (as in most provincial galleries) and other Victorians which are regaining their reputation: languid Watts nudes, Siddall's sad smile, and meticulous scenes of Raphael's death, Charles the First's burial, and the Bride of Lammermoor. One of these is even controversial—W. F. Yeames's *Defendant and Counsel;* Yeames (who came from Taganrog) gave the world no problem in *And when did you last see your Father?*, but the Bristol painting found the public anxious to know what the lady in the huge hat was being defended *for*, and one of the curators had to invent a story to go with it.

The state of painting in the city is now healthy. The Royal West of England Academy, with its exhibitions and its continuity of teaching; the Art Gallery, which houses works of Sickert and Pissarro, Matthew Smith and Ben Nicholson, along with the established Continental Renaissance masters of the glorious Schiller Bequest—including a Bellini, a da Predis, and the arresting Cranach *Luther*—and Antonio da Solario's *Withypool Altarpiece*, painted for a Bristolian; the great Chinese collection which was part of that bequest, and the priceless F. B. Abbey collection of Chinese glass; the Braikenridge collection of topographical paintings of Bristol; displays of local applied arts—Bristol delft, Bristol porcelain, Bristol glass; further homes for paintings, like the Georgian House, and for temporary exhibitions, like the Elizabethan Red Lodge; all these, in which masterpieces circulate and change their places and neighbours, keep the student and the general public aware of painting as a living force. Among contemporary painters, George Melhuish has caught the eye of public and patron as a colourist, by his portraits, air-raid scenes, snow, and architectural backgrounds, in thick layers of dynamic red, green, and yellow; Paul Feiler, an extremist, lays stress on the geometrical formula of the Golden Section; and from Corsham, Lord Methuen lends a distinguished advocacy of the arts. Two of the applied arts have kept up the old tradition—the glass of the firm of Powell, and (with a continuity back to 1642) Pountney's pottery.

Sculpture has had some publicity of late, in the rejection of the Moore *Draped Torso*; but its successor, Reg Butler's bronze of a girl peeling off her vest, has quietly settled in, proving the city's preference for semi-vested over vested interests. There are conflicting views of the Seaman under the dome of the new Council House, but the prancing golden unicorns on the roof-crests are now firmly part of the Bristol horizon; the criticism that they are over life-size is not valid. The city has the usual array of public statuary, though none (even the musing *Colston* and orating *Burke*) as pleasing as their eighteenth-century neighbour *Neptune*. The sculptors of the last century are here in some abundance, and the eclectic may even enjoy their lifeless fidelity to nature by sipping the following: Chantrey's *Mrs. Elwyn* (Cathedral) and *Henry Bengough* (Lord Mayor's Chapel); Flaxman's *Troth Blisset* (All Saints'; a poor little recumbent figure, placed too high); Branwhite's *Müller* (Cathedral); the Tyleys' striking dove-pediment at Holy Trinity, Hotwells; Bubb's admirable bas-relief and patriotic statues on the portico of the Commercial Rooms; and even, for the fun of it, Sir J. E. Boehm's *Eurydice* (Art Gallery), which has been irreverently compared with the advertisement 'I love to dance, but *oh*! my feet'. Above all, there was E. H. Baily (1788–1867), a Bristolian, whose native city owns his *Lawrence* (Art Gallery), *Southey* (Cathedral), *Justice* (Council House), and *Eve at the Fountain*, an old favourite still in the Art Gallery; the frieze of the ruined Masonic Hall is his also.

This outline of the Arts has suggested that they are fully alive in a city not oppressed by the greatness of its dead past; its famous schools train the safe hands of scholars and critics, but the 'worker' plays a part evidenced by his response to the facilities of Adult Education. At the Folk House on College Green the slogan of 'Education, Companionship, Entertainment' expresses an atmosphere in which evenings hum with pursuits from psychology to throwing pots, and from music and literature to swimming. To all the artistic endeavours of the city the advancing University gives its sanction and its support; its schools of Literature, Music, and Drama, its series of art lectures given by the highest authorities, and its creation of splendid new buildings alongside its acquisition of great Georgian houses, are at the heart of the cultural life of Bristol. And there is obvious health in a city whose chief place of secular assembly, the Colston Hall, is as packed out for symphony concerts as it is for wrestling.

BOOKS FOR FURTHER READING

COTTLE, J. *Reminiscences of Samuel Taylor Coleridge and Robert Southey*. London, 1847.
GARLICK, KENNETH. *Sir Thomas Lawrence*. London, 1954.
HUTTON, S. *Bristol and its Famous Associations*. Bristol, 1907.

LATIMER, J. *The Annals of Bristol in the Nineteenth Century*. Bristol, 1887 and 1902.
LITTLE, BRYAN. *The City and County of Bristol*. London, 1954.
POWELL, G. RENNIE. 1919. *The Bristol Stage*. Bristol, 1919.
ROSS, JAMES. 'An Eighteenth Century Playhouse: The Theatre Royal, Bristol', 1945. *Essays by Divers Hands, Being the Transactions of the Royal Society of Literature*. . . . London, new series, vol. 22, pp. 61–85.
Ten Bristol Artists. Bristol City Museum and Art Gallery, 1934.

PART THREE

CHAPTER SEVENTEEN

BRISTOL'S ARCHITECTURE, PAST AND PRESENT

BRISTOL, Treasure City of the West, is rich with Victorian brilliants in dulled mountings, cut stones of Norman and medieval craftsmanship in quiet settings, Edwardian paste, Georgian and Regency sparkling gems, modern glass in shiny chromium, Elizabethan pieces jet and ivory; all gathered in a thousand years, lumped together in delightful confusion and now to be displayed in ordered array.

Bristol is a city of proud spires and beautiful churches, historic hostelries and bonded warehouses, squares, a triangle, a polygon, and a paragon, noble towers, a university, colleges and schools, chain stores, little shops, almshouses, hospitals, Council Houses old and new, warm 'pubs' and buildings for cold storage, Georgian and Regency terraces, promenades, trees, gardens, open spaces, built-up areas, streets, avenues, and groves, extensive housing estates the result of skill, industry and resolution, banks, offices, commercial rooms, industrial buildings, Pie Poudré Court, houses rich with linings of Elizabethan and Georgian panelling, another lined with the rich panelling from a famous liner.

Beautiful buildings, ugly buildings and nondescript buildings, all share party walls or stand side by side to express the spirit of a long tradition—'Bristol fashion'.

There are no important architectural remains from Saxon times, but the carved stone depicting the 'Harrowing of Hell', now placed in the Cathedral, would be an outstanding achievement of any period.

Norman work is to be found at St. James's Church, near the Horsefair, and at All Saints' Church, City. At the Cathedral there is the splendid Chapter House and Abbey Gateways. Of the castle, the centre of Norman control over Bristol and the surrounding countryside, no contemporary structure remains above ground but an Early English stone-vaulted entrance- or ante-hall to the castle survived the air raids of the Second World War when all else around was destroyed.

At the foot of Christmas Steps there is an Early English arch and niche, sadly mutilated, part of the fabric of the one-time St. Bartholomew's Hospital. (At the head of the steps is the altered and restored little chapel, a late fifteenth-century structure, dedicated to 'The Three Kings of Cologne'.) Thirteenth- and fourteenth-century work exists at the Dominican Friary, near Merchant Street. The ancient churches are the important remaining examples of the buildings erected during the medieval period.

In the year 1140 Robert fitzHarding founded a monastery of Augustinian canons and after the Dissolution in 1539 the Abbey Church became the Cathedral (see Chapter 11, p. 187). Early in the thirteenth century the Elder Lady Chapel was added to the original Norman structure. In the Early English style, it has wall arcading with trefoil arches and Purbeck marble shafts. The carvings in the arch spandrels indicate the humour and imagination of the medieval craftsmen. Early in the fourteenth century it was decided to rebuild the Abbey, starting from the east and working towards the west. The rebuilt choir and aisles are in the Decorated style and have stone vaulting, the carved bosses and other decoration showing beautiful workmanship. The aisles are the same height as the choir, and an unusual design for the aisle was evolved to counteract the thrust of the choir vaulting. Arches span the aisles and support strong stone transomes which in turn carry a springing of vault. This ingenious solution serves the purpose of a flying buttress but is an internal system and not external as at Redcliffe.

The Berkeley Chapel, the Newton Chapel, and the Decorated work of the transepts were the next stages in the reconstruction and, after a lapse of time, the central tower and the vaulting of the transepts were built during the fifteenth century. The north and west foundations for a new nave were laid down. Then came the Dissolution and about that time the original, dilapidated Norman nave was demolished, leaving a splendid but uncompleted medieval building which terminated at the western face of the beautiful central tower. The modern nave, the work of Professor G. E. Street, was completed in the year 1877 and followed the proposals of his medieval predecessors. His decision to provide twin western towers has not met with general approval.

St. John the Baptist Church was built during the fourteenth and fifteenth centuries as part of the city wall, the tower and spire being over the north gateway. The Church of St. Laurence adjoined St. John and the tower was once a central feature between the churches (St. Laurence destroyed, 1580). The church has a fine crypt and Jacobean screen and the gateway bears figures of Brennus and Belinus, the legendary founders of the city. The portcullis groove still remains. The conduit, near the gateway, is one of many formerly provided throughout the city. St. Mark's, now the Lord Mayor's Chapel, dates from the thirteenth century, and was part of the Gaunt's Hospital. The tower was built in the fifteenth century and is a blending of a red and cream stone. The fine tower of St. Stephen's, with its distinctive angle pinnacles and splendid peal of bells, also dates from the fifteenth century. All Saints' Church includes Norman work and an ancient tower which during the eighteenth century was encased in Bath stone, and later an octagonal cupola was added. This has arched openings and an order bearing urns. It is one of the finest towers in the city and composes perfectly with the nearby Corn Exchange (see Plate XXIII). The architect was Luke Henwood. The church contains the monument to Edward Colston, by James Gibbs, the figure being by Rysbrack.

Four of the churches which stood within the walls of the ancient city suffered grievous damage during the raids of the last war. St. Peter's, the mother church, has a square set tower, built of red and grey stone, the base of which includes masonry of an early period although most of the structure is fifteenth-century work. The small but shapely tower of St. Mary-le-Port is all that remains of the early fifteenth-century fabric. Temple, or Holy Cross, Church was founded by the Knights Templars, but the now burnt-out ruins date from the fourteenth century and later. The famous leaning tower was completed towards the end of the fifteenth century. The tower settled during construction and the measures taken by the builders included under-pinning and the adjustment of the poise of the upper story. St. Nicholas' has an ancient crypt, altered during the fourteenth century. The original church stood on the city wall over a gateway in a manner similar to St. John's. When the gateway was removed, in 1762, a new church was built over the ancient crypt but in a 'Georgian Gothic' style. Designed by the architect Bridges, it was completed in 1769, and was approved by Horace Walpole. The tower, spire and the walls of the nave still stand, and from this tower the curfew was sounded until the Second World War, when bell-ringing was prohibited.

St. Mary Redcliffe Church . . . 'held and deemed to be in all respects ye fairest Parochiall Church in England by reason whereof it is highly esteemed by ye inhabitants and much admired by strangers' . . . is a rebuilding of an earlier church which stood on an outcrop of red stone in the twelfth century and of which the inner north porch is the most important survival. It is of the Early English style and has typical wall arcading. In the thirteenth century the church possessed an important relic and the outer north porch was built with doorways arranged to enable pilgrims to pass through the porch when the relic was displayed. During the fourteenth century the people of Redcliffe decided to rebuild the rest of the church on a scale worthy of an abbey or cathedral. The design included double aisles to the nave, transepts, and chancel and the building of a Lady Chapel. The rebuilding, with additional improvements, was not finished until the fifteenth century and is a superb example of the Perpendicular style.

The church is vaulted in stone. In the nave the basic mouldings of the vaulting ribs rise from the bases of the piers to soar between the clerestory windows and then to arch forward in lacings and interlacings starred with gilded carvings displaying an amazing variety of detail. The walls are panelled in stone and it is still possible to trace the imprint of a number of the consecration crosses. The windows are rich with stained glass, some ancient as in the tower and inner vestry. Beneath the central window in the south transept is the canopied and painted tomb of William Canynges. It is fitting that the great benefactor should rest in his beloved church.

The early eighteenth-century wrought-iron screens and gates at the western end are the work of a Bristol smith named Thomas Edney, and are of outstanding design and craftsmanship. The undercroft is modern and reproduces the simple vaulting of the ancient crypt. The graceful spire set on the well-proportioned tower is a famous landmark, and with the body of the church makes a fine composition from every viewpoint. The slender piers between traceried windows, the curve of flying buttresses, the verticality of crocketted pinnacles, constitute a vital expression of load, thrust and counterpoise. A skilful deployment of carved detail relates structure and ornament. By their genius and their craftsmanship the men of the Middle Ages made Redcliffe a beautiful and fitting setting for the worship of God.

By the end of the sixteenth century the wealthy merchants inhabited substantial residences built of stone. The rooms were lined with oak panelling, beautifully moulded, tenoned and mason-mitred, and had ceilings of richly decorative plaster-work. The Oak Room at the Red Lodge (*c.* 1590) is a splendid example. The room has an internal porch-type entrance and a magnificent fireplace bearing a coat of arms. The extension to the Red Lodge, known as the Wigwam, is a reproduction of an ancient tythe barn. Fine period fireplaces have been set within the walls, and one bears a motto which is now a 'Savage' Grace.

Building activity during the seventeenth century was limited because of the part played by Bristol during the Civil War. The Hatchet Inn, Frog Lane, now Frogmore Street, (*c.* 1606), is a typical half-timbered building showing a minor use of the timbers in decorative shapes. The range of three houses (five before the last war) in King Street includes the famous Llandoger Trow, *c.* 1664. The freedom in the design of the ground floor is regularized by the treatment of the two floors above it. Here is established a pleasant rhythm of projecting bay windows, one bay or two, arranged alternately. Each house culminates in a gable punctuated by a single opening. The patterning of the surface is achieved by means of the half-timbering infilled with stucco. Thus the basic construction is exposed to view and, being scaled to the fenestration, provides a unified design. The sash windows are of a later date. These buildings are perfect examples of their period.

During the course of many centuries benefactors have made themselves responsible for the care of the aged and for the safeguarding of widows and children. Bristol has a number of ancient almshouses (see Chapter 20, pp. 295–6) of which the following are typical examples:

St. Nicholas Almshouses (*c.* 1652) are among the earliest buildings to be erected in King Street. They are gabled and have mullioned windows.

The almshouses at the foot of St. Michael's Hill (see Plate XXX) are one of the benefactions of Edward Colston who purchased the land in 1690. Making a delightful composition, they are planned around three sides of a forecourt. The building is two stories in height with honey-coloured walls. The roofs, covered with pantiles, are warm in colour and of a pleasing texture. The two wings are formed by a repetition of a well-designed domestic unit and lead the eye to the chapel, which is the central feature of the third side. The chapel maintains the perfect scale and is accentuated against the roof by a simple pediment above which, at ridge level, is placed a charming bell-cote.

The almshouses erected by The Society of Merchant Venturers are situated in King Street (see Plate XXXI). They were badly damaged during the raids which destroyed the Merchants' Hall. This was a stately building of great architectural merit. The almshouses were rebuilt and extended in 1696 and during the early years of the following century, for the use of poor sailors, or the widows and daughters of sailors. From the portion which remains it is possible to appreciate the charm of the original group of buildings. The perfect domestic scale, the horizontal lines of the fenestration, strings, cornice and roof line, all express rest and peace.

The Merchant Tailors' Almshouse was built in 1701 for the widows and daughters of the members of the Company. This smaller building has much in common with the Colston Almshouses. The main entrance doorway has a shell-hood above which is a panel containing the carved arms of the Tailors. Although this building lies within the modern shopping precinct, now being developed, it is to be preserved.

The buildings erected in, and around, Bristol during the eighteenth century shew that the wealthy citizens appreciated fine architecture. For the greater part of the century the cup of prosperity overflowed. Within the city there was demolition and rebuilding, and developments took place outside the ancient boundaries. New streets and squares were planned, subject to either official or private control, which determined the observance of continuous skylines, the placing of focal points of interest, and the achievement of architectural harmony.

In 1702 work was started in Queen Square and continued through the years. Two of the original red-brick houses exist at the extreme south-west corner. The Square, which was named after Queen Anne, still lives despite the devastation caused by the riots of 1831, the construction of an arterial roadway and the damage in air raids. The dignified Customs House and other buildings were rebuilt after the Riots and the statue of William III is a brilliant example of the work of Rysbrack. St. James Square and Orchard Street were built *c.* 1716. Most of the buildings in St. James Square were destroyed by enemy action, but Orchard Street remains as a perfect example of the period. The houses in this street are three-storied, built in brick, with doorways and other features in stone all of which are now painted. The elevations are controlled but each house has been given individuality in architectural expression. Gaunt House is the finest house in the street. It has an entrance doorway with a broad architrave flanked by graceful Doric pilasters above which carved trusses, or corbels, support a curved 'broken' pediment. At an earlier date this may have contained a sculptured bust or figure. The flatly-carved grotesques forming the keystones to the well-proportioned sash windows are typical of those to be found in Hotwells, Queen Square, and Guinea Street, Redcliffe. There is a fine entrance hall and staircase. Most of the important rooms are panelled. In Orchard Street there are excellent examples of Georgian railings, footscrapers, and door furniture. Dowry Square (*c.* 1730) and the neighbouring streets were developed to meet the needs of visitors to the Hotwell. Most of the houses are of brickwork with distinctive Georgian detail.

John Wood the Elder, the distinguished Bath architect, designed the Corn Exchange and its ancillary buildings which stand in Corn Street (see Plate XXIII). It was completed in 1743, and is the most important building erected in Bristol during the Georgian period. It is faced with Bath stone. The broad front is eleven bays in width and rises through three stories above street level. The ground-floor level is treated as a strong base which carries an order expressed by three-quarter applied columns to the central three bays (which project) and by pilasters to each of the flanking bays. The order contains the first- and second-floor windows. The central window at first-floor level is treated in the Palladian manner; the remaining windows repeat the lesser order and carry a succession of curved and pointed pediments. The second-floor windows are square-shaped and all bear a simple architrave. The capitals of the main order are a free interpretation of the Corinthian, the necking mould being carried across the building. In the panels thus formed beneath the underside of the entablature carved 'swags' link the capitals. By this means a rich decorative effect is obtained beneath the strong lines of the entablature, which includes a modillioned cornice. The central feature has a pediment (enclosing a carved shield and supporters) bearing carved urns. The side-unit bays have parapets formed of balusters and dies. The carved work is said to be by Paty. The flanking buildings, free standing and of simple design, act as a foil to the Exchange. Strong lines of iron railings flank the main entrance, which is arched. The baluster-shaped metal tables, or 'nails', outside the Exchange were used in connexion with the buying and selling of corn. Hence, Bristolians say, the term 'paying on the nail'.

Coopers Hall, King Street, designed by William Halfpenny, was built in 1744 for use by the Coopers (or Hoopers) Company, and is evidence of the dignity attaching to the ancient companies. The main elevation to King Street is faced with Bath stone and is dramatic in scale. Above a strong base the hall proper is expressed by a central feature of applied columns of the Corinthian order and high double-hung sash windows surmounted by pediments. The columns carry a well-designed entablature above which a central attic story contains three windows and culminates in a pediment displaying the carved arms of the company. This fine building has been put to many uses for which it was not intended and the interior has suffered in consequence.

The New Room in the Horsefair was established in 1739 and was rebuilt and enlarged in 1748 (see Plate XXVIII). It is famous as the first Methodist chapel founded by John Wesley. Originally the building was approached by means of long narrow alley-ways and the enclosed site offered little scope for the architectural development of the elevations. The Broadmead courtyard was formed when the building was restored in 1929, and the Horsefair courtyard in 1954. The statues of John and Charles Wesley are the work of G. A. Walker, A.R.A. The New Room is at ground-level with quarters for students on the first floor. Bath stone columns carry the upper floor and the gallery. The detailing of the mouldings of the joinery is refined and the delicately cut balusters are perfect examples of their period. The architect is unknown but he designed a building beautiful in its simplicity.

The Theatre Royal, King Street, was opened in 1766. The auditorium expresses the elegance and gaiety of fashionable society in Bristol at the time. It has slender columns supporting galleries, the curves of which unite stage and auditorium. The decorative plasterwork of the ceiling and gallery fronts is refined in detail and is skilfully placed. After many vicissitudes the theatre was the subject of an expert and sympathetic restoration. Christ Church with St. Ewen was designed by William

Paty (1790). It has a well-proportioned tower and spire in the Wren city church tradition. Internally there is carving by Paty and his sons.

Domestic architecture in and around Bristol includes many important houses. Typical examples: Church House, Clifton (1711); Kings Weston House, by Sir John Vanbrugh (1714); Goldney House (1720); Redland Court, by John Strachan (*c.* 1735); Clifton Hill House, by Isaac Ware (1747); Royal Fort House, by James Bridges (1760); the 'Georgian House' (1791).

Redland Court, now Redland High School, was designed by John Strachan for John Cousins and was built on the site of an older house commanding extensive views.

'The Owner's Mansion on a gentle rise
Appears a palace to th' admiring eyes.'

It consists of a central block with low side-wings which are possibly of a later date. The eastern wing was increased in height in 1887. The elevations are faced with Bath stone and are of an elegant design, the south elevation being particularly pleasing. The principal feature is an Ionic order, which carries a pediment infilled with a carved coat of arms supported by cupids. The entrance hall (see Plate XXVII) is floored with Portland stone inlaid with tile diapers; the walls are panelled and there is a Doric cornice. The doorway to the main reception room is developed with a full Doric order. The stair-cases are curved, the handrails wreathed, and the cut balusters are arranged in pairs. The principal rooms have mahogany doors and marble fireplaces, the surrounds of which bear classical detail. The southern gateway has fine piers carrying carved urns, and the wrought ironwork of this gate and also of the smaller western gate is of excellent design and craftsmanship.

At Redland Green, on ground near the northern boundary of his estate, John Cousins erected a chapel. The design is attributed to John Strachan but he may not have supervised the actual erection, which was completed *c.* 1743. Halfpenny was connected with the work. The chapel is faced with Bath stone. Much thought must have been given to the design of this building, particularly to the cupola and gadrooned dome. Internally there is original panelling and other woodwork. The delicately undercut carvings in lime wood are the work of Thomas Paty.

The Royal Fort House built in 1760 from the designs of James Bridges stands in gardens laid out by Humphrey Repton. The three-storied house is faced with Bath stone and the elevations are developed in a fine Georgian style. The main entrance is flanked by wrought ironwork including lamp standards and torch extinguishers. There is a splendid entrance hall and beyond it a main staircase with 'hanging treads'. The decorative work from a master hand is beautiful and the treatment of the staircase walls is superb. On the flat plaster is superimposed a tracery of elegant tree-forms bearing delicate flowers, fruit and leaves enlivened by butterflies, birds and the smaller animals. There are well-proportioned rooms lined with panelling, beautifully moulded, and in a ground-floor room a strip of the original hand-painted wallpaper has been preserved.

Clifton, lying outside the Bristol boundaries, was not developed until the Regency period. During the early part of the eighteenth century the Hotwell had become popular with 'the Quality' but was reached by means of the road which followed the northern bank of the Avon. The houses of Dowry Square and its immediate neighbourhood were built at the base of the Clifton slopes. At the top of Clifton Hill, near the hamlet of Clifton, there were a few large houses standing in their own grounds. This left undeveloped a magnificent site curving away from the entrance to the Avon Gorge and formed by a series of slopes falling away to the south. Individual speculators and syndicates, who appreciated the possibilities of the site, developed Clifton as a spa. The buildings, faced either with stucco or with Bath stone, are in the form of terraces laid out to follow selected contours. Where necessary curved or crescent shapes were planned to observe the site conditions. The use of well-considered designs, with unbroken roof-lines, enable the terraces to express at high level the basic contours determining their line on plan. This gives a natural and satisfying result not only when the unit terraces are viewed from ground-level but more particularly when the whole hillside development is appreciated from a distance.

The earlier buildings set a standard which was maintained until the middle of the nineteenth century (as at Codrington Place and Worcester Terrace), after which detached houses became popular.

Certain terraces are formed by the repetition of a single living-unit two, three, or four stories high. At Royal York Crescent the living-unit is expressed in elevation and the possible monotony of the long front is relieved by projecting balconies. In the case of the smaller Paragon the repeated unit is softened by the treatment of the entrance porches, which are semi-circular on plan and introduce an interesting interplay of light and shade. Royal York Crescent is set out as a flat curve above a wide terraced walk. The Paragon is a smaller layout with a definite crescent curve. Other examples are Princes Buildings, Windsor Terrace, The Polygon, and Cornwallis Crescent. Some terraces were developed as straight-fronted formal layouts as at the lower end of Clifton Park, the West Mall, Harley Place, and Caledonia Place.

The terraces and houses of Clifton display a wealth of architectural detail; balconies with curved or flat hoods carried by delicate supports of wrought iron, some showing motifs derived from the Greek, as at Clifton Vale, iron window-boxes, railings of wrought or cast iron, lamp standards and brackets, many variations in iron or brass door furniture and fanlights of intricate design.

Further developments carried residential Clifton to the edge of Durdham Downs and eastwards to a line established by the turnpike linking Park Street and the Downs (now Whiteladies Road and Blackboy Hill).

Among the buildings in Clifton designed at a later date are some of the Gothic Revival style, such as the famous Clifton College, and others are Italianate in character.

In the seventeenth and eighteenth centuries important industries concerned with cocoa, tobacco and porcelain had been established in Bristol and grew in importance during the nineteenth century. In 1840 the railway from London reached the ancient Temple Meads and in the following years Bristol was to play her part in the new Age of Industrialism.

During the nineteenth century many new buildings were erected to serve industry and education, and to meet the needs of a population which was increasing rapidly. Much of the new work was designed in the Gothic style. Some Bristol architects favoured the 'Venetian', others the 'Romanesque', and for a short period developed a local style now defined as 'Bristol-Byzantine'.

This break with the eighteenth-century tradition began in the middle years of that century (St. Nicholas's, 1769). Horace Walpole had sponsored work at his house in a 'Gothic' style now known as 'Strawberry Hill'. St. Paul's, Portland Square, was built in 1794 and in 1796 James Wyatt designed Fonthill Abbey. The runners were spreading from Strawberry Hill. The eminent classicist, John Nash, designed the romantic Blaise Hamlet for his friend Harford (*c.* 1809). Pugin published his *Specimens of Gothic Architecture*, and other folios of measured drawings of Gothic buildings became available for reference by those who favoured a Gothic revival. They were, however, destined not to have their own way as another movement was taking place in favour of the 'Greek'.

At a national level most of the leading architects took part in the 'Battle of the Styles', which was to last well into the nineteenth century. The Classic tradition had been broken and there followed a bewildering succession of 'styles'. The streets of Bristol display many examples of buildings designed under the influences affecting architectural appreciation during the nineteenth century.

Sir Robert Smirke, one of the leaders of the Greek revival, designed St. George's Church, Brandon Hill (1823), and the old Council House (1827). The church is built on a steep slope and the main entrance is approached from the lower level by means of a dramatic flight of steps. These lead to a Greek Doric portico fronting an otherwise simple building. The portico is surmounted by a circular domed cupola set on a square base. The building is faced with Bath stone and is the work of a master. Professor Cockerell favoured the Greek style and was responsible for three Bristol buildings: Holy Trinity Church, Hotwells (1829); The Philosophical and Literary Institution (later the Freemasons' Hall), Park Street; the Bank of England in Broad Street (1844). The first two buildings were badly damaged by enemy action, but their restoration is planned. The Bank of England building has an elevation of great dignity and is a worthy member of the family of the 'Old Lady', who must approve of the personal appearance of her provincial offspring. The Commercial Rooms, an elegant building in Corn Street, was designed by C. A. Busby (1810); the Royal Western Hotel (later the Hydro, and now offices) has a tall classical colonnade and was designed by R. S. Pope (1839) who was responsible for St. Mary's-on-the-Quay (1840). Charles Dyer designed the Victoria Rooms, the foundation stone of which was laid in 1838. The main external feature is a portico of tall Corinthian columns, which support a pediment containing a vigorous sculpture 'The Advent of Morning'. The main entrance leads to the octagon which is the centre of the corridor system, and has clerestory windows beneath a saucer-dome, delicately detailed. The major axis of the main hall is set at right angles to the approach axis and is entered as from the octagon. The hall was well designed but conventional in detail. It was gutted by fire in 1934. The present main hall is an outstanding example of architectural design of the period between the wars and is in harmony with the original building.

The new building for the ancient Queen Elizabeth's Hospital (1844) on the lower slope of Brandon Hill was designed in a Gothic style; Brandon Hill stone was used. There is an underlying classical formality in this design and there is drama in the stepped approach. The Diocesan Training College, Fishponds (1854), is an academic example of Gothic revivalist design including the careful use of local materials as advocated by Ruskin, for example, the roofs covered with Pennant stone slabs. The Royal West of England Academy building was completed in 1858. Externally in the Italian style, internally in the Greek, the original design included external staircases, which were cleared away during the remodelling of the building. E. W. Godwin designed 106 Stokes Croft as a warehouse (*c.* 1860). It is understood to be the first commercial building in Bristol designed to achieve the maximum window area possible within the limitations imposed by contemporary construction. The elevation is of stone, three floors in height, expressed by continuous string courses. The ground floor has five arched openings, the first and second floors having ten. There is a simple but adequate cornice at skyline level. The proportioning of the arcades at each stage, the depth of reveals and a reticence in the use of mouldings are all factors contributing to the effect of this building. There is a clever use of local stone to achieve scale, texture and pattern. The infillings of the ground-floor arcade are modern and the original tie-bar system carrying decorative ironwork has been removed. During the following ten years buildings of this type, and with distinctive ornament, were erected in the city. Selected examples are said to constitute a local style, 'Bristol-Byzantine'. A building in which the Assyrian or Byzantine influence is more obvious is the one erected in Redcliffe Street for W. D. and H. O. Wills. In this design the basic construction is expressed by the deep recessing of the window units. The Granary on the Welsh Back is of brick, the detailing of which is distinctive. Other examples are to be found in Victoria Street. The old City Museum was built about 1871. The architects were Foster and Wood, who designed a number of Bristol buildings, including the Colston Hall, and the rebuilt Foster's Almshouses, at the head of Christmas Steps. The Museum is 'Venetian', built of stone with special brick for the upper portion. The circular windows were infilled with 'plate-tracery'. Only the walls remained after the air raids. New buildings for the ancient Grammar School are built in a Gothic style, of Brandon Hill stone. The University College buildings in University Road, built 1879–83, are 'Gothic' and are the first permanent buildings to be erected in that part of Bristol now defined as the University area. A number of churches and chapels were built in Clifton, Redland and Bishopston as these districts developed. The Cabot Tower, Brandon Hill, the result of an architectural competition, was erected four centuries after the discovery of the continent of North America. The Prudential Building in Clare Street (1899) is by Alfred Waterhouse, R.A., one of the greatest architects of his time.

Towards the end of the nineteenth century architectural thought returned to the Classic and during the early years of the following century buildings were designed in a modified Georgian style. Some employed brick as the dominant material as at Fuller's Coachworks (now School of Commerce), St. George's Road, and Fry's Factory, Tower Lane; others were built of Bath stone and show an ingenious and academic use of classical detail as in the case of the 'Sun Building' and the 'Scottish Provident', both in Clare Street. During later years many notable buildings were erected, including the Museum and Art Gallery (1905), the Bristol Co-operative Society Building (1906), and in Broad Street a gallant attempt to display joy and colour near the Law Courts. The Bristol Central Library (1906) is the perfect example of good manners in architecture; of outstanding design, this fine building is in complete harmony with the Cathedral. The University Chemical Wing, the Western College and the Bristol Baptist College, if stylistic in their design, are 'scholarly' buildings and excellent compositions on difficult sites. The Royal Infirmary (1912) is one of the most important buildings in the city in that the fine architecture is based on theories not generally adopted until twenty years later. The designs for the main buildings and tower of the University were prepared before the First World War and the foundations laid, but the outbreak of the war brought the work to a standstill.

Bristol buildings designed during the years between the two world wars follow a national pattern, as most of those erected before, say, 1930 were 'Period' designs, whereas many of the buildings of a later date show the change which was taking place in the approach to architectural design. This involved a simplification in form, the sparing use of detail and decoration, and in some buildings a stressing, visually, of the constructional frame. Buildings erected during the period include: the Bristol Homoeopathic Hospital; housing estates at Sea Mills and at Hillfields; the University main buildings; St. Monica Home of Rest; The Henry Herbert Wills Physics Laboratory; Cotham School; Wills Hall; Midland Bank, Corn Street; National Provincial Bank, Corn Street; 16 and 18 Clare Street; Manor Hall; The Central Police and Fire Station; The Evening World Building; Eagle House, Colston Avenue; Bristol Gas Company (now S.W. Gas Board); Friends' Provident Building; several swimming baths; extensions at Southmead Hospital; St. Stephen's House; University Botanical Wing and Library extension; the Dental Hospital. The Electricity Offices (now S.W. Electricity Board) and the new Council House were in course of construction at the time of the outbreak of the Second World War.

During the war Bristol suffered widespread damage, several thousand homes were destroyed and many thousands left in need of repair. A large number of buildings were lost including irreplaceable architectural treasures. The Wine Street—Castle Street shopping centre was wiped out, leaving a devastated area which in ancient times had been the site of the castle and much of the walled town.

The main effort since the war has been the development of numerous housing estates to meet the needs of the population. Most of the land available around the city has been used for this purpose and certain built-up areas are now being replanned to accommodate blocks of flats, some many stories in height.

The authorities decided that the main shopping centre should be rebuilt in the Broadmead area and that the higher ground around Wine Street should be retained for public buildings. The new shopping precinct is in course of development.

Well-designed churches, chapels, schools and shops have been built, or are in course of erection, on the various housing estates. Large buildings rise in the city, and the dignified new Council House will, in the near future, be the centre of civic ceremony. Bombed churches are being rebuilt, the new Church of St. Francis of Assisi, at Ashton Gate, setting a high standard in design.

Pre-stressing, pre-fabrication, synthetic materials, new theories as to design, and the advent of the 'Transparency style', are all factors that will affect the appearance of the Bristol yet to be built during the twentieth century.

CHAPTER EIGHTEEN

ENGINEERING IN BRISTOL

TO the lay visitor, Bristol is not a city of engineers; merchant venturers, maybe, university students, perhaps, wine importers, yes, but hardly engineers. Even a British engineer visiting the city for the first time will have difficulty in recalling much more than a connexion with the Great Western Railway and with Brunel, and thence a memory of the Clifton Suspension Bridge, and, as a disconnected modern episode, the Bristol Aeroplane Company. He may add to these thoughts at the sight of the shipping in the City Docks or of Wills's tobacco stores, but the slave trade and cigarettes will be in his mind rather than any engineering efforts associated therewith.

Some towns and districts have clear-cut large-scale engineering activities, like Coventry and cars, or Clydeside and ships, or Merthyr Tydfil and coal, but Bristol is not one of these. Its character, in the engineering sense as in many other senses, has something of the range of London; a London in little, but without the smog. How then can one produce anything like an ordered account or commentary on its engineering activities? Are there any themes running through its engineering history on which to hang such an article—real themes, that is, and not ones only to take the passing fancy of a publicity officer?

Bristol has been made, like many another ancient English city, by its geographical position as a seaport and bridgetown near the mouth of a river. Unlike many and more than most towns, however, its early importance as a transport centre has grown with the years. From ships to aeroplanes, Bristol has not just played its part and then forgotten; it has rather in each case made an original contribution and then hung on to some part of the business thus engendered. Ships still ply in the City Docks and are still built there; the aeroplane company, which earlier made electric trams and petrol-engine buses, retains a hand in the car business. There is no doubt of the love of the Bristolian for transport activities and this applies to her engineers too.

There is, however, in Bristol a secondary and less obvious influence on her engineering activities. In a small way the mineral wealth of the Bristol district has always had its influence. Lead, and perhaps rumours of iron, brought the Romans here. The stonemasons of Bath and Bristol have always enjoyed peculiar advantages. The clear waters of the surrounding hills have encouraged a paper trade that is quite astonishing to the diligent inquirer. Even the coal mining in the district has sometimes reaped the advantages of the peculiarly town-cum-country atmosphere pervading all that Bristol does.

In setting out then to discuss something of engineering in Bristol and of its engineers, it will be both convenient and natural to group the subject-matter under the two heads of transport and natural resources, though many engineering activities naturally relate to both, and most attention must be given to the former.

The archives of engineering in Bristol provide items of interest from early times. One could go back to the medieval builders and observe the work of the able and influential stonemasons of Bristol and Bath, recalling such men as Richard of Farleigh, who lived at Keynsham in 1350 and became the master mason of Salisbury Cathedral; or to the farsighted dock engineers of a century earlier who first diverted the Frome to improve Bristol Harbour. But engineering to most of us has a more modern connotation associated with metals and the industrial revolution, and we will here tend to concentrate on this late period, which covers roughly the last two hundred years.

Ships and docks must come first under our transport head. Until the expansion of Liverpool early in the nineteenth century, Bristol was the second largest port of the kingdom; nevertheless, it was till that time a port of wooden ships using docks that were little better than firm mud banks, giving point to the phrase 'shipshape and Bristol fashion'. But in 1765, the city fathers, alive to the growing competition of Liverpool and elsewhere, called in Smeaton to advise on enlarging and improving the docks. Smeaton had at that time already acquired fame for his Eddystone Lighthouse and was the leading 'gentleman' among civil engineers of that period, who were wont to meet at a coffee house in Westminster the better to attend upon Parliament and push their projects along. Smeaton in due course submitted his report, and the city authorities thanked him with the resolution: 'that the thanks of the gentlemen present be given to Mr. Smeaton for his plan now offered, and for his diligence and attention in this matter', and took no action. It awaited another generation to effect the much-needed improvements, when Jessop, a pupil of Smeaton's, carried out an extensive reconstruction scheme that by 1809 brought into being the present floating docks of the city and most of the ancillary features familiar to us to-day. Cumberland Basin, at the entrance to these docks, was originally his work, though the lock gates are modern; the smaller of the swing bridges there is still as it was built to the designs of I. K. Brunel. The tubular flanges of the wrought-iron plate girders of this small bridge are reminiscent of the much greater efforts by the same hand at Chepstow and Saltash.

The docks at Avonmouth are much later, major contributors to their design being Sir John Wolfe Bary and Sir Benjamin Baker—names popularly associated with the Tower Bridge and the Forth Bridge respectively—who completed their work in 1908. Baker had a local interest in undertaking this work. He was born at Keyford, a small Somerset village near Frome, and educated at Dean School, Cheltenham. He had previously, in 1880, essayed a design for a 1,580-ft. span suspension bridge across the Severn near Aust—one of many precursors to the current debate—and happily came back, at the end of his life, to help at Avonmouth.

Bristol's enthusiasm for shipping has not been limited to its own docks in the city and at Avonmouth. In the second half of the nineteenth century the growing steamship trade with the West Indies, and no doubt local aspirations raised by the success of the *Great Western,* led to the idea of a 'Trans-Atlantic' port at Brean Down, near Weston-super-Mare. The sheltered deep waters on the north side of this seemed hopeful for the creation of a new port on a large scale. A 'Brean Down Harbour Company' was formed, parliamentary approval obtained, and the first stone laid in 1862. But in spite of Government interest—the War Office built a small fort there—the work went slowly and a great storm in 1872 destroyed most of the first jetty. All that remains is part of the fort, which was rebuilt in the recent war for some coastal protection batteries; the Down itself is now, perhaps more happily, a bird sanctuary.

Reference to the *Great Western* recalls a great period of engineering effort in the Bristol shipyards. When one of his directors was complaining of the excessive length of the railway line from London to Bristol, I. K. Brunel made the quiet retort 'Why not make it still longer and have a steamboat to connect Bristol with New York, and call it the *Great Western*?' The incident might have passed as just a verbal quip, but it happened that one of the railway directors, T. R. Guppy, was interested in shipping and after the meeting took young Brunel aside and urged upon him the idea of a regular steamboat line to New York. Guppy came of a family long connected with Somerset; two of his ancestors, William and Justinian, had been in the Monmouth rebellion of 1685 and were deported to Barbados; he and Brunel pushed on with the project in William Patterson's Yard on the Avon, just above the present site of Hill's Yard on the west bank. Brunel designed the ship as an oak paddle-wheel steamer of 1,340 tons, an immense size in those days, with the aim of giving her a power and coal capacity permitting of continuous steaming across the Atlantic. The British Association met at Bristol in 1836 while she was in the making, and a Dr. Dionysius Lardner read a paper not only condemning the project as unworkable, like a journey to the moon, but presenting the now-famous argument that no ship could carry enough coal for the journey. It was left to an Irishman to agree to the full with Lardner's technical conclusions and yet to add 'the effort, nevertheless, will be made; the genius of English enterprise will hazard the consequences, and every honest spirit that shall hear of the brave British crew, which will embark upon that perilous expedition, will feel his heart beating high for the merchant sailor whom nothing can deter'. The ship was launched in 1837 and, after fitting out, made her maiden voyage in April, 1838. Thus started her famous career; her portrait is on the silver trophy held by winners of the Atlantic Blue Riband and one hundred years later her success was immortalized by the phrase 'the heart of the *Great Western* still beats in the *Queen Mary*'. What a triumph for her young designer, who was yet only thirty-two years old!

Brunel had now become really interested in the building of big ships, and the Great Western Steamship Company, founded in 1835 by Mark Whitwell—a name still associated with shipping here—saw its chance of further success and commissioned a new large ship from Patterson's Yard, again to be designed by Brunel.

Brunel was nothing if not boldly experimental. His bridge experience with wrought iron led him to contemplate an iron ship and he set about this by starting on extensive experiments with iron plating and riveted joints. For propulsion, he had become interested with Froude in screw propellers in place of paddle wheels and designed the first large propeller system for his new ship. Thus came into being the first iron ocean-going screw-propelled steamship in the world, the *Great Britain.* It was launched in 1843 by Prince Albert, who had incidentally arrived by train in the then record time from London of 3 hours 20 minutes, and raised the reputations of Brunel and of Patterson's Yard to international fame.

Shipbuilding in Bristol reached a new peak; three yards were now in being—Pattersons, Hills and Hydes—and in energetic competition. Between 1843 and 1875, and excluding the *Great Western* and the *Great Britain,* the maximum tonnage of ships constructed in their yards rose steadily from 500 to 1,500 tons, and by the end of the period iron ships had become common and screw propulsion usual.

To the middle of this period belonged Samuel Plimsoll, who was born in Bristol in 1824 of poor parents and yet lived to leave his mark on shipping throughout the world, apparently for ever. He prospered in middle life and became a Member of Parliament for West Derby. He long had an interest in shipping and saw, with its increase, the evils of careless maintenance and the apparent disregard of some owners for the dangers run by their seamen. Continual agitation culminated in a heated but effective debate in Parliament, and the Plimsoll Line, beyond which the loading of a ship is prohibited, came into being. This major outcome of his life is commemorated by a tablet at the harbour end of the City Centre.

Less well known, but of more fundamental scientific interest, is the fact that Froude, the founder of modern ideas regarding the water's resistance to ships and the use of model experiments on ships, was a west countryman. He was born at Dartington in 1810 and did much of his famous experimental work at Torquay. During the years of Brunel's greatest shipping activity, Froude worked under him on the best shape for the *Great Britain* and, later, the *Great Eastern* built in London, and on the design of the screw propellers for these ships. It thus came about that not only did Bristol develop as a port, but it also played a major part in the advancement of ships and shipping throughout the world.

It is curious that, although modern Bristol is obviously the centre of a network of important roads, none of these are nationally famous. Even the road from London to Bristol, which for centuries joined the two major ports of the country and formed the background to so much history, has been for several centuries known as the Bath Road. If we look further back into history at the ancient Fosseway we see that it misses Bristol by some ten miles, keeping to the hills of Cotswold and Mendip.

Bristol and Bath between them have nevertheless contributed in an interesting, and indeed characteristic, manner to the history of roads and road transport. The rise to fashion of Bath in the eighteenth century brought with it a tide of aristocratic coach traffic from London that produced both the demand and the influence to render the Bath Road fit for travel in comfort. With the same traffic came the need for postal facilities which, initiated by Ralph Allen and John Palmer, both of Bath, brought the Royal Mail into being. Public coach services followed and the Bath Road achieved a status, on a modern scale, which had long previously been held by the Dover Road to the Continent.

It was thus no accident that John McAdam, the Scottish engineer since known as the 'Father of English Roads', became Road Inspector of the Bristol Turnpike Trust in 1818, and as such was largely responsible for the reconstruction and maintenance of the roads of the district. McAdam's system of road building, characterized by its emphasis on the importance of maintaining, by drainage and covering, a dry natural foundation, and its use of only small stones thereon, eventually spread through the country and even, by 1830, superseded the earlier continentally famous system of Tresaguet of France. Telford himself, who was a contemporary of McAdam's and is believed to have built a few roads in the district (one is the winding hillside road along the beautiful Limpley Stoke Valley, south-east of Bath), could not challenge McAdam's reputation locally or nationally, and the name became part of the language of road builders throughout the world. It is a curious commentary on this career to notice, on the one hand, in the lanes of Somerset to-day the older road menders reconstructing a stretch of lane in the manner of Telford, with its edgewise or end-on large basestones, rather than that of McAdam and, on the other, the more modern county authorities constructing new by-passes in the same region, with all McAdam's care for the natural subsoil and his belief in carpets of small stones. A passage from McAdam's report of 1820 to the then Board of Agriculture is, to the eyes of a student of soil mechanics, astonishingly modern:

'The roads can never be rendered perfectly secure, until the following principles be fully understood, admitted and acted upon: namely, that it is the native soil which really supports the weight of the traffic; that while it is preserved in a dry state, it will carry any weight without sinking, and that it does in fact carry the road and the carriages also; that this native soil must previously be made quite dry, and a covering, impenetrable to rain, must then be placed over it, to preserve it in that dry state; that the thickness of a road should only be regulated by the quantity of material necessary to form such impervious covering, and never by reference to its own power of carrying weight.'

The annual rainfall of Bristol approaches 35 in., and that of Mendip is up to 45 in., as compared with the 25 in. of the London district and 100 in. or more of the Scottish Highlands; it is not unnatural that a Scottish engineer, battling with the carriage traffic from London, Bath and Bristol moving over the rich soils of the West Country, found the secret of modern road construction.

McAdam was a road maker, but Telford was much more, and became specially famous for the bridges and viaducts he built to carry his roads over rivers and estuaries. It is believed, but not certain, that the lovely masonry viaduct carrying the Limpley Stoke road over the Midford Valley is one of the few local examples of his bridge work. However that may be, his real local influence derived from his fame as the designer of the Menai Suspension Bridge, finished in 1824, and the inspiration this provided for the Clifton and other local suspension bridges.

It is not generally realized, even among bridge engineers, that some eight suspension bridges have been built across the Bristol Avon. Most of these have been small ones, but some have been very original and had an influence on suspension bridge design quite out of proportion to their local importance. When Brunel, at the age of twenty-four, won the design competition for the Clifton Bridge he succeeded not only against Telford, who was then his senior by some forty years, but also against two local competitors, Motley and Dredge, who later proved, albeit on smaller projects, to be highly original suspension-bridge designers. The Clifton Bridge itself, its abortive start, stopping at the building of the piers in 1836, the construction of the chains and their first use by Brunel in London for the Hungerford Footbridge, and the final completion of the work by John Hawkshaw and W. H. Barlow in 1864, after Brunel's death, serves as a memorial to him and as a fitting end to his 'first love'; all this, and the return of the original chains from London, is too well-known nationally, and among bridge engineers, internationally, to be repeated at length here. All these delays over the Clifton Bridge, together with the stories of the unsatisfactory behaviour of Telford's Menai Bridge in high winds, gave Motley and Dredge their chance. Motley was accustomed to the then common form of construction of timber railway viaducts by supporting the deck structure on a series of timber trusses with struts spreading out and up fanwise; he conceived the notion that suspension bridges should properly be viewed as simple inversions of this form of construction, with no catenary cable proper but with suspension rods fanning out to the deck girder from the top of each tower, itself tied back to land by suitable anchorage cables. He proceeded to demonstrate his principle by the construction of a 120-ft. span suspension bridge across the Avon at Twerton, just below Bath. This was completed in 1838, and was at once seen to be remarkably stiff as well as strong enough for its road traffic. Six years later, an inspecting engineer was able to comment: 'As regards my opinion, generally, of the principle of construction, I have no hesitation in stating that, under general circumstances, it is equally strong with the best-proportioned suspension bridge with curved chains, and vastly superior to it in stiffness, and the absence of all undulating, every part being supported by direct tension.'

At about the same time, Dredge, realizing that the tension in a suspension cable is less at the centre than at its ends, proposed to incline the usually vertical suspension rods from the main catenary cable, and so, as he said, 'taper' the construction from ends to centre. In some senses the resulting form of construction was thus midway between the classical form of the Clifton Bridge and the trestle or fan 'bracket' form of Motley's bridge. Dredge was a native of Bath and built his suspension bridge of 150-ft. span there in 1836, where, as the Victoria Bridge, it still stands, though now reduced in function to foot traffic only. Both Motley and Dredge were critical of Telford's and Brunel's designs and sought to be allowed to build the Clifton Bridge. As the following extract from the beginning of a letter from Lord Weston to Lord

Melbourne shows, Dredge was not slow to use every influence open to him: 'My dear lord, having heard that the Government is about to expend a further sum of money on the reparation of the Menai Bridge, which is said to be in a perilous state, I cannot refrain from entreating your attention to the vast improvement that has been made in the construction of suspension bridges by Mr. Dredge, of Bath. During a recent residence of two months in that city, I have had an opportunity of seeing often the bridge that has been built by him across the Avon; it is a beautiful structure, and at once commands admiration of its beauty and confidence in its stability.' And later in the same letter it appears that Dredge claimed to be able to build the Clifton Bridge better than Brunel's design at only one-third the cost.

These are echoes of an old battle, fought round the early suspension bridges of this country, when we were in the van and the American giant bridges were yet to come. The effects of the debates around the Avon bridges were later evident in those built over the Thames, where, thirty or forty years after, Peter Barlow's Lambeth Bridge and Ordish's Albert Bridge, showed some of the features introduced by Motley and Dredge. But gradually roads, for the transport of really heavy goods, were largely superseded by railways, and for railways suspension bridges were eschewed by English engineers as a result of some bitter early experiences in the north.

It is impossible to discuss the development of railways, and least of all in the West Country, without reverting once again to Brunel, so long the chief engineer to the Great Western Railway. Brunel was only twenty-seven years old when, in 1832, the first successful Bristol company was formed to construct a railway from Bristol to London via Bath. A previous company, initiated in 1824, had considered a route via Mangotsfield that had been proposed by McAdam, one of the directors and already famed for his roads, but nothing had come of it. The new company was a much more influential and representative one and, impressed by Brunel's work on the Clifton Bridge design, boldly appointed him as engineer. Thereafter, the company directors, later merged with a London group to form the Great Western Railway Company, had the privilege and excitement not only of creating a leading railway but also of dealing with the most enterprising and spirited young engineer of his time. There is no need to tell again the story of the construction of this famous railway, but as one stands in the old Temple Meads terminus (Plate XXII), still largely in its original form alongside the newer station, one can readily recall the Battle of the Gauges, the difficulties and doubts surrounding the Box Tunnel or the Maidenhead Bridge and, in doing so, perhaps contemplate a feature of the whole story which is insufficiently commented upon or realized. Brunel, in the ups and downs of his relationships with his directors and with his fellow engineers, such as John Hawkshaw and George Stephenson, was, in effect, forging the future status and customs of the professional engineer. Two classical extracts from his letters of the 1850s to the railway directors indicate his difficulties and his approach: 'I really cannot consent to forego in this case the rule I lay down for myself in my professional business, which is to yield as far as I comfortably can to the mere wishes of Directors in the mode in which I direct the works they may order, but not beyond this point—and if the Directors or anybody claim the right to control the staff which I think necessary to carry on my work, I concede the right at once, and resign the direction of that staff.'

'A Board of Directors has a perfect right to dispense with the services of an engineer, or to lay down any rules of conduct they may think fit, and to engineer the works themselves, either as a body or by appointing one of their members, if they think fit, but if they desire to have the advice and responsibility of a respectable engineer—at all events, if they wish to have mine—they must place the usual amount of confidence in me; and as long as I am an engineer they must leave me to conduct the engineering, and must act as if they assumed that I was more able to advise the Board upon all the usual practical questions of engineering than anyone of the Directors.'

We are reading here the letters of an engineer struggling to set himself and his fellows in an effective professional position, a position which for the century since perhaps has done as much to bring influential ability into English engineering as any other single factor.

A smaller matter seldom touched upon in this railway story is the extent to which experimental activities were allowed on the railways in the early years. Modern engineers engaged in pioneer activities are accustomed to meeting university professors and other consulting research workers about their works, and are perhaps tempted to think of this as a modern innovation. But it is not so; Telford encouraged David Gilbert, the then President of the Royal Society, to dabble in suspension bridge theory for the benefit of his Menai Bridge. The Great Western Railway was no stranger to academic men; Professor Babbage, of early computing fame, was allowed experimental facilities on the line, being apparently permitted to order out his locomotive at Paddington at will; Dr. Dionysius Lardner, unpleasant and inaccurate critic though he was of Brunel's work, was given experimental facilities which on one occasion led to the death of one of his pupils. One cannot say that these academic activities played a leading part in the development of the railway, but perhaps pioneers then, as now, were sometimes able to sharpen their wits on academic persons and recruit some of their best students.

This certainly happened in the case of the most recent transport development in the district, the aeronautical one now represented by the Bristol Aeroplane Company at Filton. Sir George White, the founder of the original company in 1910, had already proved himself a pioneer in transport in the electric traction enterprise of his earlier Bristol Tramway Company, and, looking round for young recruits for his new venture, hit upon F. S. Barnwell, a young graduate of Glasgow who, with a brother, had already proved himself in aviation by building and flying two experimental aeroplanes. Barnwell remained with the company, except for an interlude during the 1914–18 war with the Royal Flying Corps, until his death in a flying accident in 1938. Of the many successful aeroplanes that he designed the most famous was the *Bristol Fighter*, which achieved a position in the First World War comparable with that of the *Hurricane* and *Spitfire* in the Second. His contributions to the aeroplanes of the second war were largely through the efforts of the able young team that grew up around him, and two of them, L. G. Frise and A. E. Russell, both Bristol graduates, have since become chief designers in their own right. *Blenheims*, *Beauforts*, the *Brabazon*, and now the *Britannia*, have since flown from these Filton works and the firm has become especially famous for its skill and enterprise in the field of aircraft structures.

Aeronautics is as much a matter of mechanical as of structural engineering. The Engine Division at Bristol was founded in 1920 and at once made its name with the 355-h.p. nine-cylinder *Jupiter* radial engine. Gradual development of this culminated, in the hands of Sir Roy Fedden, himself a product of Clifton College and the old Merchant Venturers Technical College, in the 1,000-h.p. *Pegasus* engine. Overlapping this development came the sleeve-valve engines, allowing higher compression ratios, of which the best known was the *Hercules* of 2,100 h.p. Finally, with F. M. Owner and now Dr. S. G. Hooker succeeding Sir Roy, the firm moved into the field of gas turbines, producing first the *Theseus* and then the *Perseus* for the propeller-turbine plants that are becoming so popular for high-speed civil use. The company as a whole is now the largest engineering undertaking in the district and one of the largest aircraft firms in the country. This might well have been a handicap to the smaller miscellaneous engineering activities of Bristol, but since the firm represents a pioneering national activity and presents, for all in the district to see, a high standard of workmanship, its work must in fact be an inspiration to local engineers.

The smaller engineering firms in the Bristol district range in size from Stothert and Pitt in Bath to small family businesses, and in total size outweigh the aeroplane company. In fact, to the surprise of most Bristolians as well as of our visitors, the number of persons employed in engineering activities in the city is now greater than in any other one trade. To most of those participating, the smallness of the units is not a disadvantage; in most cases it permits of the efficiency associated with live family businesses, and the size of the city is such that, as the heads of most of the firms were at school together, the units they represent work well alongside each other, the one helping the other in its speciality. This is of course not unique; what is unusual is its extent and its effectiveness in Bristol.

The rise of this sort of activity, which has taken place largely during the past hundred years, is associated both with the natural resources of the district and its position as a centre of transport. The lead ore mined from Roman times on Mendip was largely smelted there locally, but gradually gave rise to lead works in Bristol, of which Sheldon Bush's at Redcliffe, with its old shot tower, is an honoured representative. In the eighteenth and nineteenth centuries, the mining of copper ore led to smelting activities in Bristol on which the Bristol Brass Wire Company, famous in its time both for its work and its Quaker persuasion, was founded in 1702. With these activities were associated the Fry family, so well known for its chocolate business, now centred locally near Keynsham, and also the Darby family, later of Coalbrookedale Ironworks, one of whom built over the Severn below Shrewsbury the first cast-iron bridge in the world. Calamine, an ore of zinc, was mined on Mendip, and around its use and that of the lead and copper ores, the smelting firm of Capper Pass grew up. That all these activities, with their early roots in Mendip, where now no mining is, have survived and developed in the modern world, is typical of the Bristol characteristic of continuity previously noted in relation to transport and has perhaps the same root cause—that people who develop their skill and earn their living in Bristol really like it, and they and their families, with their skills, tend to stay there.

The tobacco trade of Bristol, associated with the Wills family, grew naturally out of Bristol's sea link with the Americas, and around it, as also around the chocolate trade, has grown a number of small engineering firms specializing in the production of appropriate machinery. In the same way, and often provided for by the same small firms, the large paper and printing trades of the district, of which the biggest are E. S. & A. Robinson and Mardon, Son & Hall, have created needs for specialized mechanical equipment. As a result, Bristol engineering firms are known throughout the world for such machinery; it comes as a surprise to realize that many of the automatic machines in London as, for example, the Underground ticket machines, are made in Bristol; while on the larger scale the cranes of Stothert and Pitt and the rams and presses of Fielding and Platt, of Gloucester, are known the world over.

The British Association has always been so interested in education, and in engineering education in particular, that it would be wrong here to omit this aspect of engineering in Bristol. As one would expect from the foregoing outline, Bristol has always been interested in the training of engineers. The first formal school was initiated by the Society of Merchant Venturers in 1856 and this gradually grew to university stature early in the present century. A second major step was taken with the foundation of University College in 1876, where provision was made for some aspects of engineering, mainly civil, as well as for science. On the foundation of the University in 1909, the engineering work of the two centres was continued in the Merchant Venturers Technical College, civil engineering from University College joining mechanical and electrical engineering there. The University agreement with the Society of Merchant Venturers providing for this merger terminated in 1950, and the vital and formal part hitherto played by the latter then lapsed, a change commemorated in the new engineering building in the University precincts. The Sir George White Chair of Aeronautical Engineering was added to the earlier three Chairs in 1947, and the four departments thus developed, together with a Department of Theoretical Mechanics that sprung from the mathematics side of the old Merchant Venturers College, comprise the University Faculty of Engineering.

With the cessation of the Merchants College in 1950, non-university technical college work that had been housed partly in the same building took on a new name and stature, the Bristol City College of Technology, and started to move to its large new premises at Ashley Down.

In the course of this history of about a hundred years, some names of eminence among engineers have naturally arisen from this academic work. Sylvanus P. Thomson, famous as an electrical engineer and beloved of all students first struggling with the calculus, was Professor of Experimental Physics at University College, and moved thence to become Principal of the old Finsbury Technical College that later grew into the City and Guilds College of South Kensington. T. E. Stanton, later the Superintendent of the Engineering Department of the National Physical Laboratory, was a Professor of Engineering in University College; so also was Hele Shaw, best known for his ingenious work on fluid motion. Reginald Stradling, one time Superintendent of the Building Research Station and later first Principal of the Royal Military College, Shrivenham, was a student of the Merchants College. Bristol as a University is too young, however, for many of her sons to have become eminent in the engineering world without being handicapped by the anonymity imposed by the fact that they are still alive.

BOOKS FOR FURTHER READING

BRUNEL, I. *Life of I. K. Brunel*. London, 1870.
GOUGH, J. W. *The Mines of Mendip*. Oxford, 1930.
HILL, J. C. G. *Shipshape and Bristol Fashion*. Liverpool, 1951.
JACKMAN, W. T. *The Development of Transportation in Modern England*. Cambridge, 1916, 2 vols.
MACDERMOT, E. T. *History of the Great Western Railway*. London, 1927–31, 2 vols.
NOBLE, C. B. *The Brunels, Father and Son*. London, 1938.
RAISTRICK, A. *Dynasty of Ironfounders*. London, 1953.

CHAPTER NINETEEN

RELIGIOUS MOVEMENTS IN BRISTOL SINCE THE REFORMATION

IT is often stated that more churchgoing is practised in Bristol than in any other English city. The statement is beyond proof; but it is certain that Bristol religious life exhibits much more vigour than is usually to be found in these days, whether we judge from the attendance at inter-faculty lectures on theology and at beginning-of-term services in the University, or from the regular meetings for prayer and discussion of a large group of city councillors before their civic deliberations, or from the amount of space given to religious activities by the local papers, or (and this is the truest criterion) from the existence of large closely knit worshipping communities of all denominations in many parts of the city. There are many and diverse causes of this continuing vigour, and among them must certainly be named the still-surviving effects of the many powerful religious movements which have either originated in Bristol or found a useful base of operations here; yet, although we must allow due credit to reformers and revivals, we cannot doubt that a large part in keeping Christian traditions alive and healthy has been played by many congregations and parishes which have faithfully maintained the practice of corporate worship without the aid of outstanding leaders and preachers, and do not normally find a place in written history. Since we begin our survey from the Reformation, it is bound to be in considerable measure the tale of divisions and disagreements, multiplied for several centuries and continued until the present day. But at the end of it we come to the beginning of *rapprochements* and co-operation between the denominations; and whether they be divisions within the One Church of Christ (which is how the Ecumenical Movement is teaching us to think of the relations between the major denominations of the world), or breakings-off of small, self-righteous sects from the main body of Christendom, schisms do at least serve to draw attention to aspects of Christian doctrine which might otherwise be neglected, and provoke the exercise of virtues (as well as of vices) which might otherwise lie dormant.

Bristol's religious life does not seem to have been at all distinctive in the period immediately preceding the Reformation; it produced no great saints and no notable scandals, though the younger William Canynges (d. 1474), merchant prince turned priest, great benefactor of St. Mary Redcliffe and Westbury College, stands well above the common run of later medieval clergy in genuine piety and austerity. Nor did the doctrinal issues raised by Martin Luther and beginning to be noticed in England in the 1520s greatly disturb the city fathers or the city clergy. William Tyndale preached Reformed doctrine on College Green before the Augustinian Abbey in 1522; but any stir that he created was soon laid to rest. It was the controversy about the divorce of Henry VIII and Catherine of Aragon that caused the first real fluttering in the ecclesiastical dovecotes. And even about this the rank and file of clergy and laity could for a time afford to remain indifferent. Bristol was a long way from London in more ways than one. The dispute was, surely, just one more in the long series between the Pope and the English King, and would be made up by the use of the usual diplomatic channels in a year or so. Meanwhile things went on much as before in the churches and religious houses of the city; there was the same Mass celebrated by the same parish priest who, occasionally, but not often, preached after the Gospel, and as far as a layman could see there was nothing to worry about.

The higher clergy however could not take so easygoing a view. In 1533 Hugh Latimer, Rector of West Kington in Wiltshire, preached three provocative sermons in Bristol in the King's interest, taking occasion to undermine the Pope's authority by stating that the Virgin Mary needed to be saved by Christ and that the pains of Purgatory are not very formidable after all. The learned men of the city were quickly divided into two camps; John Hilsey, Prior of the Dominicans, and Edward Powell of Salisbury supplied the scholars' arguments for the defence of the Pope, and Hubberdin, an eccentric but effective preacher, roused the emotions of the waverers. Hilsey was won over to Latimer's side, but the city for three months was not free from the din of theological dispute. In 1535 Latimer became Bishop of Worcester, and his far-flung diocese included Bristol as its most populous area. Verbal strife, of course, flared up again. Some of the clergy murmured that their bishop was a heretic and the King's lackey; the Dominicans took their Bishop's side, but the Grey Friars had nothing good to say about him.

The chief event of Latimer's four years' episcopate was the fall of the religious houses. This was the happening that really changed the religious landscape of England and brought home to the ordinary man the fact that a revolution was in progress. The Bristol monasteries were not notable for either vice or virtue; numerically most of them were weak. The hardships caused by the Dissolution were no doubt shocking to many Bristol citizens; others were quite prepared to make money out of it. In fact, there emerged from it a small but powerful group of *nouveaux riches*, who received grants as a reward for supporting the King, and could add to these in various ways. Notable among these was Sir William Sharington, Treasurer of the Bristol Mint and responsible for the making of coinage out of the city's church plate; the coins were made, but much of the silver intended for them went into Sharington's private coffers. The Guild Chapels went to the Crown, and the guilds became purely secular.

Henry's measures were therefore a mixed blessing to the city. Nor did non-residence and pluralism decrease. But he did give Bristol a bishopric. In 1538 a suffragan bishop of Bristol was appointed, to work under the authority of the Bishop of Worcester. This arrangement lasted only until 1541, when Bristol became part of the new diocese of Gloucester. Fortunately for local pride this arrangement was even shorter-lived; in 1542 Bristol gained a Bishop in its own right, and St. Augustine's Abbey became the Cathedral. Yet from the start, and for centuries to come, both the Cathedral building, which lacked a proper nave,[1] and the Bishop's stipend, which compelled any self-respecting Bishop to hold other preferments at the same time, were quite inadequate to the dignity of an important city. During the reigns of Edward VI and Elizabeth I the diocese's resources were often tapped for royal purposes, and the see was several times left vacant. Most, if not all, of the holders of the see for the next two or three centuries regarded it as a stepping-stone to higher office, and this cannot have furthered the spiritual interests of the citizens. It may even be that the weakness of Bristol's episcopal status assisted the growth of nonconformity in the seventeenth and eighteenth centuries.

The Edwardian reforms and the Marian reaction flowed fairly kindly over the Bristol churches, though changes of incumbent were frequent. One non-resident priest was executed under Edward, five lay Protestants under Mary. The Elizabethan Settlement meant that if a man and his family were willing to attend the services of the Book of Common Prayer, no one would inquire very carefully into his private beliefs; and we may take it that the great majority of Bristolians were perfectly content with this arrangement, with the services in English, which they could claim to understand, with the clergy's vestments, which were seemly and dignified without lending colour to superstition, and with the good English compromise between the excesses of Rome and Geneva.

There were, however, two groups in the city who were not by any means content. The convinced and faithful adherents of the old religion found their form of worship proscribed and their religious and political intentions, especially after the Pope's excommunication of Elizabeth in 1570, highly suspect. They took the only course open to them, and went underground. We hear nothing of their activities for nearly two hundred years. The other group was of those who thought that the reformation of the Church in England had not gone nearly far enough. John Calvin, they believed, had laid bare the real nature and the true ordering of the Church as the New Testament describes them. They found no place for bishops and priests, for sacred vestments, for such legacies of the superstitious past as the sign of the Cross in Baptism. The true government of the Church was by elders and the Church Session; in the centre of true worship was the preaching of the Word of God. For the time being they were forced to conform to the laws of Elizabeth, and to wait until God should raise up some prophet to reform the English Church according to the Word of God; but they waited impatiently, and the dream of a Presbyterian Church of England was rarely absent from their minds. While they waited, some of them began to be attracted by the writings and the deeds of men like Robert Browne and Henry Barrow, who called for reformation 'without tarrying for any', denied the scriptural basis of any connexion between Church and State, and found the Church of Christ,

[1] The Norman nave was ruinous at the time of the Dissolution, and was pulled down soon afterwards. A new nave was not built until 1877.

not in the amorphous collection of people, good, bad and indifferent, who happened to live within a certain geographical area which formed a parish, but in the 'gathered' assembly of those who had made their personal covenant with God. The members of such an independent assembly had, in their view, full right to order their own Church life for themselves, without let or hindrance from any bishop or civil authority, subject only to the 'Crown Rights of the Redeemer'.

The Presbyterians and Independents in Bristol did not show their hand during the reign of Elizabeth. But the accession of James I, and their disappointment with his refusal to abolish the episcopate and with his objection to being called 'God's silly vassal', decided some of them that the time for mere conformity was past. For twenty years until his death in 1633 William Yeamans, Vicar of St. Philip's but perhaps an Independent, or at least a Presbyterian, at heart, encouraged and conducted 'prophesyings', held outside the canonical times of service in three private houses in the city—one of them in the castle grounds, which were legally an island of Gloucestershire territory in mid-Bristol, and therefore free from the interference of Bristol magistrates. After his death occasional Independent services were held for the flock which Yeamans had gathered by William Wroth, pastor of an Independent congregation in Llanvaches, near Chepstow. It was the commanding personality of Dorothy Hazzard, a member of Yeamans' congregation married to the Vicar of St. Ewen's, that inspired the foundation of Bristol's first open and public Independent congregation in 1640. Mrs. Hazzard had at first attended her husband's ministrations in the parish church, though she used often to enter the church just before the sermon; then even the sermon proved uncongenial, and she drew up and carried out the plans for a separatist Church. This Church survives to-day in full vigour as Broadmead Baptist Church, but it was not Baptist at its beginnings, that is, it did not practise the rite of Believers' Baptism. The first Puritans in Bristol to argue that since Baptism, according to the New Testament, is the rite of initiation into the Church, and since a man enters the Church in virtue of a covenant made between him and God, therefore Baptism should be administered only to those who exhibit and profess conscious faith, formed a community in the Pithay soon after the foundation of Broadmead.[1] But the attractive power of their opinion soon exercised its influence in Broadmead, and in 1653 the congregation there became a mixed one of Baptists and Paedobaptists. From this time forward its proportion of Paedobaptists steadily dropped, though nearly two hundred years elapsed before it became a purely Baptist Church. The oldest surviving Independent (now Congregational) Church came into existence within the Castle grounds about 1650, and is still called Castle Green, though now located in Greenbank.

Meanwhile the clergy and laity of the Established Church pursued a less intensive course of devotion than these small and zealous groups. But it was not so very placid a life for them either. The national disputes about King and Church and Parliament could not leave them unmoved, and though many of them had no wish to be drawn

[1] Now represented by Old King Street Baptist Church. Ernest Bevin developed many of his powers of thought and speech in the Sunday afternoon discussion class here.

into controversy, not a few became Puritan in sympathy, while others fortified themselves for the struggles which were to come by the diligent perusal of Lancelot Andrewes and George Herbert, who sought to restore in England the beauty and comprehensiveness of the Catholic Church as it was before the corruptions of Rome. And while William Laud was Archbishop of Canterbury (1629–40) no clergyman, whether of high or low degree, could feel himself safe from the archiepiscopal passion for moral and liturgical reform and administrative uniformity.

The days of the Civil Wars and the Commonwealth were halcyon ones for the Puritans and the Nonconformists. It really began to look as if their dream of a genuinely reformed Church of England was going to come true; in fact, for the Presbyterians and the Independents successively it did come true—for a few brief months. But in Bristol, as in other places, just at the time of the highest hopes of the Independents, there entered a complicating factor, in the person of the Quakers. After a brief reconnaissance visit in July, 1654, John Audland, a Friend from Westmorland, came back to Bristol in the following September with John Camm, also of Westmorland, and began a period of successful evangelistic activity which rapidly established the nucleus of a strong Meeting in the city. According to the custom of the Quakers, they preached first to the congregations of Independents and Baptists already gathered, and sought out the little company of 'Seekers' who were already looking for a personal knowledge of God. Thus the first Quaker Meeting was partly gathered out of existing congregations, and this may account for the antipathy which developed and persisted between the Quakers and the Broadmead Baptists in spite of their theological affinities; perhaps the Baptists' insistence on the Sacrament which gives them their name helped to alienate the two groups from each other.

The Friends preached an absolutely spiritual religion. They rejected sacraments, Churches, liturgies, priests and all professional ministers, and all even mildly material aids to the worship of God; they claimed immediate access to Him, and the possession of an inward Light which, rightly nurtured, gave them direct knowledge of the Truth. This is heady doctrine, especially if taken by itself and unmodified by the practical wisdom and spiritual maturity of men like George Fox and the other strong leaders whom the Society of Friends has produced in abundance. The preaching in Bristol caused emotional ferment as well as spiritual illumination; the magistrates, like their prototypes in the New Testament, paid more attention to the former than to the latter, and from the first the Quakers in Bristol had to contend with opposition both official and unofficial, and had many opportunities of declaring that they proposed to obey God rather than men. It must be confessed that they brought not a little of this upon themselves by disturbing public worship both in 'steeplehouses' (which was their name for parish churches) and in Broadmead Baptist Chapel, and by 'going as a sign', that is, going through the streets in sackcloth in token of the doom deserved by a wicked city.

Neither Bristol Quakerism nor the body of Quaker teaching is to be held responsible for the strange doings of James Nayler which brought the Bristol Quakers into long-continued discredit. This brilliant preacher and devout man of God fell pitifully from grace by failing to distinguish adequately between the reverence due to the Word of God and the respect due to himself as the bearer of that Word. In 1656 he allowed himself to be the central figure in a Messianic entry into Bristol (rather spoiled by the rain), during which certain corybantic women sang 'Holy, Holy, Holy, Lord God of Sabaoth'. Neither he nor his maenads had any permanent connexion with Bristol, and they were disowned by Bristol Friends. But the reproach stuck. Nayler was cruelly and humiliatingly punished by the Commonwealth government, and came to acknowledge fully and sincerely the error of his ways.

It is more pleasant to record that George Fox made Bristol an important base of his operations in the west, and on 27 October 1669 married Margaret Fell in the Broadmead Meeting House. They spent a week in Bristol, went to Olveston, outside the city, and parted on preaching tours for several months. In the next year the Friends began to acquire the buildings once possessed by the Dominican Friars near Broadmead (see Plate XXIX). They have met there regularly almost until the present day, but now the property is passing into the hands of the Bristol Corporation.

The Restoration of Charles II and the ecclesiastical legislation which followed it ended the last hopes of a Puritan national Church, and made the Presbyterians into permanent Dissenters like the rest of the Puritans. It cannot be said that the victors, either in Church or State, used their victory with moderation. In Bristol the penal laws against Dissenters were carried out with strictness, and sometimes with savagery. This does not mean that clergy and civil officials all engaged in the campaign of repression with equal enthusiasm. There were reasonable and compassionate men among them who carried out the laws as humanely as possible, or found an excuse for not carrying them out at all; there was a period of about ten years, from 1668 to 1678, during which persecution seems to have virtually ceased. But until the accession of William III the Dissenters went in perpetual danger of imprisonment and worse, and things happened from time to time which have left a permanent scar on the memory, and still make it quite difficult for some whose forebears suffered to enter into easy relations with Anglicans. Let it be added that there is no reason to suppose that the victory of any other party would have led to an entirely different policy.[1]

The details of repression are not edifying. Suffice it to say that the Quakers suffered most, perhaps because they tended to court persecution by such things as the disturbance of public worship even at the height of feeling against them; they were herded into insanitary prisons and several died of spotted fever. The Baptists and Independents also passed through many terrifying experiences, and their ministers spent many years in prison. The Baptists were not willing to give up their worship even at the worst times, and when necessary resorted to the open air, not least at Hanham Mount, which was a few miles outside the city and offered a reasonable chance of immunity.

[1] One of the chief inciters to persecution was Sir John Knight, whose motives were probably partly political. He was obnoxious to the Dean and Chapter as well as to the Dissenters.

Prominent among the Baptists at this time was Edward Terrill, a 'scrivener' and a man of importance in the city—so much so that on at least one occasion his fine was paid for him. He was able to open his house for Baptist meetings, and help his friends by legal advice and ingenious devices for evading the vigilance of the authorities. His 'Broadmead Records' give much invaluable evidence for the history of nonconformity in Bristol during the first seventy five years of its existence. He left the bulk of his property to support the Broadmead minister and enable him to instruct young men who were likely to be future ministers; thus he laid the foundations of the future Bristol Baptist College, which still trains men for the Baptist ministry and has made a particularly large contribution to the missionary work of the Baptist Church.[1]

The Act of Toleration in 1689 gave freedom of worship to the Dissenters, but it did not restore to them their social and intellectual rights; it took them two hundred years to regain these. Thus it did not end the cleavage which has run through English religious and social life since the Civil Wars and is only now being healed. In spite of this, the Dissenters were gradually integrated into the ordinary life of Bristol during the eighteenth century. The Quakers gave up their aggressive evangelism and their taste for controversy, and began to play that astonishingly large (in proportion to their numbers) part in commercial life and the furtherance of good causes which has distinguished them ever since. The other Dissenters settled down to the blessings of undisturbed worship—settled down too comfortably, perhaps—and took their share, too, in commercial and philanthropic developments as time went on.[2] Among them the Presbyterians tended to fall out of the picture, or to become Unitarians; some of the Independents went the latter way before the century was over. For certain periods the Unitarians exercised a strong influence on civic affairs.

Dissent, of course, held no monopoly of public beneficence. Edward Colston (1636–1721) was a merchant prince and a High Anglican who, for living purposes, preferred the comforts of Mortlake and London to those of Bristol. But he showed his affection for his native city by many munificent foundations (see Chapter 20).

The Church of England has no exciting achievements to record from the eighteenth century, but the standard of Church life was at least as high in Bristol as in most places, and in some respects higher. Joseph Butler, Bishop from 1738 to 1750, stands out as intellectually the ablest, and morally among the best, of eighteenth-century Anglican dignitaries. He was brought up as a Presbyterian, and educated at Tewkesbury Academy. His 'Fifteen Sermons', preached in his late twenties, assert 'enlightened self-interest' to be the key to Christian morality. Just before coming to Bristol he published the *Analogy of Religion*, in which he sought to reconcile the claims of reason and revelation, and produced the most effective contemporary answer to the prevalent rationalism. He was very active as a diocesan bishop in Bristol, and did much more than fill in the time until his translation to Durham.

[1] The College library possesses the great treasure of the one complete copy of Tyndale's Bible, bequeathed to it by Andrew Gifford, assistant librarian at the British Museum.

[2] The founder of J. S. Fry and Sons was a Quaker; of E. S. and A. Robinson's a Baptist. W. D. and H. O. Wills's is Congregationalist in origin.

Without question it was John Wesley who created the greatest stir in the religious life of Bristol during the century. He was a faithful, but severe and self-regarding, Christian before his 'evangelical conversion' in 1738, when he 'felt his heart strangely warmed', and that he 'did trust in Christ, Christ alone, for salvation'; after that the enormous energies of mind, spirit and body which he had devoted to his own eternal welfare were turned outward to the evangelization of England. At the invitation of his fellow-Methodist,[1] George Whitefield, he came to Bristol in the spring of 1739. His main purpose at first was to preach to the colliers of Kingswood and Hanham, wild creatures neglected with good excuse by civic and religious authorities. This he did with extraordinary success, often at Hanham Mount, where the harassed Baptist preachers had operated sixty years before. In Bristol itself he was almost equally successful, and soon decided to make the city one of the focal points of his plan for 'spreading scriptural holiness throughout the land' by means of his own specially constituted Religious Societies within the general framework of the Church of England. It was for this reason that he built first the Old Room, and then the New Room, in the Horsefair (see Chapter 17, p. 262; and Plate XXVIII), to be both a preaching-place and a rest-house and lodging for himself and his travelling preachers. It was to the care of the Society there that Charles Wesley, John's hymn-writing and almost equally eloquent brother, betook himself in 1749 after his marriage.

It was in Bristol that many of the characteristic institutions of Methodism were thought out and tried out. Wesley began Watchnight services on Saturdays to keep the Kingswood colliers from the ale-houses; they are held now only on New Year's Eve. To pay the debt on the New Room the Bristol Society was divided into groups of twelve, including a leader; each member was to pay a penny a week. This was the origin of the Class Meeting, which soon came to be used for religious fellowship of an intimate kind. In Kingswood, after an abortive attempt by Whitefield for the colliers' children, Wesley founded a boarding-school for Methodists, with a strict discipline and a wide curriculum, which was meant to put to shame the lax public schools of his day. It was later limited to the sons of preachers, but has in this century been thrown open, and has a nation-wide fame. He held many conferences of his preachers in the New Room, including the second one to be held; and it was in Dighton Street, Bristol, in 1784, that he took the fateful step of ordaining men for pastoral work in America, after being convinced for nearly forty years that a presbyter like himself had as much right to ordain as a bishop, but holding back in order to avoid a breach with the Church of England.

Wesley at all times preached and defended the orthodox doctrine of the Church of England, with a definite emphasis on the value of personal experience, and had no wish to separate from that Church. But his preaching created many undesirable emotional upsets among the simple Kingswood miners (more than among any other of his converts, and there only for the first few years), and he had no licence to preach

[1] The name 'Methodist' was first applied to Wesley and his friends in Oxford, long before his 'conversion'; it was retained by the public for the very different groups of people that formed Wesley's later Societies.

in the diocese. It was natural, therefore, that Bristol, clerical and lay, should offer him some fierce opposition (which gradually died down), and that Bishop Butler should summon him to his presence. The conversation that ensued reveals the attitudes of the two men. 'Sir,' said Butler, 'the pretending to extraordinary revelations and gifts of the Holy Spirit is a horrid thing; yes, Sir, it is a very horrid thing.' Here Butler was wrong. Wesley pretended to no private revelations. He preached what he believed the Bible to say. 'Sir,' said Butler, 'you have no business here; you are not commissioned to preach in this diocese: therefore I advise you to go hence!' Wesley replied that his Fellowship of Lincoln College gave him the right to preach where he willed. Here Wesley was wrong; he had no such right by Anglican law.

In the wake of the Methodists came the Moravians. These were the English members of the Bohemian and Moravian Protestant community, known as the Church of the Brethren, which had found refuge from persecution in the Saxon estates of Count Zinzendorf. The Count himself initiated a powerful religious revival among the refugees, and their preachers in England exerted a deep influence on John Wesley. Wesley later parted company from them, but one of his early helpers, John Cennick, established a Moravian Church in Bristol in 1748 which has taken an active part in the city's religious life ever since, and has always exerted itself on the side of Christian unity.

The Evangelical Revival which Whitefield and the Wesleys began had its permanent results, not only in the formation of the Methodist Church (which became separate from the Church of England in 1795, four years after John Wesley's death), but also within the bounds of the national Church. Here, as in Methodism, it always awakened an intense interest both in personal salvation and in the spiritual and temporal welfare of others. The second interest stopped short of any desire to change the structure of society, but it issued in large works of philanthropy. In the Bristol area the chief practical exponent of Anglican evangelicalism was the brilliant and literary Hannah More (see Chapter 16, p. 244), the friend of Sheridan and David Garrick. Converted under the influence of John Newton (ex-captain of a slave ship, evangelist, hymn-writer and friend of William Cowper), and closely collaborating with William Wilberforce, she opened schools for miners' children in Cheddar and the Mendip villages, and saw to their evangelization at the same time; she also started many beneficent works in Bristol, her native city, and her epitaph at Wrington combines fulsomeness with truth to an extent which must be rare in English epigraphy.

The opening of the nineteenth century found the Church of England, apart from its Evangelical section, still in the doldrums, and the diocese of Bristol no better than any other. The prevailing atmosphere in Anglican circles, there as elsewhere, was strongly opposed to reform; Prebendary Sydney Smith's sermon on toleration on Guy Fawkes' Day, 1828, had a very unfriendly reception. The burning down of the Bishop's Palace in the Bristol Riots of 1831 (the Cathedral narrowly escaped) cannot be said, however, to represent with accuracy the feeling of Bristol towards its Bishop. No doubt all Bristolians mourned with the dignitaries of the Church when the see of Bristol was combined with that of Gloucester in 1836, to finance the new sees of Manchester and Ripon.

Bristol lost its full diocesan status in 1836, but it gained an outstanding Bishop. James Henry Monk, Bishop of Gloucester from 1830 and of Gloucester and Bristol from 1836 to 1856, was a courageous man of deep piety and wide influence, and the Horfield Trust, for the upkeep of parsonages and the payment of curates, is a permanent memorial to his interest in and love for Bristol. Life now flowed more richly in the Bristol churches, not least after the teaching of the Tractarians had helped to raise both the standard of worship and the concept of churchmanship. Between 1830 and 1880 thirty-two churches were built and five enlarged, to meet the needs of the growing population, and it was a sign of the times that early-morning celebrations of Holy Communion in the Cathedral began in 1869. In 1897 the see of Bristol was at last restored, this time presumably *in perpetuum.*

Catholic Emancipation brought the Roman Catholics once again into the main stream of Bristol life. Permission had been reluctantly granted by the Corporation in the middle of the eighteenth century to open a chapel for Flemish workers who would not come to the city unless they could practise their religion, and the Mass was being celebrated secretly in 1765 somewhere in St. James' Backs. In 1790 the Trenchard Street Chapel and a school were opened, under the care of the Franciscans. A small Chapel was opened in Clifton in the 1830s; after years of penury and trouble of all sorts it became a pro-Cathedral just in time for the installing and enthroning in 1850 of the first Roman Catholic Bishop since the Reformation. The Jesuits had just taken over the Trenchard Street Chapel as a school and nuns had come to teach in Westbury-on-Trym in 1835. Churches and schools have been steadily opened ever since. Whereas in 1807 there was only one Roman priest in the city, assisted by two French *émigré* priests who made a living by teaching French 'in the best circles', in the middle of the twentieth century there are fifteen Roman Catholic churches and thirty-five priests, a large Roman Catholic hospital in Clifton and many schools throughout the city, and there is Roman Catholic representation on the local Education Authority.

The Free Churches shared the general prosperity of religion in the nineteenth century, and numerous large chapels, not always in the best of taste, sprang up all over the city. Their number was unfortunately increased by a serious split in the Methodist ranks throughout the country in the middle of the century; one of the principal centres of disturbance was Kingswood. Prominent among the personalities who expressed and increased the vitality of Free Church life was the German, George Müller. Converted from what he described as a luridly reprobate life in 1828, he made his home in Bristol. In 1834 he founded the 'Scriptural Knowledge Institution for Home and Abroad', and in 1835 the Orphan Home (transferred in 1849 from Wilson Street to Ashley Down), modelled on the remarkable work of the Moravian, A. H. Francke, in Halle at the end of the seventeenth century (see Chapter 20, p. 300). Müller remained narrow in his devotion to his particular interpretation of biblical truth, would not work with any of the regular denominations and refused

PLATE XXVII. *Entrance hall of Redland Court,* c. 1735.

to beg for money even on behalf of the most necessitous of his causes. But he was large in his ideas and his love for children, and has given great inspiration to many. His zeal and his narrowness are both continued in many of the smaller Protestant sects which still flourish in the city.

Some idea of the state of religion in Bristol towards the end of the nineteenth century can be gained from a census taken by the *Western Daily Press* of all those (as far as possible) who attended churches or chapels on Sunday, 30 October 1881. The population of Bristol then was 266,000. On the Sunday in question 48,596 people went to worship in the morning, 60,856 in the evening; school children are not included. These 109,452 are made up of 45,518 Anglicans, 15,363 Methodists, 11,588 Congregationalists, 10,146 Salvationists, 9,127 Baptists, 3,432 Roman Catholics; the rest belong to the smaller Protestant groups. On a Saturday night in December of the same year, as ascertained by a similar, but less complete, census, 98,226 people (including 12,440 children) were to be found in public houses between seven and eleven p.m.

The prosperity of Bristol's churches was rudely disturbed by the First World War. It was this event, coupled with the comparative failure of the Church at large to deal with post-war scientific and political questionings, that started the rot in church attendance and religious faith among ordinary people; the Second World War, besides destroying a great number of important and beautiful church buildings, accentuated and perhaps completed the process. The Church in Bristol to-day, at least partly conscious of its failures in the past, is taking steps to recover its losses. Rebuilding of what has been destroyed has to occupy much of its attention, but priority even over this has gone to the building of new churches in the housing areas which have leapt into existence round the city; and all church building is sensibly guided by a committee representing all the main denominations. The Church of England, because of the shift of population and the shortage of clergy, has taken bold steps in the reorganization and uniting of parishes, not without causing pain to those who hold that beautiful and historic buildings should be kept open for worship however few be the people who take advantage of the opportunity. Methodism is rearranging its 'circuits', or groups of churches, in order to implement the union of the Methodist Churches in 1932, and use its money and manpower economically. It has also brought a theological college from Didsbury, Manchester, and placed it in a fine new building on Henbury Hill; there are now five theological colleges in the city—Bristol Baptist College, Western College (for Congregationalists, founded in 1752 and settled in Bristol in 1901), two Anglican Colleges, Clifton and Tyndale Hall, both of strong evangelical tendency, and Didsbury. A new effort is being made by all the Churches to teach the Christian faith in the language, and apply it to the needs, of the industrial workers who form the largest element in the city's population.

We have spoken above of 'the Church in Bristol', as if there were only one Church, whereas Bristol is known as the home of nonconformity and schism. In recent years the denominations in Bristol have grown quite notably towards the consciousness of belonging together to the one Church of Christ. Under the leadership of successive

---

PLATE XXVIII. *John Wesley's Chapel, Broadmead, Bristol.*

PLATE XXIX. *Quakers' Friars, Rosemary Street.* (*By permission of the Religious Society of Friends.*)

bishops, the Bristol Council of Christian Churches, founded in 1925, one of the oldest Councils of Churches in the country and now including more than 120 congregations, has worked powerfully to this end. The 'United Front' in Redfield is the most conspicuous and successful embodiment of this new spirit; here all the churches engage in many joint activities of worship and social service as a regular and integral part of their life. It is now the normal thing for the leaders of Church life in Bristol to consult and act together in all matters of religious and public importance. As part of the post-war alliance between Bristol and Hanover, the Bristol churches have entered into close relationship with the Church of Lower Saxony, and its Bishop, Hanns Lilje, once imprisoned by the Nazis, is a welcome and frequent visitor to the city. In these and many other ways Bristol seeks to play a worthy part in the Ecumenical Movement, the one religious movement of our time which is likely to change the face of Christendom.

BOOKS FOR FURTHER READING

Child, R. L. and C. E. Shipley. *Broadmead Origins*. London, 1940.
Darby, J. H. (Ed.) *Diocese of Clifton*, 1850–1950. Bristol, 1950.
Fletcher, R. J. *A History of Bristol Cathedral*. London, 1932.
Raistrick, A. *Quakers in Science and Industry*. London, 1950.
Historical Tablets in John Wesley's Chapel. London, 1930.

CHAPTER TWENTY

BRISTOL CHARITIES, PAST AND PRESENT

BRISTOL has been called a City of Churches and Charities, and the number, variety and antiquity of both bear witness to its mercantile importance over the centuries. Charities may be divided into two main classes: first, educational charities, which include the great and ancient schools of Bristol which are dealt with in Chapter 22; and second, eleemosynary charities, which term includes the endowed, as well as the un-endowed charities, and with which we treat.

In the Middle Ages, although rich merchants such as William Canynges the younger (1399–1474), who restored and partially rebuilt St. Mary Redcliffe, gave liberally to the poor—indeed, he added to the endowment of an almshouse at Westbury-on-Trym, which was then some two to three miles outside Bristol—the only charities of consequence were the monasteries, hospitals and other religious houses and guilds. This was due to the fact that in general terms they were the only bodies with corporate rights and perpetual existence. Thus they were capable of holding the endowments which in the main were real property and so provided a means of continuing the objects of the charities. There were eight monasteries or friaries in Bristol, many of which were destroyed on the Dissolution, but fortunately the great Abbey of St. Augustine was spared to become the Cathedral Church. Its name is perpetuated in St. Augustine's Parade, which is nowadays known as the Tramways Centre. In addition to the monasteries there were four hospitals, the most important of which was the Hospital of St. Mark, Billeswick, generally called The Gaunt's Hospital. At the time of its dissolution in 1539 this hospital was providing food and accommodation for fifteen poor men who resided there, whilst over a hundred poor people called at the hospital daily for food. The site and the greater part of its possessions were sold to the Corporation in 1541, and the Chapel of the Hospital, which stands at the bottom of Park Street facing College Green and the Cathedral, still remains the property of the city. The ownership of a chapel by a municipality is unique, and the Lord Mayor's Chapel is well worth visiting.

Of course, in medieval times the word 'hospital' had a different meaning from that current to-day, and four other hospitals of ancient foundation still exist in Bristol, namely, Trinity Hospital, Old Market Street, and Temple Hospital (both almshouses); the Colston's Boys' School, which was formerly called Colston's Hospital, and Queen Elizabeth's Hospital—known as the City School—which is a day and boarding school for boys, the boarders of which are a familiar sight in Bristol wearing their Elizabethan dress (see Chapter 22, p. 313). The change in meaning of the word 'hospital' has not always been appreciated by the authorities. Thus, during the coal shortage in the period after the end of the Second World War, the writer, who acts as Clerk to the Governors of Queen Elizabeth's Hospital and also in a similar capacity to the Governors of Bristol Grammar School and the Red Maids' School, could not understand for some time why Queen Elizabeth's Hospital was allotted a bigger coal ration. It was subsequently discovered that the rationing authority was under the impression that Queen Elizabeth's Hospital was a hospital and not a school, and it had accordingly been allocated the invalid's ration scale!

The two other hospitals referred to above have interesting histories. Trinity Hospital, which is situated in Old Market Street and is divided into Trinity Hospital North on one side of the street and Trinity Hospital South, with its chapel, on the other side, was founded in 1395 by John Barstaple, Sheriff and three times Mayor of Bristol, who died in 1411. This almshouse has had a continuous existence since the time of its foundation, and still occupies the original sites, and now houses fifty old people. The founder intended one of the buildings to be an almshouse and the other a fraternity or guild. The original charter granted by Richard II has been lost, but the date of the foundation of the hospital is referred to in a later grant of letters patent by Henry IV in 1408. In 1399 John Barstaple obtained a letter from Pope Boniface IX inhibiting under pain of excommunication anyone from interfering with his Will by which he proposed to endow the hospital. However, the intention of endowing the hospital was not carried out, and soon after his death it was transferred to the Mayor and Commonalty of Bristol, who were responsible for its administration until 1836, when it was handed over to the Trustees of the Bristol Municipal Charities. The memorial brasses of the founder and his wife still remain in the chapel, which incidentally has been rebuilt three times. Barstaple's Merchants' Mark is engraved on his brass.

Temple Hospital, which almost adjoins Temple Church with its leaning tower, was founded by Dr. Thomas White, a native of Bristol, in 1613, for ten poor men and women, and endowed by him with capital which brought in £92 per annum. Dr. White was Vicar of St. Dunstan's-in-the-West, Fleet Street, London, Canon of St. Paul's, Treasurer of Salisbury Cathedral, Canon of Christ Church, Oxford and of St. George's Chapel, Windsor, holding all these offices in plurality. He was a noted preacher of his day, and died a rich man, being buried in the Church of St. Dunstan's of which he had been vicar for nearly fifty years. He left bequests to Bristol Corporation, Sion College, the Dean and Chapter of St. Paul's, and the University of Oxford. In addition to providing almshouses in Bristol and London (Sion Hospital), his bequests included marriage portions for poor maidens, repairs to roads, and loans to tradesmen, and for sermons; and in his will he expressly asked that the prisoners of Newgate be taken to St. Dunstan's-in-the-West every Sunday to hear a lecture, and that as an example the men should be chained hand to hand on one iron chain, and the women similarly chained on another. Dr. White's Temple Hospital in Bristol was rebuilt in 1882.

In all, there are at present sixteen almshouses in Bristol, including Trinity Hospital and Temple Hospital, although some have been damaged by enemy action and are empty, but will it is hoped be repaired shortly, for example, St. Nicholas Almshouse in King Street, near the Theatre Royal. The most interesting are perhaps Foster's Almshouse in Colston Street at the top of Christmas Steps; the Merchants' Almshouse in King Street (see Plate XXXI); and Colston's Almshouse, St. Michael's Hill (see Plate XXX). Foster's Almshouse was founded by John Foster in 1492, and attached to the almshouse is the Chapel of the Three Kings of Cologne, above the doorway being three empty niches evidently meant for statues of Caspar, Melchior and Balthazar. The dedication of the chapel is believed to be unique in this country. John Foster in his will of 6 August, 1492, directed his executors to find a priest to sing in the chapel for his soul, and left estates in Somerset and Gloucestershire to be sold and the proceeds used to buy the King's licence to found a perpetual chantry in addition to endowing the almshouse. Dr. George Owen, physician to Henry VIII and the holder, one would think, of a difficult appointment, augmented the endowment in 1553 by providing for payment to the Mayor and Corporation of such a sum as would provide 7*d.* a week each to ten poor persons who were to be provided with accommodation at his cost. Incidentally, the almshouse now provides accommodation for twenty-eight residents, and the Lady Mayoress has the right to nominate four poor persons to vacancies should she so desire. The present almshouse was built in 1873 in a Burgundian Gothic style, the architects being Messrs. Foster and Wood of Bristol, and it is modelled on a hospital at Beaune in France. The entrance, part of the wall and some of the roof timbers are all that remain of the original chapel.

Colston's Almshouse in St. Michael's Hill was founded and endowed by Edward Colston, who lies buried in All Saints' Church, Corn Street, where there is a large monument to him which gives details of his benefactions and which bears an effigy by Rysbrack. He has been described as the greatest philanthropist of his age. In one year he contributed anonymously £20,000 to a relief fund in London, and he sometimes spent up to £4,000 in clearing debtors' prisons. Colston, who remained a lifelong bachelor, replied to a friend who advised him to marry, 'Every helpless widow is my wife, and distressed orphans my children.' He endowed charities in Surrey, Lancashire, Devon, and other parts of England. In Bristol his benefactions included the endowment of schools (for example, Colston's Boys' School—see Chapter 22, p. 314), hospitals, and the repair of churches. The almshouse in St. Michael's Hill was erected in 1691 at a cost of about £2,500, and its management was entrusted to the Society of Merchant Venturers.

Part of another almshouse administered by the Society of Merchant Venturers for Bristol sailors and their widows or daughters is at the corner of Marsh Street and King Street. This almshouse was at the back of the Merchant Venturers' Hall, which was destroyed by enemy action in 1941. The inscription on the front of the almshouse reads:

'Freed from all storms the tempest and the rage
Of billows here we spend our age.
Our weather-beaten vessels here repair,
And from the Merchants' kind and generous care
Find harbour here: no more we put to sea
Until we launch into Eternity.
And lest our widows whom we leave behind
Should want relief they too a shelter find.
Then all our anxious cares and sorrows cease
Whilst our kind guardians turn our toils to ease.
May they be with an endless Sabbath blest
Who have afforded unto us this rest.'

Another almshouse building which is preserved but has long ceased to be used for its original purpose is the Merchant Tailors' Almshouse in Merchant Street, in the midst of the new shopping centre, which was built in 1701 but sold to the Corporation, who use it as offices for the Weights and Measures Department.

It might be of interest to note that although no official figures exist it is understood that there are approximately 2,500 almshouses in England and Wales, which provide accommodation for over 40,000 old people.

By virtue of their corporate entities, and even before the dissolution of the religious houses, charities which were endowed by merchants were administered by the Corporation or the guilds. By far the most important guild was the Society of Merchant Venturers, which probably derived from the Bristol Guild Merchant. Indeed, it might be said that the control of Bristol trade from the fifteenth to the eighteenth centuries was in the hands of the Corporation and the Merchant Venturers. The Merchant Venturers, however, administered their own charities quite separately from those administered by the Mayor and Corporation. We have seen that from the early fifteenth century the Corporation administered Trinity Hospital, and the following century saw the foundation by Bristol merchants of the Grammar School in 1532; Queen Elizabeth's Hospital in 1590, and the Red Maids' School in 1634. Mention might also be made of the gift in 1566 by Sir Thomas White, founder of St. John's College, Oxford, of sums sufficient to provide free loans of £100 per annum each to two young men (preferably clothiers) to be repaid without interest within eight years and thereafter lent again in perpetuity on the same terms. All these foundations and their endowments were under the control of the Corporation. Indeed, with the Reformation and the abolition of the religious houses charities ceased to have a religious significance and became secular. In the Statute of Charitable Uses enacted in 1601 in the reign of Elizabeth I, charitable endowments were defined. They included: relief of aged and poor persons; maintenance of sick and decayed soldiers and mariners; education and apprenticeship of orphans; schools, and maintenance of scholars at universities; marriage of poor maidens; provision of houses of correction; repair of bridges, churches, roads. In summary, it might be said that the charitable activities of the monasteries, hospitals and guilds were re-enacted without religious control.

In the sixteenth, seventeenth and eighteenth centuries, there was great distress amongst the poor, and the Corporation made attempts from time to time at its alleviation. As early as 1617 a workhouse was formed by the city authorities for poor boys, but it was short-lived; whilst in 1623 the House of Correction (Bridewell) was enlarged to provide a workhouse for unemployed, and a Master installed and provided with £200 to buy flax and hemp in order that the pauper residents could make nets. This enterprise lasted only a year. In 1697 Parliament decreed that all persons receiving parish relief should wear a red or blue badge with the letter P and the initial letter of the parish, the penalty for non-observance being a whipping and three weeks' hard labour. St. Stephen's Vestry (St. Stephen's is the church with the magnificent tower just off Corn Street) in August of that year, resolved that the poor of the parish should wear badges with the letters

'T.P.
S.S.'

Despite the severity of the Poor Laws, Bristol was ahead of the times, and it was due to the energies of John Carey, an enlightened Bristol merchant, that an institution called 'The Incorporation of the Poor' was founded; and on his instigation a petition was presented by the Bristol citizens to Parliament and an Act passed in 1696 'for erecting hospitals and workhouses within the City of Bristol, for the better employment and maintaining of the poor.' This was the first local Act in the country relating to the administration of the Poor Law, and provided for the election of guardians by the ratepayers of each ward and for the pooling of resources to provide a central workhouse. In 1698 the central workhouse in Bristol was set up in the Mint, afterwards renamed St. Peter's Hospital (which was destroyed by enemy action in 1940) and a 'manufactory' for spinning wool and cotton yarn and doing certain other work was started. Additional buildings were erected in 1709, when girls were admitted and later an infirmary and a schoolroom were added; it being considered that as there was not enough work a little education would not come amiss for the little paupers!

The Bristol scheme of the central workhouse was copied by other towns such as Tavistock, Norwich and Exeter. Despite this, however, the administration of Poor Law relief was, to say the least, callous, and must have prompted the foundation of many Bristol charities, as in the sixteenth, seventeenth and eighteenth centuries a large number were formed and their administration entrusted to the Corporation, in addition to the schools to which reference has already been made. Robert Kitchen, who was born in Kendal, made a large fortune in Bristol. He became Mayor, and left to his successors by his will dated 19 January 1594 his mansion house and £1,000 for the relief of the poor, and directed that £3 be paid for ever at Lady Day and Michaelmas to his or his wife's poor kindred. These half-yearly payments are still paid to proved descendants of his poor kindred of the late sixteenth century.

Alderman John Whitson (see Plate XXXII), in addition to founding the Red Maids' School, left substantial sums for poor men and women, and also for lying-in gifts. Thomas Holbin in 1619, Humphrey Brown in 1629, and Joseph Jackson by his will of 1658, all endowed sermons and gifts to the poor, and others left substantial bequests to the Corporation or to the parochial charities. Thomas White, George White and Richard Holworthy all left money to provide gifts for prisoners in gaol.

The endowment of sermons was no doubt due to the puritanical Corporation in the seventeenth century continually stressing their importance as opposed to the liturgical services of the Church. The Corporation had a considerable difference of opinion with the Bishop in 1605 because it had induced the Dean and Chapter to agree to the erection of a 'convenient structure' in the Cathedral where the Mayor, Alderman and Councillors and their wives might sit and hear services on 'Sabbaths' and festival days. The Archbishop of Canterbury at the request of the Bishop ordered the removal of the 'structure', which the Bishop said made the Cathedral look like a playhouse. The Archbishop did, however, give the Mayor and Corporation permission to hear as many sermons as they liked and where they wished; whereupon the Mayor and Corporation forsook the Cathedral and took to attending St. Mary Redcliffe, which was outside the Bishop's jurisdiction, to hear sermons.

In 1727 Dr. Charles Sloper left part of his estate to the Corporation in order that bibles could be given to the poor; whilst in 1768 Mrs. Mary Ann Peloquin left to the Corporation £19,000, the interest on which was to be utilized in the payment of gifts to decayed freemen, their widows or daughters, lying-in gifts and payments to the Rector of St. Stephen's Church, in which there is a tablet to her memory.

In 1784 John Merlott gave in his will £3,000 to the Corporation to provide pensions for the blind, and this charity was augmented by gifts of £5,000 from Richard Reynolds, the Bristol philanthropist, in 1809, and £4,000 from Miss Elizabeth Merlott. Richard Reynolds (1735–1816) was born in Bristol. He left the city when young and settled in or near Coalbrookedale where he amassed an enormous fortune. He returned to Bristol in 1804, and devoted himself to charitable work. In 1812 he founded the Bristol Prudent Man's Friend Society, which was the forerunner of the Bristol Trustee Savings Bank. During his life he was known to have given to charity over £200,000. He died in Cheltenham, and is buried in the graveyard attached to the Quakers' Friars in the centre of Bristol. It is interesting to note that Merlott's Charity has never had any restrictions as to place of birth or residence of the applicants. In almost all Bristol charities applicants must be natives or residents of Bristol.

The above gifts are but a few of those which were made. Considerable sums were left to Queen Elizabeth's Hospital by William Bird, Lady Mary Ramsey, Edward Colston, James Gallop, Samuel Hartnell, John Barker and others, to augment the foundation and provide additional accommodation for poor boys. As a result of the endowment of so many charities, the Corporation became owners of a considerable amount of property, and Lords of the Manor of Burnett and Congresbury in Somerset, and also of the advowsons; and jointly with the Trustees of Sion Hospital and St. Paul's, London, Lords of the Manor of Bradwell in Essex. The administration of the charities took up a considerable amount of the Corporation's time, and in the seventeenth century the Council appointed annually several of their number to manage the charities. Four aldermen were appointed keepers of the keys of the city chests; four councillors managed the loan-money charities, whilst others managed or supervised Queen Elizabeth's Hospital, the Grammar School, Trinity Hospital, gifts and road money charities. Six aldermen or councillors were appointed auditors, who were the only persons empowered to hold office connected with the charities for more than two years at a time. In the case of Dr. White's Temple Hospital, however, the control was in the hands of the four 'Ancientest' aldermen, and it remains so to this day.

The administration of the charities by the old closed Corporation was, to say the least, not as efficient or disinterested as it might have been. In spite of this the charities continued to be endowed, and in the nineteenth century the following, among others, endowed charities and named the Mayor and Corporation as their trustees or executors—Miss Elizabeth Ludlow, Pensions to Women (1805); Thomas Bonville's Pension Charity for poor housekeepers (1817) and Thomas Bonville's Charity for poor lodgers (1822). Another notable benefactor was Samuel Gist, a wealthy planter in Virginia, who had been educated at Queen Elizabeth's Hospital in Bristol. He died in London in 1815 and left £10,000 to educate poor boys and girls, and the Court ordered that the income of this bequest be shared by Queen Elizabeth's Hospital and the Red Maids' School. It is of interest to note that Samuel Gist in his will directed that his three hundred slaves be freed, and he made provision for their maintenance and education and religious training and for their descendants should they require it.

In the early nineteenth century there was a considerable outcry throughout the country that the municipal corporations of England, which numbered nearly 250, were misapplying their funds, including charitable funds under their jurisdiction, or using them for political purposes. After the Reform Act of 1832 it was inevitable that reform of the municipal corporations would follow, and after several parliamentary enquiries and commissions, and in particular the Commission of 1833, the Municipal (Reform) Act of 1835 was passed, which brought the old closed corporations to an end. This Act affected 178 boroughs, including Bristol, where there was much bitter controversy. Under the Act of 1835 the Lord Chancellor could appoint independent trustees of charities on petitions from boroughs affected by the Act, and as a result of a petition by Mr. R. Ash and Mr. G. E. Sanders, the Lord Chancellor confirmed the appointment of independent trustees of the charities administered by the Corporation of Bristol other than Dr. White's Temple Hospital.

The Trustees, on their appointment, discovered that the Corporation had diverted large sums from their original purpose, particularly in the case of the endowments of Queen Elizabeth's Hospital, the Grammar School, Dr. Owen's Charity and Trinity Hospital. In the case of Queen Elizabeth's Hospital the Trustees claimed that over £240,000 was due to the charity. The Corporation put in counter-claims, and after legal actions instituted by the Trustees a compromise was reached and considerable sums paid over to the Trustees in full settlement of their claim.

These proceedings did not affect in any way the charities administered by the Society of Merchant Venturers, or any of the funds administered by the parochial charities. The parochial charities in Bristol are considerable, and are administered by the parish vestries, although of course, with the destruction of the centre of Bristol by enemy action it has meant that the income of the parochial charities, which largely derives from land and buildings in the parishes, has been considerably reduced.

In 1836, when local feelings as regards charities were extremely bitter, the Reverend George Müller, who was born in Prussia in 1805, founded a home for orphans in Bristol. He was almost entirely without means, yet despite this, and without asking anyone for donations, this remarkable man founded and maintained the Ashley Down Orphanage, or more correctly, Orphanages, in Bristol, which housed over 2,000 orphan boys and girls and which cost over £75,000 to build. Müller lived for many years in 55 (formerly 21) Paul Street, Kingsdown, and a plaque is affixed to the outside of the house. He died in 1898, aged 93, and although over £1,000,000 had passed through his hands from voluntary efforts his total estate was sworn at only £160. 9*s*. 4*d*. From 1836 to 1955, without any appeal for funds, £3,048,000 were received for maintaining the 17,317 children admitted into the various homes—a truly remarkable achievement. The Orphanage was moved from Ashley Down to more convenient and smaller homes in Somerset and the outskirts of Bristol after the Second World War.

In 1853 the Charity Commissioners were appointed, with jurisdiction and powers over charities which had hitherto been exercised by the Court of Chancery. In 1869 and 1870 Acts were passed establishing the Endowed Schools Commissioners, to which trustees of obsolete charities might apply for the application of their endowments for charitable purposes. The Trustees of the Bristol Municipal Charities in 1875 obtained permission for the endowments of certain obsolete loan money and other charities to be transferred to Bristol Grammar School. The legal doctrine of *cy près* (which might be described as the application for charitable purposes as near as possible to the wishes of the grantor or benefactor when it is impossible to carry out the original intention) did not apply in these cases, as among the obsolete charities transferred for the benefit of Grammar School boys were certain prison redemption charities for the benefit of prisoners in gaol! Subsequently, the Endowed Schools Commissioners were merged with the Charity Commission, and in 1902 the jurisdiction over the educational charities was passed to the Board (subsequently the Ministry) of Education.

This chapter would be incomplete without reference to the medical charities, and in this connexion one of the earliest infirmaries supported by voluntary subscriptions in this country[1] was founded in Bristol in 1737 on a plot of land adjoining

[1] The Westminster Hospital was founded in 1719, Guy's in 1721 and St. George's in 1734. Bristol set the fashion outside the capital and other towns soon followed its lead.

Magdalen Lane, mainly through the energies of Mr. John Elbridge, Deputy Controller of Customs, who gave £1,500 for its equipment, and on his death the following year bequeathed £5,000 to the institution. (One of the earliest rules was that 'No person shall be admitted who has not been resident in the parishes of St. James and St. Philip's for the space of six months except mariners or in the case of casualties in the City or out-parishes.') It is interesting to note that this example was followed by similar movements in Bath, Edinburgh, Exeter and York. In 1782 the buildings were condemned and the medical staff strongly urged that the hospital be moved to the Red Lodge in Park Row. Mr. T. Tyndall, however, who lived in the Royal Fort, objected to the establishment of a hospital so close to his park, so it was rebuilt on the old site, and completed in 1786, the cost being defrayed out of invested capital. For some extraordinary reason the whole building was coated with black plaster, which must have presented a remarkable appearance, as Prince Puckler Muskau, who visited the city in 1828, compared the place to 'an enormous mausoleum'. It was not until some thirty years later that this depressing coating was removed. 1834 saw the foundation of the Bristol Medical School, with which the Infirmary has had a long and close connexion, and in 1850 Queen Victoria consented to its being known as the 'Royal Infirmary'. It was enlarged in 1876 and again in 1910, and continues its work to-day on the same site which it has occupied for nearly 220 years.

The infirmary in the nineteenth century was considered to be a stronghold of Toryism, which partly accounts for the foundation of the Bristol General Hospital in Guinea Street in 1831 by a committee which was largely composed of Whigs and Nonconformists, the founders being of opinion that the infirmary had not kept pace with the growth of the city's population. The hospital owes a great deal to the benefactions of Mr. William Proctor Baker (President 1872–1907), Joseph Storrs Fry (Treasurer 1891 and President 1908–13), Lord Winterstoke, Sir George Wills, Bt. (President 1913–28) who gave £60,000, and Sir Vernon Wills (President 1928–31). Mr. Fenwick Richards, who died in 1927, also bequeathed £60,000 to the hospital.

The Bristol Homoeopathic Hospital, which now stands at the top of Cotham Hill, was founded as a Free Dispensary for poor people in Queen Square in 1852, where it was carried on until 1883, when it moved to Brunswick Square, where it stayed until 1920, moving to Cotham House in that year. It did not become a hospital until 1903. In 1925, thanks to the generosity of the late Mr. Melville Wills, it moved to its present site. He presented the buildings as a memorial to his son Bruce Melville Wills, who died during the First World War.

Mention might also be made of the Children's Hospital, which was founded in 1866 at the top of St. Michael's Hill, and which still occupies the same site.

All the above hospitals have formed part of the State medical service since 1948, and subsequently some of the smaller medical charities, such as the Bristol Dispensary, have devoted their funds to helping the necessitous poor.

Reference has already been made to Merlott's Charity for the Blind, and to the fact that Bristol has always been in the forefront of social reforms. In the case of the blind asylums, Liverpool was first in the field by two years. In 1793 a few

Bristol Quaker philanthropists founded the Blind Asylum in Callowhill Street in a disused chapel. In 1803 it was removed to more adequate accommodation in Lower Maudlin Street near the Royal Infirmary. In 1832 the Trustees of the Blind Asylum obtained an Act of Parliament permitting them to buy and hold land within two miles of the Corn Exchange, and six years later the Asylum moved to a new building at the top of Park Street, on what is approximately the present site of the main building of the University. In 1905 a second Act of Parliament was obtained which authorized the purchase of land within three miles of the Corn Exchange, and as a result a large site was bought at Westbury-on-Trym, and the School for the Blind built there, whilst the workshops and administrative offices were removed to Museum Avenue (now St. George's Road) where they still are. In Bristol all kinds of work connected with the blind are carried on—education, adolescent training, employment and welfare; and for the past 160 years the city has been in the forefront of this kind of charitable undertaking.

The prosperous nineteenth and twentieth centuries saw the establishment of many new charities in Bristol, mainly for the provision of pensions. Mention, however, might be made of one notable exception, namely, the purchase of the Red Lodge in Park Row by Lady Byron in 1854 for a reformatory for girls. This was placed in the sole control of that remarkable educationalist and social worker, Miss Mary Carpenter (1807–77). Miss Hannah Ludlow (1863), Mr. Edward Phillips (1879), Miss Hannah Marriott (1887), Mrs. C. M. Castle (1905), Mr. H. H. Wills (1920), are among the many who founded pension charities which are administered by the Trustees of the Bristol Municipal Charities. In addition, however, other pension charities were formed under other bodies of trustees, as, for example, Peter Herve (1807), the Bristol Benevolent Institution (1869). The latter is for widows and dependants of business or professional people who have carried on business or a profession in Bristol for at least seven years. But the benefactions of the various members of the Wills family stand out among all others in variety and amount. In addition to the magnificent benefactions to the University, schools, and the city, various members of the Wills family gave large sums to the hospitals, to which reference has already been made. The late Mr. H. H. Wills built and endowed the St. Monica Home of Rest, Westbury-on-Trym, some thirty years ago, as a memorial to his wife, Dame Mary Monica Wills, and the fine buildings at the edge of the Downs were built to the design of the late Sir George Oatley, architect of the University; and this benefaction might be said to be the most important in Bristol in modern times. The Society of Merchant Venturers are Trustees of this charity. Another member of the Wills family, Lord Dulverton, has recently established the Dulverton Trust, from which notable contributions for the preservation of almshouses and churches throughout the country, as well as to charities, have been made. The Dulverton Trust is administered from London.

In 1911, Bristol University Settlement at Barton Hill was founded, which continues to do excellent work among the poor of that neighbourhood.

Visitors to Bristol in the first fortnight of each November will see three of its prominent citizens in the Corn Street area moving between the Commercial Rooms, The Bristol Club and The Constitutional Club, wearing morning clothes. They are the Presidents of the three Colston Societies collecting subscriptions for their societies, namely, the Dolphin Society (established 1749), the Anchor Society (established 1769) and the Grateful Society (established 1758). These societies were founded in memory of Edward Colston and to commemorate his many benefactions; and they elect a new president every year. Two of these societies were political in origin, the Dolphin Society being Tory and the Anchor Whig. The Grateful Society has always been non-political. Each of the societies makes annual collections which in total now amount to nearly £10,000 a year, and these collections are used to provide grants and annuities to those in need. The Dolphin Society from the date of its foundation has collected and dispensed in this way some £175,000, and the other societies have collected and made grants of similar amounts. There is one other society known as the Parent Colston Society, which is the oldest of the societies founded in memory of Edward Colston, but its funds are devoted to the maintenance of the Redcliff Schools.

In 1948 the Welfare State came into being with the passing of the National Assistance Act, the object of which was to amend the Poor Law and to abolish poverty. That, as a result, poverty has been alleviated, no-one can deny; nevertheless, the demand for private charity continues to be large. There are long waiting lists for all the almshouses, owing to the housing shortage, whilst with the depreciation of money, people with fixed incomes which were adequate to live on before the last war, now find that they cannot make ends meet, and it is this section of society in particular which the various pension charities can assist. In addition, it should be stressed that the National Assistance scales make provision for necessities only, and do not provide for any comforts; and as the National Assistance regulations give authority for incomes of up to 10*s*. 6*d*. a week from charities to be disregarded when determining need, the receipt of a small charitable pension can make a great deal of difference to a person who is receiving National Assistance. Thus the charities of Bristol continue to play an important part in the life of the city, and their administration is the concern of many of Bristol's most prominent citizens.

BOOKS FOR FURTHER READING

LATIMER, J. *Annals of Bristol*. Bristol. 4 vols.: sixteenth century, 1908, seventeenth century, 1900, eighteenth century, 1893, nineteenth century, 1887 and 1902.

MANCHEE, T. J. *Bristol Charities*, 2 vols. Bristol, 1831.

SAMPSON, W. A. *Life of the Rev. Thomas White, D.D.* Bristol, 1912.

SMITH, G. MUNRO. *History of Bristol Royal Infirmary*. Bristol, 1917.

SYMES, J. ODEY. *Short History of Bristol General Hospital*. Bristol, 1932.

TILL, ROGER. *Wills of Bristol*. Bristol, 1954.

TOVEY, S. G. *Colston, The Philanthropist*. 1863.

Social Services in Bristol. Bristol Council of Social Service Inc. Bristol, 1952. Contains a list of most of the Bristol charities.

Trans. Bristol and Gloucestershire Arch. Soc.—in particular: vols. 36, 67, 68, 71 and 72.

Victoria County History of Gloucestershire. Vol. ii. London, 1907.

CHAPTER TWENTY-ONE

MUSEUMS OF THE WEST

FOR the purposes of this brief survey the West is taken to include the counties of Gloucestershire, Somerset and Wiltshire. It is typically an area of countryside intensely varied both geologically and topographically, with Bristol as the largest industrial centre. Against such a background are set the individual museums, in all of which an attempt has been made to illustrate objectively the local environment and history from the earliest times. These museums are under different types of control—municipal, society or trustee—and all endeavour in one way or another to initiate and maintain display on modern educational lines.

So gradual and yet so effective has been the revolution in museums during the last decade that it is realized only by a relative few what tremendous changes in policy and organization have taken place. For many years museums carried out the function of collecting, but now emphasis is on the proper display of this accumulated material in order that it may be of maximum educational advantage and recreational interest to the community. New techniques of display and arrangement have helped to bring about this change and the public has certainly shown its appreciation of the new liveliness and vitality. Museums are no longer mausoleums but living organizations serving the community and performing a real function in any social unit. Especially in the smaller towns the museum performs extra-mural functions and acts as a local cultural centre on the same plan that has proved so manifestly successful in Sweden.

Moreover, museums are now regional in character, faithfully portraying the human history and natural history of their own particular environment. Gone are the days of omnivorous acquisition with its resulting miniature national museums scattered over the country. The policy of every committee or body of trustees is to acquire material according to a restricted and definite policy, and thus to interest the citizens in their own district and others in the area they are visiting. The twin policies of education and the interpretation of a restricted area are now the guiding principles in the West.

The British Association is meeting in Bristol this year and we can thus start our survey with the museums in that city. The complicated history of the City Museum is too long for inclusion in this article but it is interesting to note that it was taken over by the municipality as early as 1894. Unfortunately in the Second World War the museum was partly destroyed and the remaining shell of the building was subsequently purchased and adapted by the University for use as a Senior Common Room and students' refectory. The City Museum is now housed in the Art Gallery building where under the same roof separate administration was initiated in 1945. The museum seeks to portray the natural history, history and archaeology of the West. The earlier vast ethnological collections are in process of being reduced in favour of the expansion of the local archaeological material. The public has shown its appreciation of this change of emphasis and local excavations are news. Alfred the gorilla captures the imagination of the visitor as much as he did when living. Branch museums have been established at Blaise Castle House, Georgian House and Red Lodge. At the first, the exhibits illustrate English life during the last three or four hundred years and the rudiments of a Folk Park can be seen in an eighteenth-century corn-grinding water-mill, a gypsy wagon and a thatched dairy. The Georgian House, administered by the City Art Gallery, is so arranged to take the visitor back to the spacious and elegant days of Georgian England. The Red Lodge, also administered by the City Art Gallery, is an Elizabethan house of distinction famous for its well-preserved Oak Room. Although not available to the public, the Departments of Botany, Geology and Zoology in the University house important museums in addition to teaching collections. Also in the University buildings is the Museum of the Spelaeological Society now slowly acquiring its post-war material after extensive war damage to its original collections.

We can now pass to Gloucestershire, where the museums of Cheltenham, Cirencester, Gloucester and Stroud deal with the northern two-thirds of the county. Founded in the early part of this century and always administered by a committee of the local Council, the museum at Cheltenham has specialized in local archaeology and bygones. With the rich hinterland of the Cotswolds so close to the town this was a natural development and the Museum has taken every advantage of its geographical position.

In a similar manner the Urban District Council at Cirencester established the attractive Corinium Museum in 1938 and in the subsequent years has been successful in maintaining the Roman character of the collections, thus reflecting the essential history of Cirencester and its neighbourhood.

The museum at Gloucester originated in one of those virile and popular literary and scientific associations and was transferred to the Corporation in 1896. The City Museum contains local natural history and archaeological collections, the latter illustrating chiefly the Roman occupation of Glevum and now displayed according to the most recent technical advances. Near the Cathedral is the sixteenth-century building known as Bishop Hooper's Lodging, where the Bishop is reputed to have spent his last night and which is now a Folk Museum. This was opened in 1935 and illustrates life in Gloucestershire especially during the last four hundred years. Workshops and living rooms give an intimate and realistic setting to the exhibits. The Regimental Museum was opened as late as 1948 in an adjoining Elizabethan house and the collections cover the history of all battalions of the Gloucestershire Regiment.

PLATE XXX. *Colston almshouses, St. Michael's Hill.*

PLATE XXXI. *Merchants almshouses, partly destroyed in* 1940. (*Society of Merchant Venturers.*)

26

Aº DNI 1629
ÆTATIS 72
NQUAM DESPERABO DE
RICORDIA TUA DOMINE

The Cowle Museum at Stroud, delightfully situated in a typical valley in the heart of the Cotswold country, contains collections of local natural history, and also possesses exhibits of historical and archaeological value. The reptilian remains from the Oolite and some pottery dated 50 B.C. to A.D. 200 from Eastington are exceptionally fine. The museum has recently acquired a third room and a complete rearrangement of the exhibits is in progress.

South of Bristol, the museums of Somerset are fairly evenly scattered over the whole county with the exception of Exmoor and the Quantock Hills. In all the emphasis is now far more on display than acquisition, though all the governing bodies would admit with gratitude that they are thankful to their predecessors for their zeal in collecting. Treating the museums alphabetically, the first to be noticed is the small society museum in the ancient town of Axbridge. Founded in 1950 and backed with the energy and vitality of real enthusiasts, this museum already occupies its second home. Archaeological and Pleistocene material from local sites is well displayed and evidence of the days when Axbridge had a Mayor and Corporation is included.

The museums of Bath are unfortunately scattered with no central administration or building to serve as a focus. The Holburne of Menstrie Museum, administered by a Board of Trustees, contains works of art of all kinds including paintings, drawings, silver, porcelain, lace, textiles and coins. Some continental examples are shown for comparative purposes. The Victoria Art Gallery is controlled by a municipal committee and the collections include porcelain, Bristol delft and Elton ware. The Roman Baths Museum, also administered by the City Council, adjoins the Roman Baths and has recently been entirely reassembled. It contains various architectural fragments including the pediment of the Temple of Sul-Minerva and other objects of Roman age. Unfortunately the Museum of the Royal Literary and Scientific Institution is in store as the rooms are still occupied by the Admiralty. In pre-war days local natural history, archaeology and the important Moore collection of Somerset fossils were shown.

A small museum at Bridgwater occupies the house in which Admiral Robert Blake was born and includes much interesting personalia associated with the Duke of Monmouth and the Battle of Sedgemoor. A few local archaeological 'finds' complete this small but interesting municipal museum.

The museum in the town of Glastonbury, in the Fenland of Somerset, is naturally rich in material from the nearby and justly famous lake-village dwellings. It is administered by the local antiquarian society and was founded in 1880 when work on the lake villages started. In the same town, some architectural fragments from the Abbey are shown in the Abbot's Kitchen Museum.

The small museum at Shepton Mallet founded in 1900 and under the control of the Urban District Council contains some excellent local fossils, which have recently been relabelled by a member of the staff of the University of Bristol, and some local archaeological material. It is interesting to note how the theme of illustrating local

PLATE XXXII. *John Whitson, a contemporary portrait by an unknown artist.* (*Trustees of the Bristol Municipal Charities.*)

PLATE XXXIII. *Admiral Sir William Penn, from a portrait by Lely.* (*National Maritime Museum.*)

natural history, geology and archaeology is so consistently shown in these small museums which nestle under the southern slopes of Mendip.

Thanks to the initiative of the United Kingdom Carnegie Trustees and with the active co-operation and support of the Pilgrim and Dulverton Trusts the county museum at Taunton has been largely rearranged on modern lines. It was in 1874 that the Somerset Archaeological and Natural History Society removed its museum to the castle and since that date the collections have continued to expand. The Great Hall of the castle where Judge Jeffreys held the famous Bloody Assize in 1685 was crowded with material of exceptional quality. With the installation of modern casing and display this has been transformed into a gallery that has become the pattern of museum technique at least in southern England. The superb quality of the archaeological material is well known and in the more recent past many local bygones have been acquired.

With its frontage to the Cathedral Green and at right angles to the famous thirteenth-century West Front the museum at Wells is probably the most delightfully situated in Great Britain. The collections, due to the unique honorary curatorship of Mr. H. E. Balch, over a period of sixty years, are intensely regional in character and deal faithfully with the prehistory of the nearby Mendip area. At the present time the museum is undergoing extensive rearrangement on modern lines.

Although rather overshadowed by the public library at Weston-super-Mare the museum has in the recent past been extensively modernized and is now making a definite appeal to the influx of summer visitors at this well-known resort on the Bristol Channel. Local geology, archaeology, and natural history are represented and of exceptional interest are the prehistoric remains from Worlebury Camp.

As at Weston-super-Mare, the Wyndham Museum at Yeovil opened in 1926 is controlled by the local Council. Local antiquities predominate and the museum is noted for the Stiby collection of firearms.

The three main museums in Wiltshire are so spaced geographically that each illustrates the natural history and historical aspects of its own area. In the southern part the society-supported museum at Salisbury was founded in 1860 and owes much to the generosity and foresight of Mr. William Wyndham. The bygones—chiefly from the neighbouring countryside—are of exceptional quality and gain much by being portrayed in ‘habitat’ groups with naturalistic settings. The period figures are extremely lifelike. As to be expected there are maps, plans, prints and many objects from Stonehenge in addition to other archaeological material from well-known sites.

At Devizes, in the middle of the county, we again find a society-controlled museum with a wealth of local archaeological, natural history and geological material. The collections form a valuable series from the Stone, Bronze and Early Iron Ages and there is much material from the Roman occupation. As is now the accepted policy in so many museums, bygones are fully represented and have been acquired at an increasing rate in the last few years.

Swindon is the only municipally controlled museum of the trio. The emphasis here is on fossils and minerals though early musical instruments, coins and ceramics are present both in quality and quantity. The museum has recently been rearranged. In contrast is the small museum at Avebury, administered by the Ministry of Works and entirely devoted to the famous prehistoric remains in the immediate area.

Viewed in one way the museums of the West may appear as isolated units each ploughing a lonely furrow and endeavouring to portray the many aspects of their environment. To a great extent this was the state of affairs until 1931 when the South-west Group of Museums and Art Galleries was founded. Since then, mutual co-operation between committees and staffs has been the keynote in the museum world, and it is not without significance that this organization is termed a Group rather than a Federation.

Any account of museums would be incomplete without a word of tribute to the Carnegie Trustees who have done so much to stimulate modern display and raise the standard of museums in this country. The West has shared fully in this progressive movement and many museums, especially Taunton, have benefited themselves and the public they serve by the helpful reports from the Trustees and by the award of substantial grants.

Individually and collectively, the museums of the West are faithfully portraying their local environments and the long story of human habitation. It is a stimulating task, of benefit alike to resident and visitor, and of direct educational and recreational value to the community.

CHAPTER TWENTY-TWO

BRISTOL'S SCHOOLS

WHEN Queen Elizabeth I visited Bristol in 1574, she was ceremoniously greeted by the boys of the Grammar School: one of them, 'Salutacion', declaimed eighteen verses of poetry; he was followed by 'Gratulacion' with twenty; 'Obedient Goodwill' had packed his piece into eight verses—but the Queen could not wait. Nearly 400 years later it is still much easier to be exclamatory than to marshal the facts about Bristol schools in such a way that a reader will remain long enough to finish this chapter.

Bristol's schools have originated in six main ways. There are the ancient grammar schools, founded to provide intellectual training for future leaders in Church, State and the professions; there are the 'hospitals', founded as boarding schools for orphans and other socially handicapped children; there are the 'elementary' schools for working-class children, mostly founded by denominational interests in the nineteenth century, though some of Bristol's go back a whole century earlier; there are the schools founded by the nineteenth-century middle class for their own children; there are those founded by the private enterprise of able teachers; and there is the largest, and in many ways the most important, group of all, which owes its origin and maintenance to the work of elected bodies, dependent on public funds. A survey of a city's educational history with origins so diverse cannot lack colour; but neither can it display any balanced pattern. While, however, generalization is difficult, there are five major pieces of national legislation which have been important to some or all of the Bristol schools existing at the present time.

Throughout the three centuries prior to 1836, Bristol Corporation had a bad record in the administration of the educational endowments for which it was trustee. Things improved when, following the general parliamentary reform of municipal government in 1835, the Bristol Municipal Charity Trustees were established in 1836. But in the years following 1875, Parliamentary Commissioners again intervened in the affairs of educational charities, revising the terms of old foundations and trying to relate them to the needs of secondary education in a rapidly advancing industrial society. Meanwhile, from 1870 onwards the local School Boards took statutory responsibility for the development of elementary schools for all. After 1902, the Board of Education and local-authority education committees extended their statutory interest in the field of secondary education and began also to negotiate on a new basis for scholarship places in the old grammar schools. And after 1944 the pattern has changed again. Withal, the Bristol schools have gone robustly on, preserving and developing characters of their own.

Bristol has two ancient grammar schools, the continuous history of which is obscure; but both were refounded in the sixteenth century, the Grammar School in 1532 and the Cathedral School in 1542. The patrons of the former were the brothers Robert and Nicholas Thorne, successful Bristol merchants. For the first three hundred years of its existence the school ran as chequered a course as most such foundations. There were good headmasters who served the city and boys well, sending poor but able scholars into posts of distinction, especially at Oxford; but there were long spells of mismanagement and, indeed, under two sinecurist headmasters who held office, between them, from 1764 to 1844, the number of boys fell first to one (known as Lee's Chick) and finally, after a feeble revival, to none at all. Recovery came after 1836 under the government of the Bristol Municipal Charity Trustees. The school reopened in 1848 and quickly grew in strength with numbers reaching 201 by 1860. At this point there was a move to make it a public boarding school; but the Trustees, after appeal to the Master of the Rolls (who observed that 'the existence of free grammar schools without boarders provides the necessary instruction for the lower classes of the community'), turned against this course, thus leaving the way clear for the successful foundation of Clifton College in 1862. The mid-Victorian age brought as headmaster (1860–83) a vigorous autocrat, John William Caldicott, and under him it became an important day school. It won high academic repute for its scholars in classics and mathematics; its numbers soared to 400; and in 1879, as a result of the Endowed Schools Act, it entered the buildings at Tyndalls Park which it occupies to-day. In this era its pupils came overwhelmingly from the middle class; for it offered few places to the poor, and the wealthy preferred Clifton.

After Caldicott's retirement decline came again with numbers tumbling to less than 200 by 1906. The causes of this were in part personal, in the failings of the headmaster and in the weakness of the contemporary governors. Yet they also reflected the educational trends of an age which brought competition from public schools at one end of the social scale and from the higher-grade elementary ones at the other. An attempt to halt the decline was a much-publicized scheme of 1888, which proposed to widen the curriculum by including commercial subjects like book-keeping and colloquial foreign languages; yet little came of the plan. During this dark period, however, high standards of scholarship were maintained among a few boys in the upper forms; one of the boys was T. R. Glover, probably the most distinguished Old Bristolian scholar.

In 1906, almost by a fluke, the school's greatest headmaster, Cyril Norwood, was appointed at the age of thirty. Two forces aided him—the increase of State aid after the Balfour Act of 1902, and the generosity of local benefactors, particularly those whose wealth came from the tobacco industry. The extent of the buildings more than doubled; science took its place alongside the older disciplines; organized games became for the first time an effective reality; societies flourished; numbers rose from 185 to 528. When in 1916 Norwood laid down his charge he had made the Grammar School one of the outstanding day schools of the land—a position firmly maintained through all the difficulties and educational vicissitudes of the middle twentieth century. It now has about 930 boys in the upper school, of whom about 250 are in the sixth form. Of the boys entering the main school 50 per cent. come with reserved or free places from the local education authorities of Bristol, Gloucestershire and Somerset. For some years now, its scholars have been pre-eminent in winning open awards at Oxford and Cambridge, and in 1954 it ranked second among the nation's schools in this respect.

The other ancient grammar school, the Cathedral School, was refounded in 1542 by Henry VIII, on the lines of St. Paul's School, and is the counterpart of the King's Schools at such places as Canterbury, Ely, Rochester and Peterborough. Like the Grammar School, it suffered much during the first three centuries of its existence from the lack of funds and indifference of its governors, in this instance the Dean and Chapter, and it is only over the last hundred years that it has steadily raised the quality of its work to a good level, with about 45 of its 285 boys in the sixth form. Its character is marked by a strong sense of being an intimate Christian community. It has a good university record; one of its old boys recently appeared at the head of the Civil Service Examination list. It was not founded as a choir school, though for the last hundred years its boys have provided the cathedral choristers. The 1944 Act might have created difficulties, but with mutual goodwill it has been possible to arrange with the Bristol Education Committee to select entrants with good voices and to arrange for suitable nine-year olds to be admitted.

The two grammar schools were founded as places of learning for the education of boys who, by reason of brains or inherited status, might expect to become leaders. The next three were all 'hospitals', established to provide orphans and the like with a residential education.

John Carr, a Bristol soap-boiler who died in 1586, was the founder of Queen Elizabeth's Hospital on the model of Christ's Hospital in London. The Hospital opened in 1590 with 12 boys; the numbers increased to about 40 and remained at this level for the next two hundred years. In its early years the Hospital served as a grammar school and some of its boys went on to Oxford. But prior to 1836, it drifted on as a charity boarding school providing elementary instruction for boys who would become artisans. The boys in their blue-coat uniform were picturesque bodies for civic occasions and at one period in the seventeenth century the school earned £1 a time by supplying boys as attendants at important funerals. From 1709 to 1838, its masters were appointed for only one year at a time and it was not until this latter date that the first university graduate for over a century was appointed master with permanent tenure and the number of boys was increased from 45 to 120. In 1847 the present substantial building on the side of Brandon Hill was erected. In 1875, admission by nomination gave way to admission by examination from the elementary schools. One of the entrants was Richard Gregory, President of the British Association 1939–46. At the same time the Peloquin Scholarships were founded which made it possible for the ablest boys to go on to the Grammar School and thence to the University. After some years of strenuous educational effort the Hospital became a direct grant grammar school in 1921, with 110 boarders and some day boys on the foundation. It now has 370 with a sixth form of 70. Like the Grammar School and Red Maids, the majority of its governing body is appointed by the Municipal Charity Trustees.

The next of the hospitals was for girls, and in that respect was highly original. Indeed in providing a residential education for girls unbrokenly for over three hundred years, it is one of the oldest girls' boarding schools in the country. The Red Maids' School, as it came to be known, from the colour of the girls' dresses, was founded in 1634, in conformity with the will of Alderman John Whitson (see Plate XXXII). There was to be a 'fit and convenient dwelling-house . . . for the continued abode . . . of one grave, painful and modest woman of good life and conversation . . . and for forty poor woman children' of deceased or decayed citizens.

In proposing to give girls a substantial training, Whitson was well ahead of his time. But there was a weakness in his scheme. The girls were required to be bound apprentice to the woman in charge, and since the Governors made very meagre allowances for the maintenance of the pupils it was more usual for her to exploit the girls' labour than to bother with their education. After 1836 the new Trustees quickly put an end to the farming out of the girls but it was not until after the re-organization in 1876, carried out under the Endowed Schools Act, that much educational progress was made. Then 80 girls were admitted by competition from the elementary schools of Bristol and were given a 'sound and liberal education' up to the age of fifteen, and they began to enter for the Cambridge Locals. In 1880 telegraphy was introduced as a subject and the pupils often took Post Office jobs. During the 1880s, though it did not yet send girls to universities, a large number went to teachers' training colleges. After 1906, Red Maids' broadened out into a grammar school; in 1911 it moved to new buildings at Westbury-on-Trym, and for the last thirty years has been sending a steady stream of students to the university. It now has 70 foundation boarders, 10 paying boarders and 120 day girls on its roll.

The third of the hospitals was the creation, in his own lifetime, of one of the most remarkable of Bristol's benefactors, Edward Colston (see Chapter 20, p. 295). In 1702 he made a large contribution to the rebuilding fund of Queen Elizabeth's Hospital and proposed to endow places there for about 50 boys. But the latter proposal came to nothing, probably because the Corporation, as governors, were not prepared to accept Colston's condition that no child of a Dissenter should be admitted.

Defeated at Queen Elizabeth's Hospital, Colston asked the Society of Merchant Venturers to act as the managers of a new and independent foundation which he proposed to establish for 50 boys (increased almost at once to 100) at St. Augustine's Back, where the Colston Hall now stands. It was a school unprecedented in scale: it cost him £11,000 in capital cost and an endowment income of over £1,300, huge sums for those days. The boys were to be admitted between the ages of seven and ten and were to stay for seven years, working at a curriculum of reading, writing and arithmetic and the church catechism. Colston's ideas on education included the discouragement of nonconformity. In 1715, he ordered that boys should be expelled for attendance 'at any conventicle or meeting on pretence of religious worship'; in a letter to the Society of Merchant Venturers in 1718, complaining of their resistance to his intentions, he urged them to see that no boy was ever apprenticed to a Dissenter as they would be 'answerable for breach of their trust at the last and great tribunal'. However, the school survived the prejudices of its founder.

In 1861 it moved out to its present site at Stapleton. Thenceforward it ceased to be a charity institution with a limited curriculum, and fee-payers as well as the 100 boys on the foundation were admitted. It is, however, only over the last fifty years that it has begun to win recognition as a public school. A majority of its governing body is appointed by the Society of Merchant Venturers. Colston's Boys' School now has 35 foundation scholars, selected by open competition, among its 200 boarders and 100 day-boys.

The next foundation to be considered is what is now the oldest of the city's own grammar schools. It began very humbly as a diocesan elementary school in 1821, when the movement for Church parochial schools was in its infancy. By 1850, however, the latter movement had got into its stride and there was no obvious need for a diocesan school of the same type. While the managers were wondering what to do with their premises, Canon Moseley, F.R.S., suggested that they should transform themselves into a Diocesan Trade School, offering to the abler boys from the parish schools a 'special course of a *practical kind*, having reference to the mechanical and manufacturing callings and the trade of Bristol' with 'the purpose of teaching the scientific principles upon which trade and manufactures are based'. The scheme was adopted and the institution was opened as the first of its kind in England. It was highly successful, and when it needed more money for development it was the Merchant Venturers who came to its rescue, merging it with their Navigation School. In 1885 the Society housed the primary, secondary, and evening classes sections in good new premises in Unity Street and the whole thing was renamed 'The Merchant Venturers School'. As time went by the Society concentrated on the adult work (which, in the end, became the Engineering Faculty of the University and the College of Technology), and in 1920 the secondary school was taken over by the city and moved to its present situation, and since 1944 has been known as Cotham Grammar School.

Next comes an establishment whose origin lies in pure private enterprise. Though more than 200 years junior to Red Maids', Badminton is still one of the oldest girls' boarding schools in the country. Its founder in 1858 was Mrs. William Badock, who had to earn a living adequate to maintain an invalid husband and three children. In 1859 she issued a prospectus in which she offered a course including 'French (which is made the medium of conversation) with a sound English education, comprising Writing, Arithmetic, Grammar, Composition, Elocution, Biblical Knowledge, Geography, Ancient and Modern History, Natural Philosophy, Botany, Astronomy, Calisthenics, Deportment, Plain and Fancy Needlework.' The fees were fifty guineas per annum for boarders and twelve guineas for day pupils. The services of a laundress were available for three guineas, a seat in church for one guinea, and each girl had to take a silver fork and spoon. Mrs. Badock's scheme prospered, for two years later a larger house was taken over and the fees went up to sixty-five guineas for boarders and sixteen guineas for day pupils. The cost of laundry was also increased by $33\frac{1}{3}$ per cent., and the girls had now to bring two silver forks and spoons; but a seat in church remained at one guinea. The next move was to Badminton House, Clifton in 1868; a little later, a gymnasium was built—one of the earliest. When Mrs. Badock retired in 1893 there were about 55 pupils.

The school continued to thrive. In 1923, it was transferred to its present site just beyond the Downs, and in 1931, it became a public school, whose strong international interests were symbolized by the appointment of Lord Cecil as Visitor and Professor Gilbert Murray as President. It offers its 300 girls an unusually wide and original curriculum.

The next three schools typify the demand of the Victorian middle class for educational establishments whose academic quality would forthwith be equal to that of the better public schools. The first of them was Clifton College, founded in 1862, on the interest of Clifton business men in having for their sons a varied, up-to-date curriculum, taught at a high level by a first-rate staff, at a reasonable cost. The first headmaster was Percival, subsequently President of Trinity College, Oxford, Headmaster of Rugby and Bishop of Hereford. Appointed at the age of twenty-eight, he was one of the great educational leaders of the second half of the nineteenth century. During his seventeen years at Bristol, he established the tremendous record of Clifton College as a place of learning and education, and was also a central figure in the establishment of Clifton High School for Girls, and the University College. Afterwards he was the first president of Somerville College, Oxford, and he was one of the main figures in the development of Redland High School. But Clifton College is his outstanding creation and from his day onwards it has not only proved its strength in the older disciplines of classics and mathematics but at one time or another has done pioneer work in the teaching of natural science, modern languages and music.

In this place, it is appropriate to write especially of the school's record in the teaching of science. Between 1867 and 1877 the science staff included A. M. Worthington, H. Debus, J. Perry, G. H. Wollaston and M. J. Barrington-Ward. It was Worthington who appointed Richard Gregory as a laboratory boy at Clifton in 1884. Shenstone (who made the first specimens of silica glass apparatus in the College Laboratory with a small blowpipe and a lot of patience), Tilden and Rintoul were other remarkable science teachers of the first decades. By 1910, the laboratories were badly overcrowded, but it was not until the mid-1920s that under the leadership of two Old Cliftonians, Field-Marshal Earl Haig and J. H. Whitley, then Speaker of the House of Commons, £50,000 was raised by Old Boys for the building and equipping of the present Science School, which was planned by E. J. Holmyard and W. C. Badcock. Biology was housed over-modestly, and still is, but this has not prevented a great expansion of biological teaching in the years since the close of the Second World War. The Science School also houses the 'Stone Memorial Science

Library', quite the most remarkable school institution of its kind. At present, seven scientific chairs in English universities are held by Old Cliftonians. But the College also maintains its distinguished record of scholarship in the older disciplines and with 580 boys in the senior school is amongst the top dozen in gaining open awards year by year at the ancient universities.

At twelve meetings held in Percival's house in 1877, plans were worked out for opening a school in 1878 which should 'supply to girls on moderate terms, General Instruction of the highest class'. The first headmistress, Miss M. A. Woods, worked on three principles—that the school should be open to all girls of good character without social discrimination; that it should accord religious freedom to staff and pupils, and that it should be non-competitive.

The school flourished. Within a year numbers were up to 160 and larger premises were taken. Boarders were accepted. The first university scholarship was won at Lady Margaret Hall in 1883 and the second at Somerville in 1885. Some science was taught but laboratories were slow in coming. A specialist mistress for physical training was appointed in 1887. Cricket was introduced, and among the girls were the daughters of W. G. Grace. By 1892 the orchestra was meeting regularly on Saturday mornings and a little later the school was actively engaged in social work. Numbers passed 200 in 1889, and in 1905 Sir William Ramsey, F.R.S., opened a laboratory block. Shortly after this Clifton High School was given direct-grant status by the Board of Education.

Throughout this century it has continued to grow in scale, distinction and the width of its interests. It has offered a warm welcome to girls compelled to seek refuge in this country from Europe. By 1924 the numbers were over 400 (of whom 10 per cent. came on with free places from the elementary schools) and now the total is 670. Academically its girls have done outstandingly well in the humanities and science. A former pupil with a horticultural diploma is head gardener at Chequers. In status the school is now independent, having voluntarily given up direct grant in 1946.

Redland High School was founded five years after Clifton, though it began in 1880 as a private venture. In 1882 it was taken over by a committee for £800: there were then about 55 girls. Two prominent members of the Committee were the Rev. Urijah Thomas, a Congregational Minister, and Mr. Prideaux, the Vicar of St. Saviour's.

The early curriculum included 'The elements of Physical and Moral Science' as well as Latin and German. But the salaries of the assistant staff were too low and in order to raise them it was decided to dismiss the Drilling Master and to save on French and science. Nonetheless a few months later, the head was given authority to negotiate for chemistry lessons at 10*s*. an hour or 15*s*. for a double period.

In 1883, the governing body was widened. Percival, now President of Trinity College, Oxford, became President, while the Mayor of Bristol and the Chairman of the Bristol School Board became Vice-Presidents. Before accepting office Percival asked for and got 'an assurance that in the event of his becoming President of the

Council he should have a voice in the management of the Company's affairs'. From Oxford, Rugby and Hereford over the next twenty years Percival was immensely active, coming to Bristol to preside at meetings, demanding at speech days the good education of girls and arranging for the school to be thoroughly examined annually by the ablest of the Clifton College assistant staff. In 1885, the school moved into its present lovely eighteenth-century house, Redland Court (see Plate XXVII).

By 1887, numbers were over 200: in September of that year a dividend of 2½ per cent. tax free was declared on the shares; in 1889 the headmistress took a party of girls to the Paris Exhibition. In 1892, Bristol Town Council gave the school £500 'Whiskey money' plus an annual grant for special science teaching; in return Redland gave scholarships for girls from elementary schools. And in 1893, one of its pupils won the first of many Oxford open scholarships. The vigour of its first ten years did not diminish over the next sixty though dividends ceased long ago. During its middle years its chairman was Canon Gamble, another of Bristol's great educational leaders, who was responsible for the science wing, completed in 1932. Since 1946, Redland High School has been independent. Of the 550 pupils in the junior and main schools, over 70 are in the sixth form, which offers an unusually wide choice of courses.

The Clifton schools and Redland were established by the middle class for their own children. Colston's Girls' School sprang from the wrangle about the reorganization of the ancient Bristol educational endowments in the 1870s. The Commissioners withdrew their proposal for the virtual abolition of free boarding places in the three 'Hospitals' but in return Bristol agreed to establish a new grammar school for girls, with low fees and a substantial number of free places. It was opened in 1891, under the governorship of the Merchant Venturers. It acquired direct grant status early in the new century, but surrendered this after the Second World War. The senior school has maintained high academic standards in the sixth form, and at the same time has provided post-certificate training for girls who ultimately become key secretarial workers in the city's commercial and professional life. Of nearly 600 girls in the school well over 100 are in the sixth form, and there is a strong science side. In 1908 Colston's inherited a fine library of 8,000 books particularly suitable for sixth-form work. The kindergarten and junior school were distinguished for the interest and originality of their work in the decades before 1940 and especially during the war years. For some years it carried a Froebel Training Department affiliated with the University Department of Education. After the war the primary department was transferred to the local authority, under whom, and in quite unbelievably difficult physical conditions (due to the blitz), it continues to provide primary education of outstanding quality for boys and girls.

Most of Bristol's grammar schools owe their origin to the gifts of wealthy men, or to the imagination and drive of middle-class men and women who had themselves had a privileged education. The Grammar School of St. George originated quite differently.

It was the establishment of School Boards under the Education Act of 1870 that first gave elected local representatives access to public funds for the creation and maintenance of popular schools. Bristol's Gloucestershire suburb, St. George, was a School Board District on its own, which went to work with a will; by 1884, the Board had 4,000 children in its elementary schools, and by 1890, 6,000. Already by 1881, the School Board had begun to think about the educational needs of children with more ability and ambition than could be satisfied in the elementary schools; but a largely working-class suburb, where a penny rate produced only £270, had to move carefully if it was to provide elementary education for all and higher for some. Throughout the 1880s the School Board declined to lower its sights by the offer from Westminster and Gloucestershire of partial schemes. Nothing less than a well-established higher-grade school would do, and in 1891, the St. George School Board felt itself strong enough to apply to the Government for permission to borrow money and build an 'Organized Science School'. On this proposition the men of the School Board fought and won the triennial election. The opponents of the scheme won the support of the local secretary of the Miners' Union, and called large and noisy public meetings which passed a resolution 'That the erection of a higher-grade school is not required'. Nonetheless the School Board persisted and precipitated a fresh storm when it passed over the lowest tender from a St. George builder in favour of a slightly higher one from a Bristol contractor with more experience of building schools. By the autumn of 1894 a building for 500 children had been completed at a cost of £14,000 and a graduate headmaster at a salary of £275 a year rising by £5 to £300 had been appointed. Twenty-five per cent. of the places were to be free and for these 125 vacancies there were 595 applicants. The remaining 375 pupils paid 5*d.* a week. All available places were soon taken. In 1897 the district of St. George was absorbed into Bristol and in due course its 'white elephant', as its opponents called it, was elevated into a mixed secondary school run by the Bristol Education Committee. Its birth owes nothing to wealth or to educational tradition, and everything to elected men of the people. The seven men who bore the brunt of the struggle were a bootmaker, a coachbuilder, a Congregational minister, a draper, two grocers and a master tailor. Their £14,000 school building lacks charm and even convenience: but its life has had the educational robustness of its birth.

Bristol itself had two counterparts to St. George, though slightly later. The earlier was Merrywood co-educational Higher Grade School, opened to serve south Bristol, in 1896. In 1906, it became Merrywood Secondary School, and continued as such until 1937 when new and more adequate buildings were opened in Novers Park. But it had been decided to abandon co-education and therefore the boys' and girls' Merrywood Grammar Schools exist side by side but separate. They are only now reaching full development with about 500 children each.

The second of Bristol's Higher Grade Schools was Fairfield, opened in 1898. Like Merrywood it became a Secondary School in 1906, but it has maintained its co-educational character. It has developed along much the same lines as many other good municipal secondary schools elsewhere and, like them, it is now outgrowing its accommodation with 600 pupils.

But it is not *just* like other schools. Even in a city where music flourishes, Fairfield's musical work is outstanding. About a quarter of its pupils are in a school choir which has broadcast a number of times; this is the kind of work which gives a fine foundation to the cultural life of Bristol.

Before leaving the Grammar Schools, brief reference must be made to three others. St. Brendan's is a Roman Catholic direct-grant school for over 600 boys. It was founded in 1896 and is run by the Christian Brothers. It has an excellent all-round standard of achievement. Among its distinguished old boys are the present Archbishop of Birmingham and Field-Marshal Sir William Slim. The Roman Catholic Girls' Grammar School also has direct-grant status. It was founded in 1905, but was taken over by the Sisters of La Retraite in 1924. It has about 360 girls. The latest of Bristol's grammar schools is Rose Green High School, formerly a local-authority secondary-commercial school recruiting girls at the age of thirteen. Since 1952 it has been a fully-fledged grammar school, recruiting at the age of eleven and offering certain special commercial courses.

Bristol was already providing elementary education for children of the working classes early in the eighteenth century. Temple Colston, in the foundation of which Edward Colston played an important part, is sometimes said to be the first elementary school in the country—meaning by that a school established, not for profit, by a group of people who took responsibility for seeing that efficient elementary instruction was provided for children whose parents could not afford to pay for it. Temple Colston was founded in 1709. The parochial school at Fishponds, of which Hannah More's father was head in 1745, was a later establishment of the same type. With the growing pace of industrialization and the growing concern at the anti-social habits of the less well-instructed members of society, the move to set up elementary schools, especially by the Christian denominations, also grew. By 1870, when School Boards were established with power to run elementary schools under secular auspices from public funds, Bristol had 34 Church schools, 7 undenominational and 9 provided by smaller religious bodies. These offered about 21,000 places to the 27,000 children of school age in Bristol, but the average attendance seems to have been only about 13,000. By 1873, average attendance of those on the registers was about 70 per cent. By 1900, there were 29,000 children in the schools of the School Board and 20,000 in denominational schools—and among them all the average attendance was about 85 per cent. In the 3 years, 1898–1900, the Board provided over 8,300 places in sixteen newly opened schools. These figures show the energy with which elected bodies were capable of tackling universal education. But it was not mere numbers with which they were concerned. For the abler pupils they fought fiercely with the Board of Education in London for the recognition of 'higher-grade' and 'science' schools, such as Merrywood and Fairfield.

Education for the blind in Bristol began well before the middle of the nineteenth century. It received an impetus from the 1870 Act and the advent of braille to this country. In the 1880s and 1890s special schools or classes for the deaf, and for backward children, were established, and for children with other serious physical handicaps in 1900, but not without a battle with Whitehall for grants. In 1875, cookery classes for girls in the elementary schools were begun and in 1890 an itinerant science teacher was appointed. In 1887 an elementary school was built which included a swimming bath.

After 1902 the City Council became responsible, through its Education Committee, for the provision of both elementary and secondary education for the whole Bristol population. It is too early yet to try to describe with a due sense of perspective the policies and achievements of the Bristol Education Committee over the past half-century. But it is a safe guess that, while this present chapter is mainly about the long struggle to get academically able children to the university regardless of parental income, the corresponding chapter written for a British Association Meeting in Bristol about fifty years hence will almost certainly have a great deal to say about the mid-twentieth century efforts to do a good educational job among average and less-academically able children. They are the concern of education committees in a way that they never were before the responsibility for the schooling of all was assumed by public bodies. It may be, for instance, that some of the very enterprising work done in some secondary modern schools, especially among girls, will reveal ways in which this type of education may win a respect from the public comparable with that which is now given to grammar schools. Perhaps the use of libraries in secondary modern schools may open up possibilities at present only hoped for. Infant school methods that are at present a matter of controversy may lead to developments of great importance for other age groups. The use of unorthodox climbing gear may give to town-children the important sense of experimental physical achievement that is a normal part of growing-up in the lives of country children and of those with big trees in their own gardens. The visitor to Bristol schools finds no dull uniformity. Plenty of schools have plenty of ideas, not least the schools which, in whole or in part, concern themselves with educationally sub-normal children.

But while it is still too early to do more than hint at some aspects of the educational work that is going on in the Authority's schools, it is possible to report on the way in which Bristol has responded to the post-war demand. There are now 17,000 more children in the city's schools than there were in 1946, even though 22 schools with 8,000 places were lost by bombing. The Committee has put its main effort into new buildings in preference to patching-up old ones. So far, it has managed to build about 40 new schools with over 13,000 places; another dozen are under construction and 9 more are at the planning stage. Fortunately, Bristol attracts teachers, so that in spite of the accommodation troubles and the increase of children by over one-third since 1945, it has been possible to diminish the average size of class. With 1954, the pressure of sheer numbers begins to lift in the infant schools, and there is real hope of fundamental improvement in the conditions in which the younger children are educated.

Now the crisis of numbers moves into the secondary group. By 1959, there will be

8,000 more children in Bristol secondary schools than there were in 1953—an increase of 40 per cent. The 8,000 children in the age group will include all ranges o ability and aptitude and the development policy of the Education Committee has latterly been in the comprehensive direction. The new secondary schools are all being opened on a bi-lateral basis (grammar/modern). Two, at Hengrove and Lockleaze, were opened in 1954, and four more will open in 1955.

The problem of how best to provide grammar school education in Bristol will remain a singularly difficult one. Since 1902, the authority has developed its own schools for able children by raising the academic level of St. George, Merrywood, Fairfield and Rose Green and by assuming responsibility for Cotham Grammar School from the Merchant Venturers, and most recently and in a more limited way, for Colston's Girls. But in a city where the names and traditions of particular schools mean much in terms of status, it will be some years yet before there is complete understanding and agreement on how Bristol's grammar school places can best be used, having regard to the abilities of children, the aspirations and means of parents and the development plans of local-authority and independent governors. The existence in the city of a large number of direct-grant and independent schools is a commentary on the educational enterprise of Bristol hitherto. Status and selection, equality of opportunity and the value of fine tradition, willingness and ability to pay, legitimate longing but inability to pay—these are some of the matters with which parents, teachers, governors, committees and educational administrators must wrestle in the years to come.

ACKNOWLEDGEMENTS

I should like to thank all those in the schools and educational administration of Bristol who have supplied me with notes for this chapter, as well as to acknowledge my debt to the published and unpublished accounts of some of the schools.

PLATE XXXIV. *Victorian cricket match; Clifton High School.*

PLATE XXXV. *Physical education in a city nursery school in the* 1950s.

CHAPTER TWENTY-THREE

A UNIVERSITY IN BRISTOL

THERE are still traces at Westbury-on-Trym and at the Cathedral School of the two medieval colleges at Bristol; indeed it was Matthew of Bristol who was appointed to instruct the young Edward III in 'letters and all noble conduct'. In Chapter 22 it has been shown that the early traditions of learning never died out. But the immediate origins of the University owe a more particular debt to science. In 1797 Dr. Beddoes lectured in chemistry at the Red Lodge, Park Row, and worked in his Pneumatic Institution in Dowry Square, where his assistant Humphry Davy made his researches into the properties of 'laughing gas', emerging, it is said, to take moonlight walks in the more sublime parts of Clifton Down and along the banks of the Avon, composing poetry while breathing from his 'excellent air bag'.

Medical opinion did not entirely support the Beddoes system of curing consumption by the inhalation of the breath of cows brought into the bedroom for the purpose, but Bristol acquired a considerable reputation as a health resort to which invalids came in large numbers (see Chapter 8, pp. 138–41). In 1828 a few distinguished men set up the Bristol Medical School to provide formal courses and a wider culture for the numerous students already engaged in practical training. Bob Sawyer and Ben Allen, for example, portrayed as practising in Bristol at about that time, were already in need of such courses, and it is perhaps regrettable that Mr. Pickwick did not persuade them to join.

Though hopes had been expressed in 1840 that Bristol might become the seat of a 'Medical University', a project of wider appeal was clearly necessary as a basis upon which to build a University. The first practical step in this direction, the foundation of a university college, was taken at a meeting in the Victoria Rooms in 1874. Perhaps the most interesting feature of this meeting was the new attitude to the education of women, then a highly controversial question. Owens College, Manchester, the pioneer of the civic university movement and the model on which later universities were based, imposed a complete bar on the admission of women until 1883 and others followed their lead. But here, in 1874, Prebendary Percival saw in the College an opportunity to continue work that he had already helped to initiate in Clifton for the higher education of women and to admit them to classes in arts and science—though not yet in medicine—on an equal footing with men.

Percival was strongly supported by Benjamin Jowett, Master of Balliol. Jowett was impressed by 'several elements of a university already existing in Bristol' and by 'the great advantages of a college being placed in so ancient and interesting a

PLATE XXXVI. *A study window.*

city as Bristol.' He brought with him offers from two Oxford colleges, his own and New College, of annual grants of £300 each for five years, conditional on the admission of women to the College. The principle was accepted and Jowett remained a Governor for the remainder of his life.

It was the President of the British Association, Professor A. W. Williamson, who moved the main resolution 'that it is desirable to establish in Bristol a university college which shall provide . . . advanced teaching in the sciences applicable to the industries of the district, and in such other subjects as form the staple of a university education.' Williamson may well be pardoned for expressing a doubt whether the target—a capital sum of £25,000 and an annual income of £5,000 for three years—was really adequate for the purpose. But the promoters were encouraged by offers from the Worshipful Company of Clothmakers and other donors and made a start even before they had reached their target.

The start in 1876 was modest indeed, in a Georgian house in Park Row rented at £50 per annum, with a Professor of Chemistry and one of English and History and four lecturers who included Silvanus Thompson, promoted in the following year to a Chair in Physics and Electrotechnics. Four years later the first permanent building was erected at a cost of £5,100 on the brow of the hill above Park Row in a region of green fields which had not yet fallen into the hands of builders. But considering the precarious financial foothold of the College, the accretion of potential winners to its staff within its first decade was quite remarkable. First there was the well-known political economist Alfred Marshall and his wife, herself trained in this field. Mrs. Marshall in her reminiscences records that when her husband was invited in 1877 to the post of Professor and Principal of University College, the prospect of an atmosphere of sex equality in education that Bristol offered played no small part in his decision to accept it. Another, Hele Shaw, first joined the staff when the Professor of Mathematics was permitted to engage one of his students as an assistant, upon the understanding that the College 'is put to no expense in the appointment'. Three years later Hele Shaw became the first Professor of Engineering as a separate subject in Bristol.

Geology in 1878 was placed in the hands of W. J. Sollas, a celebrated figure in that subject in his day. In 1880 William Ramsay arrived and was joined two years later by Sidney Young, to found so famous a partnership in physical chemistry that it is difficult to realize that their association as colleagues lasted only five years. Finally, in 1884, came Lloyd Morgan, a biologist in his classical work on animal behaviour, but also a psychologist and philosopher. After an initial appointment in geology and zoology he became Principal, to pilot the College for over twenty years through to university status, and then to return to the life of teaching and research as a member of Senate. On his bicycle, with his long beard at the mercy of the wind, he was a familiar figure in the streets of Bristol, and not without his own propaganda value in that respect.

In the meantime, a scheme of association with the Medical School was already in operation, and so it may be said that the future faculties of arts, science, medicine and engineering were already in embryo; indeed, if occasional classes for articled pupils in law may be included, the remaining faculty of the University of to-day was also represented.

It is interesting to note that the training of teachers was not one of the specific objects which the founders of the College in 1874 had in mind. National education was then far less widespread than it is to-day and the supply of teachers was generally derived from other channels. But within a few years special classes to this end were started, leading later to an intermediate stage of affiliated training colleges. Now there is a University Department of Education as the central member of a regional Institute of Education with which the various training colleges are associated.

The early records of the College show evidence of the use made of local conditions by the academic staff in furtherance of teaching or of investigations in their special subjects. William Ramsay, by his lectures in chemistry in the clothmaking towns of Stroud, Trowbridge and Frome, provided an early example of extra-mural education for which the University now has such large responsibilities in Bristol and over the whole of Gloucestershire, Somerset, Wiltshire, and half of Dorset. Lloyd Morgan and others, then and since, found on their arrival in Bristol a group of enthusiastic amateurs, members of the Bristol Naturalists' Society, whom they actively fostered and supported in much valuable observational work on the geology and natural history of the district. The Society still meets in the University and publishes its own *Proceedings*. The surrounding country, so accessible and varied, encouraged from the earliest days studies in the field as part of routine teaching in geology and biology. Indeed Professor Leipner, the first occupant of the Chair of Botany, obtained the permission of the owner of fields surrounding University College to conduct field classes therein. With the aid of a small grant and donations of plants from friends, he started a small botanical garden in waste land near his laboratory. The whole garden, appreciably extended to-day, is now named after Hiatt Baker who did so much for it and for all the garden properties of the University.

Yet by the middle 1880s the University College was struggling in troubled waters. The initial wave of enthusiasm had lost much of its momentum and the effects of shortage of both capital and income were becoming apparent. It was also discouraging to lose the interest of the Society of Merchant Venturers when that body of influential citizens decided to promote technical education as a basis for entry into industry.

In seeking a cause for this early divergence in interest between the Society and University College, it must be remembered that, in the past, public service has often been associated with a political background. Thus the Victoria Rooms was built originally as a meeting centre for the Conservative Party, whereas the Colston Hall, in an earlier form, was the home of the Liberals. Again, the main teaching hospital of the University arose from a late amalgamation of two older voluntary hospitals, the Royal Infirmary and the General Hospital. At the time when the former received its Royal Charter, a wag is reported to have said that 'in search of a sovereign remedy you should go to the Infirmary, whereas the Hospital provides a radical cure'.

Possibly, therefore, the fact that some of the staunchest supporters of the early University College movement were ardent Liberals, may have led the Society to refrain from identifying itself closely with the project, and induced it to strike out on a different line of educational experiment.

It was clear, therefore, that though the Society at the outset had made a contribution of £1,000 to the capital fund of the College, no more could be looked for from that source. And when in 1893 the 'Merchant Venturers Technical College', which by then had arisen, offered courses in science and engineering for the degrees and diplomas of the University of London, a somewhat bitter rivalry developed. Wiser counsels were to prevail in the end and all differences were healed in united action when a joint appeal was made in 1908 to the Privy Council for a university charter. But in the middle 1880s, from whatever cause, student numbers and fee income in University College actually began to fall; cuts in salary were necessary and at one stage payments at the end of the term were only possible by the Chairman of the Governors, Albert Fry, acting as personal guarantor of its overdraft at the bank. There were also signs of strained nerves on the staff in a request by the Principal for an additional room 'because the arrangement whereby the Professors of Physics and Engineering both occupied the same lecture room necessitated great forebearance on both sides'. Within its walls the nickname 'Adversity College' was coined, and the teaching staff noted with approval the omission of two letters by a compositor in a local paper when he described them as 'aching'.

That the College survived this financial crisis, and minor ones to follow, was due to the loyal support of a small group of men led by Albert and Lewis Fry, who between them occupied the chair of the Council of the College and later that of the University for thirty-four years. Indeed, the family of Fry has an unbroken record of active service on the Council from 1876 to the present day.

With the immediate crisis past, a satisfying recognition of the quality of the academic work came with the grant (the first of its kind) of £1,200 per annum from Her Majesty's Treasury in 1889. In subsequent years capital grants from the City and from various benefactors followed, until in 1899 the College accounts balanced for the first time in its history.

From the end of the century, there are still some living who, like the writer, can speak with memories of the College as it then was; of Sidney Young in chemistry whose researches would never have been possible but for his skill in scientific glassblowing, unsurpassed anywhere in his day; of Chattock in physics, ingenious and original in experimental investigation, and a source of inspiration to all his students; of Reynolds busy in field work with hammer and camera, and willing to take anyone to the Avon Gorge as an introduction to geology; of Fawcett, Professor of Anatomy for forty-one years and Dean of Medicine for twenty-eight, building large wax models of specimens from the appearance of sections under the microscope, or studying the architectural features of the churches of Bristol and Somerset in anatomical detail, and with a memory not only of every medical student but also of anyone who missed a catch off his bowling; of George Hare Leonard, the physical embodiment of sweetness and light, speaking of our heritage of literature, history and art to all and sundry in lectures and discussion classes throughout the city.

Research work at that time was carried out under conditions very different from those of to-day. In the field of experimental science members of staff received little of that support in apparatus, young collaborators and technical assistance that is now available to them from a variety of sources. Not only had they to finance much of their work from their own purses but they often had to acquire personal skill in more than one recognized craft in order to construct their apparatus. But enthusiasm is a great spur to action. One woman scientist then living in Cheltenham has recorded how in all weathers she cycled the forty-four miles to Bristol every Friday afternoon and back again on Monday, in order to use the chemical laboratory during the week-end. Incidentally she recalls that she was then the fastest and often for miles the only traveller on the road; annoyed when the first motor-car appeared upon it to pass her on the level, but with self-esteem restored when she overtook it going up the next hill.

The last year of the century also marks a chapter in the history of the College in that a step was taken which within a few years was to raise the hopes of all College supporters. As has been mentioned in another Chapter, there had been societies in Bristol for more than a century bearing the name of a seventeenth-century merchant venturer and philanthropist, Edward Colston; and once a year their members meet to dine and subscribe money to charity. In the spring following the 1898 meeting of the British Association in Bristol, at which the application of science to the solution of national problems received much attention, a Bristol printer, James W. Arrowsmith, took a leading part in founding the University College Colston Society, which his nephew and great-nephew have since guided. It is believed that this Society, now the Colston Research Society, has no parallel in university history. It has supported special investigations in various departments and faculties and in recent years has acted as host to an annual symposium, international in character, in some field of current interest; the proceedings of these symposia are also published under its auspices. In its first ten years the Society not only brought money and new friends to the College, but through a succession of guest speakers, it helped to convert the pipe-dream of a future university in Bristol into a live issue. A stimulus to local action was provided by an impressive speech to the Society in 1902 by R. B. Haldane, a champion of the civic university movement who later as Lord Haldane was Chancellor of Bristol University from 1912 until his death in 1928. A few years afterwards Morris Travers, the discoverer with Ramsay of neon and other rare gases, drew up a scheme of requirements for a university in Bristol; public interest grew, donations increased, additional land was purchased and the support of the Merchant Venturers was secured. It was therefore fitting that the munificent gift of £100,000 by Henry Overton Wills—the final act leading to a University charter—should have been announced at the Colston dinner in 1908 by his son George, the President for the year.

Under the terms of the Charter, an agreement with the Society of Merchant

Venturers was reached whereby the Faculty of Engineering was housed in the Technical College and supported from the educational trust funds of the Society. For this historical reason the Engineering Faculty, from 1909 until recent months, has been separated geographically from the other faculties of the University.

After the close of the last war the increased demands of technical education in the city and of the Faculty itself, and the change in the value of money, all combined to bring this arrangement to an end. The City Council has taken over the whole responsibility for general technical education and the Faculty has now moved into the magnificent new building which is approaching completion on a site close to other laboratories of the University. But the pioneering work of the Merchant Venturers Society through these past years in support of the Faculty will remain memorable in the history of the University.

All these associations in the creation of the University are commemorated in its arms 'Argent on a cross quadrate gules the arms of the City of Bristol between in pale a sun in splendour (for Wills) . . . and in fesse to the dexter a dolphin embowed (for Colston), and to the sinister a horse courant (for Fry), both of the third.'

The University opened for its first session in October, 1909, with responsibilities greatly increased by elevation in status. In its first few years, largely through inexperience, the new machinery did not work too smoothly and some unwise actions aroused public criticism. Even when the sons of the founder, George and Henry Herbert (Harry) Wills, showed their faith in the new institution by providing for the erection of new central buildings a sum which ultimately topped half a million pounds, there were still a few who remarked that 'bricks and mortar do not make a university'. Such comment, however, showed little knowledge of the meagreness of the university resources at the time, and still less of the working of the academic mind. An able scholar, though not unmindful of salary considerations, is not likely to be tempted to accept a post in an institution which does not provide facilities necessary to his researches. It may therefore be useful as well as agreeable to record some of the main gifts of members of the Family of Wills in order to emphasize how much they have contributed to the primary needs of the University.

The original £100,000 gift of H. O. Wills at the Colston dinner was used mainly to endow certain existing chairs. With the exception of new laboratories for chemistry and physiology—models of their kind at that time—few of the buildings then existing had been originally constructed for the purpose for which they were used; there were, for instance, no permanent quarters even for the meagre library that the University inherited from the College. Many of the lecture rooms were already overcrowded, and there was also negligible provision of private rooms for the staff and for tutorial work. Administration and the Faculty of Arts were housed in rooms urgently needed for the expansion of the scientific teaching and research laboratories. An adequate assembly hall was also a necessity to any university worthy of the name.

The building which the two brothers provided to the design of Sir George Oatley, with an endowment fund for its maintenance and extension, not only fully met the needs of that day, but was of great dignity and constructed to stand the test of centuries; and in the tradition of the ancient guilds it was wrought and carved in its detail by craftsmen selected from all over the country and given an opportunity for individual skill and initiative seldom granted in modern days. One of these men engaged on hand-carving and fixing the linenfold oak panelling in the Great Hall was asked how long he expected his work to last. He replied that he was doing it to last for ever. Alas! less than a quarter of a century later, all his work and that of his colleagues, including the beautiful hammerbeam roof, was destroyed by incendiary bombs. So far it has only been possible to restore the Great Hall to use by a temporary ceiling and brick wall supports. The Library, at the time thought to be adequate for many years, has since been extended by an additional wing but its accommodation for readers is already again overcrowded.

With the inauguration of the University, George Wills also provided an important requisite of student life, an athletic ground and pavilion; the pavilion was subsequently burnt down by suffragettes, but rebuilt on an improved plan. Similarly, after the First World War, he again came to their aid by purchasing the Victoria Rooms, which were adapted as a Students' Union and Club.

Another gift, having very important consequences, was received during the First World War when Harry Wills purchased the Royal Fort estate, adjoining other University property but on the crown of the hill. Without damage to its eighteenth-century mansion and Humphrey Repton's landscape garden, this property has since provided sites for the new Engineering Building, the Hiatt Baker Botanical Garden, the Departments of Music and Education, and additional laboratories for physiology and pharmacology. At the same time Harry Wills gave £200,000 to erect on the same site the physics laboratory which bears his name and with which many distinguished physicists have since been associated; while some years later, in 1930, his brother Melville endowed a second chair of physics for £25,000 to comply with the terms of an offer of £50,000 from the Rockefeller Foundation for the establishment of a research fund in that subject.

The provision of more halls of residence became the next objective. After the First World War Harry Wills bought about twenty-five acres of land flanking Durdham Downs upon which his brother, George, built Wills Hall, as the first of several residential halls for men students. Some fifty-five acres adjoining, including four houses used as annexes, have since been acquired, providing land to house in residence at least 1,300 students, when the necessary halls are available.

On his death in 1922 Harry Wills bequeathed to the University a large capital sum for future building and endowment. This donation and the interest accruing from it has enabled progress to be made in a number of other directions. Firstly it defrayed the cost of Manor Hall, a second hall of residence for women students opened in 1932 to supplement Clifton Hill House which had already been in use since 1909. The high ground overlooking the city from the north, on which both these halls are sited, was chosen as suitable to plan a group of women's residences in Clifton similar to those for men near Durdham Down. Secondly from the same benefaction a fully equipped Dental Hospital has been built adjoining the Royal Infirmary. Lastly just before the outbreak of war the Departments of Botany and Zoology, previously confined to some of the earliest buildings of University College days, were extended and modernized by the addition of a new wing.

Such references do not complete the list of generous donors in the Wills family, one of whom, the present Lord Dulverton, recently created a fund for the restoration of the organ in the Great Hall and for the purchase of oak timber ultimately to be used in the restoration of the Hall itself.

But munificence from one family must not be allowed to mask generous contributions from other donors, even though in this brief survey only passing reference can be made to some of them by the posts or objects with which their names are specially associated. The Stanley Badock Chair of Music, the Leverhulme Chair of Physical Chemistry, the George White Chair of Aeronautical Engineering, the Exley, Worsley, and Wiglesworth Libraries, the Hiatt Baker Botanical Garden; and from the coming session a Chair in Accounting, within the framework of the Department of Economics, from the joint gifts of the Imperial Tobacco Company, the Bristol Aeroplane Company and Messrs. Arthur Guinness, Son and Co.

The existence of the Fry Home Students Society and of the annual Lewis Fry Memorial lectures is a constant reminder of the inestimable services, to which reference has already been made, of members of the Fry family from the days of University College until the present time. There are also some named open entrance scholarships and post-graduate fellowships. Among the latter, reference may be made to the gratifying support given to research in the Zoological and Botanical Departments by the Council of the Clifton Zoological Society which controls the local Zoological Gardens.

Lastly, by gifts great and small, many friends of the University in Bristol and the surrounding counties have recently responded generously to an appeal issued in 1946 in honour of the Chancellor of the University, Sir Winston Churchill. This fund now approaches the £300,000 mark, and with its help the University has started upon the foundations of the first instalment of a 'Churchill Hall' of residence for men; it is intended to follow it later with one for women students. By these means another step will have been taken towards the ideal of a fully residential University, so strongly advocated between the wars by the Chairman of Council, Sir Stanley Badock, and the Vice-Chancellor of that period, Dr. Thomas Loveday, with the support of Council and Senate.

Although the University is essentially an institution of national scope and importance, it has always kept in mind the part that it can play in the life of the city and in support of the special interests of the counties around it.

In some respects the most interesting of these is the Long Ashton Agricultural and Horticultural Research Station. Fifty-two years ago a National Fruit and Cider Institute was established at Long Ashton on the outskirts of Bristol, as an experimental station particularly concerned in the scientific problems of the cider industry.

Some years later under Government auspices the Long Ashton Agricultural and Horticultural Research Station was formed, in which the Cider Institute was absorbed as part of an organization of much wider scope of enquiry, though still with the problems of fruit culture and the practical control of diseases and pests as its special interest. The University accepted the invitation of the Board of Agriculture of that day to make itself responsible for its administration, though not without a mild protest from one lay member of Council who asked 'whether the University was proposing to open a jug-and-bottle department'. The station has now a world-wide reputation.

Another major development was of much later origin. Shortly after the war the Ministry of Agriculture and Fisheries accepted the conclusions of a special committee that, in the interests of livestock problems in Britain, the quality and status of veterinary education in the country should be raised by improved facilities for teaching and research. The University accepted the Ministry's offer of financial support for the establishment of a degree curriculum in veterinary science, involving the erection of pre-clinical laboratories in anatomy and physiology adjoining similar laboratories in medicine; and of clinical laboratories associated with an experimental farm elsewhere for the later stages of the course. To-day in the pre-clinical departments in Park Row, and the clinical laboratories and farm attached to Langford House in Somerset, the University possesses, in staff and facilities for teaching and research, a veterinary centre which is accepted as second to none in the Commonwealth. The first batch of students to complete the five-year course required for the degree of B.V.Sc. passed out as members of the profession, with the right to practise, last autumn.

In medicine, in origin the oldest faculty in this University, it is naturally the individual animal as a human being and not as one of the herd upon which attention is focused. In passing, it may be noted that the introduction of a State medical service has greatly extended the influence of the only 'teaching hospital' in the western region, reaching from Swindon to Barnstaple, and from Tewkesbury to Land's End. In the great developments in post-graduate training throughout the region which have accompanied the Health Act, members of the Faculty of Medicine have played a very important part.

To complete the picture, reference must be made to other interests which have arisen naturally in a city rich in tradition and in valuable archives of the commerce and municipal life of earlier centuries. Thus *The Great Red Book*, rich in details of legal procedure in the medieval courts of Bristol, has been a subject of research in the Faculty of Law. Members of the University also play their part in the Records Society. Again, as Gateway to the Empire with a tradition for overseas trade since the days of Elizabeth I, Bristol is a natural home of a Chair in Imperial History, a centre of activity in the field of Dominion and colonial studies, and the maintenance of special links with the Commonwealth.

Finally, in this review of projects which, though of national importance, have also a natural local setting, it may be pardonable to include one more. Reference has already been made to the Theatre Royal (Chapter 15, p. 239) but here it is appropriate to mention that in 1949 Bristol was the first university in the country to raise drama to the status of a subject which may be selected in a degree curriculum. The function of the Department of Drama is in no sense to give a professional qualification for a career in the theatre; it figures as having a part in a liberal Arts education, in which the study of dramatic literature and the art of the theatre are conducted in close association with literature in a wider sense. In an age in which both sound radio and television are being increasingly used for the presentation of drama this experiment—as to a certain extent it still is—has aroused the interest of the Rockefeller Foundation, which has presented grants to the department for a research fellowship and for the equipment of a studio theatre.

Some of the salient points in the growth of the University and its earlier College since 1876 may be brought out by reference to a graph of student population throughout these seventy-nine years. The numbers given are for full-time students, that is to say, undergraduates and graduates pursuing full-time studies for first degrees, higher degrees and diplomas. In the early years of University College, curricula were less formalized than they were later, and the figures given for, say, the first ten years, may be a little too high for that reason.

After a fairly promising start with nearly 170 students in the first session the curve shows a dip, even on this scale, for the doldrums of the middle 1880s and a halt and a temporary regression again in the 1890s. But the first decade of the century is characterized by the steady rise in numbers accompanying new hope of approaching university status. The point O marks the opening of the first University session. The graph continues with approximately the same slope until the outbreak of the First World War; the drop in population during the war and the post-war bulge afterwards are both clearly shown. It is interesting to note that, after the post-war bulge, the graph has an upward slope of about the same value as before the war. From the dotted line connecting the two portions, it might be postulated that the war was a cataclysm which had no permanent influence on the growth of the University. But the effects of a world war can hardly be so lightly dismissed; indeed, the corresponding period associated with the Second World War shows features of growth which are entirely different.

In the late 1930s the University seemed to be settling down around the 1,000 student mark. This was due partly to the natural action of supply and demand for University-trained men and women, and partly to deliberate policy. A thousand was a number relatively easy to handle administratively, and, in course of time, to accommodate entirely in halls of residence. It was also of a size which favoured an intimate mixture of the Faculties and that friendly atmosphere within the University that is a valuable asset of traditional College life. But national needs brought entirely new factors into play after the late war and created a situation from which there is no retreat, even if it were desirable. Owing to the reservation of students in science, medicine and engineering for specialized training, a drop in numbers during the

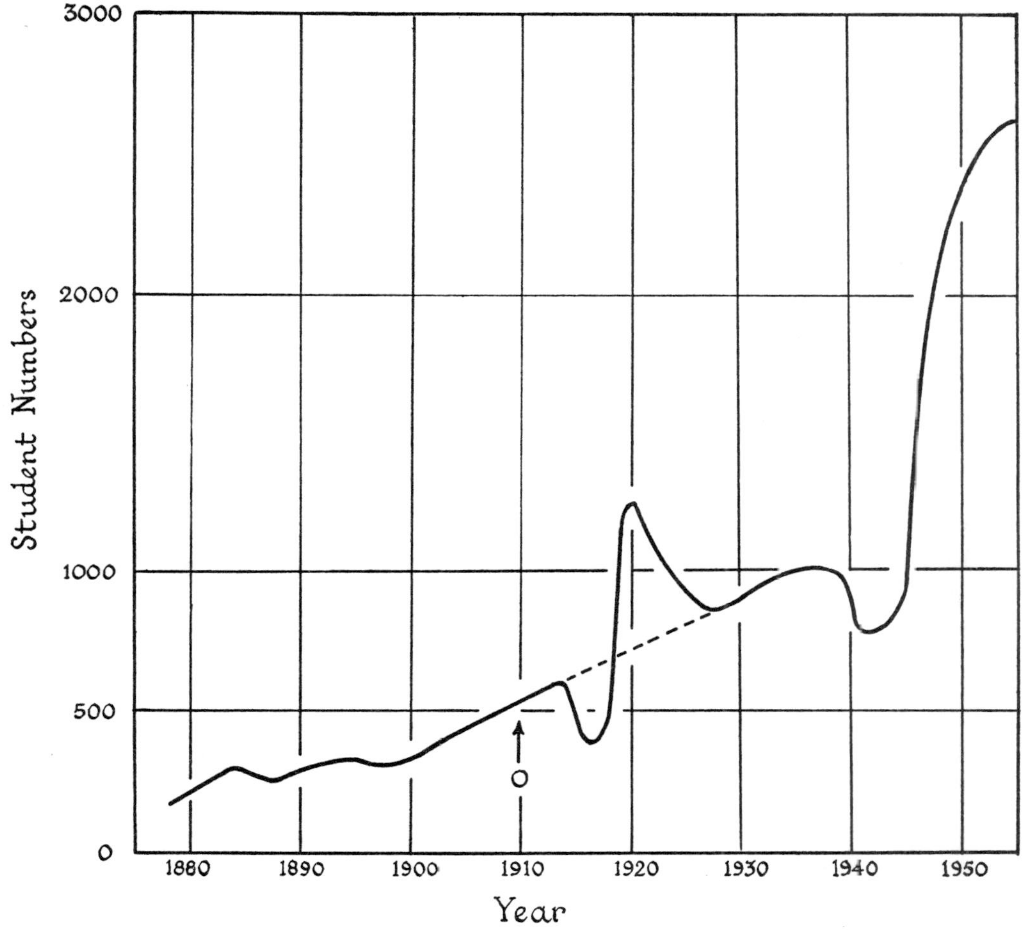

FIG. 24. *Growth of student population.*

war occurred only in arts and law. True, there were problems of accommodation resulting from the evacuation to Bristol of the greater part of King's College, London, for four years, but these were solved by methods of mutual co-operation. But after the war the rise in numbers which occurred has taxed all the resources of the University. To increase the number of students in halls, if not yet to maintain the same percentage, two smaller halls of residence were established and a number of houses purchased as annexes to existing halls. Also semi-permanent laboratories were erected to supplement existing accommodation in chemistry, biology and physiology, extensions to the Departments of Medicine and Surgery were similarly provided at the Royal Infirmary, while the purchase and adaptation of several properties in the neighbourhood of the main building has brought welcome additions to arts and administration. Finally, the transfer of the Faculty of Engineering to the imposing pile arising below the Royal Fort must rank as a major event in the history of the University.

But the policy of restricting numbers still remains though at a much higher level and for different reasons. From the graph it would appear that the post-war rise is now sensibly over. Though this may be a sympton of approaching saturation of national demands, applications for entry in many subjects still far exceed the number of places available, and a satisfactory balance is secured only by the determination of Senate to see that crowded lecture rooms and laboratories do not react upon the standards of instruction. At the same time stability in numbers provides a period in which the University can consolidate its position and prepare the way for future developments in which it may expect to be called upon to play its part.

To meet this large post-war increase in numbers of students and in the size of the staff additional amenities for social and bodily comfort were provided by the purchase of the blitzed City Museum building. Erected now within its old walls is a refectory in which 1,100 lunches have been served in one day. Above it a Senior Common Room with Dining Hall for the academic staff, which lay members of Council are also eligible to join, has done much to preserve those happy and cordial relations between members which have now existed for so many years, and which help to secure for Bristol University a reputation for life and study under the best conditions.

Finally, in reviewing the work of the early founders with their vision, however misty, of a future University in mind, it would seem that in one important respect they built better than they knew. Living, as most of them did, in country and residential areas on the high ground north of the industrial city, and seeking a site for the College, they would naturally have looked for some open space on that side of the city. Schools already existed there which might provide fee-paying students, and in days of limited transport this was an important consideration. And so it is that the University buildings of to-day stand on the old Windmill Hill from which in the Civil War the City was once defended. From several vantage points among them, the city may be seen stretched out beneath and beyond, and far less likely to be obscured by industrial smoke than many cities of its size. A turret of the tower of the Wills Physical Laboratory is the highest standing-point in Bristol, and affords an uninterrupted view of the city and country in all directions to the Cotswolds and Severn on the one hand, to Bath and Mendip on the other.

Moreover, throughout its life, lovers of natural and architectural beauty, both lay and academic, have seen to it that in the growth of the University in an industrial era, every effort was made to preserve and provide a setting for it worthy of a city of such traditions: the mansion and grounds of the Royal Fort; the eighteenth-century residence of Addington Symonds at Clifton Hill House; Wills Hall with its delightful quadrangle and its annexes set in sixty acres of wood, field and garden; and of these the garden of The Holmes in particular. Even the laboratories, the factories of the

University, are architecturally satisfying. Lastly when the freshman seeks enrolment in the University, his first impression of it may be the Tower with its ten-ton bell, Great George, sounding deep E flat. Under it he passes into the high vaulted entrance hall, up the stately staircase to the Reception Room. He can see for himself that he is to become a 'citizen of no mean city'.

The period covered in this chapter has seen the development from a somewhat rudimentary and skilfully improvised University College to a well-equipped, mature University. Through all the chances and vicissitudes there has always been a friend in need and a suitable person to solve the really difficult problems as they arose. The counties of Gloucestershire, Somerset and Wiltshire, and the cities of Bath and Gloucester as well as the City and County of Bristol itself have risen to its support by annual grants, and successive generations of men and women have taken advantage of the kindly environment which Bristol provides and have seen to it that the epithet 'Redbrick', coined some years ago by a somewhat harsh and unfriendly critic of civic universities, is singularly inappropriate when applied to Bristol. The University as it now is approaches its jubilee, internationally accepted, national in scope and character, but attractively regional in sentiment. During the years growing-points have been encouraged and developed in many directions and it now finds within its five faculties, room for the majority of the subjects which are accepted as being of concern and importance to a university. The confident hopes for the future to which its present condition gives rise are due to work well done in the past by many people who, being different in their gifts, were united by the conviction that a real university could arise in the City of Bristol. But the challenge of the present makes complacency impossible and the future of the University depends upon the continued existence of the same resourcefulness and determination in their successors serving it to-day.

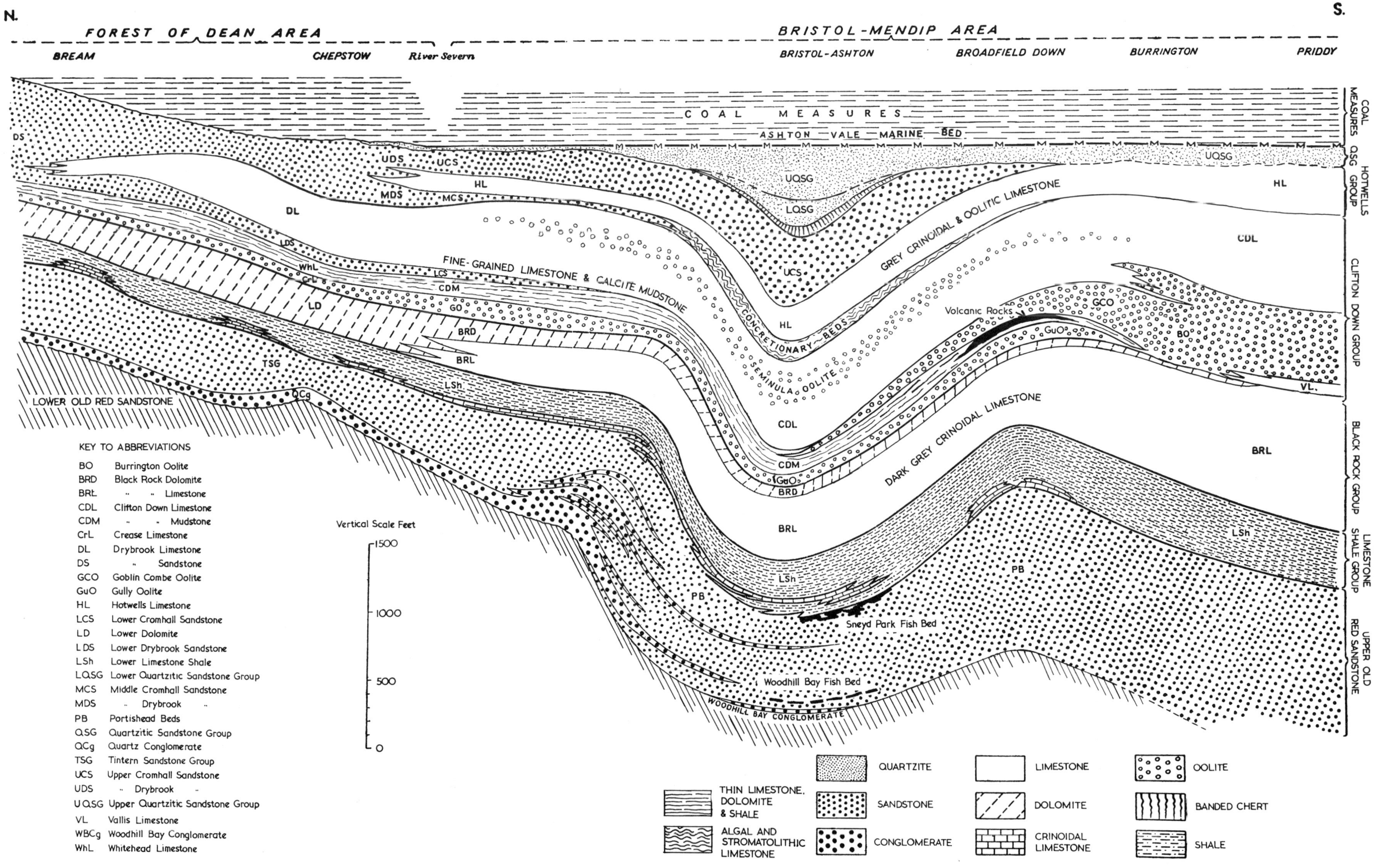
N.
S.
FOREST OF DEAN AREA
BRISTOL-MENDIP AREA
BREAM
CHEPSTOW
River Severn
BRISTOL-ASHTON
BROADFIELD DOWN
BURRINGTON
PRIDDY
COAL MEASURES
ASHTON VALE MARINE BED
DS
UDS
UCS
MDS
MCS
HL
DL
UQSG
LQSG
GREY CRINOIDAL & OOLITIC LIMESTONE
CDL
LDS
WhL
CrL
LCS
CDM
GO
FINE-GRAINED LIMESTONE & CALCITE MUDSTONE
CONCRETIONARY BEDS
SEMINULA OOLITE
Volcanic Rocks
GCO
BO
GuO
VL.
LD
BRD
BRL
TSG
LSh
LOWER OLD RED SANDSTONE
QCg
DARK GREY CRINOIDAL LIMESTONE
PB
Sneyd Park Fish Bed
Woodhill Bay Fish Bed
WOODHILL BAY CONGLOMERATE
COAL MEASURES
QSG
HOTWELLS GROUP
CLIFTON DOWN GROUP
BLACK ROCK GROUP
LOWER LIMESTONE SHALE GROUP
UPPER OLD RED SANDSTONE
KEY TO ABBREVIATIONS
BO Burrington Oolite
BRD Black Rock Dolomite
BRL " " Limestone
CDL Clifton Down Limestone
CDM " " Mudstone
CrL Crease Limestone
DL Drybrook Limestone
DS " Sandstone
GCO Goblin Combe Oolite
GuO Gully Oolite
HL Hotwells Limestone
LCS Lower Cromhall Sandstone
LD Lower Dolomite
LDS Lower Drybrook Sandstone
LSh Lower Limestone Shale
LQSG Lower Quartzitic Sandstone Group
MCS Middle Cromhall Sandstone
MDS " Drybrook "
PB Portishead Beds
QSG Quartzitic Sandstone Group
QCg Quartz Conglomerate
TSG Tintern Sandstone Group
UCS Upper Cromhall Sandstone
UDS " Drybrook "
UQSG Upper Quartzitic Sandstone Group
VL Vallis Limestone
WBCg Woodhill Bay Conglomerate
WhL Whitehead Limestone
Vertical Scale Feet
1500
1000
500
0
THIN LIMESTONE, DOLOMITE & SHALE
ALGAL AND STROMATOLITHIC LIMESTONE
QUARTZITE
SANDSTONE
CONGLOMERATE
LIMESTONE
DOLOMITE
CRINOIDAL LIMESTONE
OOLITE
BANDED CHERT
SHALE

APPENDIX

APPENDIX

CHAPTER 4

NOTES

p. 70, line 7. There is little or no evidence of rendzinas under woodlands on plateaux sites on the Jurassic limestones; they occur, however, on steep wooded limestone screes.

p. 71, line 25. The Evesham series now includes similar soils developed on all Jurassic clays.

p. 72, line 7. Little use has since been made of the Honeybourne series, these slightly gleyed brown earths where of loamy texture are referred to the Isle Abbotts series or the Podimore series, if of clayey texture. Gley soils of loamy texture are the Holwell series and if of clayey texture are called Rowsham series.

p. 72, para. 2. For a fuller account of the soils of Exmoor Forest see 'Soils of Exmoor Forest' by L. F. Curtis.

BIBLIOGRAPHY

1. *The soils of the West Midlands* (with map at 10 m. to 1 in.). D. Mackney and C. P. Burnham. General information with useful chapters on soil formation, description and classification; includes several relevant soil series.
2. *Publications on Soil Survey.* Titles of publications, including soil maps, by the Soil Survey and of contributions to journals etc. by members of the staff describing their work.
3. *Soil Survey Reports*, 1950—. Annual reports from each region on many aspects of the soils in the areas being surveyed together with reports on researches made during the previous year.
4. *Land Use Capability Classification.* J. S. Bibby and D. Mackney. Application of soil maps and reports to the classification of land for various purposes.
5. *The soils of the Mendip district of Somerset* (with 2 maps). D. C. Findlay. Description of the geology, climate, vegetation and soils of the 500 sq. miles covered by O. S. 3rd Edn. 1 in. sheets 279 (Weston-s-Mare) and 280 (Wells).
6. *The soils of the Glastonbury district of Somerset* (with map). B. W. Avery. Similar description of 216 sq. miles covered by O.S. 3rd Edn. 1 in. sheet 296 (Glastonbury).
7. *Soils of Exmoor Forest* (with map). L. F. Curtis. Describes the soils shown on a composite map (scale 1:25,000) of parts of sheets SS 73, SS 74, SS 83 and SS 84.

8. An account of the soils around Bath and Malmesbury is in preparation; the O.S. 3rd Edn. 1 in. sheets 251 (Malmesbury) and 265 (Bath) will be included. Progress reports of this survey begin in *Soil Survey Report No. 18*.
9. A soil map on O.S. 1:25,000 sheet SO 82 (Norton) is complete and a report on this area north of Gloucester is in hand.
10. Surveying is being continued on O.S. 1:25,000 sheets SP 12 (Stow-on-the-Wold), SU 05/06 (Devizes) and SU 03 (Wilton).

Soils occurring in the three counties also appear elsewhere in England and enquiries about relevant publications and maps should be addressed to The Soil Survey, Rothamsted Experimental Station, Harpenden, Herts.

D. A. OSMOND

CHAPTER 5

No extensive accounts of the local fauna have been added in recent years beyond the sort of contributions indicated on pp. 88–90—notably on birds in the local journal and from the Wildfowl Trust, while the newly formed and active mammal section of the Bristol Naturalists Society reports regularly.

However the modern attitude to the environment has invited attention particularly to estuaries and estuarine regions, and there is a good deal of stir in the Severn area. A few comments have been made for example in the *Marine Pollution Bulletin*, but a good deal more may be hoped for in the immediate future from the Sabrina organisation at Bristol University, from the other Channel Universities and Colleges, from pollution authorities such as the Severn River Board, and from the Natural Environment Research Council through the Institute for Marine Environmental Research.

R. BASSINDALE

CHAPTER 6

p. 93, l. 4 up. The Mediterranean rush *Juncus subulatus* was found, new to Britain, in this salt marsh in 1957 (Willis and Davies, 1960).

p. 94, Table XII. First column: for B.C. 10000, read 8000; for 5500, read 3500. Second column: for Late Boreal–Atlantic, read Atlantic. These changes result from radiocarbon datings (Godwin, 1960a, p. 294; 1960b, p. 1). Top of second column: 'Post-glacial' is better termed 'Holocene'. Foot of Table: fresh investigation of the Romano-British deposits casts doubt on the occurrence of a separate marine transgression at that time (Hawkins, 1973).

p. 95, l. 25. Add: Recent excavations have been concerned with wooden trackways at a much lower level in the peat and belonging to the Neolithic period (Coles *et al.*, 1968, 1970).

p. 95, penultimate para. See amendment note for p. 94, foot of Table XII.

p. 96, l. 25. The text implies poorer growth of *Peucedanum palustre* than is found. The vegetation described here is that of Shapwick Heath, since studied more fully by Hope-Simpson, Newton and Ricketts (1963).

p. 96, l. 3 up. A fen area of special floristic interest has been described by Willis (1967).

p. 96, last line: for 7,000 read 5,000. *p. 97, l. 1:* for 4,000 read 2,000. These approximate time-periods have been altered as a result of radiocarbon dating (Godwin, 1960b, p. 28).

p. 97, l. 3. *Andromeda polifolia* was found in one area in 1970, 50 years after the last record for the peat moors.

p. 97, top para. Add at end: Mechanized peat-extraction has been rapid in recent years and expanses of open water may well be left (Somerset C.C. Planning Department, 1967). A few of the semi-natural areas have been secured as nature reserves.

p. 97, middle para. (Gordano Valley). The ecological factors and plant communities have been studied by Willis and Jefferies (1959). The peat deposit, investigated by Jefferies, Willis and Yemm (1968), partly overlies Late-glacial lake mud and is fen peat throughout; these differences from the history of the Wedmore–Polden peat moors reflect the quite different topographical situation.

p. 100, l. 13. Barkham (1968), studying similar beechwoods beyond (N.E. of) Stroud, considered that most if not all of them may result from planting; hence beech may not be a natural climax.

p. 102, l. 11 (Cephalanthera rubra). Add at end of line: "and, very locally, the Chilterns (found 1955)".

p. 102, l. 18. Delete *Dryopteris spinulosa*, mentioned in error.

p. 102, l. 21. The distribution of the bryophytes of north Somerset is reported fully by Appleyard (1970).

p. 104, l. 5 up. Delete the allusion to Lower Limestone Shale.

p 104, l. 4 up. The 'podsol' of the upland heath described is one type (soil Series) of peaty gleyed podzol (Findlay, 1965).

p. 105, l. 10–6 up (excl. footnote). The rare *Sorbi* of the Avon Gorge have now been thoroughly examined by Mr. P. J. M. Nethercott. The most plentiful is *S. bristoliensis* (endemic to Avon Gorge); also present, in much smaller numbers, are *S. wilmottiana* (endemic), *S. anglica*, *S. eminens* and *S. porrigentiformis*. In addition *S. torminalis* occurs sparsely on limestone and other soils on the Somerset side.

p. 106, l. 17 up. After "*Sorbus bristoliensis*" insert "and *S. wilmottiana*".

p. 106, l. 4 up. The results of a recent floristic survey of Cheddar Gorge are reported by Gravestock (1970). In *l. 3–2 up*, the statement about *Hieracia* should now read as follows: "among them *H. stenolepiforme*, *H. cyathis*, *H. strumosum*, *H. maculatum*, *H. angustisquamum* and *H. schmidtii*. The first of these is endemic to Cheddar".

p. 107, l. 24. Add: A substantial further colony of *Linosyris vulgaris* was found on limestone in north Somerset in 1965.

p. 108, Table XIII. For *Carex humilis*, add + for Crook Peak.

p. 109. After l.4, add a new section as follows:

NATURE CONSERVATION

In the Bristol region as elsewhere, nature conservation has gathered momentum greatly since about 1960. Within the area covered by this chapter, some 23 nature reserves have been established, of diverse size and status. In more than half of them woodland predominates, but they also contain scrub, limestone grassland and rock, old lead workings, heath and peat moor.

NEW REFERENCES

APPLEYARD, J. 1970. A bryophyte Flora of North Somerset. *Trans. Br. bryol. Soc.*, **6**, 1.

BARKHAM, J. P. 1968. *The ecology of the ground flora of some Cotswold beechwoods.* Ph.D. thesis, University of Birmingham.

COLES, J. M. and F. A. HIBBERT. 1968. Prehistoric roads and tracks in Somerset, England: 1. Neolithic. *Proc. prehist. Soc.*, **34**, 238.

COLES, J. M., F. A. HIBBERT and C. F. CLEMENTS. 1970. Prehistoric roads and tracks in Somerset, England: 2. Neolithic. *Proc. prehist. Soc.*, **36**, 125.

FINDLAY, D. C. 1965. *The Soils of the Mendip District of Somerset.* Mem. Soil Surv. Gt Br. Harpenden.

GODWIN, H. 1960a. The Croonian Lecture: Radiocarbon dating and Quaternary history in Britain. *proc. Roy. Soc.*, B, **153**, 287.

GODWIN, H. 1960b. Prehistoric wooden trackways of the Somerset Levels: their construction, age and relation to climatic change. *Proc. prehist. Soc.*, **26**, 1.

GRAVESTOCK, I. F. 1970. The botany of Cheddar Gorge. *In* Cheddar Gorge Survey, by M. H. Rogers and others. *Proc. Bristol Nat. Soc.*, **31**, 645.

HAWKINS, A. B. 1973. Sea level changes around South-West England. In *Marine Archaeology* (ed. D. J. Blackman); *Colston Papers*, **23**, 67. Bristol.

HOPE-SIMPSON, J. F., S. E. NEWTON and M. J. RICKETTS. 1963. Plant communities on Shapwick Heath, Somerset. *Proc. Bristol Nat. Soc.*, **30**, 343.

JEFFERIES, R. L., A. J. WILLIS and E. W. YEMM. 1968. The Late- and Post-glacial history of the Gordano valley, north Somerset. *New Phytol.*, **67**, 335.

SOMERSET COUNTY COUNCIL PLANNING DEPARTMENT. 1967. *Peat in Central Somerset: a Planning Study.* Taunton.

WILLIS, A. J. 1967. The vegetation of Catcott Heath, Somerset. *Proc. Bristol Nat. Soc.*, **31**, 297.

WILLIS, A. J. and E. W. DAVIES. 1960. *Juncus subulatus* Forsk. in the British Isles. *Watsonia*, **4**, 211.

WILLIS, A. J. and R. L. JEFFERIES. 1959. The plant ecology of the Gordano valley. *Proc. Bristol Nat. Soc.*, **29**, 469.

J. F. HOPE-SIMPSON & A. J. WILLIS

CHAPTER 7

p. 111

	Total area '000 acres	*Area of Crops and Grass '000 acres*	*Area of Rough Grazing '000 acres*	*Number of Holdings*
Gloucestershire	601	578	148	4,919
Somerset	829	779	40	8,552
Wiltshire	683	621	52	3,644
Dorset	488	448	32	3,304

p. 112 (Gloucestershire)

(*a*) There is currently less emphasis on break crops in Gloucestershire because of the difficulty of expanding the 'break' acreage of suitable crops in the context of a vastly increased cereal acreage. The importance of herbage seed production and seed potatoes is much reduced.

(*b*) Cocksfoot leys have been almost entirely replaced by perennial ryegrass swards.

(*c*) Recent years have seen a rapid run down in the number of dairy herds but a considerable expansion of cow numbers has taken place; each year sees a rise in the average size of herd and there are now many containing 150–200 cows.

(*d*) The majority of the lambs produced are now sold off fat from the ewes.

(*e*) There are fewer Kerry ewes; they have been replaced mainly by Welsh Half-Breds.

p. 112/p. 113 (Somerset)

(*f*) The major sheep breeds on Exmoor are now Exmoor Horn, Devon Closewool, Scotch Blackface and various half-breds.

(*g*) Fewer roots are grown with the greatly expanded increase in silage making.

p. 114 (Somerset)

(*h*) The predominant dairy breed is the Friesian: Ayrshire herds are now very few in number.

(*i*) Few folded sheep flocks remain in the South Petherton area. Sugar beet is no longer grown there.

p. 115 (Wiltshire)

(*j*) Cereal growing has expanded from 143,000 acres in 1955 to 252,000 acres in 1971.

(*k*) The average dairy herd size is 56 with a large proportion consisting of over 100 cows.

(*l*) Milk yields have risen from 665 to 850 gallons in 1972.

p. 116

(*m*) Wiltshire is tuberculosis free and brucellosis eradication is in progress on a voluntary basis.

(*n*) Pig farming has become specialised and concentrated in a small number of large units breeding mainly from Large White and Landrace crosses.

p. 117 (Dorset)

(*o*) The cattle population of Dorset is 234,000, the vast majority being Friesian.

(*p*) All Dorset herds are T.B. free.

(*q*) The sheep population has risen to 83,000 which includes 31,000 ewes. (Gloucestershire)

(*r*) The area of horticultural land in Gloucestershire has declined, but there is now 100 acres of glass.

WILTSHIRE

Between the years 1955 and 1971 the trends previously described have continued with emphasis on intensification of farming systems. Cereal growing has expanded from a total acreage of 143,000 in 1955 to 252,000 acres in 1971. Yields have not increased so dramatically as in the previous decade but they have been maintained in spite of the greater risk of disease associated with the larger acreage and the crop is now handled by a much smaller highly mechanised labour force. Grain drying and storage capacity have been increased proportionately and there is a trend towards co-operative grain marketing.

On dairy farms the average herd size has increased to 56, with a large proportion of herds of over 100 cows. The total number of herds has dropped to about 1,700 with the Friesian as the dominant breed. Heavy capital expenditure on fixed equipment has been necessary to allow the remaining manpower to cope with larger herds. Milking parlours and bails now total 1,200, with only 500 cowsheds remaining in use. Bulk tanks have replaced churns on more than one third of the dairy farms. The scheme to control tuberculosis has been successfully completed and Brucellosis eradication is now in progress on a voluntary basis.

Pig farming has become specialised and concentrated in a small number of large units breeding mainly from Large White and Landrace crosses.

The Poultry industry has developed rapidly, mainly concentrated in a small number of large-scale units. Currently there are about 1½ million layers, 2 million broilers and nearly half a million breeding stock.

CHAPTER 8

ADDITIONS TO BIBLIOGRAPHY

Under *botany*

BANKS, Joseph, Journal of an Excursion to Eastbury and Bristol, &c., *Proc. Bristol Naturalists' Soc.*, N.S. **9** (1), 1898, 6–37.

Under *geology*

EYLES, V. A., John Woodward, F.R.S., F.R.C.P., M.D. (1665–1728): a bio-bibliographical Account of his Life and Work, *Jnl. Soc. for Bibliography of Natural History*, **5** (6), (1971), 399–427.

BRADSHAW, R. Bristol Diamonds. *Proc. Bristol Naturalists' Soc.*, **31** (4), (1968), 439–450. An historical account of the use of the term, and a description of the mode of occurrence of the so-called diamonds.

VALLERIUS, G. A Description of a Cliff . .[Aust Cliff]. *Proc. Bristol Naturalists' Soc.*, **31** (6), (1970), 615–624. A description of the geology of Aust Cliff made by a Swedish mining engineer in 1710. Translated by H. D. Hedberg and H. Isaaksson; and annotated by R. Bradshaw and S. C. Matthews.

EYLES, J. M. William Smith: some Aspects of his Life and Work, in *Toward a History of Geology*, Ed. C. J. Schneer, Cambridge, Mass., and London, (1969), 142–158. Deals especially with Smith's work in Somerset, from 1791–1799, while working on the Somerset Coal Canal.

V. A. EYLES

CHAPTER 9

This chapter was published in 1955. Much knowledge has been accumulated in the succeeding 18 years. It is reprinted as a summary of knowledge and ideas of

1955. To bring the chapter up to date would involve an extensive re-writing and this is not possible. A few major amendments are noted and a short list of papers, dealing with the subject, that have appeared since 1955 are listed.

AMENDMENTS

p. 148, para. 2, p. 160, para. 2. There was no rock sill in the River Avon but only a man-made ford, possibly of Roman date.

p. 154, para. 2. The stone circle was not at Abbot's Leigh but at Leigh Down, Winford. ST 542638.

p. 154, para. 3. The Priddy Circles have been proved to be henge monuments.

p. 161, para. 3. The Glastonbury Lake Village was not destroyed by fire.

REFERENCES

ApSimon, A. M., Donovan, D. T. and Taylor, H. 1961. The Stratigraphy and Archaeology of the Late-Glacial and Post-Glacial Deposits at Brean Down, Somerset. *Proc. Univ Bristol Spelaeol Soc.*, **9** (2), 67–136.

Brailsford, J. 1958. Early Iron Age 'C' in Wessex. *Proc. Prehist. Soc.*, **24**, 101–119.

Coles, J. M. and Hibbert, F. A. 1968. Prehistoric Roads and Tracks in Somerset, England. 1. Neolithic. *Proc. Prehist. Soc.*, **34**, 238–258.

Coles, J. M., Hibbert, F. A. and Clements, C. F. 1970. Prehistoric Roads and Tracks in Somerset, England. 2. Neolithic. *Proc. Prehist. Soc.*, **36**, 125–151.

Donovan, D. T. 1955. The Pleistocene Deposit at Gough's Cave Cheddar, including an account of Recent Excavations. *Proc. Univ Bristol Spelaeol Soc.*, **7** (2), 76–104.

Dowden, W. A. 1957. Little Solsbury Hill Camp. *Proc. Univ Bristol Spelaeol Soc.* **9** (1), 18–29.

—. 1962. Little Solsbury Hill Camp. *Proc. Univ Bristol Spelaeol Soc.* **9** (3), 177–182.

Godwin, H. 1960. Prehistoric Wooden Trackways of the Somerset Levels. Their construction, age and relation to Climatic Change. *Proc. Prehist. Soc.* **26**, 1–36.

Grinsell, L. V. 1971. Somerset Barrows Pt. II. North and East. *Somerset Archaeol. Natur. Hist. Supplement.* **115**, 44–137.

Heal, C. J. 1970. A New Pleistocene Mammal Site, Mendip Hills. *Proc. Univ Bristol Spelaeol Soc.* **12** (2), 155–57.

O'Neil, Helen and Grinsell, L. V. 1961. Gloucestershire Barrows. *Trans. Bristol Gloucestershire Archaeol Soc.* **79** (1), 4–148.

Rahtz, P. A. 1957. Kings Weston Down Camp, Bristol, 1956. *Proc. Univ Bristol Spelaeol Soc.* **8** (1), 30–38.

Rahtz, P. A., and Brown, J. Clevedon. 1959. Blaise Castle Hill, Bristol, 1957. *Proc. Univ Bristol Spelaeol Soc.* **8** (3), 147–171.

Tratman, E. K. 1964. Picken's Hole, Crook Peak, Somerset. A Pleistocene Site. *Proc. Univ Bristol Spelaeol Soc.* **10** (2), 112–115.

—. 1967. The Priddy Circles Mendip, Somerset. Henge Monuments. *Proc. Univ Bristol Spelaeol Soc.* **11** (2), 97–125.

—. 1970. The Glastonbury Lake Village. A Reconsideration. *Proc. Univ Bristol Spelaeol Soc.* **12** (2), 143–168.

Tratman, E. K., Donovan, D. T. and Campbell, J. B. 1971. The Hyaena Den, Wookey Hole, Somerset. *Proc. Univ Bristol Spelaeol Soc.* **12** (3), 245–280.

E. K. TRATMAN

CHAPTER 10

Page 163 (last paragraph). Disregard 'three', 'In the Cotswolds. . . at this time', and 'by it'. 164 (first paragraph). Settled conditions took time to establish. There were small forts manned by auxiliary forces at Ham Hill, Gloucester, Cirencester and possibly Bath. The early wooden buildings at Cirencester seem to have belonged to the fort or the civil settlement associated with it, and a town emerged there no earlier than at Bath. 166 (first paragraph). Other villas may have escaped the havoc of A.D. 367 because they were remote from the river valleys used by the raiders. 168 (middle). At least one other important building at Bath has since come to light. 168–9. It now seems probable that the Great Bath was covered from the start, at first with a timber roof, and later with a massive tunnel vault. Recent excavations illustrate the variety of bathing facilities that gradually came to be provided. The temple stood to the N.W. of the baths in an adjoining precinct. The altar stood east of the temple and north of the hot spring, thus associating the two. 169 (below). The 'Via Julia' notice board has been removed. 170–1. An early auxiliary fort preceded a legionary fortress at Kingsholm, Gloucester, on the same site, the fortress being established by the Twentieth Legion from Colchester. About A.D. 66 the Second Legion replaced the Twentieth and occupied a new fortress on higher and drier ground. Recent excavations have shown that it was on the site of this second fortress that the colony was built. The forum has now been found to underlie and straddle Southgate Street. 171–2. The early auxiliary fort discovered at Cirencester in 1961 was found to have been occupied until A.D. 60–65. The forum and town hall were built only in the Flavian period. The town defences were originally an earth rampart, probably erected in the mid-second century. Here, as elsewhere, this was cut back in the third century and a stone wall inserted. Discoveries of large houses continue to testify to Corinium's prosperity, and a special style of mosaic is now thought to have developed there. 173–4. Annual excavations carried out at Gatcombe by the Department of Classics, University of Bristol, have revealed bakeries and workshops, but nothing as yet resembling dwellings or a town plan. Gatcombe may have been a late fortified industrial estate. 174. A temple sited impressively above the sea at Brean Down was excavated in 1958–59. Its inner area and ambulatory form concentric squares. The use of the temple as such was dated A.D. 330–367. 175. From air and ground surveys at Charterhouse an irregular street plan for the settlement, as well as a fort or forts, has been diagnosed.

SELECT BIBLIOGRAPHY

General:

BRANIGAN, K. *The Romans in the Bristol Area*, Bristol, 1969.

Bath:

CUNLIFFE, Barry, *Roman Bath*, London, 1969.

Gloucester:

Current Archaeology, no. 26 (1971).

Cirencester:
Antiquaries Journal, vols. 41–44 (1961–64).
Gatcombe:
Current Archaeology, no. 25 (1971).
Brean Down:
Proc. Univ. Bristol Spelaeological Society, vol. 10 (1964–65).
Charterhouse:
Britannia, vol. 2 (1971), p. 278.

D. E. EICHHOLZ

CHAPTER 13

The most recent addition to the considerable literature which has appeared since this chapter was written is Frank Walker's *The Bristol Region*, 1972, which is a valuable examination of the area by an historical geographer. John Latimer's monumental *Annals of Bristol* was reprinted in three volumes in 1970. Bristol Record Society has published two volumes (XX and XXIII) edited by W. E. Minchinton dealing with trade and economic organisation in the eighteenth century; a volume by the late Dorothy Livoch on municipal finance in the sixteenth and seventeenth century (XXIV); a volume by Elizabeth Ralph and Mary Williams on the inhabitants of Bristol in 1696 (XXV); and the First Minute Book of the Society of Friends in Bristol, 1667–1686, edited by Russell Mortimer (XXVI). Two very useful articles on plans for improvement of the port and on the construction of the Floating Harbour, one by Alan Williams and the other by R. A. Buchanan, appeared in the *Transactions of the Bristol and Gloucestershire Archaeological Society*, Vols. LXXXVI and LXXXVIII. In the *Transactions*, LXXXVII, 1969, P. T. Marcy examined Bristol's communications 1740–1780. The Bristol Branch of the Historical Association has published thirty pamphlets. Those dealing with the eighteenth century, see Note on Chapter 15. To these must be added Kathleen Barker, *The Theatre Royal: Decline and Rebirth 1834–1943*; Grahame Farr, *The Steamship Great Western* and *The Steamship Great Britain*; R. J. Saywell, *Mary Carpenter*; John Cannon, *The Chartists in Bristol*; C. M. MacInnes, *Ferdinando Gorges and New England* and *Captain Thomas James and the North-West Passage*; Herbert Byard, *The Bristol Madrigal Society*; Russell Mortimer, *Early Bristol Quakerism, 1654–1700*; R. A. Buchanan, *The Industrial Archaeology of Bristol*; P. Marshall, *The Anti-Slave Trade Movement in Bristol*; David Quinn, *Sebastian Cabot and Bristol Exploration*; P. McGrath, *John Whitson and the Merchant Community of Bristol*; R. A. Buchanan, *Nineteenth Century Engineers in the Port of Bristol*; Grahame Farr, *Bristol Shipbuilding in the Nineteenth Century*; E. E. Butcher, *The Bristol Corporation of the Poor 1696–1898*; and L. V. Grinsell, *The Bristol Mint.*

The much-neglected history of Bristol in the nineteenth century is now receiving more attention from students and a number of books are in course of preparation.

The face of Bristol has changed still further, not for the better, in the last eighteen years. Tower blocks of flats and offices are changing it out of all recognition, the threat from proposed new roads grows greater, and the City Docks appear to be doomed. In 1973, the historic City and County of Bristol will celebrate the six hundredth anniversary of its Charter of 1373 and will then be merged in 1974 in the new local government area of Avon.

PATRICK McGRATH

CHAPTER 15

Mr. Reginald James has died since the volume was first published but if he had lived, he would no doubt have wished to include the following supplementary material which has appeared since he wrote his stimulating and provocative chapter. *The Complete Works of Thomas Chatterton* were edited in two volumes in 1971 by D. S. Taylor and B. B. Hoover. Linda Kelly's *The Marvellous Boy: the Life and Myth of Thomas Chatterton* appeared in the same year. *The Correspondence of Edmund Burke* has been edited in nine volumes by T. W. Copeland between 1958 and 1970.

Bristol Branch of the Historical Association has published eight pamphlets relating to the eighteenth century: Vincent Waite, *The Bristol Hotwell*; P. T. Underdown, *Bristol and Burke*; Kathleen Barker, *The Theatre Royal: The First Seventy Years*; Walter Minchinton, *The Port of Bristol in the Eighteenth Century*; Basil Cottle, *Thomas Chatterton*; C. M. MacInnes, *Bristol and the Slave Trade*; P. T. Marcy, *Eighteenth Century Views of Bristol*; P. Marshall, *The Anti-Slave Trade Movement.* These were published in 1972 (David and Charles) in one volume, edited by Patrick McGrath.

For further references, see Notes to Chapter 13.

PATRICK McGRATH

CHAPTER 16

p. 243, para. 2. The top portion of the imitation High Cross is now well sited in Berkeley Square, and the Hogarth reredos in the City Museum; the Godwin reredos has been removed, giving a vista into the brilliant new glass of the Lady Chapel.

p. 246, para. 3. Another best-selling novelist was Emma Marshall, who lived at Woodside, Leigh Woods; from 1861 to her death in 1899 she wrote over 200 wholesome novels, many with a historical background which had been carefully studied.

p. 247, para. 2. The University's new Vandyck Theatre is splendidly equipped.

pp. 248–249. The musical situation is far happier than in 1955. The place of the defunct Bristol Philharmonic is now better filled by the Bournemouth Symphony Orchestra, based on Bournemouth but serving Wessex and governed by the Western Orchestral Society, with Bristol among the tributary towns; the Sinfonietta, likewise, is Bournemouth-based but applies to the whole South-West. A praiseworthy local growth, assimilating the old Paragon, is the Bristol Sinfonia, founded by Sidney Sager, which gives regular chamber concerts at the Colston Hall in the winter season; sections of the strings are led by members of the Dartington String Quartet, who from 1972 are to be attached to the University, teaching in the Department and giving nine recitals in their first academic year. The Bristol Bach Choir, conducted by Adrian Beaumont, is now five years old and already eminent; the Bristol Opera Company has also earned a high reputation. The Colston Hall now has an immense organ, and so has the University Great Hall.

p. 251, para. 3. The Art Gallery, which now changes its exhibits far more dynamically, has acquired a splendid Taddeo Gaddi and many other masterpieces since 1955.

p. 252, para. 2. The Masonic Hall (by C. R. Cockerell) has been rebuilt.

p. 252, para. 3. The Folk House is in new premises off Park Street.

BASIL COTTLE

CHAPTER 17

pp. 258–259. The Cathedral and St. Mary Redcliffe have been the subjects of extensive repair externally. Sympathetic washing and cleaning reveals the beauty of the ashlar and carved work. The upper level of the tower of St. Stephen's Church has been rebuilt. The blitzed Church of St. Nicholas is re-roofed and, after internal alterations and adaptations have been completed, will become a museum.

The castle precinct is in course of development as a public open area with arranged contours and tree planting. The western portion is given over to two new buildings, the Bank of England and the Norwich Union. The tower of St. Mary-le-Port is adjacent to the latter building. The tower of St. Peter's Church will also be retained as a feature and excavation has reclaimed certain foundation walls of the Castle. The whole development, taken in conjunction with the nearby river walk, will be a delightful amenity to the City.

p. 261. The few remaining houses of St. James' Square have been demolished and their sites absorbed in a large office development.

p. 262. The Theatre Royal and the Cooper's Hall now form part of a splendid complex in which both buildings are preserved and enhanced. The nearby St. Nicholas Almshouses and other ancient buildings in King Street have been restored.

p. 263. Kings Weston House has been repaired and now has an assured future.

p. 265. St. George's Church, Brandon Hill, is re-decorated in accordance with Smirke's design. Holy Trinity Church, Hotwells and the Freemasons' Hall, Park Street, have been restored and adapted and the Bank of England in Broad Street has had its stonework cleaned. Thus, all three of Cockerell's buildings are restored to their original dignity.

p. 267. Fry's Factory in Tower Lane and the Sun Building, Clare Street, have been demolished and large office blocks occupy their sites. Major developments have taken place in the University and Hospital Zones situated on either side of

St. Michael's Hill. The Georgian houses on the Hill are restored and in Queen's Road the University Great Hall has been reinstated, with certain modifications.

p. 268. A number of tower blocks, either for offices or residential units, have risen in the central area. From certain viewpoints, these compete with or confuse the delicate silhouettes of ancient spires and towers, which for centuries have punctuated the low roof lines of the city, particularly when viewed from the surrounding rim of hills. Bristol was a late starter in the development of high office blocks. Most of the important central area is now subject to strict controls and it is unlikely that further tower blocks will arise to impose the extreme adverse conditions already suffered by less fortunate 'manhattaned' communities. The local societies concerned with conservation and civic values have become increasingly active. A department of the Ministry for the Environment occupies a vantage point in one of the new office towers.

Taking into account the opportunities alleged to have been lost, the many gains and the hoped-for achievements, it can be said that the Bristol of the year 2000 may prove to be a fine Regional City.

RALPH H. BRENTNALL

CHAPTER 18

Most of the changes in the engineering activities of Bristol since 1955 have arisen from transport developments. The pattern of shipping has changed and container traffic is developing. Avonmouth has lost its banana trade but is still busy, while the city docks are now little used and await closure within a decade. After years of political wrangle, work has started on a great new dock system near Portbury alongside the west bank of the Avon.

The railways around Bristol are now depleted by the closure of a number of local lines as well as of the old Somerset and Dorset Railway to Bournemouth. Meanwhile great motorways have come to the Bristol area; the M4 from London to South Wales passes just a few miles to the north of the city and is already busy; construction of the M5 from Birmingham to the South-West is well advanced. These major roads have spurred the railways to speed their main-line passenger traffic, so that journeys to London, Birmingham and the North are all faster than ever before.

These changes have involved many civil engineering works around Bristol, vying in modern terms with those of Brunel. The nineteenth century achievement of the Clifton Suspension Bridge has been matched by the twentieth-century Severn Suspension Bridge.

Amid these transport developments the aeroplane works at Filton have not been inactive, and their achievements of the past have been eclipsed by the design and production of the Concorde. Much of the overall design work and all of the engine development has been due to the works at Filton, though they are now parts of larger national aeronautical groups.

In other fields of industry, changes have added to earlier Bristol activities rather than reduced them. At Avonmouth, cattle food and various chemical activities have expanded, and great smelting works have come into being. The shoe industry continues in the Kingswood district, transformed by modern machinery and new materials.

Changes in engineering education have appeared mainly in technical college work. After the old Technical College moved to Ashley Down it became a College of Advanced Technology, only to become a few years later the Bath University of Technology centred at Claverton Down on the outskirts of Bath. And now technical education in Bristol itself is grouped into the new Bristol Polytechnic.

A. G. PUGSLEY

CHAPTER 19

Since 1955 many of the high hopes of Christian unity in Britain have been disappointed, most of all by the failure of the General Synod of the Church of England to give a sufficiently large vote in favour of the scheme for Anglican-Methodist unity. Bristol has remained in the forefront of the movement for unity, though it has been joined in this position by other cities. In no area was the way more fully prepared for the union of the Church of England with the Methodist Church. The Christians of the city were all the more bitterly grieved by the failure of the scheme. Because of the prospect of organic unity, several Anglican and Methodist ministers and congregations had begun to co-operate on a large scale. Now, in the wake of the Church of England's refusal to approve the scheme, many of these have persisted in their efforts to achieve at least local unity, and they have been joined by others, and by Churches of other denominations. A notable feature of recent developments has been the participation of Roman Catholics in ecumenical activity, made possible by the Second Vatican Council.

Add footnote to page 281, 'on 'St. Mary Redcliffe':

We have to rely on Thomas Chatterton's perhaps exaggerated narrative for our knowledge of Canynges' gifts to St. Mary Redcliffe, except that we know from other sources that he endowed a chantry there. But it seems not improbable that a man so generous to Westbury College gave much to his own parish church also.

Add footnote to p. 291, on 'Didsbury', 7 lines from the end:

This was the situation in 1955. But since then Western College has been removed to Manchester, Didsbury College has received Wesley College, Headingley, Leeds, and been re-named Wesley College, and Clifton College and Tyndale Hall have been amalgamated with Dalton House, a training college for women Church workers, to form Trinity College. Thus there are now only three theological colleges in Bristol.

CORRIGENDUM

Note to be added at the end of the article:

It is stated on p. 284 that the first Puritans with 'Baptist' views 'formed a community in the Pithay soon after the foundation of Broadmead'. This is shown to be incorrect by the *Broadmead Records*. From these it must be inferred that the 'Baptist' community was already in existence in 1640, when Broadmead was founded, and was active in 'the Fryers' from its foundation until 1699, when it bought an 'old sope house' in the Pithay for £168. I owe this correction to Mr. Cecil Beaven. It should be added, in view of the footnote to p. 284, that the community has now moved from Old King Street to Cairns Road, Redland.

RUPERT E. DAVIES

CHAPTER 20

p. 297; (a)'—it being considered that as there was not enough work a little education would not come amiss for the little paupers!'

(*b*) 'administration of Poor Law relief was, to say the least, callous, and must have prompted the foundation of many Bristol charities, as in the sixteenth, seventeenth and eighteenth centuries a large number were formed and their administration entrusted to the Corporation. . . '

No comment on the operation of Poor Law relief can be entertained without prior reference to the two major studies on this subject. These are:

(1) 'Bristol Corporation of the Poor 1696–1834', a volume of extracts by Bristol Record Society, 1931.

(2) 'Bristol Corporation of the Poor 1696–1898', a study by Bristol Branch Historical Association, 1972.

In both of these the studies are by Miss E. E. Butcher.

Examination of these two authorities causes quotation (a) to be viewed as an ill-considered remark and is accordingly dismissed as such.

In (*b*), it is pointed out that there was no real organized attempt to deal with problems of poverty till 1696 and after that date benefactors would be unlikely to leave funds to a public body financed by a compulsory levy any more than they would today—hence the use of Bristol Corporation as public trustees.

The accusation of 'callous' is dubious since operations were conducted in the light of current thought—the actions of one decade are not acceptable to its successor.

The actions of early administrators appear kid-gloved when compared to the tyranny of Work House Masters and Relieving Officers of the 1880/90s.

Miss Butcher notes in her 1972 work, that the Corporation of the Poor justified their creation, and places squarely the blame on ratepayers themselves who were only interested in poor relief when it touched their pockets and notes that it was their opposition to providing accommodation which caused a deplorable mortality rate during epidemics.

This attitude doubtless prevailed pre-1696; hence the failures of sporadic attempts in earlier days.

Not to be forgotten—many of the benefactors of charities were actuated not so much by welfare of the poor as by the idea that a generous action might make things more agreeable to themselves in after life. John Whitson is a case in point.

CHAPTER 21

p. 305. Changes in museum display have been greatly accelerated since 1955 by the introduction of new techniques and the appointment of staff especially trained in design.

p. 307. Certain changes have taken place in the administering bodies for museums. The Royal Literary and Scientific Institution, Bath, has been disbanded and its collections in Queen Square transferred to the City of Bath, and the Museum at Glastonbury, Somerset is now housed in the Tribunal and is under the Ministry of Public Buildings and Works. The collections at Taunton have been transferred to the County of Somerset.

p. 309. The South West Group of Museums and Art Galleries is now called a Federation instead of a Group in order to establish a uniform nomenclature throughout Britain. It meets informally twice a year to discuss matters of mutual interest and exchange information.

In addition, the Area Museum Council for the South West was formed in 1959, to promote closer co-operation amongst the museums of the area, and especially to provide advisory, display and technical assistance.

F. S. WALLIS

CHAPTER 22

Since this article was written, there have been major changes in the organization of the secondary schools for which the Bristol Education Authority is responsible. In general and in principle, the local authority secondary system is 'comprehensive' in nature; the former municipal grammar schools have become or will become part of this system.

This change has also been reflected in the L.E.A.'s use of and attitude to the Direct Grant Schools and to Colston's Girls' School. Redland High School has resumed its Direct Grant status; Colston's Girls' School has become independent.

One school, not referred to in the original article, has since grown to national importance. St. Christopher's School is largely a residential school for very seriously handicapped or retarded children. A short sketch of its history and special nature will be found in the oration delivered when the Principal was presented for an honorary degree in the University in July 1971 (reprinted in the Collected Volume of Minutes of Senate, 1970–71).

ROGER WILSON